Margaret Y. MacDonald, D.Phil.
(University of Oxford), is professor,
department of religious studies,
St. Francis Xavier University, Antigonish,
Nova Scotia. She is the author of *The
Pauline Churches* (Cambridge, 1988)
and *Early Christian Women and
Pagan Opinion* (Cambridge, 1996).

COLOSSIANS AND EPHESIANS

Sacra Pagina Series

Volume 17

Colossians
and
Ephesians

Margaret Y. MacDonald

Daniel J. Harrington, S.J.
Editor

A Michael Glazier Book
THE LITURGICAL PRESS
Collegeville, Minnesota
www.litpress.org

A Michael Glazier Book published by The Liturgical Press.

Cover design by Don Bruno.

1   2   3   4   5   6   7   8

Library of Congress Cataloging-in-Publication Data

MacDonald, Margaret Y.
    Colossians and Ephesians / Margaret Y. MacDonald ; Daniel J. Harrington,
editor.
        p.   cm. — (Sacra pagina series ; vol. 17)
    "A Michael Glazier book."
    Includes bibliographical references and indexes.
    ISBN 0-8146-5819-9 (alk. paper)
    1. Bible. N.T. Colossians—Commentaries. 2. Bible. N.T. Ephesians—Com-
mentaries. I. Harrington, Daniel J. II. Title. III. Sacra pagina series ; 17.

BS2715.3.M327 2000
227'.5077—dc21   00-027615

CONTENTS

EPHESIANS

Indexes

EDITOR'S PREFACE

Sacra Pagina is a multi-volume commentary on the books of the New Testament. The expression *Sacra Pagina* ("Sacred Page") originally referred to the text of Scripture. In the Middle Ages it also described the study of Scripture to which the interpreter brought the tools of grammar, rhetoric, dialectic, and philosophy. Thus *Sacra Pagina* encompasses both the text to be studied and the activity of interpretation.

This series presents fresh translations and modern expositions of all the books of the New Testament. Written by an international team of Catholic biblical scholars, it is intended for biblical professionals, graduate students, theologians, clergy, and religious educators. The volumes present basic introductory information and close exposition. They self-consciously adopt specific methodological perspectives, but maintain a focus on the issues raised by the New Testament compositions themselves. The goal of *Sacra Pagina* is to provide sound critical analysis without any loss of sensitivity to religious meaning. This series is therefore catholic in two senses of the word: inclusive in its methods and perspectives, and shaped by the context of the Catholic tradition.

The Second Vatican Council described the study of the "sacred page" as the "very soul of sacred theology" (*Dei Verbum* 24). The volumes in this series illustrate how Catholic scholars contribute to the council's call to provide access to Sacred Scripture for all the Christian faithful. Rather than pretending to say the final word on any text, these volumes seek to open up the riches of the New Testament and to invite as many people as possible to study seriously the "sacred page."

DANIEL J. HARRINGTON, S.J.

PREFACE

No two works in the Pauline corpus resemble each other as closely as Colossians and Ephesians. Thus it makes sense to study them together and seek to understand the relationship between them. Colossians and Ephesians present commentators with many challenges, however, besides that of unraveling the nature of the relationship between them. The literature on these works is full of discussions of authorship. The debate (which is especially intense with respect to Colossians) concerns whether these documents were composed by Paul himself or by a close associate or disciple of the apostle. Moreover, with respect to Colossians there has been great speculation concerning the identity of false teachers (2:8-23). With regard to Ephesians the lack of reference to specific community issues has proved to be especially frustrating. The situation is compounded by the fact that we cannot even be sure that Ephesians was originally intended for Ephesus. The words "in Ephesus" (1:1) are missing from some ancient manuscripts.

Like commentators before me, I have grappled with these classic problems of interpretation. I have examined the evidence and explained why I believe that Colossians was written by a close associate or disciple of Paul while the apostle was in prison or shortly after his death. Similarly, I have outlined why I believe Ephesians is dependent on Colossians and is also best understood as deutero-Pauline. I hope that I have contributed in some significant ways to the debates concerning the false teaching in Colossae and the purpose of Ephesians. However, in many respects I have sought to illustrate how preoccupation with only a few central issues in the interpretation of these documents has led to the neglect of other important features of the works. Moreover, by paying attention to subtle differences between Colossians and Ephesians I have aimed to shed light on the distinct perspectives of these works.

In keeping with the usual format of *Sacra Pagina*, this commentary includes my own translation of the Greek text. For the sake of clarity of exposition I have tended to offer fairly literal translations, inserting additional English words only when absolutely necessary. The notes include the usual linguistic and grammatical analysis and offer historical explanations. As for the interpretations of the various passages, I was invited to employ a relatively new method of biblical interpretation: social-scientific analysis. In brief, I have drawn upon sociological and anthropological insights when appropriate in order to shed light on the text. My methodological perspective means that there are aspects of Colossians and Ephesians that do not receive the same detailed attention in this book that might be found in other commentaries. Instead I have concentrated especially on the relationship between these documents and the social life of NT communities. This has manifested itself in three main ways. First, I have sought to understand how passages reflect ancient cultural values. In other words, I have attempted to clarify the texts by illustrating their roots in a first-century Mediterranean world. Secondly, I have explored the relationship between the works and particular aspects of community life such as worship. Finally, I have paid close attention to the connection between the shape of the works and the development of community life in larger terms—the issues faced by groups as they formed institutions and interacted with the society around them.

My social-scientific perspective has frequently alerted me to the religious significance of Colossians and Ephesians. For example, by exploring the impact of ritual forms on the shape of Colossians and Ephesians I have been able to underscore the importance of liturgical influences. The experience of baptism is at the heart of both of these epistles and both draw heavily upon hymnic material to teach believers about Christ. Ephesians has long been recognized as displaying a great interest in ecclesiology. But to study Ephesians from a social-scientific perspective helps one to see that this great interest in the identity of the church is fundamentally tied to the struggles of a community to survive and maintain a distinct identity in first-century society.

With this commentary I have been able to build on my earlier work in *The Pauline Churches: A Socio-Historical Study of Institutionalization in the Pauline and Deutero-Pauline Writings* (Cambridge: Cambridge University Press, 1988). Roughly one third of *The Pauline Churches* was devoted to the study of Colossians and Ephesians. This commentary has afforded me the opportunity to revisit some of my earlier conclusions and to conduct a much more thorough analysis of these documents. I have been working on this commentary on and off since 1992, but have devoted the whole of my sabbatical year (July 1998–August 1999) to its completion. The intensive work required to produce a commentary has sometimes proved to be enormously difficult, but I have also often rejoiced in the privilege of getting to know these works so intimately. Any commentary relies heavily on the work of past interpreters. Among previous commentators on Colossians, I have been influenced especially by the work of Mary Rose D'Angelo,

James D. G. Dunn, Murray J. Harris, Eduard Lohse, and Petr Pokorný. For Ephesians I have been influenced especially by Markus Barth, Andrew T. Lincoln, Pheme Perkins, Heinrich Schlier, and Rudolf Schnackenburg. Studies on Colossians and Ephesians by Clinton E. Arnold have also figured prominently in my study.

During the final stages of my work I received research funding both from St. Francis Xavier University (Antigonish, Nova Scotia) and from the Social Science and Humanities Research Council of Canada. I am grateful to both of these organizations. The careful reading and wise editing of my manuscript by Daniel J. Harrington, S.J. deserves special mention. I could not have produced this commentary without the patience and understanding of husband Duncan, and children Delia and Jake. On many occasions they forgave me for spending yet more time in my study instead of being with them.

I dedicate this volume to my lifelong friend, Carolyn Humphreys Baldwin.

MARGARET Y. MACDONALD

ABBREVIATIONS

Biblical Books and Apocrypha

Gen	Nah	1-2-3-4 Kgdms	John
Exod	Hab	Add Esth	Acts
Lev	Zeph	Bar	Rom
Num	Hag	Bel	1-2 Cor
Deut	Zech	1-2 Esdr	Gal
Josh	Mal	4 Ezra	Eph
Judg	Ps (*pl.*: Pss)	Jdt	Phil
1-2 Sam	Job	Ep Jer	Col
1-2 Kgs	Prov	1-2-3-4 Macc	1-2 Thess
Isa	Ruth	Pr Azar	1-2 Tim
Jer	Cant	Pr Man	Titus
Ezek	Eccl (*or* Qoh)	Sir	Phlm
Hos	Lam	Sus	Heb
Joel	Esth	Tob	Jas
Amos	Dan	Wis	1-2 Pet
Obad	Ezra	Matt	1-2-3 John
Jonah	Neh	Mark	Jude
Mic	1-2 Chr	Luke	Rev

Other Ancient Texts

Abot R. Nat.	*Abot de-Rabbi Nathan*
Adv. Haer.	Irenaeus, *Against All Heresies*
2-3 *Apoc. Bar.*	Syriac, Greek *Apocalypse of Baruch*
Ant.	Josephus, *Antiquities of the Jews*
Apoc. Elijah	*Apocalypse of Elijah*
Apol.	Justin Martyr, *Apology*
Asc. Isa	*Ascension of Isaiah*
Barn.	*Barnabas*
Bell.	Josephus, *Bellum Judaicum* (Jewish War)
Ber.	*Berakhot*
C. Apion	Josephus, *Against Apion*
C. Cels.	Origen, *Contra Celsum*
CD	Cairo Genizah copy of the *Damascus Document*
Cher.	Philo, *The Cherubim*
1–2 *Clem.*	1–2 *Clement*

Clem. Al. *Paed.*	Clement of Alexandria, *Paedagogus*
Clem. Al. *Strom.*	Clement of Alexandria, *Stromateis*
Conf. Ling.	Philo, *On the Confusion of Tongues*
Const. Sap.	Seneca, *On the Constancy of the Wise Man*
Cyr.	Xenophon, *Cyropaedia*
Decal.	Philo, *On the Decalogue*
Dial. Trypho	Justin Martyr, *Dialogue with Trypho*
Did.	*Didache*
Diogn.	*Diognetus*
Diss.	Epictetus, *Discourses*
1–2–3 Enoch	Ethiopic, Slavonic, Hebrew *Enoch*
Ep. Arist.	*Epistle of Aristeas*
Exeg. Soul	*Exegesis on the Soul*
Gig.	Philo, *The Giants*
Gos. Phil.	*Gospel of Phillip*
Gos. Thom.	*Gospel of Thomas*
Her.	Philo, *Who is the Heir of Divine Things?*
Herm. Man.	*Hermas, Mandate(s)*
Herm. Sim.	*Hermas, Similitude(s)*
Herm. Vis.	*Hermas, Vision(s)*
Hist.	Tacitus, *Histories*
Hist. Alex. Magni	Pseudo-Callisthenes, *Historia Alexandri Magni*
Hyp. Arch.	*Hypostasis of the Archons*
Hypoth.	Philo, *Hypothetica*
Ign. *Eph.*	Ignatius, *Letter to the Ephesians*
Ign. *Magn.*	Ignatius, *Letter to the Magnesians*
Ign. *Pol.*	Ignatius, *Letter to Polycarp*
Ign. *Smyrn.*	Ignatius, *Letter to the Smyrnaeans*
Ira.	Seneca, *On Anger* (in *Moral Essays*)
Jub.	Jubilees
LXX	Septuagint
Mart. Pol.	*Martyrdom of Polycarp*
Medit.	Marcus Aurelius, *Meditations*
Midr.	*Midrash*
NT	New Testament
Odes Sol.	Odes of Solomon
OT	Old Testament
Pol. *Phil.*	Polycarp, *Letter to the Philippians*
Praec. Conj.	Plutarch, *Advice to the Bride and Groom*
QL	Qumran Literature
Quaest. In Ex.	Philo, *Questions and Solutions in Exodus*
1QH	*Thanksgiving Hymns*
1QM	*War Scroll*
1QpHab	*Pesher Habakkuk*
1QS	*Rule of the Community*
Rhet.	Aristotle, *Rhetoric*
Rom. Ant.	Dionysius of Halicarnassus, *Roman Antiquities*

Spec. Leg.	Philo, *On the Special Laws*
T. Dan	*Testament of Dan*
T. Iss.	*Testament of Issachar*
T. Job	*Testament of Job*
T. Jud.	*Testament of Judah*
T. Levi	*Testament of Levi*
T. Reub.	*Testament of Reuben*
Vg	Vulgate
Vita Cont.	Philo, *On the Contemplative Life*

Periodicals, Reference Works, and Serials

AB	Anchor Bible
ACNT	Augsburg Commentary on the New Testament
ACW	Ancient Christian Writers
AnBib	Analecta biblica
ANF	The Ante-Nicene Fathers
ANRW	*Aufstieg und Niedergang der römischen Welt*
ANTC	Abingdon New Testament Commentaries
BAGD	Walter Bauer, *A Greek-English Lexicon of the New Testament and Other Early Christian Literature*, edited by William F. Arndt, F. Wilbur Gingrich, and Frederick W. Danker (Chicago: University of Chicago Press, 1979)
BDF	Friedrich Blass, Alfred Debrunner, and Robert W. Funk, *A Greek Grammar of the New Testament* (Chicago: University of Chicago Press, 1961)
BibSac	*Bibliotheca Sacra*
BTB	*Biblical Theology Bulletin*
BU	Biblische Untersuchungen
BZNW	Beihefte zur *ZNW*
CBQ	*Catholic Biblical Quarterly*
CGTC	Cambridge Greek Testament Commentaries
CNT	Commentaire du Nouveau Testament
EC	Epworth Commentary
ExpTim	*Expository Times*
FRLANT	Forschungen zur Religion und Literatur des Alten und Neuen Testaments
HR	*History of Religions*
HThKNT	Herders theologischer Kommentar zum Neuen Testament
HThR	*Harvard Theological Review*
Int	*Interpretation*
ICC	International Critical Commentary
JAAR	*Journal of the American Academy of Religion*
JBL	*Journal of Biblical Literature*
JETS	*Journal of the Evangelical Theological Society*

JR	*Journal of Religion*
JRH	*Journal of Religious History*
JSNT	*Journal for the Study of the New Testament*
JSNT.S	JSNT Supplements
JSOT	*Journal for the Study of the Old Testament*
LCL	Loeb Classical Library
MSSNTS	Society for New Testament Studies Monograph Series
NAB	New American Bible
NCBC	New Century Bible Commentary
NEB	New English Bible
NICNT	New International Commentary on the New Testament
NIGTC	New International Greek Testament Commentary
NIV	New International Version
NJB	New Jerusalem Bible
NRSV	New Revised Standard Version
NT	*Novum Testamentum*
NT.S	*Novum Testamentum* Supplements
NTOA	Novum Testamentum et Orbis Antiquus
NTS	*New Testament Studies*
ÖTK	Ökumenischer Taschenbuch-Kommentar
PGrM	Karl Preisendanz (ed.), *Papyri graecae magicae*
RB	*Revue biblique*
REB	Revised English Bible
RV	Revised Version
SBL.DS	SBL Dissertation Series
SBL.MS	SBL Monograph Series
SBS	Sources for Biblical Study
StNT	Studien zum Neuen Testament
Str-B	[Hermann Strack and] Paul Billerbeck, *Kommentar zum Neuen Testament aus Talmud und Midrasch.* 6 vols. (Munich: 1922–61)
SUNT	Studien zur Umwelt des Neuen Testaments
TDNT	Gerhard Kittel and Gerhard Friedrich, *Theological Dictionary of the New Testament*, 10 vols. Translated by Geoffrey W. Bromiley (Grand Rapids: Eerdmans, 1964–76)
TNTC	Tyndale New Testament Commentary
TU	Texte und Untersuchungen
ThZ	*Theologische Zeitschrift*
UBS	*The Greek New Testament*, edited by Kurt Aland, et al. (New York and London: United Bible Societies, 1975, corrected 1983, 1993)
WBC	Word Biblical Commentary
WMANT	Wissenschaftliche Monographien zum Alten und Neuen Testament
WUNT	Wissenschaftliche Untersuchungen zum Neuen Testament
ZNW	*Zeitschrift für die neutestamentliche Wissenschaft*
ZThK	*Zeitschrift für Theologie und Kirche*

INTRODUCTION

I. A SOCIAL-SCIENTIFIC APPROACH

During the past few decades new approaches to the interpretation of biblical literature have arisen, complementing and to a certain extent challenging the dominant historical-critical approach. Of these new approaches one in particular, social-scientific criticism, will play a central role in this commentary. In the analysis of particular documents the historical-critical approach has been employed to explore the meaning of a given author's work in light of the author's circumstances and context. The goal is to discover a document's occasion and purpose. Social-scientific criticism of the NT is also very much concerned with context, but context is generally understood much more broadly. Rather than concentrating on the unique circumstances underlying a particular document, social-scientific interpreters seek to understand the place of the document within the broader society and thus pay attention to the social mechanisms at work both within the particular group where the document was produced and in the interplay between the group and the wider social order.

Although much important work has been done on Colossians and Ephesians to date, it is also the case that both the nature of the scholarly discussions about these documents and the shape of the findings illustrate the limitations of traditional methods. Work on Colossians has concentrated heavily on discovering the identity of the false teachers (2:8-23), but the striking number of scholarly theories about the matter is testimony to the fact that their identity remains rather nebulous. Likewise, the occasion and purpose of Ephesians have proved to be remarkably elusive. The document has a majestic tone, is heavily influenced by liturgical forms, and quite simply makes no explicit reference to particular community concerns. These historical problems, coupled with a preoccupation with the question of the authenticity of documents (see further below), has meant that many interesting facets of Colossians and Ephesians have not received the attention they deserve. It is my hope that a commentary that makes explicit use of social-scientific insights will draw attention to previously neglected features of Colossians and Ephesians and contribute to our understanding of the significance of these fascinating documents.

Social-scientific interpretation of the NT has now progressed to the point where whole books are devoted to discussing the theoretical implications of the methodology and exploring its impact (e.g., Holmberg [1990]; Elliott [1993]; Esler [1994]; Rohrbaugh). The earliest examples of social-scientific interpretation of the NT from the 1970s and early 1980s elicited a mixed reaction from scholars. Among the most widely recognized benefits of the approach is that it brings the hitherto implicit assumptions of researchers into the open. Drawing upon models and theories rooted in the social sciences renders the interpreter's frame of reference easily recognizable and facilitates discussion about the appropriateness of the frame of reference and resulting conclusions. Among the most frequently heard criticisms is that practitioners of social-scientific interpretation of the NT filled in gaps from the past based on observations of modern groups in society (e.g., Judge 210). But social-scientific work on the NT has become increasingly sophisticated over time and interpreters have become increasingly conscious of the possibilities and limits of the approach. One of the main goals of those who draw upon the findings of cultural anthropology, in particular, is to guard against ethnocentric interpretations of the NT. They warn against a natural tendency to assume that NT believers acted and thought like modern people of North Atlantic cultures, and draw upon studies on modern Mediterranean cultures in the hope of shedding light on the values that shaped the NT world (here the work of Bruce J. Malina has been especially influential). Studies illustrating how the core Mediterranean values of honor and shame operate in NT texts have had a major impact on NT studies generally, and they also figure prominently in this commentary (e.g., see the notes and interpretation on Col 1:3-8; 3:5-17; Eph 4:17–5:20; 5:21–6:9). For example, the treatment of marriage in Eph 5:22-33, including the use of the symbol of the pure bride to describe the identity of the church, takes on new significance when examined in light of these values.

While it is true that social-scientific interpretation of the NT has gained a new level of sophistication in recent years, it must be admitted that those who employ this methodology do not always agree on which social-scientific models and theories are appropriate for NT analysis. For example, Bruce J. Malina has argued that Max Weber's theories concerning charisma and its routinization are too closely tied to nineteenth-century Germanic and/or northern European culture to be valuable for investigating the rise of Christianity in an ancient Mediterranean context (Malina [1984] 56; see also Elliott [1993] 97). But other NT scholars are convinced that with appropriate methodological caution and historical correction Weber's analysis can act as a valuable heuristic device for understanding particular aspects of NT works, especially questions of authority and power (e.g., Holmberg [1980]; M. Y. MacDonald [1988]; Blasi; Williams). An extensive body of sociological work that can assist with this task has arisen from the classic Weberian theories. Moreover, because Weber discusses the problems created by the death of a charismatic leader it is especially valuable to consider the implications of his findings for the continuation of Pauline Christianity. In short, his theories can shed light on the function of deutero-Pauline works (assuming, as is argued in this commentary, that Colossians and Ephesians are deutero-Pauline).

To write a commentary on Colossians and Ephesians is to deal with the question of change and development within Pauline Christianity and the transfer of a legacy to a new generation. Often discussion of these documents has been dominated by comparison to the undisputed letters of Paul, and some features of these works have been judged as somehow inferior to the "real" Paul (see, e.g., Ernst Käsemann's views concerning the "early catholic" tendencies of the author of Ephesians [1968] 290). In this commentary judgments concerning progress or decline with respect to the nature of Colossians and Ephesians in comparison to the undisputed letters of Paul are avoided. Insights from Weberian sociology are employed to help us comprehend the challenges faced by the Pauline circle in the face of the imprisonment and death of its central leader (see the notes and interpretation on Col 1:1-2; Eph 1:1-2). In our effort to understand this aspect of the communal context and as a complement to the Weberian insights we will also make use of Peter Berger and Thomas Luckmann's work on "institutionalization" from the perspective of the sociology of knowledge (e.g., see the notes and interpretation on Eph 1:3-14; 2:11-22).

This commentary will include the grammatical, linguistic, and historical analysis that has traditionally been central to NT exegesis. But it will also draw upon insights from the fields of sociology and cultural anthropology. In a commentary on two NT books one inevitably has to deal with many different subjects and types of exhortation. The choice of social-scientific material has been dictated largely by the matter under discussion. To give an obvious example, the importance of baptism in both Colossians and Ephesians has led me to turn to social-scientific studies of ritual in general and rites of initiation in particular. Since a commentary is probably not the place to test the usefulness of new theories and models, I have here deliberately appealed to social-scientific material that has been widely employed and judged to be useful by NT interpreters. In addition to the works of Weber and of Berger and Luckmann highlighted above I have made use of the studies of Bryan Wilson on religious sects (see the notes and interpretation on Col 1:9-13; 4:2-6; Eph 1:3-14; 2:1-10; 3:14-21; 4:17–5:20; 5:21–6:9), and the works of Clifford Geertz, Victor Turner, and

Arnold Van Gennep on ritual (see the notes and interpretation on Col 1:15-20; 2:8-15, 2:16-23; 3:1-4; Eph 3:14-21). In addition I have drawn upon the anthropological studies of modern Mediterranean societies that have been so usefully employed to shed light upon the NT world by Bruce J. Malina, Jerome H. Neyrey, John J. Pilch and others (see the notes and interpretation on Col 1:3-8; 1:9-13; 1:21-23; 1:24–2:7; 3:5-17; Eph 3:1-13; 4:17–5:20; 5:21–6:9).

II. *READING COLOSSIANS AND EPHESIANS TOGETHER*

Along with Philemon and Philippians, Colossians and Ephesians are prison letters. They claim to have been composed by Paul while he was in captivity. But many scholars believe that both Colossians and Ephesians are deutero-Pauline; that is, while they purport to have come directly from Paul they may have been composed by a follower or close associate of Paul while he was in prison or after he had died. There are many reasons for this theory, which are examined in more detail below, but among the arguments in favor of the deutero-Pauline authorship of Ephesians is the very close relationship between the two epistles. Of all the letters in the Pauline corpus, no two works are so closely linked. Although it has sometimes been argued that Colossians constitutes an abridged version of Ephesians, the vast majority of commentators favor the priority of Colossians. (Note, however, that Ernest Best has recently questioned many of the traditional arguments in support of the idea that the author of Ephesians used Colossians and their value for demonstrating the deutero-Pauline authorship of Ephesians; see Best [1998] 20–36; on Best's position see also the notes and interpretation on Eph 6:21-24 in this volume.) Indeed, it seems that the author of Ephesians was very familiar with Colossians, drawing upon the epistle's language, style, and concepts. In fact, more than one third of the words found in Colossians are also in Ephesians. For this reason alone it makes sense to study these two epistles together.

Among the most striking parallels between Colossians and Ephesians are Eph 1:7 || Col 1:14; Eph 2:5 || Col 2:13; Eph 3:2 || Col 1:25; Eph 3:9 || Col 1:26; Eph 4:16 || Col 2:19. The nature of the interdependence is somewhat intriguing. No long passages in Colossians are repeated in Ephesians word for word. The general impression one gets is that the author of Ephesians reproduced many of the main ideas of Colossians from memory. There is one passage in Ephesians in particular, however, that suggests the author may actually have had access to a written copy of Colossians. There is extended verbatim agreement between the recommendation of Tychicus in Eph 6:21-22 and Col 4:7-8. This agreement has figured prominently in theories concerning the deutero-Pauline authorship of Ephesians (see the notes and interpretation on Eph 6:21-24).

If the striking literary relationship between Colossians and Ephesians offers the basis for reading these works together, there are other reasons for doing so that flow from this literary relationship. This commentary includes a special focus on the social context of the epistles. The operating assumption is that the author of Ephesians reproduced much of Colossians because its language and concepts were of particular relevance to the community. In other words, Colossians and Ephesians disclose a similar world view, reflect some of the same community concerns, and generally represent a similar stage of development in Pauline Christianity (see further below). For example, the term *plērōma* (fullness) plays a key role in the distinctive theological visions of Colossians and Ephesians, which stress the expansion and filling up of the universe with divinity (cf. Col 1:9; 2:9; Eph 1:10, 23; 3:19; 4:13). Both Colossians and Ephesians carry Paul's notion of Christ as ruler of the cosmos (Phil 2:6-11) to new heights. The cosmological significance of Christ as the "image of the invisible God" and mediator of creation who is above all powers and alone guarantees salvation is underlined in the hymn of Col 1:15-20 (cf. Eph 1:20-23). Ephesians develops the familiar Pauline theme of the unity of Gentile and Jew, but leaves historical relations largely behind in favor of a cosmic depiction of the reconciliation between the two groups (Eph 2:11-22). In comparison to the undisputed letters of Paul, the symbol of the body of Christ appears transformed in Colossians and Ephesians (e.g., Col 1:18-20, 21-22; 2:9-10, 19; 3:15; Eph 1:22-23; 4:14-16; 5:23, 30). The symbol of the body of Christ sometimes becomes the vehicle for describing the cosmic reconciliation that has taken place through Christ. Now explicitly called the church, the symbol is also articulated in a new way: Christ is the head and the community makes up his body. In both works this type of focus on Christ's authority seems to be related to the development of social structures that stress the authority of the head of the household in family life (Col 3:18–4:1; Eph 5:21–6:9). Both epistles pay detailed attention to ethics (Col 3:5–4:6; Eph 4:1–6:20) and seek to encourage an appropriate way of life through remembrance of baptism (Col 1:12-14; 2:5-9; 3:1-3, 10-11; Eph 1:11-14; 2:1-6; 4:4-6, 22-24, 30; 5:8-14, 25-27).

To make a case for reading Colossians and Ephesians together is not to suggest that there are not important differences between the works. There are a significant number of passages in Colossians that have no parallels in Ephesians (e.g., Col 1:6-8, 15, 17; 2:1-2, 5, 9, 11, 16-18, 20-23) and a great many passages in Ephesians that are without parallel in Colossians (e.g., 2:4, 7-11, 17-20, 22; 4:4-5, 7, 9-12, 14, 17, 21, 26-28, 30; 5:21, 26, 28-29, 31-33; 6:2-3, 10-17, 23-24). Both Colossians and Ephesians refer to *oikonomia* (stewardship), but the term is not used in precisely the same way in these epistles. In Colossians it refers to the commission that God gave Paul to become an apostle (Col 1:25), but in Ephesians it is closely associated with God's plan for the universe (Eph 1:10; 3:2, 9). The Holy Spirit plays a central role in Ephesians (e.g., Eph 1:13-14, 17; 2:18; 4:4-6; 5:18-19), but only a relatively minor role in Colossians (e.g., Col 1:8, 9; 3:16). In any treatment of Colossians we will need to pay special attention to the description of the content of the false teaching in 2:8-23—material that is largely unique to Colossians and very important for discerning the particular circumstances that inspired the epistle. In any treatment of Ephesians we will want to reflect carefully on the significance of the detailed treatment of marriage in Eph 5:22-33, which departs significantly from the brief discussion of marriage in Col 3:18-19. Sometimes subtle differences between parallel texts in Colossians and Ephesians can be most revealing when it comes to discerning the differences of perspective between the two documents. For example, comparison of Col 4:5-6, which speaks of walking in wisdom towards outsiders, to the parallel texts of Eph 5:15-16, which makes no reference to outsiders at all, offers one indication of the decreased interest in dialogue with nonbelievers in Ephesians and the cautious attitude toward outsiders generally (see the notes and interpretation on Col 4:2-6 and Eph 4:17–5:20).

III. *COLOSSIANS*

Who Wrote Colossians?

The authorship of Colossians remains hotly debated. There have been major commentaries that argue for deutero-Pauline authorship (e.g., Lohse; Pokorný), but many commentators still favor Pauline authorship (e.g., Wright; Thurston). In his recent commentary James D. G. Dunn has argued that the solution to the problem of the authorship of Colossians lies somewhere in between. Concluding that Colossians is substantially different from the undisputed letters of Paul, Dunn has argued that Colossians is actually a type of "bridge" document between the undisputed letters of Paul and the later post-Pauline works of Ephesians and the Pastoral Epistles. He suggests that the document may well have been written by Timothy (1:1) while Paul was in prison. According to Dunn, Paul was probably still alive in prison when Colossians was composed and he probably approved of the general substance of the letter, but added only the briefest of conclusions with his own hand (Dunn 269; see my response to Dunn in the notes and interpretation on Col 4:7-18). It is possible here only to give a brief summary of the issues involved in arguments for and against Pauline authorship, but many of these issues are examined in greater detail in the main body of the commentary.

The structure of Colossians closely resembles Paul's letters. Like many of those letters it deals with concrete community concerns. In particular a type of false teaching has evidently taken hold in the community (2:8-23). The author's response to this teaching is reminiscent of Paul's approach in Galatians. Perhaps the most significant argument in favor of the Pauline authorship of Colossians is the nature of the closing remarks in 4:7-18. The fact that they are so personal and seem to speak to concrete community concerns (cf. Eph 6:21-24) adds weight to the case in favor of Pauline authorship. Moreover, these remarks closely resemble Phlm 23-24. This has led to the conclusions that both Onesimus and his master Philemon were from Colossae and that Colossians and Philemon were written at roughly the same time (on the complicated relationship between Philemon and Colossians see the notes and interpretation on 4:7-18).

The authenticity of Colossians has been questioned on the basis of language, thought, and style. For example, Colossians includes many long sentences and demonstrates a tendency to heap synonyms together. In comparison to the undisputed letters it contains a greater number of relative clauses and is notably heavily infused with liturgical influences. As is also true of Ephesians, Colossians lacks the address "my brothers [and sisters]," which appears frequently in Paul's letters and underlines the personal relationship between the apostle and his communities (e.g., Rom 7:4; 1 Cor 1:11; 2 Cor 1:8; Gal 1:11; Phil 4:1; 1 Thess 1:4). In addition, Colossians lacks some key Pauline concepts such as righteousness and justification. The cosmological significance assigned to the Christ event (1:15-20) exceeds what is found in the undisputed letters and Colossians concentrates almost exclusively on the present salvation of believers (e.g., 3:1-3). As for the relationship between Colossians and Philemon, while it may suggest that the apostle was still alive, it might also be explained by a context in which Paul had only recently died. In fact the list of greetings in Colossians is longer and more vivid than the similar list in Philemon, and this can be explained in terms of an attempt to gain a hearing for the letter as a message from Paul. The exhortations concerning Paul's fellow workers in 4:7-18 seem to reflect an awareness that Paul will never again visit Colossae, Hierapolis, or Laodicea and are generally indicative of a changed situation in contrast to the undisputed letters (see the notes and interpretation on Col 4:7-18).

In my opinion some of the most telling evidence in favor of the deutero-Pauline authorship of Colossians comes sharply into view with the aid of a social-scientific perspective. Max Weber has pointed to a crisis caused by the death of the charismatic leader and the subsequent efforts of the "staff" of the leader to secure the survival of the group. Taken together, 1:6-8 and 4:7-18 reflect an effort to reinforce the authority of Paul's co-workers (especially Epaphras and Tychicus) and to emphasize their connection with the apostle (see the notes and interpretation on 1:3-8 and 4:17-18). Perhaps the strongest evidence of the need to exert authority in community life in a new way, however, is the use of the household code in Col 3:18–4:1. The household code teaching is not completely incompatible with Paul's earlier teaching on marriage and slavery (cf. 1 Corinthians 7; 11:2-16; Philemon), but nowhere in the undisputed letters do we find such a code of rules, so clearly embracing the conventional household ethics of the Greco-Roman world. The use of this code is typical of Pauline Christianity in the latter decades of the first century and the beginning of the second century; similar teaching is found in Ephesians, the Pastoral Epistles, and even the writings of some Apostolic Fathers (see the notes and interpretation on 3:18–4:1). These rules seem intent on quieting the desire for a marriage-free life that was typical of Paul, the Corinthians, and many other early Christians. Both the code of 3:18–4:1 and the response to the ascetic false teaching in 2:8-23 offer indications that the author of Colossians stands at some distance from the Paul of 1 Corinthians 7 who preferred celibacy— the ultimate sign that the world was passing away! In this commentary I argue that the household code is an integral part of the author's response to a type of false teaching that threatens to undermine tenuous relations with the outside world. The household code recommends a way of life that allows believers to be physically integrated within the urban centers of the Greco-Roman world, but the symbolism of Colossians, replete with images of a cosmic Christ and a heavenly reign of believers, reminds the recipients that they ultimately belong to another world (see the notes and interpretation on 2:8-15; 2:16-23; 3:18–4:1; 4:2-6).

As many commentators have pointed out, viewing Colossians (or Ephesians) as deutero-Pauline should not be mistakenly understood as meaning that these documents are simply examples of forgery. For example, to write in the name of a philosopher who was one's patron could be seen as a sign of honor bestowed upon that person. The whole process of writing was probably not the same individualistic process that it is today and it may often have involved the active input of a secretary. Paul's ministry was a collaborative enterprise and, like many of Paul's letters, Colossians opens with a statement of co-authorship (on Timothy see the notes and interpretation on 1:1-2). To some extent the deutero-Pauline authorship of Pauline epistles may have flowed from this collaboration. The probable pseudonymous nature of Colossians must be viewed against the extensive body of pseudepigraphal literature produced by Jews and Gentiles in the ancient world (see the excellent summary and discussion of major works on this question in Kitchen 22–29). Ancient pseudepigraphies often reveal the desire to heighten the reputation of religious figures and to circulate their teaching. This desire to enhance Paul's position and reputation can certainly be seen in 1:24–2:7. Moreover, it is important to realize that deutero-Pauline authorship does not inevitably undermine the recognition of Colossians as Scripture (Kitchen 22).

To Whom, When, and Where Was Colossians Written?

Colossians is addressed to "the saints . . . at Colossae." Colossae was located in the Roman province of Asia, and more specifically in the Lycus Valley (now in modern Turkey). Colossae was in close proximity to the two other cities mentioned in the Epistle, Laodicea and Hierapolis (2:1; 4:13-16). There is evidence to suggest that by the first century C.E. Colossae had declined in importance in comparison to these last two cities. The community at Colossae was apparently founded by Epaphras (1:7-8) and Paul was not personally known in the churches of the Lycus Valley (2:1). Given the presence of Jewish elements in the false teaching described in 2:16-23 it is important to note the evidence for a significant Jewish minority in the cities of the Lycus Valley (see discussion of the evidence in Dunn 21–22). It seems that these cities contained several house churches. Colossians 4:15 refers to Nympha and the church in her house. Because of the reference to Laodicea in the same verse it seems most likely that Nympha's church was located there, but Hierapolis and even Colossae itself cannot be ruled out as possible locations for the church in her house (see the notes on 4:15). On the basis of the mention of Onesimus in 4:9 (the runaway slave described in Philemon), Philemon has usually been understood as the leader of a house church in Colossae. But if Colossians was intended for the group that met in this house it is particularly puzzling that Philemon is never mentioned in Colossians (it is similarly strange that Tychicus is never mentioned in Philemon). The instructions in 4:16 for the letter to the Colossians to be read in the church of the Laodiceans and for the Colossians to read the letter to the Laodiceans suggest considerable exchange between the churches—an exchange greatly facilitated by their geographical proximity (on the letter to the Laodiceans see the notes on 4:16).

Gaining historical information about Colossae is hampered by the fact that the site has never been excavated. We know that the Lycus Valley was struck by an earthquake in 60–61 C.E. (Tacitus, *Annals* 14.27.1 mentions the destruction suffered by Laodicea but not Colossae.) This would tend to suggest that the letter must have been written before the event. However, it is impossible to determine the extent of the damage suffered by Colossae. Commentators who argue in favor of Paul's authorship tend to link the letter to the final stages of Paul's career, between about 57 and 63 C.E. The dependency of Ephesians on Colossians has led scholars who argue for deutero-Pauline authorship to favor earlier dates for the epistle (generally before 80 C.E.). If the link between the list of greetings in Philemon and at the end of Colossians reflects historical reality and is not merely an attempt to bolster the authority of Colossians, the date of the deutero-Pauline letter must also be during the last stages of Paul's career (i.e., during his imprisonment) or shortly after his death.

Although it is not of crucial significance for the interpretation of the work, one of the most difficult questions to answer about Colossians is where the epistle was written. The importance one attaches to this question depends to a certain extent on whether one thinks Paul composed the letter. If the epistle was composed after the apostle's death, the imprisonment of Paul (cf. 4:3, 10, 18) functions as a setting that allows him to speak to a community facing his absence and in need of encouragement. Among scholars who treat the letter as composed by Paul there are two locations that have emerged as the probable location of Paul's imprisonment while he composed Colossians: Ephesus (mentioned in a Marcionite prologue) and Rome (the later manuscript tradition includes the subscript that Colossians was written from Rome; see the notes on 4:18 in Metzger 627). Decisions on the matter have depended on the reconstruction of events based on the relationship between Colossians and Philemon and on how the chronology of the letters has been understood. A point in favor of an earlier Ephesian imprisonment is that Ephesus is closer to Colossae than Rome and, consequently, the movement of Onesimus implied by the relationship between Colossians and Philemon becomes easier to understand. (Caesarea is also sometimes suggested as the location for the composition of Colossians and also has proximity in its favor.) In this case both Colossians and Philemon would have been written at about the same time, evidently before 2 Corinthians and Romans. However, the transformed nature of the theology of Colossians points to a time of composition very near the end of Paul's career, and thus suggests Roman imprisonment (see summary of possible scenarios in Dunn 39–41). As noted above, I am convinced that Colossians is deutero-Pauline. In my view the epistle was composed either at the very end of Paul's career, when the circumstances of his imprisonment meant that it was impossible for him to write to his communities, or relatively shortly after his death. Therefore Paul may have been in prison in Rome and it is possible, as Dunn suggests (40), that Timothy wrote in his name (1:1). But this is by no means certain and it is equally possible that Paul was already dead and we, therefore, simply cannot determine the location of the epistle's composition.

The Opponents

With the possible exception of the problem of the authorship of the letter, no issue has received as much attention as the identity of the Colossian opponents that are treated in 2:8-23. But after decades of detailed analysis scholars have failed to arrive at a consensus about the shape of the Colossian "philosophy" (2:8). Some commentators have felt that it was a product of Judaism (e.g., Wright [1986]; Dunn), but others have argued that it was a syncretistic movement, combining Jewish elements with aspects of Paganism (e.g., Lohse). Some have looked to mystery religions (e.g., Dibelius) or Gnosticism (e.g., Pokorný [1991]) for an explanation of the phenomenon. Philosophical traditions such as Stoicism, Pythagoreanism, and, most recently, Cynicism (T. W. Martin) have also figured in theories concerning the identity of the Colossian opponents. The difficulty of determining their identity arises, at least in part, from the fact that the teaching appears to combine a variety of Jewish practices (e.g., the references to food taboos and to the cultic calendar in 2:16) with pagan religious elements (e.g., the use of terminology associated with mystery rites such as *embateuein* in 2:18). In my view the recent work of Clinton Arnold (1995) on the local evidence, including the archeological evidence and inscriptions, has tipped the balance in favor of syncretism (not understood here in any way as the corruption of "pure" religious traditions, but instead as a combination of religious traditions). Arnold's investigation has led him to conclude that the Colossian philosophy was a combination of Phrygian folk belief, local folk Judaism, and Christianity. His work on the meaning of the phrase "the worship of angels" in 2:18 (one of the characteristics of the false teaching) has been especially important. Many recent commentators, influenced by the work of Fred O. Francis, have come to believe that this phrase refers to the participation of believers in some type of angelic liturgy (the worship belonging to angels), but Arnold's research has settled the debate concerning the meaning of this phrase quite conclusively in favor of "worship directed at angels" (for grammatical considerations and other issues related to interpretation of this phrase see the notes on Col 2:18). Moreover, Arnold has demonstrated that the term "angel" was central in the religious life of the people of Asia Minor; the invocation of angels was a common means of protecting people against evil and helping them deal with the affairs of daily life (Arnold 89; for detailed examination of Arnold's work see the notes on Col 2:18 and the notes and interpretation on Col 2:16-23).

I believe that Arnold's work has substantially furthered our understanding of the social context of Colossians, yet it is important to note that, although he has done a good deal to illustrate how the Colossian "philosophy" shares many aspects with the local evidence, the difficulty of making the philosophy fit any one religious group known from antiquity has not been completely eradicated. Rather than seeing the Colossian false teaching as reflecting one syncretistic movement, I am inclined to favor the proposal put forward by some commentators that Colossians is responding to tendencies that may have been shared by a variety of groups (e.g., D'Angelo 319). This is not to suggest that I am convinced by the argument that Colossians does not respond to specific false teachers and there is no real crisis involving false teaching (see especially Hooker 315–31; see also Wright [1986] 26–28; Dunn 24–25). In comparing Colossians to Galatians in particular, some scholars have been struck by the calmer tone of Colossians. For example, the confidence in the faith of the community that is expressed in Col 2:5 has seemed incompatible with the type of crisis situation we know from Galatians. But while Colossians is clearly less "fiery" than Galatians, I am convinced that the threat of false teaching was real and that the document reflects grave concern about the problem of deviance. This can be seen especially in the way it depicts adherence to the false teaching as a type of regression into the world. Adherence to the false teaching means living as though one still belongs to the world (2:20). The Colossian "philosophy" is associated with what is purely human (cf. 2:8, 22). One can, in fact, discern a good deal about the author's views on the problematic nature of false teaching by paying close attention to what is said about the sinful world and the interaction between the community and the broader society (see the notes and interpretation on 4:2-6). I argue in this commentary that the response to false teaching in 2:8-23 is based on the fact that the very boundaries of the community are at stake. But, on account of the difficulty of determining the precise identity of the Colossian opponents, it seems safer to remain open to the possibility that Colossians is responding to several groups that share similar characteristics rather than to one specific group.

The fact that so much energy has gone into attaching the correct label to the problem in Colossae may, in fact, have diverted attention away from the basic issue of why the teaching was so threatening. Although it is possible that 2:8-15 reveals evidence of the language and/or slogans of the opponents, commentators have been confident that we may actually derive information about the content of the false teaching from 2:16, 18, 20-23. Despite the diverse elements of the teaching that are revealed in these verses, they nevertheless share an important point in common. All of them contain polemic against rites and physical markers associated with an ascetic response to the world (see the notes and interpretation on 2:16-23). For example, Col 2:16 and 2:23 refer to dietary regulations and/or fasting. The references to "self-abasement" in 2:18 and 2:23 clearly refer to some type of ascetic practice and perhaps specifically to fasting (see the notes on 2:18). In my view the ascetic component of the Colossian false teaching needs to receive far more attention than it has thus far received; here it is useful to draw upon the extensive research that has been undertaken on asceticism in the ancient world (see the notes and interpretation on 2:16-23). In 2:16-23, with considerable irony, physical markers of identity including fasting and other ascetic practices are depicted as futile and worldly. They have been rendered irrelevant through Christ. The author of Colossians feels that in a profound sense the world must be rejected by believers, but this does not require physical acts of world rejection. It is not surprising that such a strong statement against ascetic false teaching is found in a document that also introduces the household code into Pauline literature for the first time—a code that permanently assigns an important role to marriage in Pauline Christianity (3:18–4:1).

In order to remind believers of what Christ has accomplished and to make the point that the measures recommended by the false teachers are irrelevant, the author of Colossians concentrates on the meaning of baptism. Baptism figures prominently in Colossians and is especially important in chapter two of the epistle (e.g., 2:11-13, 20). An appeal to baptism serves the author well in an attempt to rebuke the repetitive rituals and practices of the opponents because it instills a sense of finality and completion. No further initiatory rites are required. Because of the importance of baptism for Colossians as a whole and for the specific response to the false teaching in 2:8-23 it is likely that the meaning of baptism was central to the dispute with the opponents. Perhaps the relationship between baptism and other rites was in question (see the notes and interpretation on 2:16-23). Social-scientific analysis of ritual, in particular the studies of Victor Turner and Arnold Van Gennep, is employed in this commentary to explore how the meaning of ritual might figure in a community dispute. Such studies can help us understand the role of ritual in constructing a religious vision and the issues involved in the transition from powerful experiences in the midst of ritual to the world of everyday events (see the notes and interpretation on 2:8-15 and 2:16-23). Against an earlier tendency to view religious ideas as always at the heart of disputes in early Christian texts, many scholars are now looking carefully at ritual and social life to explain conflict. There is no doubt that christology is central in Colossians (e.g., 1:15-20) and indeed it plays a key role in the response offered to the opponents. But this focus on christology may well have been part of a larger strategy to outlaw specific ritual and ascetic practices that were understood as incompatible with Christ. It is by no means clear that the opponents had a radically different understanding of Christ than did the author of Colossians (see D'Angelo 320; Attridge 498). In fact, in this commentary it is argued that the "Paul" of Colossians may well share much of the same understanding of Christ as the opponents (see, for example, discussion of "putting off the body of flesh" in the notes on 2:11).

Religious Significance

Any attempt to address the question of the religious significance of Colossians must consider the fact that this document introduced the household code (3:18–4:1) into Pauline Christianity. In our modern context, where many are keenly aware of injustice, it is important to acknowledge that the application and interpretation of this text (particularly its teaching on slavery) produced a legacy of oppression. It is not enough simply to say that the text reflects a first-century way of life. While there is a certain amount of truth to this, we must still grapple with the fact that the author of Colossians appropriated conventional ethics instead of calling for the radical transformation of relations between people. This is especially surprising given the fact that the author speaks of Christ's defeat of cosmic powers with symbolism that prepares the way for a radical questioning of the structures of society (e.g., 2:15). The author may have given these ethics new meaning "in the Lord," but the choice to include them in the work meant that priorities were being articulated in a new way in the Pauline churches. What are we to make of this appropriation of conventional ethics? How can we understand the message of Colossians in light of this appropriation?

First, it is important to acknowledge that NT works that come from the latter decades of the first century and the beginning of the second century C.E. are rooted in an emerging religious group that was becoming increasingly visible in an urban context. It must be admitted that radical transformation of social structures by believers who were part of a minority religious group that was experiencing increasing tension in its relations with the broader social order was really not within the realm of possibility (see the notes and interpretation on 3:18–4:1; 4:2-6). Among the strongest challenges to Greco-Roman social order put forward by some early Christians was their determination to remain unmarried in a society where such efforts elicited mixed reactions at best. Within the broad spectrum of Pauline Christianity, the second-century apocryphal *Acts of Paul and Thecla* reflects the hostility and violent societal reaction that such efforts could produce—especially if undertaken by women who were part of pagan households and whose unwillingness to embrace marriage was interpreted as rebellion (see M. Y. MacDonald [1996]). On the basis of Col 3:18–4:1 one may reasonably conclude that the author of Colossians was not in favor of believers undertaking such challenges to the social order. In fact, the author's response to the false teaching in 2:16-23 suggests that acts of physical renunciation were generally viewed as detrimental to the life of the community.

Second, it is important to realize that Pauline Christians believed that the society surrounding them was profoundly evil (cf. 1:21; 2:13; 3:5-7; this sense of evil becomes even more pronounced in Ephesians). The members of the Colossian community had encountered teachers and/or fellow members of the community who felt that the evil world could only be escaped by means of ascetic practices and rituals (2:16-23). According to these proponents of "philosophy," physical bodies were symbols of a world that had to be overcome. But for the Paul of Colossians the body is not an obstacle to be overcome; it has already been transformed in baptism and believers have already been exalted (2:12-13; 3:1-4). With transformed bodies believers can participate in a new cosmic harmony—one that is free from any cosmic upheaval (2:20).

In my view the central aspect of the religious significance of Colossians is that it offers a vision of human victory in the face of an evil that can reach cosmic proportions. The hope that the author of Colossians holds out to believers would be especially prized in such an apparently hopeless situation. This author calls believers to lead a virtuous life, but also to maintain conventional household existences; at the same time, believers are reminded that they ultimately belong to another world. The dominant social order is ultimately rejected, even though visible and physical signs of world rejection are described as irrelevant. Colossians holds out an image of the cosmic Christ. Explicitly equated with the church (Col 1:18-24), "the body" is also ruled by its head, Christ (1:18; 2:10, 19). But the church and the cosmos merge to a certain extent in Colossians—the church becomes a spiritual and cosmic assembly transcending earthly problems and disputes. Christ is the head not only of the church, but also of every ruler and power (2:10). He holds all things together and restores cosmic harmony (1:15-20). Through the polemic against false teaching in 2:8-23 Colossians reminds believers of the ultimate reality. The visible and physical measures of the false teachers are only a "shadow"; the "reality is the body of Christ" (2:17). No human or heavenly power will thwart the growth of the body, for it is expanding by means of divine intervention (2:19). It is filling the world (1:18-20; 2:9; 3:15).

IV. *EPHESIANS*

Who Wrote Ephesians?

In the early church the authorship of Ephesians was not disputed, but for more than a century the question of whether or not Ephesians was composed by the apostle Paul has been extensively debated. Those who are in favor of Paul's authorship understand the work to have been composed late in his career while he was in prison, probably in Rome (cf. Acts 28:16-31). Differences between the undisputed letters of Paul and Ephesians are accounted for in terms of a change in Paul's thought and style as the end of his career approached. Those who are convinced that the work is pseudonymous, however, believe that the linguistic, stylistic, and theological features of Ephesians cannot be accounted for in this way. Among the most commonly noted features include the use of many words that are not found elsewhere in the Pauline corpus (e.g., "the heavenly places"; cf.

1:3, 20; 2:6; 3:10; 6:12), very long sentences (including much repetition and piling together of synonyms), and an ecclesiology that prefers to speak of the church always as universal and never as the local congregation. Commentators such as F. F. Bruce and Markus Barth have argued that the epistle was composed by Paul, but others such as C. L. Mitton, Rudolf Schnackenburg, and Andrew Lincoln have favored deutero-Pauline authorship. The majority of commentators today consider Ephesians to be deutero-Pauline and this is the position being taken in this commentary. (For the practice of writing pseudonymously in the ancient world see the introductory remarks on Colossians above.)

The many literary parallels between Ephesians and other letters in the Pauline corpus (especially Colossians; see discussion above) have been judged to be especially significant in establishing the deutero-Pauline nature of the epistle. Moreover, such texts as Eph 2:11-22 and 4:1-16 appear to offer a summary of Pauline teaching. Key Pauline themes such as "the unity of Jew and Gentile in one church" and "the many gifts in one body" are taken up and shaped to address what seems like a broad social context. In fact, in Ephesians it seems as if Paul is made to speak to a changed situation. Moreover, the epistle looks back to "the apostles and prophets" (2:20; cf. 3:5) and, in keeping with Jewish pseudepigraphy in particular, seems to construct an image of Paul as an authoritative figure from the past (see Kitchen 28; cf. 3:1-13). The attempt to present an adequate summary of Paul's teaching and to offer the apostle's direction in a new context has been judged by some as central to the purpose of the work. For E. J. Goodspeed (1933) this aspect of Ephesians seemed so crucial that he put forward the theory that the author of Ephesians was the collector of Paul's letters and that Ephesians was actually written as an introduction to the corpus. The specific details of Goodspeed's theory are impossible to verify, but it has had a broad impact on how Ephesians has been understood. Many commentators have accepted the general idea that Ephesians did spring from a relationship between the other letters in the Pauline corpus and that one purpose of the work is to provide guidance on the meaning of Paul's message for a new day. It should be noted that even within the NT itself we have evidence that Paul's teaching was subject to a variety of interpretations and led to controversy (2 Pet 3:15-16). It is no exaggeration to say that Ephesians constitutes the first interpretation of and guide to Pauline tradition in light of the disappearance of Paul. While in all likelihood Colossians was the earliest deutero-Pauline writing, Colossians does not reflect the same sustained effort to summarize Paul's teaching as we find in Ephesians. The frequent allusions to Jewish Scripture (though there are very few direct quotations), the many parallels with the Qumran Library, and the interest in clarifying the relationship between the Gentile church and Israel (cf. 2:11-22) are factors that have led many commentators to conclude that the author was a Jewish Christian member of the Pauline churches.

To Whom, When, and Where Was Ephesians Written?

Ephesians presents its readers with many interpretative puzzles. The very intention of the author of Ephesians to write to a community in Ephesus cannot be taken for granted. In the translation of the epistle offered in this commentary the words "who are in Ephesus" are placed in square brackets to indicate that manuscript variations with respect to this verse make it impossible to draw firm conclusions about geographic specificity. The words "in Ephesus" *(en Ephesō)* are missing from several important witnesses. Moreover, the superscription "To the Ephesians" was not part of the original document, with definite evidence for its use coming only at the end of the second century C.E. It is most likely that the words "in Ephesus" were originally missing (see the detailed discussion in the notes on 1:1). Scholars have come up with several theories to explain this gap, but all of them remain highly speculative. Among the most famous is the notion that Ephesians was an encyclical designed to reach several churches. The NT itself offers examples of documents that were intended for several congregations (cf. 1 Pet 1:1; Rev 1:4). Recently Andrew Lincoln (1990), taking up some of the suggestions of A. van Roon, has argued on the basis of the grammatical difficulties in the address that it originally included two place names. He suggests that because of the close link between Colossians and Ephesians these names were in all likelihood Hierapolis and Laodicea (Lincoln [1990] 3–4; cf. Col 2:1-3; 4:15-16). Moreover, the early church author Marcion designated the epistle as "To the Laodiceans" (for more detailed discussion see the notes and interpretation on 1:1-2).

Despite the impossibility of proving the various theories about the intended audience of Ephesians, the general tone of the document does suggest that it was meant for more than one church community. When Ephesians is compared to the other letters of the Pauline corpus it quickly becomes apparent that the document lacks the usual references to particular community concerns. The references and greetings to members of the community customarily found at the end of letters are virtually absent (cf. 6:21). In this way Ephesians is significantly different from Colossians, which includes extensive material concerning Paul's fellow workers and associates (cf. Col 4:7-18). In short, it is by no means easy to discern the specific circumstances that inspired the letter (see further below). About the only thing we can conclude with certainty about the letter's recipients is that they were predominantly Gentiles (2:11). The author sometimes distinguishes "we" (Jewish Christians associated with the author) from "you" (the Gentile recipients of the letter; but for other possible interpretations and full discussion of this distinction see the notes on 1:12).

Those who argue that Paul wrote Ephesians usually understand both Colossians and Ephesians to have been composed late in the apostle's career. Frequently Paul's imprisonment in Rome is understood as the original historical context of composition. Those in favor of deutero-Pauline authorship offer suggestions about dating based on the dependence of Ephesians on Colossians and indications of development within the text itself. For example, the perspective of Ephesians is of a "built-up" church looking back to its origins (e.g., 2:19-20). It seems that the Pauline churches have made a transition into a new generation. Frequently a date in the latter decades of the first century C.E. has been suggested (80–90 C.E.). If indeed Ephesians is deutero-Pauline, it is impossible to determine where it was composed. However, the traditional association of the document with Ephesus, the connection with Colossians, and the general ethos of the document suggest that we should look toward the cities of Asia Minor as providing the setting for the epistle's composition.

The Nature and Purpose of Ephesians

Like the question of the identity of the Colossian false teachers, the nature and purpose of Ephesians have been the subject of extensive debate. The lack of reference to specific church matters, coupled with a liturgical-catechetical style, has led to the suggestion that it is perhaps best to view the work mainly as a liturgical tract or a sermon rather than as a letter in the usual sense—that is, as a theological work merely cast in the form of a letter. It has been argued, for example, that the first three chapters might be viewed essentially as one long thanksgiving (e.g., J. T. Sanders). But it should be noted that in most respects Ephesians keeps to the usual form of a Pauline letter. There is the customary salutation (1:1-2), thanksgiving for the good conduct of believers (1:15-23), and a conclusion, including a blessing (6:21-24). As in some of the other Pauline letters, including Colossians, a section containing ethical exhortations (4:1–6:20) follows a more theological section (1:3–3:21; although this section is heavily influenced by liturgical forms). Therefore it is probably best to view the work as a letter that has been greatly influenced by liturgy rather than as a liturgical tract or sermon per se.

The extensive liturgical influences on Ephesians have been understood by some commentators as the key to unlocking the purpose of the epistle. Nils A. Dahl (1951), for example, argued that Eph 1:3-14 is rooted in a blessing uttered before baptism, and that Ephesians is best understood as giving Gentile believers instructions on the meaning of their baptism. Similarly, J. C. Kirby focused on the importance of baptism in

Ephesians, investigating the relationship between early Christian rites and Jewish liturgical traditions. It is probably fair to say that theories linking the purpose of Ephesians with liturgy have somewhat fallen out of favor. However, in this commentary it is argued that rituals were of key importance to the community life of the recipients and central to shaping the message of the letter. Not only is baptism important to consider (the influence of baptism is less explicit in Ephesians than in Colossians where it clearly figures in the dispute with false teachers), but we must also address the influence of Spirit-inspired hymns, songs, and rites that may well have involved heavenly visions (see, for example, the notes and interpretation on 1:15-23; 5:18-20).

Biblical scholars have probably turned most frequently to Eph 2:11-22 in the hope of shedding light on the communal context of Ephesians (e.g., Käsemann [1968]; Sampley). Commentators have sometimes understood this passage as a lesson directed at Gentile Christians who were in danger of divorcing themselves from Jewish origins (cf. Rom 11:17-32). The teaching was intended to smooth away tense relations between Jews and Gentiles; thus the accomplished unity of Jew and Gentile is proclaimed. But as has been frequently noted, there are problems with this theory that surpass even the obvious fact that there is no specific mention of tension between Jews and Gentiles in the church. In the first place, the recipients are described as Gentiles (2:11) and the author goes so far as to equate Israel with the church without acknowledging the presence of Jews outside the church who are part of the historical Israel (see the notes and interpretation on 2:11-22). This is particularly puzzling given the fact that most commentators believe that the author of Ephesians was a Jewish Christian who employed categories of thought reminiscent of the QL (see, for example, the notes and interpretation on 1:3-14; 3:1-13; 4:17–5:20). Ephesians clearly moves in the direction of the establishment of Christianity as a separate religion even though it views Christian history as rooted in Jewish heritage. To think of a serious problem between Jewish and Gentile believers underlying Ephesians is to go beyond the constraints of the evidence. But an examination of the relationship among Ephesians, 1 Peter, and Acts—the last two being works that come from the same approximate period and have much in common with Ephesians—suggests that it is certainly within the realm of possibility that Eph 2:11-22 spoke in general to the realities of a community comprised of a Gentile majority and a dwindling Jewish minority (see the notes and interpretation on 2:11-22).

Three remaining theories concerning the occasion of Ephesians should be considered here. As noted above, some commentators have argued that the purpose of Ephesians is essentially to summarize and interpret Paul's teaching for a new generation (e.g., Goodspeed; Mitton). The recipients of the letter can hear Paul's voice, feel his presence, and gain his direction. In this commentary the tremendous authority granted to Paul as the sole author of Ephesians (unlike most of Paul's letters, the work is not co-authored) is analyzed from a sociological perspective. By concentrating on the efforts of Paul's fellow workers the author of Colossians put measures into effect that would allow the Pauline churches to survive beyond the death of the charismatic leader, Paul. In contrast, Ephesians highlights the role of *the* Apostle to the Gentiles (cf. 1:1-2; 3:1-13). But Paul's role is cast as forming part of an apostolic foundation and there are indications that new leadership structures are forming in the community to deal with the disappearance of Paul and with the other challenges experienced by the church as it made its way toward the second century. In particular there is increasing emphasis on the role of the teacher (see the notes and interpretation on 4:1-16).

It has sometimes been argued that Ephesians responds to a particular group of false teachers. For example, Michael D. Goulder has argued that Ephesians responds to Jewish Christian visionaries (see my detailed response to Goulder in the notes and interpretation on 1:15-23). But Gnostic opponents have most frequently been suggested (e.g., Schlier [1957]; Pokorný [1965]). Second- and third-century Gnostic writers appealed to Ephesians and there are some parallels between the images found in Ephesians and later Gnostic thought (see, for example, the notes on 5:23, 32). However, there is no direct evidence of the use of specifically Gnostic terms or concepts. Moreover, the view that Ephesians is responding to a particular group of opponents is difficult to support since only in one place is there a general reference to false teachers (4:14). The contrast with Colossians here is particularly striking, especially given the dependence of Ephesians on Colossians and the extensive parallelism. The most that can be claimed about false teaching underlying Ephesians is that this threat was one of many issues community members were warned to guard against.

Finally, any survey of the theories concerning the nature and purpose of Ephesians would not be complete without considering the contribution of Clinton Arnold (1989) to our understanding of this letter. Arnold's theories are constructed on the basis of an Asia Minor context and, in particular, on the importance of Ephesus as a center for magical practices. Arnold argues that the recipients of Ephesians felt threatened by the influence of hostile spiritual powers, and that the author reassures them of the supremacy of Christ over any such powers. Although Arnold has been criticized for concentrating too exclusively on one particular theme (Lincoln [1990] lxxxi), he has made an extremely valuable contribution in highlighting the importance of the theme of power in Ephesians.

I count myself among a growing number of commentators who are reluctant to make one proposal to explain the entire context of the letter (e.g., Barth; Lincoln [1990]; Thurston). The best solution to the dilemma seems to be to affirm that the work had more than one purpose. In the most general terms Ephesians responds to the situation of a community dealing with the disappearance of Paul and the increased dangers of deviant behavior that come with the incorporation of a new generation.

Analyzing the author's response from a social-scientific perspective has, however, helped me to gain a greater understanding of the context. In particular it has helped me to appreciate a central challenge facing the recipients of Ephesians that has received very little attention from commentators. Recent work highlighting the extensive parallels between Ephesians and the QL (e.g., Perkins) has drawn my attention to the fact that Ephesians reveals a stronger introversionist sectarian response than the other Pauline epistles, including Colossians (see the notes and interpretation on 1:3-14; 1:15-23; 2:1-10; 3:14-21; 6:10-20). Community members feel threatened by spiritual powers that shape an evil outside world (e.g., 1:21; 2:2; 6:10-20). These spiritual powers are understood as inseparably linked to the evil that believers witness in their everyday lives (2:2). Believers are urged to set themselves apart from those around them as saints (holy ones) —in essence to turn into the church and away from the non-believing world. Despite an awareness of the goal of church expansion and the importance of universal mission, Ephesians displays very little interest in dialogue between believers and non-believers. Instead the evil of the Gentile world is described in uncompromising terms and the boundaries of the community are reinforced (2:1-3; 4:17–5:20; 6:10-20). The attention paid to the identity of the church in Ephesians is intended to strengthen the community (2:11-22; 4:1-16). Believers are depicted as dwelling with Christ already, having undertaken a journey of heavenly ascent (2:6). They have largely escaped the everyday world though they remain integrated within society in household units determined to demonstrate the highest virtue (4:17–6:9). Virtue is the armor that will protect them against all menacing forces (6:10-20). It would be to go beyond the constraints of the evidence to suggest that community members are being persecuted, but they are almost certainly experiencing some hostility at the hands of outsiders (see the notes on 2:12; 5:6, 12, 18; 6:16; see the interpretation on 2:11-22; 6:10-20).

Religious Significance

As in the case of Colossians, the presence of the household code in Eph 5:21–6:9 poses particular problems for determining the religious significance of Ephesians. Ephesians concentrates on the marriage relationship (5:22-33). While this relationship is infused with religious significance by the Christ-church and husband-wife comparison, there is no doubt that hierarchical relations in marriage are reinforced. Those who seek to explain the meaning of Ephesians in a modern context need to warn against the interpretative difficulties raised by the marriage metaphor. The association of Christ with the husband should not be taken to mean that the husband is more closely aligned with divinity than the wife (who is the image of the human church community). It should be noted, however, that marriage receives an unqualified endorsement as valuable for Christian life in Ephesians; it mirrors the very nature of the relationship between humanity and the divine.

The conventional household ethics of Ephesians take their place in a document that reflects an even stronger sense of evil in the world than does Colossians (cf. Eph 2:1-3; 4:17–5:20). But the salvation of believers could not be expressed in stronger terms. The author of Ephesians concentrates so directly on God's gift of salvation that the themes of election and predestination come to the fore (e.g., 1:3-14). In Eph 3:19 we have what may well be the strongest expression in the NT of the desire for human union with God. While the notion of a future deliverance is by no means eclipsed (e.g., 1:13-14; 6:13), believers are depicted as already seated with Christ in the heavenly places (2:6). Ephesians announces the possibility of a human church community participating in heavenly citizenship. It promises a safe haven in a world tormented by evil spiritual powers (e.g., 2:2).

Perhaps more than any other NT writing Ephesians concentrates on the identity of the church. This is not, as is sometimes claimed, at the expense of christology. The universal church exists on the basis of what God has accomplished through Christ (cf. 1:3-14). In my view the most enduring legacy of Ephesians is the way it establishes peace, love, and unity as priorities for the church. The church is the place where peace is made manifest through the blood of the cross—the place where all barriers must be broken down (2:13-14). Love in imitation of Christ is the virtue that actualizes Christ's sacrifice and shapes community life (e.g., 5:2, 25). Unity is the product that results from God's interaction with the world. The unity of Jew and Gentile is God's mystery revealed in the world (3:4-6). Unity should characterize the smallest cell of believers—the household (5:21–6:9; see especially 5:31-32)—and extend to the universal church (e.g., 2:15-16). Through the unified church God's wisdom will be made known to the spiritual powers in the heavenly places (3:10).

GENERAL BIBLIOGRAPHY

More specialized references are included in the bibliographies that follow each section of the commentary. Books listed below and in the section bibliographies are referred to in an abbreviated form in the Introduction and throughout the commentary.

Commentaries:

Aletti, Jean-Noël. *Saint Paul. Épître aux Colossiens.* EtB. Paris: J. Gabalda, 1993.

Barth, Markus. *Ephesians.* 2 vols. AB 34, 34A. Garden City, N.Y.: Doubleday, 1974.

Barth, Markus, and Helmut Blanke. *Colossians: A New Translation and Commentary.* AB 34B. New York: Doubleday, 1994.

Best, Ernest. *Ephesians.* ICC. Edinburgh: T & T Clark, 1998.

Bouttier, Michel. *L'Epître de Saint Paul aux Ephésiens.* Commentaire du Nouveau Testament 9b. Geneva: Labor et Fides, 1991.

Bruce, F. F. *The Epistles to the Colossians, to Philemon, and to the Ephesians.* NICNT. Grand Rapids: Eerdmans, 1984.

Caird, G. B. *Paul's Letters from Prison.* Oxford: Oxford University Press, 1976.

Conzelmann, Hans. "Der Brief an die Epheser" in Jürgen Becker, Hans Conzelmann, and Gerhard Friedrich, eds., *Die Briefe an die Galater, Epheser, Philipper, Kolosser, Thessalonicher und Philemon.* Göttingen: Vandenhoeck & Ruprecht, 1976, 86–124.

D'Angelo, Mary Rose. "Colossians," in Elisabeth Schüssler Fiorenza, ed., *Searching the Scriptures 2. A Feminist Commentary.* New York: Crossroad, 1993, 313–24.

Donelson, Lewis R. *Colossians, Ephesians, First and Second Timothy, and Titus.* Louisville: Westminster/John Knox, 1996.

Dunn, James D. G. *The Epistles to the Colossians and to Philemon: A Commentary on the Greek Text.* NIGTC. Grand Rapids: Eerdmans, 1996.

Gnilka, Joachim. *Der Epheserbrief.* Freiburg: Herder, 1971.

_____. *Der Kolosserbrief.* HThKNT 10/1. Freiburg: Herder, 1980.

Harris, Murray J. *Colossians and Philemon.* Exegetical Guide to the Greek New Testament. Grand Rapids: Eerdmans, 1991.

Hendriksen, William. *New Testament Commentary: Exposition of Ephesians.* Grand Rapids: Baker Book House, 1967.

Horgan, Maurya. "The Letter to the Colossians," in Raymond E. Brown, Joseph Fitzmyer, and Roland Murphy, eds., *The New Jerome Biblical Commentary.* Englewood Cliffs, N.J.: Prentice Hall, 1990, 876–82.

Houlden, J. L. *Paul's Letters from Prison.* Pelican New Testament Commentaries. London: S.C.M., 1977.

Johnson, E. Elizabeth. "Colossians," in Carol A. Newsom and Sharon H. Ringe, eds., *The Women's Bible Commentary.* Louisville: Westminster/John Knox, 1992, 346–48.

_____. "Ephesians," in Newsom and Ringe, eds., *The Women's Bible Commentary* (1992) 338–42.

Kobelski, Paul J. "The Letter to the Ephesians," in Brown, Fitzmyer, and Murphy, eds., *The New Jerome Bible Commentary* (1990) 883–90.

Lightfoot, J. B. *St. Paul's Epistles to the Colossians and to Philemon.* London and New York: Macmillan, 1879.

Lincoln, Andrew T. *Ephesians.* WBC 42. Dallas: Word Books, 1990.

Lohse, Eduard. *Colossians and Philemon.* Hermeneia. Philadelphia: Fortress, 1971.

MacDonald, Margaret Y. "Ephesians," in William R. Farmer, et al., eds., *The International Bible Commentary: A Catholic and Ecumenical Commentary for the Twenty-First Century.* Collegeville: The Liturgical Press, 1998, 1670–86.

Martin, Ralph P. *Colossians and Philemon.* NCBC. London: Oliphants, 1974, 53–66.

Masson, Charles. *L'Epître de Saint Paul aux Colossiens.* CNT 10. Neuchâtel: Delachaux, 1950.

Mitton, C. Leslie. *Ephesians.* London: Oliphants, 1976.

Moule, C. F. D. *The Epistles of Paul the Apostle to the Colossians and to Philemon.* CGTC. Cambridge: Cambridge University Press, 1957.

O'Brien, Peter T. *Colossians, Philemon.* WBC 44. Waco, Tex.: Word Books, 1982.

Patzia, Arthur G. *Ephesians, Colossians, Philemon.* Peabody, Mass.: Hendrickson, 1984.

Perkins, Pheme. *Ephesians.* ANTC. Nashville: Abingdon, 1997.

Pokorný, Petr. *Colossians: A Commentary.* Peabody, Mass.: Hendrickson, 1991.

Schlier, Heinrich. *Der Brief an die Epheser.* Dusseldorf: Patmos, 1957.

Schnackenburg, Rudolf. *Ephesians: A Commentary.* Translated by Helen Heron. Edinburgh: T & T Clark, 1991.

Schweizer, Eduard. *The Letter to the Colossians.* London: S.P.C.K., 1982.

Tanzer, Sarah. "Ephesians," in Elisabeth Schüssler Fiorenza, ed., *Searching the Scriptures 2. A Feminist Commentary,* 325–47.

Taylor, Walter F., and John H. P. Reumann. *Ephesians, Colossians.* ACNT. Minneapolis: Augsburg, 1985.

Thurston, Bonnie Bowman. *Reading Colossians, Ephesians, and 2 Thessalonians: A Literary and Theological Commentary.* New York: Crossroad, 1996.

Wolter, Michael. *Der Brief an die Kolosser. Der Brief an Philemon.* ÖTK 12. Gütersloh: Gerd Mohn; Würzburg: Echter, 1993.

Wright, N. T. *The Epistles of Paul to the Colossians and to Philemon: An Introduction and Commentary.* TNTC. Grand Rapids: Inter-Varsity, 1986.

Yates, Roy. *The Epistle to the Colossians.* EC. London: Epworth, 1993.

Studies:

Aletti, Jean-Noël. *Colossiens 1:15-20.* Rome: Biblical Institute, 1981.

Arnold, Clinton E. *Ephesians, Power and Magic: The Concept of Power in Ephesians in the Light of its Historical Setting.* MSSNTS 63. Cambridge: Cambridge University Press, 1989.

————. *The Colossian Syncretism: The Interface between Christianity and Folk Belief at Colossae.* Tübingen: J.C.B. Mohr (Paul Siebeck), 1995.

Attridge, Harold A. "On Becoming an Angel: Rival Baptismal Theologies at Colossae," in Lukas Bormann, Kelly Del Tredici, and Angela Standhartinger, eds., *Religious Propaganda and Missionary Competition in the New Testament World: Essays Honoring Dieter Georgi.* Leiden: E. J. Brill, 1994, 481–98.

Balch, David L. "Household Codes," in David E. Aune, ed., *Greco-Roman Literature and the New Testament*. Atlanta: Scholars, 1988.

Berger, Peter L., and Thomas Luckmann. *The Social Construction of Reality*. Garden City, N.Y.: Doubleday, 1966.

Best, Ernest. *One Body in Christ. A study in the relationship of the Church to Christ in the Epistles of the Apostle Paul*. London: S.P.C.K., 1955.

Blasi, Anthony J. *Making Charisma: The Social Construction of Paul's Public Image*. New Brunswick, N.J.: Transaction, 1991.

Boer, Martinus C. de. "Images of Paul in the Post-Apostolic Period," *CBQ* 42 (1980) 359–80.

Bony, Paul. "L'Epître aux Ephésiens," in *Le ministère et les ministères selon le Nouveau Testament*. Paris: Editions du Seuil, 1974, 74–92.

Brown, Peter. *The Body and Society: Men, Women, and Sexual Renunciation in Early Christianity*. New York: Columbia University Press, 1988.

Brown, Raymond E. *The Churches the Apostles Left Behind*. London: Geoffrey Chapman, 1984.

Bujard, Walter. *Stilanalytische Untersuchungen zum Kolosserbrief als Beitrag zur Methodik von Sprachvergleichen*. SUNT 11. Göttingen: Vandenhoeck & Ruprecht, 1973.

Cameron, Averil. *Christianity and the Rhetoric of the Empire: The Development of Christian Discourse*. Berkeley: University of California Press, 1991.

Caragounis, Chrys C. *The Ephesian Mysterion: Meaning and Content*. Lund: Gleerup, 1977.

Carr, Wesley. *Angels and Principalities: The Background, Meaning and Development of the Pauline Phrase "hai archai kai hai . . . exousiai."* MSSNTS 42. Cambridge: Cambridge University Press, 1981.

Conzelmann, Hans. "Die Schule des Paulus," in Carl Andresen and Gunter Klein, eds., *Theologia Crucis, Signum Crucis. Festschrift für Erich Dinkler zum 70. Geburtstag*. Tübingen: J.C.B. Mohr (Paul Siebeck), 1979.

Countryman, L. William. *Dirt, Greed, and Sex: Sexual Ethics in the New Testament and Their Implications for Today*. Philadelphia: Fortress, 1988.

Crouch, James E. *The Origin and Intention of the Colossian Haustafel*. Göttingen: Vandenhoeck & Ruprecht, 1972.

Dahl, Nils A. "Adresse und Proömium des Epheserbriefes," *ThZ* 7 (1951) 241–64.

_____. "Anamnesis: Memory and Commemoration in the Early Church," in idem, *Jesus in the Memory of the Early Church: Essays*. Minneapolis: Augsburg, 1976, 11–29.

Deichgräber, R. *Gotteshymnus und Christushymnus in der frühen Christenheit*. Göttingen: Vandenhoeck & Ruprecht, 1967.

Dibelius, Martin. "The Isis Initiation in Apuleius and Related Initiatory Rites," in Fred O. Francis and Wayne A. Meeks, eds., *Conflict at Colossae*. Missoula: Scholars, 1975, 61–121.

Dubisch, Jill. *Gender and Power in Rural Greece*. Princeton, N.J.: Princeton University Press, 1986.

Eisenstadt, S. N., ed. *Max Weber on Charisma and Institution Building; Selected Papers*. Chicago and London: University of Chicago Press, 1968.

Eliade, Mircea. *Rites and Symbols of Initiation: The Mysteries of Birth and Rebirth.* Translated by Willard R. Trask. New York: Harper & Row, 1958.

Elliott, John H. *A Home for the Homeless: A Sociological Exegesis of 1 Peter, Its Situation and Strategy.* London: S.C.M., 1982.

_____. *What is Social-Scientific Criticism?* Minneapolis: Fortress, 1993.

Esler, Philip F. *Community and Gospel in Luke-Acts.* Cambridge: Cambridge University Press, 1987.

_____. *The First Christians in Their Social Worlds: Social-Scientific Approaches to New Testament Interpretation.* London and New York: Routledge, 1994.

Evans, Craig. "The Colossian Mystics," *Biblica* 63 (1982) 188–205.

Feldman, Louis H. *Jew and Gentile in the Ancient World.* Princeton, N.J.: Princeton University Press, 1993.

Fischer, Karl Martin. *Tendenz und Absicht des Epheserbriefs.* FRLANT 111. Göttingen: Vandenhoeck & Ruprecht, 1973.

Fox, Robin Lane. *Pagans and Christians in the Mediterranean World from the Second Century AD to the Conversion of Constantine.* Harmondsworth: Penguin, 1988.

Francis, Fred O. "Humility and Angelic Worship in Col 2:18," in Francis and Meeks, eds., *Conflict at Colossae,* 163–95.

Furnish, Victor P. *Theology and Ethics in Paul.* Nashville: Abingdon, 1968.

Gager, John G. *Kingdom and Community: The Social World of Early Christianity.* Englewood Cliffs, N.J.: Prentice Hall, 1975.

Geertz, Clifford. "Religion as a Cultural System," in Michael Banton, ed., *Anthropological Approaches to the Study of Religion.* Association of Social Anthropologists Monographs 3. London: Tavistock, 1966, 1–46.

Gilmore, David, ed. "Introduction: The Shame of Dishonor," in *Honor and Shame and the Unity of the Mediterranean.* Washington, D.C.: American Anthropological Association, 1987, 5–8.

Goodspeed, Edgar J. *The Meaning of Ephesians.* Chicago: University of Chicago Press, 1933.

Goulder, Michael D. "The Visionaries of Laodicea," *JSNT* 43 (1991) 15–39.

Holmberg, Bengt. *Paul and Power: The Structure of Authority in the Primitive Church as Reflected in the Pauline Epistles.* Philadelphia: Fortress, 1980.

_____. *Sociology and the New Testament: An Appraisal.* Minneapolis: Fortress, 1990.

Hooker, Morna D. "Were There False Teachers in Colossae?" in *Christ and Spirit in the New Testament.* Edited by Barnabas Lindars and Stephen S. Smalley in honour of Charles Francis Digby Moule. Cambridge: Cambridge University Press, 1973, 315–31.

Judge, Edwin A. "The Social Identity of the First Christians: A Question of Method in Religious History," *JRH* 11 (1980) 201–17.

Käsemann, Ernst. "A Primitive Christian Baptismal Liturgy," in idem, *Essays on New Testament Themes.* London: S.C.M., 1964, 149–68.

_____. "Ephesians and Acts," in Leander E. Keck and J. Louis Martyn, eds., *Studies in Luke-Acts.* London: S.P.C.K., 1968, 288–97.

Kiley, Mark C. *Colossians as Pseudepigraphy.* Sheffield: JSOT Press, 1986.

Kirby, John C. *Ephesians: Baptism and Pentecost: An Inquiry into the Structure and Purpose of the Epistle to the Ephesians.* London: S.P.C.K., 1968.

Kitchen, Martin. *Ephesians.* London and New York: Routledge, 1994.

Kuhn, Karl G. "The Epistle to the Ephesians in the Light of the Qumran Texts," in Jerome Murphy-O'Connor, ed., *Paul and Qumran.* London: Geoffrey Chapman, 1968, 115–31.

Lafontaine, Jean S. *Initiation: Ritual Drama and Secret Knowledge Across the World.* Harmondsworth: Penguin, 1985.

Lindemann, Andreas. *Die Aufhebung der Zeit: Geschichtsverständnis und Eschatologie im Epheserbrief.* Gütersloh: Gerd Mohn, 1975.

Lincoln, Andrew T. *Paradise Now and Not Yet.* MSSNTS 43. Cambridge: Cambridge University Press, 1981.

Lincoln, Andrew T., and A. J. M. Wedderburn. *The Theology of the Later Pauline Letters.* Cambridge: Cambridge University Press, 1993.

MacDonald, Margaret Y. *The Pauline Churches: A Socio-Historical Study of Institutionalization in the Pauline and Deutero-Pauline Writings.* MSSNTS 60. Cambridge: Cambridge University Press, 1988.

_____. *Early Christian Women and Pagan Opinion: The Power of the Hysterical Woman.* Cambridge: Cambridge University Press, 1996.

_____. "Citizens of Heaven and Earth: Asceticism and Social Integration in Colossians and Ephesians," in Leif Vaage and Vincent L. Wimbush, eds., *Asceticism and the New Testament.* New York: Routledge, 1999, 269–98.

Malina, Bruce J. *The New Testament World: Insights from Cultural Anthropology.* Atlanta: John Knox; London: S.C.M., 1981.

_____. "Jesus as Charismatic Leader," *BTB* 14 (1984) 55–62.

Malina, Bruce J., and Jerome H. Neyrey. "Honor and Shame in Luke-Acts: Pivotal Values of the Mediterranean World," in Bruce J. Malina and Jerome H. Neyrey, eds., *The Social World of Luke-Acts: Models for Interpretation.* Peabody, Mass.: Hendrickson, 1991, 25–65.

_____. *Portraits of Paul: An Archaeology of Ancient Personality.* Louisville: Westminster/John Knox, 1996.

Martin, Dale B. *Slavery as Salvation: The Metaphor of Slavery in Pauline Christianity.* New Haven and London: Yale University Press, 1990.

_____. *The Corinthian Body.* New Haven and London: Yale University Press, 1995.

Martin, Troy W. *By Philosophy and Empty Deceit: Colossians as Response to a Cynic Critique.* JSNT.S 118. Sheffield: Sheffield Academic Press, 1996.

Meeks, Wayne A. "In One Body: The Unity of Humankind in Colossians and Ephesians," in Wayne A. Meeks and Jacob Jervell, eds., *God's Christ and His People: Studies in Honour of Nils Alstrup Dahl.* Oslo, Bergen, and Tromsö: Universitetsforlaget, 1977, 209–21.

_____. *The First Urban Christians: The Social World of the Apostle Paul.* New Haven and London: Yale University Press, 1983.

Metzger, Bruce M. *A Textual Commentary on the Greek New Testament.* Stuttgart: United Bible Societies, 1975.

Miletic, Stephen F. *"One Flesh": Eph 5.22-24, 5.31: Marriage and the New Creation.* AnBib 115. Rome: Pontifical Biblical Institute, 1988.

Mitton, C. Leslie. *The Epistle to the Ephesians.* Oxford: Clarendon Press, 1951.

Moule, C. F. D. *An Idiom Book of New Testament Greek.* 2nd ed. Cambridge: Cambridge University Press, 1971.

Moulton, J. H. *A Grammar of New Testament Greek.* 3 vols. Vol. 2: J. H. Moulton and Wilbert Francis Howard; Vol. 3: Nigel Turner. Edinburgh: T & T Clark, 1908–63.

Percy, Ernst. *Die Probleme der Kolosser-und Epheserbriefe.* Lund: Gleerup, 1946.

Pokorný, Petr. *Der Epheserbrief und die Gnosis.* Berlin: Evangelische Verlagsanstalt, 1965.

Robinson, John A. T. *The Body.* Philadelphia: Westminster, 1952.

Rohrbaugh, Richard, ed. *The Social Sciences and New Testament Interpretation.* Peabody, Mass.: Hendrickson, 1996.

Roon, A. van. *The Authenticity of Ephesians.* Leiden: Brill, 1974.

Rosaldo, Michelle Zimbalist. "The Use and Abuse of Anthropology: Reflections on Feminism and Cross-Cultural Understandings," *Signs* 5 (1980) 389–417.

Rosaldo, Michelle Zimbalist, and Louise Lamphere, eds. *Woman, Culture, and Society.* Stanford: Stanford University Press, 1974.

Rowland, Christopher. "Apocalyptic Visions and the Exaltations of Christ in the Letter to the Colossians," *JSNT* 19 (1983) 73–83.

Sampley, J. Paul. *"And the Two Shall Become One Flesh": A Study of Traditions in Eph 5:21-33.* Cambridge: Cambridge University Press, 1971.

Sanders, E. P. "Literary Dependence in Colossians," *JBL* 85 (1966) 28–45.

_____. *Paul, the Law, and the Jewish People.* Philadelphia: Fortress, 1983.

Sanders, J. T. "The Transition from Opening Epistolary Thanksgiving to Body in the Letters of the Pauline Corpus," *JBL* 81 (1962) 348–62.

_____. "Hymnic Elements in Ephesians 1–3," *ZNW* 56 (1965) 214–32.

_____. *The New Testament Christological Hymns.* MSSNTS 15. Cambridge: Cambridge University Press, 1971.

_____. *Schismatics, Sectarians, Dissidents, Deviants: The First One Hundred Years of Jewish-Christian Relations.* Valley Forge, Pa.: Trinity Press International, 1993.

Schille, Gottfried. *Frühchristliche Hymnen.* Berlin: Evangelische Verlagsanstalt, 1965.

Schlier, Heinrich. *Christus und die Kirche im Epheserbrief.* Tübingen: J.C.B. Mohr, 1930.

Schüssler Fiorenza, Elisabeth. *In Memory of Her: A Feminist Theological Reconstruction of Christian Origins.* New York: Crossroad, 1983.

Sumney, Jerry. "Those who 'Pass Judgement': The identity of the Opponents in Colossians," *Biblica* 74 (1993) 366–88.

Tannehill, Robert C. *Dying and Rising with Christ: a Study in Pauline Theology.* BZNW 32. Berlin: A. Topelmann, 1967.

Theissen, Gerd. *The Social Setting of Pauline Christianity: Essays on Corinth.* Philadelphia: Fortress, 1982.

Turner, Nigel. *Grammatical Insights into the New Testament.* Edinburgh: T & T Clark, 1965.

Turner, Victor. *Drama, Fields, and Metaphors: Symbolic Action in Human Society.* Ithaca, N.Y.: Cornell University Press, 1974.

Valantasis, Richard. "Constructions of Power in Asceticism," *JAAR* 63 (1995) 775–821.

Valantasis, Richard, and Vincent L. Wimbush, eds. *Asceticism.* New York: Oxford University Press, 1995.

Van Gennep, Arnold. *The Rites of Passage [Les Rites de Passage].* Translated by Monika Vizedom and Gabrielle Caffe. Chicago: University of Chicago Press, 1960.

Vermes, Geza. *The Dead Sea Scrolls in English.* Sheffield: Sheffield Academic Press, 1995.

Verner, David C. *The Household of God: The Social World of the Pastoral Epistles.* SBL.DS 71. Chico: Scholars, 1983.

Weber, Max. *Economy and Society: An Outline of Interpretative Sociology.* 3 vols. Ed. Guenther Roth and Claus Wittich. Berkeley: University of California Press, 1978.

Wild, Robert A. "The Warrior and the Prisoner: Some Reflections on Ephesians 6:10-20," *CBQ* 46 (1984) 284–98.

Williams, Ritva H. *Charismatic Patronage and Brokerage: Episcopal Leadership in the Letters of Ignatius of Antioch.* Doctoral Dissertation, University of Ottawa, 1997.

Wilson, Bryan R. *Patterns of Sectarianism.* London: Heinemann, 1967.

_____. *Magic and the Millennium.* St. Albans, U.K.: Paladin, 1975.

Wimbush, Vincent L., ed. *Ascetic Behavior in Greco-Roman Antiquity: A Sourcebook.* Minneapolis: Fortress, 1990.

Wright, N. T. "Poetry and Theology in Col 1:15-20," *NTS* 36 (1990) 444–68.

Zeilinger, Franz. *Der Erstgeborene der Schöpfung: Untersuchungen zur Formalstruktur und Theologie des Kolosserbriefes.* Vienna: Herder, 1974.

COLOSSIANS

TRANSLATION, NOTES, AND INTERPRETATION

1. *Greeting* (1:1-2)

1. Paul, an apostle of Christ Jesus by the will of God, and Timothy the brother, 2. to the saints and faithful brothers in Christ at Colossae: Grace and peace to you from God our Father.

NOTES

1. *Paul, an apostle of Christ Jesus by the will of God, and Timothy the brother:* The opening words of Colossians are identical to 2 Cor 1:1. The Greek term *apostolos* (apostle) can sometimes mean "emissary" (the one who is sent) in Paul's letters (e.g., Phil 2:25; 2 Cor 8:23), but it is clearly used here in the special titular sense evident in 1 Cor 15:5-7 (cf. 1 Cor 9:1; Gal 1:15-16). Paul's work stems from his being chosen by the will of God (cf. Gal 1:12) to belong to a particular group of witnesses to the resurrection (1 Cor 15:5). Timothy is a fellow worker who is frequently mentioned along with Paul in the salutations of epistles (e.g., 2 Cor 1:1; Phil 1:1; 1 Thess 1:1; 2 Thess 1:1; Phlm 1). In an effort to interpret the meaning of the literal Greek reference to Timothy as the brother *(ho adelphos),* the REB translates the term as "our colleague." Timothy may have served as Paul's amanuensis (secretary), but the significance of his appearance with Paul should be understood as extending beyond the role of literary assistant (see interpretation below). Paul's ministry is a collaborative effort involving a network of relationships. This is suggested by the familial language in vv. 1-2 uniting Paul, Timothy, and the community members together as brothers. Tychicus (4:7) and Onesimus (4:9) are both also called brothers in the epistle. Given the likelihood that the letter was not actually composed by Paul (see Introduction), it has been suggested that Timothy was the actual author. He may have written the letter with Paul's approval (see Dunn 37–41; see the notes and interpretation on 4:7-18). It is rather surprising, however, that Timothy is never mentioned again in the epistle. According to Acts 16:1-5, Timothy was a native of Lystra. He was the son of a Jewish mother and a Greek father, and

Paul had him circumcised. The warm tribute paid to him in Phil 2:19-24 offers an indication of the important place he occupied among Paul's fellow workers (Yates 4).

2. *to the saints and faithful brothers in Christ at Colossae:* The Greek words *tois hagiois* translated as "the saints" might equally be rendered as "the holy ones." They refer to those who belong to the people of God. The saints and faithful brothers are the same people—those who are members of the church community. The NIV understands *hagiois* to be adjectival, thus translating as: "To the holy and faithful brothers." Departing from the literal Greek, the NRSV opts for the more inclusive translation in this instance and elsewhere to communicate Paul's intent to address the whole community: "To the saints and faithful brothers and sisters." In contrast to the Thessalonian correspondence, the Corinthian correspondence, and Galatians, the term *ekklēsia* (church) does not appear in the address, but "faithful brothers" recalls the opening of Romans and Philippians. The nature of believers' commitment and membership is defined by means of the characteristic Pauline formula "in Christ" (*en Christǭ*). There has been much scholarly discussion concerning the meaning of the Greek expression, which sometimes seems to suggest incorporation into the body of Christ (e.g., Phil 3:9), but at other times refers to the agency of salvation (e.g., 1 Cor 1:4). In the latter case the concern is salvation that comes through Christ. In Col 1:2 the phrase does appear to be largely incorporative, but the idea that salvation comes through attachment to Christ and through his power is certainly not precluded (cf. 1:4, 14, 16, 17, 19, 28; 2:3, 6, 7, 9, 10, 11, 12; 3:18, 20; 4:7). Faithful commitment to Christ, incorporation into his body, and membership in a holy community are central Pauline notions that are intertwined in the brief opening of the letter to the Colossians. Although the community in the ancient city of Colossae is singled out in the address, later references in the letter to the neighboring cities of Laodicea (2:1; 4:13-16) and Hierapolis (4:13) suggest that the letter speaks to the broader context of believers in the region of the Lycus Valley (on these cities see Introduction).

Grace and peace to you from God our Father: This is the greeting found consistently throughout Paul's letters (Rom 1:7; 1 Cor 1:3; 2 Cor 1:2; Gal 1:3; Phil 1:2; 1 Thess 1:1; Phlm 3). It is here offered with notable brevity, (cf. 1 Thess 1:1) which probably explains why some witnesses (Textus Receptus, ℵ A C G I 88 614 *Byz Lect al*) add "from the Lord Jesus Christ" to the greeting from God the Father. This formula may reveal the influence of the characteristic Greek salutation: "greetings" (*chairein,* though the related key Pauline term *charis* occurs here). It may also have been influenced by the traditional Jewish greeting, "peace" (*shalom*). Some Jewish salutations refer to "mercy and peace" (cf. 2 *Apoc. Bar.* 78:2).

INTERPRETATION

The opening address of this letter corresponds to those of the other Pauline epistles, but its weight should nevertheless be measured in relation to the particular circumstances that inspired Colossians. Here it is useful to compare the opening of Colossians to the opening of Galatians. Both letters are inspired by the need to counter false teaching with the authority that comes directly from God. The nature of Paul's apostleship is central to his efforts to establish divine sanction for his teaching. In Gal 1:1-4 the greeting is more elaborate and there is far greater insistence on apostleship being the result of divine and not human agency; however, such considerations are also operative in the arguments of Colossians (see the notes and interpretation on 1:24–2:7).

In Col 1:1-2 the assertion of Paul's authority as "an apostle of Christ Jesus by the will of God" is especially important. A social-scientific perspective invites one to consider the means being employed to establish Paul's authority in these verses. Although its value for understanding the NT world has not gone unchallenged (see Introduction), the classic work of Max Weber on charisma and its routinization has figured prominently in the attempts of NT scholars to understand the nature of Paul's authority (e.g., Blasi; Gager; Holmberg [1980]; M. Y. MacDonald [1988]; Williams [1997]). In the language of Weber, Paul's authority may be defined as "charismatic authority." In contrast to other types of authority that are sanctioned on the basis of institutionalized offices and/or traditions, his authority is based on charisma, defined by Weber as:

> A certain quality of an individual personality by virtue of which he is considered extraordinary and treated as endowed with supernatural, superhuman, or at least specifically exceptional powers or qualities. These are such as are not accessible to the ordinary person, but are regarded as of divine origin or as exemplary, and on the basis of them the individual is treated as a "leader." (241–42; cf. 246–54)

The description of Paul as "an apostle of Christ Jesus by the will of God" resonates with the assertions of Paul's charismatic authority found in the undisputed letters. While he obviously appeals to tradition, especially Jewish Scripture, to justify his position and explain his teaching, ultimately Paul's assertions rest upon the conviction of his having been chosen by God. It is clear that Paul understands his own authority as centered in his claim to be an apostle (cf. 1 Thess 2:6; Gal 1:1; 1 Cor 1:1; 9:1-2; Rom 1:1). For Paul, being an apostle involves a commission from the risen Lord (1 Cor 15:8-9); his work as Apostle to the Gentiles is authorized by revelation (Gal 1:15-17). Paul was set apart by God (Gal 1:15; Rom 1:1) and given responsibility concerning the Gentiles. At some points in Paul's letters the implication is that God is ultimately the speaker (1 Thess 2:2-4, 13; 4:15; 1 Cor 14:37; 2 Cor 5:18-20). To deny Paul's teaching is to reject God (1 Thess 4:8; Gal 1:8). In addition to the references to his divine commission, the indications of Paul's Spirit endowment bolster his charismatic authority.

Miracles are a definite sign of an apostle (Rom 15:19; 2 Cor 12:12). Pneumatic acts are involved in his transmission of the gospel (cf. 1 Thess 1:5; 1 Cor 2:4). He possesses several spiritual gifts including tongues (1 Cor 14:18; cf. 1 Cor 2:13), prophecy (1 Thess 3:4; 1 Cor 15:51; Rom 11:25-27), and various signs and wonders (2 Cor 12:12; Gal 3:5; Rom 15:19).

While it may seem to be based exclusively on the special qualities of an individual, it is important to remember that Weber's definition of charismatic authority depends on the presence of a community that acknowledges the charisma of the leader. A charismatic leader establishes his or her authority "solely by providing his powers in practice. He must work miracles. . . . He must perform heroic deeds. . . . Most of all, his divine mission must prove itself by bringing well-being to his faithful followers; if they do not fare well, he obviously is not the god-sent master" (Weber 1114; cited in Williams [1997] 28). Thus there is a sense in which charisma is larger than any one person. Anthony Blasi has offered the following insightful remarks about the communal nature of charisma:

> The individual who has a charisma is not only a person but a personage, a public character in a public drama who receives and imparts legitimacy. That drama is a process rather than an entity. It not only takes a processual form such as narrative, lending itself to reenactment, imitation, and recitation, but also is a process in the sense of itself having to be constituted and reconstituted in history. (5–6)

When one reads such epistles as Galatians or 2 Corinthians one senses the tenuous nature of Paul's authority in the face of several challenges to his understanding of what it means to be an apostle; his authority is dependent on a communal acknowledgement of his role. The fact that in Colossians Paul's authority is asserted with greater confidence, and in a somewhat stereotyped fashion in keeping with other deutero-Pauline works, is an indicator of a changed situation (see the notes and interpretation on 1:24–2:7). Nevertheless, the continuing validity of Paul's authority in the churches of the Lycus Valley depends on the community's acknowledgment of the power of his words to speak to such community realities as the problem of false teaching (2:8-23) and on the ability of coworkers to mediate Paul's authority in his absence (cf. 1:3-8; 4:7-18).

Particularly relevant for understanding the context of Colossians are Weber's assertions concerning the inherent instability of charisma. The problems surrounding the death of the charismatic leader give rise to a routinization process whereby, for example, charisma can be transformed into an objective, transferable entity in order that it may become embodied in traditions, successors, and bureaucracies. It may, for example, be transmitted from one bearer to another by means of rituals such as the laying on of hands associated with ordination (Weber 1139–41; see M. Y.

MacDonald [1988] 13–14). Weber argues that the interests of the charismatic leader's "staff" in guaranteeing the survival of the group often provide the impetus for the routinization process (246–51, 1121–48; Eisenstadt
54). Underlying Colossians one detects the struggles of Paul's fellow
workers to cope with the problem of his absence (see the notes and interpretation on 1:3-8 and 4:7-18).

Paul was a charismatic leader at the center of a movement, but his
leadership was often exercised in collaboration with associates and by
making use of the communication routes that existed in Greco-Roman
society. Networks of communication existed in the Pauline churches to
facilitate ministry. Travel and letter-writing allowed for contact between
Paul and the communities. Sociological investigation of the roles of the
local leaders and collaborators mentioned by name in Paul's letters has revealed that leadership was related not only to such obvious talents as
good teaching and inspired prophecy (cf. 1 Cor 12:4-11), but also to the
ability to travel and the capacity to host church gatherings in the home
(see Theissen 73–96). Paul clearly relied on assistants such as Timothy
(1 Cor 4:17; 16:10; 1 Thess 3:1-6; Phil 2:19-24) to maintain ties with his communities. The frequent references to Timothy in the Pauline epistles suggest that he was among the most important of Paul's collaborators. He is
presented as the co-sender of Colossians, but there is good reason to understand 1:1 also as a reference to his role as secretary (cf. 4:18).

Attempts to understand the full impact of the role of the secretary in
Pauline correspondence have pointed to various levels of possible secretarial activity, including the formal composition of letters from "short-
hand" notes (see Richards). In the case of Colossians it has even been
suggested by some who believe that the letter is deutero-Pauline that Timothy's secretarial role developed naturally into full authorship (see the
notes on 1:1). Even in the case of the undisputed letters it is perhaps somewhat misleading to think of Paul composing every word of his writings.
The legacy of the Pauline literature is clearly the result of the efforts of a
group. It is at times even difficult to distinguish between the leadership of
local communities and the roles of such assistants as Timothy, Sosthenes,
Silvanus, and Titus. These collaborators were fellow-travelers with Paul
and participated in such tasks as co-authorship of letters, establishment of
communities, reinforcement of Paul's teaching, and organization of community affairs, including collections (2 Cor 1:19; 1 Thess 3:2, 6; 2 Cor 8:6,
16-24). For example, Prisca and Aquila seem to have combined the roles of
protector and host of Paul and of local house church assemblies with
travel and evangelization (Acts 18:26; see Meeks [1983] 133–34). In Colossae, Epaphras was clearly an important local leader who appears also to
have been the missionary founder of the community. Tychicus and Onesimus traveled to Colossae bearing Paul's letter and personal information

about Paul; their presence in the community may well extend to offering Pauline guidance on the problem of false teaching (see the notes and interpretation on 1:3-8 and 4:7-18).

In addition to the evidence of collaboration between Paul and his coworkers, several terms are employed in the greeting that reinforce the sentiment of belonging to a group. In the reference to "brothers" we find the characteristic Pauline usage of familial language to address members of the community. Such terminology should be read in relation to the physical organization of Pauline churches as groups that met in houses (Col 4:15). Although the focus is less on intimacy than on election, the reference to the "saints" or "holy ones" also reinforces identity. In addition, the expression "in Christ" reinforces the boundaries separating the body of those who will be saved from those on the outside; it connects the revelation of Christ with the existence of a community of believers. Believers are incorporated into Christ. There is clearly an element of exclusivity here, but if we consider the letter as a whole it becomes clear that this must be held in tension with a tremendous confidence in universal salvation (1:6, 15-20, 23).

FOR REFERENCE AND FURTHER STUDY

Barrett, C. K. *The Signs of an Apostle*. Philadelphia: Fortress, 1972.
Best, Ernest. *One Body in Christ. A Study in the Relationship of the Church to Christ in the Epistles of the Apostle Paul*. London: S.P.C.K., 1955.
Blasi, Anthony J. *Making Charisma: The Social Construction of Paul's Public Image*. New Brunswick, N.J.: Transaction, 1991.
Holmberg, Bengt. *Paul and Power: The Structure of Authority in the Primitive Church as Reflected in the Pauline Epistles*. Philadelphia: Fortress, 1980.
Lieu, Judith M. "'Grace to you and Peace': The Apostolic Greeting," *BJRL* 68 (1985) 161–78.
Richards, E. Randolph. *The Secretary in the Letters of Paul*. WUNT 2nd ser. 42. Tübingen: J.C.B. Mohr, 1991.
Stowers, Stanley K. *Letter Writing in Greco-Roman Antiquity*. Philadelphia: Westminster, 1986.
Wedderburn, A.J.M. "Some Observations on Paul's Use of the Phrases 'in Christ' and 'with Christ,'" *JSNT* 25 (1985) 83–97.

2. *Thanksgiving for the Colossians* (1:3-8)

3. We always give thanks to God, the Father of our Lord Jesus Christ when we pray for you 4. because we have heard of your faith in Christ

Jesus and of the love you have for all the saints, 5. on account of the hope that is stored up for you in heaven and of which you have previously heard in the word of the truth of the gospel 6. that has come to you. Just as in the whole world it is bearing fruit and growing, so also it has been doing so among you since the day you heard it and came to know the grace of God, in truth. 7. You learned this from Epaphras our beloved fellow slave who is a faithful minister of Christ on our behalf, 8. and who indeed informed us of your love in the Spirit.

NOTES

3. *We always give thanks to God, the Father of our Lord Jesus Christ when we pray for you:* The thanksgiving section of the letter begins with the use of the verb *eucharistoumen* (we give thanks). Prayer and thanksgiving go together in Colossians (cf. 1:12-14; 2:7; 3:15-17; 4:2-3). Philemon 4-7 offers the closest parallel in Pauline literature to Col 1:3-8 (cf. Phil 1:3-11). Commentators have pointed to the inclusion of thanksgivings to God (the gods) in the letters of Jews and pagans in antiquity (see, e.g., 2 Macc 1:10–2:18, discussed by Lohse 12–13). Thanksgivings are found in all Pauline epistles with the exception of Galatians, 1 Timothy, and Titus. The plural subject "we" here is probably an example of "epistolary plural" (replaced by the singular in 1:23) where there is no difference in meaning between it and the singular; here Paul himself is the subject, or perhaps Paul and Timothy as co-authors (see the notes on 1:1). As is the case elsewhere in Pauline works, God is identified as the Father of the Lord Jesus Christ (2 Cor 1:3; Eph 1:2 has "God our Father and the Lord Jesus Christ"). The more usual expression in Colossians, however, is Christ Jesus (e.g., 1:1; 2:6).

4. *because we have heard of your faith in Christ Jesus and of the love you have for all the saints, 5. on account of the hope that is stored up for you in heaven and of which you have previously heard:* While in English the phrase immediately calls to mind faithfulness and loyalty, it is probably closer to the meaning of *tēn pistin hymōn en Christǭ Iēsou* to think in terms of the sphere in which the faith of the Colossians operated (see the notes and interpretation on 1:1-2). The parameters of the community of those who have been incorporated into Christ are being announced. Note the greater focus on Christ as the object of faith implied by the language in 2:5, which refers to the firmness of the faith of the Colossians in Christ: *to stereōma tēs eis Christon pisteōs hymōn* (Harris 16). Verses 4-5 introduce the classic Pauline triad of faith, love, and hope (cf. 1 Corinthians 13; 1 Thess 1:3; Col 3:14). Hope here has a special significance. It is less an attitude to foster than an object to be seized. In essence the term functions as a synonym for eternal life. Where to locate salvation is a central concern of Colossians. The notion of a heavenly store of eternal life fits with the cosmological interests of the letter and probably also reflects the nature of the conflict at Colossae; the "false teaching" seems to have included heavenly visions, and community members evidently debated how the present fruits of salvation

should be lived out on a daily basis in the earthly realm (see the notes and interpretation on 2:8-23). The use of the verb *apokeimai* here refers to what is put away or stored up (BAGD 92; cf. 2 Tim 4:8). The transition from v. 4 to v. 5 is awkward because of the Greek term at the beginning of v. 5 (*dia* + accusative), translated literally here as "on account of." It is not certain if the hope that is laid up in heaven provides the grounds for the thanksgiving (i.e., one more reason for giving thanks), though grammatical considerations suggest otherwise (see Harris 17). It is more likely that in v. 5 hope (eternal life) acts as the basis for faith and love. The rather fluid translation offered in the REB and NEB probably best captures the true meaning: "both [faith and love] spring from that hope stored up for you in heaven." Love *(agapē)* is mentioned again in v. 8.

in the word of the truth of the gospel 6. that has come to you: The translation of this phrase is the same as that adopted by the NRSV and the NIV, but it has been rendered otherwise by some translators: "when the message of the true gospel" (REB; NEB). The difficulties of translation involve several issues including: (1) *en* could be spatial (in), instrumental (through), or temporal (when); (2) the word *logos* is translated variously in English as "word," "message," or "preaching"; (3) it is not entirely clear whether "of the truth" refers specifically to the gospel or to the word that constitutes the gospel (see Harris 18). None of these variations, however, alters the sense dramatically. The important point is that the Colossians have previously heard of the true word/message, that is, the gospel (cf. Eph 1:13). The insistence on truth is no doubt related to the false gospel preached by certain teachers (cf. Col 2:8, 16-23). The importance of truth is stressed a second time in v. 6.

Just as in the whole world it is bearing fruit and growing, so also it has been doing so among you: The Greek words *kathōs kai* are repeated twice in this verse and are used to convey comparison ("in the same way too"). There is an awkwardness in the language used to compare the arrival and growth of the gospel in Colossae to its expansion throughout the world. Some copyists sought to alleviate the awkwardness by inserting an extra *kai* before the words *estin karpophoroumenon* (it is bearing fruit), but the reading adopted here is both early and well attested (Metzger 619). The central idea is clear: the presence and growth of the gospel among the Colossians reflects a cosmological reality. The verbal construction "it is bearing fruit and growing" points to more than a single occurrence in the present; it refers to ongoing action (Harris 19). Both in the community and in the whole world the gospel is engaged in a process of expansion and production. Growth is a very important theme in Colossians, with respect both to the theological ideas articulated in this epistle and to the social reality experienced by community members. (For more detailed discussion of this expression see the notes on 1:10 below.)

since the day you heard it and came to know the grace of God, in truth: The Colossians have come to know the grace of God. The verb meaning "to come to know" here is *epignōskō* in contrast to the more common term *ginōskō*. Thus some assign weight to the prefix and translate it as "comprehend" (NRSV) or "understood" (NIV). But a comparison of this passage to 2 Cor 8:9 reveals that there is no necessary difference in meaning between the compound verb and the simpler form (see Harris 20; on the importance of knowledge in Colossians see the notes on 1:9). This is the second reference to grace in the epistle (cf. 1:2). "The grace of God" in this instance is a reference to the true message of salvation, the gospel. The NRSV captures the heart of the meaning of this phrase by rendering the reference to truth as an adverb that modifies the verb "came to know or comprehended": "from the day you heard it and truly comprehended the grace of God." However, the more literal translation here allows the repetition of the concept of truth in vv. 5-6 to stand out more clearly (see also the notes on 1:5).

7. *You learned this from Epaphras our beloved fellow slave:* Clearly an important member of Paul's circle of fellow workers, Epaphras is depicted in Colossians as being with Paul in prison (cf. 4:12; Phlm 23). The reference to the Colossians learning of the gospel from Epáphras (v. 7) means that he founded the community. While it is possible to translate the term *doulos* in a more neutral way as "servant," it is increasingly being recognized that the metaphorical use of the term "slave" in Pauline Christianity is related in complex ways to the actual shape of the institution of slavery in the Greco-Roman world. Because Epaphras is described as both a fellow slave and a faithful minister of Christ, it is possible that what is meant is that both he and Paul are fellow slaves of Christ. Epaphras is in fact described as a slave of Christ in 4:12. Since being enslaved to members of the upper class was a form of possible upward mobility in the ancient world, to be a slave of Christ (1:15: the image of the invisible God, the firstborn of all creation) would mean that one participated in Christ's supremacy. Thus the term "slave" could function to enhance Epaphras' authority in Colossae. It is also clear, however, that Paul can speak of himself as a slave in a manner that calls to mind self-abasement and the language used by popular leaders of the time to reinforce their solidarity with the masses, their enslavement to their followers. In 1 Cor 9:19-23 Paul speaks of having become a slave to all in order to benefit some. He has even become weak in order that he might win the weak (see Dale B. Martin [1990]). Such considerations may also underlie v. 6 since it is evident that Epaphras is bound to the Colossian community and goes to extraordinary lengths to foster its growth (Col 4:12-13). At any rate there are indications in the text that the institution of slavery required careful attention in Colossae (see the notes and interpretation on 3:18–4:1).

who is a faithful minister of Christ: The word "minister" here is the same Greek term as was later used to refer to the established church office of deacon (*diakonos*). The term does not imply that Epaphras occupies an institutionalized office, but it is nevertheless a title reserved for leaders. Local community leaders in Philippi (Phil 1:1) are given the same title along with another designation, overseer, which would later refer to the office of bishop (*episkopos*). Paul can also describe himself as a minister of Christ (e.g., Rom 15:15-16 [the Greek term for minister here is *leitourgos*]). In 1:23 he is called a minister of the gospel. Another member of the Pauline entourage, Tychicus, is called a faithful minister in 4:7, and in 4:17 Archippus is instructed to fulfill the ministry that he has received in the Lord (see also the notes and interpretation on 4:7-18). Recent work on the concept of *diakonos* in the ancient world has high-lighted the use of the word to refer to the role of messenger, spokesperson, go-between, or authorized representative (see Collins 71–191, 195–210). It is likely that both descriptions of Paul and Epaphras are intended to convey the notion that they are messengers on assignment from God or Christ (cf. 1 Cor 3:5; 2 Cor 3:5-6; 6:4; 11:23), but there is also a sense in which Epaphras is on as-signment from Paul. Epaphras is in fact the founder of the community (1:7-9; 2:1; 4:12-13).

on our behalf: The strong evidence for both "on our behalf" *(hyper hēmōn)* and "on your behalf" *(hyper hymōn)* among the textual witnesses has made it diffi-cult for translators to arrive at a conclusion about this verse. The NIV favors the former while the NRSV prefers the latter. However, the goal here seems to be to do more than establish Epaphras' connection with the Colossians; it is, apparently, to formalize Epaphras' authority over the Colossians by reinforc-ing his association with Paul (cf. 4:12-13). Thus "our behalf" is the preferred translation. Epaphras acts on Paul's behalf; in essence he acts in his place. The translation adopted here best captures this sense (see Harris 22). The words carry an especially strong weight if Colossians is deutero-Pauline; in Paul's absence his authority is mediated through the apostle's fellow worker who is well known to the Colossians.

8. *and who indeed informed us of your love in the Spirit:* While the term spirit *(pneuma)* can sometimes refer to the human spirit in Pauline literature, in this case the meaning is probably God's Spirit: love (cf. 1:4) has been awakened or engen-dered in the Colossians by God's Spirit. That the verse refers more generally to the Colossians having a spiritual love appears less likely. There is, however, very little in Colossians about the Holy Spirit. The Spirit figures much more prominently in Ephesians.

INTERPRETATION

In Greek, Col 1:3-8 is one long sentence that offers reasons for thanking God. These reasons extend from the origins of the community to its ultimate goal. As is also the case with other Pauline thanksgivings, these verses in-troduce themes and concerns that are taken up again later in the letter. To praise the community for a faith that is publicly known is also a typical feature of the opening of Pauline works. In other letters such praise makes explicit the universal scope of the gospel message (e.g., 1 Thess 1:7-10; Rom 1:8) and this consideration probably also shapes Colossians.

Read social-scientifically, Paul's praise takes on new significance as an assertion of the legitimacy of the church mission. In an honor-shame so-ciety like the first-century Mediterranean world the public demonstration of reputation is vital to the establishment of identity. In recent years NT scholars have turned to anthropological studies of Mediterranean societies in order to shed light on the values embraced by ancient Mediterranean people (e.g., Malina [1983]; Malina and Neyrey [1991]; M. Y. MacDonald [1996]). An understanding of the core Mediterranean values of honor and shame has proved to be especially fruitful. A leading anthropologist of Mediterranean societies defines honor and shame as "reciprocal moral values representing primordial integration of individual to 'group.' They reflect, respectively, the conferral of public esteem upon the person and the sensitivity to public opinion upon which the former depends" (Gilmore 2). In essence the apostle's praise recognizes that the Colossian community has been endowed with honor: its worth has been publicly acknowledged. In order for the community to have a credible identity such acknowledgment is vital.

It is easy for a modern person to miss the weight of such a brief testimony to the public success of early Christianity as is disclosed by the reference to the apostle having heard of the faith of the Colossians. Its importance is far greater than simply a passing reference to church growth and exemplary church life. The faith that binds the community members together in Pauline Christianity and forms them into one body must be externally manifested (see Malina [1993] "Faith–Faithfulness," 68). Such considerations help explain why community members are instructed to conduct themselves wisely toward outsiders (4:5). All exchanges with the outside world involve the precarious commodity of community honor (see the notes and interpretation on 4:2-6).

In these dense few verses a good deal is communicated about the priorities of the letter. The basis of salvation is at stake. The fact that this basis is described in terms of hope which is stored in heaven may reflect the interest of the false teachers, examined below, in heavenly bodies and cosmic speculation (see the notes and interpretation on 2:18-23). The author may be correcting interpretations by making use of the language that has become controversial in Colossae.

The spatial language that appears at the beginning of the epistle has been judged by scholars who understand Colossians to be deutero-Pauline because it represents a shift in meaning in relation to the "authentic" Paul: hope changes from something with a temporal-eschatological orientation into a concept with spatial characteristics. The change in priorities is made even more apparent in v. 6 where the process of entering the church is described as knowing the grace of God in truth. The association between knowledge and truth has been judged as characteristic of later NT writings (e.g., 1 Tim 2:4; 2 Tim 3:7; see Lohse 18, 21). Petr Pokorný (1991) describes the shift as follows: "The 'spatial' interpretation of Christian hope [cf. the "above" in Col 3:1] relativizes the dimension of the future fulfillment, which is rarely the case in the main letters of Paul [cf. Titus 2:13]. In place of a future fulfillment we read in 3:4 of a future unveiling of the content of hope (of eschatological praise and of being with Christ)" (41). Pokorný notes, however, that the notion of a heavenly deposit can be found in Jewish apocalyptic literature (4 Ezra 7:14) and in Jesus' sayings (Matt 6:20-21, par.; Mark 10:21, par.), and he points out that it is not completely foreign to Paul (1 Cor 2:7).

There are clearly strong elements of continuity between the undisputed letters of Paul and Colossians, but there are also some changes of emphasis. A social-scientific perspective allows us to make greater sense of these changes of emphasis that emerge in Colossians. In their famous treatise on the sociology of knowledge Peter Berger and Thomas Luckmann described a dialectical relationship existing between the symbolic universe (a canopy of ideas offering meaning to the individual and the group) and the actors in a given social context. The symbolic universe is continually shaped by social experience and continually shapes what is experienced. According to their analysis contact with "deviants" or "heretics" leads to legitimations of the symbolic universe (attempts to justify a particular perspective, perhaps by making use of the language of the perceived deviants). These legitimations are incorporated into the symbolic universe and the symbolic universe is ultimately transformed (Berger and Luckmann 125; see the full discussion in M. Y. MacDonald [1988] 10–18).

When Colossians is understood as the result of a dialectical relationship between social actors and the symbolic universe its cosmological perspective emerges as fundamentally tied to the realities of community life. Everything is pushed upward and outward in Colossians: Hope is laid up in heaven; Christ is above, seated at the right hand of God; the gospel is bearing fruit and filling the world; Christ is the head of the church (cf. Col 1:5-6; 1:18; 3:1). Such beliefs are articulated first and foremost in relation to the problem of false teaching (2:8-23), but other social factors should be considered such as the growth of the Pauline churches, the disappearance of the apostle, and especially rising tension between the church community and the outside world (see the notes and interpretation on 4:2-6). In these opening verses of Colossians the assertion of Paul's authority as an apostle and over the Colossians is intended to ensure that they continue to be established securely in the faith (cf. 1:23). Just as in Galatians (cf. Gal 1:6-9), there is value in stating what has been known to be true from the beginning: the gospel is the same gospel of which they have previously heard and that is now bearing fruit among them. It is the same gospel that has a universal scope and that promises heavenly treasure. The strategy to ensure adherence to the gospel in v. 7 turns to the concrete matter of the leadership of Epaphras.

Epaphras is presented in vv. 7-8 as an intermediary between Paul and the Colossian community. The church at Colossae is clearly part of the

Pauline sphere of influence, but the Colossians did not receive the gospel from Paul himself. Epaphras founded the community and the letter presents him as now with Paul and as having brought news about the life of the community to the apostle. Epaphras is perhaps the most important of Paul's fellow workers mentioned in Col 1:7 and in the list of greetings in Col 4:7-17, but Onesimus and Tychicus also play a significant role in community affairs. These verses reveal an attempt to bolster the reliability of Paul's fellow workers and emphasize the centrality of their role in maintaining communication between the apostle and the community. The reliability of the associates of the apostles is stressed in other NT works as well. In a manner that calls to mind the exhortation in Col 4:7-8 a promise is made in Eph 6:21 that Tychicus will communicate all things to the addressees. The Pastoral Epistles are not addressed to communities in the first instance, but exhort church groups through Paul's delegates, Timothy and Titus. A particularly interesting exhortation is found in 1 Pet 5:12, which suggests a link between the bolstering of the apostles' associates and the writing of pseudonymous epistles. Silvanus is not only a faithful brother to the community, he is also the one through whom Peter is said to write. All these texts come from the latter decades of the first century and the early second century when particular problems arose due to a vacuum in leadership created by the death of the earliest witnesses and authorities in early Christianity (see Brown [1984]).

As discussed in the comments on Col 1:1-2, Paul's authority is charismatic; it has been bestowed upon him by a divine encounter with Christ and revealed through his miracles and wonders, and above all by means of his ability to convince others to accept the gospel and attain salvation. By establishing a strong link between Paul and Epaphras, who brought the gospel to the Colossians, the author of Colossians leaves no doubt that community members participate in the divine benefits—the hope that is laid up in heaven—delivered through the Pauline mission. Because Epaphras is clearly the one who preached the gospel originally in Colossae and perhaps also in Laodicea and Hierapolis (4:13) it may be accurate to consider Epaphras also as a type of charismatic leader, but his leadership is clearly dependent on Paul's. In Weberian terminology, Epaphras is part of the staff of the charismatic leader. The disappearance of the original charismatic leader creates the problem of succession: to whom will we now listen? Those who are closely associated with the charismatic leader, the fellow workers, will naturally need to secure their own leadership positions and reinforce their authority among the body of followers (mediated through a connection to the central leader; see the notes and interpretation on 1:1-2; and see M. Y. MacDonald [1988] 11–16). Whether Paul is imprisoned or dead, fellow workers like Epaphras would need to secure the continued existence of the Pauline movement by defending their own leadership. The problems created by the proponents of the "false teaching" (see the notes and interpretation on 2:8-23) make even more critical the reinforcement of the authority of the one who originally preached the gospel in Colossae. If Colossians is deutero-Pauline, then it would most likely be individuals like Epaphras who would seek to make Paul speak to the community by writing in his name. They would make his presence felt and bring comfort in his absence.

There is no doubt that the disappearance of Paul would have been traumatic for those who worked closely with him. However, the continued existence of Pauline Christianity beyond the disappearance of the apostle was related to the practices and social structures of Greco-Roman society. The very act of composing a document in Paul's world inevitably involved a group effort in a way that is no longer the case in the modern world (see the notes and interpretation on 1:1-2). It may well have seemed natural for Paul's fellow workers to continue to spread the truth of Pauline Christianity by taking on his persona. Certainly the practice of composing pseudonymous works is one that early Christians shared with Jews and pagans in the ancient world and it should not be understood as simply an effort to deceive (see Introduction). If we think of the authorship of Pauline works as a communal enterprise undertaken by Paul and his entourage, the sharp distinction between authentic and inauthentic epistles is significantly reduced.

The potential for Paul's assistants to continue to exercise their authority in Paul's absence was also strengthened by the system of patronage that permeated relationships in Greco-Roman society. Whether in the context of political, economic, or religious arenas, the system of patronage imbued non-kinship relationships with the flavor of relations in the hierarchical household (see Malina [1993] "Patronage," 133–37). The patron acted very much like the head of a household. Patrons bestowed material benefits on their "clients" and in return expected to receive honor and loyalty. These material benefits were not simply financial but included all kinds of economic resources (such as access to a house for church meetings). Patrons allowed clients to have access to social advantages as well: the client shared in the prestige of the patron. In the context of Paul's churches we can easily see how the prestige associated with particular patrons becomes the subject of conflict when Paul censures the Corinthian community for dividing into parties: "each of you says, 'I belong to Paul,' or 'I belong to Apollos,' or 'I belong to Cephas,' or 'I belong to Christ'" (1 Cor 1:12 NRSV). Sometimes a third party facilitated the relationship between patron and client. "Brokers" or "mediators" provided access to the patron. In many respects Paul's fellow workers acted as brokers, mediating between Paul and the "client" communities.

Scholars are increasingly coming to recognize that an understanding of the system of patronage in the ancient world sheds light not only on the general nature of the relationship between Paul and his communities but also on the interaction between the apostle and the individuals mentioned in his correspondence. Although most often it is Paul who is cast in the role of patron, it is increasingly acknowledged that the balance of power varied considerably from relationship to relationship. That in Rom 16:1-2 Phoebe is recommended by Paul to the community indicates that she will benefit from Paul's prestige. Like Epaphras she is called *diakonos*, minister or deacon. But Paul in this text also describes Phoebe as his patron, indicating his dependency on her in certain circumstances (see Whelan). The relationship between Epaphras, Paul, and the Colossians turns out to be complex when it is evaluated in terms of the ancient structures of patronage, for in the few verses where Epaphras is mentioned he is shown as functioning in all three roles: patron, broker, and client.

As is made clear by the description of Epaphras as a minister to the Colossians "on our behalf," Epaphras is a mediator figure, providing the Colossians with access to Paul's benefaction and communicating their loyalty to the apostle (Col 1:7-8). Epaphras is also a patron to the Colossians: having founded the community, he continues his prayers and hard work to sustain it (Col 1:7; 4:12-13). Implicit in such commendations of Epaphras is probably an encouragement to respect his authority—to honor him with loyalty and obedience. But Epaphras can also stand with the Colossians in their relationship with Paul as "clients before the patron Paul," for Epaphras is described as "one of them" (Col 4:12). The flexibility of the role of Epaphras (and other fellow workers) probably contributed to the survival of Pauline Christianity beyond the disappearance of the main charismatic leader. Paul may have been absent, but his assistants were in place to provide access to the Pauline legacy. Their solidarity with local communities was reinforced because they, along with other community members, had been Paul's clients. Participation in Paul's mission and the privilege of sharing in Paul's prestige as "fellow slaves of Christ" prepared them to become patrons of local communities.

When they are understood as deutero-Pauline, Colossians and Ephesians are usually associated with a transitional period between the height of the leadership of the Apostle to the Gentiles and the establishment of the church offices of bishop, presbyter, and deacon, at the beginning of the second century when the apostle's fellow workers would themselves have died. One senses a void of leadership in the social setting of Colossians and Ephesians. To become aware of the influence of the system of patronage on social relations in Greco-Roman society enables us to see more clearly the structures that would have been in place to allow Pauline Christianity to continue beyond the disappearance of Paul.

FOR REFERENCE AND FURTHER STUDY

Brown, Raymond E. *The Churches the Apostles Left Behind.* New York: Paulist; London: Geoffrey Chapman, 1984.

Collins, John N. *Diakonia: Re-interpreting the Ancient Sources.* New York and London: Oxford University Press, 1990.

Crafton, Jeffrey A. *The Agency of the Apostle: A Dramatistic Analysis of Paul's Response to Conflict in 2 Corinthians.* JSNT.S 51. Sheffield: JSOT Press, 1990.

Malina, Bruce J. *The New Testament World: Insights from Cultural Anthropology.* Atlanta: John Knox, 1981; London: S.C.M., 1983.

_____. "Faith–Faithfulness" in John J. Pilch and Bruce J. Malina, eds., *Biblical Social Values and Their Meaning: A Handbook.* Peabody, Mass.: Hendrickson, 1993, 67–70.

_____. "Patronage," in ibid. 113–17.

Marshall, Peter. *Enmity in Corinth: Social Conventions in Paul's Relations with the Corinthians.* Tübingen: J. C. B. Mohr, 1987.

Martin, Dale B. *Slavery as Salvation: The Metaphor of Slavery in Pauline Christianity.* New Haven and London: Yale University Press, 1990.

O'Brien, Peter T. *Introductory Thanksgivings in the Letters of Paul.* NT.S 49. Leiden: Brill, 1977.

Saller, Richard P. *Personal Patronage under the Early Empire.* Cambridge: Cambridge University Press, 1982.

Schubert, Paul. *Form and Function of the Pauline Thanksgivings.* BZNW 20. Berlin: A. Töpelmann, 1939.

Whelan, Caroline F. "*Amica Pauli:* The Role of Phoebe in the Early Church," *JSNT* 49 (1993) 67–85.

Witherington, Ben III. *Conflict and Community in Corinth: A Socio-Rhetorical Commentary on 1 and 2 Corinthians.* Grand Rapids: Eerdmans, 1995.

3. *Prayer on Behalf of the Colossians* (1:9-14)

9. Because of this we also, from the day on which we heard it, have not ceased to pray on your behalf, asking that you may be filled with the knowledge of his will in all spiritual wisdom and understanding, 10. so that you may walk in a manner worthy of the Lord, pleasing to him in every respect, bearing fruit in every good work and growing in the knowledge of God, 11. being strengthened with all the strength, in accordance with his glorious might, for all endurance and patience, while joyfully 12. giving thanks to the Father, who has made you fit to share in the inheritance of the saints in the light, 13. who delivered us out of the power of darkness and transferred us into the kingdom of his beloved son 14. in whom we have redemption, the forgiveness of sins.

9. *Because of this we also, from the day on which we heard it:* This construction rein-forces the close connection between vv. 9-14 and the preceding verses. Each section constitutes one long sentence in Greek and they share many words and phrases. Thanksgiving and intercession both flow from the report the apostle has received from Epaphras concerning the Colossians (1:7-8). This re-port is central to the nature of the apostle's relationship with the Colossians at present and it shapes the instructions he is about to give. The term *kai* in the Greek text here means "also" and it is employed to communicate the fact that not only does Paul offer thanksgiving to God for the Colossians, but he "also" intercedes on their behalf (see Harris 29).

have not ceased to pray on your behalf, asking: What is being stressed by the use of the verbs "[not] cease" *(pauō)*, "pray" *(proseuchomai)*, and "ask" *(aiteō)* is unin-terrupted intercession on behalf of the Colossians. Paul's never-ceasing inter-cession is also highlighted in 1:3—an indication of the close connection between this section and the thanksgiving of 1:3-8. In 4:3 Paul asks the com-munity to pray for him. Prayer is portrayed as an important feature of com-munity life in Colossae (cf. Col 4:2, 12).

that you may be filled with knowledge of his will: This phrase explains the content of the apostle's intercession on behalf of the Colossians. Paul asks God to fill the Colossians with knowledge of his will ("his" refers to God's will). The compound noun translated as knowledge here, *epignōsis*, can mean full or complete knowledge or insight (see the translations in NJB; REB). But it seems more likely that the addition of *epi* to the general term *gnōsis* in this case serves the grammatical purpose of expressing knowledge directed toward a particu-lar object, i.e., God's will (see Harris 30; see also the notes on 1:6). This view of knowledge is also found in the writings of the Qumran community (e.g., 1QH 4:9-12; 1QS 5:8-10; 11:15-20). The triad of "knowledge, wisdom, and under-standing" in this verse recalls the gifts that are granted to those who live their lives under the direction of the Spirit of Truth (1QS 4:1-6; for a full discussion of parallels with QL see Lohse 25). Knowledge of God is an important concept in Colossians (cf. Col 1:6, 9, 10; 2:2, 3; 3:10). How one attains such knowledge is at the heart of the dispute involving the false teachers. The use of the verb *plēroō* ("fill") as a means of describing the process of spiritual transformation is intriguing. A similar use of the term is found in 2:10. The related term "full-ness" *(plērōma)* is employed to describe the means by which God infuses the universe through Christ (1:19; 2:9). This terminology is even more extensive in Ephesians (cf. Eph 1:10, 23; 3:19; 4:10, 13; 5:18); it plays a vital part in the unique christologies/theologies of these documents.

in all spiritual wisdom and understanding: "In" *(en)* should probably be under-stood as referring to instrument: the means through which God's knowledge is both attained and made manifest (cf. NIV). (On the relationship between wisdom and understanding [insight or discernment] in Jewish writings see Deut 4:6; Dan 2:21; cf. Bar 3:23.) "Spiritual" *(pneumatikos)* may refer to what re-lates to the human spirit or to what is given by the Spirit—the gifts of the

Spirit (cf. Rom 1:11; 1 Cor 2:12-13; 12:1, 4; 14:1-2). In order to make this latter
meaning clear Eduard Lohse renders the phrase as "in all wisdom and insight
worked by the Spirit" (27). Given the extensive recognition that wisdom and
understanding come only from the Spirit (cf. Exod 31:3; 35:31; Isa 11:2; Wis
9:17-18; Sir 39:6; Philo, *De gigantibus* 22-27; 4 Ezra 14:22, 39-40; cited in Dunn
71), it is likely that this thought is taken up here as well. The ability to discern
is especially critical because of the problem with false teaching in the community (cf. 2:8-23). It is valuable to contrast the positive evaluation here of the
role of wisdom in Christian existence with the negative evaluation of the
claims to wisdom by those who adhere to false teaching. The measures adopted
by the opponents have only the appearance of wisdom (2:23). The first chapter
of Colossians contains many instances of the term *pas* (all, every). The occurrence in this verse is the first in a cluster (1:9-11; cf. 1:4, 6): Wholeness, completeness, and fullness are closely related themes that run throughout this
epistle.

10. *so that you may walk in a manner worthy of the Lord, pleasing to him in every respect:*
The verb *peripateō* refers to how one lives the whole of one's life. Hence most
modern translations refer to "living a life" or "leading a life" that is worthy of
the Lord. But the more literal translation "walk" better captures the active dimension of the concept. The verb also occurs in 2:6, an important text summarizing the teaching in the first part of the epistle and offering a transition to the
discussion of false teaching. In 3:7 the verb *peripateō* is used to draw attention
to the way of life of nonbelievers, which has now been rejected by community
members, and in 4:5 it refers to how believers should conduct themselves in
relation to nonbelievers. Paul frequently employs this verb to describe the
conduct of believers (e.g., Gal 5:16; 1 Cor 7:17; 2 Cor 5:7), apparently influenced by the metaphorical reference to walking in Jewish thought (e.g., Exod
18:20; Deut 13:4-5; Ps 86:11; Prov 28:18). The life that is worthy of the Lord involves walking in the world and visibly demonstrating the fruits of Christian
existence. The verb *peripateō* occurs in a very similar expression in 1 Thess
2:12. It is also central to the ethical exhortations in 1 Thess 4:1-12, which highlight the contrast between the morality of believers and the standards of the
outside world and offer advice as to how one should interact with the nonbelieving world. In Rom 8:4 Paul employs the term to describe the identity of believers as those "who walk not according to the flesh but according to the
Spirit" (NRSV; see interpretation below). The noun "pleasing" *(areskeia)* occurs only here in the NT (cf. LXX Prov 31:30). In the wider Greek literature it
most often carries negative connotations: obsequiousness (BAGD 105), but
here it is clearly used in a positive sense. Paul frequently makes use of the related verb "to please" *(areskō)* to refer to pleasing God (e.g., Rom 8:8; Gal 1:10;
1 Thess 2:4, 15; 4:1).

bearing fruit in every good work and growing in the knowledge of God: Bearing fruit
and growing are the first two of four participles describing the characteristics
of walking in a manner that is worthy of the Lord. To bear fruit in every good
work ("all kinds of good deeds"; BAGD 405; cf. 2 Cor 9:8) is to demonstrate
what has transformed one inwardly. In Pauline Christianity good works seem

to be understood as central to the community's interaction with the outside world. This can be seen especially clearly in Rom 13:3 where good works are viewed as contributing to the approval of believers by civic authorities. In Gal 6:10 Paul lays special emphasis on benefiting the members of the household of faith, but also speaks of the necessity of working for the good of all people. In some texts the verb "to bear fruit" *(karpophoreō)* refers to "practical conduct as the fruit of inner life" (BAGD 405; Philo, *Cher.* 84; *Odes Sol.* 11.23; cf. Rom 7:4; Pol. *Phil.* 1:2). Growth—an important theme in Colossians—is mentioned here, as in 1:6, but the meaning is slightly different. In 1:6 growth is the expansion that occurs as the gospel is spread throughout the world; it refers to outward expansion. Growth in 1:10 refers to the intensifying experience of God shared by believers; this is inward expansion. It is important to note, however, that an alternate understanding of this phrase is grammatically possible, as is made clear by Lohse's translation: "that you bear fruit in every good work and grow through the knowledge of God." In this case the knowledge of God is the means through which the bearing fruit and growing take place rather than being the subject of growth itself (see Lohse 28–29). On knowledge see the notes on 1:9.

11. *being strengthened with all the strength, in accordance with his glorious might:* "Being strengthened" is the third of four participles describing the characteristics of walking in a manner that is worthy of the Lord (v. 10). This participle is a cognate of the noun "power" or "strength" *(dynamis),* which also occurs here and is closely related in meaning to the term here translated as "might" *(kratos).* The focus on God's power in Colossians is in keeping with the significance attributed to God's transcendence and rule of the universe. The same power through which God reigns also infuses Christians (cf. 1:29). These ideas become even more important in Ephesians (Eph 1:19; 3:16, 20; 6:10). According to Eph 3:16 believers are strengthened in power by the Spirit.

for all endurance and patience: "Endurance" *(hypomonē)* means fortitude and perseverance especially in relation to an external threat or enemy. In 2 Cor 1:6 Paul reinforces his solidarity with the Corinthians by speaking of the kind of endurance that must persevere in hope through suffering: "if we are being afflicted, it is for your consolation, which you experience when you patiently endure the same sufferings that we are also suffering" (NRSV; see Lohse 30–31). There are indications in Colossians that believers are experiencing hostility or the threat of hostility at the hands of outsiders (see the notes on 4:5-6). Under such circumstances their commitment requires great fortitude and patience *(makrothymia).* Patience is a gift of the Spirit in Paul's letters (cf. Gal 5:22; 1 Cor 13:4). In 3:12 believers are called to clothe themselves with patience.

while joyfully: A more literal translation of the phrase would be "with joy" (see NAB). It has been rendered here as "while joyfully" (as in the NRSV) because the phrase fits more naturally with the following verse: "while joyfully giving thanks." A very similar construction is found in Phil 1:4. Lohse views vv. 12-14 as a summons to give thanks that has been influenced by traditional liturgical language of prayer, thanksgiving, and celebration. He believes that vv. 12-14 have been placed before the Christ-hymn to serve as a type of introit, introducing the hymn sung by the community. The singing of the hymn by the community should open with the sound of joy (cf. 1 Thess 5:16-18; Phil 4:4-6; see Lohse 32–33). On the relationship between the Christ-hymn of 1:15-20 and this section see also the notes on 1:13 below.

12. *giving thanks to the Father:* Giving thanks is the final participle describing the characteristics of walking in a manner that is worthy of the Lord (v. 10). It has sometimes been judged to be the equivalent of an imperative: "Give thanks with joy" (see Lohse 32; Taylor and Reumann 122–23). The interests of the thanksgiving in 1:3-8 are reiterated here. This verse is subject to a variety of variant readings (see Metzger 620). These seem to have been caused by the unusual designation of God simply as "the Father" *(tō patri)* when Christ has not been named. This led some copyists to modify the phrase, adding either "of Christ" *(tou Christou),* or in some cases "God" *([tō] theō).*

who has made you fit to share: As is made clear by the alternate readings proposed by the NRSV there are two textual variants to consider here. The unusual expression "made fit" *(hikanoō)* is strongly attested (e.g., 𝔓[46] A C D[c] K L P), but the alternate term "called" *(kaleō)* is also contained in several Western manuscripts (e.g., D* F G 33 436 1175 it[d,g] cop[sa] goth arm eth). The unusual use of the phrase "to make fit" or "to qualify" may have led copyists to choose the more common term. In the NT *hikanoō* is found elsewhere only in 2 Cor 3:6. In addition, several manuscripts refer to "us" (e.g., A C D G K P Ψ 33 614 *Byz Lect* it vg syr[p,h] cop[bo] *al*) rather than "you" (e.g., ℵ B 1739 syr[hmg] cop[sa] goth arm eth), but the substitution was probably the result of an attempt to harmonize v. 12 with v. 13 (see Metzger 620).

the inheritance of the saints in the light: This phrase should be compared to Acts 26:18 (cf. Acts 20:32)—a summary of Paul's teaching that contains both the term "inheritance" or "lot" *(klēros)* and a reference to those who are sanctified (i.e., the saints or holy ones; a cognate of the expression *hoi hagioi* occurs). It has been suggested, based largely on the Qumran evidence (e.g., 1QS 11:7-8; 1QH 11:11-12), that *hoi hagioi* refers to the angels that figure prominently in the religiosity of Colossians (e.g., 2:18; see Lohse 36; Taylor and Reumann 123–24; see also BAGD 9). But the fact that "saints" is usually used in the more general sense, referring to those who belong to the people of God (cf. 1:2, 4, 26, etc.; see the notes on 1:2), as well as the similar terminology in Acts have led others to argue that this interpretation is unlikely (see Harris 34–35). It is not easy to decide the matter, but the fact that apocalyptic thought includes the notion of fellowship with angels or the righteous being in communion with angels tips the balance in favor of "saints" referring to angels (*1 Enoch* 51; Matt 22:30; cf. 1QS 4:20-23; Pol. *Phil.* 12:2; cited in Dunn 52; see also the notes on Eph 1:18; 2:1). On "the inheritance" see the note on 3:24 (cf. Eph 1:14, 18; 5:5). The reference to the light is probably to the nature of the kingdom in which the believers now dwell. This is the kingdom of God's beloved Son mentioned in v. 13—the antithesis of the power of darkness. Similar concepts occur in the QL (cf.1QM 13:4-18; for further parallels and more extensive discussion of this relationship see Lohse 35–37).

13. *who delivered us out of the power of darkness:* Verses 13-14 are sometimes taken together with vv. 15-20 (see REB; NJB). They are in fact closely related to the christological hymn of vv. 15-20. With these verses the focus is shifted toward the Son and away from the Father in the first instance, but vv. 15-20 have often been viewed as an independent unit (see below). Moreover, vv. 13-14 continue the interests of previous verses in spelling out the grounds for offering thanksgiving to the Father, and the reference to "darkness" in v. 13 clearly offers a parallel to the focus on light in the previous verse. Thus vv. 13-14 are best read as closely related to vv. 9-12, but acting as transitional verses in relation to the next section (this sense of transition is clearly visible in v. 14). The notion of deliverance here recalls the Exodus (Exod 6:6; 14:30; Judg 6:9, 13) and God's rescue of God's people generally (e.g., Judg 8:4; Ps 77:11-15). The preposition *ek* is usually rendered in this case as "from" (from the power of darkness). Yet "out of the power of darkness" captures more forcefully the sense of rescue and deliverance from an existence that is devoid of hope. *Ek* in this case refers to "situations and circumstances out of which someone is brought" (BAGD 234). There is a very strong sense of transference from one realm to the other. The term *(exousia)* translated here as "power" is a central concept in Pauline thought. It is used elsewhere clearly to establish Christ's reign; Christ conquers all other powers—even those that rule in the spiritual world (cf. 1:16; 2:10, 15). *Exousia* can carry a wide variety of meanings in the NT, including publicly recognized power that sets one apart as an authority (such as in the case of apostolic authority; cf. 2 Cor 10:8; 13:10). In 1:13 the term should be read in relation to the concept of kingdom. It refers to the realm or domain in which power is exercised (BAGD 278). This domain is characterized by darkness (on the similarity between this language and concepts in the QL see the notes on 1:12). That this "power of darkness" is meant as the most negative and menacing of all dominions is made clear by the use of the same expression in Luke 22:53, which offers Jesus' reaction to those who wish to arrest him: "When I was with you day after day in the Temple, you did not lay hands on me. But this is your hour, and the power of darkness!" (NRSV).

and transferred us into the kingdom of his beloved son: Both the verbs "deliver" and "transfer" emphasize the Father's initiative in securing the salvation of the Colossians. The Father has led believers into a new domain; their citizenship is now in a new kingdom. This language recalls the powerful experience of baptism for believers. The emphasis is on the present reality of existence and their present participation in the kingdom. A similar emphasis on the present is found in Eph 5:5 where believers are described as sharing the inheritance in the kingdom of Christ and of God (cf. 2 Tim 4:1, 18). The kingdom clearly belongs to both Christ and God. The reference to the kingdom of Christ is quite unusual in the NT; the usual expression is "kingdom of God." That the kingdom is said to belong to Christ (or in this case, to "his beloved Son") seems to stem from the notion of the Son's agency in establishing the Father's rule (cf. 1 Cor. 15:23-25; and see Harris 36). The use of the concept of "kingdom" here as the domain of present salvation is very much in keeping with the theology of Colossians. Outside of the synoptic gospels, however, references to the kingdom of God are comparatively rare. In the undisputed letters of Paul the notion is frequently employed with a clear future dimension (e.g., 1 Cor 6:9-10; Gal 5:21). Although it is possible that v. 14 should be understood as referring to the Son who is begotten of the Father's love *(tou huiou tēs agapēs autou),* it is much more likely that the reference to love should be understood as qualitative, as is made clear by the translation "beloved Son" (NRSV; NAB), "dear Son" (REB), or "the Son that he loves" (NJB; see Harris 36; cf. Mark 1:11; 9:7; 12:6).

14. *in whom we have redemption:* Verse 14 clearly sets the stage for the Christ-hymn below (see the notes on 1:13). "In whom" refers to incorporation into Christ as in 1:2 (see discussion of "in Christ" in the notes on 1:2). The term for "redemption" or deliverance here *(apolytrōsis;* cf. Eph 1:7, 14; 4:30) literally means release (cf. Heb 11:35), drawing its origin from the notion of "buying back a slave or captive, making him free by payment of a ransom" (BAGD 96). One can detect the close connection with release from slavery in Paul's use of the term in Rom 8:23. In Rom 8:21-23 slavery serves as a metaphor for that from which Christians have been delivered. There is a significant amount of language of bondage and release in Colossians (see the notes on 2:14, 15). This is particularly interesting since the condition of slaves is one of the social issues addressed by the letter (Col 3:23-25). Although the reading is not well attested, some manuscripts have "redemption through his blood," harmonizing the text with Eph 1:7.

the forgiveness of sins: Redemption is defined as the forgiveness of sins. This precise formula does not occur in the undisputed letters of Paul; the closest parallel is in Rom 3:24-25. It may seem like an overly brief description of salvation, but it is most likely meant to encapsulate the powerful transformation that occurs in baptism. In the Acts of the Apostles "the forgiveness of sins" acts as a formula for the content of salvation (Acts 5:31; 10:43; 13:38; 26:18). The relationship between this concept and baptism can be seen clearly in Acts 2:38, where the forgiveness of sins is identified as the purpose of baptism: "Repent, and be baptized every one of you in the name of Jesus Christ so that your sins may be forgiven; and you will receive the gift of the Holy Spirit" (NRSV). The phrase is a particularly apt definition of redemption for Colossians since the meaning of baptism is in all likelihood central to the dispute between the author and the false teachers (see the notes and interpretation on 2:8-15).

INTERPRETATION

The prayer on behalf of the Colossians is very closely related to the thanksgiving of vv. 3-8. Similar concepts and terminology shape both sections. This is made clear by v. 12, which returns once again to the theme of thanksgiving. Both sections draw upon the language of prayer and worship, with liturgical influences especially evident in vv. 9-14. Taken together they prepare the way for the citation of the Christ-hymn in vv. 15-20, which is of central importance to the shape of the letter. One subtle difference between vv. 3-8 and vv. 9-14, however, is that to a great extent the latter section leaves behind the concrete concerns of community life (such as the relationship between the community and Paul's fellow workers; cf. 1:7), instead concentrating mainly on the nature of the Colossians' relationship with God—the basis of their salvation. That Colossians 1:9–2:23 pays close attention to the doctrinal foundation of community life has often been recognized. In fact, the letter has frequently been viewed as divided rather neatly between doctrine (chs. 1–2) and ethics (chs. 3–4). While this distinction is correct in very general terms, it is also somewhat artificial. In the section presently under discussion, for example, ethical concerns are clearly evident in v. 10 where believers are instructed to walk in a manner worthy of the Lord, bearing fruit in every good work. It should also be noted that while Colossians (like Ephesians) has a very interesting doctrinal component it needs to be examined as integrally related to the way of life of community members, involving both ethical comportment and ritual practices.

Part of the reason why commentators have emphasized doctrine at the expense of other features of the work is that the conflict with false teachers (2:8-23) appears to be fundamental to the document's purpose (see Introduction). Moreover, traditionally the tendency among scholars has been to value theological ideas above all other features of NT works. Thus the conflict at Colossae has been viewed as mainly about beliefs. An interest in identifying the precise shape of heretical ideas has dominated interpretation of the work, even the interpretation of verses that are not explicitly concerned with responding to heretical beliefs. Commentators have evaluated a section like this one, for example, examining the concepts and terms in the hope of finding indirect evidence of the nature of the false teaching by means of the response. Those who argue in favor of the opponents being Gnostic (or proto-Gnostic) in orientation might, for example, wonder if the focus on knowledge in vv. 9-10 is an attempt to respond to opponents who argue that salvation is based on a special claim to higher knowledge. The main difficulty with such an interpretation is that the manner in which knowledge, wisdom, and understanding are treated in these verses is very much in keeping with contemporary Jewish literature (see Pokorný [1991] 47) and by no means necessarily reflects a particular teaching of the author in response to the opponents (see the notes on 1:9). As is explained below, in 1:9-14 it is in fact possible to detect the author's strategy for responding to opponents, but it is not possible to infer from these verses any information about the doctrines at the heart of the dispute between author and opponents.

Despite the considerable information revealed about features of the opponents' stance in 2:16-23 there has been no consensus among scholars about their identity. New work on the contemporary evidence, including ancient inscriptions, has demonstrated that key elements of the teaching were present in local groups, including local Jewish groups, but many questions remain (see, e.g., the discussion of the work of Clinton Arnold [1995] in the Introduction, and the notes and interpretation on 2:16-23). In the face of a wide variety of theories (see Introduction) concerning the identity of the Colossian opponents, ranging from Judaism to Gnosticism to such philosophical schools as Cynicism and Pythagoreanism, some scholars now believe that it is best to think of the document as responding to "a set of traditions widely affirmed and practiced" rather than to the position of one particular party (see D'Angelo 319). Moreover, recent work has stressed the probability that the author of Colossians and the opponents may have shared core Christian beliefs (D'Angelo 320; see also Attridge 498). But if beliefs were not at the heart of the conflict at Colossae, what was causing the problems? Social-scientific criticism has helped interpreters to understand that community conflict can result for reasons other than purely doctrinal debates. As is argued throughout this commentary, it is best to think of the conflict at Colossae as centered in the significance of what is experienced in the midst of ritual. In particular the transition from the anti-structured liminality experienced during central religious rituals such as rites of passage (e.g., baptism) to the world of social structures that frames the living out of experience in everyday life has proved problematic (for a full discussion see the notes and interpretation on 2:8-15). At the heart of the conflict is how to live out the meaning of the profound experiences that lead one into the community and continue to foster commitment.

Colossians 1:9-14 reflects the author's strategy for responding to the problems among the Colossians. It is a strategy of remembrance: it recalls for believers the core experience of God they attained during baptism and that they sense in the midst of prayer and worship. The recollection of baptism seems especially central to the author's response to the problems in the community (cf. 1:12-14; 2:9-15; 3:1-3, 10-11). The hope seems to be that if community members are brought back to the joy they experienced in baptism they will see the futility of the strongly ascetic measures adopted by the false teachers (2:8-23).

As is made clear by the phrase "growing in the knowledge of God" (1:10), the author is aware that intense religious experience is central to the life of the Colossians. But the prayer on behalf of the Colossians is for discernment (1:9). Believers have shared in the powerful experience of God, but they must know how to live with and worship God. Ethical deportment is a priority. Walking (*peripateō*) in the manner that is worthy of the Lord clearly refers to interaction between believers, but it is important to realize that the ethical stance demanded of believers also involves interaction with nonbelievers and the world in general. The use of the term *peripateō* in 3:7 and 4:5 reveals this dual perspective clearly (see the notes on 1:10).

It is interesting to compare the use of the term "to walk" (or "to live") in 1 Thess 4:1-12 with the usage in Col 1:10. The former passage begins with general exhortations to live *(peripateō)* and to please God (1 Thess 4:1) that resemble those in Col 1:10. Throughout 1 Thess 4:1-12 the ethical standards of the community are defined with reference to the life of nonbelievers. Even marriage between believers is described with a view to the standards of the nonbelieving world (1 Thess 4:4-5; see the alternate translation of the Greek text in the notes on 4:4 in NRSV). The Thessalonians passage culminates in the instruction that believers should behave *(peripateō)* "properly" toward outsiders (v. 12). An ethical standard that calls for "proper" or "reputable" behavior in relation to outsiders is surprising to modern readers, especially considering the abundance of NT texts that stress the need to set aside the concerns of the world and even to separate oneself from the evil world. In fact sometimes NT interest in the reaction of outsiders appears at first glance to be motivated by little more than a concern for social respectability (e.g., 1 Tim 3:7). But two aspects of the social setting of an early church community need to be kept in mind when we seek to understand such priorities. First, living in an honor-shame society (see the notes and interpretation on 1:3-8), first-century community members defined their identities to a great extent through public acknowledgment of their reputation. Second, the general cultural concern for gaining public acknowledgment was played out in a group that combined a call for a clearly distinguishable identity with a commitment to universal mission. An attempt to balance these two elements is reflected in 4:5-6 where believers are instructed in how to walk *(peripateō)* in relation to outsiders.

As illustrated by the discussion in the notes on 1:10, the reference to good works probably also should be understood as pertaining not only to works (or deeds) that are part of the interaction between community members, but also to works involving interaction between believers and nonbelievers. In the deutero-Pauline letters the authors seem particularly aware of the visibility of good works, their potential for revealing commitment and for demonstrating the value of faith (e.g., Col 3:17; Eph 2:10; for full discussion of several parallel texts see Lohse 29–30). In the Pastoral Epistles "good works" are an attribute of pious women (1 Tim 5:10). There is good reason to believe that in these documents the interest in directing the behavior of women is in response to public criticism of the behavior of believing women (see M. Y. MacDonald [1996] 154–78). In contrast, the error of false teachers is revealed, for they are unfit for any good work (Titus 1:16). Similarly, the previous life of the Colossians involved doing evil deeds (Col 1:21). As the Pauline communities developed beyond the first generation of their existence they were troubled both by internal deviance and by increasing hostility from outsiders. A broad reference to the model conduct of Christians in daily life such as is contained in the phrase "every good work" needs to be understood in light of this background. The author's prayer for the Colossians is that they may be strengthened by an all-powerful God and be granted patience and endurance. That the deeds of community members are gaining a new significance in an increasingly tense atmosphere (cf. Col 4:5-6) is further suggested by the development of the household code (3:18–4:1), which introduces into Pauline Christianity a series of rule-like ethical exhortations governing daily life.

The prayer for the empowerment of the Colossians in v. 11 is followed immediately by a thanksgiving for what the all-powerful God has accomplished in Christ in vv. 12-14. These verses recall baptism and give thanks for the new citizenship of believers; believers have been transferred into the kingdom of God's beloved Son. Verses 12-14 may in fact constitute a doxology that was once part of a baptismal liturgy. The themes of authority and empowerment continue in these verses from v. 11 on, even if the language is not explicit. Believers have been rescued and have received redemption. God is the ultimate authority. Such language may well have conjured up images of release from bondage (see the notes on 1:14) and spoken powerfully to the slave members (cf. 3:22-25) of the community (see also the notes on 2:14, 15).

As in the undisputed letters of Paul, one of the main ways in which the identity of believers is communicated in Colossians is through language of belonging and language of separation (see M. Y. MacDonald [1988] 32–39, 98–100; Meeks [1983] 87–90). NT interpreters who draw upon insights from the social sciences have noted the importance of such language in maintaining a sectarian identity—a very strong commitment to create a community that is set apart from the outside world. The reference to "sharing in the inheritance of the saints in the light" is language of belonging, boldly announcing that believers ultimately belong to a transformed world. But strong language also expresses what has been rejected; believers have separated themselves from the power of darkness. Yet to say that the Colossian community has a "sectarian" identity should not be taken to mean that the community had no interest in relations with outsiders. On the contrary, Colossians displays considerable interest in a universal mission (e.g., Col 1:6, 18-20, 23; 2:19; 3:15). In fact the Pauline churches display the type of tension between the desire to win new members and the need to remain separate that has been noted in modern "conversionist" sects. This tension generally exposes the community to certain difficulties; for a full discussion of this topic see the notes and interpretation on 4:2-6, as well as M. Y. MacDonald [1988] 97–102. (On sectarian identity in Ephesians see the notes and interpretation on Eph 2:1-10.)

Colossians 1:13-14 offers an excellent example of the language of belonging-separation typically found in Colossians and Ephesians. In these documents language of belonging-separation takes the form primarily of a remembrance of conversion—a remembrance of transference from the evil world outside into the realm where salvation is now to be found (cf. 1:21-23; Eph 4:17-24). Typically remembrance of the initial acceptance of the gospel and baptism is followed by ethical exhortations setting the behavior apart from that of internal enemies and nonbelievers. Colossians 1:13-14 might be viewed as a particularly succinct statement of a sentiment that runs from 1:1–2:7. Taken as a whole this longer unit proclaims the reconciliation of the estranged, explains the significance of the Christ event, and celebrates Paul's role. It recalls for believers all that has taken place and the means through which God has transformed the universe. This longer section culminates in the following summary statement, which draws upon many of the ideas found in 1:9-14: "As therefore you received Christ Jesus the Lord, walk in him, rooted and built up in him and established in the faith as you were taught, abounding in thanksgiving" (2:6-7). Having undertaken this remembrance, the author turns specifically to the problem at the heart of the dispute with false teachers in 2:8-23.

FOR REFERENCE AND FURTHER STUDY

Attridge, Harold A. "On Becoming an Angel: Rival Baptismal Theologies at Colossae," in Lukas Bormann, Kelly Del Tredici, and Angela Standhartinger, eds., *Religious Propaganda and Missionary Competition in the NT World: Essays Honoring Dieter Georgi*. Leiden: E. J. Brill, 1994, 481–98.

Benoit, Pierre. "Qumran and the N.T.," in Jerome Murphy-O'Connor, ed., *Paul and Qumran*. London: Geoffrey Chapman, 1968, 18–24.

_____. "*Hagioi* en Colossiens 1:12; hommes ou anges?" in Morna D. Hooker and Stephen G. Wilson, eds., *Paul and Paulinism. Essays in Honour of C. K. Barrett*. London: S.P.C.K., 1982, 83–99.

Dahl, Nils A. "Anamnesis: Memory and Commemoration in the Early Church," in idem, *Jesus in the Memory of the Early Church*. Minneapolis: Augsburg, 1976, 11–29.

Käsemann, Ernst. "A Primitive Christian Baptismal Liturgy," in idem, *Essays on New Testament Themes*. London: S.C.M., 1964, 149–68.

Martin, Dale B. *Slavery as Salvation: The Metaphor of Slavery in Pauline Christianity.* New Haven and London: Yale University Press, 1990.

Sullivan, M. Kathryn. "Epignosis in the Epistles of St. Paul," in *Studiorum Paulinorum Congressus Internationalis Catholicus 1961*. AnBib 17, 18. Rome: Pontifical Biblical Institute, 1963, 2:405–16.

Wiles, Gordon P. *Paul's Intercessory Prayers*. MSSNTS 24. Cambridge: Cambridge University Press, 1974.

4. *The Christ-Hymn* (1:15-20)

15. He is the image of the invisible God, the firstborn of all creation, 16. for in him were created all things in heaven and on earth, the visible and the invisible, whether thrones or dominions or rulers or powers—all things have been created through him and for him. 17. He is before all things and in him all things hold together, 18. and he is the head of the body, the church. He is the beginning, the firstborn from the dead, in order that he might come to hold first place in all things. 19. For in him all the fullness was pleased to dwell, 20. and through him to reconcile all things to himself, making peace through the blood of his cross (through him), whether the things on the earth or the things in heaven.

Notes

15. *He is the image of the invisible God:* The translation adopted here is identical to that found in the NRSV and the NAB. Literally, it could be rendered as "who is the image." The use of the relative pronoun "who" *(hos)* is identical to that in v. 13 ("who delivered us"). The phrase has been rendered in English as the start of a new sentence since it clearly marks the beginning of the self-contained unit, vv. 15-20. "He" refers to the beloved Son in whom believers have their redemption (vv. 13-14). The image of God might mean the image belonging to God (genitive of possession), but it most likely refers to the notion of Christ "imaging" God (objective genitive). The term "image" *(eikōn)* may mean simply "resemblance," but that the word refers to "complete likeness" is much more likely because of the close identification between the Son and God implied by 1:9 (cf. 2:9; and see Harris 43). In a similar manner Christ is referred to as the image of God in 2 Cor 4:4. In Colossians the notion of image also figures in the description of baptism in 3:10 where the believer as a new person is said to be renewed in full knowledge according to the image of the creator (see the notes and interpretation on Col 3:10-11; cf. 1 Cor 15:49). The description of God as the invisible *(aoratos)* God is in keeping with other NT texts where the same word occurs (Rom 1:20; 1 Tim 1:17; Heb 11:27); 1 Tim 1:17 offers an especially apt parallel in language of praise. As in Colossians, the unseen, transcendent God is in view: "To the King of the ages, immortal, invisible, the only God, be honor and glory forever and ever" (NRSV; cf. 1 Tim 6:16). The notion of Christ making known an unseen God is prominent in John's gospel (cf. John 1:18; 12:45; 14:9). In 1:16 the notion of invisible is also applied to a portion of God's creation (see the notes below).

the firstborn of all creation: The concept of the firstborn is important in the Hebrew Bible (e.g., Gen 48:18; Num 18:15). The term is employed in Luke's description of Mary giving birth to Jesus (Luke 2:7; cf. Matt 1:25). In some texts the term refers not only to birth order, but also to preeminence in rank as in the description of the Davidic king in Psalm 89:27 (see Harris 43). In fact, scholars consider it probable that when the term "firstborn" *(prōtotokos)* was used in NT times the force of the second half of the term (born, from *tichtō*, to give birth to) was lost unless it referred literally to a birth (as in Luke 2:7). In other words, the term could refer to rank, rather than birth or origin (see BAGD 726; Michaelis, *TDNT* 6:878). Certainly the emphasis in 1:15 is clearly on Christ's preeminent place in the created order. Similarly in 1:18 Christ is referred to as the firstborn from the dead (cf. Rev 1:5). These texts should be compared to Rom 8:29-30 where Christ is described as the firstborn of a new community of believers that is to be glorified: "For those whom he foreknew he also predestined to be conformed to the image of his Son, in order that he might be the firstborn within a large family. And those whom he predestined he also called; and those whom he called he also justified; and those whom he justified he also glorified" (NRSV). In Colossians the glorification of believers is also in view (Col 3:1-4). The concepts of creation (or every creature; cf. 1:23) and of God creating (cf. Col 1:16; 3:10) are central in Colossians. It is grammatically possible to translate the phrase less literally as Lohse has done: "the firstborn before all creation" (taking the Greek phrase to be a genitive of comparison rather than an objective genitive implying simply superiority, i.e. Christ is over all creation). Lohse believes that the phrase is a characterization of the preexistent Christ who is called "firstborn" before creation in a manner that accords with Jewish speculation about wisdom. Wisdom was created before all other things (e.g., Prov 8:22; Sir 1:4). Wisdom praises herself: "Before the ages, in the beginning he created me, and for all the ages I shall not cease to be" (Sir 24:9 NRSV; cf. Wis 9:4, 9; on the possible connection of this hymn with feminine imagery of God see interpretation below). Even though Lohse adopts a translation that highlights Christ as created before all creatures he argues that the main point is not time, but rank: "The point is not a temporal advantage but rather the superiority which is due to him as the agent of creation who is before all creation. As the first-born he stands over creation as Lord" (Lohse 48–49). Thus while it may seem at first glance that the reference to Christ as "firstborn" implies that Christ belongs to the created order as the first created being, this is most likely not the case (though it should be noted that the Arian controversy in the fourth century concerned the status of Christ as independently created by the Father rather than co-existing with the Father). The focus is on Christ's primacy; as the following verse makes clear, he stands beyond the created world as the agent through which everything came into existence.

16. *for in him were created all things in heaven and on earth, the visible and the invisible:* "For" *(hoti)* here means "because" and the verse goes on to explain why Christ reigns supreme over all creation and to highlight his unique position. The NIV translates the expression *en autō* as "by him" (see also the notes for NRSV). This more closely captures the meaning of the expression, but it has been rendered here as "in him" in order to draw attention to the fundamental connection between this phrase and the characteristic Pauline formula "in Christ." As is the case here, the formula can sometimes be employed in Pauline literature to refer to Christ as "agent" (see the notes on 1:2). In 1:16 Christ is viewed as the agent of creation. The expression "all things" *(ta panta)* recalls the reference

to "all creation" in v. 15; there is greater attention given in v. 16, however, to the separate spheres of existence (heaven and earth, the visible and the invisible) and the individual things (thrones, dominions, etc.) which make up the whole collectivity. The main point here is that nothing is excluded.

whether thrones or dominions or rulers or powers: In all likelihood this is a reference to cosmic powers that are viewed as subordinate to Christ. They may very well have been understood in the Colossian community as angelic beings. The terminology is associated with angels in Jewish literature (cf. *2 Enoch* 20:1; *2 Enoch* 61:10). According to *T. Levi* 3.8 in heaven "there are thrones and dominions in which they always offer praise to God." The author of Colossians stresses the superiority of Christ over these supernatural beings, but the proponents of the false teaching in Colossae may have believed that these beings were Christ's rivals or, what is more likely, they may have thought that veneration of these beings provided additional access to the benefits of salvation (cf. the notes on 2:10, 15 and the interpretation below.) In the NT this is the only place where throne *(thronos)* refers to a supernatural being. Dominion *(kyriotes)* refers to spiritual powers in Eph 1:21 (cf. 1 Cor 8:5). Rulers (sometimes translated as "principalities") and powers are quite frequently associated with the cosmic realm in the NT and often are listed together. For "ruler" *(archē)* see Rom 8:38; 1 Cor 15:24; Eph 1:21; 3:10; 6:12. For "power" *(exousia)* see 1 Cor 15:24; Eph 1:21; 3:10; 6:12; 1 Pet 3:22. The language used here with respect to the cosmic entities can also appear in the NT to refer to earthly authority and rule (e.g., Luke 20:20; 2 Pet 2:10; Jude 8).

all things have been created through him and for him: Verse 16 contains one of several examples in the hymn of chiasmus, the A-B-B-A pattern found frequently in the NT ("were created all things . . . all things have been created"). The change of verb tense from the aorist to the perfect form indicates creation's ongoing existence. In other words, not only were all things created but they also remain in their created existence through Christ and for Christ. The passive voice that runs through the verse indicates that God is the creator. God creates, but Christ is the agent of creation: "through him." "For him" *(eis auton)* may refer to Christ's glorification, but it most likely describes Christ as the final goal: all things are created toward him. In speculation about Wisdom (see the note on 1:15 above) she was depicted not only as present at the beginning of creation but also as bringing the world to its final goal. According to *1 Enoch* 49:1-4, Wisdom will reappear in the last times and her spirit will dwell in the Son of Man and he will execute judgment. In this hymn and in Colossians generally Christ is the agent who mediates creation and the final fulfillment of the universe. Similar notions are contained in 1 Cor 8:6: "yet for us there is one God, the Father, from whom are all things and for whom we exist, and one Lord, Jesus Christ, through whom are all things and through whom we exist" (NRSV).

17. *He is before all things:* The "he" in this case is most likely emphatic. It means he himself—he and no other. To say that Christ is before all things is a reference to preexistence. Although *pro* most often refers to temporal priority, it is also sometimes employed in the NT to refer to priority of importance (see Jas 5:12;

1 Pet 4:8; and see BAGD 702). A focus on the superiority of Christ over the universe would be in keeping with the use of "firstborn" in 1:15 (see the notes above; cf. 1:18). It is most likely that the notions of temporal priority (Christ existed before the creation of the universe) and supremacy work together.

and in him all things hold together: The NRSV notes include the alternate translation of the characteristic Pauline formula "in him" as "by him." This would be the instrumental sense as in 1:16. But the locative sense seems more appropriate here than in 1:16: the universe is subsumed under Christ and contained within Christ (see the notes on 1:2). Christ fills the universe with his power. Such notions would act as an appropriate transition to use of the symbol of the body of Christ in 1:18. The main point is that not only does Christ act as the agent of creation but also creation is maintained in him. The term "to hold together" *(sunistēmi)* suggests coherence, unity, and stability, which occur in Christ. It is a term employed in Platonic and Stoic philosophy to designate the unity of the cosmos.

18. *and he is the head of the body, the church:* As in 1:17 the opening "he" is emphatic: he himself, he and no other. "And" here *(kai)* has the sense of also: Not only is the universe centered in Christ, so also is the church *(ekklēsia)*. In the undisputed letters of Paul the community of believers is also described as Christ's body *(sōma;* e.g., Rom 12:4-8; 1 Cor 12:12-17), but in Colossians and Ephesians the body of Christ symbolism has been transformed. First, the body of Christ (as in this verse) is *explicitly* equated with the church, i.e., the *ekklēsia* is called body (cf. 1:24; Eph 1:22-23; 5:23). Second, the symbol has been augmented: Christ has become the head while the believers make up his body (1:18, 24; 2:10, 17, 19; Eph 1:22; 4:4, 15; 5:23). There is a close connection in 1:15-20 between Christ as head of the universe and Christ as head of the church. His body becomes the vehicle of cosmic reconciliation (see the notes on 1:19, 20 below). Moreover, the body of Christ symbolism that is anticipated in v. 17 (see the notes above) and continues throughout vv. 18-20 reveals an underlying equivalence between the universe and the church that is probably tied to the experience of universal mission (see the interpretation below). The notion of "head" *(kephalē)* establishes this equivalence. In 2:10 Christ is called head of every ruler and authority (see the notes on 1:16 for an explanation of these terms)—an expression that clearly establishes Christ's cosmic reign. The comparison of the whole cosmos to the body is well attested in ancient Greek sources (see, e.g., Plato, *Timaeus* 28B) and can also be found in Hellenistic Judaism. In a manner that recalls Christ's role here, Philo of Alexandria, for example, spoke of the body *(sōma)* of the cosmos needing the eternal *logos* of God who is the head of the universe *(Quaest. in Ex.* 2.68; for other examples see Lohse 53–54; on the body in Greco-Roman culture see Dale B. Martin [1995] 15–34). Many scholars believe that the expression "[of] the church" was added to the hymn (originally an independent unit) as an editorial gloss by the author of Colossians (see the interpretation below).

He is the beginning, the firstborn from the dead: Calling Christ the beginning *(archē)* could well be a reference to his preexistence. In Jewish literature Wisdom is called the beginning: "In the beginning *(archē)*, before the ages he established me" (LXX Prov 8:23; see Lohse 56; and see the notes on 1:15 above). But the reference to the beginning might also simply be a means of introducing the expression that follows. As in 1:15, Christ is named as the firstborn, but the focus is not on his role in creation but on his role in saving humanity. "Firstborn from the dead" is clearly a reference to the path to salvation made possible by Christ's death and resurrection. Christ is the "first-fruits" and others now share in the hope of resurrection: "Christ has been raised from the dead, the first-fruits of those who have died" (1 Cor 15:20 NRSV; cf. Rom 8:29; Rev 1:5). It is interesting to note that sometimes the expressions "firstborn" and "beginning" occur together in Jewish literature to describe the founder of a people (see LXX Gen 49:3; LXX Deut 21:17; and see Lohse 56). Similarly, these verses explain how Christ is founding a new community; he is re-creating a people.

in order that he might come to hold first place in all things: This is a purpose clause: in order that he might come (*hina genētai*, aorist, middle subjunctive of *ginomai*). Because Christ is the beginning and "the firstborn from the dead" he therefore became first in all things. While the verb *ginomai* often means simply "is" *(eimi)*, there may be special significance attached to the use of the verb here. It may be employed in contrast to the "is" *(eimi)* of v. 17a. It is probably best to translate *genētai* here as "become" (REB: "to become in all things supreme") or as is the case here (and in NRSV): "that he might come to hold first" (see Harris 48–49). Verse 17 refers to Christ's place in the universe where he is and always has been supreme. Verse 18 refers directly to what Christ has accomplished through his death and resurrection and to the existence of the church (see the notes above). This phrase reveals an awareness of a particular moment in history when Christ's supremacy in relation to the church was revealed. Specific attention is paid to events that occurred in order that he might come to hold first place in all things (see Harris 49). As in v. 17 and v. 18a, "he" is emphatic (he himself, he and no other). The verb "to be first" *(proteuō)* represents a further emphasis on Christ's preeminence that is closely related in meaning to the expression used twice in the hymn: "firstborn" (v. 15, v. 18) and "he is before all things" (v. 17). "In all things" is a further example of a notion occurring frequently in the hymn (see vv. 16-17). It refers to the whole of the universe, to both the visible and the invisible. But there is a particular focus on the church here as being part of this totality and perhaps even an underlying equivalence between the universe and the universal church that fills the universe as Christ's body (see the notes above).

19. *For in him all the fullness:* This verse supplies the reason why Christ is supreme in both creation and universe. "For" *(hoti)* has the sense of "because." This is the third occurrence of "in him" in the hymn. Here the Pauline formula is clearly used in a locative sense: fullness dwells within Christ (see the notes on 1:16, 18; cf. 1:2). The main translation question arising from the Greek text is whether "God" should be supplied as the implied subject even though the term does not appear. It is grammatically possible to translate the verse as in the NIV: "because God wanted all fullness to be found in him" (cf. NJB; REV). This translation allows for a smoother transition to v. 20 (i.e., God makes

peace). A major difficulty with this option, however, is that Christ is consistently the subject throughout the hymn, with God not having been mentioned since v. 15. Thus it is probably best to take "fullness" *(plērōma)* as the subject (cf. NAB). The NRSV also adopts this option, but rather than taking the subject as impersonal (simply as "the fullness"), it conceives of the subject personally, as "the fullness of God" (see Harris 49–50). This translation has no doubt been influenced by 2:9 where occurs the expression "the fullness of the deity" (see BAGD 672). Despite the possible differences in meaning and the grammatical ambiguities, however, the main point is clear: God dwells within Christ. The fullness refers to the fullness of God in its totality. The use of the term "fullness" *(plērōma)* in Colossians helps to shape the distinctive theological vision of this document (cf. 1:9; 2:9; Eph 1:10, 23; 3:19; 4:13). The significance of the term "fullness" within this verse has been extensively debated by scholars; see summary of possibilities in Aletti [1981] 78–81). In non-technical usage it refers straightforwardly to that which fills or that which makes something complete. The term was sometimes employed in a more technical sense. For example, it figured prominently in second-century Gnostic thought. Among the Valentinians the concept referred to the totality of emanations that came forth from God. The eons emanating from God filled the space in the uppermost spiritual realm—the place closest to God. This spiritual or heavenly realm was understood as separated from the cosmos by a boundary (for background on this concept see Lohse 56–77; Delling, *plērēs, plēroō, TDNT* 6:283–311).

Although it has sometimes been argued that such ideas have influenced the theology of the author of Colossians (see Käsemann 158–59), most commentators only go so far as to say that the false teachers (and not the author of Colossians) may have been influenced by proto-Gnostic tendencies. The false teaching at Colossae seems to have included speculation concerning the heavenly realm and ascetic measures designed to guarantee access to the heavenly realm; supernatural powers (including Christ) may have been understood as intermediaries who required veneration on an ongoing basis. Behind the Christ-hymn probably lies an attempt to bring the false teaching to an end with the argument that Christ is the only mediator between God and the world; God dwells fully within Christ alone (see the notes and interpretation on 2:8-23).

was pleased to dwell: The reference to the fullness (of God) being pleased to dwell calls to mind Jewish Scripture where a connection is expressed between God's choosing and God's dwelling place. In LXX Ps 67:17, for example, Zion is identified as the mountain on which it pleased God to dwell (for further examples see Lohse 58). Some have seen here an echo of the baptismal language of Mark 1:11: "You are my Son, the Beloved; with you I am well pleased" (NRSV). Similarly the verse calls to mind the reference to the incarnation in John 1:14: "the Word became flesh and dwelt among us" (NRSV). But rather than being a reference to a specific point in salvation history the verse probably pertains to the whole of the salvific work accomplished through Christ.

20. *and through him to reconcile all things to himself:* As in v. 16, we find here the expression "through him" used to refer to Christ's agency. Creation occurs through

Christ and the broken harmony of the universe has been restored through Christ: there has been a cosmic reconciliation. The expression "to himself" *(eis auton)*, however, is ambiguous in Greek. Some commentators believe that it refers to God and not to Christ because of the way reconciliation consistently occurs "to God" in other Pauline works (Rom 5:10; 2 Cor 5:18-20; Eph 2:16; see Harris 50). We might compare the verse to 2 Cor 5:19: "in Christ God was reconciling the world to himself, not counting their trespasses against them, and entrusting the message of reconciliation to us." The NRSV understands "to him" as referring to God, as the translation makes clear: "and through him God was pleased to reconcile to himself all things." The verb "to reconcile" *(apokatallassō)* is not a term that occurs frequently in Pauline literature (1:20, 22; Eph 2:16; *katallassō:* Rom 5:10; 1 Cor 7:11; 2 Cor 5:18, 19, 20). The close association of the related term *katallassō* with the notion of rupture is made clear by the use of the term in 1 Cor 7:11. Here it is used with respect to the breakup of a husband and wife: "if she does separate let her remain unmarried or else be reconciled to her husband" (NRSV). Underlying 1:20 is the notion of rupture and restoration on a cosmic level. "All things" refers to the whole of the universe.

making peace through the blood of his cross: This verse explains how the reconciliation occurred. It is the only place in the NT where the verb "to make peace" *(eirēnopoieō)* is found, though a cognate of the term occurs in the well-known Matthean beatitude: "blessed are the peacemakers" (Matt 5:9). This phrase is striking in a hymn devoted to celebrating Christ's triumph and cosmic reign. It reminds believers that Christ's suffering and death are central to the salvation of the universe. Historical and physical experiences are fundamental to redemption. The cross is mentioned again in 2:14 in order to make the point that the measures adopted by the false teachers are not necessary: the death and resurrection have changed the shape of the universe. Colossians 1:20 is in keeping with Paul's theology of the cross (1 Cor 1:18), which is revealed especially clearly in 2 Corinthians. It is interesting to note that 2 Cor 5:11-21 brings together elements of this theology with the notion of reconciliation that is also central to Col 1:20 (see 2 Cor 5:14-21). In 2 Cor 5:19 Paul speaks of the message of reconciliation—"the word of reconciliation"—in a manner that parallels his famous expression "the word of the cross" (1 Cor 1:18). Many scholars believe that the expression "through the blood of his cross" was added to the hymn (originally an independent unit) as an editorial gloss by the author of Colossians (see the interpretation below).

(through him), whether the things on the earth or the things in heaven: There is some manuscript variation related to the expression in brackets (through him). This expression is awkward and is missing from some manuscripts. It is retained in brackets, however, in the standard version of the Greek NT (UBS 4; see Metzger 621) and in some translations (e.g., NAB). Commentators have suggested that the repetition of "through him" supports the theory that the expression "through the blood of his cross" was inserted into the hymn as an editorial addition to a traditional hymn (see the interpretation below). The expression may be superfluous, but it may also be emphatic: "through him alone" (NEB); if indeed it

represents emphasis it should probably be taken as referring back to "through him to reconcile" at the beginning of the verse rather than being directly related to "making peace" (see Harris 51–52). The reference to things on earth and in heaven is a further means of emphasizing that the whole of the cosmos is involved. The expression complements the reference to "all things" at the beginning of the verse and the similar sentiments in v. 16.

INTERPRETATION

With the possible exception of the texts that deal specifically with the content of the false teaching (2:8-23), the Christ-hymn of Col 1:15-20 has received the greatest attention among passages in Colossians. Scholars have come to believe that these verses constitute a hymn (comparable to Phil 2:6-11) for several reasons, including the frequent repetition of terms, the presence of non-Pauline expressions and *hapax legomena*, the concentration of relative constructions, the shift in pronouns (vv. 15-20 are in the third person, while vv. 13-14 are in the first person and vv. 21-23 are in the second and first persons), and the use of rhetorical devices such as chiasmus (A-B-B-A pattern; for a chart illustrating three interlocked instances of chiasmus see Harris 42; see also the notes on 1:16). The consensus is that these verses represent an independent unit that was inserted into the letter, but there have been many technical debates concerning the structure, precise shape, and origin of the hymn. While the majority of commentators believe that the hymn begins at 1:15, it has been argued that it actually begins at 1:12. (For a list of scholars on both sides of the debate see Horgan 879.) Moreover, there are two major theories concerning how the hymn should be divided in terms of stanzas. According to Lohse there are two strophes, each beginning with the Greek relative clause *hos estin* (he [who] is) at 15a and 18b. These stanzas are divided according to the themes of Christ's role in creation and Christ's role in reconciliation—cosmology and soteriology (Lohse 42). While Lohse's view is probably the most widely held, Ralph P. Martin (following Eduard Schweizer) argues in favor of a tripartite theory. According to Martin there are three stanzas: 1:15-16; 1:17-18a; 1:18b-20. He argues that the second of these partly resumes the thought in the first, but also asserts that Christ acts as the unifying principle, holding the universe together as its head (Ralph P. Martin [1974] 55).

While there has generally been consensus that Col 1:15-20 represents an independent unit, the question of who composed the hymn remains. Most scholars believe that it represents traditional liturgical material that was edited by Paul or the deutero-Pauline author. It is widely accepted that the author of Colossians made two short interpretative additions to the hymn. First, the identification of Christ as the head of the body, the church, found at the end of the cosmological strophe suggests that the statement "of the church" was added by the author. The cosmos was frequently compared to a body in the ancient world, and headship of the cosmos was associated with God's reign in Hellenistic Jewish literature (see the notes on 1:18 above). Second, the peculiar repetition of the expression "through him" in 1:20 (see the notes) leads one to believe that the expression "through the blood of his cross" was probably also added by the author of Colossians. These two additions seem to have been made in order to give solid historical reference to a hymn with a clear cosmological flavor. Believers are reminded that the reconciliation of the whole cosmos took place through *the death of Christ*. Christ expresses his reign to *the present reality of the church*, his body (cf. Col 1:21-23).

As for the background, the body symbolism and the idea of the universe "holding together" call to mind certain philosophical concepts of the ancient world (see the notes on 1:17). In seeking to understand the origins of the hymn scholars have drawn attention to the syncretistic environment in first-century Asia Minor. They have also pointed to similarities between the hymn and Gnostic redeemer-myth material. But the most frequently proposed background for the hymn is the Jewish Wisdom tradition. In speculating about the background of the hymn Mary Rose D'Angelo has recently noted that it may have originated as a hymn to Sophia or as a pre-Christian hymn attributing the characteristics of Wisdom to the divine (male) *logos*. Because Wisdom was personified as feminine, D'Angelo has attempted to translate vv. 15-20 with the pronouns transposed to the feminine gender:

> She is the image of the unseen God (Gen 1:26-27; Wis 7:26),
> firstborn of all creation (Prov 8:22; Sir 24:9)
> in/by her was created everything
> in the heavens and on earth (Wis 7:22; 9:2-4; Prov 3:19-20; 8:22-30)
> seen and unseen:
> whether thrones or principalities, rules or authorities.
> All things were created through her and for her,
> And she is before all and the all subsists through her;
> She is the head/source of the body the church/assembly;
> She is the beginning/rule,
> that she might be preeminent among all
> Because in her the *plērōma* was pleased to dwell,
> And through her to reconcile the all to her
> Whether on heaven or on earth.

According to D'Angelo this translation, including the transposition of pronouns to the feminine gender, illustrates the relationship of the hymn not only to the Jewish Wisdom tradition, but also to Gnosticism:

In this context (as in Col 2:9), *plērōma* refers to the totality of divine reality; in Gnostic materials it designates the totality of spiritual beings and emanations. If Sophia was the original subject of the hymn, it acclaims her because her preeminent role in creation enables her to mediate the reunion of the lesser divine realities (like thrones and principalities, rules and authorities) into one full spiritual reality *(plērōma)* (D'Angelo 317–18).

The Christ-hymn of Col 1:15-20 anchors traditions about divine Wisdom firmly in history by stressing the relationship between the death of Christ and the reconciliation of the universe, and by highlighting the indwelling of Christ in the church. But as D'Angelo's reconstruction makes clear, it is important to acknowledge that the background to this hymn probably included the use of feminine imagery for divine Wisdom.

While there is great debate among scholars concerning the form, structure, and origin of the Christ-hymn, there is wide agreement that the hymn was inserted within the letter to set the stage for and even reinforce the major arguments presented. The principal themes of Colossians are announced via this hymn. The focus on Christ's preeminence and on what has been accomplished through Christ in the universe lays the foundation for the arguments against the false teaching in 2:8-23. The notion of the reigning Christ prepares the way for the proclamation that believers have been raised with Christ, and for the ethical implications of this heavenly enthronement (Col 3:1–4:1). Body symbolism is introduced into the hymn, which is central to the vision of cosmic and social integration in Colossians. Even the way the hymn articulates its message with reference to polarities (heavenly-earthly, invisible-visible) and presents Christ, ironically, as the image of the invisible God reflects the social predicament of believers: Believers find themselves in the ironic situation of living on earth while experiencing a strong sense of heavenly citizenship (see the notes and interpretation on 2:8-23; 3:18–4:1; Eph 2:1-10).

That the author of Colossians would use a hymn that believers may often have sung to act as the foundation for the major theological arguments of the epistle may seem surprising; yet recalling the experience of worship is clearly considered the best way to make points about the errors of false teaching, to proclaim the true identity of Christ, and to ensure that believers live as members of the body of Christ. The author of Colossians in fact alludes to the function of hymns, psalms, and spiritual songs in Col 3:16. (It is impossible to differentiate precisely among these three types of singing; see the notes on 3:16.) They seem to be encouraged because they lead to instruction of the community. Paul's instructions with respect to worship in 1 Corinthians 14 come immediately to mind.

The hymns we associate with worship are an example of what social scientists call ritual. The anthropologist Clifford Geertz defines ritual simply as "consecrated behavior"—behavior set apart for contact with the sacred. What Geertz has said about ritual can shed light on the importance of the Christ-hymn for Colossians as a whole. While we might be inclined to think that religious beliefs precede worship and that worship merely articulates and celebrates belief, Geertz's thought in fact suggests that this unidirectional theory is far too simplistic. According to Geertz ritual functions not only as a model for what is believed, but also as a model for believing it. In other words, ritual is involved in the very process of generating religious conviction. In the midst of ritual, authorities that transform human experience are acknowledged (in the language of Christianity, the lordship of Christ is acknowledged). In essence, in the midst of ritual people attain their faith as they portray it. Geertz also notes that ritual involves learning (see Col 3:16 where teaching is closely associated with psalms, hymns, and spiritual songs) and shapes how one will behave in the future: "Even within the same society, what one 'learns' about the essential pattern of life from a sorcery rite and from a commensual meal will have rather diverse effects on social and psychological functioning" (Geertz 39). I argue throughout this commentary that the ethical implications for what is experienced in the midst of ritual are at the heart of the conflict in Colossae.

✓   The Christ-hymn of Col 1:15-20 serves as an effective basis for the arguments in the epistle because it recalls the ritual context: it draws believers back into the arena of worship where they discover and renew their experience of the lordship of Christ. It may well be the case that the hymn was part of baptismal celebrations (see Käsemann [1964]). In hearing the hymn within the context of a letter, believers will come to realize who Christ is in the universe and in the church if they are reminded of the transformation they have experienced. (Note that Käsemann [1964] suggested that the hymn formed part of the baptismal liturgy.) Just as Christ holds all things together in the universe, he ensures the cohesion of the community. Community members no doubt have often sung this hymn, but by taking it out of its context in worship or prayer and placing it in an epistle the author invites focus on the content of the hymn and the view of the world and ethical deportment it presupposes. A focus on the content of the hymn seems especially important in a community threatened by "empty deceit" (Col 2:8).

Social-scientific theory concerning ritual can help us understand why the hymn occupies such a central position in Colossians. Insights from the sociology of knowledge are particularly useful, however, in elucidating the relationship between the content of the hymn and the social world of Colossians. In this commentary it is being argued that three community problems underlie Colossians: the issue of Paul's death or imprisonment (see the notes and interpretation on 1:1-2; 1:3-8; 4:7-18); the false teaching that threatens the community (see the notes and interpretation on 2:8-16; 2:16-23); and hostile reactions to the church by nonbelievers (see the notes and interpretation on 4:2-6). The symbolic universe (a "canopy" of meanings shaping the lives of individuals and groups) created under Paul's leadership is being threatened and requires efforts to ensure its maintenance. In developing their theories concerning the sociology of knowledge Berger and Luckmann have noted that when problems such as heresy arise in community life, theorizing becomes necessary for the maintenance of the symbolic universe. They describe this type of theorizing broadly as legitimation: the means by which the institutional world is both explained and justified. In the process of theorizing, the symbolic universe is both expanded and transformed (see Berger and Luckmann 79; 102–103; 124–25; and see the notes and interpretation on 1:3-8; M. Y. MacDonald [1988] 10–18). Debates concerning the cosmological speculations, visionary experiences, and ascetic measures that formed part of the false teaching (cf. 2:16-23) may well have affected both the choice to include the hymn and the structure of the hymn itself—especially the editorial glosses in 1:18 and 1:20. In response to teaching that stresses present heavenly fulfillment and ascetic departure from the world by means of various practices and rituals these editorial glosses stress history and physicality (see the notes). But in Col 1:15-20 we also find evidence that the symbolic universe reflected in Paul's undisputed letters is being pushed beyond its original form. Although notions concerning Christ as ruler of the cosmos can also be found in the undisputed letters (e.g., Phil 2:6-11), the cosmological significance given to the Christ event here and elsewhere in Colossians far exceeds what is found in the undisputed letters. Similarly the body symbolism in which Christ is represented as the "head" reflects a simultaneous appeal to existing symbolism and transformation of the tradition to fit a new situation (see the notes on 1:8).

The effect of the Christ-hymn of Col 1:15-20 at the level of social interaction is to encourage cohesion and integration. The cosmic imagery and body symbolism in Colossians is fundamental to the process of maintaining the Pauline symbolic universe in the face of the problems of community life. Scholars have often noted a possible correlation between the hierarchical notions implicit in the symbolism (Christ is head of the body; Christ reigns supreme in the universe) and the hierarchical structures that define the ideal Christian household in Col 3:18–4:1 (e.g., D'Angelo 320). Thus it is important to recognize that the strategy adopted by the author of Colossians to restore harmony in community life introduced a new style of governance into Pauline Christianity with articulated concepts of the rulers and the ruled (see the notes and interpretation on 3:18–4:1). However, it is also important to keep in mind the function of the correlation between body-cosmic symbolism and authority structures within church life: it no doubt fostered a strong sentiment of the integration of God, community, and individual (see Cameron 69–70). Believers were part of a harmonious totality.

That the hymn must have spoken very powerfully to believers in the first century C.E. is also suggested by Dale B. Martin's recent work on the body in Greco-Roman culture. Martin notes that "in the ancient world, the human body was not *like* a microcosm; it *was* a microcosm—a small version of the universe at large" (Dale B. Martin [1995] 16). To sing about Christ's body as the locus for the reconciliation of the universe (v. 20) was no mere pious sentiment; it was a proclamation of the incredible power that had been made known through the blood of the cross and the ultimate justification of a universal mission (cf. 1:23).

For Reference and Further Study

Aletti, Jean-Noël. *Colossiens 1:15-20*. Rome: Pontifical Biblical Institute, 1981.

Benoit, Pierre. "L'hymne christologique de Col 1:15-20. Jugement critique sur l'état des recherches," in Jacob Neusner, ed., *Christianity, Judaism and Other Greco-Roman Cults: Studies for Morton Smith at Sixty*. Leiden: Brill, 1975, 1:226–63.

Best, Ernest. *One Body in Christ. A Study in the Relationship of the Church to Christ in the Epistles of the Apostle Paul*. London: SPCK, 1955.

Cameron, Averil. *Christianity and the Rhetoric of the Empire: The Development of Christian Discourse*. Berkeley: University of California Press, 1991.

Carr, Wesley. *Angels and Principalities: The Background, Meaning, and Development of the Pauline Phrase hai archai kai hai exousiai*. MSSNTS 42. Cambridge: Cambridge University Press, 1981.

Johnson, Elizabeth A. *She Who Is: The Mystery of God in Feminist Theological Discourse*. New York: Crossroad, 1992.

Käsemann, Ernst. "A Primitive Christian Baptismal Liturgy," in idem, *Essays on New Testament Themes*. London: S.C.M., 1964, 149–68.

MacGregor, G.H.C. "Principalities and Powers: The Cosmic Background of Paul's Thought," *NTS* 1 (1954–55) 17–28.

Martin, Dale B. *The Corinthian Body*. New Haven and London: Yale University Press, 1995.

Martin, Ralph P. *Colossians and Philemon*. NCBC. London: Oliphants, 1974, 53–66.

Moule, C.F.D. "The Corporate Christ," in idem, *The Origin of Christology*. Cambridge: Cambridge University Press, 1977, 47–96.

Overfield, P. D. "Pleroma: A Study in Content and Context," *NTS* 25 (1979) 384–96.

Robinson, John A. T. *The Body*. London: S.C.M., 1952.

Wright, N. T. "Poetry and Theology in Col 1:15-20," *NTS* 36 (1990) 444–68.

5. *Application of the Hymn to the Situation in Colossae* (1:21-23)

21. And you who were once alienated and hostile in mind because of your evil deeds, 22. but now he has reconciled you in the body of his flesh through his death, to present you holy and blameless and irreproachable before him, 23. provided that you continue in the faith, firmly grounded, steadfast, and never being dislodged from the hope of the gospel which you heard, which has been proclaimed to every creature under heaven, of which I, Paul, became a minister.

NOTES

21. *And you who were once alienated:* Beginning at this verse we have a change of focus from the cosmic condition to the immediate situation of the Colossians. This is forcefully conveyed by "and you" (*kai hymas;* the accusative case and the direct object of the verb "to reconcile" in v. 22). A present participle (*ontas*) of the verb "to be" (*eimi*) works together with a perfect passive participle (*apēllotriōmenous*) of the verb "to alienate or to estrange" (*apallotrioō*) to convey the continuous state of alienation from God of the Colossians prior (*pote*) to reconciliation (a continuation of the theme of v. 20). Both the NEB and the NIV attempt to make the implied sense clearer by rendering the phrase as "alienated from God" (see Harris 56).

and hostile in mind because of your evil deeds: With very strong language the Gentile past (cf. 1:27) of the Colossians is recalled; they were "hostile." While it is rendered here and in many translations as an adjective, the term *echthrous* might also be translated as the noun "enemies" (e.g., REB; cf. Rom 5:10; 11:28). It is interesting to note that in the LXX "mind" (*dianoia*) is usually the translation offered for the Hebrew word for "heart" (cf. Gen 8:21; 17:17; 24:45; for further examples and discussion see Lohse 62–63). In Ephesians "mind" is employed to describe the enmity of the Gentiles toward God (Eph 2:3; 4:18). In the NT the Greek terms "heart" (*kardia*) and "mind" (*dianoia*) are found together to refer to the whole thinking, mentality, emotions, and intentions of the person (e.g., Luke 1:51; Heb 8:10). In keeping with this tendency the REB offers the following translation of Col 1:21: "Formerly you yourselves were alienated from God, his enemies in heart and mind." That active opposition to God is in view is made especially clear by the reference "because of your evil deeds." The *en* found in the Greek text of this expression seems to be causal (because of; cf. NIV; NAB), but it might also refer to how alienation from God was expressed. The translators of the REB prefer this latter sense: "as your evil deeds showed." The expression "evil deeds" is not found elsewhere in the Pauline letters (cf. John 3:19; 7:7), but the notion of enmity toward God translating into evil deeds is clearly apparent in Rom 1:18-32. Probably in an effort to communicate a strong sense of active opposition to God, some translators phrase the hostility in terms of attitude: "You were once estranged and of hostile intent through your evil behavior" (NJB).

22. *but now he has reconciled you:* This verse contains syntactic irregularity and is characterized by textual variation. In the first place, the phrase is made somewhat awkward by the presence of the object of "he has reconciled" at the beginning of v. 21: "you" (see the notes on 1:21). This was probably done in order to emphasize the appeal to the community directly and to highlight the shift from the cosmic hymn to its application to the local context. With respect to textual variation, preference is usually given to the best-attested reading, as is the case here: "he has reconciled *(apokatēllaxen)* [you]," but some translators have opted for the textual variation found in a few early manuscripts where the verb to reconcile *(apokatallassō)* is in the passive, "you have been reconciled" *(apokatēllagēte,* preferred by Metzger 622), for it more easily explains the rise of other readings. In this case "and you" in v. 21 would be taken with "all things" and as the object of "to reconcile" in v. 20. This does not seem likely, however, given the clear shift away from the cosmic "all things" and toward the human community in 1:21-23 (see Taylor and Reumann 130–31; for textual issues raised by this verse see also Lohse 64; Metzger 621–22; Harris 57–58). "But" *(de)* sets up an opposition between now *(nyn)* and then (see v. 20), between the present reality of believers and the past life of estrangement.

in the body of his flesh through his death: The expression "the body of his flesh" is sometimes rendered less literally as "his fleshly body" (NRSV; NAB), mortal body (NJB), or physical body (NIV). There is clearly a parallel here with the notion found in the hymn of the reconciliation occurring through the blood of the cross (v. 20). Hence we have the fluid translation adopted by the REB: "But now by Christ's death in his body of flesh and blood God has reconciled you to himself." The body here clearly refers to the physical body of Christ, which underwent suffering, and not to the cosmic entity—the church—that fills the universe with Christ's glory as in v. 18. But the intent of the author may well be to draw a parallel between the two. The body as church and the physical suffering of Christ are very closely associated in 1:24 (see also the interpretation below). The phrase "body of flesh" occurs in the QL (1QpHab 9:2; see Lohse 64).

to present you holy and blameless and irreproachable before him: This phrase announces the goal of reconciliation. As is the case with "he reconciled" (v. 22a), God is the implied subject of "to present" *(parastēsai).* This verb is associated with sacrifice (cf. Rom 12:2), as indeed are the adjectives "holy" and "blameless" (cf. Heb 9:14; 1 Pet 1:19; Exod 29:37-38; Num 6:14), but the immediate context does not suggest a primary interest in sacrifice. The verb "to present" is also used in legal language and with reference to judgment (cf. Rom 14:10; 2 Cor 4:14). Once again, however, it is not immediately clear whether the forensic use of the term can shed light on this verse. An interesting use of the verb appears in Jude 24-25 where the worship of the community is linked to its presentation before God: "Now to him who is able to keep you from falling, and to make you stand without blemish in the presence of his glory with rejoicing, to the only God . . ." (NRSV). While there is no direct interest in liturgy in Col 1:22, a liturgical influence is suggested by the use of the verb in conjunction with the adjective "holy" in Eph 5:25-27, where baptism is clearly in view. It has been suggested that the verb "to present" in 1:22 functions as roughly the equivalent of "to make" or "to render" (BAGD 628; cf. Eph 5:27; 2 Tim 2:15). In fact this straightforward interpretation points to a common theme running through the sacrificial, legal, and liturgical use of the verb "to present" as highlighted above: public demonstration of the worth of the community. In the language of cultural anthropologists, this verse reflects the values of honor and shame: the community is rendered honorable before God. (On honor and shame see the notes and interpretation on 1:3-8.) It is holy (see the notes on 1:2); it keeps all that is shameful on the outside; it is blameless and irreproachable (Phil 2:15; Eph 5:27; for "without shame" see the interpretation below). This verse is sometimes compared to 1 Cor 1:8: "He will also strengthen you to the end, so that you may be blameless on the day of our Lord Jesus Christ" (NRSV). The focus in 1:22, however, is clearly on the present and not on the future Day of the Lord. But future considerations are not ruled out altogether, as the following verse makes clear. Living in God's presence requires commitment and a particular way of life. The "him" (*autou*) found in the expression "before him" probably refers to God and not Christ as in the first instance of the word "him" in this verse. The NJB aims to alleviate any ambiguity by translating the passage as "to bring you before himself holy, faultless, and irreproachable."

23. *provided that you continue in the faith, firmly grounded, steadfast:* The grammatical construction here clearly indicates that the presentation of the Colossians before God is tied to a specific condition. They must continue in the faith, but this continuance requires active, ongoing commitment, as the two adjectives that follow make clear. Both "firmly grounded" and "steadfast" should probably be taken as closely related to "the faith." *Pistis* is sometimes translated simply as "in faith" (REB; cf. NIV) rather than "in the faith" (NRSV; NAB). Taken as "in faith," the phrase is understood as meaning personal faith, the basis of Christian commitment. Taken as "in the faith," the expression is understood as being equivalent to the content of the gospel mentioned later in the verse. In Jude 3, 20 and Acts 6:7 the expression refers to "the faith" in the sense of the entire content of a religious movement, involving doctrine, Scripture, and a way of life that clearly sets believers apart from outsiders (cf. Eph 4:5). Given the interest in distinguishing between truth and false teaching in Colossians (which includes an erroneous way of life) such attempts at self-definition might also inform Col 1:22. This verse draws upon architectural symbolism. In Jewish Scripture *themelioō* (to ground firmly, to lay a foundation, or to establish) is associated with the founding of God's city on Mount Zion (LXX Ps 47:9; LXX Isa 14:32; 44:28; LXX Hag 2:18; LXX Zech 4:9; 8:9). In keeping with the notion of the community as God's building found in the QL (e.g., 1QS 5:6; 7:17; 8:7-8; see Lohse 66), early church authors used the image of the building to describe the Christian community (Eph 2:19-22; 1 Cor 3:10-17; 1 Tim 3:15; 1 Pet 2:4-10; Matt 7:24-27). For other texts where the notion of being firmly grounded and steadfast appears see 1 Cor 15:58; Eph 3:17.

and never being dislodged from the hope of the gospel which you heard: There is a great deal of emphasis here on the Colossians not departing from an original message they had received. "The hope of the gospel" refers to the hope that is based on the gospel (BAGD 253). However, the association between gospel and hope is so close here that the meaning comes close to being "the hope that is the gospel." The emphasis on the present is so strong in Colossians that even the object of hope is characterized largely as something to which one presently has access—the content of salvation (cf. 1:5). In 1:27 the center of salvation, Christ, is himself proclaimed as the hope of glory.

which has been proclaimed to every creature under heaven: This phrase describes the universal mission of the early church. The expression *en pasę ktisei* is sometimes translated as "in the whole of creation" (REB) instead of "to every creature" (NRSV; NAB; NIV; NJB). As in 1:6 the focus of attention is on preaching the gospel to the inhabited world, but the translation adopted here better reflects the shift in focus away from the cosmic arena, where all things in heaven and earth were reconciled, to Paul's human mission. Every creature is the equivalent of every human being. To refer to every creature "under heaven" is another way of saying every creature on earth (BAGD 594). It is important to note, however, that while from v. 20 to vv. 21-23 there is a move from the cosmic to the earthly, the spheres are viewed as inseparably linked. Universalism permeates 1:15-23. The arch of heaven may represent the boundary between the earthly realm and the realm of spiritual beings; but all things under or above are transformed by Christ and his gospel.

of which I, Paul, became a minister: Paul is a minister *(diakonos)* of the gospel. The first-person singular voice ("I, Paul") is in contrast to the "we" of the thanksgiving (Col 1:3-14) and emphasizes Paul's apostolic authority. Similarly, when read in relation to the notion of "minister of the church" (v. 25), the expression "minister of the gospel" highlights the importance of apostolic authority. Neither expression occurs in the undisputed letters. *Diakonos* is a fluid term that is rendered variously in English. The NRSV, NIV, and NJB, for example, opt for the translation "servant." But greater emphasis on Paul's leadership role appears to be at play here than is usually suggested by the English term "servant." *Diakonos* is also translated in a more titular sense to refer to a church office, that of the deacon (e.g., see NRSV: Rom 16:1; 1 Tim 3:8-13). A recent study suggests that *diakonos* was used frequently in the ancient world to refer to an agent of a high-ranking person who acted as messenger, diplomat, or intermediary in commercial transactions (see Collins, *Diakonos*). As a *diakonos* of the gospel Paul was an agent of God, a mediator or broker of the mystery of God, that is, Christ himself (Col 2:2; cf. Rom 1:1; 15:16; 2 Cor 11:23). As in the undisputed letters, Paul can use the term to refer to local community leaders (Phil 1:1; cf. Rom 16:1) and to his coworkers on the mission route (1 Thess 3:2). It should be noted that in Colossians *diakonos* appears as a designation for both Epaphras (Col 1:7) and Tychicus (4:7)—individuals who play an important role in the Colossian community. If Colossians is in fact deutero-Pauline, the use of the same designation for Paul and local leaders may be especially significant; it may represent an attempt to reinforce the connection between Paul and leaders known to the community whom the author views as Paul's representatives (on *diakonos* see also the notes and interpretation on 1:7).

INTERPRETATION

Colossians 1:21-23 is very closely related to the Christ-hymn of Col 1:15-20; it offers an interpretation of the hymn, including its application to community life. Many of the themes found in the hymn are repeated, such as reconciliation, universalism, the body, and the salvific importance of Christ's physical death. In fact, 1:21-23 is also loosely connected to 1:13-20; a focus on redemption is maintained from 1:13-23. Moreover, v. 23 reiterates four themes of the thanksgiving of vv. 4-6: faith, hope, and the spread of the gospel throughout the world (see Harris 56).

Like vv. 13-14, vv. 21-23 offer a very good example of a pattern of exhortation that permeates Colossians (cf. Eph 4:17-24). There is a remembrance of "conversion"—a recollection of the process of transference from the evil outside world into the church community. The goal of this remembrance is to ensure that the beliefs, practices, and ethical deportment of believers are clearly distinguishable both from those who adhere to false teaching and from unbelievers. The link between remembrance of conversion (receipt of the Gospel and baptism) and the call to the right way of life is clearly evident in Col 2:6-7 and 3:1-4, but the connection informs the author's approach throughout the epistle (see also the notes on 1:13-14). In sociological terms the remembrance of conversion constitutes language of separation from the outside world. It should be noted, however, that in Colossians characterizations of the outside world are found largely in remembrance of a past way of life and reminders of the dangers of slipping back into evil ways rather than in explicit condemnations of the outside world. Because of this it is very easy to underestimate the strength of the opposition to the nonbelieving world (or sectarian response) revealed by the work (see the notes and interpretation on 1:9-14 and 4:2-6). In fact, the language is very strong (cf. Col 2:13; 3:5-7; Eph 2:12; 4:18). The description of the community's past alienation from God as having been "hostile in mind because of your evil deeds" recalls the strong sectarian response of the Fourth Gospel in which the world is denounced categorically: "And this is the judgment, that the light has come into the world, and the people loved darkness rather than light because their deeds were evil" (John 3:19 NRSV; cf. 7:7).

As we move from the Christ-hymn to its interpretation in 1:21-23 we see how the tragedy of a divided cosmos without Christ is replicated in the tragedy of the estrangement of the nonbeliever from Christ. The universe has been transformed and believers enjoy present glory, but they are still subject to dangers, as the conditional statement in v. 23 implies (cf. 3:5-9; esp. v. 6). The "you were once . . . but now" construction that shapes the exhortation in vv. 21-22 is a typical formula in Pauline epistles and probably reflects the language of worship: hymns and baptismal proclamations (Col 2:11-23; Eph 2:1-10, 11-22; Rom 6:17-22; 7:5-6; 11:30-31; 1 Cor 6:9-11; Gal 4:8-10; cf. 1 Pet 1:14-25; 2:10). There is a simultaneous call for and celebration of a new identity.

An understanding of the core values of honor and shame in the ancient Mediterranean world is essential to a full appreciation of how this new identity is envisioned in Col 1:21-23. (See the notes and interpretation on 1:3-8.) The goal of God's reconciliation of the Colossians is announced in v. 22 as "to present you holy and blameless and irreproachable before him[self]." This phrase might seem strange to the modern reader. Why would salvation be described as God presenting a pure community before himself? God here is understood as acting like an honorable Mediterranean male who protects the reputation of his bride (the community) and presents her worth to the world outside. The ideal community is characterized in much the same way as a Mediterranean woman who displays appropriate shame (concern for reputation). Although gender categories are not explicit in Col 1:22, this text is frequently compared to Eph 5:25-27 where similar language occurs and gender categories are explicit (cf. 2 Cor 11:2). In Eph 5:25-27, Christ is viewed as the principal actor in relation to the church-bride; human marriage is understood as a metaphor for the relationship between the human community and the divine: "Husbands, love your wives, just as Christ loved the church and gave himself up for her, in order to make her holy by cleansing her with the washing of water by the word, so as to present the church to himself in splendor, without a spot or wrinkle or anything of the kind—yes, so that she may be holy and without blemish" (NRSV). In this text the values of honor and shame work together with allusions to baptism and to the ritual bath of purification taken by Jewish women before marriage in order to ensure that the community behaves in a manner that is worthy of Christ's redemptive acts. Similar considerations underlie Col 1:21-23. God is the protector of the community and guarantees its honor (it is blameless and irreproachable), but the community must guard its reputation carefully, remaining ever steadfast—a solid house of faith (on architectural imagery see the notes above).

Awareness of the cultural values of the biblical world can also shed light on the immense claim that the gospel "has been proclaimed to every creature under heaven" in v. 23. Hyperbole is often recognized in this verse, but its significance is not clearly understood. The statement is probably a reflection of what has been called "dramatic orientation" (exaggeration, over-assertion) in Mediterranean culture (see Pilch 47–49). Dramatic orientation is a means by which the core values of honor and shame are maintained and enhanced. It can take the form of hyperbole, eloquence, boasting, heroic gesture, or speaking of a deed as if it has already been accomplished. Colossians 1:23 calls to mind Paul's similarly astonishing claim in Rom 15:19: "from Jerusalem as far round as Illyricum I have fully proclaimed the good news of Christ" (NRSV). Paul claims to have conquered a huge geographical area when in reality he must only have begun small cells of Christians in strategically located cities. Such statements are probably not intended to be taken literally, but they represent a technique necessary for securing the reputation of the speaker as an honorable Mediterranean male. That the statement in Col 1:23 about the gospel having been proclaimed to every creature is intended to enhance Paul's authority is further indicated by the shift to the first person singular at the end of the verse: "I, Paul, became a minister [of this gospel]."

Reading Col 1:21-23 in relation to 1:15-20 reveals how the situation in the local community of believers was viewed as intimately related to the situation in the whole cosmos. The earthly and heavenly, the local and universal domains sometimes merge to such an extent that they become indistinguishable. Early church members were caught up in a drama in which cosmic events became replicated in human experiences. The modern proclivity to endeavor to understand the relationship between earthly existence and the universe as a whole based on cause and effect is strikingly absent. With a dramatic orientation the author tends to speak as though deeds have already happened. All creatures have already received the good news. Believers have already been raised with Christ (Col 3:1). The past serves as a window into a world that must be profoundly rejected and acts as a foil for a glorious "now." The present dominates and the future fades from view.

FOR FURTHER REFERENCE AND STUDY

Collins, John N. *Diakonia: Re-interpreting the Ancient Sources.* New York: Oxford University Press, 1990.

Dahl, Nils A. "Anamnesis: Memory and Commemoration in the Early Church," in idem, *Jesus in the Memory of the Early Church.* Minneapolis: Augsburg, 1976, 11–29.

Malina, Bruce J. "Eyes–Heart," in John J. Pilch and Bruce J. Malina, eds., *Biblical Social Values and Their Meaning: A Handbook.* Peabody, Mass.: Hendrickson, 1993, 63–67.

Martin, Ralph P. "Reconciliation and Forgiveness in the Letter to the Colossians," in Robert Banks, ed., *Reconciliation and Hope: New Testament Essays on Atonement and Eschatology Presented to L. L. Morris on his 60th Birthday.* Exeter: Paternoster; Grand Rapids: Eerdmans, 1974, 104–24.

Pilch, John J. "Dramatic Orientation (Exaggeration, Over-Assertion)," in Pilch and Malina, eds., *Biblical Social Values and Their Meaning: A Handbook,* 47–49.

6. Paul's Authority in Colossae and Laodicea (1:24–2:7)

24. Now I rejoice in my sufferings for you, and in my flesh I am filling up
what is lacking in Christ's afflictions, on behalf of his body, which is the
church, 25. of which I became a minister, according to the stewardship of
God given to me for you, to bring the word of God to completion, 26. the
mystery which has been hidden throughout the ages and from generations. But now it has been revealed to his saints, 27. to whom God wished
to make known the extent of the riches of the glory of this mystery
among the Gentiles, which is Christ in you, the hope of glory. 28. It is he
whom we proclaim, warning every person and teaching every person in
all wisdom, in order that we may present every person perfect in Christ.
29. For this also I labor, struggling with his energy powerfully working
within me. 2:1. For I wish you to know how great a struggle I am having
on your behalf and on behalf of those in Laodicea, and on behalf of all
those who have not seen me face to face, 2. in order that their hearts may
be encouraged, united together in love, so that they might have all the
riches of fully assured understanding, for the knowledge of the mystery
of God, that is, Christ himself, 3. in whom are hidden all the treasures of
wisdom and knowledge. 4. I am saying this so that no one may deceive
you with persuasive speech. 5. For though I am absent in the flesh, yet I
am with you in spirit, rejoicing to see your order and the firmness of your
faith in Christ Jesus. 6. As therefore you received Christ Jesus the Lord,
walk in him, 7. having been rooted and being built up in him and being
established in the faith as you were taught, abounding in thanksgiving.

NOTES

24. *Now I rejoice in my sufferings for you:* The link with v. 23 is established by the
continuous use of the first person singular in vv. 24-25. From the end of 1:23 to
2:5 the focus is directly on Paul's apostleship and its importance for the recipients. "Now" is probably not merely conveying transition as in "now then,"
but refers to the present situation: "as things now stand." The aim is to discuss
the immediate situation of the apostle in prison (see BAGD 545; Harris 65).
There is some ambiguity, however, presented by the Greek text: *tois pathēma-
sin.* It might be rendered simply as "the sufferings" rather than "my sufferings," thus raising the possibility that Paul is rejoicing in the sufferings of
Christ rather than in his own sufferings. But the fact that the suffering is "for
you" rather than "for us" and other grammatical considerations make this unlikely (Harris 65; cf. 2 Cor 1:5-7). In Paul's letters and in Acts suffering is presented as a sign of an authentic apostle (e.g., 1 Cor 4:9-13; 2 Cor 11:23-33; Gal
6:17; Acts 9:15-16; 20:19-23). The suffering of the apostle is a key element in the
picture of Paul in Colossians and Ephesians (Col 1:24; 4:3, 10, 18; Eph 3:1, 13;
4:1; see the interpretation below).

   *and in my flesh I am filling up what is lacking in Christ's afflictions, on behalf of his
   body, which is the church:* This phrase raises numerous problems of interpreta-

tion as well as doctrinal questions. Literally meaning "to fill up," the verb *antanapleroō* is sometimes translated as "to complete" (NRSV; NEB). *Ta hysterēmata* refers to whatever lack may still exist (BAGD 73). At first glance the phrase seems to imply that Christ's sacrifice was somehow insufficient and that Paul was completing it. But commentators have noted that this cannot be the meaning since the NT is consistent in understanding reconciliation as having been thoroughly accomplished through the death of Christ and, indeed, this is a central argument in Colossians. To view the expression as meaning literally that something was lacking in the suffering of Christ would contradict 1:13-14 and 1:22. Paul's sufferings *(pathēma)* are identified with Christ's afflictions *(thlipsis)*, but it is sometimes argued that special attention should be given to the meaning of "Christ's afflictions." Commentators frequently note that the term *thlipsis* is never applied to Jesus' suffering in the NT, but that it is regularly used by Paul to describe the hardships of those who proclaim the gospel (Rom 5:3; 8:35; 2 Cor 1:4, 8; 2:4; 4:17; 6:4; 7:4). This has led some to conclude that the afflictions in view are actually Paul's and not Christ's. The expression "the afflictions of Christ" would thus be functionally equivalent to the expression "the circumcision of Christ" (cf. 2:11; i.e., not literally Christ's circumcision but the metaphorical circumcision belonging to the church community; see Horgan 880). Filling up what is lacking in Christ's afflictions would be a means of expressing the suffering that is deemed a necessary step in the completion of what is required for the growth of the church and the completion of Paul's mission. It has also been suggested that the expression "the afflictions of Christ" reflects the Jewish apocalyptic notion of "messianic woes," which would precede the end of the age (cf. Mark 13:1-27; Matt 24:1-31; *1 Enoch* 47:1-4; *2 Apoc. Bar.* 30:2; see Lohse 71). Through his suffering Paul is vicariously fulfilling the affliction that God's people must undergo before the end. If such considerations do inform Col 1:24, they have been significantly reformulated to fit a new context; Colossians reveals virtually no interest in the imminent expectation of the end, and in fact, displays little interest even in the future (though see the notes on 1:27).

Perhaps what the extensive comment on this verse reveals above all is that the phrase should not be pressed too hard for logical (and doctrinal) consistency in modern terms. We may nevertheless be confident that we understand the author's general patterns of thought. In the verse Christ's body is explicitly identified with the church. The identification between Christ and the community in Colossians is so close that it may have seemed quite natural to speak of Christ continuing to suffer just as believers (and most importantly Paul) continue to suffer (despite the doctrinal issues of temporality and such questions as whether suffering is merely exemplary or fully expiatory). In Colossians, Christ's body is also identified with the universe and Paul's mission is universal. There is a great deal of spatial terminology, including the very notion of "filling up" Christ's body. Colossians 1:24 offers a window into the intense religious experiences of an early church community: one detects a profound sense of interconnectedness among believers, community, cosmos, and Christ. (For a full discussion of this difficult verse see Lincoln and

Wedderburn 38–39; see also the discussion of the cultural values of ancient Mediterranean society in the interpretation below.)

25. *of which I became a minister, according to the stewardship of God given to me for you:* Paul here is described as a "minister *[diakonos]* of the church" (see v. 24); this precise expression is not found in the undisputed letters of Paul. "Minister of the church" is very closely related to "minister of the gospel" in v. 23, as is made clear by the interest in evangelization that permeates v. 25. *Diakonos* is an important title in Colossians, conferring authority on both Paul and his fellow workers (see the notes on 1:7 and 1:23). *Oikonomia* (stewardship) is often also translated as "commission" (NRSV; NIV; see Michel, *Oikonomia, TDNT* 5:151–53). In Colossians, the term appears only in this verse. Some have also suggested that the expression *oikonomia tou theou* should be understood as a qualifying genitive meaning "the office of God," that is, "divine office" (see Lohse 72). However, given that the expression is followed immediately by "given to me," it seems better to take it as a genitive of origin, meaning "the stewardship or commission God gave me." In the end, however, both possibilities point to Paul receiving a divine appointment to be an apostle. The expression recalls the way Paul is described in Col 1:1 (cf. Gal 1:12-24). In 1 Cor 4:1-2 Paul describes himself (and other apostles) as stewards of God's mysteries—a management role that carries with it many responsibilities (cf. 1 Cor 9:17). In speaking of his commission as an apostle Paul frequently employs the term "grace" (*charis*; e.g., Gal 2:9; 1 Cor 3:10; 15:10; Rom 1:5; 12:3, 6; 15:15) and in 1:25 *oikonomia* seems to function as its equivalent. *Oikonomia* has a different sense in Ephesians, however, where it refers to God's plan for the history of salvation (cf. Eph 1:10; 3:2, 9). "For you" repeats the thought found also in 1:24; cf. 2:1. Everything the apostle is doing is for the sake of the Colossians.

to bring the word of God to completion: Here the verb *plēroō* means to bring to completion, but it can also mean "to fill up" or "to fulfill" (BAGD 671; see Delling, *plēroō, TDNT* 6:286–89). In the NT the verb is often employed for the fulfillment of a promise announced in Scripture (e.g., Mark 14:49; Matt 1:22; 2:15; Luke 4:21; 24:44; John 13:18; 17:12). Paul has received a divine commission (see the notes above) fully to proclaim the gospel (here defined as the word of God; cf. Col 1:5). The verb is used in the same sense in Rom 15:19 where Paul states: "from Jerusalem as far round as Illyricum I have fully proclaimed the good news of Christ" (NRSV; see the interpretation of 1:21-23). Both in its cosmology and in the way the roles of actors are defined, the language of Colossians suggest limits that must be filled up. In order to instruct Archippus to pay attention to his office (or duty) the author of Colossians instructs him to fulfill *(plēroō)* his ministry (4:17; cf. Acts 13:25; 14:26). The expression here, *ton logon theou* (the word of God), anticipates its usage in the Fourth Gospel, where it comes to refer specifically to Christ (cf. John 1:1-18). As the description of Paul's apostleship is further developed in 1:26-27 we see that the word of God is described as the mystery that is identical to "Christ in you."

26. *the mystery which has been hidden throughout the ages and from generations. But now it has been revealed to his saints:* In Greek the sentence breaks off quite sud-

denly, with a new sentence beginning at "But now." Yet the concepts of mystery *(mystērion)*, to hide *(apokryptō)*, and to reveal *(phaneroō)* reflect a revelation schema (what was previously hidden is now proclaimed publicly) occurring repeatedly in Pauline literature. This schema may well draw its origins from a ritual setting where the contrast between one's past life and one's new life was experienced and celebrated (cf. 1 Cor 2:6-16; Rom 16:25-27; 1 Tim 3:16; cf. Lohse 73–74). Those of Gentile background who received Colossians would have been familiar with the concept of "mystery" (see Bornkamm, *Mysterion* 4:819–24). In the plural form the term is used to refer to the mystery cults of Greco-Roman society ("the mysteries"). Gentiles would not have been surprised by the notion that the mystery needed for salvation was hidden. The concept of mystery is also well attested in Jewish literature (here too the concept is often in the plural) and the use of the concept of mystery in Pauline literature is closely related to this usage. In Jewish literature God's secret purpose for Israel's destiny is called "mystery"; the wise and the pious are sometimes granted a view of God's plan (cf. LXX Dan 2:28; Wis 2:22; 1 Enoch 63:3; 104:11-13; 4 Ezra 14:26). In the QL the mystery is revealed only to such persons as the teacher of righteousness (e.g., 1QpHab 7). In Colossians the mystery is equated with the word of God and explicitly defined in v. 27 as "Christ in you, the hope of glory." In essence the mystery is Christ—the apex of Christian commitment. The term "mystery" occurs frequently in Colossians and Ephesians (Col 1:26, 27; 2:2; 4:3; Eph 1:9; 3:3, 4, 9; 5:32; 6:19). In Ephesians the "mystery of Christ" is defined more precisely and the relationship between the term and Jewish notions of God's plan for the world stands out even more sharply. In Eph 3:6 the nature of the mystery is described as follows: "the Gentiles have become fellow heirs, members of the same body, and sharers in the promise of Jesus Christ through the gospel" (NRSV; cf. 3:3-9). It has sometimes been suggested that "from" *(apo* + genitive) has a "local" sense: from the ages and generations (i.e., from the people of former generations and ages). Similarly it has been argued that the author has in mind the principalities and powers that are under dispute in Colossians or perhaps even personified eons (BAGD 28) because of the fact that in 1 Cor 2:6-13 Paul refers to the "rulers of this age." But grammatical considerations, especially the use of "now," make a straightforward temporal meaning more likely: "throughout" (NRSV and above) or "for long ages and through many generations" (NEB). There is no thought of a future event lying hidden in God's plan informing this verse; the focus is on the present. All the saints—all the believers—have access to the mystery (see the notes on 1:2) and it is being proclaimed throughout the world. When placed in the context of the section as a whole the last phrase suggests the type of tension between openness and introversion that is typical of Pauline Christianity. Language that reinforces a distinct identity as the elect holy ones (cf. 3:12) is held in balance with language announcing a mission to the whole world (1:25, 27).

27. *to whom God wished to make known the extent of the riches of the glory of this mystery among the Gentiles:* The reference to "God wishing to make known to the saints" here repeats the notion of revelation found at the end of the previous

verse. If one compares various translations one sees several variations, but only subtle differences in meaning are revealed. Used with a noun denoting quality or quantity (riches or wealth), the pronoun *ti* may mean "what sort of" (BAGD 819), or it may mean "the extent of," "how great" (NRSV). The focus on the grandeur of the mystery throughout this verse makes the latter possibility more likely. "The riches of the glory" may mean "the glorious riches" (NIV) or the phrase may be taken as possessive, that is, the riches belonging to the glory. Although it is sometimes taken as modifying "to make known" (NIV: to them God has chosen to make known among the Gentiles) it is less awkward to view the prepositional phrase "among the Gentiles" as modifying "the riches of this mystery" (see Harris 70–71). "Riches and glory" are mentioned together in the OT (e.g., LXX Gen 31:16; 1 Kgs 3:13; 1 Chr 29:28; etc.). Romans 9:23 offers a close parallel and literary dependence has sometimes been suggested as the most likely explanation (see E.P. Sanders [1966]), but it is also possible that Paul and the author of Colossians are drawing upon traditional phrases. In describing the scope of the mystery in Ephesians, that author places special emphasis on revelation not only among the Jews, but also among the Gentiles. In contrast, in Colossians "among the Gentiles" seems to function as the practical equivalent to "throughout the world" (Eph 3:3-9; see the notes on 1:26 above).

which is Christ in you, the hope of glory: Here mystery is explicitly defined as "Christ in you" and identified with "the hope of glory." It is possible to read the article *ē* before "hope" as denoting possession—"your hope of glory" (NJB), but most translations have "the hope of glory." Because of the grammatical parallel between "among the Gentiles" and "in you" (the preposition *en* occurs in both instances) some have argued in favor of the translation "among you" (see Lohse 76), contending that the expression refers to the proclamation of Christ among the nations and, more specifically, among the recipients of the letter. But a more mystical understanding of "in you" cannot be excluded here (cf. 2 Cor 13:5; Rom 8:10; Eph 3:17). Religious experience is of central importance in the community; how powerful experiences of Christ should be lived out in community life seems to be at the heart of the dispute with the false teachers (2:16-23). This phrase should be compared to Eph 1:13-14 where the indwelling of the Spirit is defined as "the pledge of our inheritance," the visible manifestation of hope. In 1:27 hope points toward the final consummation (cf. Col 3:4), but clearly also shapes the present (cf. 1:5).

28. *It is he whom we proclaim, warning every person and teaching every person in all wisdom:* In v. 28 there is a change from the first person singular to the first person plural. (The first person singular is used again in v. 29.) This change probably reflects the fact that Paul's fellow workers are being included with him. The apostle does not know the Colossians personally; his fellow workers brought the gospel to them and continue to guide the community (e.g., 1:7-8; 4:12-13). The plural voice could be intended even more broadly to refer to all apostles and teachers considered legitimate by the apostle, but excluding the false teachers. The participles "warning" and "teaching" may refer either to the means of proclamation or to its accompanying circumstances, "while we

admonish and teach." That the latter possibility (which recognizes a greater distinction between the verbs) is more likely is suggested by the way in which the three functions of proclamation, warning, and teaching seem to be replicated in the structure of the epistle itself: 1:1–2:5 proclaims Christ or recalls the initial proclamation of the gospel; 2:6-23 warns against false teachers; 3:1–4:6 teaches Christian living (see Thurston 32). In Paul's letters *kattaggellō* (to proclaim) refers to missionary preaching (e.g., Phil 1:17; 1 Cor 9:14; cf. Acts 13:5; 17:3, 13, 23). *Noutheteō* (to admonish or to warn) and the noun, *nouthesia* (admonition) are regularly used by Paul to correct or offer helpful advice on community matters (e.g., 1 Thess 5:12; 1 Cor 4:14; cf. Acts 20:31). In 3:16 the task of the whole community is described as teaching and admonishing. The expression *panta anthrōpon* (every person) occurs three times in 1:28; the focus is on inclusivity. "In all wisdom" might mean "by means of wisdom" (dative of instrument), but the way in which the NIV translates the phrase seems more probable: "with all wisdom" *(en pasę sophią)*, indicating the circumstances, mode, or manner of the apostolic admonition and instruction. Moreover, it is highly unlikely that "in all wisdom" refers to the specific content of the teaching because of the grammatical construction of the phrase; in that case one would expect the object of teaching to be expressed in the accusative (see Harris 73). In Colossians wisdom and understanding are important qualities of Christian life (see the notes on 1:9; cf. 4:5).

in order that we may present every person perfect in Christ: The goal of Paul's proclamation is announced here: Christian perfection (cf. 4:12; Matt 5:28). The adjective *teleios* (perfect) means "having attained the end or purpose, complete or perfect" (BAGD 809). In Pauline literature the adjective sometimes refers to full-grown or mature individuals (mature in faith). This is true of the example in Eph 4:13 where the expression "mature man" *(andra teleion)* occurs (cf. 1 Cor 14:20). Thus some versions opt for the translation "mature in Christ" (cf. NRSV; NEB). In mystery religions *teleios* was regularly employed as a technical term, referring to one initiated into mystery rites—one made perfect. This more mystical sense seems to be in view here (cf. Phil 3:15). Some have seen an indirect response to the false teaching (2:16-23) in this phrase. The proponents of the false teaching may have claimed special knowledge and access to divine power that rendered them perfect. In turn Colossians responds with its own understanding of perfection (cf. Col 4:12; see Lohse 78). The use of the adjective in conjunction with the verb "to present" recalls Col 1:22. The notion of presenting believers as perfect before God in light of the final judgment may well be in play, but present perfection is an even greater priority. Since Paul's apostolic role is central to the context, the presentation of the believers as perfect offers an outward demonstration of Paul's legitimacy. It is a visible demonstration of the apostle's honor (see the notes and interpretation on 1:22). The expression "in Christ" here ties together the notion of a "perfect" person with a perfected community (the body of Christ). The NEB translation favors the communal dimension of the language especially strongly: "so as to present each one of you as a mature member of Christ's body." On the notion of "in Christ" see the notes on 1:2.

29. *For this also I labor, struggling:* After a series of plurals in v. 28, v. 29 returns to the singular voice. The intention is probably to focus again specifically on the apostle's role and not to speak of the ministry he shares with his fellow workers (see the notes on v. 28). It is not completely clear whether Paul is laboring in the first instance in order to present every person perfect in Christ or more broadly for the proclamation, admonition, and teaching that culminate in such perfection. Paul uses the verb "to labor" *(kopiaō)* to refer to the difficult work he conducts as a messenger of the gospel (cf. 1 Cor 15:10). This use of the verb should not be viewed as distinct (*contra* Lohse 78–79) from the usage of the term to refer to the manual work Paul does to support himself (1 Thess 2:9; 1 Cor 4:12; 2 Thess 3:8). In recent years scholars have become increasingly convinced that the social circumstances of home and work fostered the growth of the church community and should be viewed as directly connected to the process of mission. The participle *agōnizomenos* might be translated as "struggling" or "striving" (NEB: I am toiling strenuously). The same term is used of Epaphras' activities on behalf of the Colossians in 4:12 (see also the notes on 2:1). Here the author draws on athletic imagery, but the association of the term with competition or contest is not nearly as apparent as in 1 Cor 9:25.

with his energy powerfully working within me: The Greek term rendered as energy *(energeia)* might be translated more literally (but more awkwardly) as "the working" or "the operation." The word has the same root as the participle of the verb found here: *energeō* (to be at work or to operate). God energizes Paul. His apostleship is based upon God operating in him. The use of the Greek term *kata* is stronger than that implied by the translation "in accord with the exercise of his power" (NAB). Rather the term denotes "reliance upon," "with the energy he (Christ) supplies" (see Harris 74). Such a strong connection between the apostle's work and the power of Christ is suggested by the way Paul speaks elsewhere about being strengthened and energized by God's power (e.g., Phil 2:13; 4:13). The Greek text might be rendered more literally as "working with me in power" *(en dynamei);* it could mean "with power," but it is usually translated in the adverbial sense ("powerfully") as above. The power of God working in Paul is the basis of charismatic leadership (see the notes and interpretation on 1:2-3; and see the interpretation below; cf. 2 Cor 12:9).

2:1. *For I wish you to know how great a struggle I am having:* A long sentence in Greek spanning three verses begins here. "Struggle" *(agōna)* is a cognate of the participle *agōnizomenos* in 1:29 and the use of the two terms establishes a firm connection between the two verses (see the notes on 1:29). By stating that he "wishes [or wants] the recipients to know" the author is making a strong assertion and probably initiating a transition into the direct discussion of the problem with false teaching beginning at 2:8 and anticipated in 2:4. Similar formulas occur in Rom 11:25; 1 Cor 10:1; 11:3; 12:1; 1 Thess 4:13 (see Horgan 880). It is useful to compare this verse to Rom 1:13 where a similar expression occurs: "but I would not have you ignorant." This expression is followed as in Col 2:1 by an attempt to reinforce the bond between the apostle and community members he does not know personally.

on your behalf and on behalf of those in Laodicea, and on behalf of all those who have not seen me face to face: It is clear that the teachings in Colossians concern not only the people in Colossae, but also believers in other cities of the Lycus Valley. In addition to Laodicea (cf. Rev 3:14-22), 4:13 mentions Hierapolis, which explains why some later manuscripts add Hierapolis to 2:1. Colossians 4:16 instructs the Colossians and the Laodiceans to exchange letters (on these cities see the Introduction). It seems that most of the recipients do not know Paul personally; they received the Pauline message via Epaphras (cf. 1:7). Literally the Greek text speaks of "those who have not seen my face in the flesh"; it refers to all those who have not seen Paul face to face, that is, do not know him personally. The fact that the author is writing to people he does not know personally is especially significant if, as is being argued in this commentary, the letter is deutero-Pauline (see the interpretation below).

2. *in order that their hearts may be encouraged, united together in love: Hina* (in order that, so that) introduces the reasons for Paul's struggle on behalf of the believers in the Lycus Valley. The use of the third person "their" rather than "your" is probably due to the fact that the nearest antecedent in 2:1 is "those who have not seen me face to face." That the author is especially concerned with the situation of those who do not know him personally is further suggested by 2:5. To speak of the heart in the ancient Mediterranean world is to refer to the whole of the human capacity for thought, judgment, and emotion. The verb *parakaleō* may mean "admonish" in Pauline literature (cf. 1 Thess 4:1; 2 Cor 5:20; 10:1; Rom 12:1), but in this verse it is probably being used in the complementary sense of encouragement or comfort (cf. 2 Cor 2:7; 4:1, 6; 7:6, 13). There is an absence of grammatical sequence between the aorist participle *symbibasthentes* (united together; from the verb *symbibazō*) and what comes before, thus raising some questions about how it should be understood (see the summary of the complicated textual issues in Harris 80–88). However, the interpretation offered by the NAB is probably correct: the encouragement and uniting are viewed as contemporaneous ("as they are brought together in love"; cf. RSV). The verb *symbibazō* can also mean "to instruct" (1 Cor 2:16; Acts 9:22; 19:33). Thus the Vg understood it as "being instructed in charity." Because the verb so clearly refers to uniting or bringing together in Col 2:19, most modern commentators prefer that rendering also in this case (cf. Eph 4:16). However, the focus on understanding, wisdom, and knowledge in 2:2-4 suggests that comforting, uniting, and teaching are closely related in the apostle's work.

so that they might have all the riches of fully assured understanding: This refers to the result of the encouragement and uniting, or more broadly, it continues to define the purpose of Paul's struggle (v. 1). The reference to riches recalls 1:27. The Greek text literally refers to "the riches of the full assurance of understanding." *Plērophoria* does not occur frequently in the NT (Col 2:2; 1 Thess 1:5; Heb 6:11; 10:22). It can mean full assurance, certainty, or fullness (BAGD 670). Here the term is taken as descriptive of understanding (cf. 1:9) but it is also possible on grammatical grounds to understand the phrase in the sense of the NEB: "the full wealth of conviction which understanding brings."

for the knowledge of the mystery of God, that is, Christ himself: "Knowledge" may serve as a parallel term for "understanding," but the use of the Greek term *eis* (for) suggests that special significance is attached to knowledge of the mystery of God as the ultimate goal of Paul's struggle (see Harris 81). The Greek term for knowledge here is *epignōsis* and it could refer to "full knowledge" (see the notes on 1:9; cf. 2:3). The reference to God's mystery recalls 1:26-27 and offers the key to the best explanation of the phrase, "that is, Christ himself." In Greek the phrase contains juxtaposed genitives *(tou theou Christou)*, literally meaning "of God, of Christ." The terseness of this phrase probably explains the numerous manuscript variations including the one found in the marginal notes of the NRSV: "of the mystery of God, both of the Father and of Christ" (for an excellent summary of these see Lohse 82). The reading adopted here is preferred because it best explains the numerous variations (see Metzger 622). The expression has given rise to considerable comment. Some have argued that Christ should be viewed here as explicitly equated with God (the mystery of God who is Christ), but such a strong statement of equation is not found elsewhere in the NT. Rather the meaning is suggested by 1:27: Christ is God's revealed mystery.

3. *in whom are hidden all the treasures of wisdom and knowledge:* All the treasures of wisdom and knowledge are hidden in Christ (or in God's mystery, equaling Christ [see v. 2]). "All" excludes every other source of wisdom and knowledge (perhaps in response to the false teaching that is viewed as relying upon other founts of knowledge). The "treasures" recall the "riches" mentioned in the previous verse. Wisdom *(sophia)* and knowledge *(gnōsis;* cf. Col 2:2; and cf. 1:9 where the term is *epignōsis)* appear as a unit here and this is in keeping with Jewish tradition (e.g., Eccl 1:16-18; 2:26; Sir 21:13). With its focus on wisdom, knowledge, and understanding (v. 2), Col 2:2-3 takes up ideas from Col 1:9-11 (cf. Rom 11:33; see the notes on 1:9). The notion of the treasure being "hidden" *(apokryphos)* in Christ is especially interesting. It serves to highlight the fact that true knowledge is only available to those who recognize Christ; treasure is to be found only in him. It reflects the notion that the mysteries of God's revelation are revealed only to God's elect (cf. *1 Enoch* 46:3). Similarly 1:26 speaks of the mystery as having been previously hidden, but now revealed to God's "saints" (see the notes above). The notion of treasure lying hidden in Christ also recalls the description of the Gospel in 1:5 as the hope laid up in heaven. Underlying Colossians is a strong sense of the precious being invisible, otherworldly, and heavenly. Believers likewise carry marks of identity that are not physically visible and this poses some challenges with respect to maintaining a distinct identity in the Greco-Roman world (see the notes and interpretation on 2:16-23).

4. *I am saying this so that no one may deceive you with persuasive speech:* The term "this" probably refers to the previous statements about Christ being the apex of God's revelation and of Christian identity. Although most translators understand the purpose clause as it is rendered here, it is also possible to translate it in an imperative sense: "What I mean is this: let no one deceive you" (Harris 86–87). This verse anticipates the more direct treatment of the

issue of false teaching that begins in 2:8. The Pauline message is understood as equipping believers with the necessary defenses against deception. *Pithanologia* (persuasive speech) refers to the art of persuasion: the rhetorical techniques used by orators in the ancient world to convince their audiences. The term occurs only here in the NT and it is clearly used in a pejorative sense as is made clear by the use of the verb *paralogizomai* (to deceive or delude; cf. Jas 1:22). In the Corinthian correspondence Paul displays a strong awareness of the dangers of deception in relation to artful speech. In 1 Cor 2:4 he writes, "My speech and my proclamation were not with plausible words of wisdom, but with a demonstration of the Spirit and of power" (NRSV). In 2 Corinthians Paul deals at length with the problem of the luring speech of false apostles. Deception is perceived as a major problem in the NT; it is often framed in terms of the problem of outward demeanor and behavior not matching inner nature (e.g., Matt 6:2, 5, 16). The expectation of deception was widespread in the ancient Mediterranean world and played a role in strategies for protecting one's honor and bringing shame upon one's enemies (see Neyrey, "Deception" [1993] 38–42). The identification of deception as a danger among the Colossians is related to the attempt to establish the apostle's honor in 1:24–2:7.

5. *For though I am absent in the flesh, yet I am with you in spirit:* This phrase explains why the Colossians should not be led easily astray by deception. The apostle's presence is a continuing reality in the community. "Absent in the flesh, yet with you in spirit" means that the apostle is physically absent but spiritually present (cf. 1 Thess 2:17; 1 Cor 5:3; Phil 1:27; cf. Moule [1971] 46). "In the spirit" refers to the presence of the inner self (one's thinking, will, and emotions) as distinguished from the physical body. (It is possible to translate *tē sarki* [in the flesh] as "in the body"; e.g., NRSV.) Some commentators, however, argue in favor of "in the Spirit" (e.g., Lohse 83; Patzia 47). The Holy Spirit is the basis of the apostle's unity with the community. Later in the verse the community is described as sharing a common faith in Christ; according to Rom 8:9-11 to be in Christ is to be in the Spirit.

rejoicing to see your order and the firmness of your faith in Christ Jesus: The expression *chairōn kai blepōn* (rejoicing and seeing) should be taken together as one phrase: "rejoicing to see" (BDF 471.5). Both "order" *(taxis)* and "firmness" *(stereōma)* appear in ancient descriptions of military organization. Order refers to the orderly arrangement of an army of soldiers and "firmness" can describe a bulwark or fortification (for examples in ancient literature see Lohse 84). It has been suggested that the experience of Paul's imprisonment may have led him (or the deutero-Pauline author) to adopt military metaphors; however, the use of the term *taxis* in 1 Cor 14:40 suggests a more general sense: "but all things should be done decently and in order" (NRSV). Both Paul's employment of the word here and the military usage point to the connection of such language with the values of honor and shame. The community is praised on account of its public display of honorable behavior (see the interpretation). At the same time it is reminded in general terms of the ideals of community life that must be preserved. When the passage is read in relation to v. 4 one senses the threat of a new teaching in relation to a previously unswerving community.

The praise is intended to encourage the community and no doubt to remind them of the solid foundation of the Gospel message they received from Epaphras (cf. 1:7, 23). They are strengthened by their faith in Christ Jesus (cf. 1 Pet 5:9; Acts 16:5).

6. *As therefore you received Christ Jesus the Lord, walk in him:* Colossians 2:6-7 is sometimes taken to be more closely related to what follows than to what precedes these verses. There may be an attempt to draw a contrast between the authentic message that was received and the false teaching that is condemned as human tradition in 2:8 (see Thurston 38). Yet these verses are more directly tied to previous verses for a variety of reasons. First, the Greek term *oun* probably draws a connection with what comes before it. Secondly, many of the terms that form the first part of the epistle are brought together here (e.g., "walk," "be rooted"). In fact, the admonition in 2:6-7 may well serve as the conclusion to all of Col 1:1–2:5, a long proclamation of the reconciliation of the estranged, underlining the significance of the Christ event and Paul's role in proclaiming the message of salvation. The bridge from 2:5 to 2:6-7 offers an excellent example of the remembrance-ethical exhortation pattern that characterizes Colossians as a whole (see the notes and interpretation on 1:13-14 and 1:21-23). However, it is also important to note that 2:6-7 is transitional in nature, summarizing the essence of the previous message and setting the stage for what is to come. The verb "to receive" *(paralambanō)* reflects rabbinic concepts used to describe the reception and transmission of tradition (see Lohse 93). The notion of communicating the content of a tradition is central in these verses, but it is closely related to the notion of receiving the person of Jesus whose presence lives on in the community. To walk in Christ Jesus *(peripateō,* to live one's life in Christ Jesus; cf. NRSV) refers to ethical deportment (see the notes on 1:10; cf. 3:7; 4:5).

7. *having been rooted and being built up in him:* There are four participles in v. 7 all relating to the verb "to walk" in the previous verse. Because of the close association with the imperative "walk" some translations cast the participles as virtual imperatives: "Be rooted in him, be built in him, grow strong in the faith as you were taught; let your hearts overflow with thankfulness" (NEB; cf. NJB). But it is probably better to take the participles as adverbial, describing the manner in which an action takes place (see BDF 418.5); in this case four typical characteristics of Christian "walking" (behavior; cf. Harris 89) are enumerated. "Having been rooted [cf. Col 1:6, 10] and being built up" may be a mixed metaphor (combining the ideas of being firmly fixed and yet growing), or it may reflect a tendency to combine agricultural and architectural imagery (cf. 1 Cor 3:6-15; Eph 3:17). Both participles, however, imply the notion of a strong foundation in Christ; both are directly connected to the "in him." Special attention should be given to the change in tense. "Having been rooted" *(errizōmenoi)* is a perfect passive participle implying a previous rooting and an ongoing state of rootedness. "Being built up" *(epoikodomoumenoi)* is a present passive participle implying an ongoing process. Together these participles connect the past with present, ongoing reality.

and being established in the faith as you were taught, abounding in thanksgiving: Bebaioumenoi is a participle of the verb meaning "to establish or confirm" *(bebaioō)*, further supporting the idea of a solid anchoring. Faith here seems to refer more directly to the object or content of belief (as is further suggested by the reference to teaching) than to the act of believing. The expression *tȩ pistei* might be a dative of instrument ("by your faith"; cf. NJB) or a dative of reference ("with respect to your faith"), but most translators now prefer the locative sense (in the faith; e.g., NRSV; REB; NAB; NIV). This verse probably recalls the original teaching given by Epaphras (1:7; cf. 2:6). The participle "abounding" *(perisseuontes)* is one of many terms in Colossians that suggest "filling up" (see the notes on 1:25). Thanksgiving *(eucharistia)* is an important theme in Colossians (cf. 1:3, 12; 3:15, 16, 17; 4:2). Although the term implies gratitude the verse should probably be taken as encouraging worship in ritual forms that were deemed acceptable by the author (see the notes and interpretation on 3:16-17; 4:2). There is a strongly attested variant reading of this verse *(perisseuontes en autȩ en eucharistią,* where *en autȩ = en pistei)* meaning "overflowing with faith and thanksgiving," but it is most often regarded as a copyist's assimilation to 4:2. Similarly, *perisseuontes en autǭ en eucharistią* (abounding in Christ with thanksgiving) seems to have arisen under the influence of the previous occurrence of *en autǭ* (in him) in the verse (see Metzger 622; Harris 90).

Interpretation

This section of Colossians appears at first glance to be a digression triggered by the personal remark concerning Paul's apostleship at the end of 1:23 (see Thurston 38). It is true that, after the letter has addressed the situation of the Colossians, the nature of the Gospel, and the significance of Christ in 1:1-23, we can imagine the author offering the summary in 2:6-7 and/or turning directly to the issue of false teaching in 2:8. But when we focus intently on the relationship between Colossians and its social context we quickly realize that the discussion of Paul's apostolic role is not really a digression, but is absolutely vital to securing a hearing for the epistle's message.

If one is familiar with Paul's impassioned defense of his Gentile mission in Galatians (Gal 1:15-17; 2:7-9) or his bitter dispute with rival apostles in 2 Corinthians (chs. 10–13), the apostle's comments in Col 1:24–2:7 may strike one as both confident and staid. Much of what is said here about Paul is also found in the undisputed letters of Paul, but it does not appear to be necessary for him to defend his apostleship in the same way. False teaching is a menace to which Paul must respond, but there is no direct evidence in Colossians of rivals who are undermining his claim to the title "apostle." As is also the case in Ephesians, there is no evidence of doubt surrounding Paul's role as an apostle (cf. Eph 3:1-13). Rather, in keeping with the interests of the letter as a whole, his apostleship is depicted in cosmic terms. In 1:23 Paul is viewed as a minister of a universal gospel—a gospel preached to every creature under heaven. Colossians 1:24–2:7 builds on this, highlighting the fact that Paul is bringing "the word of God to completion" (1:25) and being the mediator of the revelation of the mystery of God to the Gentiles (*ta ethnē;* 1:26-27; 2:2). But as is discussed below, while Colossians reveals little doubt about Paul's identity the letter does contain indications of concern about the continuing influence of his authority in community life.

As in the undisputed letters, Paul's authority is presented in Colossians as charismatic authority (see the notes and interpretation on 1:1-2). Phrases such as "minister according to the stewardship of God" reveal the basis of his authority in divine commission (v. 25). The energy powerfully working within Paul (v. 29) is God's power revealed in the apostle's word and deed. Paul has been especially chosen by God; he is the revealer of mysteries. In important respects the acceptance of Paul's authority means an acceptance of authority that is not sanctioned by convention and tradition, even though Paul's letters do obviously appeal to the norms and values of Jewish and Greco-Roman culture in order to make their claims intelligible to their audiences. When comparing Colossians to the undisputed letters, however, one detects a greater reliance on tradition and convention. Paul's authority is proclaimed in terms of an emerging image of what constitutes a true apostle in early church communities. This image works in conjunction with culturally appropriate means of gaining a hearing from an ancient audience (see below). Something is changing in the Pauline churches: Paul's charismatic authority is becoming increasingly routinized.

Scholars have paid close attention to the way Paul's person and achievements are presented in deutero-Pauline literature. It has been argued, for example, that a legend of Paul became current after his death, but prior to any widespread knowledge of his letters (indeed, it is interesting to note that the Acts of the Apostles makes no reference to Paul's letter writing, but operates with a clearly articulated vision of his authority). In investigating Colossians, Ephesians, Acts, and the Pastoral Epistles, Martinus de Boer has identified six common images of Paul that appear to have been central to this legend (370). Paul is (1) *the* apostle (or, in Acts, *the* missionary) (2) to the Gentiles or nations (*ta ethnē*) (3) who brought the gospel to the whole world (4) and suffered to make this possible. He is (5) the redeemed persecutor and (6) the authoritative teacher of the church. The above discussion makes it apparent that categories (1) to (3) are applicable to the Paul of Colossians. Category (5) is absent from Colossians, but is clearly attested in Ephesians (cf. Eph 3:8). As is illustrated below, categories (4) and (6) are central to the picture of Paul in Colossians.

In Colossians Paul is the suffering apostle *par excellence* (cf. Acts 9:16; Eph 3:1, 13; 2 Tim 1:8-18; 2:9). The gospel is able to penetrate the world only because Paul suffers (cf. 1:24; 4:3, 10,18). This may well have spoken directly to the situation of believers who increasingly experienced difficulties in their own interaction with the world (see the notes and interpretation on 4:2-6).

Because of the reference to Paul filling up what is lacking in Christ's afflictions, Col 1:24 has struck some as a type of glorification of suffering that is foreign to the authentic Paul (see the notes above). Rather it should be understood as a statement of the close relationship between Christ and Paul in the strongest possible terms (and reflecting the outlook of first-century Mediterranean people; see the discussion below). The word *hysterēma* (what is lacking, a deficiency) is sometimes used in Paul's letters to express "the absence of a person to whom one is consciously attached" (Lohse 71). While it is going too far to say that Christ is viewed as absent in the community (as it would be going too far to view his sacrifice as deficient), there is a sense in which Paul represents Christ to the community (Christ might also be viewed as representing God: he is the mystery of God; see 2:2). Similarly Paul is not really absent; he is with them in spirit (2:5) and he is represented by his fellow workers, Epaphras (1:7; 1:23), Tychicus, and Onesimus (4:7-9) as is suggested by the similar terminology used to describe their mission and the roles they perform (see the notes and interpretation on 1:3-8 and 4:7-18). In fact one detects a relationship between the main players in Colossians that might be characterized as follows: Christ represents God; Paul represents Christ; Paul's fellow workers represent Paul. But there are problems surrounding the preservation of this unbroken chain. In a community that longs for Paul's presence his continuing absence must be explained, and the means to keep his authority viable must be secured. Paul encourages the Colossians. The importance of what he is about to teach is underscored by the proclamation: "For I wish you to know how great a struggle I am having on your behalf and on behalf of those in Laodicea, and on behalf of all those who have not seen me face to face" (2:1).

Two direct references to Paul's physical absence are found in this passage (2:1, 5). Moreover, Paul does not announce a plan to visit the community in the future as is the case in Romans (15:24). He is imprisoned (4:18). Thus Paul's physical absence must be considered a central part of the social situation underlying Colossians. Max Weber's discussion of problems created by the death of a charismatic leader is suggestive for understanding the situation created by the death or imprisonment of Paul. (On Paul as a charismatic leader and for more information about Weber's theories see the notes and interpretation on 1:1-2 and 1:3-8.) According to Weber the death of the charismatic figure will give rise to the problem of succession: to whom will we now listen? It will often trigger attempts on the part of the followers or "staff" of the leader to ensure the continuation of the movement and to secure their own positions. This is one of the means by which charisma becomes routinized: access to charisma becomes defined by tradition and by clearly articulated authority structures. In the case of the disappearance of Paul, his fellow workers may naturally have claimed special access to charisma (God's favor bestowed as a gift of grace; cf. Eph 3:7) based upon their close connection with Paul. They may have written in his name and reinforced their own authority in the local Pauline churches based upon their association with Paul. In light of the problems created by Paul's indefinite absence the fellow workers' success depended on their continuing ability to convey the apostle's voice.

The controversy created by the false teaching (2:8-23) made it especially important for Paul to speak to the community. In keeping with the sixth image of Paul identified by de Boer, Paul is presented as the authoritative teacher who stands firmly against any deviation from the truth he teaches, ready to warn and protect believers (2:4, 8-15). In Col 2:2-4 the verbs "to encourage" *(parakaleō)* and "to join together" *(symbibazō)*, along with the emphasis on understanding, knowledge, and wisdom, reinforce this image (see the notes on 2:2). Once again it is important to consider the relationship between Paul and his fellow workers who are similarly presented in a teaching capacity. The Colossians did not receive the gospel from Paul himself, but from Epaphras (Col 1:7). The connection between Paul and Epaphras is strongly reinforced in Col 1:23 and 2:6-7: the purpose of Paul's instructions is to remind them of what they have already been taught. Similarly Tychicus' mission with respect to the community is presented as being identical to Paul's mission: He is to encourage *(parakaleō)* their hearts (Col 4:8). The relationship between Paul and his fellow workers has sometimes been described in terms of a Pauline "school." In the ancient world the relationship between disciple and teacher was understood as being far closer than the modern professional arrangement of instruction. Disciples were viewed as shaped by their teachers. In "schools" an individual teacher's identity became encapsulated in the group identity: "To know the teacher or mentor was to know the disciple" (Malina and Neyrey [1996] 161; see also 27–28, 160–61). The attempt to speak in Paul's name should be understood in light of this phenomenon.

For an awareness of the full significance of Paul's comments concerning his apostolic role it is important not only to place his comments against the background of the social conditions faced by the community, but also to seek to understand why an ancient audience would have found Paul's assertions of authority convincing. In order to appreciate what may have moved an ancient audience, a recent study of Paul's letters by Bruce J. Malina and Jerome H. Neyrey (1996) combines a rhetorical analysis with an anthropological appreciation of ancient Mediterranean values. In recent years scholars have become increasingly interested in analyzing Paul's letters in light of the fact that people in the ancient world were schooled in rhetoric—conventional forms that were seen as essential to public speaking and the persuasion of others. In fact, in the text presently under discussion the author displays an awareness of "the rules of the game" when he expresses his fear that the Colossians will be deceived by persuasive speech (see the notes on 2:4). Despite the negative portrayal of human tradition in Col 2:8, scholars are increasingly convinced that Pauline thought was influenced by the conventional categories of ancient rhetoric. (There is, however, debate about the extent of such influence and about whether it is appropriate to think of Paul using such conventions in a formal way.) Paul's self-descriptions may, for example, be analyzed in light of the *encomium*, the ancient speech of praise (involving such fixed categories as origin and birth, nurture and training, accomplishments and deeds [of the body, of the soul, and of fortune] (see Malina and Neyrey [1996] 23–64; see also 219–24 for examples of *encomia* found in ancient literature). Such an analysis may shed light on how Colossians' assertions were shaped by conventional categories. To understand how the *encomium* might illuminate Colossians it is particularly useful to compare the text to 2 Corinthians, where many similar concepts occur.

Eschewing many of the traditional sanctions of authority, Paul appeals to the charismatic basis of his authority (1:1; 1:25-27), but this appeal is nevertheless reinforced by elements of tradition, conventional categories, and commonly held values. In Colossians Paul makes little reference either to his origins or to his education (cf. Gal 1:13-14, 15-16; Phil 3:2-11), although the reference to the "stewardship of God" points to Paul receiving a divine commission from God (see the notes on 1:25) in much the same way as the origins of prophets were determined by divine choice (see Malina and Neyrey [1996] 39-41). As in 2 Corinthians 10–13, the focus in Col 1:25–2:7 is primarily upon Paul's accomplishments and deeds. As in 2 Cor 11:23, Paul calls himself *diakonos* (minister, servant) in Col 1:23 (of the gospel) and in Col 1:25 (of the church). The term *diakonos* was frequently employed in the ancient world to refer to the service rendered by an individual as an agent of a high-ranking person (an intermediary in commercial transactions, a messenger, or a diplomat; see Collins 77–95, 169–76; see also the notes on 1:23). Brokerage or agency is an important concept to keep in mind when analyzing Paul's authority in Col 1:24–2:7, but as 1:25-27 illustrates, in his ministry to the church Paul is no earthly functionary; he is acting as God's agent; he does nothing less than make known the mystery of God (= Christ) to the world. Paul's honor is enhanced even further by the reference to various deeds of the body. In his suffering he is filling up what is lacking in Christ's afflictions (1:24). With the use of athletic imagery we hear of his struggles and labor in 1:29–2:1; this recalls Paul's use of the catalogue of hardships in 2 Cor 11:23-33 and elsewhere in 2 Corinthians. Several similar catalogues have been found in the literature of Paul's day. An ancient audience would no doubt have been impressed by Paul's courage while in chains. They might well have understood the reference to the power Paul enjoys as an example of a "deed of fortune"—an indication of divine favor showered upon Paul. (Other deeds of fortune that were commonly listed in ancient *encomia* include wealth, friends, children, fame, etc.; see Malina and Neyrey [1996] 31–33, 59.) Paul's power demonstrates that God has bestowed upon him this favor or grace (see the notes on 1:29; cf. 2 Cor 12:9 where grace [*charis*] and power [*dynamis*] are listed together). In essence, God is Paul's patron. He operates through him in power (see Malina and Neyrey [1996] 55–60; on patronage see also the notes and interpretation on 1:3-8).

After the accomplishments of a person were highlighted, speeches of praise in antiquity sometimes included comparisons (some of which praised one candidate while blaming another; cf. Malina and Neyrey [1996] 48–50). Second Corinthians clearly seeks to praise Paul and depicts the "superapostles" as misguided at best. A comparison between Paul and his opponents is announced in Col 2:4 and developed fully in 2:8-23. Colossians 2:4 leaves little doubt, however, that the art of persuasion is at the heart of the dispute. One senses the struggle to win an audience. The magnitude of Paul's mission, his close relationship with Christ, and his heroic deeds as the suffering apostle are stated in such strong terms that it almost appears to be over-assertion to enhance honor (see the notes on 1:23). The shame of being deceived by an artful speaker is recalled for an audience only too familiar with the dangers of being duped. The only honor is to be found in adhering to the original Pauline gospel that was preached among the Colossians. It is only then that a Christian may be presented as perfect in Christ (1:28)—publicly displayed before God as a perfect creation (the new self, according to the image of its creator; cf. 3:10).

As an ancient person Paul (or the author of Colossians) was a group-oriented person rather than an independent, individualistic person as modern Western people tend to be. Malina and Neyrey (1996) have described the general outlook of the group-oriented people in Paul's world as follows:

> First century Mediterranean persons were strongly group-embedded, collectivist persons. Since they were group-oriented, they were "socially" minded, as opposed to "psychologically" minded. They were attuned to the values, attitudes, and beliefs of their in-group, with which they shared a common fate due to generation and geography. Thanks to their in-group enculturation, they were used to assessing themselves and oth-

ers in terms of stereotypes often explained as deriving from family "history" and the geographical location of their group. (16–17)

Thus when one reads statements concerning the nature of Paul's role such as those found in Col 1:24–2:7 it is important to keep in mind that group-oriented people tended to view themselves as subject to the control of forces greater than themselves and were dependent on group expectations to a far greater extent than are modern Western people. Such an outlook shapes even the way salvation and the apostle's role as a mediator of salvation are described. The way the relationship between Paul, Christ, and the church is described in 1:24 may seem strange and even doctrinally flawed to modern readers, but it was a culturally appropriate means of describing Paul's ultimate dependence on Christ and God (cf. 1:29; cf. Phil 4:13-19), and his embeddedness in the community, the church. Ancient Mediterranean people viewed themselves as embedded in others such as their teachers and patrons. Paul's description of himself as "a minister [or servant], according to the stewardship of God given to me for you" (1:26) is rooted in such a cultural understanding. Throughout the passage Paul is presented as a steward of God's mystery. God is Paul's patron (and ultimately his only teacher: cf. Col 1:1). He "brokers" God's mystery (the person of Christ) in the Colossian community. Having been chosen by God to be a servant of the gospel (1:24-26), he in turn teaches the community so that they might have "all the riches of fully assured understanding" and "the knowledge of the mystery of God, that is, Christ himself" (Col 2:2).

FOR REFERENCE AND FURTHER STUDY

Boer, Martinus C. de. "Images of Paul in the Post-Apostolic Period," *CBQ* 42 (1980) 359–80.

Brown, Raymond E. *The Semitic Background of the Term "Mystery" in the New Testament*. Philadelphia: Fortress, 1968.

Collins, John N. *Diakonia: Re-interpreting the Ancient Sources*. New York: Oxford University Press, 1990.

Coppens, Joseph. "Mystery," in Jerome Murphy-O'Connor, ed., *Paul and Qumran: Studies in New Testament Exegesis*. Chicago: Priory, 1968, 132–58.

Fitzgerald, John T. *Cracks in the Earthen Vessel: An Examination of the Catalogues of Hardships in the Corinthian Correspondence*. Atlanta: Scholars, 1988.

Malina, Bruce J., and Jerome H. Neyrey. *Portraits of Paul: An Archaeology of Ancient Personality*. Louisville: Westminster/John Knox, 1996.

Meeks, Wayne A. "In One Body: The Unity of Humankind in Colossians and Ephesians," in Wayne A. Meeks and Jacob Jervell, eds., *God's Christ and His People: Studies in Honour of Nils Alstrup Dahl*. Oslo, Bergen, and Tromsö: Universitetsforlaget, 1977, 209–21.

Moir, W. R. G. "Colossians 1:14," *ExpT* 42 (1930–31) 479–80.

Neyrey, Jerome H. "Deception," in John J. Pilch and Bruce J. Malina, eds., *Biblical Social Values and Their Meaning: A Handbook.* Peabody, Mass.: Hendrickson, 1993, 38–42.

_____. "Eyes–Heart," in ibid. 63–67.

Pfitzner, Victor C. *Paul and the Agon Motif: Traditional Athletic Imagery in Pauline Literature.* Leiden: E. J. Brill, 1967.

Pokorný, Petr. *Colossians: A Commentary.* Peabody, Mass.: Hendrickson, 1991.

Proudfoot, C. M. "Imitation or Realistic Participation? A Study of Paul's Concept of Suffering with Christ," *Interpretation* 17 (1963) 140–60.

Reumann, John. "*Oikonomia*-terms in Paul in Comparison with Lucan *Heilsgeschichte*," *NTS* 13 (1966–67) 147–67.

Rigaux, Béda. "Révélation des Mystères et Perfection à Qumran et dans le Nouveau Testament," *NTS* 4 (1957–58) 237–62.

Schenke, Hans-Martin. "Das Weiterwirken des Paulus und die Pflege seines Erbes durch die Paulus-Schule," *NTS* 21 (1974–75) 505–18.

7. Debate with the Opponents: The Power of the Risen Christ (2:8-15)

8. See to it that no one takes you captive through philosophy and empty deceit according to human tradition, according to the elements of the universe and not according to Christ. 9. Because in him dwells all of the fullness of the deity bodily, 10. and you have your fulfillment in him who is the head of every ruler and power. 11. In him also you were circumcised with a circumcision made without hands, by the putting off of the body of the flesh, by the circumcision of Christ. 12. You were buried with him in baptism, in which you were also raised with him through faith in the power of God who raised him from the dead. 13. And when you were dead because of the transgressions and the uncircumcision of your flesh, he made you alive together with him, forgiving us all of our transgressions, 14. wiping out the bond that stood against us with its legal demands; he has also set it aside, nailing it to the cross; 15. stripping the rulers and powers, he made a public example of them boldly, triumphing over them in him.

NOTES

8. *See to it that no one takes you captive through philosophy and empty deceit:* When the verb "to see" *(blepō)* is followed by the future indicative as it is here (literally, see to it that there shall be no capturing) instead of the aorist subjunctive as is usually the case (cf. Matt 24:4), an especially urgent warning is intended (cf. Heb 3:12; Harris 91; Moulton 178). The verb *sylagōgeō* (to rob, to take as

captive, to carry off as booty; BAGD 776) occurs only here in the NT; it is one of several uses of concepts associated with slavery in Colossians that may have spoken poignantly to a community where many had direct experience of slavery (see the notes and interpretation on 3:18–4:1). To adhere to the false teaching is to be enslaved. The false teaching is here called a philosophy (*philosophia*; see Michel, *TNDT* 9:172–79). Although it occurs only here in the NT, "philosophy" was a broad concept in the ancient world used to refer to the teachings and points of view of a variety of groups. It could be used as a positive term designed to win respect. Josephus, for example, explained that within Judaism three philosophical schools existed simultaneously: the Pharisees, Sadducees, and Essenes (*C. Apion* 1.54; *Bell.* 2.119; *Ant.* 18.11). Associated with "empty deceit" (on deception see the notes and interpretation on 2:4), the term is clearly used in a negative sense (for a negative philosophy see also 4 Macc 5:11).

according to human tradition, according to the elements of the universe and not according to Christ: Colossians 2:6 reflects the idea of conveying authentic tradition (see the notes above). In contrast, here "human tradition" is inauthentic tradition. It is ultimately teaching associated with the evil world outside the church (see the interpretation below). It is not according to Christ. The meaning of the expression "elements of the universe" *(stoicheia tou kosmou)* has been extensively debated by scholars (cf. 2:20). The word *stoicheon* refers simply to a member or element in a series, but could be used to describe such diverse elements as the letters of the alphabet, fundamental principles, or even the signs of the zodiac. The precise meaning of the expression as it appears in Colossians is by no means clear. Three possible meanings have most commonly been suggested by scholars. The expression may simply refer to the elementary teachings of this world: "based on the principles of this world" (NJB; cf. REB)—a world that is clearly judged negatively (cf. Col 2:20). The most common interpretation is made clear, however, by the translations offered by the NRSV, REB, NAB, and others: "elemental spirits of the universe." Here the elements are viewed as spiritual forces or heavenly powers. Commentators have understood them to be identical to the rulers and powers (1:16; 2:10, 15; e.g., Arnold [1995] 193–94). Moreover, some have argued that the elements are associated with the "worship of angels" (2:18; see Lohse 128). In general it has been argued that the opponents sought to establish a proper relationship with spiritual beings by means of certain ritual and ascetic acts in the hope of participating in divine fullness (2:16-23). In support of this interpretation is Paul's use of the expression "elements of the universe" in Gal 4:3, 9 where it appears to refer to personalized forces; in 4:8-9 they are closely associated with the gods the Galatians had previously rejected (see also evidence from Jewish apocalyptic that spoke of spirits controlling the elements; cited by Dunn 149).

But arguing in favor of a third way of understanding the expression Eduard Schweizer (1988) has noted that the philological evidence from the first century strongly suggests that these elements are the four elements of the universe (i.e., earth, water, air, and fire; cf. 2 Pet 3:10, 12; Wis 7:17). Though they had originally been in harmony, in this period these elements were thought to threaten the universe by their strife and continuous interchange. Against such upheaval the resurrected Christ of Colossians is presented as reconciling all things once and for all. In other words, in referring to the elements of the universe the author may have been seeking primarily to stress the error of the false teaching by exaggerating its connection with worldly (or cosmic), unstable, and in the author's opinion ultimately base phenomena. In short, it is impossible to be certain that the *stoicheia* played a part in the rituals of the opponents. If indeed the *stoicheia* figured in the worship of the Colossians' opponents they must have done so in a negative way; that is, measures must have been taken to control these hostile powers rather than to venerate them. The author of Colossians expects that his audience will share the negative evaluation of life according to the elements of the universe: no further justification is necessary.

9. *Because in him dwells all of the fullness of the deity bodily:* The term "because" *(hoti)* introduces two reasons, based on the identity of Christ, why believers must turn away from the false teaching. "In him" is the first of three uses of the expression "in Christ" in vv. 9-11 (see the notes on 1:2). The expression clearly has a locative sense, but the use of the verb "to dwell" *(katoikeō)* renders this sense even stronger than usual; it refers to residing or settling down in a permanent way (see BAGD 124). This verse is very similar to 1:19. Indeed, this section of Colossians takes up again many of the ideas found in the Christ-hymn of 1:15-20. In contrast to 1:19, however, the nature of the fullness *(plērōma)* is defined explicitly. (For the significance of the concept of *plērōma* for the theology of Colossians see the notes on 1:19.) It is the "all of the [or the whole of the] fullness of the deity" (sometimes translated as "Godhead," e.g., REB) that dwells in Christ. The eternal dwelling of God in Christ is in view here. But in keeping with the theology of Colossians, which relates the cosmic Christ to the incarnation and sees what Christ has accomplished physically as enormously significant, the deity is described as dwelling bodily *(somatikōs)* in Christ. This may well reflect a response to proponents of the false teaching who require various physical measures in the form of rituals and ascetic acts for full access to the "fullness" (cf. 2:16-23).

10. *and you have your fulfillment in him who is the head of every ruler and power:* Literally the Greek text speaks of believers "having been filled" *(peplērōmenoi).* The verbal construction includes a perfect passive participle of the verb *plēroō* that means to fill, to bring to completion, or to fulfill. This verbal construction, which addresses the present state of the Colossians, clearly relates the completeness of believers to the fullness of the deity in the previous verse. Like 2:9 it probably also recalls 1:19. (On echoes of Col 1:15-20 in this section see the notes above.) Similarly, the expression "the head of every ruler and power" recalls 1:18 ("head") and 1:16 ("ruler and power"). In all likelihood this is a reference to cosmic powers that are viewed as subordinate to Christ. Some have understood these rulers and powers as identical to the elements (elemental forces or spirits) of the universe mentioned in 2:8. The rulers and powers may very well have been understood in the Colossian community as angelic beings. The veneration of these beings may have been recommended by the pro-

ponents of the false teaching as a means of securing greater access to the benefits of salvation. Perhaps the rulers and powers were viewed by some in the community as evil spiritual powers who needed to be placated (see Arnold [1995] 193–94; on the meaning of this expression see the notes on 1:16; see also the notes on 2:18). Colossians 2:15 makes it very clear that the author of Colossians viewed these forces as evil.

11. *In him also you were circumcised with a circumcision made without hands:* Verses 9-10 contain the heart of the explanation for why the false teaching should be rejected: it is not according to Christ. The deity dwells in Christ and believers have received ultimate fulfillment in him. Verses 11-13 extend this argument by reminding believers of the means by which they achieved such completeness: the experience of baptism. In order to understand the meaning of v. 11 we must read it in conjunction with v. 12 where the equivalence between baptism and circumcision is made clear. The Greek text literally refers to a circumcision made without hands that the NRSV interprets as a "spiritual" circumcision. This verse speaks of circumcision of the heart (a transformation affecting the inner self that bears no visible, physical signs and is intimately connected to the experience of baptism). Indeed the term "circumcision" is used in a figurative sense in vv. 11-12. It should be noted that circumcision had already been discussed figuratively in the Hebrew Bible (Deut 10:16; Jer 4:4; Ezek 44:7) and in Paul's letters (Rom 2:28-9; Phil 3:3), but the explicit association of circumcision with baptism occurs for the first time in Colossians. Since the Colossian false teaching clearly included Jewish elements (2:16-23), it is possible that the references to circumcision are an indication that the rite was practiced by the opponents, even if this is never stated explicitly. It is also possible, however, that the term "circumcision" was employed by the proponents of the false teaching to refer either to a certain rite of initiation or to an alternate understanding of baptism (see the notes and interpretation on 2:16-23). It is being argued in this commentary that the meaning of baptism is at the heart of the dispute with the false teachers (see the interpretation below; see also Attridge).

by the putting off of the body of the flesh, by the circumcision of Christ: The expression "putting off the body of flesh [*sarkos*]" invites comparison to Gal 3:26-27 and other texts from early Christian literature where garment imagery is employed in conjunction with baptism (see the interpretation below). It also invites comparison to the polemical discussion of the practices involved in the false teaching in vv. 16-23. Colossians 2:23 makes reference to the severe treatment of the body that is recommended by the opponents and to various measures that are deemed of no value in checking the indulgences of the flesh (*sarkos*; see the notes and interpretation on 2:23). It may be that "putting off of the body of the flesh" is a priority shared by both the author of Colossians and the proponents of the false teaching, but the author clearly disagrees with the measures adopted by the opponents to guarantee such a stripping away. (On the notion of putting off see also 2:15 and 3:9-10.) It is probable that "the body of the flesh" refers to one's sinful nature, which is removed at baptism. (On the relationship between "flesh" and "body" in Pauline thought see Robinson.)

Similarly, "the circumcision of Christ" likely refers to baptism by which one participates in the death and resurrection of Christ (see Lohse 103), but the meaning of this phrase has been the subject of considerable debate (see Harris 102). Some have taken the phrase to refer specifically to Christ's physical nature—not to his literal circumcision (Luke 2:21), but to his death (cf. Rom 7:4), where he stripped off his physical body (see Dunn 158). Similarly, "the putting off of the body of the flesh" has sometimes been taken to refer to Christ's death (in 2:15 similar terminology is used to refer to what Christ has accomplished through his death and resurrection), but if it did indeed refer to Christ's death one would expect the presence of the possessive "his" as in 1:22 (see O'Brien [1982] 116–17; Moule [1957] 96; and the response to Moule in Lohse 103).

12. *You were buried with him in baptism:* The verb "you were buried with him" agrees with the verb "you were circumcised" in v. 11 and refers either to simultaneous action (circumcision and burial occurring together at baptism) as is implied by the NRSV translation "when you were buried" or to subsequent action (spiritual circumcision: inner transformation, followed by burial with Christ in baptism; see the notes on 2:11). There is strong manuscript support for two variant readings of this phrase. Some manuscripts employ the more usual NT term for the rite of baptism *(baptisma),* while others employ a term that usually refers to "dipping" or "ritual washing" *(baptismos;* cf. Mark 7:4; Heb 9:10). Because it is a much less usual term for baptism in the early church it is more likely that copyists would alter it to conform to the usual usage than vice versa. A similar usage of *baptismos* to refer to the rite of baptism occurs in Heb 6:2: "instruction about baptisms" (NRSV; see Metzger 623). It is possible that the opponents, with their focus on ritual purity (2:16-23), used this less common term and that the author cites it in order to illustrate the true meaning of baptism. In this section, and repeatedly throughout Colossians, we find the expression "with *(syn)* Christ" (cf. 2:12, 13, 20; 3:1, 3, 4). In the undisputed letters of Paul "in Christ" is by far the most frequent formula. "With Christ" can be employed by Paul to refer to the present union of believers with Christ (e.g., Rom 6:4-6), but Paul also clearly speaks of being made alive with Christ as a future event (e.g., Rom 6:8; 8:17; 1 Thess 4:17). Only in Col 3:4 does the experience of being with Christ have a future component. In the remainder of the cases the focus is on the experience of the death and resurrection in which believers have already shared through baptism.

in which you were also raised with him through faith in the power of God who raised him from the dead: The expression *en hǭ kai,* which is translated here, in keeping with most modern translations, as "in which" (referring to the baptism in which they were raised) might also be translated as "in him" (referring to Christ). Thus Lohse translates the phrase as "in him you were also raised with him" (92). But several factors count against this possible translation including the awkwardness of "in him" being followed immediately by "with him" (see Harris 104). *En* is usually taken to be locative (in which), but might also be instrumental ("by which" as in NJB). The verb "you were raised [with]" *(synēgerthēte)* is an aorist passive indicative with God the implied agent. The emphasis is clearly on something that has already occurred shaping present existence. This verse naturally invites comparison to Rom 6:4-14, where the notion of dying and rising with Christ in baptism also occurs (see especially 6:4-5, 8-11, 13). But, as has frequently been noted by commentators, in Romans 6 being united with Christ in resurrection has a strong future dimension: "Therefore we have been buried with him by baptism into death, so that, just as Christ was raised from the dead by the glory of the Father, so we too might walk in newness of life. For if we have been united with him in a death like his, we will certainly be united with him in a resurrection like his" (Rom 6:4-5 NRSV). Although some commentators have seen a radical transformation of the understanding of the resurrection in Colossians in comparison to the undisputed letters of Paul (see, for example, Lohse 104–105), it is probable that Colossians reflects merely a change in emphasis rather than a radical shift. The encounter with the Colossian opponents may have led the author to adopt an almost exclusive focus on the present in order to ward off perpetual efforts to guarantee access to the mystery of God. (On the notion of the power of God see also 1:29 where similar terminology occurs.) The power of God works through Christ, Paul, and ultimately all believers. It is what moves the universe in a harmonious process toward union with God.

13. *And when you were dead because of the transgressions and the uncircumcision of your flesh:* "You" probably refers to the Gentile identity of the Colossians in contrast to the "us" later in the verse that most likely refers to the totality of believers: Jews (including Paul) and Gentiles. The expression *nekrous ontas* (literally, "and you being dead") might also be rendered as "although you were dead" as in the case of the NEB. "Death" refers to the spiritual death caused by sin (cf. Rom 7:9-10). (On death being used in a figurative sense in the NT see Luke 15:24, 32; Rev 3:1; James 2:17-26.) *En* is understood here as causal (because of; see also NJB and REB), but it might also be understood in the locative sense ("dead in the transgressions"). This amounts, however, only to a slight difference in meaning. The expression "the uncircumcision of your flesh" calls to mind 2:11 where the believers are said to have put off the body of the flesh in a circumcision made without hands. The removal of the body of flesh in 2:11 refers to the putting off of a sinful nature; ultimately the uncircumcision of the flesh here also refers to this sinful nature. However, it is possible that physical circumcision is more directly in view here than in 2:11: physical uncircumcision *(akrobystia)* might be a symbol of Gentile alienation from God (cf. Eph 2:11-12). Paul frequently employs the term "uncircumcision" as a designation for Gentiles (e.g., Gal 2:7; Rom 3:30).

he made you alive together with him, forgiving us all of our transgressions: "You" is absent from some manuscripts and other manuscripts have made "us" alive. The absence of "you" from some manuscripts was probably caused by the perception of superfluity, and a replacement of "you" with "us" may well have been caused by a desire to harmonize the person with that used at the end of the phrase, "our transgressions." Thus the reading offered above is preferred (see Metzger 623). The NRSV alleviates any ambiguity by making the implied subject of the phrase explicit: "God made you alive." Literally the

Greek text refers only to "he" as it appears above and in most modern translations; thus the phrase might mean that Christ made believers alive together
with himself. That God is the implied subject is supported by the use of the
passive verbs in 2:12 where God is the implied agent and by the parallel text
of Eph 2:4-5. The shift from "you" at the beginning of this phrase to "us" at the
end has been taken as a sign that traditional expressions (possibly hymnic influences) underlie 2:13c-15 (see the notes below). The experience of baptism
appears also to be connected to the forgiveness of sins in Col 1:13-14 (see the
notes) and such an association is found elsewhere in the NT (cf. Acts 2:38; Matt
6:9-15 *par.*).

14. *wiping out the bond that stood against us with its legal demands:* Beginning at v. 13c
to v. 15 the focus moves once again to what God has accomplished through
Christ. The unusual terminology and the linking together of several participles (e.g., forgiving, wiping out, nailing, etc.) have been viewed as indications
of the use of traditional hymnic formulations (see the notes above). The term
cheirographon (bond, certificate of indebtedness, record of debt) occurs nowhere else in the NT. It refers literally to something that is written by hand and
more specifically to the certificate of indebtedness issued by the debtor in his
or her own hand as an acknowledgment of debt. The term occurs in the LXX in
Tob 5:3 and 9:5. The relationship between God and humanity in Judaism
sometimes is envisioned as that between a creditor and a debtor; God's mercy
leads to the blotting out of transgressions (e.g., LXX Isa 43:25; for full discussion see Lohse 108). Although the specific term is not used, the concept of a
certificate of indebtedness is reflected in the following text from Paul's letter
to Philemon where Paul refers to the possible wrongdoing of Philemon's runaway slave, Onesimus: "If he has wronged you in any way, or owes you anything, charge that to my account. I, Paul, am writing this with my own hand: I
will repay it. I say nothing about your owing me even your own self" (Phlm
18-19 NRSV). One wonders whether the language of 2:14 would have spoken
strongly to the slave members of the community who were likely to have
stood literally under debtors' bonds. It should be noted that the precise meaning of the term *cheirographon* in the context of Colossians has been widely debated. Theories range from that of Tertullian and Origen who thought that the
bond referred to a deal between the devil and humanity, to a heavenly record
book kept by God concerning human sin (cf. Rev 5:1-5). It has even been argued that the term refers to Christ's body itself based on the notice nailed to
the cross of Christ (Mark 15:26; 2 Cor 5:21). It is clear that the notion of a bond
here is linked to the concept of legal demands *(tois dogmasin),* but the grammar
of the phrase makes the precise relationship difficult to determine (see Harris
108–109). Most modern versions, however, now favor the dative of accompanying circumstances made clear by the term "with" (e.g., NRSV: erasing the
record that stood against us with its legal commands; cf. NIV; NJB; NAB; REB).

The mention of legal demands is often viewed as a reference to the Mosaic
Law (cf. Eph 2:15, the only other place in the Pauline corpus where *dogma* occurs). The implication appears to be that human beings were unable to keep
these commands and Christ's death was required to cancel the bond; the

record of transgressions has been erased. It is also possible that the expression "legal demands" was inserted within traditional formulations concerning the forgiveness of sins in an effort to respond directly to the opponents as is implied by the use of the related verb in 2:20, *dogmatizō*, to refer to the ordinances to which the opponents submit. In the Greek text the negative character of the bond with its legal demands is stressed to such an extent that the sentence seems overloaded. Two repetitive expressions occur: "that was against us" *(to kath' hēmōn)*, and "that stood against us" *(ho ēn hypenantion hēmin)*, but the repetition may well be an interpretative device to highlight hostility. The NIV translation aims to capture this emphasis: "having cancelled the written code, with its regulations, that was against us and stood opposed to us." Clearly the bond that was wiped out was condemnatory.

he has also set it aside, nailing it to the cross: Most commentators have viewed God as the subject in vv. 13-15. However, there is some ambiguity raised by the Greek text. Believing that *apekdysamenos* must refer to Christ divesting himself in v. 15 (see the notes below), some commentators have argued in favor of a change of subject from God to Christ either at "he set it aside" or at the beginning of v. 14, "wiping out." Most translators accept a temporal relationship between the setting aside of the bond and the nailing to the cross: God set it aside, having nailed it to the cross. It is possible, however, that the nailing refers directly to the means by which the debt is cancelled as is suggested by the NJB rendering: "he has destroyed it by nailing it to the cross." The verb "to nail" *(prosēloō)* occurs nowhere else in the NT. As in the Christ-hymn of 1:15-20, the significance of the physical death of Jesus is highlighted.

15. *stripping the rulers and powers:* The participle of a rarely used middle verb *(apekdyomai)*, "stripping," occurs in the NT only here and at 3:9 (see the use of the cognate in 3:11). It means to strip, divest, or renounce (the middle voice refers to reflexive or reciprocal action as is also clearly the case in 3:9, which refers to believers having stripped off their old selves). Viewed as a middle proper, the expression has sometimes been rendered in the manner proposed as the alternate translation in the notes to the NRSV: "he divested himself of." Sometimes, however, the middle voice will be used where an active is expected and this is probably the case here (see BDF 316.1). Thus the participle should be understood as referring to the activity of stripping or disarming the rulers and powers. It recalls the public shame of being stripped of all honor, being rendered naked before friend and foe alike. The active sense appears to fit better with the ongoing role of God as the subject in vv. 13-15, but it should be noted that some have seen Christ as the subject in v. 15. In the early church it was widely held that Christ was the subject in this verse. The Latin Fathers, for example, presupposed the addition of "his physical body" as is reflected by the alternate translation included in the margins of the REB: "he stripped himself of his physical body, and thereby made a public spectacle of the cosmic powers and authorities." Here the "powers and authorities" (translated in this commentary as rulers and powers) are viewed as the object of the verb "to make a public spectacle (or example)." This view has not gained wide acceptance. The rulers and powers are most often taken as the object of "stripping"

—the evil forces have been rendered powerless by God (see the discussion in Harris 110; Lohse 111). On the meaning of the expression "rulers and powers" see the notes on 1:16 and 2:10.

he made a public example of them boldly, triumphing over them in him: The implied subject here is probably God and the object is "rulers and powers" (see the notes above). The verb "to make a public example of them" *(deigmatizō)* refers to public humiliation and shame, occurring only here in Pauline literature. Its usage in Matt 1:19 makes its strong meaning clearly apparent: "Her husband Joseph, being a righteous man and unwilling to expose her to public disgrace, planned to dismiss her quietly" (NRSV). The sense is strengthened in the Greek text by the repetitive qualifier "in the open" (probably meaning boldly; *en parrēsią*). The verb "to triumph over" or "to lead in triumphal procession" *(thriambeuō)* occurs in the NT only here and in 2 Cor 2:14. The expression recalls the triumphal procession of military rulers who displayed the spoils of war. Captured slaves, women, and children were likely to be prominent among the displayed spoils and this imagery may well have spoken powerfully to these members of the community. In this case the powers and not the enslaved peoples have been placed in the position of humiliation; God plays the role of the triumphal victor. "In him" probably refers to Christ (God triumphs over them in Christ). It is also possible to translate the Greek expression *(en autǭ)* as "in it," most likely referring to the cross (e.g., NRSV). If Christ is taken as the subject in v. 15 (see the notes above), *en autǭ* must refer to the cross. *En autǭ* can be either locative (in him or it) or instrumental (through/by him or it) and the various possibilities are reflected in modern English translations.

INTERPRETATION

Although it is alluded to in 2:4, the author of Colossians begins his response to the false teaching in earnest at 2:8. The response is in fact two-pronged, with christology being at the center of 2:8-15 and the specific practices of the opponents critiqued in 2:16-23. There is consensus among scholars that we may confidently draw information about the content of the false teaching from 2:16, 18, 20-23, but many have also argued that the language of the opponents also shapes 2:8-15. Among the key words of the opponents that have been postulated by scholars are "philosophy" (v. 8), "the elements of the universe" (v. 8), "fullness" (vv. 9-10), "rulers and powers" (vv. 10, 15), "circumcision" (vv. 11-13), "putting off the body of flesh" (v. 11), and "legal demands" (v. 14). But as the discussion of the meaning of the phrase "elements of the universe" (see the notes on 2:8) makes clear, it is often very difficult to be certain that the author is actually quoting the opponents in this section; other explanations of the terminology are possible. In interpreting Col 2:8-15 we are confronted by a problem that shapes interpretation of the whole letter: that of separating polemic against the opponents from the actual content of the false teaching. In conducting our analysis we should keep in mind that it is important to remain open to the discovery of perspectives that the author and opponents may have shared.

The problems of understanding the relationship between Col 2:8-15 and the false teaching are heightened by the uncertainty surrounding the identity of the false teachers and the actual shape of the false teaching. There is no consensus among scholars (see the Introduction, and the notes and interpretation on 2:16-23). The best explanation seems to be that Paul is responding to a "syncretistic" movement native to the Lycus Valley that combined Jewish elements with tendencies found in pagan religious groups. It is also possible that the author of Colossians is responding to widespread tendencies found among groups in the local environment and not to one specific group. Against an earlier tendency to view doctrines (especially christological doctrines) as being at the center of the controversy in Colossae, scholars are increasingly looking to ritual and social life to explain the conflict. Many now believe that ascetic practices and visionary experiences lie at the center of the author's objections, rather than a distinctive christology that sets the author apart from the opponents. Such conclusions have been inspired by a better understanding of the pluralistic environment of the Roman empire and a greater knowledge of social history (often informed by the social sciences). In general NT scholars have moved away from the tendency to see religious ideas as being the only aspect of religious life important enough to lead to debate in the church: early church life is now viewed as a rich composite of beliefs, rituals, ethics, and values.

There is no doubt that theological ideas concerning the identity of Christ are central to the response to the opponents offered in Col 2:8-15. However, this focus on christology forms part of the author's strategy to prevent deviance—especially deviant *praxis*—by reminding community members of what is central to their lives. When read in relation to 2:16-23 (see the notes and interpretation below) 2:8-15 reveals indications that the "Paul" of Colossians may well share much of the same understanding of Christ as the opponents (see, for example, the discussion of "putting off the body of flesh" in the notes on 2:11). On account of Christ, believers have put off their bodies of flesh (Col 2:11). They have triumphed with Christ over all the cosmic forces—rulers and powers (2:12-15). The true focus of believers' aspirations is the heavenly realm (Col 3:1-4). Both the stance adopted by the author of Colossians to critique the opponents (Col 2:8) and the ascetic measures propounded by the opponents (Col 2:16-23) indicate a profound commitment on the part of both parties to rejection of the present order (although it is lived out in different ways: see the notes on 2:16-23 and 3:18–4:1); both parties seek to live out an alternative mode of existence in relation to the dominant social order. Colossians 2:8-15 captures the attention of the audience with a "for or against Christ decision" and the stakes are clearly very high. Yet it is important to understand that this decision, which may at first glance appear to be mainly about holding the right doctrines concerning Christ, was probably part of a larger strategy to outlaw specific ritual and ascetic practices mentioned in 2:16-23 that were understood by the author as incompatible with life in Christ.

When we are seeking to understand the relationship between Col 2:8-15 and the conflict in the community there is wisdom in trying to discern the author's main arguments (moving away from too exclusive a focus on the identification of the opponents' slogans). At the outset the author seeks to convey the message that adoption of the false teaching means no longer living in Christ (2:6); it carries one back into the outside world. The false teaching is labeled variously as "philosophy," empty deceit, according to human tradition (cf. 2:22), according to the elements of the universe, and not according to Christ. In effect these categories work together as a broad generalization labeling the false teaching as evil—associated with an unbelieving world (despite the possibility that the adherents of the philosophy may themselves have insisted on the centrality of Christ to their experiences). The author expects that the recipients will want to choose Christ rather than the traditions of the world that they have previously rejected. Paul reminds them of the meaning of their baptism (the significance of which is probably under dispute). In 2:11 Paul reminds believers that they have already removed their bodies of flesh—their sinful natures associated with an unbelieving past—in the circumcision of Christ. The reference to "circumcision" may indicate circumcision was among the practices being recommended by the false teachers; these practices clearly included many Jewish elements (2:16-23). But it is also possible that other rites of initiation were under dispute, and indeed the second chapter of Colossians has often been investigated against the background of initiation into mystery rites in the ancient world (see Lohse 130).

An appeal to the experience of baptism in 2:11-13 serves the author well in the attempt to rebuke the repetitive rituals and practices of the opponents because it instills a sense of finality and completion among the recipients. The description of baptism in terms of burial and resurrection with Christ recalls how baptism in the early church could serve as a dramatic re-enactment of salvation attained through Christ's body—the place where the fullness of the deity has come to dwell (2:9; see also the notes and interpretation on 3:10-11). Perhaps through reference to a well-known hymn (see the notes on 2:13-15), believers are reminded that baptism marks the forgiveness of sins, the end of legal demands, the ultimate triumph over rulers and powers (2:13-15). In short, the importance of baptism for life in Christ is stated in Colossians in the strongest possible terms: baptism is essential to salvation. No further initiatory rites are required.

Both the importance of baptism for Colossians as a whole and its significance for the response to the false teaching in ch. 2 mean that baptism was at the heart of the conflict at Colossae. It may be that competing visions of baptism were under dispute. The opponents seem to have attached great significance to other rites (see the notes and interpretation on 2:16-23) and the relationship between these rites and baptism was probably central to the conflict. The focus on "circumcision" in 2:11-13 may mean that proponents of the false teaching were arguing that this Jewish initiatory rite should actually replace baptism as the means of entry into the group (cf. Galatians 2), or it is possible that the label "circumcision" was metaphorically applied to rites commemorating the "putting off of the body of flesh" by the opponents. In response the author applied the term "circumcision" to the rite of baptism, calling it "the circumcision of Christ" (2:11).

Early Christian literature reveals that baptism was a powerful but somewhat ambiguous ritual that was interpreted in various ways (see the notes and interpretation on 3:10-11). Social-scientific thought on ritual can help us understand how ritual can figure prominently in social conflict. Victor Turner's concept of *communitas* sheds light on the situation underlying Colossians:

> The bonds of communitas . . . are anti-structural in the sense that they are undifferentiated, egalitarian, direct, non-rational (though not irrational), I-Thou relationships. In the liminal phase of [African] Ndembu rites of passage, and in similar rites the world over, *communitas* is engendered in ritual humiliation, stripping of the signs and insignia of preliminal status, ritual leveling, and ordeals and tests of various kinds, intended to show "that man thou art dust!" In hierarchical social structures *communitas* is symbolically affirmed by periodic rituals . . . in which the lowly and the mighty reverse social roles. In such societies too . . . the religious ideology of the powerful idealizes humility, orders of religious specialists undertake ascetic lives, and *per contra,* cult groups among those of low status play with symbols of power and authority. (53)

Turner's thought points to what I believe is at the heart of the conflict at Colossae: the transition from anti-structured liminality back to social structure. (Turner adopted the concept of liminality from the famous study of Arnold Van Gennep, *Les Rites de Passage.* Liminality refers to an unstructured egalitarian condition on the peripheries or margins of everyday life—often a sacred condition.) What is at stake in Colossians is how one lives out this powerful experience in everyday life: How should the experience affect one's ethics in general and even one's attitude toward such basic facets of life as eating and sexuality? How should one rekindle the powerful experience that led to building an alternate community—in

Turner's language, the experience of *communitas?* The ascetic and ritual practices of opponents are visible signs of their identity, indicators of *communitas.* In Col 2:8-15 Paul argues that baptism alone is what transforms the individual, creating identity in Christ. Psalms and hymns celebrate that identity and teaching brings it to maturity (Col 3:16-17), but the new life shared by believers ultimately depends on baptism, when one becomes clothed with the new self (3:10). Social scientists have noted that ritual is fundamental to the process of creating the boundaries of the social group. It should come as no surprise, therefore, that despite indications of considerable convergence between the position of Paul in Colossians and the false teaching, the opponents are condemned as essentially belonging to another society. They subscribe to human tradition and belong to the evil world outside (2:8, 20-23).

Finally, the nature of the symbolism closely associated with the description of baptism in 2:8-15 should be noted. Once again Turner's analysis is helpful. In the notes on 2:8, 14, and 15, the relationship between religious imagery and the social condition of slaves is explained. What we find in these texts is the use of the experience of slavery to highlight the reversal of social standards that occurs when the bonds of *communitas* are formed. Freedom is attained in Christ and adherents to the false teaching risk returning to a state of subjugation: the philosophy will hold them captive (v. 8). It is those in the world outside (including the errorists) who are enslaved; for believers—those who accept Paul's gospel—the debtors' bonds have been canceled (v. 14). Particularly striking is the image of the rulers and powers—ultimately all that is against God in the universe—being displayed as captives of war (v. 15). To be on the side of Christ is to be on the side of triumph. One is no longer captive; public humiliation is over. Symbols of power and authority are used to reverse the experience of low status on the social plane. But does such a vision in the Colossian community lead to transformation of social structures? The presence of hierarchical household ethics in Col 3:18–4:1 has led to the opinion that there exists a certain incongruity between the symbols of empowerment in Colossians and the way of life prescribed for believers who were subordinate members of households (see, e.g., D'Angelo 320–23; on the relationship between symbolism that seeks to deny subjugated status and household ethics in Colossians see the notes and interpretation on 3:18–4:1).

FOR REFERENCE AND FURTHER STUDY

Arnold, Clinton E. *The Colossian Syncretism: The Interface between Christianity and Folk Belief at Colossae.* Tübingen: J.C.B. Mohr [Paul Siebeck], 1995.

Attridge, Harold A. "On Becoming an Angel: Rival Baptismal Theologies at Colossae," in Lukas Bormann, Kelly Del Tredici, and Angela Standhartinger, eds., *Religious Propaganda and Missionary Competition in the New Testament World: Essays Honoring Dieter Georgi*. Leiden: E. J. Brill, 1994, 481–98.

Blanchette, O. A. "Does the *Cheirographon* of Col 2:14 Represent Christ Himself?" *CBQ* 23 (1961) 306–12.

Feuillet, André. "Mort du Christ et Mort du chrétien d'après les épîtres pauliniennes," *RB* 66 (1959) 481–513.

Robinson, John A. T. *The Body*. Philadelphia: Westminster, 1952.

Schweizer, Eduard. "Slaves of the Elements and Worshipers of Angels: Gal 4:3, 9 and Col 2:8, 18, 20," *JBL* 107 (1988) 455–68.

Sumney, Jerry. "Those who 'Pass Judgement': The Identity of the Opponents in Colossians," *Biblica* 74 (1993) 366–88.

Turner, Victor. *Drama, Fields, and Metaphors: Symbolic Action in Human Society*. Ithaca, N.Y.: Cornell University Press, 1974.

8. Debate with the Opponents: Warnings against Ascetic Practices (2:16-23)

16. Let no one, therefore, pass judgment on you in matters of food and drink, or with respect to festivals, or new moons, or sabbaths. 17. These are a shadow of what is to come, but the reality is the body of Christ. 18. Do not let anyone cheat you of your prize, delighting in self-abasement and the worship of angels, entering into the things that he has seen, vainly puffed up by his fleshly mind, 19. and not holding on to the head from whom the whole body, supported and held together by its joints and sinews, grows with a growth that is from God. 20. If you died with Christ to the elements of the universe why do you submit to regulations as though you were living in the world, 21. "Do not hold, do not taste, do not touch"—22. referring to things that all perish with use; they accord with human injunctions and teachings? 23. These have indeed the reputation of wisdom in self-imposed worship and self-abasement and the severe treatment of the body. They are of no value against the indulgence of the flesh.

NOTES

16. *Let no one, therefore, pass judgment:* This phrase includes an imperative construction referring to an action that must always be avoided (see Harris 117–18; and see the similar construction in 2:8). The verb *krinetō* means to "pass unfavorable judgment upon" (BAGD 452). The term is very closely

related to the notion of being disqualified in v. 18. "Therefore" *(oun)* links this exhortation definitively to what comes before. On the basis of Christ's role as ruler of the cosmos (v. 15; cf. vv. 8-15) believers should not let the adherents to the Colossian "philosophy" pass judgment on them. (For other texts in the NT that warn against judging see Rom 14:3-13; Matt 7:1 *par.;* cf. Jas 4:11.)

on you in matters of food and drink: The Greek text refers more literally to eating and drinking, but it is clear that dietary prohibitions are involved. The text invites comparison to possible references to fasting in 2:18 and 2:23 (see the notes). This phrase is usually taken as evidence that the teaching of the opponents included Jewish elements (see also the notes on the next phrase). However, the extent to which the philosophy was actually Jewish remains a subject of debate. According to Lohse this "philosophy" made use of Jewish concepts that "had been transformed in the crucible of syncretism" (116). Wright, on the other hand, argues that in Colossians Paul's polemic is aimed at Judaism ([1986] 26–28). Dunn argues that "the first item of the particularities envisaged here points fairly firmly to an essentially Jewish faction who were deeply critical of Gentile Christian failure to observe Jewish food laws" (174).

or with respect to festivals, or new moons, or sabbaths: In Greek the references to festivals and new moons are in the singular and the phrase is sometimes literally translated as such (e.g., NAB: with regard to a festival or new moon or sabbath). But it is also possible that the nouns are generic singulars and therefore can be translated as they are here in the plural (cf. NRSV). The reference to "new moons" *(neomēnia;* translated either as "new moon" or first of the month) is probably to a festival celebrated by Jews and Gentiles (see also *Barn.* 2:5; 15:8; Jub. 6:34-38; Justin, *Dial. Trypho* 8.4; Num 28:9-15; Ezek 45:17). Sabbath appears here in the plural form *(ē sabbatōn),* but both in the singular and in the plural the term *sabbatōn* can refer either to the seventh day of the week in the Jewish calendar marked by special religious observances, or simply to a week (e.g., Luke 18:12; Mark 16:9; Matt 28:1). The former meaning is more likely in this case and is usually preferred by translators, but the latter cannot be ruled out completely (in which case the phrase would refer to weekly, monthly, and probably annual festivals [cf. Gal 4:10; see BAGD 739]). As is the case with the previous phrase, this expression is often taken as evidence that the Colossian philosophy included Jewish elements (see the notes above). It should be noted that together with the food taboos mentioned above, the ritual practices of the various festivals involve visible markers of identity. According to the author of Colossians, such visible markers of identity are rendered irrelevant through Christ (see the interpretation).

17. *These are a shadow of what is to come:* "These" most likely refers to all the categories mentioned in v. 16 (food, drink, and festivals) rather than simply to sabbaths. The term "shadow" might mean "shade," "shadow," or it might refer to a foreshadowing in contrast to reality (see BAGD 755). In order to highlight the notion of contrast some English translations refer to "only" a shadow (NRSV; NJB) or "no more than a shadow" (REB). The term appears only here in the Pauline epistles, but a similar usage occurs in Heb 8:5 and 10:1. More literally "what is to come" might be translated as "of the things coming" *(tōn*

mellontōn). Because the reality, Christ (to which the shadow corresponds), has already arrived, some versions translate the participle as "what was to come" (REB) or "what was coming" (NJB) or "the things that were to come" (NIV). In Colossians the greater emphasis on the past than on the future might suggest that the renderings offered by the REB and NJB are to be preferred. However, the future is not ruled out entirely in Colossians; a very similar conflation of the present and future occurs in 3:3-4 (cf. Rom 5:14). In Colossians the past, present, and future merge to a certain extent under the dominion of Christ. The more straightforward rendering offered here is therefore preferable (cf. NRSV; NAB). It is not clear whether the food regulations and festivals are understood as foreshadowing "what is to come" or whether these things are a shadow cast by future events (see Harris 119).

but the reality is the body of Christ: The Greek term *sōma* is usually translated as "body." Many modern versions translate it simply as reality (NIV; NAB; REB) or substance (NRSV: the substance belongs to Christ). In ancient literature *skia* (shadow) sometimes appears opposite to *sōma* in order to distinguish the shadow from the reality or substance (e.g., Philo, *Conf. Ling.* 190; on *skia* see BAGD 755). Note, however, that the more common means of distinguishing the true reality from the outer appearance, especially in Platonic philosophy, was to speak of the *skia* (shadow) and the *eikōn* (form, image, or achetype). No doubt the main intent in 2:17 is to set up a contrast with the food regulations and festival rites of the opponents that are being rendered insignificant. Nevertheless, the most common modern translations mask the fact that the same term here is used elsewhere in Colossians to refer to the body of Christ and to the church as the body of Christ. Christ's body and notions of the physical body figure prominently in the debate with the opponents in 2:8-23 (cf. 2:11, 19, 23). Colossians 2:17 may well be intended to introduce an idea that receives further elaboration in 2:19. In many respects the debate with the opponents is about rival understandings of the body (see the interpretation). Thus, in line with the NJB, the above translation is preferred. It should be noted that the genitive construction "of Christ" *(tou Christou)* might mean "belongs to Christ" (NRSV; REB; NAB), "is found in Christ" (NIV), or "is [the body of] Christ" (NJB and above).

18. *Do not let anyone cheat you of your prize:* Using slightly different language, this verse repeats the warnings against judgment in v. 16. The verb *katabrabeuō*, however, has a slightly different meaning. Frequently translated as "to disqualify" (e.g., NRSV; REB), it has also been rendered as "to condemn" (e.g., Lohse). In ancient literature it refers to being robbed of a prize one justly deserves (see Stauffer, *TDNT* 1:637–39). The simple verb *brabeuō* can have the straightforward meaning of awarding a prize in a contest (for a metaphorical use of this verb where wisdom is depicted as an umpire see LXX Wis 10:12). Here the prize under dispute is clearly salvation (cf. 2 Tim 4:7-8; 1 Cor 9:24; Phil 3:14). Rendering the verse as above (see also NJB) better captures the sense of competition that is integral to these verses.

delighting in self-abasement: It is possible that the participle *thelōn* (delighting or insisting on) should be taken with the previous phrase in an adverbial sense.

Thus it would read: "Do not let anyone *willfully* cheat you of your prize" (see BDF 148.2). However, because of the position of the participle and the content of the phrase most interpreters have taken it in a modal sense. The opponents are "insisting on" (cf. NRSV) or "delighting in" (cf. NIV; NAB) self-abasement and the worship of angels. Pokorný explains the rationale for this dominant interpretation as follows: "That the opponents wanted to rob the recipients of their prize is the opinion of the writer and not the opponents' intention, whose desire it was to help the recipients to attain what they considered to be the true prize" ([1991] 146). Many have sensed the influence of the Septuagint in this verse, where the verb *thelein* is used to translate the Hebrew (to find pleasure in; see Pokorný [1991] 146; cf. LXX 1 Sam 18:22; 2 Sam 15:26; 1 Kgs 10:9; Pss 111:1; 146:10; Schrenk, *TDNT* 3:45, n. 13). The notion of "delighting in" also captures the centrality of the ascetic practices to patterns of religiosity that are opposed by the author of Colossians (see the interpretation). The term *tapeinophrosynē*, rendered here as "self-abasement," can also be used in a positive way by the author of Colossians to refer to the virtue of humility (cf. Col 3:12). Here, however, it clearly refers to a type of self-denial the author judges negatively. Many commentators have understood *tapeinophrosynē* to be part of the vocabulary of the false teachers: a technical term referring to ascetic practices. In the early church the term could indeed be used to refer to fasting (e.g., *Herm. Vis.* 3.10.6; *Herm. Sim.* 5.3.7). The connection of "self-abasement" with visions and worship in the passage has led scholars to compare it to Jewish texts where fasting (or other rigors of devotion) is linked to visions (e.g., Dan 10:2-9). According to Lohse the focus on worship in this passage is so strong that he prefers the translation of *tapeinophrosynē* as "readiness to serve" by means of cultic conduct (see Lohse 118). Rowland has argued that it is possible on the basis of the Greek text that "self-abasement/humility" in the verse refers to the activity of the angels and not human practitioners, but this view has not been widely accepted (see Rowland 75; response to Rowland by Arnold [1995] 90).

and the worship of angels: The meaning of the phrase *thrēskeią tōn angelōn* has been the subject of considerable scholarly debate because of ambiguity introduced by the Greek text. Traditionally the expression has been taken to mean "worship directed at angels" (an objective genitive). However, especially influenced by the work of Fred O. Francis on literary evidence for angelic liturgies in Judaism (the QL, *Ascension of Isaiah, Testament of Job, Apocalypse of Abraham, 3 Enoch,* and the Arabic *Testament of Isaac*), many scholars have come to translate the phrase as "angelic worship," that is, participation in some type of angelic liturgies (a subjective genitive). It has been argued that practitioners of the supposed Colossian "heresy" may have sought to participate in, or behold, angelic liturgies in the heavenly realm (i.e., the angels themselves are not the object of veneration; instead, God is the unexpressed object; see *1 Enoch* 71:1-17; *2 Enoch* 22:4-7; *3 Enoch*). However, the recent work of Clinton Arnold (1995) may have caused the pendulum to swing once again in the direction of the more traditional interpretation. Arnold has noted that the actual textual support for translating the phrase as a subjective genitive (angelic worship) is rather weak. *Thrēskeia* typically occurs with a subjective genitive when people are doing the worshiping (i.e., the worship of the Jews, e.g., 4 Macc 5:7 and Josephus, *Ant.* 12.5.4), but a survey of ancient literature fails to turn up a single instance where *thrēskeia* is employed with a subjective genitive to refer to divine beings or typical objects of worship (see Arnold [1995] 91). Moreover, Arnold has paid particular attention to local religious traditions, examining closely the inscriptions and archeological evidence from Phrygia, Lydia, Caria, and Asia Minor. He concludes that the Colossian false teaching is best understood as a type of syncretism (a blending of a variety of Jewish and pagan religious traditions); it represents a combination of Phrygian folk belief, local folk Judaism, and Christianity. In the process he notes that the magical papyri (where angels known from Judaism figure prominently) and the angel inscriptions of Asia Minor are especially significant; he argues that Col 2:18 refers to the magical invocation of angels to provide protection from harm—especially the evil forces that threaten life in the here and now.

Since Judaism appears to be central to the Colossian "philosophy," and indeed to Arnold's (1995) own theories concerning the influence of syncretism in Colossae, he must contend with the scholarly debate concerning whether there was a strand of Judaism involved in worshiping angels. He argues that there is strong evidence to suggest that within Jewish circles where magic was practiced, angels were venerated. The discovery of amulets indicates that angels were invoked privately and such works as the *Testament of Solomon* and *Sepher Ha-Razim* suggest the possibility of group involvement. Arnold qualifies his assertion, however: "In spite of the fantastic concentration on angels in this material, one can still say that in most instances monotheism is retained. God has become more remote, but he is still supreme—above all angels. The angels are seen as more accessible and easily moved to action if one has sufficient knowledge, viz. their names and the appropriate rites and formulas" ([1995] 60). According to Arnold (1995) the evidence from Jewish inscriptions in Asia Minor confirms this type of angel veneration. The phrase "worship of angels" might be part of the vocabulary of the opponents or, as Arnold (1995) believes, a polemical condemnation of "magical" practices by the author of Colossians. (On the identity of the Colossian opponents see the Introduction and the interpretation below.)

entering into the things that he has seen: This is a literal rendering of a phrase whose meaning is by no means clear. The NRSV translates the phrase as "dwelling on visions," the REB refers to "access to some visionary world," and the NIV speaks of a person "who goes into great detail about what he has seen." In addition to meaning "to enter" or "to set foot upon," the verb *embateuō* can mean entering into a subject so as to investigate it closely (e.g., NIV). However, it is likely that something closer to the REB's translation is actually in view. In an important essay Martin Dibelius drew attention to the fact that *embateuō* could serve as a technical term in mystery religions and thus has often been viewed as a catchword of the Colossian opponents. It refers to the process whereby the candidate undergoes an initiation rite, enters a chamber, and receives an oracle. The inscriptions from the Apollo Temple at Claros are particularly significant. (For a summary of the evidence see Lohse 119–20.) It is likely that the expression in Col 2:18 refers to initiation rites during which the individual experienced ecstatic visionary experiences, perhaps including ascent into heaven. Lohse believes that the evidence of correlations between Col 2:18 and the inscriptions is so strong that he translates the expression as follows: "as he has had visions of them during the mystery rites."

A somewhat different interpretation of the expression has been proposed by Fred O. Francis. His interpretation is based on Jewish apocalyptic literature in which fasting prepares the seer for a visionary ascent into heaven and participation in angelic liturgies. Both explanations highlight the significance of ecstatic visionary experience. In setting aside the influence of mystery rites in favor of Jewish apocalyptic literature, however, Francis fails to account for the absence of the term *embateuō* as a technical term for heavenly ascent in the latter (but see 1 Enoch 14:9 where Enoch speaks of entering heaven). There are variations in the manuscript tradition for this verse. The reading that is given here is strongly supported by many early witnesses. The alternate reading includes a negative "not entering" *(ouk:* F G; *mē:* ℵ^c C D^c K P Ψ 614 it[g, 61, 86] vg syr[p,h] goth arm *al).* The reason for the alteration was probably that scribes did not understand the expression or sought to sharpen the attack against the opponents: they had not in fact seen authentic visions. The negative would be in keeping with the phrase that follows it immediately (see Metzger 623). It should also be noted that the difficulties raised by this Greek expression have on occasion led interpreters to posit conjectural emendations (see Bruce [1984] 120–21, n.130).

vainly puffed up by his fleshly mind: Here the author calls the proponents of the false teaching arrogant: inflated with their own importance (cf. 1 Cor 5:2; 8:1). The expression calls to mind Paul's language in Rom 7:8. *Nous* (mind, intellect, outlook) was an important concept in Gnostic systems where it could be associated with the divine principle and the journey of the soul to full understanding. Scholars who have understood the Colossian philosophy in terms of nascent Gnosticism have suggested that the term *nous* may be employed polemically against the false teachers (see the summary of Gnostic evidence in Pokorný [1991] 148). The expression "fleshly mind" refers to purely physical existence—existence that is dominated by the senses and is thus worldly. One of the main techniques used by the author to condemn the false teaching is to highlight endeavors that are designed to induce "other-worldly" experiences and confirm heavenly status, and label them definitively as "this-worldly" (cf. 2:8, 23; see the interpretation below).

19. *and not holding on to the head:* The verb here carries the strong meaning of "holding fast to someone or something" or "remaining closely united to it, him, or her" (cf. BAGD 448e). Thus those who have turned to a worldly existence (see the previous phrase) have severed a vital connection. The head *(kephalē)* here as in 1:18 is Christ: he is the head of his body, the church (cf. 1:24; 3:15; cf. Eph 4:1-16). The term "head" stresses Christ's authority: in 2:10 Christ is described as the head of every ruler and power.

from whom the whole body, supported and held together by its joints and sinews: The body is completely dependent upon its head. In keeping with stress on the whole, fullness, and Christ's rule filling all in Colossians, here we have the whole and complete body with no part excepted. It is implied that the body is the church (see the previous phrase). The use of the verb *epichorēgeō* (to support or to nourish) is interesting, given the household ethics of Col 3:18–4:1. It can often be used to refer to the support that a husband gives a wife (see the summary of evidence in Lohse 122, n. 62). In the early church writing called *1 Clement* the verb is employed to exhort the rich man to support the poor man (*1 Clem.* 38:2). We have here an image of the church as provider/patron of believers with Christ as the ultimate source of benevolence. The expression "joints and sinews" appears in ancient medical writings (see Lightfoot 196–98).

grows with a growth that is from God: The common interpretation takes the genitive here as a genitive of source (growth that is from God). Very closely related in meaning is the possible rendering of the verse as a subjective genitive: "growth given by God" (NJB). The REB, however, takes the expression to be a genitive of reference: "grows according to God's design" (see Harris 124). The ideas of dependence on Christ as head of the church and of God as the source of growth for the church are very closely related in this verse. The notion of growth is of central importance in Colossians (Col 1:6, 23; cf. Eph 1:23; 3:9-10; see the interpretation).

20. *If you died with Christ to the elements of the universe:* "Dying with Christ" is a reference to the experience of baptism, which is recalled throughout the epistle. It is sometimes described more fully as dying and rising with Christ (2:12-13; 3:1-4; cf. Rom 6:3, 5, 8). The elements of the universe *(stoicheia tou kosmou)* are elements or forces associated with the previous existence of believers. They may refer to the four elements of the universe (earth, water, air, and fire). It was believed in this period that the elements had lost their original harmony and were thereby threatening the universe with their upheaval. The reign of Christ frees believers from the effects of this strife, for the universe has been reconciled through him (Col 1:15-20). The meaning of the phrase *stoicheia tou kosmou* has, however, been extensively debated by scholars. Some have argued that they are spiritual forces associated with the "worship of angels" (2:18; on the meaning of this phrase see the notes on 2:8). It is evident that the author of Colossians expects that his audience will share the negative evaluation of life according to the elements of the universe.

why do you submit to regulations as though you were living in the world: The regulations are clearly those listed in v. 21. The acceptance of false teaching—portrayed here not as a potential threat but as a real and present danger—is depicted as a type of regression into the world. Such notions are found elsewhere in Pauline literature (e.g., Gal 4:3-11). Like Col 2:8, this verse presents hearers with a categorical "for or against" Christ option. The false teaching is associated with the world *(kosmos)* that was previously rejected (in Col 2:8, where it is labeled as "human tradition"). As part of the strategy to lead believers to reject past patterns of existence once and for all the author labels all that is outside of the church as evil. It is important to recognize the very real possibility, however, that the adherents to the "philosophy" may have insisted upon the centrality of Christ to their experience and may have seen the "regulations" as a means of living out the process of leaving the old world behind (see the interpretation).

21. *"Do not hold, do not taste, do not touch"*: The regulations mentioned in the previous verse are described here sarcastically in a series of "do nots." They may actually reflect the prohibitions of opponents, but they might be intended sarcastically, to categorize their rules as prohibiting *everything*. The first and last prohibitions are very closely related in meaning and both refer to a type of "touching," but the first probably refers to more substantial contact, often conveyed in modern translations as "holding" or "handling" *(haptō)*, as opposed to superficial "touching" *(thigganō*; see Harris 128–29). The first prohibition uses a derivative of the same Greek verb *(haptō)* as is found in the slogan of the ascetic Corinthians that Paul quotes at the beginning of 1 Cor 7:1: "It is well for a man not to touch *(haptesthai)* a woman." This may be an indication that sexual asceticism is involved in the Colossian false teaching (see the interpretation). The second prohibition adds support to the notion that the ascetic practices critiqued by the author of Colossians involve fasting and/or food and drink taboos (see the notes on 2:16 and 2:18).

22. *referring to things that all perish with use; they accord with human injunctions and teachings:* That none of these regulations is of any value whatsoever is emphasized by the term "all" *(panta)*: all the objects whose handling and tasting is forbidden are destined for destruction in any event: they perish with use. Since v. 22a appears to be parenthetical, acting as an incidental remark, v. 22b probably refers back to 2:21—to the regulations specifically cited that accord with human injunctions and teachings *(kata ta entalmata kai didaskalias tōn anthrōpōn)*. However, it is also possible to take v. 22b as loosely connected to the whole passage running from 2:20-22 (see REB: "That is to follow human rules and regulations"; see Harris 129–30). "Injunctions and teachings" are closely related in meaning and tied grammatically (they share a single preposition and article). The language here is very similar to that in LXX Isa 29:13, which is cited by Jesus in response to the ritual requirements of the tradition of the elders: "In vain do they worship me, teaching human precepts as doctrines" (NRSV Mark 7:7 *par.*; cf. Titus 1:14). The notion of perishable things calls to mind Jesus' strong statement concerning unclean foods: "Do you not see that whatever goes into a person from outside cannot defile, since it enters, not the heart but the stomach, and goes out into the sewer?" (NRSV Mark 7:18-19 *par.*; on what is perishable see also 1 Cor 6:13 and Acts 8:20). The fact that these injunctions and teachings are categorized as merely "human" (literally "of men") recalls the similar statement in Col 2:8 about "human tradition" (cf. 2:20).

23. *These have indeed the reputation of wisdom:* This verse is one of the most difficult to translate in the NT, with some commentators concluding that it cannot be translated satisfactorily. The ending is particularly perplexing (see the notes below). Many scholars have argued that the text must have been corrupted

very early in its manuscript tradition. There has been much conjecture concerning how certain additions might clear up the ambiguous sentence. Yet with very few exceptions the manuscript evidence has consistently preserved the obscure arrangement of words (for a full discussion of the problems of translation and relevant scholarly theories see Lohse 124–26). Moreover, theories concerning an early corruption of the text are difficult to support since one then must explain why textual oddities would be introduced by scribes. The problems of understanding the verse are compounded by the fact that it is likely that actual catchwords are cited together with satirical condemnations of the false teaching and it is by no means easy to distinguish between the two. Because v. 22a seems to be a parenthetical remark it is likely that "these" refers to the human injunctions and teachings and not directly to the things that perish with use. Wisdom *(sophia)* is a term that occurs frequently in Colossians and is deeply valued by the author (1:9, 28; 2:3; 3:16). But the wisdom claimed by the false teachers has the "reputation" or the "appearance" of wisdom (e.g., NIV; NRSV) only. The translation of the expression *logos* (literally "word," though it is a concept that can take on many different meanings; see BAGD 477) as "reputation" is closer to the value system of an ancient context. What is at stake is the public demonstration of wisdom and ultimately the honor of the community (see the interpretation).

in self-imposed worship and self-abasement and the severe treatment of the body: With the listing of these three concepts we have a strong indication of the close connection between asceticism and ritual. The term "in" *(en)* is probably locative, meaning "in the sphere of " or "in promoting" (NRSV), but the grammatical construction could also be a dative of instrument where *en* means "through" or "with" (NIV). *Ethelothrēskia* is a term that can be translated roughly to mean "self-imposed" or "self-chosen" worship or piety. It has often been taken to be a polemical attack on the false teaching: a sarcastic designation by the author in order to label the worship of the opponents purely human and worldly. However, because "self-abasement" and "severe treatment" have often been judged to come from the language of the opponents (although this is not beyond dispute; see below), it is also possible that *ethelothrēskia* was used by the group as a self-designation, expressing confidence in their achievements. In this case the term would mean "self-chosen" worship: the opponents had freely and proudly chosen to participate in these religious rites. The verse contains the second reference to "self-abasement" *(tapeinophrosynē)* in the epistle (cf. 2:18). The second "and" *(kai)* in the phrase is omitted from a substantial number of early manuscripts, and therefore it is inserted in brackets in UBS 4 and in some modern translations (e.g., NAB; see Metzger 624). If the alternate reading is preferred, then the phrase could read "self-abasement, that is, severe treatment of the body" (see Harris 33).

The concept of "severe treatment of the body" *(apheidia sōmatos)* is a general reference to austerity, and it leaves open the possibility of a variety of ascetic performances involving physical renunciation. These are understood by the author of Colossians as threatening to the life of the community. It is not entirely clear whether "severe treatment of the body" was used by practitioners of the false teaching to express confidence in their own pursuits or whether it is the author's own characterization of what they were doing. The expression invites comparison with Col 2:11, where believers are said to have put off the body of flesh in the circumcision of Christ (see the notes and interpretation on 2:11). This putting off the body of flesh figures in an argument designed to convince the Colossians to remain faithful to Christ and to reject the competing "philosophy." The use of similar terminology raises questions about points of contact between the author's attitude to renunciation and that of the opponents; it may be an indication that the false teaching and the way of life recommended by the author were not as disparate as they first appear (see the interpretation).

They are of no value against the indulgence of the flesh: This Greek phrase is highly ambiguous. In the margins of the NRSV one finds the alternate translation: "are of no value, serving only to indulge the flesh." In other words, what looks like rigorous piety in fact amounts to self-indulgence. N. T. Wright has summarized the problems with this alternate translation (arguing in favor of the one adopted here) in a clear and useful manner:

> [The alternate reading] involves reading most of the verse as a parenthesis: "which are (though possessing a reputation for wisdom with their self-imposed worship, abject grovellings and harsh physical discipline, all of no value) merely a way of gratifying the flesh." This may ease the grammatical problem in the first part of the verse, where the main verb "are" *(estin)* is followed almost at once by an accusative participle "having" *(echonta)*, but at the cost of straining the rest of the sentence unbearably. . . . It is safest overall to follow NIV (and RSV): they (i.e., these regulations) lack any value in restraining sensual indulgence. This takes the clause as a single whole, understanding *pros plēsmonēn tēs sarkos*, literally "towards the gratifying of the flesh," as modifying *timē*, value. ([1986] 127–28)

One of the major problems in interpreting this verse is that there is no Greek word in the verse for "restraining" (NIV) or "checking" (NRSV). The term *pros* can imply results (i.e., leading to indulgence of the flesh). But the term can also mean "in relation to" or "against" (or implicitly, checking or combating indulgence of the flesh). It is important to recall that the author of Colossians has already described baptism (spiritual circumcision) as leading to the removal of the body of flesh (2:11). It is probable that both the author of Colossians and those who accept the false teaching strive to contain the indulgence of the flesh. Yet the Paul of Colossians disagrees with the methods of containment recommended by the opponents. Acceptance of the gospel and baptism are the basis of a life that holds the dangers of the flesh at bay. The measures prescribed by the false teachers are not only superfluous; they are also completely useless in checking the indulgence of the flesh. The Greek term for "value" *(timē)* might be translated literally (but very awkwardly in English) as "honor." The term suggests that public appraisal and concern for reputation are central in evaluating the ascetic measures recommended by proponents of the Colossian "philosophy" (see the interpretation).

INTERPRETATION

Colossians 2:16-23 is closely related to Col 2:8-15. These two passages contain the heart of the response to the false teaching. Although some have detected evidence of the language and/or slogans of the opponents in Col 2:8-15 (see the notes and interpretation on that section), there exists scholarly consensus that we may draw information about the content of the false teaching from 2:16, 18, 20-23. It is virtually beyond dispute that in this section the author of Colossians is citing some of the phrases and catchwords of the false teaching. For example, 2:18 has often been understood as citing these terms extensively: "self-abasement," "the worship of angels," "entering the things that he has seen." But it is important to recognize that the extent to which the author of Colossians is quoting from false teaching remains a subject of debate even with respect to this particular verse (see the notes on 2:18; see also the notes on 2:21 and 2:23). It is especially difficult to be certain whether the Paul of Colossians is quoting the opponents directly or engaging in polemical attack against the "philosophy." For example, while it seems more likely that we should understand the reference to "self-imposed worship" in 2:23 as the author's sarcastic designation of the rituals of the opponents, it is also possible that the Greek term means "self-chosen worship" and could, therefore, be part of the vocabulary of the opponents (see the notes on 2:23). We must even be open to the possibility of points of contact between the position of the author of Colossians and that of the opponents that may be somewhat masked by the polemic. For example, it is likely that both the Paul of Colossians and the opponents strive to contain the indulgence of the flesh (2:23) by putting off the body of flesh (cf. 2:11). According to the author of Colossians this putting off the body has been accomplished once and for all through baptism: in baptism, believers died with Christ (Col 2:20). In contrast, the proponents of the false teaching continue to engage in "severe treatment of the body." The various measures they adopt are said to be "of no value against the indulgence of the flesh" (Col 2:23).

There has been a good deal of scholarly discussion concerning the identity of the Colossian errorists, which has resulted in a vast array of theories (see the Introduction). The position taken in this commentary is that two scenarios are most likely. The recent work of Clinton Arnold (1995) on the local evidence, including archeological evidence and inscriptions, has strengthened the case for syncretism (this should not be understood as a corruption of "pure" religious traditions but as a combining of religious traditions). Although scholarly reconstructions have sometimes concentrated only on one side of the equation, many have understood the false teaching to be a blending of a variety of Jewish (e.g., the reference to food taboos and to the cultic calendar [2:16]), and pagan religious traditions (e.g., the use of terminology associated with mystery rites such as *embatuein* in 2:18). The problem is that until recently theories concerning syncretism have remained somewhat vague. Arnold's (1995) work on the local evidence has led him to conclude that the Colossian philosophy represents a combination of Phrygian folk belief, local folk Judaism, and Christianity (see the notes on 2:18). Probably Arnold's (1995) most important contribution has been to place the phrase "the worship of angels" within its social context and to settle the exegetical debate concerning the meaning of the phrase quite conclusively in favor of "worship directed at angels" rather than "angelic liturgy" (see the notes on 2:18). According to Arnold (1995), the local inscriptional evidence demonstrates that "angel" was an important term in the religious life of the people in Asia Minor:

> Our texts point to a specific kind of angel veneration, viz. calling on angels, invoking them, praying to them. The purpose of these invocations was largely apotropaic: people called on angels as divine mediators to protect them or their properties from various forms of evil, including evil angels who could bring them harm, grave robbers, etc. They also may have called upon angels to help them with the affairs of daily life (success in business, healing, bringing vengeance on enemies, etc.). While much of the evidence we have examined would have been used privately, some may have been used in a corporate context. (89)

Increasingly NT scholars conduct their scholarship with an appreciation of the Greco-Roman context in which Christianity was born. There is a growing awareness that early Christian groups articulated their identity while being both influenced by and in competition with other religious groups. Such awareness is especially vital to the task of explaining the conflict at Colossae.

The second most likely explanation for the identity of the false teachers threatening the Colossian community arises from the difficulty of making the philosophy "fit" the known religious groups in antiquity. It has been argued that the false teaching might not have been the position of one party, but rather "a set of traditions widely affirmed and practiced" (D'Angelo 319). This theory would not in fact be negated by the evidence uncovered by Arnold (1995), but would lean in the direction of a variety of groups threatening the community rather than one specific syncretistic movement. If, indeed, Colossians is pseudonymous, it might have suited the author to respond broadly to all the religious currents in the surrounding environment that seemed dangerous. The similarity between Colossians and Galatians (where the problem is a return to Jewish practices; see, for example, Gal 4:3-11 where "elements of the universe" are also in view) might even be a deliberate means of assuring the authenticity of the message in a new context.

There is in fact a unifying element among the otherwise quite diverse practices and traditions that are repudiated in Col 2:16-23. Our textual study has revealed a sustained interest in discouraging ascetic practices. Colossians 2:16 and 2:23 refer to dietary regulations and/or fasting. The references to self-abasement in 2:18 and 2:23 clearly allude to some type of ascetic practices and might refer specifically to fasting (see the notes on 2:18). The reference to severe treatment of the body calls to mind a variety of forms of physical renunciation. These verses might also contain evidence of sexual asceticism. The command not to hold in 2:21 employs the same Greek terminology as the Corinthian ascetics whom Paul quotes at the beginning of 1 Cor 7:1: "It is well not to touch a woman" (NRSV; see the notes on 2:21). There is no explicit and indisputable evidence in Colossians that the avoidance of sex was part of the false teaching, and therefore the idea has not won wide support among scholars. However, it is important to note that in early church literature and in the ancient world generally fasting and sexual asceticism often went together (cf. 1 Tim 4:3; see Philo of Alexandria's description of the Therapeutae, a Jewish monastic community, in *Vita Cont.* 34–35). Moreover, the terminology found in this section, especially the reference to severe treatment of the body in 2:23, is broad enough to allow for sexual asceticism. In our analysis of Col 3:18–4:1 we will discuss how the household code, with its unmistakable legitimation of Christian marriage, functions in relation to the ascetic currents in Colossae. Finally, in seeking to understand the centrality of asceticism in Col 2:16-23 it is important to note that reference to the "angelic" is a means of conceptualizing ascetical life in early Christianity (see Attridge 489–90).

Many modes of existence in the ancient world have been called ascetic, and asceticism has been described as the property of a variety of religious groups (Jewish, Christian, and pagan). The terminology derives from the Greek term *askēsis*, which means self-discipline. In popular discourse it has come to mean austerity, physical renunciation, and abstinence from physical pleasure—an attitude to the physical body that seems to be at the heart of the Colossian false teaching. But to gain a better understanding of the conflict at Colossae it is valuable to consider some recent scholarly theories of asceticism. Defining asceticism as a multi-faceted phenomenon, Vincent Wimbush asserts that "ascetic behavior represents a range of responses to social, political, and physical worlds often perceived as oppressive or unfriendly, or as stumbling blocks to the pursuit of heroic personal goals, life styles or commitments" (20). A second useful definition of asceticism by Richard Valantasis calls for a broad application of the concept: "Asceticism may be defined as performances within a dominant social environment intended to inaugurate a new subjectivity, different social relations, and an alternative symbolic universe" (797). When asceticism is defined in this way it becomes clear that the concept can shed light not only upon the activities of the false teachers but also on the perspective of the author.

With respect to the dominant social environment the author of Colossians is clearly calling for the acceptance of an alternate symbolic universe. (On the notion of a symbolic universe see the notes and interpretation on 1:3-8.) Colossians makes extensive use of "language of separation" that functions in the process of self-definition. The conversion of members is recalled: their transference from the evil world outside into the "body" where salvation is to be found (e.g., Col 1:13-14, 21-23; cf. Eph 4:17-24). But there is a mode of world-rejection that is condemned by the author of Colossians, one that involves physical indicators and visible signs of identity. In 2:16-23 physical markers of identity, including fasting and other ascetic practices, as well as various religious observances are depicted as futile and worldly. They have been rendered irrelevant through Christ. Yet the author also believes that the world must be rejected in a profound sense. In order to have a fuller understanding of the author's response it will be important for us to consider below the implications of believers adopting a way of life that involves such practices. Here a social-scientific perspective can further our understanding of what is at stake.

To understand the author of Colossians as waging a battle on two fronts—against the dominant social environment and the particular ascetic performances of the false teachers—can alert us to the irony inherent in the response given in Col 2:16-23. The main strategy adopted by the author in this section is to single out practices that are designed to induce "other-worldly" experiences, to confirm their heavenly status and to label them as "this-worldly." From Col 2:18 it is impossible to figure out precisely what the proponents of the false teaching were recommending, but their practices included some types of self-abasement (probably fasting), an initiation rite whereby the candidate experienced visions (implied by the phrase "entering the things that he has seen"), and "the worship of angels" as a means of warding off the evil forces that threaten daily life. While the precise shape of and relationship between these elements of the teaching is impossible to determine with certainty, studies of this verse against the Jewish and pagan background of the ancient Mediterranean world suggest that we can be confident in seeing a connection between ritual, visionary experience, and ascetic practices in the Colossian false teaching. The false teachers recommend measures designed to induce intense religious experiences and participation in the spiritual realm such as one finds in the mystery religions of the ancient world, but instead such a teacher is called "vainly puffed up by his fleshly mind." Their arrogance is described as groundless as it is based on an existence dominated by the senses and is purely worldly. In Col 2:20 the irony of the attraction to the false teaching by some members of the community is emphasized further by the notion of regression back into the world. The requirements of the false teaching are associated with the world that was previously rejected (cf. Col 2:8) by means of a sharp question: "Why do you submit to regulations as though you were living in the world?" The references to "perishable things" and "human injunctions and teaching" that have only "the reputation of wisdom" (vv. 21-23) serve to reinforce the point. But the ultimate irony is expressed at the end of v. 23. The Colossians seek access to the spiritual realm, not the earthly realm. Their old fleshly selves have been transformed into new selves (cf. Col 3:1-11). Through baptism they have died with Christ (2:20) and removed the body of flesh (Col 2:11). Yet they now accept practices that "are of no value against the indulgence of the flesh!"

It is valuable to approach Paul's response to the false teaching in Col 2:16-23 with an awareness of the values of ancient Mediterranean society. Such awareness is especially useful in allowing us to see that the response to the false teaching is not only about silencing errorists, but also about drawing the boundary between those who have been raised with Christ and nonbelievers. First, it is interesting to note that the term translated here as "value" in Col 2:23 *(timē)* might be rendered more literally as "honor." Because of the significant research of scholars on the value of honor in the biblical world (see the notes and interpretation on 1:3-8), it is important to consider how the concept of honor might shed light upon the text. To a greater extent than in modern Western society the personal identity of ancient Mediterranean people was bound up with social identity. A high value was placed upon public appraisal and concern for reputation (consider, for example, how the author of Colossians labels the false teaching as having "the reputation of wisdom" in v. 23). In studying Pauline literature it is important to remember that even the process of separating oneself from the dominant social environment might be validated by the judgment of outside observers. In 1 Corinthians Paul demonstrates a particularly acute concern for reputation with respect to the ritual setting of the community. Witnesses to early church meetings could condemn or glorify (1 Cor 14:23-25; cf. 1 Cor 11:2-16). The cyclical rites that formed part of the Colossian false teaching were visible indicators of identity, and therefore may have been treated as strong indicators to the outside world of the honor of the community.

Similarly, the ascetic measures that formed part of the teaching should be understood in light of this communal identity and concern for reputation. It is interesting to compare the reaction to asceticism in Colossians with Paul's reaction to asceticism in 1 Corinthians 7. Paul approves of celibacy for those who have this special gift. Celibacy is linked with freedom from the things of this world and with the transformation of the old order. However, marriage is what is recommended as the means of containing the immorality that threatens the community. Passion can corrupt the purity of the church (1 Cor 7:2-9, 36-38). Marriage keeps the boundary strong between what is inside the group and what should be kept out. A comparison of Col 2:16-23 with 1 Corinthians 7 raises the possibility that acceptance of the traditional arrangements of the household (Col 3:18–4:1) should be considered as part of the author of Colossians' solution to the problem of containing the indulgence of the flesh (Col 2:23). What the comparison definitely reveals, however, is the strong stance of the author of Colossians against ascetic practices involving physical and visible signs of world-rejection. This type of asceticism is rejected categorically by the author of Colossians; there is no room for the qualified approval one finds in 1 Corinthians 7. In recalling the broad definitions of asceticism listed above it is important to note that the author of Colossians approves of a type of ascetic response to the world in which believers participate in an alternate symbolic universe, but also one that insists that believers maintain a high degree of *physical* integration within the dominant social order.

The conflict between the Paul of Colossians and his opponents has to do with rival understandings of the physical body. For Paul the body is no longer an obstacle to be overcome; it has been transformed to such an extent that believers have already been exalted (Col 2:12-13; 3:1-4). With their new bodies they participate in a new cosmic harmony—one free from the upheaval caused by the elements of the universe (2:20). On the social plane this integrative view works in conjunction with traditional ethics to provide patterns of life that allow for the continuation of many aspects of conventional existence (see the notes and interpretation on 3:18–4:1), while at the same time reinforcing convictions about ultimately belonging to another world. The dominant social environment is rejected in a profound sense even though visible signs of departure from the world in the form of rituals and ascetic practices of various kinds are denounced. The notion of the body of Christ is central to this vision of Christian existence (see the notes and interpretation on 1:15-20). Explicitly equated with the church (Col 1:18-24), the "body" in Colossians is ruled by its head, Christ (Col 1:18, 2:10, 19). Christ is the head of the church, but also of every ruler and power (2:10). The error of the false teachers is that they have lost sight of the authority of Christ's headship (Col 2:19). Christ holds all things together and restores cosmic harmony (Col 1:15-20). The body of Christ symbolism in Colossians clearly articulates a vision of the church as a spiritual and cosmic assembly. The visible and physical ascetic rites of the false teachers are a "shadow"; the ultimate "reality is the body of Christ" (2:17). In 2:19 this spiritual and cosmic entity is depicted as growing by means of divine intervention. It is a growing and thriving body that is filling the world (cf. Col 1:18-20; 2:9; 3:15).

It is highly likely that the rival understandings of the physical body are rooted in differing interpretations of the experience of baptism. Baptism is discussed extensively in Colossians and figures prominently in ch. 2, especially in 2:11-13 (cf. 2:20). The focus on circumcision as a means of describing baptism in this text may suggest that the proponents of the false teaching argued that this Jewish initiatory rite should replace or augment baptism as the rite of entry into the group (cf. Galatians 2). It is also possible, however, that the term was applied metaphorically to various rites that symbolized the removal of the body of flesh (see the interpretation on 2:8-15). Here it is important to note that Col 2:18 draws upon terminology that was employed to describe initiation into the mystery rites in the ancient world (see the notes). The author stresses the definitive transformation that occurs in baptism (Col 2:20), but the proponents of the false teaching seem to have attached equal or greater significance to other rites and practices. By drawing upon insights from the social sciences we are in a better position to understand what is at stake in the rejection or acceptance of the ascetic practices and rites that are under dispute in Col 2:16-23. In particular it is interesting to consider social-scientific theory concerning initiation rites.

The classic work on initiation rites by Arnold Van Gennep, *Les Rites de Passage,* has influenced many subsequent anthropological studies. Van Gennep identified three stages of the rites of passage that function in group and societal attempts to deal with social change: separation, transition, and incorporation. In the transitional or liminal phase the individual is set apart from the conventional structures of society, often having powerful experiences such as visions (Col 2:18). It has been noted that initiation rites frequently use symbols of death and rebirth to express transformation (see 2:20; see also Eliade). Recent anthropological studies have stressed the social function of rites of passage, their importance for establishing identity and drawing boundaries between insiders and outsiders: "ritual, by regulating the relation of individual events to these basic divisions, maintains social order, locating individuals in relation to positions within it. It is a short step from recognizing this to perceiving that the effect of ritual is to maintain boundaries. The ritual transfer of individuals across boundaries is the means by which these boundaries are made manifest and reaffirmed as significant" (Lafontaine 27).

It is important to recognize that the rejection of initiatory rites, rituals, and related ascetic practices that is recommended in Col 2:16-23 might cause significant problems for the preservation of communal identity. The main theological argument in ch. 2 is that Christ's reign over the universe renders such practices meaningless. But to abolish regulations concerning food and drink or to cancel festivals, new moons, and sabbaths (Col 2:16), for example, would not be easy and critics might well look at the rich variety of practices in the religions of antiquity and wonder if the loss was indeed worth it. The proponents of the false teaching made use of Jewish practices that had a long history of contributing to the survival of a distinct group. The vision of the church that is propounded in Colossians is a spiritual-cosmic identity that largely eschews the physical markers of identity. The great advantage of such a vision, however, is that it raises the possibility of the church penetrating cities and households without arousing suspicion. The advantages of invisibility must have been increasingly cherished by a group that was not only growing, but also growing more suspect every day (see the notes on 4:2-6 and 3:18–4:1).

FOR REFERENCE AND FURTHER STUDY

Arnold, Clinton E. *The Colossian Syncretism: The Interface between Christianity and Folk Belief at Colossae.* Tübingen: J. C. B. Mohr [Paul Siebeck], 1995.
Attridge, Harold A. "On Becoming an Angel: Rival Baptismal Theologies at Colossae," in Lukas Bormann, Kelly Del Tredici, and Angela Standhartinger, eds., *Religious Propaganda and Missionary Competition in the New Testament World: Essays Honoring Dieter Georgi.* Leiden: E. J. Brill, 1994, 481–98.
Dibelius, Martin. "The Isis Initiation in Apuleius and Related Initiatory Rites," in Fred O. Francis and Wayne A. Meeks, eds., *Conflict at Colossae.* Missoula: Scholars, 1975, 61–121.
Evans, Craig. "The Colossian Mystics," *Biblica* 63 (1982) 188–205.
Francis, Fred O. "Humility and Angelic Worship in Col 2:18," in Francis and Meeks, eds., *Conflict at Colossae,* 163–95.
Fridrichsen, Anton. "*Thelōn* Col 2:18," *ZNW* 21 (1922) 135–37.
Leaney, Robert. "Colossians II. 21-23 (the use of *pros*)," *ExpT* 64 (1952–53) 92.
Muir, Steven C. *Healing and Initiation in Luke-Acts.* Doctoral Dissertation, University of Ottawa, 1998.
Rowland, Christopher. "Apocalyptic Visions and the Exaltations of Christ in the Letter to the Colossians," *JSNT* 19 (1983) 73–83.
Schweizer, Eduard. "Slaves of the Elements and Worshippers of Angels: Gal 4:3, 9 and Col 2:8, 18, 20," *JBL* 107 (1988) 455–68.
Sumney, Jerry. "Those who 'Pass Judgement': The Identity of the Opponents in Colossians," *Biblica* 74 (1993) 366–88.

9. *New Life in Light of the Resurrection* (3:1-4)

1. If then you were raised with Christ, seek the things that are above, where Christ is, sitting at the right hand of God. 2. Set your thoughts on the things that are above, not on the things that are on the earth. 3. For

you have died, and your life is hidden with Christ in God. 4. When Christ your life is revealed, then you too will be revealed with him in glory.

NOTES

1. *If then you were raised with Christ:* There is a parallel here with 2:20, where the consequences of dying with Christ are in view. Although the two concepts are clearly inseparable, the more immediate focus here is on the consequences of the resurrection. In both cases "if" *(ei)* does not convey uncertainty, but rather an assumed fact (BAGD 219). Here "if" is used in conjunction with "then" *(oun)* in order to advance the logic of the argument, recalling something that came before while at the same time marking the beginning of a new section. (Some translate the whole expression as "since" [NJB] or "since then" [NIV].) Having died with Christ (in baptism) implies resurrection with Christ (2:20; cf. 2:12-13). The aorist passive indicative compound verb "you were raised with" *(synēgerthēte)* indicates something that has already occurred (cf. Rom 6:4). Believers have already been raised. The term "with" *(syn)* here appears as a prefix to the verb (cf. 2:12-13). The word also appears in 3:3, 4. In all instances "with Christ" reinforces the notion of identification with Christ that is central in these verses. The Greek text actually refers to "the Christ" here, but the use of the article is not usually seen as significant (see Grundmann, *TDNT* 9:540–41).

seek the things that are above: The Greek expression is rendered here literally as "the things that are above." It has often been taken to refer to a heavenly realm (e.g., the REB has "realm above"). The expression is used as a means of referring to heaven in John 8:23 (cf. Gal 4:26; Phil 3:14). Verses 1-4 contain many spatial images that depict salvation as something that can be sought out and located in a particular place. The Colossians were encouraged to understand themselves as living in a new realm (see the interpretation below).

where Christ is, sitting at the right hand of God: The comma in the English translation, separating the phrase "where Christ is" from the participle "sitting," is meant to suggest the presence of two related but nevertheless distinct assertions: (1) Christ is to be found above; (2) He sits at God's right hand. The comma is absent from the NAB and the NIV. These versions have taken "is" to be connected to "sitting." However, the word order makes the rendering adopted here more likely (see Harris 137). Christ is depicted as exalted and enthroned at God's right hand, recalling Ps 110:1 (cf. Eph 1:20; 2:6). The verse may also presuppose the ascension of Christ (see Acts 1:9-11; 2:34-35).

2. *Set your thoughts on the things that are above:* In many respects v. 2 repeats the ideas of the previous verse, but there may be some differences in nuance. The reference to "seeking" places the emphasis on the goal, while the use of the verb *phoneō* (to think or to be intent on) refers to sustained devotion and general attitude. In ancient literature the verb could frequently be used to make reference to taking someone's side or espousing someone's cause (for the NT

usage in this sense see Mark 8:33; Matt 16:23; Rom 8:5; 14:6; see BAGD 866). One must strive and commit with one's whole being.

not on the things that are on the earth: There is clearly an antithesis being set up that resembles Paul's contrast between things of the spirit and things of the flesh in Rom 8:5. Similarly in Phil 3:19 Paul describes the enemies of Christ as those whose minds "are set on earthly things" (NRSV). Physical existence is not being attacked per se (cf. Col 1:16). Rather, the main point is that Christian existence is not limited by physical existence but has been fundamentally transformed by Christ. Believers share a heavenly spirituality. The antithesis takes up the ideas in 2:20-23 where physical measures that are apparently designed to grant people special access to the heavenly realm are condemned as worldly and fleeting (see the notes and interpretation on 2:20-23). The earthly is associated with a way of life that must be rejected (cf. 2:5).

3. *For you have died:* The verb here is identical to that found in 2:20 and serves as a natural corollary to "you were raised" in 3:1. The reference to dying and rising with Christ recalls the experience of baptism for believers (cf. Rom 6:2-8). To state that believers have died is to use strong metaphorical language to convey a radical change of identity. The term *gar* ("for" or "because") introduces the reason why believers are called to turn themselves toward the heavenly realm in 3:2.

and your life is hidden with Christ in God: The verb "to hide" *(kryptō)* here refers to hiding or concealing in a safe place (BAGD 454). Cognates of the term appear in both 1:26 *(apokryptō)* to refer to "the mystery that has been hidden throughout the ages and from generations" and in 2:2-3 *(apokryphos)* to refer to "the knowledge of the mystery of God, that is Christ himself, in whom are hidden all the treasures of wisdom and knowledge." Acceptance of Christ offers access to mysteries that otherwise remain hidden. The reference to what is hidden may reflect apocalyptic notions (see the notes on 3:4). No doubt believers who "died" gave up much physical security and found solace in a new life hidden with Christ. Given the discourse against the false teachers who stress ritual and physical indicators of religious identity in Col 2:8-23, it is interesting to compare 3:3 to Rom 2:29 where the cognate adjective *kryptos* (hidden, in secret) occurs: "For a person is not a Jew who is one outwardly, nor is true circumcision something external and physical. Rather, a person is a Jew who is one inwardly *[en tō kryptō]*, and real circumcision is a matter of the heart: it is spiritual and not literal" (Rom 2:28-29). In Pauline Christianity the marks of true identity could be understood as being invisible and ultimate reality viewed as hidden in the heavenly realm.

Identification with Christ is stated in the strongest possible terms. There is no question that believers are to share in the fruits of the resurrection. The use of spatial images and terminology continues with the use of the locative *(en):* in (the sphere) of God. "In God" is found only rarely in Pauline letters (1 Thess 1:1 and 2 Thess 1:1; cf. Eph 3:9), but the main point here, consistent with 1:15-20, is clearly that identification with Christ means that one is caught up with the divine power that shapes the universe (see Dunn 207). Beginning at 3b there is a clear example of chiasmus (the A-B-B-A pattern found frequently in the NT): "life . . . Christ . . . Christ . . . life."

4. *When Christ your life is revealed:* Some manuscripts have "our" life, which is preferred by some translators (e.g., NEB; RSV). It would seem to make more sense that "our" would be changed to "your" by copyists to harmonize with the rest of the verse, rather than the reverse. However, the manuscript evidence for "your" is stronger among both Alexandrian and Western witnesses and is probably to be preferred (see Metzger 624). This verse draws upon traditional apocalyptic notions of hiddenness and manifestation to refer to Christ's second coming (cf. 1 Cor 15:22; 2 Cor 5:10; 1 Thess 4:15-17). Paul usually uses the synonym *apokalyptō* to refer to the revelation at the end of time (e.g., Rom 8:18; 1 Cor 3:13), but the attempt to draw a contrast with what is hidden probably leads to the choice of *phaneroō*—a more natural choice to create the antithesis of hiddenness and revelation (cf. Rom 2:28-29; 1 Cor 14:25; see Dunn 208). The term does appear elsewhere in the NT to refer to Christ's appearance (cf. 1 John 2:28; 3:2; see also the notes on 1:26).

then you too will be revealed with him in glory: This phrase contains the third reference to being "with Christ" in this section, reinforcing the notion of identification with Christ. An explicit reference to the parousia is found only here in Colossians. In 1:26 (where the same verb *phaneroō* occurs) the revelation refers to the appearance of Christ that has already taken place. The presence of this reference is highly significant, for its absence could suggest a mentality of "realized eschatology"—believers not only fully participate in Christ's glory now, but there is no future consummation. Yet the verse prevents this conclusion. The tenses of the verbs move from the past (you were raised with Christ), to the present (you are hidden with Christ), to the future (you too will be revealed). Although believers do share in Christ's enthronement now, their glorification is clearly not yet completed. The promise of future fulfillment is the justification provided for an ethical life (3:5-17).

INTERPRETATION

This section acts as both a summary of 2:8-23 and a bridge into the ethical exhortations that follow (see Wolter 164–65). The author of Colossians is deeply concerned with the way of life of believers, their homes, their rituals, the nature of their meetings, and their ethical deportment generally. Having responded to the errors of the false teaching, the author sets out to give a theological summary of the essence of salvation before spelling out its implications. The author chooses language that will speak powerfully to the audience, for it draws upon traditional themes and resonates with the experience of baptism.

Colossians 3:1 alludes to Ps 110:1, a frequently cited text in the NT (cf. Mark 12:36 *parr.;* Acts 2:34-35; Heb 1:13): "The Lord says to my lord, 'Sit at my right hand until I make your enemies your footstool'" (NRSV). The implication of 3:1-2 is that God is on his throne in heaven and Jesus sits on a throne beside him (cf. Dan 7:9-14; see Dunn 203–204). What has fascinated interpreters most about this image of heavenly enthronement is the way it includes the present situation of believers. Emphasis on the present heavenly enthronement of believers in Colossians and Ephesians (cf. Eph 1:3; 2:6-7) sets these documents apart from the undisputed letters. There is clearly a relationship between such ideas and the proclamation of Christ's rule over the universe in Phil 2:6-11 or the description of baptism as being buried with Christ in Rom 6:3-11. But the symbolism in Colossians and Ephesians associated with present salvation is less restrained. Paul, for example, in Rom 6:3-11 does not explicitly state that believers have been raised with Christ, and 1 Corinthians seems intent on discouraging attitudes born of the notion that Christians have already been raised (e.g., 1 Cor 4:8). The notion of the future appearance of Christ is clearly present in 3:4 (cf. 3:6), but in general the perspective of Colossians has been judged to have more of a spatial orientation (above-below) than a temporal-eschatological one.

In Paul's letters hope is usually envisioned as anticipation of future consummation by means of the coming of Christ. A certain tension exists between "already" and "not yet." But in Colossians, the "not yet" fades from view. Hope is a message that believers have already received and that is prepared already in heaven: "the hope that is stored up for you in heaven and of which you have previously heard in the word of truth of the gospel" (1:5; cf. 1:23). There is a strong connection between this text and Col 3:1-4. The hope of the community is quite literally the heavenly enthroned Christ. In 1:27 Christ (or the presence of Christ in the believer) is described as the "hope of glory." Glory is also central in the verses presently under discussion. When Christ appears the Colossians will appear with him in glory (i.e., salvific events include a future dimension). Nevertheless, in Colossians this future revelation is depicted as the manifestation of a heavenly union that already exists in the present.

There has been a good deal of speculation concerning the origins of the difference between the theology of the undisputed letters of Paul and that of Colossians and Ephesians. Scholars have debated whether these documents reflect an awareness of the delayed parousia or a belief system in which the parousia is no longer given the same weight. The focus on the present access to the heavenly realm has led some to seek parallels between ideas found in Colossians and Ephesians and those of later Gnostic systems. It has been argued, for example, that contact with Gnostic (or proto-Gnostic) opponents led the author to absorb Gnostic ideas and/or take them up in order to refute them (see the Introduction). With respect to this section (and v. 2 in particular with its call for setting one's thoughts on the things that are above), Erich Grässer has argued in favor of a Gnostic influence. However, in comparing the text to *2 Apoc. Bar.* 48:42–52:7 J. R. Levison has argued that Col 3:1-4 reflects an apocalyptic perspective (see also the discussion in Dunn 202). The difficulty in determining the identity of the Colossian errorists, coupled with the often impossible task of distinguishing with certainty between the author's perspective and that of the false teachers, means that such comparisons are probably of limited value for determining the reasons for the changed perspective in Colossians and Ephesians. Moreover, given the brevity of Colossians it is impossible to draw comprehensive conclusions about the beliefs of the recipients. A more valuable approach is to seek to draw correlations between what we can know in general about the situation in the community and the author's assertions.

In examining the eschatological language in Paul's letters from a social-scientific perspective Wayne Meeks (1983) has illustrated both the many dimensions of such language and the variety of its applications to the practical concerns of community life. At times communal problems such as the need to restrain innovation in church groups lead Paul to use futuristic eschatological language, while at other times emphasis falls upon the present fulfillment of eschatological hopes (Meeks [1983] 174–79). Similarly, the emphasis in Colossians on the present nature of salvation and the use of cosmological symbolism needs to be analyzed in light of the realities of community life. In their treatise on the sociology of knowledge (the study of the relationship between human thought and the social context in which it arises), Berger and Luckmann have noted that the problem of "heresy" often accelerates the development of Christian theological thought. Greater theorizing about the "symbolic universe" is required, new implications of the tradition are identified, and ultimately the symbolic universe is pushed beyond its original form (Berger and Luckmann 78; see also the discussion of the symbolic universe in the notes and interpretation on 1:3-8 and 1:15-20).

Berger and Luckmann's study invites us to consider the relationship between the conflict at Colossae and the beliefs expressed in Colossians. The fact that the earliest witnesses and authorities in the Pauline churches were beginning to die, coupled with the dissent of once-faithful members and the threat of false teachers, meant that the relationship between Christ and the community needed to be reinforced in the strongest possible terms. Moreover, the need for a strong, direct approach may have been exacerbated by increasing tensions between the community and society at large (see the notes and interpretation on 4:2-6). Recipients were reminded that they had been raised with Christ and in 3:5–4:1 that they would be instructed concerning the life appropriate to their condition.

One of the main reasons that 3:1-4 serves as such an effective transition into the next major section of the epistle—the ethical admonition—is that it recalls the experience of baptism. (That being raised with Christ refers to baptism is made explicit in 2:12.) We have seen that the ritual of baptism is central in Colossians and the meaning of baptism is probably at the heart of the conflict between the author of Colossians and the opponents (see the notes and interpretation on 2:8-15, 16-23). Anthropologists who have studied rituals have noted their centrality for the construction of belief, for the birth of ethos, and even for the learning necessary for the integration of individuals within communities. Anthropologist Clifford Geertz has defined ritual as consecrated behavior— behavior that is set apart for contact with the sacred (see the notes and interpretation on 1:15-20). In recalling the experience of baptism the author of Colossians reminds believers of their deepest religious experience. One question that has fascinated anthropologists is how people integrate the transformation that occurs in the midst of ritual into everyday life. This question is particularly relevant for an investigation of Col 3:1-4 because this text is intent upon linking the experience of transformation to a way of life in the everyday world (3:5–4:1).

The text communicates the fact that believers have changed with very strong metaphorical language: You have died! (3:3). The work of anthropologists on initiation rites (see the notes and interpretation on 2:8-15, 16-23) has explored how rituals facilitate often disruptive social transition or change. In early Christianity an initiation rite such as baptism was central to the redefinition of social boundaries that had to occur for each new member. During baptism the believer is in a liminal or threshold state, and language describing the event often dramatizes the pre- and post-liminal states (i.e., death and rebirth; see Muir). Groups frequently make use of symbols of death and rebirth in order to express the change or transformation that is experienced in the initiatory rite. Mircea Eliade examined this feature of initiation rites in an in-depth study:

> In the scenario of initiatory rites, "death" corresponds to the temporary return to Chaos; hence it is the paradigmatic expression of the end of a mode of being—the mode of ignorance and of the child's irresponsibility. Initiatory death provides the clean slate on which will be written the successive revelations whose end is the formation of the new man. (xiii)

Eliade's findings help us to appreciate the profundity of what was experienced during baptism in these early church communities. To say that a new identity was created is no exaggeration. Indeed, this new identity is precisely what is celebrated in 3:10-11—a passage based on a traditional baptismal formula (see the notes and interpretation).

While in the first instance Col 3:1-4 does not seem to be concerned with everyday life, it nevertheless recommends an ethos that was meant to carry the believer through his or her daily interactions. This is revealed by the phrase "your life is hidden with Christ in God" and by the idea that permeates the text: ultimately one's dwelling is in the heavenly realm in unity with Christ. To state that one's mind should not be "on the things that are on the earth" evokes a sense of being a stranger in human society (a theme that is developed extensively in 1 Peter). True citizenship is in the heavenly realm (cf. Eph 2:19-21). This is not to suggest that what is being recommended is abdication from social responsibilities; even the households of believers should be organized in a certain fashion and should reflect the Lord (3:18–4:1). But to identify the object of one's longing so strongly with the invisible heavenly realm means that visible signs of status and even religious purity can be rendered irrelevant. Here it is important to recall the debate with the Colossian opponents. The conflict in Colossae involved differing understandings of the physical body (see the notes on 2:8-15, 16-23). For the author of Colossians the body is no longer an obstacle to overcome by means of various ascetic practices; in fact, the transformation that the bodies of believers has undergone is so great that they have been exalted already (3:1-4; cf. 2:12-13). Upholding ethical ideals (3:5–4:1), believers will go about their daily business in a way that allows for the preservation of many aspects of conventional life. In a society that is becoming increasingly hostile (see the notes and interpretation on Col 4:5-6), believers are strengthened by the conviction that they ultimately belong to another world. The perspective that is recommended recalls the words of Jesus in the Fourth Gospel (8:23): "You are from below, I am from above; you are of this world, I am not of this world."

FOR REFERENCE AND FURTHER STUDY

Eliade, Mircea. *Rites and Symbols of Initiation: The Mysteries of Birth and Rebirth.* Translated by Willard R. Trask. New York: Harper & Row, 1958.

Grässer, Erich. "Kol. 3:1-4 als Beispiel einer Interpretation *secundum homines recipientes*," *ZThK* 64 (1967) 139–68. Reprinted in idem, *Text und Situation.* Gesammelte Aufsätze zum Neuen Testament. Gütersloh: Gerd Mohn, 1973.

Hay, David M. *Glory at the Right Hand: Psalm 110 in Early Christianity.* SBL.MS 18. Nashville: Abingdon, 1973.

Lafontaine, Jean S. *Initiation: Ritual Drama and Secret Knowledge Across the World.* Harmondsworth: Penguin, 1985.

Levison, J. R. "*2 Apoc. Bar.* 48:42–52:7 and the Apocalyptic Dimension of Colossians 3:1-6," *JBL* 108 (1989) 93–108.

Lincoln, Andrew T. *Paradise Now and Not Yet.* MSSNTS 43. Cambridge: Cambridge University Press, 1981.

Muir, S. *Healing and Initiation in Luke-Acts.* Doctoral Dissertation, University of Ottawa, 1998.

10. *Ethical Guidelines for a New Life* (3:5-17)

5. Put to death, therefore, the parts of you that are earthly: immorality, impurity, passion, evil desire, and the greed that is idolatry. 6. Because of these things the wrath of God is coming [upon the sons of disobedience], 7. among whom you also walked then, when you lived in these things. 8. But now you must put off all of these things: wrath, rage, malice, slander and filthy language out of your mouths. 9. Do not lie to one another, for you have stripped off the old self with its practices 10. and have put on the new self, which is being renewed in full knowledge according to the image of its creator. 11. Here there is no Greek and Jew, circumcision and uncircumcision, barbarian, Scythian, slave, free; but Christ is all and in all. 12. Put on, therefore, as God's chosen ones, holy and beloved, heartfelt compassion, kindness, humility, gentleness, and patience, 13. bearing with one another and forgiving each other, if anyone has a complaint against another; as the Lord forgave you, so also you must. 14. And over all these things love, which is the bond of completeness. 15. And let the peace of Christ rule in your hearts, to which indeed you were called in one body. And be thankful. 16. Let the word of Christ dwell in you richly, teaching and admonishing each other in all wisdom with psalms, hymns, and spiritual songs as you sing with gratitude in your hearts to God. 17. And whatever you do in word or deed, do all things in the name of the Lord Jesus, giving thanks to God the Father through him.

NOTES

5. *Put to death, therefore, the parts of you that are earthly:* The pattern of moving from doctrinal assertions to ethical exhortations is frequent in Pauline correspondence (e.g., Rom 6:1-14). The reference to death echoes 3:2. The point is that the dying that occurs through baptism has consequences for ethical comportment. The problem with those who are tempted by the false teaching (see 2:8-23) is that their "dying" has not led to this required ethical comportment; they live as though they still belonged to the world (2:20). The idea of transformation of the self underlies this verse (cf. 3:10). The Greek expression *ta melē* refers to members or parts of the physical body (although the word "body" is not explicit but implied). The description of the parts as earthly (literally, the members that are on the earth) probably refers to the fact that members can be instruments of wickedness (cf. Rom 6:13; 1 Cor 6:15). Originally the Greek text did not contain "of you" *(hymōn)*, but it was implied and thus was later added to some manuscripts. An alternate interpretation of this verse has been proposed (see Masson; Turner [1965]; see also the discussion in Harris 145–46): "You, therefore, as members [of the Body], must put to death" (taking *ta melē* as vocative rather than accusative). Although it is grammatically possible, this interpretation has won very little approval because it does not seem to fit well with the content of the verses in question, requiring one to supply notions of the body of Christ that do not appear to be the immediate concern here.

immorality, impurity, passion, evil desire, and the greed that is idolatry: This list of vices is similar in content to many other descriptions of vices in Pauline literature (e.g., Rom 1:24, 26, 29-31; Eph 4:31; 5:3-5, 6:14-17). Such lists were common in the writings of Hellenistic philosophers and some Jewish writings, including the Dead Sea Scrolls (e.g., 1QS 4:2-12, 18-26). The term "immorality" *(porneia)* refers to a broad range of sexual sin, and translators have sought to make this clear (e.g., NRSV; REB: fornication; NJB: sexual vice). In his discussion of marriage and celibacy in 1 Corinthians 7 Paul speaks of immorality as a menacing threat—something that must be contained by marriage for those who do not possess the gift of celibacy. In fact, the references to impurity *(akatharsia),* passion *(pathos),* and evil desire *(epithymia kakē)* probably also carry sexual connotations. For example, in 1 Thess 4:3-5 Paul instructs: "For this is the will of God, your sanctification: that you abstain from fornication *[porneia];* that each one of you know how to control your own body in holiness and honor, not with lustful passion *[en pathei epithymias],* like the Gentiles who do not know God" (NRSV). (On "impurity" as a reference to immoral sexual conduct see 1 Thess 4:7; Gal 5:19; 2 Cor 12:21; Rom 1:24.) Sexual immorality and idolatry were frequently listed together in the descriptions of the pagan world by Jewish authors (e.g., Wisdom 13–14 [see especially 14:12-27]; see the full discussion of Jewish evidence in Dunn 213–16) and early Christian authors followed their lead. The grammatical construction, including the use of the definite article, makes it clear that only greed here is described as idolatry (see Harris 146–47). The two concepts are also listed together in Eph 5:5 and the pairing has often been seen as reflecting the sentiments of Matt 6:24 *par.:* "You cannot serve God and wealth." It seems that avarice was a problem in early church communities (e.g., 1 Tim 6:10-11; Pol. *Phil.* 11:1-2). There may be a connection between greed and sexual immorality in this verse, for greed could be depicted as unrestrained sexual appetite (Plato, *Symposium* 182D) and one senses this idea in 1 Thess 4:4-5 (see Dunn 225). But Col 3:5 may in fact reflect an awareness of some of the problems of maintaining a distinct identity in the Greco-Roman world that arise with the accumulation of wealth (see the interpretation below).

6. *Because of these things the wrath of God is coming [upon the sons of disobedience]:* "Wrath" *(orgē)* should not be understood in terms of human emotion, but is rather a way of referring to God's future judgment (BAGD 578–79; see also the notes and interpretation on 3:4). In contrast, Rom 1:18-32 concentrates on the present dimensions of wrath. A close parallel to 3:6 can be found in 1 Thess 1:10 (cf. 1 Thess 5:9). As in 1 Thess 4:3-6 (see the notes on Col 3:5), the consequences of sexual vice are described as dire. The verse may offer an indication that an expectation of an imminent end was still alive, or it may simply be a traditional formula associated with warnings against vices. The phrase "upon the sons of disobedience" is placed in brackets here (cf. NAB) because opinion is heavily divided as to whether the phrase is a later addition. The NRSV and NJB include the phrase, while it is omitted in the NEB, REB, and NIV. Commentators and translators who favor omission point to the fact that it is missing from many of the oldest manuscripts (e.g., 𝔓⁴⁶ and B) and that the phrase

may have been added in order to harmonize the verse with the parallel text of Eph 5:6 (e.g., Pokorný [1991] 167; cf. Eph 2:2). But on the other hand the shorter reading makes for an awkward transition to the next verse, which begins with "among whom" or "among which" (see Metzger 624–25).

7. *among whom you also walked then, when you lived in these things:* This Greek phrase is awkward to translate with decisions depending in part on whether one accepts the longer ending of 3:6 (see the notes above). A comparison of modern translations will reveal the variety of possibilities, none of which, however, differs significantly in meaning. *En hois* can be translated as "among whom" if one accepts the longer ending that is preferred here, but it can also mean "in which" referring back to v. 6a and ultimately back to v. 5 where the vices are listed. (Lohse translates the expression as "in these things"; cf. NAB "by these.") This latter option renders the phrase somewhat repetitive and thus some prefer to translate the second expression *en toutois* not as "in these things," but less literally as "in that way" (NAB) or "that life" (NRSV). The verb *peripateō* (to walk) refers to how one lives the whole of one's life and appears frequently in Pauline correspondence. Hence most modern translations refer to "living." But the more literal translation better captures the active dimension of the concept. In Colossians it is used with a view to the interaction of community members and the nonbelieving Gentile world (cf. 4:5; see the notes and interpretation on 1:10). Against the "among whom" translation referring to the "sons of disobedience" Harris argues that Paul does not view living among Gentiles per se as sinful (148; cf. 1 Cor 5:10). But the issue of concern here is a type of association with the Gentile world that involves taking up an entire way of life. The expression "you also" relates the former behavior of the Colossians to that of the Gentiles.

8. *But now you must put off all of these things:* Verse 7 refers to "then" and here we find the corresponding "but now." The aorist middle imperative of the verb "to put off" *(apotithēmi)* recalls the similar usage in Rom 13:12: "Let us lay aside the works of darkness and put on the armor of light" (NRSV; cf. Eph 4:22). In order to make the translation more intelligible in English many modern translators prefer to translate the verb *apotithēmi* as "to get rid of" (NRSV), "to put away" (NAB), or "to give up" (NJB). But these translations mute the powerful metaphor of putting off and putting on clothes that runs throughout 3:8-11 to describe the transformation and the creation of a new identity (for use of the verb as literally "to remove clothing" see Acts 7:58). Language of putting off and putting on clothes in Pauline literature recalled the experience of baptism (cf. Gal 3:26-28; see the notes and interpretation below) where such natural actions came to take on deep significance for the process of change that the participant experienced (see Meeks [1983] 151). The image of putting off and putting on garments was used in mystery religions with respect to the process of initiation (see Lohse 141).

wrath, rage, malice, slander and filthy language out of your mouths: If the previous list of vices (3:5) had mainly to do with sexual sins, this list is mostly about the sins of speech. The term for "wrath" *(orgē)* is the same as that found in 3:6, but this time it refers to the human emotion of anger and not to God's judgment. It is very closely related to the next term, *thymos,* and the two words frequently occur together (e.g., Rom 2:8; Rev 16:19; 19:15; Eph 4:31), but *thymos* perhaps refers to an outburst of anger (or rage; see BAGD 365). Malice *(kakia)* refers to wicked intent (cf. 1 Cor 5:8; 14:20; Rom 1:29; Eph 4:31) that manifests itself in wicked speech: slander or lying *(blasphēmia;* cf. Mark 7:22 *par.;* Eph 4:31; 1 Tim 6:4; 2 Tim 3:2). In Titus 3:2 the believer is someone who speaks evil *(blasphē-mein)* of no one. The final expression, *aischrologia* (filthy [REB], obscene [NAB], or abusive [RSV; NJB] language) is especially interesting. It is the only use of this specific term in the NT (cf. *Did.* 3:3; 5:1), but the values it reveals are very much in keeping with the ancient Mediterranean world. Mark McVann writes:

> Communication in the ancient Mediterranean region is generally reflected in the concrete images of mouth and ears. Anthropologically, these orifices are viewed as boundaries of the human body. In eastern Mediterranean culture of biblical times, in which purity concerns are intense, these boundaries are tightly regulated and subject to continuous and close scrutiny. The purity of the mouth is guarded in two ways: by censuring what comes in (food), and that which goes out (speech). (25)

For an especially good illustration of these ideas see the discourse concerning the tongue in Jas 3:1-12. Inappropriate use of the mouth could be viewed as causing serious concerns in early Christian communities, as the instructions directed toward young widows in 1 Tim 5:13 clearly illustrate.

9. *Do not lie to one another, for you have stripped off the old self with its practices:* The participle, "having stripped" *(apekdysamenoi),* and the corresponding participle in v. 10, "having put on" *(endysamenoi),* are most probably causal adverbial participles, spelling out the grounds for the injunction "do not lie" (cf. Eph 4:25; see Harris 150). Hence English translations convey this with terms such as "for" or "since" (e.g., NIV; NAB). On several occasions Paul states that he himself is not lying (e.g., Rom 9:1; 2 Cor 11:31; Gal 1:20; 1 Tim 2:7) and the avoidance of lying was of considerable concern in the early church (Acts 5:3-4; Jas 3:14; 1 John 1:6; *Did.* 3:5; *Herm. Man.* 3.2; see Dunn 220). The command not to lie to one another is a demand to treat each other honorably (see the interpretation below) and seems to summarize the previous list of ethical guidelines. The verb "to strip off" *(apekdyomai)* is a synonym of "to put off" *(apotithēmi).* The latter term occurs far more frequently in ethical exhortation (cf. Eph 4:22). The verb *apekdyomai* also occurs in 2:15 (see the notes) and a cognate of the verb is found in 2:11. The baptismal metaphor, which began at 3:8, is developed further (see the notes on v. 8 above). The expression "the old self" or "the old person" *(ton palaion anthrōpon)* corresponds to the concept of "the new self" or "the new person" *(ton neon [anthrōpon]).* The old self is a way of referring to existence prior to baptism in a manner that underscores a radical change of identity (cf. Rom 6:6; 1 Cor 5:7-8; Eph 4:22). Just as is the case with the new self (see v. 12), the nature of the old self is demonstrated by means of practices or behavior.

10. *and have put on the new self:* This idea recalls the notion of putting on Christ in Gal 3:27 (cf. Eph 4:22, 24). The contrast between the old self and the new self

makes it clear that the new self refers to the transformation of the believer in the first instance and not to Christ himself. But there are strong notions here of close identification with Christ in baptism (see the notes below). The verb "to put on" *(endyō)* was used in Pauline literature in conjunction with ethical imperatives, as is also the case in 3:12 (cf. Rom 13:12, 14; Eph 4:22, 24). The metaphor is used in Hebrew thought for the putting on of such graces bestowed by God as "righteousness" (e.g., Job 29:14) or "strength and dignity" (e.g., Prov 31:25; see Dunn 221).

which is being renewed in full knowledge according to the image of its creator: A present passive participle of the verb "to renew" *(anakainoō)* occurs here, suggesting ongoing action in the present (cf. 2 Cor 4:16). The REB aims to bring this out by translating the term as "which is being constantly renewed." Although there is greater preference for the translation of *eis* in the locative sense as "in" full knowledge or "in the sphere of" full knowledge, the term may also express direction (NJB: towards true knowledge; REB: brought to know God). *Epignōsis* (cf. 1:6) is used here as in Col 1:9, where it seems best to translate the term simply as "knowledge" (see the notes on 1:9). However, the Greek term can also mean full or complete knowledge or insight. The implied notion of moving toward a goal means that "full knowledge" is the preferred translation in this case. As in the first half of the verse, identification with Christ is central. According to Col 1:15 Christ is the image of God (on the meaning of the term *eikōn* see the notes on 1:15; cf. Rom 8:29). However, the description of the new self also appears to be influenced by Gen 1:26-27 where the human being is created in the image of God (see D'Angelo 321). By putting on the new self (or new humanity), one shares in (or returns to) the perfection of creation (see the interpretation below). The allusion to Genesis may also suggest that the reference to knowledge should be read in light of the motif of Adam and creation, and of how knowledge figured in humanity's failure (cf. Gen 2:17; 3:5, 7; see Dunn 222). In Paul's letters knowledge is a characteristic of the believer (cf. Phil 1:9). According to Dunn, the description of renewal resonates with Adam christology (see Dunn 221–23; cf. Romans 5–6).

11. *Here there is no:* There is a strong focus on ethnic divisions and perceptions of cultural inferiority here. The phrase begins with the Greek term *hopou,* "where" (referring back either to the image or the new self of v. 10), but it is translated as "here" in this case in order to render the sentence intelligible in English (as in NAB; REB). Like Gal 3:28 and 1 Cor 12:13, Col 3:11 has been understood as reflecting a baptismal reunification formula which took on slightly different shapes in different circumstances (see Meeks 1974). This formula also underlies several extra-biblical texts (e.g., Clem. Al. *Strom.* 3.13.92; 2 *Clem.* 12:2; *Gos. Thom.* 37, 21a, 22b). Of particular interest to scholars has been the absence of the male-female pair in 3:10 in comparison to Gal 3:28. (The male-female pair does appear in the manuscript tradition of 3:11, but this is clearly an attempt to harmonize the verse with Gal 3:28.) Some have understood this omission as a sign of an attempt to harmonize the baptismal teaching with the traditional ethics of the household code in 3:18–4:1 (Johnson [1992] 347). The expression "there is no" also occurs in Gal 3:28, but unlike Gal

3:28 where the first two of the pairs are linked with *oude* (nor), in Col 3:11 the first two pairs are linked together with *kai* ("and"; cf. the reference to the male and female pair in Gal 3:28); perhaps this underscores the fact that the division of humanity into two classes (Greek *and* Jew, circumcision *and* uncircumcision) is no longer appropriate (see Dunn 223). For a full discussion of the relationship between Col 3:11 and Gal 3:28, see Aletti [1993] 233–35.

Greek and Jew, circumcision and uncircumcision: In Pauline literature Greek and Jew are a way of referring to the whole of humanity (e.g., Gal 3:28; Rom 1:16). The reference to circumcision and uncircumcision simply repeats the previous thought and completes a chiasmus (the A-B-B-A pattern that occurs frequently in the NT; see Harris 154). In Gal 6:15 Paul speaks of the abolition of the difference between circumcised and uncircumcised as a new creation. (For other references to circumcision-uncircumcision in Colossians see also 2:11, 13; 4:11.)

barbarian, Scythian, slave, free: The list of terms that are juxtaposed antithetically (as in Gal 3:28) is interrupted with the mention of barbarians and Scythians. These seem to be enumerated together as representatives of stigmatized groups (see Lohse 144). "Barbarians" is a derogatory way of referring to all non-Greeks (cf. Rom 1:14), and Scythians (inhabitants of the northern coast of the Black Sea, now southern Russia) were commonly viewed as an especially barbaric race. The reference to the contrast between slave and free recalls Gal 3:28 and may have been included here simply because it was part of the baptismal tradition (cf. 1 Cor 12:13). However, this part of the proclamation may also have had special importance in the community since the detailed attention to slaves in 3:18–4:1 may indicate concerns about their status and behavior (see the interpretation below and the notes and interpretation on 3:18–4:1).

but Christ is all and in all: This is a proclamation of the recreated humanity in Christ that resembles the ending of Gal 3:28 (cf. Eph 1:23). In Gal 3:28 the unification of the community who are all one in Christ Jesus is proclaimed, and in 3:29 the fact that all are heirs according to the promise is celebrated. In Col 3:11 the contrast between the old ethnic and cultural divisions and the new cosmic reality in Christ is emphasized. The cosmic power of Christ is also celebrated in the hymn of 1:15-20.

12. *Put on, therefore:* A list of virtues here complements the list of vices in 3:5-11. The grammatical construction at the beginning of this verse is identical to that found at the beginning of 3:5. The term "therefore" *(oun)* acts as a bridge from indicative statements to the imperative voice. The same verb "to put on" is also used in 3:10. In fact, "therefore" probably ultimately refers back to 3:10 with the new self that has been put on being the basis for the ethical stance.

as God's chosen ones, holy and beloved: "As God's chosen ones" offers further justification for putting on the virtues enumerated here. The concepts resemble the language of belonging that is found throughout Paul's letters (e.g., Rom 1:7; 8:33; 1 Thess 4:3) to reinforce the boundary between believers and the outside world and to generate cohesion (see the notes and interpretation on 1:1-2). The notion of election is similar to that found in the Hebrew Bible (e.g., 1 Chron 16:13; Isa 43:20) and the QL (e.g., 1QM 12:1). The members of the early church community are described as "saints" or "the holy ones" in 1:2, 4, 26 (cf. Eph 1:1; 3:18; 5:3; see the notes on 1:2). They are called the "chosen" or "called ones" also in 3:15 (cf. Eph 1:4; 4:4). The notion of being loved by God also occurs in Eph 2:4, as does the idea of being loved by Christ (Eph 5:1-2, 25). Individual members of the community can also be called "beloved" (Col 4:7, 9; cf. Eph 6:21).

heartfelt compassion, kindness, humility, gentleness, and patience: These terms are used in Pauline literature not only to refer to human virtues, but also to the acts of God or Christ (see Lohse 147). Thus the new self's very actions emulate God or Christ. The first expression has a very close parallel in Phil 2:1. A literal translation of the Greek would be "bowels of compassion" *(splagchna oiktirmou).* The inward parts or entrails *(splagchnon)* were thought to be the seat of emotion (BAGD 763); hence we have here a reference to very strong or heartfelt (NAB; NJB) compassion. (On kindness see, e.g., Gal 5:22; 2 Cor 6:6; Eph 2:7.) Particular attention should be paid to the reference to humility *(tapeinophrosynē).* Here it is clearly used in a positive sense, but in 2:18 and 23 it probably has a pejorative meaning and it is best to translate the term in those verses as "self-abasement" (see the notes on 2:18). Many believe that in 2:18 and 23 the author of Colossians is quoting from the opponents who claimed that their ascetic activities brought them special access to divine experiences. In 3:12 the author of Colossians is encouraging the type of humility that should transform the social life of the community. Bruce J. Malina has defined humility in the biblical world as "a socially acknowledged claim to neutrality in the competition of life" ("Humility" [1993] 107). In response to a religiosity that was seen as causing competition the author of Colossians recommends a way of life that attaches no value to the flaunting of "achievements." (On meekness see Gal 5:23; 6:1; 1 Cor 4:21; Eph 4:2; on patience see Gal 5:22; 2 Cor 6:6; Eph 4:2.)

13. *bearing with one another and forgiving each other, if anyone has a complaint against another:* Both participles are grammatically dependent on the imperative "put on" in v. 12. Thus they are translated as imperatives in some versions (e.g., NRSV; REB; NJB). To put up or bear with one another (cf. Mark 9:19 *parr.;* 2 Cor 11:1, 19) is no doubt required in a community made up of people of different ethnic origins and from different status groups, especially when the reaction from society is growing increasingly hostile (see the notes on 4:5-6). God's forgiveness is in view in 2:13, but here it is the forgiveness that community members bestow on each other that is of concern.

as the Lord forgave you, so also you must: It is Christ himself who sets the example for the community. In Pauline literature "Lord" refers to Christ except in the case of the quotations from the OT (see Dunn 231), yet the reference to Christ forgiving sins is very unusual. In Col 2:13 it is God who forgives (cf. Eph 4:32). In the synoptic tradition Jesus forgives sins (e.g., Mark 2:5-7 *parr.;* Luke 7:47-49), but it is likely that the author of Colossians has in mind the relationship between the *Kyrios* as exalted Lord and his people, rather than the specific actions of the earthly Jesus (see Lohse 148). The notion that being forgiven leads one to forgive others also occurs in the synoptic tradition (e.g.,

Matt 18:23-35). Bruce has argued that the phrase contains a conscious allusion to the Lord's Prayer (Bruce [1984] 155; see Matt 6:9-15; cf. John 4:11). The variant reading of "Christ" *(Christos)* instead of "the Lord" *(kyrios)* probably developed as a result of an attempt to be more definite (i.e., the reference is specifically to Christ and not broadly to God). However, "Lord" is found in the best witnesses of the Alexandrian and Western texts. The two other variant readings of "God" *(theos)* and "God in Christ" *(theos en Christō)* probably resulted from an attempt to harmonize Col 3:13 with Eph 4:32 (see Metzger 625).

14. *And over all these things love:* This verse is grammatically dependent on the use of the verb "to put on" in v. 12 above. Thus many translators make this clear by inserting the verb before "love," even though it does not occur in the Greek text. The dressing and undressing metaphor that begins at v. 8 continues to shape the text. The term *epi* can also mean "above" (NRSV), but, given the clothing metaphor, "over" is the more appropriate translation (cf. NAB; NJB). The NJB boldly underscores the metaphor by translating the word as "over all these clothes." Love becomes the most important garment. Paul places love above all other graces (cf. Gal 5:22; 1 Cor 13:13; Rom 13:9-10). In describing ancient Mediterranean society Bruce J. Malina notes that the value of "group attachment" and "group bonding" is inherent in the concept of love ("Love" [1993] 110–11). This is somewhat in contrast to modern Western cultures in which "love is an affect of the heart which is usually experienced individualistically toward another or other individuals" (Malina [1993] "Love," 113). Thus it is not surprising that talk of love leads to description of a bond that holds the community together in harmony.

    which is the bond of completeness: Although the term for bond *(syndesmos;* cf. Eph 4:3), which means literally "that which binds together" (BAGD 785), does seem to fit with garment imagery, it does not appear to have commonly been used to refer to clothing. It is used in 2:19 to refer to ligaments of the body. Its usage in this verse finds a parallel in philosophical writings where it refers to a bond that unites virtues. The Pythagoreans are described as regarding friendship as the bond of all the virtues (Epictetus 208a; see Bruce 156). The term for completeness or perfection *(teleiotēs)* occurs only here and in Heb 6:1 (cf. Matt 5:43-48); the genitive construction might describe a bond characterized by completeness but more likely refers to the bond that results in completeness or perfect harmony (NRSV).

15. *And let the peace of Christ rule in your hearts: Brabeuō* literally meant to award prizes in contests and generally came to mean "to judge, decide, control, rule" (BAGD 146). In the biblical world the heart is viewed as more than the seat of emotion. Instead, together with the eyes, the heart is understood as the center of the human capacity for "emotion-fused thinking" (Malina, "Eyes–Heart" [1993] 64). The heart is central to how one thinks, feels, arbitrates, and evaluates. It is central to one's motives and priorities. Thus when Paul attempts to define the essence of Jewish identity he speaks of circumcision of the heart (Rom 2:29). The REB aims to bring out the notion of the centrality of Christ's peace for decision-making by translating the phrase fluidly: "Let Christ's

peace be arbiter in your decisions" (cf. Eph 4:3). In 2 Thess 3:16 peace refers to the peace that Christ gives.

to which indeed you were called in one body: "You were called" repeats the notion of God's chosen people in 3:12. This is the last of the many references to the church as the body (of Christ) in Colossians (cf. Col 1:18-20, 21-22; 2:9-10, 19). In comparison to the undisputed letters the symbol of the body of Christ in Colossians generally has a more cosmological flavor with Christ defined as the head and the community seen as the body (see the notes and interpretation on 1:15-20), but in this verse the usage closely resembles that in the undisputed letters. The reference to worship in the subsequent verses probably means that the local community is mainly in view rather than the body that fills the universe, but notions of the universal church should not be ruled out (see Dunn 235; cf. Rom 12:5; Eph 4:4).

And be thankful: The specific adjective *eucharistos* (thankful) is found only here in the NT. The term is used frequently in ancient inscriptions referring to those who were grateful to their benefactors (Harris 166). The notion of thanksgiving, however, is frequent in Pauline literature. There are subsequent references to thanksgiving in vv. 16-17 and a great interest in thanksgiving and prayer throughout Colossians (cf. 1:3-8, 12-14; 2:7; 4:2-3). Given the interest in the worship of the community, which is expressed in vv. 16-17, it is reasonable to conclude that giving thanks to God was a central part of early church liturgy. The instruction to be thankful serves as a good introduction to the discussion of liturgy.

16. *Let the word of Christ dwell in you richly:* This verse gives us one of the few precious descriptions of community worship in the NT (cf. 1 Corinthians 14; Acts 2:42). The expression the "word of Christ" is only found here in the NT. It is not surprising, therefore, that some manuscripts substitute the more common expressions "word of God" or "word of the Lord." The rendering adopted here is very well attested, and the fact that the expression is so unusual increases the likelihood that it represents the original (Metzger 625). The "word" is equated with the gospel in 1:5 (cf. 1:25); hence the REB translates the verse as "the Gospel of Christ." The expression "the word of Christ" is probably equivalent to "the word of the Lord" (e.g., 1 Thess 1:8; 2 Thess 3:1) or the "gospel of Christ" (Gal 1:7; 1 Cor 9:12; 2 Cor 2:12) and seems to correspond to the expression "the peace of Christ" in the previous verse. "The word of Christ" might refer to proclamations of the cross and resurrection (the message about Christ: objective genitive) or to the recounting of the teaching of Jesus during community gatherings (the message spoken by Jesus: subjective genitive), but the two ideas are closely related and the expression most likely refers to both. The notion of identification with Christ is continued from v. 15. The use of the verb "to live in" or "to dwell in" *(enoikeō)* suggests that the word of Christ is alive in the hearts of believers as a dynamic force (Harris 167). The expression reflects the experience of being inspired by the word during community gatherings. In much the same way as the Pauline expression "in Christ," the terminology ties together notions of close identification with Christ with the communal notion of belonging to the body of Christ. Some

translators stress this corporate dimension by translating *en hymin* not as "in you," but as "among you" (NEB; REB). Similarly the adverb *plousios* (richly) has been rendered as "in rich abundance" (Lohse 150) in order to highlight the corporate sense: "Let the word of Christ dwell abundantly among you" (Lohse 136).

teaching and admonishing each other in all wisdom: There are several punctuation issues raised by the Greek text (see Harris 167–70 for full discussion). It is grammatically possible to take "in all wisdom" with "dwell in," but most translators today are in agreement that it is more natural to take it together with "teaching and admonishing." There is far more disagreement as to whether the psalms, hymns, and spiritual songs should be taken with "teaching and admonishing" (e.g., Pokorný [1991] 174) or with "singing" (e.g., Dunn 211). In favor of the latter it has been pointed out that the three terms for songs seem to fit best with the participle "singing" (*ądontes*—even though this would weigh down the participle with several qualifying statements). However, that psalms, hymns, and spiritual songs can be a vehicle for teaching is also implied by the instruction to the addressees in Eph 5:19 to speak to one another by means of such ritual forms. It is also important to keep in mind 1 Corinthians 14 where Paul clearly values the teaching functions of the various gifts of the Spirit (especially prophecy); in 1 Cor 14:26 psalms and teaching clearly go hand in hand. In support of a close connection between exhortation and hymns, psalms, and spiritual songs is also the fact that social scientists have long observed that rituals such as singing or chanting play a central role in educating community members (see M. Y. MacDonald [1988] 65; Meeks [1983] 146; the notes and interpretation on 1:15-20). Wisdom is highly valued in Colossians (cf. 1:9; 2:3; 4:5). In contrast to true wisdom, the false teaching leads to what only has the appearance of wisdom (2:23).

with psalms, hymns, and spiritual songs: It is impossible to differentiate precisely among these words. Together they probably refer to the whole range of singing and chanting that is prompted by the Spirit (see Lohse 151; Meeks [1983] 144). The psalms, hymns, and spiritual songs were probably patterned after Jewish liturgical traditions. It is reasonable to conclude that the "psalms" included some from the biblical psalter. Such singing most likely combined traditional elements with innovative tendencies. Revelation 19:1-8 illustrates that phrases and themes from Scripture could be proclaimed in a form adapted to the current situation in a church community (see Schweizer [1976] 210). In this verse the singing is connected to the presence of the word of Christ in the community, but in the parallel text of Eph 5:18 it is seen as evidence for the presence of the Spirit. The reference to spiritual songs probably also denotes inspiration by the Spirit and may refer to the gift of tongues (cf. 1 Cor 14:15).

as you sing with gratitude in your hearts to God: Here the participle is understood as circumstantial (NIV: as you sing), but may also be taken as imperative (sing! e.g., NRSV; NJB). With the reference to gratitude or thanks (*charis;* BAGD 878), the notion of thanksgiving is taken up again from the previous verse. Although it is omitted from some witnesses, the manuscript tradition favors the inclusion of the definite article in the expression *en tē chariti* (with gratitude). The expression may be phrased this way in order to draw a connection to 1:6 where notions of grace (again *charis;* see BAGD 877) and the gospel message also appear together (cf. 4:18; see Dunn 239–40). In place of "to God" some manuscripts have "to the Lord," probably in an effort to harmonize the verse with Eph 5:19 (see Metzger 625; on the heart see the notes on 3:15).

17. *And whatever you do in word or deed, do all things in the name of the Lord Jesus:* This verse serves as a summary of the whole section (3:5-16). Not only worship but also all aspects of life (word and deed) are to be done in the name of the Lord Jesus. A similar statement is found in 1 Cor 10:31. The references to "whatever" and to "all" stress the fact that the whole of life is involved. The verse resembles similar teaching in the Jewish tradition (e.g., Sir 47:8; Mishnah *ʾAbot* 2:12) and the expression "in the name of the Lord Jesus" appears to have arisen in analogy to the phrase *bᵉšem* YHWH that frequently occurs in Jewish Scripture (see Dunn 240-1; Bietenhard, *TDNT* 5:242–83). In this verse "in the name of the Lord Jesus" suggests the idea of calling the name of the Lord as an invocation (see Harris 171), but taken together with the reference to the whole of life "in the name of" more probably means "as a representative of" (the name represents its bearer and calls his authority into play; see Bietenhard). Such ideas are at work in the notions of baptism "in the name of the Lord Jesus Christ" (1 Cor 6:11) and the passing of judgment "in the name of the Lord Jesus" in a case of church discipline (1 Cor 5:4; see Lohse 152).

giving thanks to God the Father through him: It is possible that the participle could be taken as an imperative and hence as representing a more distinct thought than the translation here allows (e.g., REB: and give thanks). However, most take the participle as circumstantial, closely related to the command "whatever you do in word or deed, do all things in the name of the Lord Jesus" (see Harris 171). All action and speech must involve thanksgiving. The notion of worship characterizing daily life is also found in Rom 12:1: "present your bodies as a living sacrifice, holy and acceptable to God, which is your spiritual worship" (NRSV). Thanksgiving is central in vv. 15, 16, and 17 and indeed to the epistle as a whole (see the notes on 3:15). A very unusual Greek expression appears to refer to God the Father, *tō theō patri,* but it is very widely supported. It appears that copyists emended the expression by inserting *kai* before *patri* in order to imitate Eph 5:20 and other passages (cf. 1 Cor 15:24; Phil 4:20; see Metzger 626). "Through him" here refers to "through Christ."

INTERPRETATION

Although a new section of the letter begins at 3:5 with specific ethical exhortations it is actually very closely linked to 3:1-4. Throughout 3:1-17 there is a balancing of indicative sentences referring back to the transformation that occurs in baptism, with imperative admonitions that point ahead to the new life that must be lived by those who have been raised with Christ (see Lohse 145). Colossians 3:1-4 serves as a summary of previous teaching concerning the opponents and a final justification for the stance that is recommended in relation to these opponents. It also leads naturally into the ethical discussion beginning at 3:5. The list of vices and virtues in 3:5-17 is given shape by baptismal garment imagery and the proclamation of a baptismal reunification formula in 3:10-11. The significance of baptism is central in this section, as indeed it is throughout most of Colossians.

It is not really surprising that the meaning of baptism figured prominently in the conflict at Colossae (see the notes and interpretation on 2:8-15 and 2:16-23). Early Christian literature provides ample evidence that baptismal experiences were powerful, but the meaning of the ritual itself was sometimes ambiguous and variously interpreted. A comparison of 3:10-11 with such texts from Paul's letters as Gal 3:27-28 and 1 Cor 12:3, and other early Christian texts from the second and third centuries C.E. illustrates the point. The similarities among these texts, such as the proclamations of unity and the abolition of differences, the naming of pairs, and the use of garment imagery have led many scholars to believe that they draw upon the same source or upon a similar traditional baptismal saying. This saying may even predate Paul. In the *Gospel of the Egyptians,* which is cited by Clement of Alexandria (not to be confused with its namesake from Nag Hammadi), the following saying is attributed to Jesus: "When you tread upon the garment of shame and when the two become one and the male with the female neither male nor female" (Clem. Al. *Strom.* 3.13.92, cited in D. MacDonald [1987] 14; cf. *2 Clem.* 12:2; *Gos. Thom.* 37, 21a, 22b). Dennis MacDonald has shown that in the branches of early Christianity known as Valentinian Gnosticism and early Syrian Christianity the ancient baptismal saying was used in conjunction with efforts to return to the perfect state of an androgynous creation when there would no longer be male and female ([1987] 1–63). (Interest in the reunification of opposites, androgyny, and the putting off of garments is also evident in Greek philosophical traditions and in Hellenistic Judaism. For example, the first-century Jewish philosopher Philo of Alexandria argued that the first account of creation in Genesis [1:1–2:4a] referred to a perfect androgynous creation; see D. MacDonald [1987] 23–30.) Such strange and somewhat shocking phrases as "treading upon the garment of shame" (Clem. Al. *Strom.* 3.13.92) and "destroying the works of the female" (Clem Al. *Strom.* 3.9.63) were essentially proclamations of a return to perfection (often imagined as more male than fully androgynous) and a strongly ascetic departure from the world. Garment imagery was used to describe the process of removing evil flesh in exchange for a transformed body. This new body was maintained on a daily basis by the avoidance of sex altogether.

When Gal 3:27-28 has been compared to Col 3:10-11 there has been particular interest in the fact the male-female pair is absent. Most often this has been seen as an attempt to harmonize the saying with the traditional teaching of the household code (Col 3:18-4:1) and ultimately to restrict possibilities for women's leadership (see the notes on 3:11; see also the discussion of Nympha in the notes on 4:15). However, the facts that the male-female pair is so prominent in the ascetic versions of the baptismal formula cited above and that ascetic practices emerge as such an important feature of the false teaching that is condemned in Colossians (see the notes and interpretation on 2:16-23), suggest that the absence of the male-female pair should be seen primarily as a response to ascetic currents. Strong ascetic currents were a problem for Paul in Corinth; he made it clear to the Corinthian rigorists in 1 Corinthians 7 that he did not support those in the community who called for a complete avoidance of sex in all circumstances, nor did he view incorporation into Christ as a return to androgynous perfection (1 Cor 11:2-16). It is interesting to note that like Col 3:10-11, 1 Cor 12:13 also omits the male-female pair. In both cases this absence may be due to the tendency for such language to be used as justification for "severe treatment of the body" (cf. Col 2:23). In an effort to shed light on the background of Colossians, Harold Attridge has recently pointed to an interpretation of baptism that emerges in the third-century Gnostic text *Zostrianos*. Of particular relevance to the situation in Colossians is the fact that in this text a series of baptisms is part of a mystical journey through which the seer eventually is transformed into a heavenly or angelic state (see the notes and interpretation on 2:18, where the worship of angels is listed as one of the characteristics of the false teaching). In everyday life the results of the mystical journey translate into celibacy, and the call to abandon a fleshly existence is expressed in terms similar to those in the early Christian texts cited above: "Flee from the madness and the bondage of femaleness, and choose for yourselves the salvation of maleness" (NHC VIII, 1:130,16–132,5; see Attridge 483–86).

That ascetic currents may have influenced the shape of the baptismal teaching in Col 3:5-17 is also implied by the fact that in one important respect the text displays greater contact with the more ascetic versions of the baptismal reunification formula than does Gal 3:27-28. Colossians 3:9-10 states that believers have stripped off the old self with its practices and have put on the new self. There is clearly a connection here between these thoughts and the notion of putting on Christ in Gal 3:27, but Colossians departs from Galatians with the assertion that the new self is being renewed in full knowledge according to the image of its creator. Colossians 1:15 describes Christ as the image of God and this would be in keeping with the idea of putting on Christ. However, Col 3:10 appears to have been influenced by Gen 1:26-27 where the human being is created in the image of God. It may well be that the author of Colossians and the proponents of the false teaching shared the belief that putting on the new humanity meant partaking in (perhaps even returning to) the perfection of creation (cf. the views of Philo cited above). Yet the way in which the baptismal teaching in Colossians is framed by ethical exhortations calling for a virtuous life, which includes harmony among various cultural groups and thereby excludes claims of spiritual superiority, suggests that this vision of recreated humanity excludes severe treatment of the body (3:23). Moreover, that 3:5-17 is followed immediately by the household code of 3:18–4:1, with its strong support of marriage, adds further support to the notion that Col 3:5-17 represents a further (albeit indirect) response to the ascetic false teaching to complement Col 2:8-23.

In addition to the absence of the male-female pair from the baptismal proclamation in 3:11, some commentators have attached special significance to the repetition inherent in the phrase "there is no Greek and Jew, circumcision and uncircumcision." Dunn, for example, has recently observed: "the distinctive doubling of the emphasis here, including the third and otherwise gratuitous reference to circumcision in the letter (2:11, 13; 3:11; also 4:11) must surely indicate, first, that the primary challenge to the Colossian believers was posed by local Jews and, second, that it presupposed a valuation of circumcision which called the Christians' standing as beneficiaries of Jewish heritage into question" (225). Other commentators, however, have been much less certain than Dunn that circumcision was of central concern in the community (e.g., Pokorný [1991] 124). Advocacy of circumcision would indeed conform to the Jewish elements of the false teaching (see the notes and interpretation on 2:16-23), yet there are no direct references to circumcision being advocated in the community and the issues of concern are far less clear in Colossians than in Galatians. Moreover, in 2:11-13 the reference to circumcision is largely metaphorical, applying to baptism and the removal of a fleshly, sinful existence prior to baptism. If indeed the term "circumcision" was part of the vocabulary of the false teachers, it may also have referred to an alternate understanding of baptism or perhaps even to a type of initiation rite that carried that label (see the notes and interpretation on 2:8-23).

We cannot know for certain whether the phrase "there is no Greek and Jew, circumcision and uncircumcision" had special significance because there were proponents of physical circumcision in the community. However, the attempt to define the true circumcision as the circumcision of Christ and the circumcision "made without hands" (baptism) in 2:11 is in keeping with the interests of 3:5-17. To say that there is no circumcision and uncircumcision is to critique a rite that sets people apart physically from one another and reinforces the boundaries of ethnic identity. The author of Colossians is deeply concerned with the rites and practices that purport to provide spiritual benefit, but are viewed by the author as bound up with limited, earthly existence (2:16-23). With the exception of the slave-free pair (see below and the notes and interpretation on 3:18–4:1), all of the pairs and categories in 3:11 deal with ethnic identity. Divisions based on such markers of identity need to be abolished. When these are placed in the context of Colossians as a whole one senses a great effort to stabilize relations among members and a more cautious attitude toward innovation than in Galatians. Within the context of the argument of Galatians as a whole, Gal 3:28 provides a justification for an innovative stance on the relations between Gentiles and Jews in Christ. The focus in Col 3:11 is on unifying community, dispelling claims of special status, and recommending a way of life that allows each member to walk (cf. 3:7) as a new self in the world. However, caution is required in dealing with outsiders (see the notes and interpretation on 4:2-6) and with respect to conventional social institutions. The reference to the slave-free pair relativizes this distinction, but in the opinion of the Paul of Colossians the new life does not lead to a revolutionary transformation of the institution of slavery (cf. 3:18–4:1).

In 3:5-17 the shape of this new life is communicated mainly by means of a list of virtues and vices. Because such lists also occurred in Greco-Roman and Jewish literature (see the notes on 3:5) scholars have often viewed them as largely conventional as opposed to reflecting information about the specific context of a given work (e.g., Horgan 882). While it is true that such a list does not tell us very much about what is unique to Colossians, analysis of its content remains vital for understanding the context of the epistle. A social-scientific perspective invites us to identify what values the epistle shares with other aspects of first-century Mediterranean society. With an appreciation of such values we will be better able to grasp the real concerns that faced the Colossians in their daily lives and even to understand the specific problems addressed in the epistle.

Although the vices are associated in v. 7 with the previous life of believers, the use of the imperative voice throughout this section implies that the danger of slipping back into old ways is very real (cf. 2:20). The list of vices in vv. 5-9 is divided roughly according to two themes: sexual sins and sins of speech. In the first-century biblical world sexual conduct —and in particular the chastity of women—was of special significance to the preservation of honor. By remaining chaste a woman demonstrated her "shame"—her concern for the honor or reputation of the house and/or community. In turn it was the male prerogative to defend this honor—to protect the chastity of the woman and, ultimately, to protect the reputation of the house-community. (On honor and shame see the notes and interpretation on 1:3-8.) Purity regulations and concerns were fundamental to maintaining honor. The maintenance of the purity of the body came to symbolize the preservation of the honor of the community. Similarly, the mouth was viewed as an orifice through which pollution could occur, resulting in the shaming of the community. The purity of the mouth was guarded both by censoring what came in (food), and what went out (speech; see the notes on 3:8). That the vices defining what must be excluded from the community are divided in terms of speech sins and sexual sins would not surprise an anthropologist of Mediterranean society. For example, describing life in rural Greece, Jill Dubisch observes: "Concern with what comes and goes in the body, with things that move from inside to out and those that go from outside to in, parallels the concern with what goes inside and outside of the house and reflects the larger preoccupation with the boundaries of the family and their protection. Through bodily orifices pollution can occur" (201–202). A particularly good illustration of Dubisch's findings comes from the Greco-Roman Jewish text *Joseph and Aseneth.* In this text, which was probably written in Hellenistic Egypt between the first century B.C.E. and the second century C.E., Joseph expresses the following concerns about becoming attached to the as-yet-unconverted Aseneth who eats idolatrous food and blesses idols with her mouth:

> It is not fitting for a man who worships God, who will bless with his mouth the living God and eat blessed bread of life and drink a cup of immortality and anoint himself with blessed ointment of incorruptibility to kiss a strange woman who will bless with her mouth dead and dumb idols and eat from their table of strangulation and drink from their libation cup of insidiousness and anoint herself with ointment of destruction. (8.5; translated by Christoph Burchard, in James H. Charlesworth, ed., OT *Pseudepigrapha* 2)

As the above notes make clear, the list of virtues and vices has much in common with Jewish ethical teaching, and the association of idolatry with sexual vice is the most striking example of this correspondence. Rather than simply being viewed as the repetition of ethical patterns, these ethical exhortations should be seen as reflecting concerns about the preservation of distinct identity that members of Pauline communities shared with Jews (even though they came to reject some of the specific practices that were central to the preservation of Jewish identity). Careful analysis of the list may even shed light upon some of the daily challenges associated with this effort to preserve a distinct identity. Here it is especially interesting to consider the reference to "greed which is idolatry" in v. 5 (cf. Eph 3:5). While this may simply be a way of linking sexual appetite with idolatry, it is possible that the phrase reflects an awareness of the temptations faced by believers in their contacts with nonbelievers. It has been suggested that the verse refers to the tendency for those who are wealthy to cultivate contact with pagans for business purposes, greatly increasing the chances of consumption of idolatrous foods at pagan banquets (Theissen 130–31). Taking the household code of 3:18–4:1 as evidence for the leadership of wealthy householders in the community, Harry Maier has argued that "the exhortation against greed will have had an important role in reminding well-to-do leaders of their primary allegiance to the church, especially when business concerns would have tempted them to form close associations with outsiders" (234). The problem of avarice was of significant concern in early church communities (see the notes on 3:5). In linking avarice to idolatry early church authors were following the lead of Jewish contemporaries (e.g., *T. Levi* 17.11; *T. Jud.* 18.2; 19.1). Indeed, preoccupation with pagan friends and the accumulation of wealth emerges as an important factor leading to apostasy in the early Christian work known as the *Shepherd of Hermas* (e.g., *Herm. Sim.* 4.5; 8.8.1-2; 9.20.1; *Herm. Vis.* 3.6.5; *Herm. Man.* 10.1.4; on the challenges faced by slaves with respect to the sexual ethics outlined in 3:5 see the interpretation of 3:18–4:1).

Jerome Neyrey has defined the strong cultural expectation of deception (cf. Matt 23:8; Mark 7:6; Luke 12:1) in the Mediterranean world as "the presumption that arises that one's world is full of disguised enemies; it is difficult to tell friends from foes and the stakes are high: loss of honor and even bodily harm and death" ("Deception" [1993] 40). Against such strong cultural expectations community members are told not to lie—clearly a very significant sign of their new identities (3:9). Their dealings with each other should not simply be as they were before. Any inclination to compete on the basis of special claims to heavenly mysteries (cf. 2:18) must be rejected in favor of humility. Any community problems stemming from cultural diversity or differences in social status (e.g., slave or free) need to be dispelled in the spirit of forgiveness. Among the virtues that God's chosen ones are to put on, love is the most important. It is the bond that holds believers together as one body—a new humanity. The vices in 3:5-17 point to a world that must continually be rejected, but the virtues are visible signs of a new world that is continually being realized.

The sins of speech listed in v. 8 find a powerful antidote in community worship: thanksgiving prayers, accounts of the "word of Christ," spiritual singing, and proclamations in the name of the Lord. Moreover, Col 3:16-17 makes it clear that worship is not an isolated event but should shape daily life: "And whatever you do in word or deed, do all things in the name of the Lord Jesus." Given that the rejection of certain rites is so central to the critique of the false teaching in 2:16-23, the inclusion of a description of ritual behavior that was viewed as appropriate to life in Christ is especially significant. These rituals all involve speech and offer no suggestion of ascetic practices (cf. Eph 4:29). Together with baptism, the experience of community gatherings is central to the author's efforts to ensure that members continue to live their lives in Christ Jesus the Lord, in the manner in which they originally received him (2:6). The author of Colossians actually uses hymns to teach (see Aletti [1981]; Deichgräber; J. T. Sanders [1971]). The most obvious example of this is the use of the Christ-hymn in Col 1:15-20 and its accompanying interpretation in 1:21-23. The author appears to have adopted a hymn that was familiar to the audience and interpreted it in order to launch the argument against the proponents of the false teaching (see the notes and interpretation on 1:15-23). In 3:16 the author recommends the same process to community members. They are to teach and admonish each other "in all wisdom with psalms, hymns, and spiritual songs."

While it may not be immediately clear to modern readers, the frequent references to thanksgiving/gratitude in 3:15-17 also would have come as powerful reminders of the priorities of the community. Such language resonates with the prominence of the system of patronage in the ancient world (see the notes and interpretation on 1:3-8). The Greek terms are all derivatives of the word *charis*, grace—translated as "gratitude" in 3:16. The specific Greek terms that are rendered in English as "be thankful" in v. 15 were often employed in the ancient world by clients who wished to express their gratitude to their patrons or benefactors (see the notes on 3:15). Such expressions of gratitude presuppose an acknowledgement of dependence on the patron and the patron's ultimate authority. Grace is a favor that God bestows on God's people (cf. 1:6). For people in the first-century Mediterranean world the receipt of God's grace would naturally imply obligations to be faithful to God and to obey God (see Malina, "Grace–Favor" [1993]).

For Reference and Further Study

Aletti, Jean-Noël. *Colossiens 1:15-20*. Rome: Pontifical Biblical Institute, 1981.
Attridge, Harold A. "On Becoming an Angel: Rival Baptismal Theologies at Colossae," in Lukas Bormann, Kelly Del Tredici, and Angela Standhartinger, eds., *Religious Propaganda and Missionary Competition in the New Testament World: Essays Honoring Dieter Georgi*. Leiden: E. J. Brill, 1994, 481–98.
Charlesworth, James H., ed. *Old Testament Pseudepigrapha*. 2 vols. Garden City, N.Y.: Doubleday, 1983–1985.
Countryman, L. William. *Dirt, Greed, and Sex: Sexual Ethics in the New Testament and Their Implications for Today*. Philadelphia: Fortress, 1988.
Deichgräber, Reinhard. *Gotteshymnus und Christushymnus in der frühen Christenheit*. Göttingen: Vandenhoeck & Ruprecht, 1967.
MacDonald, Dennis Ronald. *There is No Male and Female: the Fate of a Dominical Saying in Paul and Gnosticism*. Philadelphia: Fortress, 1987.
MacDonald, Margaret Y. "Citizens of Heaven and Earth: Asceticism and Social Integration in Colossians and Ephesians," in Leif Vaage and Vincent Wimbush, eds., *Asceticism and the New Testament*. New York: Routledge, 1999, 269–98.

Maier, Harry O. "Purity and Danger in Polycarp's Epistle to the Philippians: The Sin of Valens in a Social Perspective," *Journal of Early Christian Studies* 1 (1993) 229–47.

Malina, Bruce J. "Eyes–Heart," in John J. Pilch and Bruce J. Malina, eds., *Biblical Social Values and Their Meaning: A Handbook*. Peabody, Mass.: Hendrickson, 1993, 63–67.

_____. "Grace–Favor," in ibid. 83–86.

_____. "Humility," in ibid. 107–108.

_____. "Love," in ibid. 110–14.

McVann, Mark. "Communicativeness (Mouth–Ears)," in ibid. 25–28.

Meeks, Wayne A. "The Image of the Androgyne: Some Uses of a Symbol in Earliest Christianity," *HR* 13 (1974) 165–208.

_____. "The Unity of Humankind in Colossians and Ephesians," in Wayne A. Meeks and Jacob Jervell, eds., *God's Christ and His People: Studies in Honour of Nils Alstrup Dahl*. Oslo, Bergen and Tromsö: Universitetsforlaget, 1977, 209–21.

Neyrey, Jerome H. "Deception," in Pilch and Malina, eds., *Biblical Social Values and Their Meanings: A Handbook*, 38–42.

Sanders, J. T. *The New Testament Christological Hymns*. MSSNTS 15. Cambridge: Cambridge University Press, 1971.

11. *The Households of Believers* (3:18–4:1)

18. Wives, be subject to your husbands, as is fitting in the Lord. 19. Husbands, love your wives and do not be embittered against them. 20. Children, obey your parents in everything, for this is pleasing in the Lord. 21. Fathers, do not provoke your children, or they may lose heart. 22. Slaves, obey in everything your masters according to the flesh, not with eye-service as men-pleasers, but with simplicity of heart, fearing the Lord. 23. Whatever you do, put your whole selves into it, as for the Lord and not for human beings, 24. knowing that from the Lord you will receive the reward of the inheritance. It is the Lord Christ you serve. 25. For the wrongdoer will be paid back for what was done wrong, and there is no partiality. 4:1. Masters, treat your slaves justly and fairly, knowing that you also have a master in heaven.

NOTES

18. *Wives, be subject to your husbands:* A section devoted to household ethics begins here. Colossians 3:18–4:1 appears to be an independent unit, only loosely connected to what comes before and after. This, coupled with the fact that similar

household teaching is found elsewhere in the NT and early Christian literature, suggests that the regulations were based on earlier traditional material
(cf. Eph 5:22–6:9; 1 Pet 2:18–3:7; 1 Tim 2:8-15; 3:4; 6:1-2; Titus 2:1-10; 3:1; Ign.
Pol. 4:1–5:1; Pol. *Phil.* 4:2–6:1). This traditional material appears to draw its origins from the *topos* "concerning household management," the classical expression of which is found in the teachings of Aristotle, though it was also
common in the philosophical and moral discussions of Greco-Roman society
(see the interpretation below). The first of three pairs appears in this verse.
The structure is similar throughout with each pair being assigned reciprocal
responsibilities. In fact, a comparison of various versions of the household
code in early Christian writings reveals the use of a predictable schema. An
address is typically followed by an imperative verb. Sometimes an amplification occurs and frequently a reason clause provides motivation or theological
justification (see Verner 84–91). In this verse the first two and the last of these
elements are present. The imperative of the verb *hypotassō* occurs, meaning to
be subject to or subordinate to someone else. Its use reflects common cultural
values about the authority of the head of the household, the *paterfamilias*. In
contrast to Eph 5:21-22 the use of the verb is not softened by notions of mutual
submission. Its use in 3:18 invites comparison to 1 Cor 14:34 where the subjection of wives (as opposed to women in general) to husbands is also in view.
Some have argued that 1 Cor 14:33b-36 represents an editorial gloss (i.e., it
was not part of the original correspondence) intended to harmonize Paul's
teaching with deutero-Pauline works, especially 1 Timothy (cf. 1 Tim 2:8-15).
If this is the case, then it would add weight to the argument that the household codes represent a more "patriarchal" position with respect to women
than can be found in the undisputed epistles (see the interpretation).

as is fitting in the Lord: This clause provides the motivation or theological justification for the previous command (see the notes on the previous phrase).
There is an unexpected use of the imperfect of *anekō* to refer to the present: "as
is fitting, as is proper" *(anēken).* It may stem from an attempt to stress that "behind the present fittingness lies a past determination of what was proper" (see
Harris 178–79; see also BDF 358.2). The REB translation captures this sense:
"that is your Christian duty." (However, this much less literal translation sac-
rifices the impact of the last expression, "in the Lord," that is so central to providing theological justification for the command.) Indeed, the use of the verb
in the literature of the day was very much bound up with notions of duty (cf.
Schlier, *TNDT* 1:360; 3:437–40). The Stoic conviction that it was one's duty to
live in harmony with the natural order of things (which would have included
the natural order of the household) is evidenced in Hellenistic Jewish literature and the NT (e.g., Rom 1:20; Eph 5:4; see the citation of further evidence in
Dunn 248). Thus it is not entirely clear whether community members are
being instructed about what is naturally fitting, and hence also fitting for
those who are in the Lord, or whether "fitting in the Lord" actually implies a
distinctly Christian vision of the household. As Dunn observes, the expression
can be taken "as a qualification that only that degree of subjection to the husband which is 'fitting in the Lord' is to be countenanced" (248). Scholars differ

with respect to the weight they attach to "in the Lord" (cf. 3:20; 4:7, 17). It has sometimes been understood as an addition largely designed to Christianize the current social ethic (see Schüssler Fiorenza 253). At the other end of the spectrum it has been judged to be an indication that "the entire life, thought, and conduct of believers is subordinated to the lordship of the Kyrios" (Lohse 156). It is argued below that when understood in light of the problems in Colossae the household code reveals the strong convictions of a household transformed in the Lord even if to onlookers this household might have had a largely conventional appearance.

19. *Husbands, love your wives and do not be embittered against them:* Here husbands are enjoined to avoid any bitterness toward their wives—never to treat their wives harshly. To become bitter *(pikrainō)* is a verb that occurs only here in the Pauline correspondence, but it is used in the *Shepherd of Hermas* (a second-century Christian work) to describe a result of ill temper (*Herm. Man.* 10.2.3). The attitude that is recommended recalls 3:12-14 where love also reigns supreme and the virtues of compassion, kindness, humility, gentleness, patience, and forgiveness rule out any harshness or bitterness. Love here most likely has deep spiritual significance. The marriage relationship is infused with the special bond of love that comes with life in Christ (cf. 1:4; see the notes on 3:14). The household code of Colossians is the most succinct of all such codes in the NT. In the parallel text of Eph 5:22-33 the author develops a detailed comparison of the marital relationship and the love relationship between Christ and his church. For other uses of the verb "to love" *(agapaō)* in Pauline literature see Rom 8:37; Gal 2:20; Eph 2:4; 5:2, 25.

20. *Children, obey your parents in everything:* The verb "to obey" *(hypakouō)* is very close in meaning to the verb "be subject to" *(hypotassō)* used in v. 18. This is illustrated by the use of these verbs in 1 Pet 3:5-6 where the holy women are described as having been subject to their husbands, as Sarah obeyed Abraham. The importance of the obedience of children is rooted in the fourth commandment (cf. Exod 20:12 [cited in Eph 6:2]; Deut 5:16); it was central to both Jewish (e.g., Philo, *Spec. Leg.* 2.225-36) and Greco-Roman ethical teaching (Dionysius of Halicarnassus, *Rom. Ant.* 2.2.26.1-4; for further citations and a full discussion of the evidence see Lincoln [1990] 400–401). It is important to note here that the children are addressed directly. They were clearly present during the assembly when the epistle would probably have been read aloud. The address and imperative verb are followed by an amplification ("in everything")—a typical feature of the NT household codes (see the notes on 3:18).

for this is pleasing in the Lord: This clause provides the theological justification for the previous command. Some English translations here take the expression *en kyriǭ* (in the Lord) to be the equivalent of *tǭ kyriǭ* (to the Lord): "for this is pleasing to the Lord" (NAB; cf. NIV; NJB), but this masks the parallel with v. 18 where the expression "in the Lord" also occurs. The dative expression "to the Lord" is indeed what would be expected here, and this is what actually occurs in Eph 5:10. The usual Pauline expression is "pleasing or acceptable to God" (cf. 2 Cor 5:9; Rom 12:1; 14:18; Phil 4:18). Although it is not present in the Greek text, we should perhaps take "to God" or "to the Lord" as implied after "pleasing." Thus the reference would be to behavior that not only pleases God but also is appropriate for those who belong to the Lord or are in the Lord (cf. REB; see Harris 180). The adjective "pleasing" *(euarestos)* was used in the ancient world to refer to behavior that is in keeping with established social values (see Gnilka [1980] 220). This sense appears clearly in Titus 2:9 where the term refers to the demeanor that slaves should have in relation to their masters. The reference to behavior that is pleasing suggests bestowing honor on one's patron or master.

21. *Fathers:* In contrast to the reference to both parents in the previous verse, here we have a reference to the father only (note that the NJB takes it as referring to both parents). Since the instructions involve a warning to fathers about being too harsh, the specific reference to fathers is especially appropriate. Greco-Roman society gave extreme authority *(patria potestas)* to the father over the children. The extent of this power is shocking in comparison to modern standards. The best-known aspect of this power was the right of the father to decide the fate of a newborn. Unwanted daughters could be exposed, and "deformed" infants could be killed. A father's authority extended even over the lives of adult children. Also surprising from a modern perspective is the fact that in case of divorce the father retained possession of the children. As Dionysius of Halicarnassus wrote about fatherhood among the Romans:

> The law-giver of the Romans gave virtually full power to the father over his son, whether he thought proper to imprison him, to scourge him, to put him in chains, and keep him at work in the fields, or to put him to death; and this even though the son were already engaged in public affairs, though he were numbered among the highest magistrates, and though he was celebrated for his zeal for the commonwealth. (*Rom. Ant.* 2.26.4; cited in Lincoln [1990] 398–99)

It is not surprising, therefore, that the power of the *paterfamilias* over the child could be compared to the power of the *paterfamilias* over a slave (*Rom. Ant.* 2.27.1; note the metaphorical comparison of slaves and sons that Paul employs in Gal 4:1-7).

Within Judaism fathers did not have such rights over the lives of newborn children and pagan practices such as exposure and abortion were condemned (e.g., Philo, *Spec. Leg.* 3.108-119; *Hypoth.* 7.7; for further examples and full discussion see Lincoln [1990] 400). However, the authority of fathers was clearly also of paramount importance in Judaism (e.g., Philo, *Spec. Leg.* 2.225-27; Philo, *Decal.* 119-20, 165-67), and it included the administration of physical punishment (e.g., Philo, *Spec. Leg.* 2.232; Josephus, *C. Apion.* 2.206; 2.217; cf. Lev 20:9; Deut 21:18-21). Both Jewish and Greco-Roman authors sometimes warned against excessive severity and it is difficult to be certain how often extreme measures were actually carried out (see the detailed discussion in Lincoln [1990] 398–402). However, against such a background, at the very least the instructions found in Colossians appear to be in keeping with moderate approaches.

do not provoke your children, or they may lose heart: In contrast to 2 Cor 9:2 (the only other instance of the term in the NT), the verb *erethizō* (to provoke, irritate, or exasperate) is used negatively. Some manuscripts (A C D* F G *al*) substitute *parorgizō* (to make angry), harmonizing the verse with Eph 6:4. The reference to the possibility of losing heart or becoming discouraged *(athymeō)* actually gains new meaning when one seeks to understand it within the context of a first-century early church community. Dunn writes: "To belong to such a strange sect, a religion without a cult center, without priest and sacrifice, must have exposed the younger members of the Christian families of Colossae to some abuse from their fellows in the marketplace. Without strong parental encouragement, they could easily become 'discouraged'" (252; RSV; see also the interpretation below). In contrast to Eph 6:4, the succinct teaching in Colossians makes no reference to the role of parents in the education of their children.

22. *Slaves, obey in everything your masters according to the flesh:* The instructions concerning the slave-master pair are much more detailed than the other instructions in the household code of 3:18–4:1. However, the instructions to slaves in this verse are very similar in form to the instructions to children in v. 20. The same verb, "to obey" *(hypakouō)* occurs in both verses and in both cases it is amplified by the words "in everything" (see the notes on 3:18; on the similarities between the position of slaves and the position of children with respect to the *paterfamilias* see the notes on 3:21). As was also noted with respect to children, the fact that slaves are addressed directly offers indisputable evidence of their presence in the community. The same term is used in Greek for both Lord and master: *kyrios*. The author draws upon this linguistic relationship for teaching purposes. There is a contrast between a master according to the flesh and a master (Lord) in heaven (cf. 4:1; 3:24 has "Lord Christ"). The expression "according to the flesh" *(kata sarka)* probably means "earthly" and is often translated as such (e.g., NRSV; REB), but it could also refer to "the sphere in which the service-relation holds true" (BAGD 459). Thus the NJB translates the expression as "according to human reckoning." The contrast between the earthly and heavenly realms is central to the dispute in the community (see the notes and interpretation on 2:8-23). Colossians 3:22 contains the last of the many references to flesh *(sarx)* in the letter (it is found also in 1:22, 24; 2:1, 5, 11, 13, 18, 23), including two in the treatment of the false teaching (2:16-23). (On the institution of slavery and life in the church see also the notes and interpretation on 3:11.)

not with eyeservice as men-pleasers, but with simplicity of heart: The term *ophthalmodoulia* (eyeservice – literally enslavement to the eye, linking the condition to the situation of slaves) is found only here and in Eph 6:6 in the NT and is not found outside the NT. It is most often understood as service that is rendered while the master is watching (e.g., NRSV; NAB; NJB; NIV). But it might also refer to service that is concerned only with external appearances or service designed to catch the attention of one's masters (cf. REB). This latter possibility would link the concept very closely with the next expression: *hos anthrōpareskoi* (as men-pleasers; in the NT the term is found only here and in Eph 6:6; cf. 2 *Clem.* 13:1). Men-pleasers are slaves who act in a certain fashion in order to please people (those who curry favor; see REB; NAB; NIV). The expression *en haplotēti kardias* (with simplicity of heart) can also mean "wholeheartedly" (e.g., NRSV; NJB), "with singleness of heart" (Lohse), "with sincerity of heart" (Dunn), or even with "single-mindedness" (REB; although this translation obscures the reference to the heart in Greek). It refers to the type of single-mindedness involved in total commitment. In the biblical world, the eyes and heart were understood as closely connected; they were central to one's thinking, orientation, and commitments. They represented the zone of "emotion-infused thought" (Malina [1993] "Eyes–Heart," 64). What is being demanded here is complete commitment to one's master (on the situation of slaves who had nonbelieving masters see the interpretation below).

fearing the Lord: The verb used here is *phobeō*: to fear, be afraid, have reverence (BAGD 862–63). The participle "fearing" probably refers to the whole attitude of obedience rather than simply to the last expression, "simplicity of heart." The use of the article distinguishes the Lord Christ (cf. v. 24) from the earthly master (see Harris 183). This phrase offers motivation for slaves to obey their earthly masters. "Fearing God" is a frequent expression in the OT (e.g., LXX Exod 1:17, 21; Lev 19:14, 32; 25:17; Ps 54:20) and it is also found in the NT (e.g., 1 Pet 2:17; Rev 11:18; 14:7; 19:5). The reference to fearing the Lord, however, is unusual, suggesting that Christ must be obeyed (see Lohse 160). The expression is found only here in the NT (hence, in some mss. including 𝔓⁴⁶, it has been altered to read "fear of God"). Its use is probably related to the fact that the relationship between subordinate members of the household and their superiors is being discussed. Colossians 3:22 calls to mind 1 Peter, in which believers are also instructed to fear God (1 Pet 2:17; cf. 1 Pet 1:17). "Fear" is also mentioned in the instructions concerning marriage in 1 Pet 3:1-6. At the end of this text women (probably especially those who are married to nonbelievers) are instructed: "never let fears alarm you" (1 Pet 3:6; cf. 1 Pet 3:14 NRSV). They are instead to fear God. But the attitude they are to adopt toward their husbands is one of circumspect submission (1 Pet 3:1-2). This is in keeping with the teaching of contemporary philosophers who taught that wives were to fear their husbands (e.g., Xenophon, *Concerning Household Management* 7.25; cf. Eph 5:33). The hope is that their reverent (literally "in fear," *en phobō*) behavior—their exemplary display of what it is like to emulate the fear of God—will lead their partners to accept Christ (1 Pet 3:2; see M. Y. MacDonald [1996] 198; note that in 1 Pet 2:18 slaves are called to submit themselves in fear to their masters). Similarly in Colossians the notion of fearing the Lord points to the ultimate commitment of slave-believers to the Lord Christ, but at the same time describes that commitment as rooted in cultural expectations of appropriate behavior of slaves to their masters.

23. *Whatever you do, put your whole selves into it, as for the Lord and not for human beings:* The expression "put your whole selves into it" might be translated more literally as "work from the soul" (*ek psychēs ergazesthe*). But the soul here is not some disembodied spirit. As Dunn puts it, the "translation 'soul' easily causes confusion because of the more typically Greek idea of the soul as the real person confined within the material body" (255). In this text the soul is an inner dynamic source from which all thinking and doing proceeds. In the Bible an

individual's very life or essence is often called "soul" (see Malina [1993] "Eyes–Heart," 64). As in the previous verse, the focus here is on total commitment. The motivation is not based on human relations or institutions. Slaves are ultimately serving the Lord and not human beings. It is interesting to note that actions for the sake of what is purely human are seen as a characteristic of the false teaching that threatens the community (cf. 2:8, 22).

24. *knowing that from the Lord you will receive the reward of the inheritance:* "Knowing that" *(eidotes hoti)* is a typical way of introducing a well-known fact in the Pauline correspondence (e.g., 4:1; Rom 5:3; 6:8-9; 2 Cor 4:13-14; 5:6; see Harris 185). The term for "reward" *(antapodosis)* occurs only here in the NT and elsewhere usually refers to just punishment or retribution (e.g., LXX Jer 51:56-57; Hos 9:7; see Lohse 161), but here it is used in a positive sense perhaps in an attempt to draw a contrast between the punishments often received when one is a slave and the rewards of the Lord. There is a reversal of cultural expectations inherent in the notion that real slaves receive the reward of inheritance. With metaphorical language Paul highlights the benefits of divine inheritance by contrasting it with enslavement: "For all who are led by the Spirit of God are children of God. For you did not receive a spirit of slavery to fall back into fear, but you have received a spirit of adoption. When we cry 'Abba! Father!' it is that very Spirit bearing witness with our spirit that we are children of God, and if children, then heirs, heirs of God and joint heirs with Christ—if, in fact, we suffer with him so that we may also be glorified with him" (Rom 8:14-17 NRSV; cf. Gal 4:7). The term *klēronomia* (inheritance) occurs only here in Colossians, but a cognate of the term is also in 1:12 *(klēros).* The concept of inheritance is central in Ephesians (cf. Eph 1:14, 18; 5:5).

It is the Lord Christ you serve: Various textual witnesses sought to smooth over the abruptness of the text at the beginning of this phrase (see the list of mss. in Harris 185; some actually add *gar* [for]). Many translators understand the expression as an indicative and it is presented as such here (e.g., NRSV; REB; NJB), but it is also possible to take the phrase as an imperative (e.g., "be slaves of the Lord Christ" [NAB]). (For a full discussion of the arguments in favor of both views see Harris 185–86.) The expression "the Lord Christ" is used to distinguish the Lord from human lords (see the notes on 3:22). The only other use of the specific title "Lord Christ" is in Rom 16:18; the more common expressions are "Lord Jesus Christ" or "Lord Jesus."

25. *For the wrongdoer will be paid back for what was done wrong, and there is no partiality:* "The wrongdoer" probably refers to the conduct of slaves, since the specific teaching to masters clearly begins with the address in 4:1. The use of the verb *komizō* (get back; be requited for; be paid back) is closely related to the notion of reward in v. 24. It refers to fitting payment, and in the case of judgment, fitting punishment (cf. Prov 22:8; 2 Macc 13:8; 1 Cor 3:13; 2 Pet 2:13). The NJB aims to highlight the notion of a just recompense by translating the term as, "Anyone who has done wrong will be paid back in kind" (see Dunn 258). The term "partiality" *(prosōpolēmpsia)* is found only in early Christian literature and was formed from the Hebrew idiom "to raise [= accept] the face of a humble suppliant" (i.e., show partiality or favoritism; see Harris 187; Lohse,

TDNT 6:779–80). But with God's judgment there is no such favoritism (cf. Rom 2:11; Eph 6:9). It is likely that this statement is intended to motivate slaves not only by warning them of the dangers of non-compliance, but also by encouraging them with respect to the justice of God. They might well have heard a promise in this statement that the injustice of masters would be called to account on a day when there will be no distinction between masters and slaves (cf. Eph 6:9; see Schweizer [1982] 226–27). The verse prepares the way for the warning to masters that they themselves have a master in heaven.

4:1. *Masters, treat your slaves justly and fairly, knowing that you also have a master in heaven:* The very brief instruction to masters is in contrast to the much more detailed teaching directed at slaves. This might indicate that relatively few slaveowners were part of the community in comparison to the number of slaves, but this is far from certain. The verse does not constitute a general call for the emancipation of slaves, but rather a demand that masters not abuse their authority. The manumission of slaves in due course might form part of these just and fair actions (see the interpretation below). Being "just" *(dikaios)* and "fair" *(isotēs)* were frequently listed together in the popular philosophy and moral teaching of the day (see Lohse 162). (On the just treatment of slaves in Jewish sources see Exod 20:10; Lev 25:43, 53; Sir 4:30; Philo, *Spec. Leg.* 2.66-68, 89-91; 3.137-43; *Pseudo-Phocylides* 223–27, cited in Dunn 259). *Isotēs* can actually also mean "equality" (BAGD 381), but it is highly unlikely that it is used in this sense with respect to slaves in a first-century context. The participle "knowing" should be taken as offering the reason and motivation for encouraging masters to treat their slaves justly and fairly: they are only earthly masters (see the notes on 3:22); they themselves also have a master in heaven. (The word for lord and for master is the same in Greek.) Both slaves and masters owe obedience to the one Lord. In essence the masters are being warned that in the final judgment they will be held accountable for their treatment of slaves. While the slave-master authority structures are still in place, the last phrase clearly relativizes the status of masters within the early church community.

INTERPRETATION

The origin and function of the NT household codes have long interested scholars. The extent to which these codes represent an adoption of traditional material from society at large has been debated. Some commentators view the codes as offering insight into a specifically Christian way of life, but others have seen very little in these codes that separates church ethics from the general environment and have viewed such phrases as "in the Lord" largely as additions intended to legitimate the adoption of conventional social ethics. In the case of Colossians the role the household code plays within the broader concerns of the letter has not even seemed entirely clear; the code appears to be a self-contained unit, which was inserted into the letter rather abruptly. However, it is argued below that the code is by no means only an afterthought, but rather is integral to the message of the letter and to the stance being adopted in relation to the false teaching.

Despite ongoing debate about the extent of Christian influence on the Colossian household code, it is generally accepted today that Col 3:18–4:1 (like the other NT codes) draws its origin from the traditional *topos* "concerning household management" that appears frequently in the literature of the ancient world. The work of David Balch has been central to illustrating the connection between the NT codes and this *topos*. The most important example of the *topos* is found in Aristotle's *Politics* 1, where Aristotle states that discussion of the component parts of the state must begin with consideration of household management:

> Hence there are by nature various classes of rulers and ruled. For the free rules the slave, the male the female, and the man the child in a different way. All possess the various parts of the soul, but possess them in different ways; for the slave has not got the deliberative part at all, and the female has it, but without full authority, while the child has it, but in an undeveloped form. (I. 1260a 9-14; cited in Balch [1981] 34–35)

Offering various examples from the Stoics, Hellenistic Jews, and Pythagoreans, Balch demonstrates that this classical expression of the *topos* "concerning household management" remained at home in the moral and philosophical teachings of the Roman Empire (Balch [1981] 51–59).

When we compare the *topos* as reflected in Aristotle's thought to the Colossian household code the importance of the theme of "ruling and being ruled" stands out sharply. Moreover, the same three pairs of relationships are present: wives-husbands, children-parents, and slaves-masters. Colossians contains no direct evidence of the notion of the household as a microcosm of the state, which frames Aristotle's discussion. However, other household codes in the NT suggest this idea. For example, the household code of 1 Peter is introduced as follows: "For the Lord's sake accept the authority of every human institution, whether of the emperor as supreme, or of governors, as sent by him to punish those who do wrong and to praise those who do right. For it is God's will that by doing right you should silence the ignorance of the foolish" (1 Pet 2:13-14 NRSV; cf. 1 Tim 2:1-3; Titus 3:1-2). While it does not refer to government authorities, the household code in Ephesians develops the idea of household relations reflecting the wider social reality: the obedience of wife to husband is viewed as a reflection of the obedience of church to Christ (Eph 5:22-33). Although it is not clearly articulated in the text there is every reason to suspect that convictions concerning the significance of household relationships for the wider social reality also underlie Colossians. Both epistles stress the authority of Christ as ruler of the cosmos and highlight the identity of believers as those who are ruled by royal power. The symbol of the church as the body of Christ ruled by its head plays a key role in communicating such ideas (e.g., Col 1:18-20, 21-22; 2:9-10, 19; 3:15; Eph 1:22-23; 4:15-16; 5:23, 30) and similarly draws upon traditional ideas, including the notion of the human body as a microcosm of the universe (see Dale B. Martin [1995] 16). In recent years scholars have frequently spoken about a probable correlation between the body symbolism that emphasizes the subordination of body (church) to head (Christ) in Colossians and Ephesians and the hierarchical household structures (e.g., D'Angelo 314–15; M. Y. MacDonald [1988] 154). The work of Averil Cameron invites us to think about how this correlation might have operated within a religious vision, encouraging the integration of members into the community of believers:

> Since human society was presented as naturally ordained according to hierarchical principles, in a context in which the same ordering with Christ as the head was seen as analogous to the human body, it provided the potential for a totally integrated rhetoric of God, community, and individual. (69)

In addition to its integrative function the household code of Colossians probably served some apologetic purposes. Balch has argued that the function of the household code in 1 Peter was apologetic and many scholars have taken up his views and applied them to other household codes (note, however, that Balch has been criticized by J. H. Elliott [1982] for stressing this feature of the household code at the expense of an integrative purpose; see Elliott 215–18). According to Balch, Christians are being exhorted to behave in an exemplary fashion in order to refute those who accuse them of promoting deviant behavior. In building his case he points to the apologetic use of the *topos* "concerning household management" by Jewish authors contemporary with the NT. For example, Philo writes, "Wives must be in servitude to their husbands, a servitude not imposed by violent ill-treatment but promoting obedience in all things. Parents must have the power over their children. . . . The same holds of any other persons over whom [a man] has authority" (*Apology for the Jews* 7.3, 5 LCL; cited in Balch [1981] 54). Balch draws attention to similar ideas found in Josephus, *C. Apion* (II.199–216), a text that closely parallels the apologetic *encomium* of Rome given one hundred years earlier by Dionysius of Halicarnassus in *Roman Antiquities* (I.9–II.29; written 30–7 B.C.E.; see Balch 54–55, 74–75). In a manner that recalls the accusations made against Jews in the Roman world (e.g.,Tacitus, *Histories* 5.5), early Christians of the second century C.E. were accused of disrupting society and upsetting the order of the household. The pagan intellectual Celsus, for example, described the early Christians as follows:

> In private houses also we see wool-workers, cobblers, laundry workers, and the most illiterate and bucolic yokels, who would not dare to say anything at all in front of their elders and more intelligent masters. But whenever they get hold of children in private and some stupid women with them, they let out some astounding statements as, for example, that they must not pay any attention to their father and school teachers, but must obey them; they say that these talk nonsense and have no understanding, and that in reality they neither know nor are able to do anything good, but are taken up with mere empty chatter. (Origen, *C. Cels.* Trans. Chadwick. 3.44)

Although direct evidence of such accusations comes from the second century there are indications in the NT that similar criticisms were experienced during the first century (see M. Y. MacDonald [1996]); the household codes may have been shaped by a desire to dispel such impressions. Moreover, it is interesting to note that it has recently been argued that the Christian household codes were actually on the conservative end of the spectrum when it came to what was often being lived out by women in Greco-Roman society (Tanzer 330–31). If the group was perceived as a social irritant it may have been especially important to ensure that church members exceeded the most conservative standards of the day.

The apologetic function of the Colossian household code is not as self-evident as in the case of the household code of 1 Peter. In 1 Peter the household teaching (2:18–3:7) includes a specific reference to the impression made on the nonbelieving head of the household (3:1-2), and it is clear that the community is experiencing slander and is suffering at the hands of outsiders (e.g., 2:15; 3:15-16). Colossians, however, also reflects concerns about the impressions believers make on nonbelievers, and there is good reason to believe that the community was experiencing criticism (see the notes and interpretation on 4:5-6). Moreover, there are indications in the NT household codes that the conversion of women and slaves who were part of pagan households was a source of tension between early church communities and the outside world (e.g., 1 Pet 3:1-6; 1 Tim 6:1-2). The strong recommendations for believers to be subordinate to the pagan *paterfamilias* seem to have been made for two main reasons: a desire to limit the potentially controversial visibility of these members and a recognition of their strategic opportunities to evangelize nonbelievers within the home. The wives, children, and slaves of nonbelievers are not explicitly singled out in the Colossian household code, but their membership in the community is by no means precluded by the ethical exhortations. In fact, one wonders whether the detailed exhortation to slaves may have been inspired at least in part by the difficulties caused by the membership of slaves whose masters were nonbelievers.

Because the exhortation to slaves is by far the longest exhortation in the Colossian household code scholars have looked primarily to it for evidence of the specific circumstances in the community that inspired the rule-like statements. Crouch, for example, has argued that the Colossian household code represents a reaction against enthusiasts who appealed to such baptismal slogans as Gal 3:28 (proclaiming the abolition of distinctions between Jew and Greek, slave and free, male and female) that stimulated social unrest among slaves (126). There are some difficulties, however, with Crouch's contentions (see the full discussion in M. Y. MacDonald [1988] 111–12). First, the author of Colossians happily quotes a version of the baptismal saying in Col 3:11 that includes a proclamation of the unity of slave and free and relativizes their status in the Lord (see the notes and interpretation on 3:11). Second, while the author of Colossians does take special care to exhort slaves this does not necessarily mean that a general problem existed with slaves seeking their freedom.

The extensive recent work of classicists, ancient historians, and scholars of early Christianity on the situation of slaves in the ancient world should prevent us from jumping too quickly to the conclusion that slaves seeking their freedom were a problem in the church at Colossae and that the author of Colossians is offering what amounts to a conservative backlash. For example, having considered the extensive new findings about the lives of slaves in the ancient world, J. Albert Harrill recently argued that in the contentious text of 1 Cor 7:21 Paul is actually exhorting "slaves who are offered manumission *indeed* to avail themselves of the opportunity and to *use freedom*" (127; cf. NRSV, which interprets the text differently). Harrill's interpretation takes account of the fact that Romans viewed manumission as "the regular reward for their deserving urban slaves" and Paul made room in his theology to accommodate the institutionalized exercise of manumission (127). Thus Paul's recommendations were very much in keeping with societal expectations. According to Harrill the situation that leads to the strong stance against manumission by Ignatius of Antioch (Ign. *Pol.* 4:3) was quite different from that faced by Paul in Corinth but still in keeping with the realities of Greco-Roman society. The Bishop of Antioch writes at the beginning of the second century C.E.: "Do not be haughty to slaves, either men or women; yet do not let them be puffed up, but let them rather endure slavery to the glory of God, that they may obtain a better freedom from God. Let them not desire to be set free at the Church's expense, that they be not found the slaves of lust" (LCL). Here what was at issue was not the individual master granting manumission to a slave, but rather the expectation that the church would purchase the freedom of slaves from funds out of its common chest. According to Harrill this text should not be taken as meaning that early Christians generally opposed the manumission of slaves. Pointing to

Roman perceptions that associations tended to recruit slaves and this could lead to social problems (citing Cicero and Plutarch), he argues that Ignatius' attitude reveals "his larger apologetic stratagem for outside social respectability and internal ecclesiastical unity under his own terms as a monarchical bishop" (Harrill 195; cf. 183).

Harrill's findings can help us raise questions about the significance of Col 3:22–4:1. When the *paterfamilias* is exhorted to treat his slaves fairly and justly in 4:1 this would presumably include the granting of manumission in due course as a reward for faithful service, but there are no immediate demands placed on masters to grant manumission, and slaves owe them unquestioning obedience. As the notes above make clear, the commitment of slaves to masters is reinforced in the strongest possible terms. Harrill's conclusions about the instructions concerning slaves by Ignatius of Antioch may shed light on this strong stance. If, as is suggested by the comparatively longer exhortation, slaves formed a significant part of the congregation, it may be that suspicion about active recruitment of slaves was fueling general suspicion about an illegitimate group. The situation would be especially volatile if many slaves were actually part of nonbelieving households. The author of Colossians would probably not have been in favor of the type of corporate manumission efforts for such slaves that Ignatius denounced. But it is by no means clear in the case of Colossians that slaves were collectively seeking manumission. When this issue is considered within the broader context of the epistle as a whole one wonders whether the more immediate danger for the slaves was the threat of false teaching.

In Colossians the condemnation of false teaching focuses on rituals and physical markers of identity (see the notes and interpretation on 2:8-23)—precisely the type of practices that would make members of the church, perhaps especially slaves, visible in society at large. It is important to recall that when we are talking about the visibility of early Christian groups in this period we are largely talking about the visibility of household life—either believers meeting together in a house, seeking to build a Christian home, or struggling to preserve Christian allegiance in the house of a pagan *paterfamilias*. To counter the false teaching the author of Colossians tells believers that they have been raised with Christ and ultimately belong with him in the heavenly realm (3:1-4; cf. 2:12-15). Fleshly or earthly measures recommended by the false teachers are irrelevant. (For points of contact between the household code and the polemic against the false teaching see the notes on 3:22 and 3:23.) In comparison, it is interesting to note the rhetorical strategy adopted by the author with respect to the institution of slavery: both slaves and masters are reminded of the contrast between the master (lord) according to the flesh and the master (Lord) in heaven. Both slaves and masters ultimately serve the same

Lord and are subject to the rewards and punishments of final judgment. But daily life for slaves is to be governed by fleshly masters. Even the slaves of nonbelievers are presumably to serve their masters with simplicity of heart. One would assume that the slaves of believing masters are to turn to their masters for guidance about which teaching is to be followed, how one should relate to outsiders, and generally how to live one's life in the Lord. Leadership structures are being put into place. The *paterfamilias* is becoming not only household leader, but house church leader as well (cf. 1 Tim 3:1-7).

Colossians 3:22–4:1 does not offer the kind of evidence that would allow us to draw firm conclusions about the activities of slaves in the community, but the new research on slaves in the ancient world is leading to a growing appreciation of the complex situation of slaves in early church communities. To complement the work of Harrill discussed above, Jennifer A. Clancy has recently drawn attention to the sexual availability of slaves to their masters and the use of slaves as prostitutes. She then goes on to ask questions about whether the fact that masters had control over the bodies of slaves presented obstacles to the participation of slaves in the Corinthian church, given the teaching against immorality and prostitution in 1 Corinthians 5–7. Colossians also includes detailed exhortation against sexual vice (see the notes and interpretation on 3:1-17). Would obedience to one's master have excluded willingness to provide sexual gratification? The participation of the slaves of nonbelievers in early church communities must sometimes have presented these slaves with impossible situations. One can imagine a Christian slave attempting to refuse sex to a nonbelieving master and this leading to the discovery of the slave's Christian allegiance. The sexual ethics adopted by the Pauline Christians would presumably have meant that Christian slaveowners would need to relinquish sexual relations with slaves. But reluctance on the part of some masters to give up past patterns (cf. 1:21-23; 2:20) might have made it especially important to warn them of their accountability before the Lord (3:25–4:1).

The acceptance of the institution of slavery in the NT often seems shocking to modern readers, while historically biblical texts have been used to justify acts of oppression (see Meeks [1996]). But it is important to recognize that the opportunities to exert political pressure or work for the reform of society were not available to the early Christians as they are to those of us who live in modern social democracies (Dunn 253). It is also important to recognize, however, that with the introduction of the household codes NT authors were moving in a specifically "patriarchal" direction that was not adopted by all branches of early Christianity (Schüssler Fiorenza 251–79). Colossians represents more than acceptance of the reality of slavery but seeks to reinforce the authority of the *paterfamilias* over the subordinate members of the household in very strong terms even if he is repeatedly warned against treating subordinate members harshly. There are points of continuity between the household code and Paul's earlier teaching on women and slaves (cf. 1 Cor 7:20-24; 11:2-16; 14:34-36; Phlm 10-20), but the rule-like statements are much more categorical, leaving less room for exceptional behavior on the part of some members. Particularly striking in the case of Colossians is the tension one senses between symbolism that calls for the ultimate rejection of the standards and priorities of society and household teaching that so clearly mirrors the standards and priorities of society. Mary Rose D'Angelo has drawn attention to the potential for a message of empowerment revealed in the baptismal imagery of Colossians. She points to the notion of putting off a fleshly body (2:11), and to the references to canceling a debtor's bond (2:14), to stripping the rulers and authorities and displaying them as captives (2:15); these last two ideas would have been especially meaningful to the slave members of the community (see the notes on 2:14-15). However, given the presence of the household code in the epistle, D'Angelo concludes that "these images are likely to have encouraged double consciousness in women and slaves, demanding that they deny their subjected status in the religious realm while submitting to it in the social world" (320).

While there is no doubt that the Colossian household code functions to sustain the patriarchal order of society and may contribute to a double consciousness, it may be that this double consciousness was part of a strategy for survival for Pauline Christians in a hostile environment. If one imagines being at a first-century church gathering (in Nympha's house, perhaps; see Col 4:15) where Colossians was read, one can sense something of its impact. All members, including most notably slaves, were addressed directly. No matter what social group one belonged to, one would be guaranteed a place and provided with a guide for living. The need for reciprocity of responsibility would be powerfully impressed by the concise nature of the exhortations. Even if one were a believing woman who was coming under pressure from a nonbelieving husband, or a believing slave who lived in fear of reprisals at the hands of a pagan master, one would be reminded that from the Lord one would receive the reward of inheritance. With God there is no partiality; in the final judgment no one group, no matter how powerful in the earthly realm, would experience favoritism. By the time one heard the proclamation of the household code one would have heard of one's own heavenly exaltation with Christ and one's membership in a spiritual body ruled by Christ at its head. Yet in adopting this largely conventional ethical stance one would be embracing a way of life that would very much resemble the life of one's neighbors. It would provide one with a good deal of invisibility in the Greco-Roman urban environment.

In many respects the ethos recommended by Colossians resembles the "inner asceticism" described by Walter O. Kaelber:

> More difficult to define, but perhaps also more significant, is what may be termed an "inner asceticism," consisting of spiritual rather than physical discipline. Such asceticism involves not detachment from or renunciation of any specific worldly pleasure but rather detachment from or renunciation of the world per se. It is reflected in the biblical attitude of being "in the world, but not of it," or in the Bhagavadgita's "renunciation in action, rather than renunciation of action." (442)

In calling subordinate members to take their place in a household ruled by the *paterfamilias* the author of Colossians is ensuring that the ethical ideals in the church match those of the outside world. Believers who are repeatedly told that they are not "of this world" in previous passages are nevertheless rooted firmly "in this world" for daily living by these ethical teachings. This "inner asceticism" is in direct contrast to the asceticism recommended by the false teachers, which includes visible, physical signs of world-rejection.

Rather than representing simply general and conventional ethical exhortations that are only tangentially related to the main interests of Colossians, I believe that the household code is fundamental to the response to the problem of false teaching. The author of Colossians calls members together as the spiritual body of Christ; they are to live in a manner that allows this body to become secretly integrated within household quarters —even houses where nonbelievers live. The spiritual body is also a place where such attention-drawing acts of asceticism as sexual renunciation and fasting have no place. Rituals associated with such practices are unnecessary (see the notes and interpretation on 2:8-23). In the face of growing hostility many of the physical-social boundary markers of religion seem to be eradicated. The inner asceticism recommended by the author of Colossians may have been expedient, but it was clearly not without its challenges. The ascetic practices and rituals propounded by the Colossian opponents were physical markers that would foster a distinct identity. They included Jewish practices that had a long history of serving this purpose (see the notes and interpretation on 2:16-23). In the conflict at Colossae one senses a struggle to determine how best to live out a Christian life that is distinct but not separated from mainstream society. Indeed, this is a struggle that is close to the heart of many Christians today.

In considering the function of the household code within the broader context of the epistle we need to treat one last issue. Anthropologists working on the issue of women and gender have warned of the dangers inherent in rapidly reaching conclusions about the implications of hierarchical authority structures. They have noted that patterns of male dominance are subject to significant cultural variations and that correlations should not be drawn too quickly between ideology and the actual shape of female power (see Rosaldo; Rosaldo and Lamphere). In fact, the mention of Nympha in Col 4:15 reinforces the need to exercise caution. Nympha is a woman leader of a house church (see the notes and interpretation on 4:15) who is mentioned in the context of a letter that includes exhortations calling for the subordination of wives to husbands. How, then, are we to understand the relationship between a patriarchal ideology and the reality of a woman's life? The theoretical distinction between power and authority has emerged as important in anthropological discussions. Power is defined as "the ability to gain compliance," while culturally legitimated authority is defined as "the recognition that it is right" (Rosaldo and Lamphere 21). Thus the authority granted to the *paterfamilias* in Col 3:18–4:1 is an example of "culturally recognized authority"; it represents an acknowledgment that the power granted to the *paterfamilias* in society at large is also right within the context of the early church. But this does not necessarily mean that women do not exercise power: "while authority legitimates the use of power, it does not exhaust it, and actual methods of giving rewards, controlling information, exerting pressure, and shaping events may be available to women as well as men" (Rosaldo and Lamphere 21). Anthropologists have even noted examples in which authority structures that confine women to the domestic sphere, and are seemingly intent on denying power to women, have actually created avenues for women to exercise power (Dubisch 18; see the full discussion of these concepts and their relevance for understanding early Christian texts in M. Y. MacDonald [1996] 41–47).

These theoretical reflections can have a direct bearing on our understanding of the household codes in the NT. The household code material found in 1 Pet 3:1-6 illustrates their relevance especially well. Here obedient Christian wives are directed to display modest silence in order that their nonbelieving husbands might "be won over without a word by their wives' conduct" (1 Pet 3:1 NRSV). The authority of the husband over his wife is proclaimed in conventional terms, but the exhortation also contains an indirect acknowledgment of the power of the woman to lead her husband to the faith. This acknowledgment takes place even though according to the norms of society at large it was the prerogative of the *paterfamilias* to determine the religion of the household (cf. Plutarch, *Moralia* 140D; see M. Y. MacDonald [1996] 44–47, 195–204). Thus, when understood within their context, texts that appear only to reinforce conventional attitudes may in fact include elements that challenge the status quo. By remaining in the home of unbelievers, wives (and potentially also slaves and children; cf. *Letter* 107, Jerome to Laeta) were in a position to contribute to the expansion of Christianity. No doubt the situation was often very difficult and the cause of considerable suffering (cf. 1 Pet 3:6; 1 Cor 7:12-16). Colossians 3:18–4:1 presents a vision of a harmonious, ordered Christian household, but may well have spoken to much more complicated family arrangements including to slaves, children, and wives in the congregation who were part of nonbelieving households. In the end it is important to remember that the household codes are ethical ideals and do not tell the whole historical story; they need to be understood in light of the realities of an emerging Christianity in competition with other social groups and subject to hostility from outsiders.

FOR REFERENCE AND FURTHER STUDY

Balch, David. *Let Wives be Submissive: The Domestic Code in 1 Peter.* SBL.MS 26. Chico: Scholars, 1981.
_____. "Household Codes," in David E. Aune, ed., *Greco-Roman Literature and the New Testament.* Atlanta: Scholars, 1988, 25–50.
Barclay, J. M. G. "Paul, Philemon, and the Dilemma of Christian Slave-Ownership," *NTS* 37 (1991) 161–86.
Clancy, Jennifer A. "Obstacles to Slaves' Participation in the Corinthian Church," *JBL* 117 (1998) 481–501.
Crouch, James E. *The Origin and Intention of the Colossian Haustafel.* Göttingen: Vandenhoeck & Ruprecht, 1972.
Dubisch, Jill. *Gender and Power in Rural Greece.* Princeton, N.J.: Princeton University Press, 1986.
Elliott, John H. *A Home for the Homeless.* London: S.C.M., 1982.
Finley, M. I. *Ancient Slavery and Modern Ideology.* New York: Viking, 1980.
Harrill, J. Albert. *The Manumission of Slaves in Early Christianity.* Tübingen: J.C.B. Mohr (Paul Siebeck), 1995.
Kaelber, Walter O. "Asceticism," in Mircea Eliade, ed., *The Encyclopedia of Religion.* New York: MacMillan, 1987, 1:441–45.
Käsemann, Ernst. "Sentences of Holy Law in the New Testament," in idem, *New Testament Questions of Today.* London: SCM, 1969, 66–81.
MacDonald, Margaret Y. "Citizens of Heaven and Earth: Asceticism and Social Integration in Colossians and Ephesians," in Leif Vaage and Vincent Wimbush, eds., *Asceticism and the New Testament.* New York: Routledge, 1999, 269–98.
Malina, Bruce J. "Eyes–Heart," in John J. Pilch and Bruce J. Malina, eds., *Biblical Social Values and Their Meaning.* Peabody, Mass.: Hendrickson, 1993, 63–67.
Martin, Dale B. *Slavery as Salvation: The Metaphor of Slavery in Pauline Christianity.* New Haven and London: Yale University Press, 1990.
_____. *The Corinthian Body.* New Haven and London: Yale University Press, 1995.
Meeks, Wayne A. "The 'Haustafeln' and American Slavery: A Hermeneutical Challenge," in Eugene H. Lovering, Jr., and Jerry L. Sumney, eds., *Theology and Ethics in Paul and His Interpreters: Essays in Honor of Victor Paul Furnish.* Nashville: Abingdon, 1996, 232–53.

Origen, *Contra Celsum.* Translated by Henry Chadwick. Cambridge: Cambridge University Press, 1953.

Rosaldo, Michelle Zimbalist. "The Use and Abuse of Anthropology: Reflections on Feminism and Cross-Cultural Understandings," *Signs* 5 (1980) 389–417.

Rosaldo, Michelle Zimbalist, and Louise Lamphere, eds. *Woman, Culture, and Society.* Palo Alto, Calif.: Stanford University Press, 1974.

Schüssler Fiorenza, Elisabeth. *In Memory of Her: A Feminist Theological Reconstruction of Christian Origins.* New York: Crossroad, 1983.

Schweizer, Eduard. "Traditional Ethical Patterns in the Pauline and Post-Pauline Letters and their Development (Lists of Vices and House-Tables)," in Ernest Best and Robert McLean Wilson, eds., *Text and Interpretation. Festschrift for Maxwell Black.* Cambridge: Cambridge University Press, 1979, 195–209.

12. *Prayer, Mission, and Contact with Outsiders* (4:2-6)

2. Persevere in prayer, keeping alert in it with thanksgiving; 3. at the same time pray also for us, in order that God may open a door to us for the word, to speak of the mystery of Christ for which I am in prison, 4. in order that I may reveal it, as I must speak. 5. Walk in wisdom toward outsiders, making the most of the time. 6. Let your speech be always gracious, seasoned with salt, so that you know how you should answer each one.

NOTES

4:2. *Persevere in prayer, keeping alert in it with thanksgiving:* In Pauline letters opening prayers are typically followed by a corresponding closing prayer (e.g., Rom 1:9-10; 15:30-32; Eph 1:15-23; 6:18-20; see Dunn 261). In the NT the idea of keeping alert or watchful *(grēgoreō)* is understood to be an appropriate attitude as the end of all things draws near (1 Thess 5:6, 10; 1 Pet 4:7). The idea is also associated with the avoidance of temptation. In the famous scene in the Garden of Gethsemane where Jesus waits for his arrest with Peter, James, and John, Jesus says to Peter: "Simon, are you asleep? Could you not keep awake one hour? Keep awake *[grēgoreō]* and pray that you may not come into the time of trial; the spirit indeed is willing, but the flesh is weak" (Mark 14:37-38 NRSV). Particularly important for the context of Colossians is that an attitude of watchfulness is also associated with the avoidance of false teaching in the NT (e.g., Acts 20:21; 1 Pet 5:8). Prayer and thanksgiving are singled out as fundamental to the life of the community in 3:15-17, the text that immediately precedes the household code, and here they are mentioned immediately following the household code. (For references to thanksgiving in Colossians see also 1:12-14 and 2:7.)

3. *at the same time pray also for us, in order that God may open a door to us for the word:*
The Greek term *hama* refers to two actions that occur simultaneously or at the
same time: the Colossians' general prayer (v. 2) and the specific prayer that is
demanded here (BAGD 42). "Us" could refer only to Paul, but more probably
it refers to the evangelical efforts he shares with coworkers such as Timothy
(1:1) and Epaphras (4:12-13; see Harris 193). The author of Colossians is using
a metaphorical expression to refer to opportunities for the spread of the
gospel message and the subsequent expansion of the early church. Paul uses
the same expression to refer to the door of opportunity in 1 Cor 16:9 and 2 Cor
2:12 (cf. Acts 14:27; Rev 3:8). Given the setting of early church communities in
house churches and the importance of the conversion of household units (e.g.,
1 Cor 1:16) to the expansion of early Christianity, one wonders if the use of this
architectural metaphor was particularly meaningful in this context. Colossians presupposes an atmosphere of church growth; the word is spreading
throughout the whole world (1:5-6; cf. 1:23). The Paul of Colossians may have
been expressing a desire to be able to preach even in captivity or perhaps re-
layed his hope of being released in order to resume his mission. He may have
hoped to convince those who held him captive. It is particularly interesting to
compare this text to Phil 1:12-14: "I want you to know, beloved, that what has
happened to me has actually helped to spread the gospel, so that it has become known throughout the whole imperial guard and to everyone else that
my imprisonment is for Christ; and most of the brothers and sisters, having
been made confident in the Lord by my imprisonment, dare to speak the word
with greater boldness and without fear" (NRSV). On prison posing no hindrance for the word of God preached by the apostle see also 2 Tim 2:9. Barth
and Blanke have noted that it is grammatically possible that the reference to
the door (literally, "to us a door of the word") indicates a distinction between
"the word of Paul and his co-workers" and the subsequent reference to mystery, thus highlighting a contrast between the word of Paul and his coworkers
and the word of the Colossians described in 4:5-6. They translate the verse as
"Pray also for us, that God may open a door for our word, to proclaim the secret, the Messiah" (Barth and Blanke 453–54). This view has not been widely
accepted due to the fact that "word" and "mystery" are equated in 1:25. The
term "word" and the concept of speech also play a key role in vv. 5-6, offering
an indication that both parts of this section are closely related.

to speak of the mystery of Christ for which I am in prison: The verb *laleō* (to speak)
probably means "to proclaim" in this context; what is in view here is the
proclamation of the word. The word is equated with the mystery of Christ
(REB: secret of Christ). Christ himself is the mystery here. Christ is the center
of Christian commitment. Similar notions are found in 1:25-27. (On the use of
the term *mystērion* in Colossians see the notes on 1:26.) The reference to Paul's
imprisonment means literally "to have been bound" *(deō)* or "to be in chains"
(NJB). (On Paul's imprisonment see also 4:10 and 4:18 [cf. Phil 1:12-14 cited
above].) Colossians contains no mention of where Paul was imprisoned.
Scholars who treat the letter as genuine have frequently argued that Paul composed Colossians in Rome near the end of his life, but others have argued in

favor of an earlier Ephesian imprisonment (see Lohse 165–67; see also the Introduction).

4. *in order that I may reveal it, as I must speak:* This phrase probably offers a second purpose for the prayer of the Colossians. According to v. 3 the Colossians should pray that Paul receive the opportunity to proclaim the gospel; here the prayer is for bold revelation. The verb *phaneroō* means to reveal, to manifest, to make known (see Harris 195). The NIV seeks to bring out this sense by departing from the literal Greek in including the imperative verb: "Pray that I may proclaim it clearly" (NIV; cf. NJB). To translate *phaneroō* as "to proclaim" in this case, however, links it a little too closely with the verb *laleō* (to speak) and masks the notion of the unveiling of mysteries. The same verb, *phaneroō*, also occurs in 1:26 and 3:4, reflecting traditional apocalyptic notions (see the notes). The concepts of mystery, hiddenness, and revelation work together as a schema in Pauline literature (what was previously hidden is now proclaimed publicly). Paul sometimes describes his own apostleship to the Gentiles with a particular focus on his role as one who reveals the secrets of God's plan (Rom 11:25-26; 1 Cor 2:7; 4:1; cf. Col 1:27-29; Eph 3:7-13). One senses something of Paul's "burning conviction and sense of destiny" in the use of the expression "as I must speak" (Dunn 264). "As I must" *(hōs . . . dei)* implies a sense of duty or compulsion. A similar grammatical construction *(pōs . . . dei)*, "how you should," occurs in v. 6, offering a further indication of the close connection between vv. 1-4 and 5-6 (see the notes on 4:3).

5. *Walk in wisdom toward outsiders:* In Pauline letters concluding remarks tend to reiterate important points or treat issues that were left unsaid earlier (e.g., Gal 6:1-16; see Dunn 164, 261). Colossians 1:10 instructs believers to "walk in a manner worthy of the Lord" and 1:9 refers to wisdom; Col 2:6-7 (a key text in the epistle serving as the conclusion for all of Col 1:1–2:5; see the notes on 2:6) speaks of walking in Christ. Colossians includes a positive evaluation of the role of wisdom in Christian existence (1:28; 2:3; 3:16), but denounces the claims to wisdom by those who adhere to false teaching (2:23; on wisdom see the notes on 1:9). Community members are clearly being invited to engage in discernment. The verb *peripateō* (to walk) is often used to refer to one's behavior, life, or conduct in Pauline literature. Given the interest in outsiders here it is particularly interesting to note that the ethical teaching of 1 Thess 4:1-12 culminates in the instruction that believers should behave (walk; *peripateō*) properly toward outsiders (v. 12). Translations such as "to conduct yourselves wisely" (NRSV) or "to act wisely" (NJB) of the Greek text in Col 4:5 tend to obscure the outward and truly active orientation of the expression in a first-century Mediterranean context. Walking in the world means visibly demonstrating the fruits of Christian existence (see the notes and interpretation on 1:10). The reference to outsiders *(tous exō)* represents strongly sectarian language (see the interpretation below), seemingly drawing a definite line between those who are inside and those who are outside the community. The expression also occurs in the undisputed letters of Paul, both in 1 Thess 4:12 (discussed above) and in 1 Cor 5:12-13, a text in which Paul calls members to focus on the moral standards of the believers.

making the most of the time: Colossians 4:5-6 has consistently been understood as reflecting missionary interests (e.g., Schweizer [1982]; Taylor and Reumann). The prayer for the success of Paul's mission in vv. 2-4 strongly suggests that the difficult expression "making the most of the time" (or using every opportunity) refers to evangelism (cf. 2 Thess 3:1-2). The verb *exagorazō* normally means "to buy," "to buy up," or "to redeem" (to buy back; cf. LXX Dan 2:8; see BAGD 271). Here the reference would be to making the most of time or to an opportunity that would otherwise be lost. Noting that the term "time" *(kairos)* frequently refers to eschatological time in the NT (e.g., 1 Cor 4:5; 7:29; 2 Cor 6:2) and the eschatological urgency of Paul's mission (e.g., Rom 11:13-15; 1 Cor 4:9), Dunn suggests that there might also be eschatological overtones in 3:5. Furthermore, he argues that this phrase should prevent us from assuming a loss of imminent expectation in Colossians (Dunn 266; see also the notes and interpretation on 3:1-4).

6. *Let your speech be always gracious, seasoned with salt:* The mention of speech (literally "the word," *ho logos*) connects the exhortation concerning the Colossians' interaction with outsiders to the prayer for the success of Paul's mission in 4:3: "that God may open a door to us for the word." The reference to gracious speech is literally to speech in grace or with grace *(en chariti)*. It may recall the use of the expression in 3:16 (minus the definite article), which refers to gratitude or thanksgiving; see the notes on 3:16), and the references to divine grace in 1:2, 6. But its use in conjunction with the expression "seasoned with salt" suggests that the more immediate meaning involves conventional notions concerning appropriate speech. The phrase reflects cultural norms with respect to pleasing speech and well-chosen words. Plutarch, for example, states: "For wit is probably the tastiest condiment of all. Therefore some call it 'graciousness' because it makes the necessary chore of eating pleasant" (*Moralia* 685A; cited in Lohse 168). Similarly, Plutarch states that people try to ingratiate themselves to each other by seasoning the occupations in which they are presently engaged with the salt of conversation (*Moralia* 514E-F; cited in Lohse 168). (On the use of salt as a metaphor in the NT see Matt 5:13; Mark 9:49-50; Luke 14:34-35. On the value of salt for flavor and as a preservative in the biblical world see Job 6:6.) With this phrase the Colossians are clearly being told not to turn their backs on outsiders, but to engage in conversation with them. The phrase also acknowledges the power of words to help one ingratiate oneself with listeners. The NJB aims to bring out these ideas: "Always talk pleasantly and with a flavor of wit."

so that you know how you should answer each one: The expression *pōs . . . dei* (here rendered as "how you should") is used to define how one must act, one's duty. A very similar grammatical construction referring to the necessity of the apostle's speech occurs in v. 4 (see the notes on 4:4). Paul's duties as an evangelist are evidently related to the duties of community members in general. The parallelism adds weight to the teaching directed at community members. The previous phrase calls for the use of appropriate words, but this phrase introduces an element of prudence. The instruction that believers should know how to answer outsiders is an indirect acknowledgment that wrong responses can lead to trouble. It is interesting to compare this text to 1 Pet 3:15-16 where more perilous relations with outsiders are of concern and the community is instructed always to be ready to make a defense *(apologia)* to anyone who questions them concerning the faith. But in a manner that resembles Col 4:5-6 community members are told that their dealings with nonbelievers should be characterized by gentleness and reverence *(pace* Dunn 267).

INTERPRETATION

As the notes above make clear, the two parts of 4:2-6, vv. 2-4 and vv. 5-6, are closely related. They are held together by a common goal of the spreading of the gospel and by a sense of obligation to speak to outsiders. In order to appreciate fully what was being asked of community members it is important to keep in mind that they were instructed by a suffering apostle, an apostle who was in prison. He asked community members to pray for the success of his ongoing mission despite the hindrances raised by his arrest and by his continuing absence from the community. There was hope for an open door, yet Paul was aware that an open door always meant risks. From his base in Ephesus he wrote to the Corinthians: "a wide door for effective work has opened to me, and there are many adversaries" (1 Cor 16:9 NRSV). In light of the risks to security so vividly illustrated by Paul's imprisonment believers must have been especially anxious for direction with respect to their dealings with outsiders. The fact that these directives were included among the final exhortations in the letter highlights their importance.

Colossians 4:2-6 combines strong mission motifs with a certain caution with respect to outsiders. The reference to "outsiders" offers an especially strong indication of the "sectarian" tendencies of the Pauline churches. The manner in which early Christian groups set themselves apart from society at large has led NT scholars to compare these groups to modern sects (e.g., Elliott [1982] 73–78). The hope is that this comparison will shed light upon the social forces at play as the group sought to define its identity (see the full discussion in M. Y. MacDonald [1988] 32–39). In one type of sect labeled "conversionist" by the sociologist Bryan Wilson there is a particularly strong tension between the desire to remain distinct from the outside world and the goal of mission. The compromising of sectarian values is an ever-present danger to groups that remain open to recruiting new members and continually in dialogue with the values of the outside world. This is in contrast with more "introversionist" sects that often physically separate themselves from the rest of society in the hope of guaranteeing isolation from an evil world (see Wilson [1967] 36–41).

Paul's burning desire to found new churches in the cities dotting the eastern Mediterranean is well known. However, it is also important to acknowledge that Paul's missionary priorities could shape the teachings he directed to his communities. For example, Paul acknowledges that the community's interaction with outsiders could lead to the expansion of the church when he points to the "conversion" of nonbelievers as a possible result of their observing the worship of the Corinthians (1 Cor 14:23-25). But the tension between evangelism and separation from outsiders identified by Bryan Wilson can also be seen in his ethical exhortations. One can sense Paul aiming to strike a balance between these tendencies in recommendations that call for the avoidance of idolatry on the one hand but that also steer well clear of recommending dissociation from nonbelievers on the other hand (e.g., 1 Cor 10:14-33). Colossians 4:2-6 also reveals this tension. The expansion of the church is clearly a priority and members are invited to engage in dialogue with outsiders, but caution is also recommended in dealings with them.

Colossians does not reflect the kind of concerns about persecution that one senses in 1 Peter (e.g., 1 Pet 4:12-19) or Revelation (e.g., Rev 2:9-11). However, given the element of prudence in Col 4:6, Dunn's description of a positive relationship with the outside community is probably an overstatement: "such advice envisages a group of Christians in a sufficiently positive relation with the surrounding community for such conversations to be natural, a group not fearful or threatened, but open to and in a positive relationship to its neighbors (even as 'outsiders,' 4:5)" (267). It is important to realize that the missionary priorities of Paul (or his disciple) would probably have led him to encourage interaction with outsiders even if considerable tension existed between church members and outsiders. Moreover, if one is aware of the tension between the desire to remain distinct from outsiders and the desire to win outsiders that existed in the Pauline churches from the earliest period, Col 4:2-6 takes on new significance. Nowhere else in the undisputed Pauline letters is there such detailed attention given to how to speak to outsiders (cf. 1 Thess 4:12); this suggests that problems were arising. Colossians 4:2-6 addresses how Christians should relate to their neighbors in the marketplace, in the baths, at the meal table, and so on (see Dunn 267), yet it is important to remember that by the second century such daily interactions were clearly giving rise to rumors about the disruptive effect of Christians on society and household (see M. Y. MacDonald [1996]); it may well be that Col 4:2-6 represents an attempt to offer guidance in light of the beginning of such problems. Moreover, the presence of the household code (3:18–4:1) in the epistle may well represent an attempt to silence such rumors (see the notes and interpretation on 3:18–4:1).

In seeking to understand the context of Colossians interpreters have tended to concentrate on the problem of false teaching. However, in my view this context also included increasingly tense relations between the church and the outside world. In fact, the advice the Colossians received concerning the false teaching may well have been shaped by rising tensions between the church and the world and a desire to secure the identity of the community in light of those tensions. It is interesting to note that adherence to the false teaching is depicted by the author of Colossians as regression into the world (Col 2:20). The result of the series of labels applied to the false teaching in Col 2:8 is a categorical rejection of it as a base and purely human phenomenon, not according to Christ (cf. Col 2:22). Thus believers are told that adherence to the false teaching will in no way grant them special status or spiritual benefits, but will cause them to merge with the world once again.

The critique of the false teaching focuses on rituals and ascetic practices that are closely related to visionary experience (see the notes and interpretation on 2:8-23). The author of Colossians' rejection of such measures calls to mind Paul's ambivalence concerning visions and ecstatic phenomena; his letters reflect an awareness that such highly visible displays were subject to misunderstanding both inside and outside the church (cf. 1 Corinthians 14; 2 Cor 5:11-13; 12:1-7). Moreover, studies of such early Christian texts as *The Acts of Paul and Thecla* have illustrated how asceticism in church circles could act as an irritant in Greco-Roman society. If, as was suggested earlier in this commentary, the Colossian false teaching included the conviction that removing the body of flesh in baptism meant a return to a primordial state of perfection where there was no longer male and female, the potential for controversy would be considerable (see the notes and interpretation on 3:11). In short, there seems to have been a good deal about this false teaching that would have increased tensions between the church and the outside world. Moreover, the author of Colossians seems aware of the fact that in vying for the allegiance of the Colossians he faces the reality of competition between groups. Does the command to know how to answer outsiders suggest that the false teachers may have been the more successful evangelists? Indeed, in anticipation of the discussion of false teaching that begins in 2:8 the Paul of Colossians offers the following warning: "I am saying this so that no one may deceive you with persuasive speech" (2:4).

In keeping the above reconstruction of the social situation of Colossians in mind it is valuable to consider what is being said about the respective roles of the apostle and the Colossians in 4:2-6. Paul is clearly depicted as the evangelist *par excellence* in 4:2-4. There is no need for circumspection when it comes to his mission. He is the revealer of mysteries whose efforts should not even be hampered by imprisonment. Colossians

4:5-6 envisions the Colossians as sharing in Paul's evangelical interests and may even represent a tacit acknowledgment of the importance of daily interactions with "outsiders" as a source of new members for the church. But the bold proclamations of Col 4:2-4 are replaced with carefully chosen words in Col 4:5-6. In much the same way as in the household code of 3:18–4:1, believers are offered a pattern of living in the world that allows them to remain physically integrated within Greco-Roman urban centers. How one lives as a believer is of paramount importance in Colossians. Strengthened by prayer, the Colossians are implored to walk in wisdom. In many respects the exhortations represent a re-application of Paul's teaching in 1 Thess 4:11-12 in the face of new circumstances: "to aspire to live quietly, to mind your own affairs, and to work with your hands, as we directed you, so that you may behave properly toward outsiders and be dependent on no one" (NRSV).

FOR REFERENCE AND FURTHER STUDY

Elliott, John H. *A Home for the Homeless.* London: SCM, 1982.
MacDonald, Margaret Y. *Early Christian Women and Pagan Opinion: The Power of the Hysterical Woman.* Cambridge: Cambridge University Press, 1996.
_____. "Citizens of Heaven and Earth: Asceticism and Social Integration in Colossians and Ephesians," in Leif Vaage and Vincent Wimbush, eds., *Asceticism and the New Testament.* New York: Routledge, 1999, 269–98.
Wilson, Bryan. *Patterns of Sectarianism.* London: Heinemann, 1967.

13. *Conclusion: Personal Notes and Greetings* (4:7-18)

7. Tychicus, the beloved brother, faithful minister, and fellow slave in the Lord, will tell you all the news about me. 8. I have sent him to you for this very purpose, in order that you might know how we are and that he may encourage your hearts, 9. together with Onesimus, the faithful and beloved brother, who is one of you. They will tell you about everything here. 10. Aristarchus my fellow prisoner greets you, as does Mark the cousin of Barnabas (concerning whom you have received instructions— if he comes receive him), 11. and Jesus who is called Justus. These only are of the circumcision among my fellow workers for the kingdom of God, and they have been a comfort to me. 12. Epaphras greets you; he is one of you and a slave of Christ Jesus, always striving for you in his prayers in order that you may stand mature and fully assured in all the will of God. 13. For I testify for him that he has much labor on behalf of you and on behalf of those in Laodicea and Hierapolis. 14. Luke, the

beloved physician, greets you and Demas. 15. Greet the brothers in Laodicea and Nympha and the church in her house. 16. And when this letter is read before you, have it read also in the church of the Laodiceans, and you in turn read the one from Laodicea. 17. And tell Archippus, "See that you fulfill the ministry that you received in the Lord." 18. The greeting is in my own hand—Paul's. Remember my chains. Grace be with you.

NOTES

4:7. *Tychicus, the beloved brother, faithful minister, and fellow slave in the Lord:* This verse and those that follow contain many examples of the "language of belonging" that is typical of Pauline Christianity (see the notes and interpretation on 1:1-2). Both Tychicus (4:7) and Onesimus (4:9) are called beloved brothers. In the address of the letter Timothy is also called a brother (1:1). The description of Tychicus is very similar to that of Epaphras in 1:7-8 who is named both as a fellow slave and a faithful minister of Christ, perhaps offering an indication of their complementary roles in Colossae (see further below). The term "minister" or "deacon" *(diakonos)* should be understood as an important leadership designation, but should not be taken as referring to the institutional office characteristic of later Christianity. *Diakonos* is a leadership category that is applied both to Paul (1:23) and to his fellow workers (cf. 1:7; 4:17) in Colossians (see the notes on 1:7)—an indication of the collaborative nature of Paul's ministry. It is increasingly being recognized that the metaphorical use of the term slave *(doulos)* in Pauline Christianity is related to the actual shape of the complex institution of slavery in the Greco-Roman world. The notion of being a slave in the Lord or a slave of Christ (cf. 4:12) may have enhanced the authority of Paul's fellow workers as those who served the most important lord of all, the Christ (see the notes on 1:7). In Eph 6:21-22, which is almost identical to Col 4:7-8 (see the notes on Eph 6:21-22), Tychicus is also called a beloved brother; he is the only individual singled out in Ephesians (cf. 2 Tim 4:12 [note the considerable overlap between the names listed in Colossians and 2 Tim 4:9-12]; Titus 3:12). According to Acts 20:4 Tychicus was Paul's companion from Asia. It is striking that Tychicus is only mentioned in the letters often considered to be deutero-Pauline, perhaps offering an indication that he only became involved in the movement near the end of Paul's ministry (Dunn 272). It may be that his role became especially important after Paul's death and that the exhortations here are intended to legitimate his role as an authentic representative of the apostle (Gnilka [1980] 234–35; Pokorný [1991] 191).

will tell you all the news about me: Tychicus and Epaphras appear to have similar connections to the Colossian community. Both act as intermediaries between Paul and the community (see the notes on 1:8). The "news" (literally, "all things") may refer to the conditions of Paul's imprisonment, or to other personal details that Paul has shared with Tychicus. (For the significance of the Greek expression for "tell all the news" see the notes on 4:9.)

8. *I have sent him to you for this very purpose, in order that you might know how we are and that he may encourage your hearts:* The use of the aorist tense of the verb *pempō* (to send) gives a strong indication that Tychicus (along with Onesimus, cf. 4:9) is delivering Paul's letter to the Colossians. After the use of the future tense the author switches to a past tense projecting "himself into the situation of the recipients, for whom the sending will be in the past" (Harris 201). This use of the epistolary aorist (cf. BDF 334) can be translated into English as "I have sent" (NRSV) or as "I am sending" (e.g., REB; NAB; NJB). In this instance "this very purpose" refers not to what comes before but to what follows "that you might know." "How we are" may be intended to include Timothy (cf. 1:1; on this expression see also the notes on 4:9). Tychicus' mission with respect to the Colossian community is identical to Paul's mission: he is to encourage or comfort *(parakaleō)* their hearts (cf. 2:2). As the English translation might suggest, this should not be understood as simply providing emotional support. Given the way the heart was understood in the biblical world, it is more accurate to think of Tychicus and Paul encouraging the commitment of the Colossians and comforting them in light of their resolve (see the notes on 3:15). There are several textual variations of the phrase "that you might know how we are," including "that you might know how you are," "that he may know how we are," and "that I might know how you are." The reading adopted here most easily explains the rise of the alternative readings (see Metzger 626).

9. *together with Onesimus, the faithful and beloved brother, who is one of you. They will tell you about everything here:* Onesimus is evidently a member of the Colossian community. He is described in terms similar to Tychicus (see the notes on 4:7), but his role appears to be secondary. The mention of Onesimus raises questions about the relationship between Colossians and Philemon; Onesimus is the name of the runaway slave about whom Paul writes to Philemon (cf. Phlm 10; see the interpretation below). Onesimus has evidently traveled with Tychicus, bearing Paul's letter (see the notes on 4:8). Some translations aim to make this association clear by translating "he is coming with Onesimus" (NRSV) or "with him I am sending Onesimus" (NJB). The same verb "to tell" or "to make known" *(gnōrizō)* is used with respect to Onesimus as was used with respect to Tychicus (cf. 1:27; 4:7). The fact that the Colossians are to know all is emphasized particularly strongly. The expression *panta . . . ta hōde* (everything here) is very closely related to *ta kat' eme panta* (all the news about me) in v. 7 and *ta peri hēmōn* (how we are) in v. 8.

10. *Aristarchus my fellow prisoner greets you:* Although it is not always the case (e.g., Galatians; 1 and 2 Thessalonians), most of Paul's letters include closing greetings. The usual pattern is for Paul to send greetings to fellow workers and associates first and then to include a few greetings from others (e.g., Romans 16). But in Colossians the greetings of Paul's fellow workers are reported first and in the greatest detail. In this respect and in the precise shape of the exhortations the greetings in Colossians very closely resemble those in Paul's letter to Philemon (see Phlm 23-24; and see the interpretation below). A very interesting term is used to describe Aristarchus, who is evidently in prison with Paul. One would have expected the more usual term *syndedemenos* (cf. Heb 13:13) or

syndesmotes, but instead the text has *synaichmalōtos,* which means literally "fellow prisoner of war." (Epaphras is given this designation in Phlm 23.) Some have argued that since Paul was not a prisoner of war and may well have used the term in a figurative sense in Rom 16:7 to refer to Andronicus and Junia it is likely that that the expression here is also being used in a figurative sense (see Kittel, *TDNT* 1:196–97; Harris 206). Thus the NEB translates: "Aristarchus, Christ's captive like myself." But that Aristarchus' imprisonment may well have been literal (he was either apprehended with Paul or volunteered to share his imprisonment) is suggested by Acts. In Acts 19:29 Aristarchus is described as a Macedonian (from Thessalonica; cf. Acts 27:2) who was dragged off in the midst of the confusion in Ephesus as a result of the silversmith Demetrius' condemnation of Paul for rejection of the gods. He is also described as accompanying the captive Paul on his sea journey to Rome (Acts 27:2). In the Pauline epistles Aristarchus is mentioned only in Col 4:10 and in Phlm 24.

as does Mark the cousin of Barnabas (concerning whom you have received instructions—if he comes receive him): Mark is probably the John Mark who is mentioned in Acts 12:12 and who is frequently associated in Acts with Barnabas (Paul's collaborator whose work was central to the development of the church in Antioch; cf. Acts 11:22; 13:1; 15:35); the followers of Jesus met in the house of his mother, Mary. There were evidently tensions between Mark and Paul, as indeed there were between Paul and Barnabas (cf. Acts 12:25; 15:37, 39). Whatever disputes there had been between Mark and Paul were apparently resolved at the time when Colossians was composed. Yet one may perhaps sense a hint of lingering tension in the conditional clause, "if he comes receive him." There seems to have been some uncertainty as to whether Mark would indeed make the journey and/or whether the Colossians would be naturally inclined to receive him (Dunn 277). Mark is also mentioned in Phlm 24. We do not know the precise circumstances underlying the parenthetical statement, but it may be that the instructions were a means of introducing Mark to the Colossians. In the NT the verb *dechomai* (to receive, to take) is frequently used to refer to hospitality (e.g., Matt 10:14, 40-41; Mark 6:11; Luke 9:5, 11; 10:8, 10; 16:4, 9; John 4:45; Gal 4:14; Heb 11:31).

11. *and Jesus who is called Justus:* That Jesus who is called Justus "greets you" is implied here. Some English translations refer simply to Jesus Justus (NEB; REB; NJB). Jesus emerges as a common name among the Jews in the NT period (it is the Greek form of Joshua; cf. Luke 3:29; Matt 27:16-17; Acts 13:6). Justus appears as a surname also in Acts 1:23 and Acts 18:7 (see Dunn 278). In contrast to many of the fellow workers listed here, there is no mention of him in the parallel text of Phlm 23-24 or elsewhere in the NT.

These only are of the circumcision among my fellow workers for the kingdom of God, and they have been a comfort to me: "These only" might be rendered more literally as "these are of the circumcision, these only fellow workers for the kingdom of God." It is difficult to know exactly how to punctuate this phrase (see Harris 208). The main sense is plain, however: among Paul's fellow workers who are with him, only Aristarchus, Mark, and Jesus who is called Justus (or possibly only Mark and Jesus) are Jews (cf. Rom 4:12). It is clear that this is not a general reference to all of Paul's fellow workers, but rather a reference to this specific context, for Paul clearly had other coworkers who were Jews such as Prisca and Aquila (Rom 16:3). It may be that the reference to those who are of the circumcision is intended to make the point that among a group that is often hostile to the Pauline mission (cf. Gal 2:12; Titus 1:10) there are nevertheless some individuals who are truly supportive of the Pauline mission (see Ellis [1978] 116–28). There may also be a certain sadness in Paul's admission that is reminiscent of the emotions he expresses concerning his own people in Romans 9–11. The Greek term for fellow worker here is *synergos;* when it is used by Paul this term stresses mutual reliance and the collaborative nature of the Pauline mission (cf. 1 Cor 3:5-9). (On the kingdom of God see also 1:12-13.) The grammatical construction of the last phrase in Greek may imply emphasis (see Harris 208). Thus the NJB translates, "They have been a great comfort to me" (cf. NEB; REB). This is the only occurrence of the term *parēgoria* (comfort or solace) in the NT (cf. 4 Macc 5:12).

12. *Epaphras greets you; he is one of you and a slave of Christ Jesus:* Of all the coworkers who are singled out in the epistle Epaphras is perhaps the most important to the Colossians themselves. In 1:6-8 he is described as the one who delivered the gospel to them (see the notes). Here his connection with the Colossians is stressed in a manner similar to those coworkers who are described in 4:7-11. Like Onesimus he is one of the Colossians (see the notes on 4:9). Reinforcing the connection between the Colossians and Paul's fellow workers is a central preoccupation of this text (see the interpretation below). Like Tychicus (another key figure), he is called a "slave"—although Tychicus is described as Paul's fellow slave *(syndoulos),* while the expression here is slave *(doulos)* of Christ Jesus; yet in 1:7 Epaphras is called a *syndoulos.* (On the significance of these designations see the notes on 1:7 and 4:7.) Although "Christ Jesus" has the greatest textual support some manuscripts have simply "Christ" (cf. NEB; REB; NAB) or "Jesus Christ." In the parallel text of Phlm 23-24 the list of greetings begins with Epaphras.

always striving for you in his prayers in order that you may stand mature and fully assured in all the will of God: Once again we have a text that underscores the importance of prayer (cf. 1:9-14; 3:15-17; 4:2-4). The participle *agōnizomenos* (striving) literally means struggling or fighting and is used to describe fighting with weapons; it is also used to refer literally or figuratively to an athletic contest (cf. 1 Cor 9:25; BAGD 15). In Colossians the verb is used to refer to Paul's labor in general in 1:29 (cf. 2:1) and, as in 4:12, it is closely associated with maturity or perfection *(teleios;* cf. 1:28). Paul's work is linked very closely to that of Epaphras in Colossians. The verb "to stand" here *(histēmi)* can actually mean to stand firm (BAGD 382) and its usage, along with the notions of maturity and full assurance, suggests the need to take a firm stand against the false teaching (cf. 2:8-23). That a member of the Pauline mission who is so obviously central to church life among the Colossians would pray for this would add weight to Paul's pleas in 2:8-23. In this case the verb *plērophoreō* refers to what fills completely (BDF 172); thus, in the passive voice: "be fully assured or absolutely convinced." The NJB translates the phrase fluidly in order to capture this sense: "that you will never lapse but always hold perfectly and securely to the will of God." Recalling the usage in 1:9, "in all" refers to "every aspect of." The will of God is also mentioned in 1:9. It is not entirely clear whether the expression "in all the will of God" should be taken with both "stand mature" and "fully assured" or only with "fully assured" (cf. REB). The NIV understands the phrase as denoting attendant circumstances: "that you may stand firm in all the will of God, mature and fully assured." It is also possible that the phrase should be read more independently, with the notion of engaging in doing the will of God being implied (see Harris 210).

13. *For I testify for him that he has much labor on behalf of you and on behalf of those in Laodicea and Hierapolis:* The term *ponos* (labor or hard work) occurs very rarely in the NT (cf. Rev 16:10, 11; 21:4 where it means "pain"). Although its presence in this verse is strongly attested, other manuscripts have *kopon* (trouble, hard work) and *zelon* (zeal), *pothon* (longing), and *agona* (contest, struggle). The variations probably resulted from an attempt to substitute other words for the very rare word (see Metzger 626). *Ponon* could refer to the striving that Epaphras does in prayer (4:12), but might also refer more generally to his efforts on behalf of the Colossians (cf. 2:1). The present tense denotes Epaphras' ongoing labor for the Colossians (NRSV "he has worked hard for you"). As in the previous verse, the connection between Epaphras and the Colossians is reinforced. The almost solemn opening implies that special care is being taken to increase the stature of Epaphras in the eyes of the Colossians: "For I testify." Laodicea was a neighboring city to Colossae in the Lycus Valley; by the first century C.E. Laodicea was a large and important city (cf. Rev 3:14-21). Hierapolis was located six miles north of Laodicea and is only mentioned here in the NT (see the Introduction). No further mention is made of Hierapolis (cf. 4:16), perhaps suggesting that evangelical efforts had been less successful there.

14. *Luke, the beloved physician, greets you and Demas:* Both Luke and Demas (though in reverse order) are included in the greetings of Phlm 24. Luke is also mentioned. Only here is Luke called a physician *(iatros).* It cannot be determined on the basis of this brief reference whether the physician cared for Paul and his entourage. Later church tradition understood the physician and companion of Paul to have been the author of Luke-Acts. Demas is also mentioned in 2 Tim 4:10, but in that case Paul's coworker is presented in an unfavorable light: "for Demas, in love with the present world, has deserted me and gone to Thessalonica" (NRSV).

15. *Greet the brothers in Laodicea and Nympha and the church in her house:* Having passed on the greetings of others, the author now sends greetings of his own. The reference to the brothers is intended to include all the believers in Laodicea. The NRSV, departing from the literal Greek, translates the term inclusively: "brothers and sisters" (cf. 1:2). It is not entirely clear whether the house church associated with Nympha was part of the broader community in Laodicea that included other house churches or whether Nympha is hostess to a whole community in Laodicea (cf. Rom 16:23; in this latter case "and" would

mean "and specifically"; see Barth and Blanke 486). It is also possible that the house church was found in Hierapolis (though one would have expected further reference to it in 4:16) or even Colossae. (On the basis of the reference to Onesimus, the runaway slave described in Philemon, in Col 4:9, Philemon is generally understood to be the leader of a house church in Colossae. But Philemon is never mentioned in Colossians.) The expression "the church in her house" is in keeping with similar formulations in the undisputed letters (cf. 1 Cor 16:15; Rom 16:5; Phlm 2). In the first century C.E. believers gathered in houses. Most recent translations (in keeping with Codex Vaticanus) have adopted the reading "Nympha" (a woman) rather than the alternative "Nymphas" (a man) which is also widely attested. The Greek text has *Nymphan*, which can refer to a man or woman depending on accentuation (*Nymphan*, from the feminine nominative *Nympha*; *Nymphan*, from the masculine nominative *Nymphas*). It seems that uncertainty about the name, and probably also discomfort about a woman leader of a house church, led to the transformation of the possessive pronoun *autēs* to *autou* in some manuscripts. A third reading emerged—"the church in their [*autōn*] house" evidently in an attempt to include the "brothers" in the reference or perhaps to refer to Nymphas and his wife (see Metzger 627; Schüssler Fiorenza 51). The fact that Nympha is mentioned alone suggests that she may have been a widow as widows in the ancient world were sometimes in a position to maintain independent control of considerable resources. On the implications of Nympha's leadership role within the context of Colossians see the interpretation below.

16. *And when this letter is read before you, have it read also in the church of the Laodiceans, and you in turn read the one from Laodicea:* Laodicea was located ten miles from Colossae; exchange of correspondence must have seemed quite natural. The command to "read the one from Laodicea" most likely does not refer to a letter that the Laodiceans composed, but rather refers to a letter Paul wrote to the Laodiceans that the Colossians should also read. *Tēn* (the one) may well be possessive here: "my letter" (see Harris 214). The letter to the Laodiceans is now lost. However, an apocryphal epistle to the Laodiceans, extant in Latin but probably originally composed in Greek in the fourth to the fifth century C.E., seems to have been composed in order to fill the gap in the record of Paul's life. It has been suggested that the letter to the Laodiceans is actually Ephesians; the words "in Ephesus" in Eph 1:1 seem to have been added later, and thus the work may have not been intended for the Ephesians at all (see the notes on Eph 1:1). But the theory that Ephesians is actually the letter to the Laodiceans is purely speculative, as is the suggestion that Philemon is actually this lost letter. This verse provides solid evidence for the practice of the community reading Paul's letters aloud and for exchanges that may have preceded the process of collecting Paul's letters.

17. *And tell Archippus, "See that you fulfill the ministry that you received in the Lord":* There is no way of knowing what special duties were in view in the reference to ministry (*diakonia*; cf. Eph 4:12). It is important to recognize that the term refers to providing services for the church and not to the office of the diaconate in this period. The term can refer to a particular act of service in

Pauline literature (e.g., Rom 12:7; 15:31; 1 Cor 12:5) or more generally to sustained service (e.g., Rom 11:13; 2 Cor 4:1). The notion of having to fulfill the ministry suggests that that the author has a special act of service in mind (see Dunn 288; and see the notes on 1:7 and 4:7 for use of the cognate term "minister" *[diakonos]* in Colossians). This verse perhaps offers the strongest indication that 4:7-18 is not merely a stylized imitation of Phlm 23-25, but is actually speaking to a real community context. Almost as an afterthought—a point too important to exclude—the author sends a message to Archippus. Archippus appears as a member of the family and/or house church of Philemon and is described as a fellow soldier in Phlm 2 (cf. Phil 2:25). One detects a sense of urgency in the warning given in 4:17. There have been several suggestions made about the nature of Archippus' commission, including the suggestion that Archippus was the true owner of the runaway slave Onesimus and that his ministry had something to do with the affair of the runaway slave discussed in Philemon (Knox [1959] 49–51). But this is highly speculative and it seems best to look for suggestions within the confines of the major concerns of Colossians itself. Perhaps Archippus has a special role to play in dealing with false teaching.

18. *The greeting is in my own hand—Paul's. Remember my chains:* In keeping with the common practices of the day, Paul is presented as writing the closing with his own hand (cf. Gal 6:11; 1 Cor 16:21; 2 Thess 3:17) after the body of the letter has been dictated (cf. Rom 16:22). But if Colossians is deutero-Pauline this final greeting may have served as an especially important sign of authentication (cf. 2 Thess 3:17; 2 Thessalonians is considered by many to be deutero-Pauline). This is the third reference to Paul's imprisonment in the epistle (cf. 4:3, 10). The request to remember (*mnēmoneuō;* cf. 1 Thess 2:9; 2 Thess 2:5) is a call to reflect on all of Paul's labor, but may also be inviting the Colossians to pray for him.

Grace be with you: Paul's letters typically include this phrase in the closing. "Grace" refers to the grace of the Lord Jesus Christ (cf. 1 Cor 16:23; 2 Cor 13:13; Gal 6:18; Phil 4:23; 1 Thess 5:28; 2 Thess 3:18; Phlm 25). This closing is shorter than is usually the case in Pauline letters. Only the Pastorals contain such brief closings (cf. 1 Tim 6:21; 2 Tim 4:22; Titus 3:15). Grace is also bestowed upon the Colossians in the greeting found in the opening of the letter (cf. 1:2).

INTERPRETATION

These closing remarks underline the intimate relationship between Paul and his fellow workers. The fact that they are so personal and seem to speak to concrete concerns (cf. Eph 6:21-24) adds weight to the case in favor of the authenticity of the epistle. For example, it is difficult to accept that the rather urgent instruction to Archippus in v. 17 represents pseudonymous fiction! In discussions of how these verses should affect decisions concerning the authenticity of Colossians, the relationship of Colossians to Philemon has proven to be especially important.

We do not know for certain when or where the Letter of Paul to Philemon was written. However, the mention of Onesimus in 4:9 (see the notes), and the general overlap in names between 4:7-18 and Phlm 23-24 has led to the widely held conviction that both Onesimus and his master Philemon were from Colossae. With the exception of Jesus who is called Justus and Nympha, all of the names that appear in Colossians also appear in Philemon. Yet a comparison of the references in the two letters reveals the greater detail in Colossians in almost every case (see the chart in Lohse 175). Apart from labeling them as coworkers of Paul, Phlm 23-24 tends to include only the names of these individuals. In Colossians much more information is given about the person named (e.g., Mark, the cousin of Barnabas; Luke, the beloved physician) and generally more information about the individual's role and connection to Paul. It has been suggested that Colossians was written by one of Paul's students who knew and used Philemon, making the list of greetings more vivid to ensure that the letter would gain a hearing as a message from Paul (see M. Y. MacDonald [1988] 130).

James D. G. Dunn has recently argued, however, that Colossians represents a type of "bridge" document between the undisputed epistles and the later post-Pauline works, Ephesians and the Pastoral Epistles. He believes there is good reason to believe that the document was actually penned by Timothy (1:1) while Paul was in prison. Paul was still alive at the time of composition and he gave his approval "in substance if not in detail" (269). Dunn's views on 4:7-18 and his understanding of the relationship between Colossians and Philemon are central to his reconstruction. Although there are several complicated issues concerning the relationship between the two epistles (e.g., Colossians never mentions Philemon), Dunn argues that the most plausible solution is that Colossians and Philemon were written at about the same time. The conditions of imprisonment (in either Ephesus or Rome) meant that it fell to a secretary (probably Timothy) to speak with Paul's voice. At the time of the composition of Colossians it was only possible for Paul to add the briefest of conclusions with his own hand (4:18; cf. Dunn 37–41.).

Dunn's reconstruction of events goes a considerable distance in explaining how a letter that was probably not specifically composed by Paul nevertheless reflects contact with the characters and communities that had been influenced by Paul during his ministry. However, one may accept Dunn's theories about the "bridge" character of Colossians without accepting his view that Colossians constitutes "the last Pauline letter to be written with the great apostle's explicit approval" (41). In fact, in many respects Colossians makes the most sense as the first Pauline epistle that was composed without the benefit of the apostle's involvement. It may well have been composed while the apostle was still living and imprisoned, or he may have died very shortly before (indeed, the close relationship between Colossians and Philemon may suggest this). The author (perhaps Timothy, but it is impossible to be certain) may have been convinced that it was most natural to write in Paul's name (see the Introduction). But the exhortations concerning Paul's fellow workers in 4:7-18 seem to reflect an awareness that Paul will never again visit Colossae, Hierapolis, or Laodicea. These exhortations reflect an awareness of a changed situation that becomes even more pronounced in later deutero-Pauline works.

One of the first things that one notices in comparing the closings of the undisputed letters of Paul to the Colossians is that the list of greetings is longer than most, and that the greetings of Paul's coworkers are reported first and in greatest detail with only a few brief greetings from Paul conveyed at the end (vv. 15-17; cf. Rom 16:21-23). The closing of Philemon includes only greetings from Paul's coworkers but is strikingly brief in comparison to the similar list in Colossians (see above). Taken together with 1:6-8, Col 4:7-18 reflects an effort to reinforce the authority of the coworkers, especially Epaphras and Tychicus (perhaps also Onesimus) in Paul's absence. Colossians 4:7-18 includes numerous designations to enhance the status of these coworkers such as "beloved brother," "minister," and "fellow-slave." The work of coworkers on behalf of the community is highly praised by Paul and its value is sometimes legitimated in almost formal terms (see v. 13). In Colossians Paul's work is described in terms that correspond to the descriptions of the efforts of his fellow workers. For example, in v. 12 Epaphras' "striving" is described in a way that recalls the manner in which Paul's own struggles and efforts on behalf of the Colossians are defined in 1:9 and 1:29. Particularly striking is the consistent use of the word "minister" (*diakonos*) to link Paul's mission with the service of Paul's associates. In 1:23 Paul is described as a minister of the gospel and later both Epaphras (1:7) and Tychicus (4:7) are given that title. In light of a situation that may have been aggravated by Paul's absence one detects a certain urgency in the final instruction of the letter: Archippus is exhorted to fulfill the ministry (*diakonia*) he has received in the Lord.

The work of sociologist Max Weber on the death of charismatic leaders can help us appreciate the implications of the reinforcement of the authority of Paul's fellow workers and associates that occurs in 1:6-8 and 4:7-18 (see the notes and interpretation on 1:1-2 and 1:3-8; see also M. Y. MacDonald [1988] 11–16). Weber argued that the death of a charismatic leader creates a crisis of leadership for his or her staff that threatens the life of the group. In order to secure their own leadership, members of the staff need to legitimate their own authority in terms of the authority of the charismatic leader. Something similar may be at work in Colossians. The disappearance of Paul created a problem of governance for the communities. Paul's leadership was exercised as part of a broad group of associates during his lifetime and communities were accustomed to his influence being communicated by means of letters, emissaries, and close associates. But his imprisonment for an indefinite period and/or his death would clearly mean a loss of center. In order to receive "encouragement" from Tychicus the Colossians needed to be reassured by Paul that Tychicus could truly make Paul's presence felt (vv. 7-9). They needed to be repeatedly told that Tychicus and Onesimus would inform them about everything concerning Paul (see the notes on 4:9). The fact Tychicus was traveling to Colossae with a member of the Colossians' own community, Onesimus, would surely have heightened the sentiment of reassurance (v. 9).

Within the context of Greco-Roman society mechanisms to guarantee the continuation of the Pauline churches beyond the life of their founder would have operated within a system of patronage that permeated relationships at all levels. Acting very much like the head of a household, a patron bestowed benefits upon his clients and, in return, expected to receive loyalty and honor. Sometimes a third party, a mediator or broker, was central to providing access to the patron. In Paul's letters his fellow workers act much like brokers: they mediate between Paul and his "client" communities (see the discussion in the interpretation of 1:3-8). Epaphras acts as a mediator-figure in Colossians; he provides the Colossians with access to Paul's benefaction and communicates to Paul their loyalty to him (1:7-8). But Epaphras' role within the patronage system is also flexible—a fact that may have contributed to the ability of the movement to survive Paul's death and allowed fellow workers to take up leadership roles more easily. On the one hand he can stand with the Colossians as one of them (4:12), but on the other hand the fact that he himself brought the gospel to the Colossians and his ongoing efforts on their behalf (4:12-13) prepare the way for Epaphras to assume the role of patron himself (see the interpretation of 1:3-8). Similarly, Tychicus mediates between Paul and the Colossians. He is the one who brings news of Paul to the Colossians and who is responsible for keeping Paul's influence alive in the community. On the one hand the fact that he is traveling with Onesimus who is so well known to the Colossians reinforces the solidarity of Paul's fellow workers with the Colossians, who are all ultimately dependent on their patron, Paul (4:9). But on the other hand the commission that he received from Paul must have done a good deal to strengthen his own authority in a community that had yet to experience Paul's physical presence (4:8). In fact, the several references to Tychicus in deutero-Pauline works suggest his heightened status after Paul's death (see the notes on 4:9). In seeking to appreciate the magnitude of the role of Paul's associates it is important to keep in mind that Paul had never been to the community, and that nowhere in the letter does Paul even raise a visit as a possibility.

Colossians 4:7-18 offers us a window into a collaborative enterprise—Pauline Christianity—that had the stamina and organizational means to outlive its founder. In addition to the system of patronage described above the Colossians benefited from the services Paul's fellow workers could provide. They were a mixed group, including both Jews and Gentiles, and most likely people from a variety of social strata (Yates 84). Some had the capacity to travel (Epaphras, Tychicus, Onesimus, and Mark). They included a physician (4:14), but also a slave. Our discussion of 3:18–4:1 introduced the importance of the slave presence in the Colossian community; here the presence of Onesimus (probably the runaway slave mentioned in Philemon), carrying out an important service for the church and described as one of the Colossians, strengthens that impression (4:9).

Leadership in Pauline Christianity has been linked with the ability to provide services (see the notes and interpretation on 1:1-2). Perhaps the most important service that a first-century believer could provide for a church group was to offer a house for meetings. Thus Nympha no doubt played a key leadership role in the churches of the Lycus Valley. The church in her house may well have been in Laodicea (see the notes on 4:15). Given the hierarchical household structure implied by 3:18–4:1 the description of Nympha's role is striking. Any incongruity might be explained by the fact that the women who are exhorted in 3:18–4:1 are married, and the lack of reference to a man in 4:15 may suggest that Nympha was a widow. However, there is no way to be certain that was the case. Even if Nympha's role can in part be attributed to widowhood, it remains striking that the work that indisputably introduces a patriarchal ethic into church life contains the only unambiguous reference in the Pauline correspondence to the leadership of a house church by a woman. Prisca and Aquila clearly share the leadership of a house church (e.g., Rom 16:3-5) and the description of Phoebe as a "benefactor" strongly suggests that she may have been the leader of a house church (Rom 16:1-2). But apart from the issues raised by the textual variants, that Col 4:15 refers to a woman house church leader is indisputable (and perhaps because of this the manuscript tradition sought to masculinize the text; see the notes on 2:15). The description of Nympha calls to mind the description of Lydia, whose home becomes a site for church meetings (Acts 16:14-15, 40; cf. Acts 12:12). The reference to Nympha comes as a reminder that the adoption of traditional ethics in church groups did not negate all avenues for women's influence (see the interpretation of 3:18–4:1). Even by the second century, when the household codes were widely accepted as guides for Christian living (e.g., Ign. *Pol.* 4:1–5:1; Pol. *Phil.* 4:2–6:1), we find prominent women exercising leadership roles. The correspondence of Ignatius of Antioch includes references to Tavia, the wife of Epitropus, and Alce (cf. Ign. *Smyrn.* 13.2; Ign. *Pol.* 8:2-3).

For Reference and Further Study

Bruce, F. F. *The Pauline Circle.* Grand Rapids: Eerdmans; Exeter: Paternoster, 1985.

Ellis, E. Earle. "The Circumcision Party and the Early Christian Mission," in idem, *Prophecy and Hermeneutic in Early Christianity.* WUNT 18. Tübingen: J.C.B. Mohr (Paul Siebeck); Grand Rapids: Eerdmans, 1978.

_____. "Paul and his Co-Workers," *NTS* 17 (1970–71) 437–52.

Knox, John. "Philemon and the Authenticity of Colossians., *JR* 18 (1938) 144–60.

_____. *Philemon among the Letters of Paul.* Nashville: Abingdon, 1959.

Malina, Bruce J. "Patronage," in John J. Pilch and Bruce J. Malina, eds., *Biblical Social Values and Their Meaning: A Handbook.* Peabody, Mass.: Hendrickson, 1993, 113–17.

Olrogg, Wolf-Henning. *Paulus und seine Mitarbeiter: Untersuchungen zu Theorie und Praxis der paulinischen Mission.* WMANT 50. Neukirchen-Vluyn: Neukirchner Verlag, 1979.

Rutherford, J. "St. Paul's Epistle to the Laodiceans," *ExpT* 19 (1907–08) 311–14.

Schneemelcher, Wilhelm. "The Epistle to the Laodiceans," in Edgar Hennecke, *New Testament Apocrypha.* Edited by Wilhelm Schneemelcher. English translation edited by Robert McLean Wilson. Philadelphia: Westminster, 1965, 2:128–32.

Weima, Jeffrey A. D. *Neglected Endings: The Significance of Pauline Letter Closings.* JSNT.S 101. Sheffield: JSOT Press, 1994.

EPHESIANS

TRANSLATION, NOTES, AND INTERPRETATION

14. *Greeting* (1:1-2)

1. Paul, an apostle of Christ Jesus by the will of God, to the saints who are [in Ephesus] and faithful in Christ Jesus. 2. Grace to you and peace from God our Father and the Lord Jesus Christ.

NOTES

1:1. *Paul, an apostle of Christ Jesus by the will of God:* This opening phrase is identical to that found in Colossians and 2 Corinthians, is virtually identical to the opening of 1 Corinthians, and essentially summarizes the ideas found in the opening of Galatians. To state that Paul is an apostle (*apostolos;* on the meaning of this term see the notes and interpretation on Col 1:1-2) "by the will of God" is to stress Paul's apostolic authority. A particularly striking feature of this opening phrase, in comparison to Colossians and the undisputed letters, is that it mentions none of Paul's coworkers as co-authors of the letter (e.g., Colossians states that the letter is from Paul and Timothy). Only Romans also lacks this characteristic reference to a joint enterprise.

to the saints who are [in Ephesus] and faithful in Christ Jesus: With minor differences the salutation follows Colossians closely. Colossians refers to faithful "brothers" and to "Christ" and not "Christ Jesus" as is the case here. *Tois hagiois* (to the saints) literally refers to the "holy ones." In Pauline literature these are all believers who belong to the people of God; the phrase draws on the Hebrew Bible notion of being set apart as God's people (see also the notes and interpretation on Col 1:1-2). "Saints" is a term that is used frequently in Ephesians (cf. 1:15, 18; 3:8; 4:12) and in this case evidently refers to the same people as the faithful *(pistois);* the suggestion that the address is intended to designate two groups, Jewish Christians called saints (cf. 2:19) and Gentile believers who are also faithful (see Kirby 170 and n. 86), has won little support. Faith in Christ is central to the identity of the addressees as "saints." In Ephesians the term can be used not only to refer to the present state of believers but also with respect to the ultimate fulfillment of believers according to God's plan: "the riches of his glorious inheritance among the saints" (1:18). As a term that incorporates people into community, "saints" is closely related to the expression "in Christ Jesus" (REB; Eph 1:1: "to God's people at Ephesus, to the faithful, incorporate in Christ Jesus"). This expression is a variation of the characteristic Pauline formula "in Christ" (*en Christ̥ō*) that, found in 1:10, "in Christ Jesus," is repeated again in 2:10. (On the meaning of *en Christ̥ō* see the notes and interpretation on Col 1:1-2.)

In Pauline literature the saints are frequently described as those who are located in particular geographic locations. For example, Colossians is addressed "to the saints and faithful brothers who are in Colossae" (cf. 2 Cor 1:1; Phil 1:1). As the use of the brackets around "in Ephesus" makes clear, however, the manuscript variations with respect to this verse make it impossible to draw firm conclusions about geographic specificity. The words "in Ephesus" (*en Ephes̥ō*) are missing from several important witnesses (𝔓⁴⁶ ℵ* B* 424ᶜ 1739) as well as from manuscripts known by Basil and the text used by Origen (see Metzger 604). Marcion designated the epistle as "To the Laodiceans" (cf. the notes on Col 4:16). Some modern translations omit "in Ephesus" altogether, preferring instead to present this as an alternate reading in the notes (e.g., NJB). It seems most likely that the words "in Ephesus" were originally missing; the shorter version is the more difficult reading and therefore more likely to be closer to the original (but on the grammatical difficulties associated with the shorter reading see the extensive discussion by Andrew Lincoln [1990] 1–4). The words "in Ephesus" are nevertheless included in square brackets in recognition of the fact that, except for those listed above, all witnesses include the words and the epistle has traditionally been known as "To the Ephesians" (see Metzger 601). Note, however, that the superscription "To the Ephesians" was not part of the original document; definite proof for this superscription's existence comes only from the latter part of the second century. For scholarly attempts to account for the absence of the words "in Ephesus" see the interpretation below.

2. *Grace to you and peace from God our Father and the Lord Jesus Christ:* This is the greeting found consistently throughout Paul's letters. The greeting probably reflects the influence of the standard Greek salutation: "greetings" (*chairein*, though the related key Pauline term *charis* occurs here). It may also be influenced by the traditional Jewish greeting, "peace" (*shalom*). Some Jewish salutations refer to "mercy and peace" (e.g., 2 *Apoc. Bar.* 78:2). One of the major themes of Ephesians is the achieved unity of Jews and Gentiles (2:11-22). Thus the greeting, which seems to have blended Jewish and Gentile influences, may have had special significance in this context (Thurston 93). The reference to peace (*eirenē*) may have been especially significant: Ephesians 2:17 speaks of Christ proclaiming peace to those who were near (Jews) and those who were far off (Gentiles). The themes of grace (1:6, 7; 2:5, 7, 8; 4:7, 29) and peace (2:14, 15, 17; 4:3; 6:15) are central in Ephesians. The closing once again brings the themes of grace and peace together (6:23-24).

INTERPRETATION

Ephesians presents interpreters with many difficulties. One of the most notorious puzzles has to do with the identity of the addressees and is raised immediately at 1:1. The manuscript variations and concomitant uncertainty as to whether the document was ever intended specifically for Ephesus (see the notes above) have led scholars to suggest various scenarios concerning the nature of the document, its authorship, and its intended audience (see also the Introduction). One theory that has gained wide support is that Ephesians was originally an encyclical letter designed to reach several churches. The NT itself provides precedents for such a theory. First Peter was written for several congregations in Asia Minor (1 Pet 1:1) and Revelation also seems to have been composed with a view to reaching several congregations (Rev 1:4). There are variations on this general "encyclical" theory that aim to be more specific about the purpose of the document and the identity of the addressees. E. J. Goodspeed proposed that the author of Ephesians (most likely Onesimus), inspired by a reading of Acts, was the collector of the authentic letters and that Ephesians was written as a general letter to serve as the introduction to the Pauline corpus. Many of the particular details of Goodspeed's theory, including the idea of an "introduction," have been rejected on the basis of the tenuous nature of the proposals. However, the general notions of Ephesians as intended for a broader than local audience and of Ephesians as arising from a relationship with the Pauline corpus have won considerable support (see Mitton [1973] 29). More recently Andrew Lincoln (1990), following some of the suggestions of A. van Roon, has argued that the grammatical difficulties in the address (especially the use of *kai*) are best explained if it originally included two place names. Given the use of Colossians in Ephesians, Lincoln believes that these are most likely to have been Hierapolis and Laodicea (Lincoln 3-4; cf. Col 2:1-3; 4:15-16). This intriguing suggestion would be in keeping with Marcion's view of the letter as connected with Laodicea (see the notes above), but in the end it remains highly speculative.

If Ephesians were indeed intended for more than one church community, this would go some way toward explaining the general tone of the work. Ephesians suggests greater distance between the apostle and the audience than is usually the case in Pauline literature. It lacks the type of interest in specific community concerns that is so obvious, for example, in the Corinthian correspondence or in Colossians. Instead the doctrinal expositions and ethical exhortations seem applicable to many different contexts. In some ways the broad perspective of Ephesians resembles the approach taken by Paul in Romans, yet in an important respect Ephesians differs from Romans and from other Pauline works. The customary references to Paul's fellow workers and the greetings to and from members of the local communities (cf. Romans 16; note, however, that some scholars believe that Romans 16 was not originally part of Romans) are virtually absent from Ephesians (cf. 6:21). With respect to the specific content of the

address, the greater distance between the apostle and the audience is revealed through comparison to the very similar address in Colossians.
Ephesians 1:1-2 does not employ the familial language that was typical of
Pauline Christianity. In contrast to Col 1:1-2, there are no references to the
brothers, including Timothy. Such terminology does appear at the end of
the epistle (6:21, 23), and familial metaphors are used to describe believers
(1:5; 5:1) and the church (Eph 2:19: "household of God"), but language
that speaks of group members as if they were members of a family is less
frequent in Ephesians than in Colossians and other Pauline works. Moreover, it should be noted that the address "my brothers," which appears
frequently in the undisputed letters of Paul (e.g., Rom 7:4; 1 Cor 1:11; 2
Cor 1:8; Gal 1:11; Phil 4:1; 1 Thess 1:4), is absent from both Colossians and
Ephesians.

As we seek to understand the impact of the opening of Ephesians we
should pay special attention to the fact that Paul alone is the sender of the
letter. Among the undisputed letters of Paul this is only true of Romans.
One might argue that a parallel exists between Romans and Ephesians in
that Romans, like Ephesians, was written to a community not known personally by Paul; the similarity could be seen as strengthening the case for
the authenticity of the epistle. But, as Lincoln (1990) has pointed out, the
situation underlying Romans is unique among Pauline epistles. Not only
had Paul not been to the community in Rome; the congregation apparently did not owe its origin to Paul and his fellow workers (Rom 1:1-15).
This would certainly not have been the case for the churches in Asia
Minor to which Ephesians was probably addressed (Lincoln [1990] 5).
Moreover, Colossians addresses a community Paul has never visited (Col
2:1-5), but nevertheless includes Timothy as a co-sender of the epistle.
Taken together these factors suggest that special weight should be attached to the mention of Paul alone in the opening of Ephesians.

There is good reason to believe that insistence on the apostolic authority and teaching of the apostle is integral to the purpose of Ephesians (see
the notes and interpretation on 3:1-13). The designation of Paul as "an
apostle of Christ Jesus by the will of God" is especially significant. To draw
upon the categories of sociologist Max Weber, this is an appeal to Paul's
charismatic authority. To a great extent Paul's authority finds its sanction
outside the traditional realms of power. His authority is regarded as being
of divine origin and he displays powers and qualities that are not accessible to most people (for a full discussion see the notes and interpretation
on Col 1:1-2). Paul receives special revelations and is, in turn, a revealer of
mysteries (3:1-13). Paul is chosen by the will of God to be an apostle. Such
works as Galatians and 2 Corinthians illustrate the precariousness of such
an assertion of apostolic authority; in these epistles Paul must defend his
leadership vigorously. But in Ephesians, as in Colossians, one senses no

direct threats to Paul's apostolic claim. Instead, Paul's leadership as an apostle is asserted unhesitatingly and its cosmic proportions are celebrated (3:1-13). In the previous commentary on Colossians this new confidence was judged to be a sign of a changed situation ensuing from the disappearance of the apostle.

In deutero-Pauline literature one detects an emerging image of what constitutes a true apostle, which includes such elements as emphasis on Paul's suffering for the sake of the church (3:13) and his role as a redeemed persecutor (3:8). Paul's authority is asserted with greater reliance on convention and tradition than in the undisputed letters (see the notes and interpretation on Col 1:24–2:7). Paul's charisma is becoming "routinized": access to the divine benefits he bestows is becoming increasingly defined by clearly articulated authority structures. Paul has become *the* apostle to the Gentiles; access to the divine gifts—grace *(charis)*—depends on the acknowledgment of Paul's role and acceptance of the Pauline vision of house, church, and cosmos (4:7; cf. 4:1-16; 5:30-33). In Colossians the image of Paul works in conjunction with practical efforts to reinforce the authority of his fellow workers and to legitimate their role as intermediaries between the apostle and the community (according to Weber's analysis, effort on the part of the staff of the charismatic leader to secure their own leadership positions upon the leader's death is a central means by which charisma becomes routinized). In Ephesians such efforts play only a minor role (Eph 6:21-22). As the reference to Paul as the sole author of the epistle makes clear, the focus is on Paul's unique place in relation to God, Christ, and community. In fact it is much more difficult in the case of Ephesians than in the case of Colossians to detect practical mechanisms that are being put in place to ensure the continuation of Pauline Christianity beyond the disappearance of the apostle. Taken as a whole, however, Ephesians reveals a defensive strategy for the community to adopt in relation to the outside world. The universal character of the Pauline mission is celebrated, but the pendulum has swung in the direction of greater "introversion" than in the case of Colossians (see the notes and interpretation on Col 4:2-6). The reference to "the saints [who are in Ephesus] and faithful in Christ Jesus" reinforces the boundary between the church and the outside world and prepares the way for the very strong expressions of renunciation of the ways of unbelievers that occur later in the epistle (see the notes and interpretation on 4:17–5:20 and 6:21-24).

FOR REFERENCE AND FURTHER STUDY

Best, Ernest. "Ephesians 1.1," in Ernest Best and Robert McLean Wilson, eds., *Text and Interpretation: Studies in the New Testament Presented to Matthew Black.* Cambridge: Cambridge University Press, 1979, 29–41.

_____. "Ephesians 1:1 Again," in Morna D. Hooker and Stephen G. Wilson, eds., *Paul and Paulinism. Essays in Honour of C. K. Barrett.* London: S.P.C.K., 1982.

_____. "Recipients and Title of the Letter to the Ephesians: Why and When the Designation Ephesians?" *ANRW* 2.25.4 (1987) 3247–79.

Dahl, Nils A. "Adresse und Proömium des Epheserbriefes," *ThZ* 7 (1951) 241–64.

Goodspeed, E. J. *The Meaning of Ephesians.* Chicago: University of Chicago Press, 1933.

Lieu, Judith M. "'Grace to you and Peace': The Apostolic Greeting," *BJRL* 68 (1985) 161–78.

Stowers, Stanley K. *Letter Writing in Greco-Roman Antiquity.* Philadelphia: Westminster, 1986.

15. *Blessing* (1:3-14)

3. Blessed be the God and Father of our Lord Jesus Christ who has blessed us with every spiritual blessing in the heavenly places in Christ, 4. As he chose us in him before the foundation of the world, to be holy and without blemish before him, in love. 5. He predestined us for adoption to himself as sons through Jesus Christ, according to the good pleasure of his will, 6. for the praise of the glory of his grace with which he favored us in the beloved, 7. in whom we have redemption through his blood, the forgiveness of trespasses, according to the riches of his grace 8. that he lavished upon us in all wisdom and insight. 9. He has made known to us the mystery of his will, according to his good pleasure that he set forth in him, 10. as a plan for the fullness of time, to sum up all things in Christ, the things in the heavens and the things on the earth. 11. In whom we also have received an inheritance, having been predestined according to the purpose of the one who accomplishes all things according to the counsel of his will, 12. so that we might be to the praise of his glory, we who have already hoped in Christ. 13. In him you also who have heard the word of truth, the gospel of your salvation, and have believed in him, were sealed with the promised Holy Spirit 14. which is the pledge of our inheritance toward redemption as his possession to the praise of his glory.

NOTES

1:3. *Blessed be the God and Father of our Lord Jesus Christ:* In Greek 1:3-14 is one long sentence; there are no formal stops. In fact it constitutes the longest sentence in the NT. The syntax suggests the influence of liturgical forms that incorporated repetition of words, the use of synonyms, and redundancy. There are also many interwoven relative clauses and participial constructions. The precise relationship between phrases is sometimes impossible to determine and this has often frustrated commentators (see the interpretation), but the main ideas are clear. Blessings (sometimes called benedictions or eulogies) are also found in the opening of 2 Corinthians (1:3-4) and 1 Peter (1:3-12). The extended blessing or *berakah* that is found in the OT (e.g., 1 Kings 8:15, 56; Pss 41:13; 72:18, 19) and in Jewish worship (e.g., 1QS 11:15; 1QH 5:20) forms the background for these texts. An example of such a Jewish blessing is contained in the NT in Zechariah's prayer (Luke 1:68-79). Jewish liturgical patterns were adopted by the early Christians. That these forms were transformed to fit a new context is revealed by the fact that God is addressed as "the Father of our Lord Jesus Christ"; the same terminology is found in the texts from 2 Corinthians and 1 Peter cited above. It seems that this Jewish pattern was incorporated into letters for the first time with the NT (see the further discussion in Lincoln [1990] 10–15). Many scholars have tried to isolate an underlying hymn from 1:3-14 and others have judged the whole passage to be a hymn, setting out to identify precise strophes. It has been argued, for example, that the passage constitutes a benediction before baptism that unlocks the purpose of Ephesians as a whole: reminding new believers of the implications of their baptism (e.g., Dahl [1951]). Because of the extensive relationships among 1:3-14, Colossians, and other texts in the Pauline corpus others have argued that it is unlikely that 1:3-14 had an independent liturgical life prior to the composition of Ephesians (e.g., Mitton [1973]). Many today hold that the passage is, however, generally influenced by traditional liturgical language and traditional Pauline phrases (e.g., M. Y. MacDonald [1988] 140; J. T. Sanders [1965] 229; Lincoln [1990] 14; see the interpretation below).

who has blessed us with every spiritual blessing in the heavenly places: "Blessed us" (*eulogēsas*) is the first of six aorist verbs in vv. 3-9. Emphasis is on the things God has done for God's people. There are three instances of the Greek term *en* in this verse; it is best translated as "with" in the first case and as "in" in the remaining two cases. As is usually true in the NT, the use of the adjective "spiritual" (*pneumatikos*) refers to the presence and working of the Holy Spirit in God's blessing. Similar use of the adjective is found in 5:19. The Holy Spirit plays an important role in Ephesians (cf. 1:13-14). In ancient literature generally, the adjective *pneumatikos* refers to the inner life of the human being in contrast to bodily existence. There may be something of this meaning at work here, as is suggested by the close association of "spiritual blessing" with "the heavenly places." The earthly existence of believers has been joined to the invisible, heavenly world. The phrase *ta epourania* is distinctive to Ephesians (cf. 1:20; 2:6; 3:10; 6:12) and might be translated literally as "the heavenlies." It could refer to heavenly things or beings, but its usage elsewhere in Ephesians strongly suggests a local sense: heavenly realms or places (see Lincoln [1973]). In keeping with Hebrew thought, the NT refers to heaven in the plural. The expression "heavenly places" here is not identical, however, to the view of heaven that later came to be accepted in Christianity, for the heavenly places contain evil forces that can still trouble the life of believers (cf. 3:10; 6:12). The heavenly places are understood to be part of the universe and are inhabited by forces that continue to influence the life of believers, yet in 1:20 and 2:6 "the heavenly places" are also depicted as the realm of divine transcendence where Christ sits at God's right hand. In the new age the heavenly realms are being transformed. Ephesians 1:3 asserts God's supremacy in the heavenly places and states that believers already taste the benefits of the new age.

in Christ: The notion of dwelling in heavenly places is reinforced by the characteristic Pauline formula *en Chrisț* (in Christ; see the notes and interpretation on 1:1-2). Variations of the formula occur eight more times in this section and very frequently throughout the whole of Ephesians. In studying this terminology scholars have frequently sought to distinguish between instances where it refers to Christ as the agency of salvation and instances where it depicts Christ as the locus of salvation (salvation requires incorporation into Christ's body). Because in Ephesians there is such a tremendous emphasis on Christ as the agent through whom God carries out the divine plan it has been argued that the use of "in Christ" throughout the epistle is instrumental (e.g., Allan). But 2:6, in which God is said to have raised up believers and made them sit with him "in the heavenly places in Christ Jesus," makes it clear that the notion of incorporation into Christ is by no means ruled out in Ephesians.

4. *As he chose us in him before the foundation of the world:* Beginning at v. 4 the passage stresses the participation of believers in God's preordained plan of salvation. The conjunction *kathōs* ("as") has a causal sense and introduces the various reasons for blessing God. The verse contains the second aorist verb found in the passage, "chose" *(exelexato):* the focus is on God's initiative and what God has already accomplished. The verse reflects the influence of OT notions of God choosing a people (e.g., Deut 14:2) and also recalls the notion of "saints" or "holy ones" in 1:1. (On "in him" see the notes on 1:3.) "Before the foundation of the world" is a phrase that is also found in John 17:24 and 1 Pet 1:20. Although the terminology is not identical, similar sentiments are found in 2 Thess 2:13 and Rom 8:29, where the use of the verb "to foreknow" suggests that God's knowledge of believers precedes the creation of the world (see Lincoln [1990] 23).

to be holy and without blemish before him, in love: It is possible to take *en agapē* (in love) with the following verse. In that case it would be a reference to God's love and not human love (cf. NAB; cf. 2:4). However, the majority of subsequent references to love in the epistle (1:15; 3:17; 4:2, 15, 16; 5:2, 25, 28, 33; 6:23, 24; cf. Col 1:4, 8) point to human love. Moreover, the trio of holiness, spotlessness, and love occur together to refer to human qualities elsewhere in Pauline literature (Phil 1:9-10; 1 Thess 3:12-13; see Lincoln [1990] 17). Thus it seems best to take "in love" with v. 4 and understand it as a reference to a quality the believing community must demonstrate. The reference to believers being holy and without blemish before Christ *(hagious kai amōmous katenōpion autou)* recalls the similar expression in Col 1:22. "Holy" is a cognate of the word "saints" in 1:1. The term *amōmos* is used in Scripture to describe sacrificial animals (LXX Exod 29:37, 38; Num 6:14; 19:2), but can also be used to refer more generally to ethical blamelessness (LXX Pss 14:2; 17:23-24). It is language that draws the lines of purity. "Holy and unblemished" is also an attribute of the pure church (envisioned as a bride) who is presented to Christ (Eph 5:27). She has been cleansed through baptism (5:26; see the interpretation below, and the notes and interpretation on 5:21–6:9).

5. *He predestined us for adoption to himself as sons through Jesus Christ, according to the good pleasure of his will:* With the aorist participle *proorisas* (he predestined or having predestined us) the focus on what God has accomplished is maintained. The notion of predestination also occurs in the undisputed letters of Paul in conjunction with the theme of sonship (1 Cor 2:7; Rom 8:29-30) and in the QL (e.g., 1QH 15:15-17; cf. 1QS 3:15-23). The term *huiothesia* (adoption as sons; often translated more inclusively as "children"; cf. NRSV; REB) appears quite frequently in Paul's letters (Rom 8:15, 23; 9:4; Gal 4:5) and is associated with the experience of baptism (Rom 8:14-17; Gal 4:4-7). It also reflects the practices of the ancient world and uses terminology found in Roman law (see Lyall). In order to describe the relationship that new believers had with God, Paul called to mind the practice of a well-to-do, childless adult wanting to adopt a male heir, often a slave. As Rom 9:4 illustrates, the notion of adoption is also shaped by Israel's special relationship with God, which now becomes shared by all believers (see Lincoln [1990] 25). The expression *dia Iēsou Christou* (through Christ) stresses the agency of Christ. In the Greek text the prepositional phrase *eis auton* (to him or into him) follows immediately after this expression, but it clearly refers to God and not to the Son. The phrase "according to the good pleasure of his will" repeats the sentiments inherent in "He predestined us" and represents one of the many examples of redundancy in this hymnic passage. On "good pleasure" see also the notes below.

6. *for the praise of the glory of his grace with which he favored us in the beloved:* The repetition of genitives, "of the glory of his grace," is typical of a liturgical style. The beginning of the verse finds a very close parallel in v. 12 and v. 14: "the praise of his glory." The logic of the verse is difficult to follow, but the main idea appears to be that God bestows grace upon believers and believers in turn praise the glory of that grace. Grace is certainly the main theme of the verse (on grace see also the notes and interpretation on 1:1-2). Not only does the central Pauline term *charis* (grace) occur here, but it should also be noted that the verb *charitoō* (to favor) is a cognate of that term. In the NT *charitoō* is found only in Eph 1:6 and Luke 1:28. The mention of "the beloved" recalls the reference to the beloved son in Col 1:13. In keeping with OT patterns (e.g., Deut 33:12; Isa 5:1, 7), Paul's letters usually refer to believers as God's beloved people (1 Thess 1:4; 2 Thess 2:13; Rom 9:25; Col 3:12). Those who have stressed the liturgical and/or baptismal roots of this passage have attached special significance to the fact that Jesus is identified as the beloved *(ho agapētos)* in the baptismal scenes in the gospels (Mark 1:11 *parr.*). It should also be noted that the baptismal scene includes the use of the verb *eudokeō* (I take pleasure), a cognate of *eudokia* (good pleasure) in the previous verse (see Kobelski 886). Jesus is also called "the beloved" in the transfiguration accounts (Mark 9:7 *parr.*). The term "beloved" introduces a transition to what Christ has accomplished.

7. *in whom we have redemption through his blood, the forgiveness of trespasses:* On "in whom" ("in Christ") see the notes on 1:3. Ephesians 1:6b-7 is very similar to Col 1:13-14. Both texts, for example, refer to "redemption" (*apolytrōsis;* cf. 1:14; 4:30). Some have viewed the use of this word in Ephesians as a straightforward reference to deliverance. The only use of the term in the LXX (Dan 4:34) and many instances of cognate terms in the LXX suggest that the term could be used as a general word for deliverance from danger, and especially for deliverance from the Egyptian bondage and the Babylonian exile (Lincoln [1990] 28). The word, however, literally means release (cf. Heb 11:35) and draws its origins from the notion of "buying back a slave or captive, making him free by payment of a ransom" (BAGD 96). One can see the close connection between the experience of deliverance and release from bondage in Paul's use of the term in Rom 8:21-23—a text that has other points in common with this passage (see the notes on v. 5; see also the notes on Col 3:14). For both Jewish and Gentile recipients of Pauline epistles this word would resonate with powerful imagery. The language may have made an especially strong impression on the slave members of the community (cf. Eph 6:5-8). In contrast to this verse, Col 1:14 lacks "through his blood," but Col 1:20 does refer to "the blood of his cross" (this was in all likelihood a modification made by the author of Colossians to a preexisting hymn in order to stress the physical aspect of redemption through Christ). Another subtle difference between Col 1:14 and Eph 1:7 is that Colossians refers to the forgiveness of sins (*hamartiōn*) whereas Ephesians has forgiveness of trespasses (*paraptōmatōn;* cf. Eph 2:5). Colossians 2:13 has "forgiving (*charisamenos*) us all of our transgressions." The undisputed letters of Paul do not refer specifically to the forgiveness of sins or trespasses. In the Acts of the Apostles "forgiveness of sins" is a summary statement aiming to encapsulate the experience of salvation associated with baptism (Acts 2:38; cf. Acts 5:31; 10:43; 13:38; 26:18; see also the notes and interpretation on Col 1:14). Baptismal traditions probably also underlie the reference to the forgiveness of trespasses in Ephesians.

according to the riches of his grace 8. *that he lavished upon us in all wisdom and insight:* This is the second mention of grace in the passage (cf. 1:6 which also contains a cognate of the term: "he favored"; on grace see also the notes and interpretation on 1:1-2). On the riches bestowed by God on God's people see also 1:18; 2:7; 3:8, 16. "Riches" (*to ploutos*) and "he lavished" (*eperisseusen*) suggest that God's grace is inexhaustible (cf. 2 Cor 9:8; Rom 5:15-20). This idea is further reinforced by the use of "all" in v. 8. Interpreters are divided as to whether "in all wisdom and insight" should be seen as attached to v. 7 or whether it introduces a new thought (e.g., NRSV: "With all wisdom and understanding he has made known"; see also NAB). If the NRSV's rendering is preferred it would serve as a natural parallel to the alternate translation of vv. 4-5: "in love he destined us" (NAB; see the notes on vv. 4-5 above). In this case wisdom and understanding would be divine qualities (cf. Eph 3:10). The reading adopted here (cf. REB; NJB) seems preferable, however, because of the contents of the prayer described in 1:17 and the use of the similar phrase in Col 1:19; it is likely that the phrase refers to God's gift of grace bestowed upon humans (see the full discussion in Lincoln [1990] 17). It is virtually impossible to distinguish between "wisdom" *(sophia)* and "insight" *(phronēsis);* the use of the terms represents one of many examples of repetition in the passage. Wisdom and insight are closely associated in the LXX (Prov 1:2; 3:19; 8:1; 10:23; Jer 10:12; Dan 2:21; 4 Macc 1:18; see Lincoln [1990] 29).

9. *He has made known to us the mystery of his will:* Taken together with v. 8, this verse stresses that all knowledge and insight comes from God. The revelation of God's plan for the universe is called "making known the mystery of God's will." The term *mystērion* (mystery or secret) would have been familiar to all the recipients of Ephesians and would probably have conjured up powerful imagery. In its plural form the term was used to refer to the mystery cults of Greco-Roman society. In the NT the use of the term recalls Jewish eschatology: at the end of the age God will reveal the contents of divine mysteries. Commentators have pointed to LXX Dan 2:18 when seeking to understand the background of the concept of mystery in Ephesians (Perkins 40; Lincoln [1990] 30). In this text the Aramaic term *rāz* is translated as *mystērion.* This same Aramaic term appears in the QL to refer to the secret plan of salvation which has been revealed to members of the group (1QpHab 7:1-4, 13-14; 8:1-3). Romans 11:25-32 reveals similar ideas. In general, however, Paul uses the term *mystērion* in a variety of ways, sometimes in the plural (e.g., 1 Cor 4:1; 13:2) and sometimes in the singular (1 Cor 15:51; Rom 11:25). In Ephesians the term only appears in the singular (cf. 3:3-10; 5:32; 6:19). The use of the concept seems to have been influenced by Colossians where the mystery is defined as what was once hidden but is now fully revealed in Christ (see also the notes and interpretation on Col 1:26-27). In Ephesians the "mystery" is often defined more precisely than in Colossians (cf. 3:3-10). It is especially important to note that *mystērion* plays a key role in the ecclesiology of Ephesians (cf. 3:4-6; 5:32). In this passage the mystery that is revealed constitutes God's plan for the fullness of time: to sum up all things in Christ, things in the heavens and things on the earth. Later it is disclosed, however, that the church is Christ's body, the fullness of him who fills all in all (1:23). The Church is filling the universe! In order that they might seize this mystery, God has bestowed the gifts of wisdom and insight upon God's people (v. 8). In the Hebrew Bible wisdom is a divine quality associated with creation. Taken together, the language of vv. 8-10 invites listeners to reflect upon the grandeur of God's plan, in which Christ and the church are pivotal. A reference to God's will is also found in v. 5.

according to his good pleasure that he set forth in him: As is the case in the previous phrase, we have a repetition here of a concept found in v. 5: "good pleasure" (see the notes on 1:5). The idea of predestination is stressed once again. Many modern translations have "in Christ" in an effort to be as clear as possible (e.g., NRSV; REB; NJB). The Greek text has "in him" *(en autǭ),* but it is evident that the reference is to Christ (see the notes on "in Christ," 1:3). It is difficult to know how to translate the verb *proetheto* (from *protithēmi*) here. It can mean "to display publicly, to plan, to propose, to intend" (cf. BAGD 722). In Rom 1:13 it simply expresses Paul's intent to visit the Romans, but in Rom 3:25 it is used to describe Christ's relationship to God, which is in keeping with the perspective of Ephesians. Christ Jesus is described as one "whom God put forward *(proetheto)* as a sacrifice of atonement by his blood, effective through faith" (NRSV). In the context of Ephesians this "setting forth" is apparently understood as preordained. The NJB aims to bring out this meaning: "according to his good pleasure which he determined beforehand in Christ."

10. *as a plan for the fullness of time:* It is sometimes difficult to know how to translate *oikonomia* (plan) in the NT. In ancient literature it referred to the management or administration of a house or city. It was sometimes closely associated with an administrative office (see the use of *oikonomos* in Rom 16:23). With respect to God it would necessarily refer to God's direction of the cosmos (see Perkins 41; BAGD 559). The use of the term *oikonomia* in Ephesians differs from its meaning in Col 1:25. In Colossians it is used in conjunction with the commission or appointment Paul received from God to be an apostle: "of which I became a minister according to the stewardship of God given to me for you." In Ephesians, however, the term refers consistently to God's plan for the universe (cf. 3:2, 9). *Plērōma* (fullness) is a concept that Ephesians also shares with Colossians (Col 1:9; 2:9), but the term appears more frequently in Ephesians (cf. 1:10, 23; 3:19; 4:13). In general it refers to what fills or makes something complete, but in second-century Gnostic speculations it sometimes had a more technical meaning (see the notes on Col 1:9). The term plays a key role in the distinctive theological visions of Colossians and Ephesians, which stress the expansion and filling up of the universe with divinity. In this particular case the usage of the term differs somewhat from the usage in Colossians and in other instances in Ephesians. Rather than referring specifically to the fullness of divinity, it speaks of the fulfillment of God's eternal purposes. The plan for the universe is now coming to completion. There is a progression of periods of time (the Greek text reads literally "of the times"). Lindemann argued (95–96) that the expression refers not to a progression but to the suspension of temporal categories. Lincoln (1990), on the other hand, has noted the apocalyptic background for this verse (e.g., LXX Dan 2:21; 4 Ezra 4:37) and the points in common between this verse and other eschatological texts in the NT (e.g., Mark 1:15; Gal 4:4; see also the interpretation below, and the notes and interpretation on 1:13-14).

to sum up all things in Christ, the things in the heavens and the things on the earth: Down through the centuries there has been a great deal of interest in the use of the word *anakephalaiōsasthai* (to sum up or to gather together) in this verse. The image is one of a cosmic Christ who draws all things into himself according to God's plan (cf. Col 1:15-20). Paul uses the term in Rom 13:9 to express the idea that the Law is summed up in the commandment to love. Ephesians 1:10 was especially influential in the development of the doctrine of recapitulation among the Latin Fathers (the Greek term *anakephalaiōsis* was translated as *recapitulatio*). Irenaeus was particularly influential in the development of the doctrine that included belief in a restoration of fallen humanity to God through obedience and a "summing up" in the Incarnation of all previous revelations of God (*Adv. Haer.* ANF 1.330; 1.442-443; 1.548). "In Christ" is usually used to stress both what God has accomplished for believers through Christ's agency and also that salvation in found in his body (see the notes on 1:3). Here what Christ has accomplished reaches cosmic dimensions and the suggestion is that his body fills the whole world. The reference to "all" is elucidated by means of the reference to "the things in the heavens and the things on the earth." On "the heavens" see the notes on 1:3.

11. *In whom we also have received an inheritance:* The passive of the verb *klēroō* means literally "to be appointed by lot" (BAGD). This verb occurs only here in the NT. A cognate of the verb occurs in Col 1:12: *klēros* (inheritance or lot): "giving thanks to the Father who has made you fit to share in the inheritance of the saints in the light" (cf. Deut 10:9; 12:12; 1QS 4:26; 11:7-8; see the notes on Col 1:12). In Colossians the focus is clearly on how believers have been transformed in order to share in the lot or inheritance. In Ephesians, God's initiative is stressed even more strongly: God has simply dispensed an inheritance; God "appoints" believers in Christ. Note the close parallel in 1QH 3:22-23: "You have cast an eternal lot for man . . . in order that he might praise your name together in joy" (cited in Kobelski 887). On inheritance in Ephesians see also 1:14, 18; and 5:5.

    having been predestined according to the purpose of the one who accomplishes all things according to the counsel of his will: This repeats many of the ideas found in the previous phrase and in previous verses. References to predestination and to the will of God also occur in v. 5 (see the notes above). The noun "purpose" *(prothesis)* is a cognate of the verb "set forth or plan" *(protithēmi)* in v. 9 (see the notes above). God is carrying out the divine plan for the destiny of humanity (1 Cor 12:6; Rom 8:28).

12. *so that we might be to the praise of his glory, we who have already hoped in Christ:* This phrase is probably more directly related to "in whom we also have received an inheritance," than the phrase that immediately precedes this verse. It spells out the purpose of God's dispensation of the inheritance, repeating many of the ideas of vv. 5-6. "The praise of his glory" is also found in v. 14 and a very similar expression is found in v. 5 (see the notes above). The word *proēlpikotas* is a perfect active participle of the verb *proelpizō* (to hope before). It occurs only here in the NT. The verbal form suggests an action that has been completed with ongoing results (see Lincoln [1990] 37). A contrast begins in this verse between "we" and "you" (vv. 13-14) that commentators have struggled to explain. It has most often been understood as drawing a contrast between Jewish Christians (including Paul) who first believed and Gentile believers who also believed (e.g., Barth 92, 130–33). This would fit well with 2:11-22, which seeks to remind Gentile members of the Jewish origins of the church and perhaps most easily explains the use of the term *proēlpikotas* (note, for example, the NRSV translation: "we, who were the first to set our hope" [cf. REB; NAB; NJB]. A variation of this theory is that "we" refers to Jews who hoped in the Messiah before his coming; cf. NJB). But the problem with this interpretation is that up to this point the discussion about redemption and predestination has involved all believers. Moreover, the distinction between Jews and Gentiles has yet to be introduced in the work, though one also might argue that with this text the author is announcing a theme to be taken up later.

Others have argued that the distinction made between "we" and "you" may simply represent an attempt to distinguish the recipients of the work from Christians in general (e.g., Kobelski), with "you" in v. 13 perhaps representing an attempt to draw the recipients of the letter specifically into the discussion (see Lincoln [1990] 36–38). But with this interpretation it is somewhat difficult to account for the use of *proēlpikotas*. A third possibility has recently been put forward by Pheme Perkins. She notes that 1:12 alludes to the audience's "conversion" upon hearing the gospel and suggests that the verse should be compared to other "mission" texts in Pauline literature where the speaker is distinguished from the audience (e.g., Col 1:4-5; Rom 10:14-17). She argues that the same distinction is at work in the we/you language of 1:12-14 (Perkins 42–43). But in contrast to the texts she suggests for comparison, there is little interest in Paul's apostolic role in Eph 1:3-14. Although none of the theories accounts for all difficulties, on balance the most likely proposal seems to be the first.

13. *In him you also who have heard the word of truth, the gospel of your salvation:* On "in him" see the notes on 1:3. On the switch from the first person plural "we" (1:12) to the second person plural "you" here, see the notes on the previous verse. The series of verbs in 1:13 beginning with "you have heard" and culminating in "you were sealed" is typically used in reports of missionary success in the NT, which frequently include references to baptism (e.g., Acts 8:12-17; 10:34-48; 19:2, 10; cf. Rom 10:14-17). This phrase is very similar to Col 1:5, where the expression "the word of truth" is also equated with the gospel (see also the notes on Col 1:5). Paul speaks of "the word of truth" in 2 Cor 6:7 and generally associates truth with the gospel in several texts (e.g., Gal 2:5, 14; 5:7; 2 Cor 4:2). On truth in Ephesians see also 4:14-15, 21-24.

and have believed in him, were sealed with the promised Holy Spirit 14. *which is the pledge of our inheritance:* On the link between believing and receiving the Spirit see Acts 19:2. In Greek the reference to the Holy Spirit is literally to the "Holy Spirit of the promise" (cf. Gal 3:14). Although it could mean that the Spirit is full of promise, it is more likely that it refers to the Spirit promised to the Jewish people (see Lincoln [1990] 40). The NT describes the Holy Spirit as that which was promised or anticipated (Acts 2:17; Luke 24:49; Gal 3:14) and the OT speaks of the presence of God's Spirit in the last days (e.g., Ezek 36:26-27; 37:14; Joel 2:28-30). In keeping with v. 10, the recipients of the epistle are reminded that God's plan for the universe is unfolding as it should. If the "you" in this verse refers to Gentile Christians (see the notes on v. 12), their receiving of the Spirit is perhaps a sign of their inclusion in the people of God. The blessing of 1:3-14 concentrates on the present shape of salvation, but these words clearly assign a future dimension to salvation. Moreover, although it is not made explicit and is by no means accepted by everyone, many commentators have seen an allusion to baptism in the reference to sealing. (Cf. *2 Clem.* 7:6; 8:6; *Herm. Sim.* 8.6.3; 9.16.3-6; see also the notes on the previous phrase. See Lincoln [1990] 39–40 for a summary of the debate and interpretation below.) The Holy Spirit is a seal received during baptism that guarantees the inheritance until its full possession is acquired. Very similar language occurs in 2 Cor

1:21-22: "But it is God who establishes us with you in Christ and has anointed us by putting his seal *(sphragisamenos)* on us and giving us his Spirit in our hearts as a first installment *(arrabōn)*." The verb *sphragizō* (seal or mark with a seal) is rooted in the use of marks as a means of identification in the ancient world. For example, in the case of animals that were branded the mark denotes ownership and carries with it a guarantee of the protection of the owner (BAGD 796). In the biblical tradition the seal denotes the thing that set the people apart as belonging to God (cf. Ezek 9:4; 4 Ezra 6:5; Rev 7:1-8; 9:4).

Arrabōn can be translated as "first installment, deposit, down payment, pledge, that pays a part of the purchase price in advance, and so secures a legal claim to the article in question, or makes a contract valid" (BAGD 109). The term is used in commercial texts, but in the context of Ephesians it should not be taken to mean that humans have a legal right to a claim against God (Perkins 43–44). Within the context of the passage as a whole the term clearly refers to God's pledge to complete the process of bestowing the gifts of salvation of which believers have already received a first installment. The reference to "inheritance" *(klēronomia)* recalls v. 11, where a cognate term occurs. Colossians 3:24 speaks of the reward of inheritance *(klēronomia):* the possession of salvation that flows from being children of God (cf. 1:18; 5:5). The change from the second person plural at the beginning of the verse to a reference to "our" inheritance may be intended to highlight the fact that Jewish and Gentile believers share the inheritance. There are variant readings of the first word in v. 14 and it is very difficult to decide between them. Some manuscripts have *hos* (the masculine relative pronoun corresponding to *arrabōn*), but there is slightly greater attestation of *ho* (the neuter relative pronoun), which agrees with the gender of *pneuma* (spirit) (see Metzger 602).

toward redemption as his possession to the praise of his glory: The term "redemption" *(apolytrōsis)* also occurs in v. 7; it can refer to the buying back of a slave or captive, or it can have the more general meaning of "release" (see the notes on 1:7). That slavery may be being used as a metaphor for salvation is suggested by the use of the term *peripoiēsis* (possession or property). Believers may have achieved freedom from the malevolent forces in the universe (cf. 2:2-3; cf. Kobelski 887). It is difficult to know how to translate the phrase. In Greek it is literally "toward redemption of the possession." "The possession" could refer to what the believer possesses: the inheritance, but elsewhere in the NT where "possession" occurs it refers to God's initiative (1 Pet 2:9; cf. Acts 20:28). Thus the NRSV interprets the meaning of the Greek phrase as "toward redemption as God's own people." The final phrase, "to the praise of his glory," is only loosely connected to the previous one and acts as a final testimony to the liturgical style of the blessing. An almost identical phrase is found in v. 6 and v. 12.

INTERPRETATION

In Paul's letters the salutation is usually followed by a thanksgiving for the faith of the recipients (e.g., 1 Cor 1:4-9; Phil 1:3-11). However, in 2

Corinthians the salutation is followed by a blessing (2 Cor 1:3-11). Ephesians includes both a blessing (1:3-14) and the usual thanksgiving for the good conduct of the faithful (1:15-23). Some interpreters have viewed the liturgical-catechetical style of Ephesians as so pervasive that they have argued that it is best to understand the work as a liturgical tract merely cast in the form of a letter. But in most respects Ephesians keeps to the form of Paul's letters. For example, it includes the usual salutation (1:1-2) and conclusion (6:21-24). While 1:3–3:21 is clearly heavily influenced by liturgical forms, it nevertheless constitutes a doctrinal or theological section that, as in other letters in the Pauline corpus (e.g., Galatians, Colossians), is followed by ethical exhortations (4:1–6:20). Moreover, as with other letters in the Pauline corpus, the opening of Ephesians introduces major themes that are taken up again in the epistle, such as "mystery" (1:9; cf. 3:3-10; 5:32; 6:19) and "fullness" (1:10; cf. 1:23; 3:19; 4:13), and even the central theme of the unity of Jew and Gentile (2:11-22, if one accepts that the "you" of vv. 13-14 refers to Gentile Christians; see the notes on 1:12). It is striking that the notion of the body of Christ that fills the universe is not explicit in 1:3-14, as it plays such a central role in the remainder of the letter (cf. 1:22-3; 4:15-16; 5:23, 30). Nevertheless, it is anticipated in the description of all things being summed up in Christ (see the notes on 1:10).

There is a general consensus among interpreters that the form of Eph 1:3-14 draws its origin from the extended blessing *(berakah)* found in the OT and in Jewish worship (see the notes on 1:3). The close association with the language of worship is best experienced if one reads the passage aloud. The amount of repetition is especially striking. For example, the invocation to praise is powerfully conveyed by the three-time repetition of the phrase "to the praise of his glory" (1:12; cf. 1:6, 14). To the frustration of some commentators, the logical progression of the argument is sometimes difficult to uncover. However, the language seems to have been chosen not so much for doctrinal clarity as to instill awe in the face of the majesty of God. It has been suggested that the text itself may constitute a blessing "hymn," perhaps used in conjunction with baptism.

While the hymnic features of the text are generally recognized, attempts to isolate a hymn from 1:3-14 and/or to identify precise strophes have fallen out of favor to some extent. This is primarily because the dependence of the passage on Colossians is now widely recognized. One might consider, for example, the relationship between Eph 1:6-7 and Col 1:13-14 (see the notes on Eph 1:7). There are also many points of contact between Ephesians and the undisputed letters of Paul. For example, there are similar ideas and terminology in Rom 8:12-30, which also refers to predestination and the adoption of believers as God's children, and which stresses the role of the Holy Spirit (see also the notes on 1:5, 7). Because of the probable dependence of Eph 1:3-14 on other Pauline works it is no longer possible to hold that this section had an independent liturgical life prior to the composition of Ephesians. However, it is important not to underestimate the significance of the presence of liturgical influences in the document based upon a view of the author of Ephesians as a mere synthesizer of traditions. All of Paul's letters are influenced by ritual forms, but Colossians draws upon hymnic and baptismal language to an exceptional extent (see M. Y. MacDonald [1988]). The inclusion of much of the language of Colossians in Ephesians means that the author of Ephesians understood it as relevant for the addressees. Ephesians is written from the standpoint of one who believes that recalling what is experienced in the midst of community gatherings and worship is a central teaching strategy. The older theories of N. A. Dahl and J. C. Kirby, which saw the liturgical language in Ephesians as key to unlocking the purpose of the document, need to be revisited in light of social-scientific thought on the importance of ritual for the creation of belief and for the establishment and integration of communities (see below).

Discussion of liturgical influences and the dependence of Ephesians on Colossians raises the question of the use of tradition by the author of Ephesians. Liturgical traditions, scriptural influences, and Pauline themes are woven together masterfully throughout the work. The correlation of Ephesians with Colossians and the undisputed letters of Paul, as well as with Acts and 1 Peter (see Mitton [1973] 15–18), points to the probability that the author of Ephesians was the recipient of a body of tradition left behind by the first generation of believers in the church. In the past the use of tradition by the author of Ephesians was sometimes judged by Protestant commentators as a sign of an emerging "early catholicism." Ernst Käsemann, for example, viewed the author of Ephesians as a skilled craftsman who organized traditions in relation to carefully chosen themes. Käsemann noted that Paul also appeals to tradition in his letters. But what sets Ephesians apart from the undisputed letters is the extent of the reliance upon tradition. Unlike the undisputed letters, the document does not reflect an ability to break through the boundaries of tradition. Its main interest lies in making a particular message normative (Käsemann [1968] 288–97). Most scholars today, regardless of their background or denominational affiliation, would not accept Käsemann's judgments with respect to Ephesians. Today scholars evaluate the synthesis of Pauline themes and traditions in Ephesians in light of a greater understanding of the social setting of early church communities. An understanding of the sociological processes of institutionalization is especially useful in illustrating why it is important to judge Ephesians on its own terms rather than by means of comparison to such Pauline epistles as Galatians, which blaze with innovation.

In their treatise on the sociology of knowledge, Peter Berger and Thomas Luckmann describe "institutionalization" as the result of "reciprocal typification" that occurs in human interaction. When individuals share patterns of activity, institutions with realities of their own are formed. The institution determines that actions of type X will be performed by actors of type X (Berger and Luckmann 72; see also M. Y. MacDonald [1988] 11–12). Institutionalization can begin between only two people, but the introduction of a third party changes the situation significantly. Institutions, once easily changeable, now become increasingly hardened or crystallized. The institutions are now experienced in a way that suggests they have a life of their own: "There we go again" becomes "This is how things are done"! On a societal level Berger and Luckmann note that these mechanisms are clearly visible when a third generation is introduced into a social group. Their observations can help us understand the shape of Ephesians —a document that many scholars believe was composed about 90 C.E., the period when a new generation of believers was being introduced into the Pauline churches. They may also shed light on the more "distant" and "objective" tone of Ephesians, which has made it virtually impossible to identify the precise circumstances the document addresses (see the Introduction, and the notes and interpretation on 1:1-2). According to Berger and Luckmann institutions can only be transmitted to a new generation as part of an objective world—a symbolic universe—that confronts the individual in a manner similar to the realities of the natural world (Berger and Luckmann 76–77; on the symbolic universe see the notes and interpretation on Col 1:3-8). When Ephesians was composed the Pauline churches were the beneficiaries of the fairly "hardened" symbolic universe. In contrast, Paul's letters were composed in about 50–60 C.E.—a period when new institutions were being formed and the apostle struggled to legitimate a novel proclamation. This same creativity was not necessary, or even possible, for the author of Ephesians, who sought to bring Paul's teaching to a new situation.

The reliance on tradition is not only an important feature of Ephesians, it also reveals something about the social setting of the community. Ephesians is probably addressed to a "third generation" community: a group that looks back to an earlier time to recall its formative moments. Deviance is probably a growing concern, coupled with fear of increasing assimilation within the broader environment. The group needs to secure its survival by transmitting its time-honored traditions to new members. As will be illustrated in the discussion of 2:11-22 (the description of the union of Gentile and Jew in one church), Pauline symbols have become detached from the situation in which they were born in order to address a new situation. We can shed light upon the social setting of Ephesians by paying close attention to which Pauline symbols have achieved an "objective quality" and how they are being used to address new situations. Because Ephesians is dependent upon Colossians it will be especially important to look for subtle differences in the symbolism between the two documents as possible indicators of the specific circumstances of the composition of Ephesians.

Drawing upon ideas and symbols that are found in Colossians and the undisputed letters of Paul, the main message of Eph 1:3-14 might be expressed as follows: God has a plan for the universe that has been in existence since "before the foundation of the world" (1:4). This plan is being fulfilled and revealed through God's agent, Christ. Believers have received the Holy Spirit as a pledge of their "inheritance toward redemption." The three members of the Trinity play a part in the text: God (vv. 3-6), Christ (vv. 7-12), and the Holy Spirit (vv. 13-14). Yet despite the existence of this "trinitarian" structure (see Thurston 94), the focus on God's initiative never fades from view. In terms of the social structures of the day God is depicted here as the ultimate patron or benefactor whose contact with his dependents is mediated by his agent Christ (Perkins 36; on patronage in the ancient world see the notes and interpretation on Col 1:3-8). To praise *(eulogeō)* one's benefactor is the natural outcome of having been endowed with every blessing (v. 3). Even the term for God's plan *(oikonomia)* in this passage is closely linked to the leadership exercised by powerful patrons in the ancient world; the term is frequently used to refer to the management of a house or city (see the notes on 1:10). The conviction concerning God's preordained plan of salvation is so strong that it leads to a celebration of the special status of believers as God's chosen ones—those who have been predestined for adoption. Once again the values and practices of the ancient world become invaluable in describing what God is like. The implication of the reference to "adoption" is that God is like a powerful but childless adult who longs for heirs and identifies them among the "slaves" (see the notes on 1:5).

It is not surprising that Eph 1:3-14 has figured prominently in theories of predestination throughout history. Predestination ideas in Pauline literature draw their origins from OT notions of God choosing a people (see the notes on 1:4). Moreover, scholars have noted many parallels between the predestination language of Eph 1:3-14 and the QL (e.g., Kobelski 886–87; Perkins 37–44). Ephesians 1:3-14 is often compared to Rom 8:29-30 (cf. 1 Cor 2:7), where the idea of predestination also appears in conjunction with notions of sonship. Within the broader context of Romans 8, however, there is greater emphasis on the benefits of adoption lying in the future than is the case in Eph 1:3-14.

What leads to the more concentrated stress on the special status of believers in the here and now in Ephesians? The descriptions of God's election of the righteous and condemnation of the wicked before creation in the QL may prove helpful (e.g., CD 2:7; 1QS 1:10-11). Pheme Perkins sees a significant difference between these texts and Ephesians:

> A striking difference between the use of the predestination language in
> Ephesians and similar expressions found at Qumran is the lack of any
> reference to the wicked. Ephesians knows such language, as later refer-
> ences to "those who are disobedient" indicate (2:2-3; 5:6). But in keeping
> with the author's vision of unity, God's gracious election could not be
> expressed as the sharp division of humankind into a righteous remnant,
> the holy elect, over against a majority who will never experience God's
> grace. (39)

Perkins may have overstated the differences somewhat between the
Qumran assertions and Ephesians in this case. In 2:2-3 the expressions
"the sons of disobedience" and "the children of wrath" are in effect corol-
laries of the description of believers as predestined for adoption as sons in
1:5. Ephesians 2:2-3 speaks of the past life of believers, and the implication
is that all who are outside the church are the progeny of wickedness. Later
in the epistle the wrath of God is said to be coming upon the sons of disobedience (5:6). In 1:3-14 believers are reminded of who they are and
where they stand in relation to God. The emphasis on redemption that is
experienced in the present, the adoption language, and the references to
predestination work together to convey strong sentiments of being set
apart from all others. Like the language of the QL these concepts reinforce
sectarian identity (see the discussion of "introverted sectarianism" at
Qumran in Esler [1994] 70–91). As 1:10 makes clear, Ephesians shares with
Colossians a tremendous interest in the universal scope of salvation (e.g.,
3:8-13; 6:19-20). But it is argued in this commentary that the sectarian response manifested by the epistle is more "introversionist" than that of
Colossians. In contrast to the Colossians, the recipients of Ephesians receive no explicit encouragement to engage in dialogue with outsiders
(5:15-16; cf. Col 4:5-6; and see the notes and interpretation on Col 4:2-6). In
fact, the practical implication of much of the teaching found in Ephesians
is greater isolation from the outside world. There are strong indications in
the text that believers are feeling increasingly menaced by external forces,
both human and those that are not of flesh and blood (cf. Eph 6:12; see
also the notes and interpretation on 1:15-23; 2:1-10; 6:10-20).

As Eph 1:3-14 illustrates, Ephesians shares a "cosmological" perspective with Colossians in describing Christ's identity and the nature of what
God has accomplished in Christ (cf. Col 1:15-20). In 1:3-14 this perspective
is revealed most clearly in the majestic description of God "summing up"
all things in Christ. The passage includes the first reference to "the heavenly places" in the epistle (see the notes on 1:3). The implication is that
believers already dwell in the heavenly places, the realm of divine transcendence where Christ sits at God's right hand (1:20; 2:6). As is also the
case with Colossians, Ephesians depicts the earthly existence of believers
as already joined to the heavenly invisible world (cf. Col 3:1-4). To a great

extent Eph 1:3-14 displays a perspective of "realized" eschatology (Lincoln [1990] 35). The tendency to speak as though all salvation is already present is to be expected with the use of liturgical language and is a natural counterpart to concepts of "election," but Ephesians generally displays a greater interest in the future and in the progress of history than does Colossians. In this passage the mention of "a plan for the fullness of time" has points of contact with apocalyptic thought anticipating the end of the present age by divine judgment (see the notes above). Moreover, in vv. 13-14 the description of believers being sealed with the Holy Spirit as a pledge of inheritance clearly assigns a future dimension to salvation (see the notes). The plan involves judgment of the wicked. It is particularly significant that the second half of Ephesians culminates in a call to stand ready for the day of judgment (6:12-13). Ephesians reveals a conviction that evil forces still menace the universe but will one day be conquered (2:21; 6:12).

The eschatological perspective of Ephesians appears to be something in between belief that all salvation is already present in Christ and anticipation of a future stage of salvation (Perkins 41). Given the parallels between 1:3-14 and the QL, it is interesting to consider the following comments by Philip Esler:

> Although a belief in the destruction of the present unjust order and the dawn of the messianic age was certainly a part of Qumran ideology, I wish to suggest that this was not its central focus. That this was the case is a reflection of an introversionist outlook. Salvation has become a present endeavor, rather than a future hope. The community believed that they were already a holy and almost perfect community, a community of God, closely linked with heaven; as 1QS says: "He has joined their assembly to the Sons of Heaven to be a Council of the Community, a foundation of the Building of Holiness, an eternal Plantation throughout all ages to come" (1QS XI.7b-9a). . . . Pressures which might lead a deprived and oppressed group to generate a millennial dream and long for its fulfillment became considerably attenuated for this community given that it had effectively insulated itself from the evils of the outside world. (84)

Esler's description of a community convinced of its perfection and of its links to heaven also captures the spirit of 1:3-14 (cf. 1:3-4). Ephesians 5:27 illustrates that the description of believers as "holy and without blemish" before Christ (v. 4) is a description of human perfection in the strongest possible terms. In 5:27 the cultural association of this language with gendered roles emerges boldly. The believing community is compared to a pure bride who stands prepared for Christ. In the ancient Mediterranean a pure woman's body was a potent symbol of an honorable community and the behavior of women was an important means of demonstrating concern for the reputation of household and community to the wider society (see the notes and interpretation on 5:21–6:9). To describe believers as chosen before the foundation of the world to be holy and without blemish is to give testimony to the fact that reputation and behavior are fitting for the most intimate of unions between the human and the divine.

To return to Esler's comments above, what is less clear in the case of Ephesians in relation to the QL is whether the community was confident that it had successfully isolated itself from the evils of the outside world. It is being argued in this commentary that one of the major purposes of the work is to encourage greater isolation from the outside world and this represents a significant departure from the attitude to the world that is normally encouraged in the undisputed letters of Paul and in Colossians (see the notes and interpretations on Col 4:2-6; Eph 6:10-20). As noted above, Ephesians displays interest in the universal scope of salvation. It would be overstating the case, therefore, to suggest that Ephesians discloses an introversionist response to the world of the magnitude identified by Esler with respect to the Qumran evidence. But in relation to the remainder of the Pauline corpus Ephesians is clearly moving in that direction.

Ephesians 1:3-4 praises God for establishing a community of believers chosen in Christ—set apart—before the foundation of the world. In order to remind believers of their true identity the author of Ephesians employs language that is rich in liturgical allusions. When the recipients of Ephesians heard 1:3-14 they would probably have been reminded of the various hymns associated with community worship. For social scientists the singing of hymns constitutes ritual. Rituals have been shown to be instrumental in the solidification of beliefs, community learning, and the formation of an ethos that carries participants into everyday life (Geertz 39; see the notes and interpretation on Col 1:15-20). The value attached to such hymns by the author of Ephesians is clearly attested by Eph 5:18-20 (cf. Col 3:17-18). In this text the singing of hymns is taken as evidence for the presence of the Spirit (the parallel text of Col 3:16 refers instead to the word of Christ). Likewise, Eph 1:3-14 culminates in a reference to the Holy Spirit.

While it is doubtful that 1:3-14 was a specific hymn associated with baptism, there is every reason to suspect that similar "blessing" language was employed during baptism (see above and the notes on 1:3). Ephesians contains many direct and indirect references to baptism (1:13-14; 2:1-6; 4:4-6, 22-24, 30; 5:25-27; see the full discussion of the evidence in Kirby 150–61). Although it continues to be a subject of lively debate, a reference to baptism is almost certainly found in 1:13-14, which speaks of the believers being "sealed" with the promised Holy Spirit. Social-scientific thought helps establish the likelihood of this scenario.

First, however, it is important to examine the reasons why commentators have sometimes been reluctant to conclude that 1:13-14 refers to baptism. It should be admitted that the reference to baptism is not explicit, and definite evidence for sealing as a means of describing baptism comes from the second century (see the notes on 1:13-14). We should guard against the tendency to read later developments back into the NT era. While acknowledging that "sealing" in Eph 1:13-14 is probably closely related to baptism, Lincoln (1990) has argued (citing Caird) that it is important not to confound water baptism with reception of the Spirit, which was usually accompanied by observable phenomena (e.g., Acts 8:17, 18; 10:44-46; 19:6). He concludes that "the 'seal' of the Spirit is therefore baptism of the Spirit, to which in the conversion-initiation process baptism in water was the reverse side of the coin, an expression of the faith to which God gives the Spirit" (Lincoln [1990] 40).

Lincoln raises an important issue when he points to observable phenomena in the midst of the assembly as signs of reception of the Spirit. Anthropologists who investigate ritual have stressed the importance of the use of physiological phenomena (e.g., blood, death, birth) in the creation of symbols and ideologies that integrate the individual within the community (Turner [1974] 55–56). The mention of sealing clearly calls to mind physiological phenomena: identifying with a sign, marking with a seal, branding. It is not surprising that this terminology is used by Paul to refer to the circumcision of Abraham in Rom 4:11. Moreover, circumcision is described as a seal in *Barn.* 9:6 and in several later rabbinic texts (e.g., *Ber.* 7.13; Str-B 3.495; 4.31-33; cited in Lincoln [1990] 39). Such language is a natural choice for initiation rites. Those who argue that sealing refers to baptism in 1:13-14 frequently note the metaphorical description of baptism as circumcision in Col 2:11. Given the broad purpose of 1:13-14 as celebration of the identity of believers as those adopted by God, it is highly probable that an appeal would be made to the rite in the early church that most clearly established the boundaries of the community: baptism (Lafontaine 160). The sealing left no visible traces, but the believers had experienced a physical rite and demonstrated observable spiritual phenomena; they had been profoundly changed.

Reading Eph 1:13-14 in light of social-scientific studies of ritual suggests that it is highly likely that "sealing" is a way of describing baptism that highlights the powerful transformation of believers. (It appears also to refer to baptism in 2 Cor 1:22, which speaks also of anointing; cf. Acts 10:38 where the term "anointing" is clearly used in conjunction with baptism.) It is possible that the author had reception of the Spirit primarily in mind when he composed 1:13-14, but no doubt in meditating upon God's purpose, the universe, and their membership in a holy people, those who heard Ephesians proclaimed in the midst of the assembly would also have thought of baptism. Reception of Spirit is very closely linked to water baptism in the NT (cf. Acts 2:37-39; 8:12-17; 19:5, 6; cited in Lincoln [1990]

39). In Rom 8:14-17 (a text that has many points in common with 1:3-14) reception of the Spirit and water baptism seem to merge completely; the initiate comes out of the water crying "'Abba! Father!'" Impelled by the Spirit of God, he or she proclaims adoption as God's child.

FOR REFERENCE AND FURTHER STUDY

Allan, John A. "The 'In Christ' formula in Ephesians," *NTS* 5 (1958–59) 54–62.
Brown, Raymond E. *The Semitic Background of the Term "Mystery" in the New Testament*. Philadelphia: Fortress, 1968.
Coppens, Joseph. "Mystery," in Pierre Benoit et al., *Paul and Qumran: Studies in New Testament Exegesis*. Edited by Jerome Murphy-O'Connor. Chicago: Priory, 1968, 132–58.
Dahl, Nils A. "Adresse und Proömium des Epheserbriefes," *ThZ* 7 (1951) 241–64.
Esler, Philip F. *The First Christians in Their Social Worlds*. London and New York: Routledge, 1994.
Käsemann, Ernst. "Ephesians and Acts," in Leander E. Keck and J. Louis Martyn, eds., *Studies in Luke-Acts*. London: S.P.C.K., 1968, 288–97.
Lampe, G.W.H. *The Seal of the Spirit*. London: Longmans, Green, 1951.
Lincoln, Andrew T. "A Re-Examination of 'The Heavenlies' in Ephesians," *NTS* 19 (1973) 468–83.
Lindemann, Andreas. *Die Aufhebung der Zeit: Geschichtsverständnis und Eschatologie im Epheserbrief*. StNT 12. Gütersloh: Gerd Mohn, 1975.
Lyall, Francis. "Roman Law in the Writings of Paul—Adoption," *JBL* 88 (1969) 458–66.
Lyonnet, Stanislas. "La bénédiction de Eph 1, 13-14 et son arrière-plan judaique," in *A la Rencontre de Dieu. Memorial Albert Gelin*. Bibliothèque de la Faculté Catholique de Théologie de Lyon 8. Le Puy: Éditions Xavier Mappus, 1961, 341–52.
O'Brien, Peter T. "Ephesians 1: An Unusual Introduction to a New Testament Letter," *NTS* 25 (1979) 504–16.
Sanders, Jack T. "Hymnic Elements in Ephesians 1–3," *ZNW* 56 (1965) 214–32.
Wilson, R. A. "'We' and 'You' in the Epistle to the Ephesians," in Frank L. Cross, ed., *Studia Evangelica 2*. TU 87. Berlin: Akademie-Verlag, 1964, 676–80.

16. *Thanksgiving and Prayer* (1:15-23)

15. Therefore I also, having heard of your faith in Christ Jesus and your love for all the saints, 16. do not cease giving thanks for you, remembering you in my prayers, 17. that the God of our Lord Jesus Christ, the Father of Glory, may give you a spirit of wisdom and of revelation in full

knowledge of him. 18. I pray that, the eyes of your heart having been enlightened, you may know what is the hope of his calling, what are the riches of the glory of his inheritance among the saints, 19. and what is the surpassing greatness of his power for us who believe, according to the working of his mighty strength 20. which he worked in Christ when he raised him from the dead and seated him at his right hand in the heavenly places, 21. far above every rule and authority and power and dominion and every name that is named, not only in this age, but in the age to come. 22. And he has put all things under his feet and gave him as head over all things to the church, 23. which is his body, the fullness of the one who fills all in every way.

NOTES

1:15. *Therefore I also, having heard of your faith in Christ Jesus and your love for all the saints:* Like 1:3-14, Eph 1:15-23 constitutes one long sentence in Greek without any formal stops. For the sake of clarity it has been divided into sentences in English in the translation above. "Therefore I also" connects this section to the previous blessing, perhaps especially to vv. 13-14 where the blessings experienced by the community are specifically in view. The language of 1:15-16 is very similar to that in Col 1:3-4, but the thoughts are expressed in the reverse order. Faith in Christ has communal connotations in this text. It refers to the faith that incorporates believers into the community located "in Christ"—incorporated into his body. The community is being praised for their exemplary display of faith and love. (On "in Christ" see the notes and interpretation on Eph 1:1-2, the notes on 1:3, the notes and interpretation on Col 1:1-2, and the notes on Col 1:4. On "saints" see the notes and interpretation on Eph 1:1-2 and Col 1:1-2.) Love is a frequent theme in Ephesians (see the notes on 1:4). In 1:4 love is also singled out as a quality demonstrated by the community. The familiar Pauline triad of faith, love, and hope occurs in the parallel text of Col 1:3-5 (see the notes). Hope is not mentioned in this verse, but it has already been mentioned in 1:12 and will be again in 1:18. Some textual witnesses ($\mathfrak{P}^{46}$ ℵ* A B P 33 1739 *al*) lack the reference to "and your love" and read simply *kai tēn eis tous hagious* (and toward all the saints). Commentators in favor of the shorter reading have pointed out that the longer reading may well have been the result of an attempt to harmonize Eph 1:15 with Col 1:4. However, there are also several considerations that militate against acceptance of the shorter reading, including the fact that a failure to distinguish between faith in Christ and faith directed towards one's fellow believers would be quite unusual in a Pauline epistle (but cf. Phlm 5). The shorter reading is in fact fairly easily explained by a scribal error caused by the repetition of the definite article (*tēn*; see the detailed discussion in Lincoln [1990] 46-47 and Metzger 602). On balance the longer reading is to be preferred.

16. *do not cease giving thanks for you, remembering you in my prayers:* In including a thanksgiving, Paul kept to the pattern of Hellenistic letters that typically gave

thanks to the gods for the health of the recipients or for news about the recipients that the author had received. However, thanksgiving is also part of Jewish liturgical tradition, closely associated with "blessing." Pauline thanksgivings bring these elements together (Lincoln [1990] 48). The thanksgiving in Ephesians most closely resembles those of Col 1:3-4 and Phlm 4-5. In most respects it follows the form of the thanksgiving found in all Pauline letters with the exception of Galatians, 1 Timothy, and Titus. Yet the thanksgiving in Ephesians is particularly long. The use of the present participle *eucharistōn* (giving thanks) is unusual (cf. Col 1:3: *eucharistoumen* [we give thanks]). It is especially striking that the thanksgiving in Ephesians offers so little detail about what the apostle is offering thanks for (cf. Col 1:3-8; Kitchen 53). As in Colossians, the thanksgiving of Ephesians is closely associated with prayer. The term *pauō* (cease) is used with respect to the apostle's prayer in Col 1:9. The notion of continuous petition and thanksgiving is found throughout the Pauline epistles (cf. Rom 1:8-10; 1 Cor 1:4; 1 Thess 1:1-3, 13; 2 Thess 1:3; 2:13; Phil 1:4; Phlm 4; Col 1:3). "Remembering you in my prayers" reflects the conventional assurance of a writer's constant prayers for the well-being of the addressee in Hellenistic letters (cf. 1 Thess 1:2; Rom 1:9; Phlm 4).

17. *that the God of our Lord Jesus Christ, the Father of Glory:* Beginning at 1:16b the thanksgiving quickly moves into a prayer for spiritual wisdom and revealed knowledge. The author of Ephesians is informing the recipients of what the apostle will ask God to do on their behalf. Verses 16-17 contain many terms that are similar to those in Col 1:9-10. The expression "Father of Glory" is a Semitic phrase similar to "Lord of glory" (1 Cor 2:8) and "God of glory" (Acts 7:2; cf. LXX Ps 28:3; Lincoln [1990] 56). The mention of "glory" gives the text a liturgical flavor. "Glory" is mentioned three times in the blessing of 1:3-14 in the context of a formula with unmistakable liturgical echoes (cf. 1:6, 12, 14). The blessing of 1:3-14 emphasizes God's initiative and actions through God's agent, Christ. The same emphasis is found in this passage. Note, for example, the points of contact with the blessing: "Blessed be the God and Father of our Lord Jesus Christ" (1:3).

may give you a spirit of wisdom and of revelation in full knowledge of him: This phrase is very similar to Col 1:9 where we find mention of "spiritual wisdom and understanding." In both Colossians and Ephesians it is often not entirely clear whether "spirit" refers to human spirit and hence to human qualities or to the Holy Spirit who inspires such capacities. But the fact that the Spirit is central in 1:13-14 and the importance of the Holy Spirit in Ephesians generally suggest the latter. There is clearly a connection between this verse and vv. 7-8, which refer to "wisdom and insight." Verses 7-8 emphasize what God has already accomplished "according to the riches of his grace that he lavished upon us in all wisdom and insight." In Ephesians the prayer is for believers to seize what they have already been offered. There are several references to wisdom in Ephesians (cf. 1:8, 17; 3:10; 5:15). The notion of revelation *(apokalypsis)* also plays a key role. It refers to the disclosure of divine mystery (3:3; cf. 3:5 where the cognate verb occurs, and note also the prevalence of the synonym *gnorizō* [to make known] in Ephesians: 1:9; 3:3, 5, 10; 6:19). Elsewhere in Ephesians the author uses this type of language to refer to the special insight shared by prophets and apostles (cf. 3:3-5), but in this case it clearly designates the divine benefits shared by all believers. The phrase culminates in a reference to *epignōsis,* which can mean simply knowledge or, as is more likely in this case, full knowledge (cf. NJB; see the notes on Col 1:9). Ephesians refers to *epignōsis* also in 4:13 (cf. Col 2:2; 3:10) and to *gnōsis* (knowledge) in Eph 3:19 (cf. Col 2:3). Notions of election that were so important in 1:3-14 also underlie this text as is made clear by descriptions of the Qumran community as the pure remnant possessing the spirit of understanding, insight, wisdom, and knowledge (1QS 4:3-6).

18. *I pray that, the eyes of your heart having been enlightened:* The Greek text reads literally "having been enlightened the eyes of your heart" and there are some questions concerning the place of this participial clause in the syntax of the verse (see Lincoln [1990] 47). As noted above, 1:15-23 constitutes one long sentence in Greek. In order to make the translation intelligible in English, "I pray" has been inserted. This expresses the intent of the verse in keeping with the prayer beginning at v. 16b. In the ancient Mediterranean world the heart and the eyes were understood as the zone of human capacity for thought, judgment, and emotion (Malina [1993] "Eyes–Heart," 63–67). The specific phrase "eyes of the heart" does not appear in the OT, but the eyes and heart are closely associated in the Hebrew Bible. For example, Eccl 11:9 gives the following instruction: "Follow the inclination of your heart and the desire of your eyes, but know that for all these things God will bring you into judgement" (NRSV; cf. Job 31:7; Prov 15:30; Ps 19:8). The QL refers to illumination of the heart (1QS 2:3; 1QS 11:3-6). The use of the expression "eyes of your heart" in 1:18 is clearly tied to expressions of fundamental commitment by believers. In keeping with this focus on commitment, some commentators have argued that "enlightenment" in 1:18 refers to baptism; they note in particular the relationship between this verse and Col 1:12-13, which seems to describe baptism in terms of transference from darkness to light (e.g., Schlier [1930] 79). "Enlightenment" came to be a common way of describing baptism in the second century (e.g., Justin Martyr, *Apol.* 1.61.12; 1.65.1; *Dial. Trypho* 39.2; 122.1, 2, 6). Moreover, in line with the perspective of Colossians the prior life of the Ephesians is described in terms of darkness (4:18; 5:8). Baptism does not seem to be as immediately relevant to the context of 1:18, however, as to the context of Col 1:12-13. Rather, spiritual illumination or inner enlightenment seems to be of primary interest (cf. Lincoln [1990] 58; Thurston 100). The verb *phōtizō* (to shine or give light) also occurs in the key text of Eph 3:9 (for similar use of the verb in the NT to refer to enlightenment see John 1:9; Heb 6:4; 10:32). Visionary phenomena may well have been highly prized by the author and recipients of Ephesians (see the interpretation below). It should be noted, however, that such experiences were probably quite closely related to the experience of conversion and baptism.

you may know what is the hope of his calling: The reference to God's "calling" brings to mind the repeated emphasis on God's initiative and choosing in 1:3-14. This is the second reference to hope in the epistle (cf. 1:12, though here the action of hoping is in view). "The hope of his calling" refers to the content of salvation, what has been hoped for: membership in the people of God. In keeping with Colossians, Ephesians here presents hope as an object to be seized (cf. Col 1:5, 23, 27). Hope serves essentially as a synonym for eternal life. Although 1:12-14 makes it clear that hope in Ephesians has future connotations, here the emphasis is on hope as shaping the present lives of believers. In this verse "hope" appears to complete the familiar Pauline triad of faith, love (1:15), and hope (1:18). A very similar expression occurs in 4:4: "the hope of your calling."

what are the riches of the glory of his inheritance among the saints: This phrase repeats many of the terms found in the blessing of 1:3-14: riches (v. 7); glory (vv. 6, 12, 14); inheritance (v. 14; cf. v. 11). In Rom 9:23-24 Paul uses the expression "the riches of glory" to refer to the calling of a people from among both Jews and Gentiles. In 1:14 the "inheritance" refers to the possession of salvation that flows from being children of God. However, 1:18 speaks of "his inheritance." Even though in the end it also amounts to a description of salvation, the emphasis in this case is on God possessing a people as his inheritance (Lincoln [1990] 59). There is extensive debate concerning the meaning of the expression *en tois hagiois* (in or among the saints). As is also the case with the parallel text of Col 1:12, parallels with the QL have suggested that the saints (literally "the holy ones") are angels: "Those whom God has chosen he has set as an eternal possession. He has allowed them to inherit the lot of the holy ones" (1QS 11:7, 8; cited in Lincoln [1990] 60). In the OT the angels are called "the holy ones" (e.g., Deut 33:2-3; Pss 89:6-8; Dan 8:13; cf. 1 Thess 3:13). Thus 1:18 could well constitute a reference to believers sharing in the lot of the angels. As is also true of Col 1:12, the strongest argument against an allusion to angels is the presence of many references to saints as believers in the epistle (1:1, 15; 2:19; 3:8; see the notes on Col 1:12). This is clearly the case, for example, in 1:15 at the beginning of this section. However, in the case of Ephesians the content of 1:15-23 as a whole suggests that there may have been a shift from the reference to saints (believers) in v. 15 to a reference to the holy ones (angels) in v. 18. In this text and elsewhere in Ephesians believers are depicted as engaged in a journey of heavenly ascent (see the interpretation below).

19. *and what is the surpassing greatness of his power for us who believe, according to the working of his mighty strength:* There is a change from the second person plural (v. 18) to the first person plural here, but this does not appear to have any particular significance. With this verse the passage moves on to argue that God's power working through Christ exceeds all other powers and authorities. Christ's power is beyond all measure and reaches into infinity. The use of synonyms and the repetition serve to emphasize the point (cf. Col 1:11). While there is greater emphasis on divine power in Ephesians than in Colossians, there are texts in Colossians that prepare the way for such a focus. Colossians 1:29 speaks of God's energy powerfully working within Paul during the struggles of his apostleship. Both Eph 1:19 and Col 1:29 refer to *energeia* (the energy or the working). In Col 2:12 the same term is used to refer to the power

of God in raising Christ from the dead. The power of God works through Christ, through Paul, and ultimately through all believers.

20. *which he worked in Christ when he raised him from the dead:* Many scholars have argued that the author draws upon traditional material in vv. 20-23, perhaps creedal formulations or a hymn fragment. That these verses are subject to liturgical influences is suggested by their points in common with such NT hymns as Phil 2:6-11 and Col 1:15-20, which also mention Christ's resurrection, his exaltation, and his place at God's right hand. But attempts to reconstruct an actual hymn underlying 1:20-23 are subject to many uncertainties (see Lincoln [1990] 50–52). The verb *enērgēsen* (he worked) is a cognate of the noun "the working" in v. 19. On the similarities between this verse and Col 2:12 see the notes on v. 19. In keeping with other texts in the NT, the resurrection is depicted here as something God accomplishes, not as the accomplishment of Christ alone.

and seated him at his right hand in the heavenly places: References to Christ's resurrection and exaltation occur also in Rom 8:34, Col 3:1, and Acts 2:32, 33. With echoes of Ps 110:1, Christ is depicted as exalted and enthroned at God's right hand (cf. Col 3:1). Psalm 110 is frequently cited in the NT (e.g., Rom 8:34; Acts 2:34-35; Heb 10:12; see Hay). Ephesians 2:6 speaks of believers sitting together in the heavenly places in Christ Jesus, but omits the reference to God's right hand. The expression "the heavenly places" is distinctive to Ephesians and occurs frequently throughout the letter (see the notes on 1:3). Here as in 1:3 it refers to the realm of divine transcendence, but other instances of the expression in Ephesians indicate that it was understood as a realm subject to spiritual forces that could trouble the lives of believers (cf. 3:10; 6:12). It is interesting to note that, in contrast to the undisputed letters of Paul, the exaltation of Christ rather than the cross is the locus of power (cf. Rom 1:4; 1 Cor 6:14; 2 Cor 13:4; Phil 3:10; see Barth and Blanke 69). This shift of emphasis and the need to highlight God and Christ's power in the strongest possible terms may be related to deeply felt threats from menacing powers (see the interpretation below).

21. *far above every rule and authority and power and dominion:* Although the terms do not appear in the same order, this list of "powers" is almost identical to that found in Col 1:16 (cf. Col 2:10, 15). In Colossians *thronos* (throne) is listed first, but this term does not appear in Ephesians. Instead Ephesians speaks of *dynamis* (power). Both these terms refer to spiritual powers (cf. 3:10; 6:12). They are associated with angels in Jewish literature (see the extensive discussion of the evidence in Arnold 52–54). The proponents of the false teaching in Colossae seem to have believed that the veneration of angelic beings provided additional access to the benefits of salvation (see the notes on Col 1:16; 2:10, 15, 18). Their worship included ascetic practices designed to lead to visions of the heavenly realm (see the notes and interpretation on Col 2:8-23). In response to such tendencies the author of Colossians insisted upon the final authority and ultimate triumph of Christ over all powers. There is no doubt that the Colossians author considered these powers to be subordinate to Christ. Ephesians 1:21 reinforces this idea. Although it remains a subject of lively debate, (note,

for example, that Arnold [1989] argues that the powers are both angelic and evil [56], but Perkins [51] argues in favor of a positive use of angelic powers in 1:21), there is good reason to believe that in Ephesians the powers are actually viewed as hostile beings. The understanding of powers as hostile beings is supported especially by 6:12, but also by comparing the text to 1 Cor 15:24-26 where the rulers, powers, and authorities are enemies. Both Eph 1:21-22 and 1 Cor 15:24-26 refer to Ps 8:6 and Ps 110:1.

and every name that is named, not only in this age, but in the age to come: A reference to names also appears in the description of Christ's supremacy in Phil 2:9-11. In the ancient world the names of deities were thought to have divine power. Clinton Arnold (1989) has argued that the naming of names was central to the practice of magic in Greco-Roman society. He has drawn attention, for example, to the repeated reference to the very term "name" *(onoma)* in the magical papyri. He argues that the recipients of Ephesians would have been very familiar with magical practices and so for them this verse would convey a powerful message: Christ's name alone is enough for a successful confrontation with the powers of evil (Arnold 54–56). The reference to two ages draws its origins from Jewish apocalyptic: the present evil age and the new age when God will reign supreme (Mitton [1973] 73; cf. Matt 12:32). Ephesians leans in the direction of "realized eschatology" and stresses the present salvation of believers. However, this text offers one of several indications in the letter that the future remains of importance for the author of Ephesians (see the notes and interpretation of 1:3-14).

22. *And he has put all things under his feet:* With this citation of Ps 8:6 the author of Ephesians continues to highlight Christ's ultimate authority. Ps 110:1 has points in common with Ps 8:6. Both are cited by Paul in 1 Cor 15:24-26 (see the notes on vv. 20-21 above), and the citation reappears here in Ephesians.

and gave him as head over all things to the church, 23. which is his body: The NRSV and NJB have "made him" instead of "gave him as." But this does not adequately capture the strength of the claim. The verb *didomi* (give) occurs frequently throughout Ephesians (cf. 1:17; 3:2, 7, 8, 16; 4:7, 8, 11, 27, 29; 6:19). Barth (1974) notes that in Hebrew the verb "to give" can sometimes have the meaning of "to appoint" or "to install" (Barth 157–58; e.g., 1 Sam 8:5-6; Lev 17:11). But, with the possible exception of 4:11, the verb appears to be used in Ephesians in the usual Greek sense, meaning "to give." The claim is literally that God gave Christ to the church as head. The importance of the church in God's plan of salvation could not be stated more strongly. "All things" clearly refers to the universe (cf. 1:10). God gives Christ as cosmic Lord to the church as head. The use of the symbol of the body *(sōma)* to refer to the church is very similar in Colossians and Ephesians (see Best [1998] 189–96). This symbolism both builds upon and departs from the body symbolism in the undisputed letters of Paul (see the full discussion in the notes and interpretation of Col 1:18). In Colossians and Ephesians the church *(ekklēsia)* is explicitly equated with the body (1:22-23; 5:23; cf. Col 1:18, 24). Christ has become the head *(kephalē)*, while believers make up his body (cf. 4:4, 15; 5:23; cf. Col 1:18, 24; 2:10, 17, 19). Colossians 1:15-20 reveals a close connection between Christ as head of the universe and Christ as head of the church and an underlying equivalence between the universe and the church (cf. Col 2:10). These ideas become more explicit in Eph 1:22-23. The comparison of the whole cosmos to the body is well attested in Greek sources, including Hellenistic Jewish literature (see the notes on Col 1:18).

Comparison of Col 1:15-20 to Eph 1:22-23, however, also reveals a difference of emphasis. In Col 1:15-20 Christ's body (the church) is viewed as the vehicle of a cosmic reconciliation (cf. 1:18, 19). But Eph 1:22-23 articulates what Christ's universal reign means for the life of the church; the focus is on the majestic parameters of the *ekklēsia*. This is the first instance of the term *ekklēsia* (church or assembly) in Ephesians. As is frequently noted by commentators, in contrast to other Pauline works (including Colossians), in Ephesians *ekklēsia* always refers to the universal church and never to the local community (cf. 3:10, 21; 5:23, 24, 25, 27, 29, 32).

the fullness of the one who fills all in every way: There are several problems of translation and interpretation associated with this phrase. The use of the term "fullness" *(plērōma)* is key to the distinctive theological vision of Colossians and Ephesians (cf. 3:19; 4:13; Col 1:19; 2:9). *Plērōma* means literally that which fills or that which makes something complete, but the term took on a technical meaning among second-century Gnostics. For example, among the Valentinians it came to refer to the totality of emanations that came from God (see the full discussion in the notes on Col 1:19). In Colossians "the fullness" means the fullness of God in its totality that comes to dwell in Christ (Col 1:19; 2:9). It is sometimes suggested that the author of Colossians took up the use of the term on account of debates with the false teachers who used the term in their speculations concerning the heavenly realm (see the notes on Col 1:19). The author of Ephesians seems to have adopted the language of the author of Colossians, or the terminology may simply reflect contact with a syncretistic religious environment. In line with the meaning of "the fullness" in Colossians some commentators have argued that it refers back directly to Christ in v. 22 (him). But it makes better grammatical sense to understand "the fullness" as a second symbol for the church: The church is both the body and the fullness (Barth 158; Lincoln [1990] 73). There has also been debate as to whether "fullness" here has the more usual active meaning (that which fills; i.e., the church would be completing Christ, cf. Col: 1:24) or whether it is passive in force (that which is filled by Christ). On balance, however, the passive meaning is to be preferred (see the detailed discussion in Lincoln [1990] 76). Finally, it is not immediately clear whether the participle *plēroumenou* is passive (the one who is filled) or middle (the one who fills). Given the fact that Col 1:19 and 2:9 describe God as already dwelling fully in Christ, as well as other considerations, it is probably best to understand the participle as middle with an active force. As in the previous verse, "all things" refers to the cosmos and "in every respect" is added for emphasis (see the full discussion in Lincoln [1990] 73–78). Lincoln summarizes the author's overall thought in v. 23 as follows: "the church is Christ's fullness and Christ is the one who is completely filling the cosmos" ([1990] 77). In the end it must be admitted that v. 23

cannot be pressed too hard for doctrinal clarity. The church, Christ, and the universe are linked closely together in order to celebrate what God has accomplished through Christ among God's people. See also the notes on 4:10.

INTERPRETATION

The thanksgiving of 1:15-23 is introduced with an assertion of Paul's apostolic authority. The apostle speaks in the first person singular, recalling the greeting of 1:1-2 which states that the letter is from Paul alone and not from Paul and his coworkers as is usually the case (cf. Col 1:1-2). As the notes above make clear, the thanksgiving is structurally connected to the blessing of 1:3-14, contains many of the same terms (e.g., hope, v. 12; inheritance, v. 14), and shares many interests with the previous text (e.g., the focus on election and God working through God's agent, Christ). But 1:15-23 also contains important points of contact with what follows. The content of Paul's intercession in 1:17-19, for example, has much in common with 3:14-19. These overlaps, and the fact that the first part of Ephesians ends formally at 3:21, have led some to suggest that all of 1:3–3:21 functions as an introductory thanksgiving (e.g., J. T. Sanders [1962]). Yet it is clearly possible to identify separate units with their own purposes within this large section. For example, one of the main purposes of the thanksgiving of 1:15-23 appears to be to introduce the important theme of the universal church that is taken up again frequently in the letter.

The references to the faith and love of the recipients are intended to engender the goodwill of the recipients and to draw them into the work (cf. Col 1:3). That the apostle has heard of their faith and love means that these have been publicly demonstrated. In terms of the value system of the first-century Mediterranean world, the community has displayed honor and so is being recognized. In 1:17-19 (introduced in v. 16b) the thanksgiving moves into a report of the content of Paul's intercession on their behalf. The brevity of the specific thanksgiving in 1:15-16 and the lack of detail about the community (cf. Col 1:3-8) support the theory that the epistle was originally intended for more than one church community. In contrast, however, the content of Paul's intercession on behalf of the recipients is described in significant detail. There are two major requests: (1) that God may grant the recipients "a spirit of wisdom and of revelation" (v. 17); (2) that believers may know "the hope of his calling," "the riches of the glory of his inheritance," and "the greatness of his power" (vv. 18-19). While the prayer report of vv. 17-19 focuses specifically on believers, vv. 20-23 have a hymnic tone (see the notes on 1:20) and celebrate what God has accomplished in Christ. The focus is on Christ's exaltation, his cosmic power, and the consequences for the life of the universal church. A more specific focus on the recipients is resumed in 2:1.

The emphasis on enlightenment and the description of the experience of being a believer in 1:17-19 are among the most interesting features of the thanksgiving in 1:15-23. Given the critique of the visionary experiences of the Colossian opponents (see the notes and interpretation on Col 2:8-23), one is struck by the reference to "the eyes of your heart having been enlightened" (v. 18). There is a great interest in revelation, enlightenment, insight, and mystery throughout Ephesians (e.g., 1:3-14; 3:2-5, 8-10, 18-19). Even Paul's mission is described in terms of illumination (3:9-10). The experience of enlightenment leads to a type of "knowing" (v. 18). Here the thanksgiving builds on ideas already introduced in the blessing, where God is described as having made known the mystery of the divine will (1:9; cf. 1:8-10). In both the blessing and the thanksgiving the special insight is closely tied to receipt of the Holy Spirit (1:13-14, 17). As the notes above make clear, it is highly likely that "a spirit of wisdom and of revelation" in v. 17 is a reference to the Holy Spirit who grants special insight (cf. Col 1:9). Moreover, Eph 5:18-19 suggests that the Spirit was central to the rituals embraced by the community (see the notes and interpretation on 4:17–5:20).

Believing that the epistle was originally intended for the community at Laodicea (see the notes on 1:1 and the Introduction), Michael Goulder has argued that Ephesians was written by Paul to counter the claims of Jewish Christian visionaries. While one might contest specific features of his reconstruction (including his treatment of Ephesians as genuine), Goulder has rightly pointed to the importance of visionary phenomena in Ephesians. In placing Ephesians within the broader context of Pauline literature Goulder attaches particular significance to the ambivalence Paul displays concerning visions in 2 Corinthians 12, apparently under threat of competition from more visionary teachers. He also draws attention to the visionary component of the Colossian false teaching (Col 2:18), which operated in conjunction with various Jewish rituals and practices (Goulder 18–30; see the notes and interpretation on Col 2:8-23). According to Goulder competition from Jewish Christian visionaries persisted and Ephesians was written to counter their claims. He argues that the emphasis on revelation (*apokalypsis;* see the notes on 1:17) throughout Ephesians and especially in 3:2-21 is intended to respond to them. Goulder admits that such a vocabulary is fairly regular with Paul (e.g., Gal 1:12, 16), but correctly identifies a particular stress on hiding and revealing in Ephesians (20). In seeking to understand the background of Ephesians, Goulder points to Jewish texts including several visionary texts that mention angels. In *3 Enoch,* for example, the angels' praise of God is the climax of Enoch's vision (Goulder 19; see also 23–24). Angels are of interest in Ephesians as well. As the notes on 1:18 illustrate, sharing in the lot of the angels may well be the true meaning of the phrase "inheritance among the saints."

Goulder has made a valuable contribution in highlighting the interest in visionary phenomena in Ephesians. I find his argument that Ephesians is intended to *counter* the claims of visionaries less convincing, however. He believes that the emphasis on Christ's triumph in Ephesians is intended to respond to visionaries who make bold claims about their access to the heavenly realm (Goulder 25). Thus the argument of Ephesians is understood as similar to that of Colossians where what God has accomplished through Christ renders the visionary techniques and ascetic practices of the opponents irrelevant. But in contrast to Colossians there is very little evidence in Ephesians of polemic against false teachers (cf. Eph 4:14). I am convinced that while Ephesians certainly shares with Colossians a great interest in Christ's supremacy, it is in fact quite open to visions and ecstatic experiences of the Spirit (see the notes on 5:18). In other words, Ephesians may reflect a type of spirituality in which visionary phenomena have not become, or are no longer, viewed as problematic. One imagines that the proponents of the Colossian philosophy would have found Ephesians far more conducive to their way of life than the response they received in the letter to the Colossians! The author of Ephesians is significantly less guarded than the author of Colossians in the use of language that would have had broad appeal in a syncretistic religious environment.

Despite these reservations, Goulder's analysis alerts us to an important current running throughout Ephesians. In line with the analysis described above he attaches special significance to the distinctive use of the phrase "the heavenly places" in Ephesians (see the notes on 1:20). He draws attention to a variety of texts where the holy man journeys through the seven heavens. The journey is frequently depicted using architectural language, sometimes in terms of a succession of houses and temples and of spaces being filled (e.g., *1 Enoch* 1–36; see Goulder 29). It is therefore interesting to note the use of architectural symbolism (fused with body symbolism) to refer to the *ekklēsia* in 2:14-22. In Ephesians taken as a whole there is a sense in which believers, and indeed the universal church, are depicted as engaged in a journey of heavenly ascent. These ideas underlie the exposition of what has been accomplished through Christ in 1:20-23. In 1:20 Christ is depicted as sitting at God's right hand in the heavenly places. This prepares the way for the description of believers sitting in the heavenly places in Eph 2:6. It is difficult to imagine Paul making such a statement if his desire had been to discourage visionaries (cf. Revelation 4).

In Ephesians Christ's exaltation is closely related to the ultimate triumph of believers. They too are moving from the earthly realm to the heavenly realm. Similar ideas are found in the apocalyptic book of Daniel where the exaltation of a heavenly figure to God's throne comes to represent the ultimate triumph of God's elect (Dan 7:13-27; cf. Perkins 50). In

Daniel's vision this heavenly figure (perhaps identified with the archangel Michael [cf. Dan 10:13, 21; 12:1]) is given "dominion and glory and kingship, that all peoples, nations, and languages should serve him" (Dan 7:14 NRSV). He is identified with the "saints" or "the holy ones": "The kingship and dominion and the greatness of the kingdoms under the whole heaven shall be given to the people of the holy ones of the Most High" (Dan 7:27 NRSV). As is also the case with Eph 1:18, there is considerable debate concerning whether "the holy ones" in Dan 7:18, 21, 25, 27 refers specifically to angelic hosts or to a human community. In either case a heavenly figure comes to represent a corporate entity (and ultimately the glorification of a people) as the body of Christ comes to represent the church. In Daniel such heavenly exaltation is related to triumph over historical thrones and powers. The vision correlates heavenly enthronement to the defeat of a political threat, especially the rule of Antiochus IV Epiphanes in the second century B.C.E. (Dan 7:7-8, 23, 25). Ephesians does not share this specific historical focus. However, as the discussion of the spiritual powers mentioned in v. 21 makes clear, the author of Ephesians is certainly convinced that believers are menaced by outside forces (see the notes on 1:21).

The emphasis on Christ's victory over evil spiritual powers in 1:21 prepares the way for the admonition for believers to engage in spiritual warfare (6:10-20). That the powers are spiritual agencies and not human authorities is communicated especially strongly by 6:12 where conflict is said to be not against flesh and blood but against spiritual powers. In the NT the various terms for "powers" in 1:21 sometimes do refer to earthly authorities (e.g., Rom 13:1-7), but this is clearly not the case in Ephesians. Attempts to demythologize the terms by understanding them as representing oppressive structures of society may be valid interpretations for our time, but it is important to recognize that such an interpretation does not fit with the cosmology of the New Testament world (see Lincoln [1990] 64). The recipients of Ephesians would have understood the powers as spiritual forces of evil that could influence their lives in dangerous ways. The battle language of Ephesians suggests that these should be understood as outside forces and enemies of the community. Their presence requires nothing less than a combat stance. The recipients of Ephesians may well have employed magical practices in the past to deal with such menacing forces and were perhaps inclined to consider returning to them. For such people Eph 1:21-23 would convey an important message: Christ's power transcends these spiritual forces and fills the universe (Arnold [1989] 56).

While they do not refer to earthly enemies per se, it is important to recognize that the spiritual powers in Ephesians are understood as deeply affecting the society in which believers live. This is illustrated especially clearly by 2:1-3, where the outside world is depicted as dominated by the "ruler of the power of the air" (2:1; see the notes and interpretation on 2:1-10). This dominion causes great moral decay (2:3) and the only real defense against it is God's armor of ethical and spiritual virtues (6:14-17). Thus the way society is now understood in Ephesians as the result of a cosmic struggle that is overcome for believers by means of a new life with Christ in the heavenly places. What is experienced on the earthly plane has a cosmic referent. Furthermore, how one lives on the earthly plane finds its true significance in the heavenly places. Ephesians was in all likelihood composed in an atmosphere of great consciousness of evil and commitment to separation from outsiders. In comparison to the other writings in the Pauline corpus it demonstrates a sectarian identity that is moving in the direction of greater introversion. There is no evidence that believers are experiencing persecution from political powers, but there is good reason to believe that they are experiencing increasing hostility from nonbelievers as their forays into society at large become increasingly problematic (see the notes and interpretation on 1:3-14; 2:1-10).

An awareness of these sociological realities can shed light on the reasons for the increased emphasis on the universal church in Ephesians. It is sometimes argued that christology has been essentially swallowed up by ecclesiology in Ephesians. Some interpreters have been particularly struck by the contrast between Colossians and Ephesians in this regard, especially since these two documents display very similar theologies. But christology is actually no less important in Ephesians than in Colossians. As the thanksgiving of 1:15-23 illustrates so well, ecclesiology is the result of christology in Ephesians. Christ's exaltation has consequences for believers, and this is expressed in terms of the whole corporate entity. Ephesians spells out the implications for the life of the church of the christology it shares with Colossians. The greater interest in the identity of the church and in its universal dimensions in Ephesians is probably the result of the conviction that hostile powers threaten the community. Removed from a first century context Ephesians may well give the impression of an unhealthy "divinization" of the church, perhaps expressed most dramatically in the notion of God giving Christ to the church as head in v. 22. But the composite of metaphors for the church in v. 23 represents the hopes, visions, and dreams of a community that feels under siege. The purpose of these metaphors proclaiming the majestic boundaries of the community is twofold. First, the notion that the church shares in and gives expression to Christ's universal reign relativizes the experience of alienation and opposition that inevitably accompanies separation from a world dominated by evil; all things come under the church's domain (that which is filled by Christ). Second, while the notion of the universal church in Ephesians links the earthly community with heavenly realities it also allows believers to draw comfort from the conviction that ultimately they belong to a heavenly assembly. The heavenly places are, after all, where Christ is to be found (v. 20) and believers have now been raised with him and are seated with him (2:6).

For Reference and Further Study

Arnold, Clinton. *Ephesians, Power and Magic: The Concept of Power in Ephesians in Light of its Historical Setting.* MSSNTS 63. Cambridge: Cambridge University Press, 1989.

Carr, Wesley. *Angels and Principalities: The Background, Meaning, and Development of the Pauline Phrase hai archai kai hai exousiai.* MSSNTS 42. Cambridge: Cambridge University Press, 1981.

Ernst, Josef. *Pleroma und Pleroma Christi: Geschichte und Deutung eines Begriffs der paulinischen Antilegomena.* BU 5. Regensburg: Pustet, 1970.

Goulder, Michael D. "The Visionaries of Laodicea," *JSNT* 43 (1991) 15–39.

Hay, David M. *Glory at the Right Hand: Psalm 110 in Early Christianity.* SBL.MS 18. Nashville: Abingdon, 1973.

Malina, Bruce J. "Eyes–Heart," in John J. Pilch and Bruce J. Malina, eds., *Biblical Social Values and Their Meaning.* Peabody, Mass.: Hendrickson, 1993, 63–67.

Overfield, P. D. "Pleroma: A Study in Content and Context," *NTS* 25 (1979) 384–96.

Sanders, Jack T. "The Transition from Opening Epistolary Thanksgiving to Body in the Letters of the Pauline Corpus," *JBL* 81 (1962) 348–62.

_____. "Hymnic Elements in Ephesians 1–3," *ZNW* 56 (1965) 214–32.

Schubert, Paul. *Form and Function of the Pauline Thanksgivings.* BZNW 20. Berlin: Töpelmann, 1939.

Wink, Walter. *Naming the Powers: the Language of Power in the New Testament.* Philadelphia: Fortress, 1984.

17. *The Consequences of Life Together with Christ* (2:1-10)

1. And you were dead in your transgressions and sins 2. in which you once walked according to the age of this world, according to the ruler of the power of the air, of the spirit who now works in the sons of disobedience. 3. Among them we also all once lived in the passions of our flesh, following the wishes of our flesh and impulses and were children of wrath by nature, like the rest. 4. But God, being rich in mercy, because of his great love with which he loved us 5. even when we were dead in transgressions, made us alive with Christ (by grace you have been saved), 6. and he raised us up with him and seated us with him in the

heavenly places in Christ Jesus 7. in order that in the ages to come he might show the immeasurable riches of his grace in kindness to us in Christ Jesus. 8. For by grace you have been saved through faith, and this is not of you, it is a gift of God—9. not of works, lest anyone should boast. 10. For we are his handiwork, created in Christ Jesus for good works, which God prepared beforehand in order that we might walk in them.

NOTES

2:1. *And you were dead in your transgressions and sins:* The previous section ends with the introduction of the important theme of the universal church (1:22-23) that is taken up again in 2:11-22. However, 2:1-10 returns to the question of how God's plan for the salvation of the world is worked out through Christ (cf. 1:17-21). A connection between 2:1-10 and the thanksgiving of 1:15-23 is suggested by the use of *kai* (and; cf. Col 2:13), but this is frequently omitted from English translations (e.g., NRSV; REB; NAB). The opening clause (literally "you being dead") is actually the object of the verb *synezōopoiēsen* (made alive with) in v. 5. The subject of the verb is God (v. 4). The opening clause is repeated at the beginning of v. 5, using the first person plural instead of the second person plural. The dative expression "in your transgressions and sins" is often understood as a dative of instrument: "through your" (e.g., NRSV; cf. NJB), but because evil is depicted as a realm in vv. 1-3 it seems best to understand the expression as bringing together an instrumental meaning with a locative one. The terms "transgressions" *(paraptōmata)* and "sins" *(harmatiai)* are synonyms and are also used interchangeably in Romans (5:12-21) and Colossians (cf. 1:14; 2:13). Death is clearly a spiritual death caused by sin (cf. Rom 7:9-13). In describing the previous existence of believers the author is obviously influenced by Col 2:13, but elsewhere in Pauline literature death and sin are linked with the power of the former age (cf. Rom 5:12-21; 6:23; 1 Cor 15:56; see Lincoln [1990] 93). "Death" is frequently used in a figurative sense in the NT (e.g., Luke 15:24, 32; Rev 3:1; Jas 2:17-26). The metaphorical references to death and new life in Colossians and Ephesians are connected to the death and resurrection of Jesus. They also recall the experience of baptism (Col 2:12-13; cf. Rom 6:4-5, 8-11, 13). Verses 1-3 include the "you-we" distinction that is found throughout Ephesians. "You" in v. 1 may well be a reference to the Gentile recipients of Ephesians (cf. 2:11), but other explanations are also possible (see the notes on 1:12).

2. *in which you once walked according to the age of this world:* There are four instances of the preposition *en* (in, among) in vv. 2-3. Believers once walked in the realm of sin. The verb *peripateō* literally means "to walk," but it is most frequently translated simply "to live." The more literal translation better captures the active connotations of the word and the fact that it refers to visible behavior. In Col 4:5 it is used to describe how believers should conduct themselves in relation to nonbelievers (cf. 1 Thess 2:12; 4:1-12; see the notes on Col 1:10). The term occurs frequently in Ephesians (cf. 2:10; 4:1, 17; 5:2, 8, 15). The

attempt to distinguish the ethical comportment of believers from the non-believing world is central to its usage. The world *(kosmos)* is the realm of sin. Commentators are divided, however, with respect to how one should understand the term *aiōn* (age). *Aiōn* appears in Gnostic literature as a technical term to describe the spiritual beings associated with heavenly fullness (Perkins 56). Some commentators have therefore understood the clause "according to the age of this world" as being in apposition to the subsequent "the ruler of the power of the air." They have understood *aiōn* to mean a spiritual power or being (BAGD 26; Kobelski 887; Gnilka [1971] 114; Barth [1974] 212). However, the fact that in all other instances in Pauline literature the term is used in a temporal sense (with the possible exception of 2:7), and not in reference to a personal power, strongly suggests that it should be understood as such here. Believers once walked according to the present evil age, which stands under divine judgment (Perkins 58; Lincoln [1990] 94; cf. Eph 1:21; 2:7; 3:9). It is important to note that Paul talks of personal powers ruling this age (cf. 2 Cor 4:4; 1 Cor 2:6, 8) but does not use the specific term *aiōn* to refer to such powers (Lincoln [1990] 95).

according to the ruler of the power of the air: In ancient astrology the air was understood as an intermediate realm between the earthly and the heavenly realms, and as inhabited by various cosmic powers (stars, spiritual forces, demons, angels, etc.; cf. Philo, *Gig.* 8–18). In Eph 3:10 and 6:12 the heavenly places are viewed as subject to the influence of evil spiritual powers. It is evident that according to the cosmology of Ephesians malevolent forces inhabit all spaces, from the earth to the upper reaches of the universe. The ruler of the power of the air is the devil (4:27; cf. 6:11-12 where similar terminology occurs). In the Fourth Gospel Satan is described as the ruler of this world (cf. John 12:31; 14:30; 16:11). There is a connection between the ruler of the power of the air and the evil powers described in 1:21. The term "power" or "authority" *(exousia)* appears in both verses, and a cognate of "ruler" *(archōn)* in 1:21.

of the spirit who now works in the sons of disobedience: Most translations have simply "the spirit," but the Greek is literally "of the spirit" *(tou pneumatos)*. It is difficult to be certain how to understand "of the spirit," but clearly here it is not the Holy Spirit. It has frequently been understood as another name for "the ruler," yet the term is in the genitive and not in the accusative as one might expect (though it might be a genitive of apposition; cf. BDF 167). Other interpreters have argued that "of the spirit" is another way of saying "of the air"; this would more readily explain the use of the genitive. Lincoln has proposed that the term is actually in apposition to *exousia* (power or authority), which he translates as "realm" (cf. Col 1:13; [1990] 95–96). In that case the spirit would be a more impersonal force through which the influences of evil would be transmitted. Thus the ruler influences the full extent of the cosmic sphere. Whatever the precise relationship between the terms in 2:2, however, the cosmology clearly includes belief in the existence of evil spiritual beings that are the antithesis of the Spirit of God (cf. 2 Cor 4:4; 1QS 3:13–4:26; see Barth 215). Ephesians 6:12 refers specifically to spiritual beings *(ta pneumatika)* who are closely associated with the devil. In 1:15-23 there is great emphasis on divine power, which is said to be working *(energeō)* in Christ and among believers (1:19-20; a cognate noun of the term occurs in 1:19; cf. 1:11). The same verb appears here to speak of the forces at work among nonbelievers. It is clearly a very menacing threat. "Sons of disobedience" is a Semitic phrase that resembles QL expressions (e.g., 1QS 1:10 [sons of darkness]; 3:21 [sons of deceit]). It constitutes very strong language assigning all nonbelievers to the realm of sin.

3. *Among them we also all once lived in the passions of our flesh, following the wishes of our flesh and impulses:* In Greek vv. 1-7 form a single sentence. For the sake of clarity a new sentence has been introduced into the English translation at the beginning of v. 3. If "you" refers specifically to the Gentile recipients in v. 1 (see the notes), then "we" might be intended to include both Jews and Gentiles or perhaps simply to include the author in the general reference to the recipients. The use of the term "all" *(pantes)* strongly suggests that ultimately the author means that all humanity was once in the same state as those who are outside the body of Christ. The verb "to live" *(anastrephō)* is a synonym of the verb "to walk" in v. 2. The use of this Greek verb to refer to human conduct is associated with "the practice of certain principles" (BAGD 61). In this case the principles are principles of error (cf. 2 Pet 2:18). "Passions of our flesh" recalls Gal 5:16, 24 where Paul contrasts earthly existence without Christ and life in the Spirit in a similar manner. In Paul's letters "flesh" *(sarx)* is sometimes a general term for sinful human existence and it refers to more than simply physical existence (e.g., Rom 8:8). There are many references to flesh in Ephesians, but only here and possibly in 2:11 is flesh associated with sin (cf. 2:14; 5:29, 31; 6:5, 12). The characterization of the past existence of believers in this verse is also in keeping with Jewish characterizations of the Greco-Roman world that tended to stress idolatry and sexual immorality in particular. Paul, for example, singles out lust *(epithymia)*, as a primary characteristic of the Gentiles who do not know God (1 Thess 4:5). The word for "wish" *(thelēma)* is the same term in Greek that is translated as "will" to refer to the will of God in 1:1, 5, 9, 11. The implication is that "the wishes of our flesh and impulses" are in direct opposition to the will of God. The plural of the term *dianoia* literally means "thoughts" (NIV), but "impulses" (NAB) better captures the notion of yielding to desire that underlies this verse. Given that Paul uses the term "flesh" to refer to the whole person in opposition to God, the further qualification of sin to include impulses is interesting and may suggest that "flesh" in Ephesians refers more specifically to the sensual than it does in Paul's letters (see Lincoln [1990] 98–99). It is clear, however, that the terminology is designed to communicate the essence of a purely human orientation rather than one that is in tune with the will of God.

and were children of wrath by nature, like the rest: "Children of wrath" is a Semitic phrase similar to "sons of disobedience" in v. 2 (cf. 1QH 1:25; 1QS 1:10; 3:21). The meaning of "by nature" *(physei)* has been debated. It was later understood in light of the doctrine of original sin. While some commentators (e.g., Barth 231; Gnilka [1971] 117) see no evidence of this doctrine, others believe that the notion is not entirely alien to the verse (e.g., Lincoln [1990] 99). There are points in common here with Rom 5:12-21, which suggests that humans were in a sinful condition from the beginning. The closest parallel to the specific use of the expression "by nature" is found in Gal 2:15, where Paul states: "We ourselves are Jews by birth *(physei)* and not Gentile sinners" (cf. Gal 4:8; Rom 2:12-14). It is difficult to imagine either Paul or anyone who wrote in his name describing Jews as children of wrath by nature (Perkins 60). Taken as a whole, v. 3 probably reflects conventional Jewish notions of the Gentile world. Wisdom 13:1 describes idolaters, for example, as follows: "For all people who were ignorant of God were foolish by nature; and they were unable from the good things that are seen to know the one who exists" (NRSV; cited in Perkins 60–61). The inclusive "we" probably means that Paul and/or Jewish believers are being depicted as sharing the lot of Gentiles in their previous existence. The expression "like the rest" *(hōs kai hoi loipoi)* associates the past life of believers with those who continue to be outside the church. It is strongly sectarian language (see the interpretation below).

4. *But God, being rich in mercy, because of his great love with which he loved us:* A change of focus begins here. Thus far the passage has concentrated on the dire past existence of believers and the condition of sinful humanity. Now the grandeur of God's grace is celebrated. God is the subject of the verb "to make alive with" in v. 5 (see also the note on 2:1). The verb recalls the celebration of God's blessings bestowed on believers in 1:3-14 where love *(agapē)* and the heavenly places (cf. 2:6) are also mentioned.

   Similarly 1:7-8 refers to God's riches (cf. 1:18). The similarities with the blessing may stem from the fact that vv. 4-7 and possibly also v. 10 draw their origins from a hymn (e.g., Schille 53–60). Some scholars have understood v. 5b to be an addition to the hymn (but see also the response to this theory in Lincoln [1990] 89–90). Ephesians frequently refers to the riches bestowed by God on God's people (cf. 1:18; 2:7; 3:8, 16). Here the cognate adjective "rich" *(plousios)* occurs. On God's mercy *(eleos)* see Exod 34:6 and Ps 145:8. Love is a very important theme in Ephesians, although it usually is an attribute of the human community (see the notes on 1:4). In this text and possibly also in 1:4 divine love is in view.

5. *even when we were dead in transgressions, made us alive with Christ:* The opening clause in this verse is essentially a repetition of the opening clause in v. 1 (although there is a change from the second person plural to the first person plural). Both clauses are related to the verb "made us alive with"; God is the subject (see the notes on 2:1). The *kai* at the beginning of this verse corresponds to the opening of v. 1 (see the notes). It may simply serve a connecting function, or, as is most likely, it underlines the fact that God's love was so great that God chose to save God's people even *(kai)* in this terrible condition. The verb *synezōopoiēsen* (made alive with) is used in Col 2:11-13, which clearly refers to baptism and is very similar to Eph 2:5 (cf. 1 Pet 3:18; 1 Cor 15:22-23). The prefix *syn* (with), attached to this verb and those in v. 6, reinforces the solidarity of believers with Christ. "With Christ" language appears frequently in Paul's letters to describe how believers share in Christ's destiny (e.g., Rom 6:8; 8:17). God is the main actor here, but works through Christ. Ephesians 1:19-23 also focuses on Christ. Instead of the straightforward dative expression *tǭ*

Christǭ some witnesses have *en tǭ Christǭ* ("in Christ"; 𝔓⁴⁶ B 33 *al*). This variation is quite easily explained either by the accidental repetition of the last letters of the previous word *(synezōopoiēsen)* or by an attempt to harmonize v. 5 with "in Christ Jesus" in v. 6 (see Metzger 602).

(by grace you have been saved): The same statement is found at the beginning of v. 8. The parenthetical statement interrupts the description of what believers have experienced with Christ. The author reminds them that salvation flows from God's initiative and is based on God's free gift (grace: *charis;* on grace in Ephesians see the notes on 1:2). In v. 4 grace appears to be a synonym for mercy. This key Pauline concept was previously introduced in the opening blessing (1:6-7). *Sesǭsmenoi* (literally "having been saved") is a perfect passive participle indicating a past action with ongoing consequences. Apart from v. 8 the use of the perfect tense for this verb is unique in Pauline literature. Some scholars have judged this to be a strong indication of the deutero-Pauline nature of Ephesians (e.g., Lindemann 137). However, Lincoln has argued correctly that the significance of the use of this tense should not be exaggerated. While Paul most frequently uses the verb *sōzō* in the future (e.g., Rom 5:9), there are references to salvation as both a present and a past experience and various terms are employed in a flexible manner (Lincoln [1990] 104). It remains striking, however, that in this verse "by grace" is linked to the verb "to save," when in the undisputed letters of Paul "by grace" (also "by faith") is used in conjunction with "justification" language (cf. Acts 15:11; 2 Tim 1:9). It must be admitted that salvation and justification can sometimes act as virtual synonyms in Paul's letters (e.g., Rom 10:10; see Lincoln [1990] 104). Nevertheless, 2:5 offers the first of several indications in this passage that traditional Pauline terminology is being adapted to address a new situation (see the interpretation below).

6. *and he raised us up with him and seated us with him in the heavenly places in Christ Jesus:* This verse should be compared to Eph 1:20 where very similar terminology occurs (see the notes; cf. Col 2:12; 3:1). Comparison makes it clear that the identification of believers with Christ's destiny is being stated in the strongest possible terms: Believers presently share in Christ's exaltation. In contrast to 1:20, however, there is no reference to enthronement at God's right hand, perhaps implying that Christ's place in the heavenly realm is unique. The verbs in 1:20 are in the regular and not compound form of 2:6, where they include the prefix *syn* (with). (On the meaning of being with Christ in this passage see the notes on 2:5.) Moreover, unlike in 1:20, the phrase "the heavenly places" is followed in 2:6 by "in Christ Jesus." The expression "in Christ" is employed very frequently throughout Ephesians. It is most likely that the locative sense of this expression is being used here (believers are found in Christ—located in his body) and not the instrumental sense (through Christ; see the notes on 1:3). The phrase "the heavenly places" is found only in Ephesians. In 2:6, as in 1:3 and 1:20, it refers to the realm of divine transcendence, but elsewhere it is understood as a realm still subject to hostile spiritual forces (3:10; 6:12; see the notes on 1:3). This verse has many points in common with Col 3:1-4, but the perspective of "realized eschatology" stands out even more sharply in Ephesians (see the interpretation below).

7. *in order that in the ages to come he might show the immeasurable riches of his grace in kindness to us in Christ Jesus:* The reference to the future provides immediate balance to the strong perspective of "realized eschatology" in v. 6 (see the notes on 1:21). The meaning of the phrase "in the ages to come" *(en tois aiōsin tois eperchomenois)* has been the subject of debate. It is sometimes taken to mean "among the coming [attacking; cf. Luke 11:22] eons." (On *aiōn* see the notes on 2:2.) The *aiōsin* would then be the hostile powers and the phrase would convey similar ideas to those found in 3:9-10, which speaks of the wisdom of God being made known to the powers in the heavenly places (e.g., Conzelmann [1976] 97; Lindemann 121–29). But there are grammatical problems with this interpretation. In particular, with the alternate reading one would expect the use of the preposition *eis* (not *en*) or the dative case to refer "to those to whom something is shown" (Perkins 62). It seems best to understand the phrase in the usual temporal sense. This verse is in keeping with the emphasis on the manifestation of salvation throughout Ephesians (cf. 1:6-10; 1:18-20). Here the manifestation stretches into the future (cf. Col 3:4). The plural may signify a succession of ages (Lincoln [1990] 110–11). The verse reflects the values of the first-century world, where what is honorable is associated with what is publicly visible. The verb "to show" or "to demonstrate" *(endeiknymi)* also fits with the emphasis on visionary phenomena in Ephesians. The notion of a cosmic display appears to underlie this verse (see the notes and interpretations on 1:15-23). A reference to God's grace is also found in 2:5 and 2:8. The mention of "kindness" *(chrēstotēs)* recalls the previous references to God's mercy and love (v. 4).

8. *For by grace you have been saved through faith, and this is not of you, it is a gift of God—9. not of works, lest anyone should boast:* Those who view vv. 4-7 as hymnic often understand vv. 8-9 as an interpretation of the hymn with the hymnic material beginning again at v. 10. There is a shift from the generalized "we" of vv. 4-7 to "you" in vv. 8-9, with a shift back again in v. 10 (see the notes on 2:1). The reference to saving by grace repeats v. 5b with the addition of "through faith." Some have viewed vv. 8-10 as the most concise summary of Pauline theology in the NT. It is not entirely clear whether "this" *(touto)* refers to grace, salvation, faith or all of these. But the main message of vv. 8-9 is clear: faith (which leads to salvation) is a gift *(dōron;* used only here in the Pauline corpus, though the related term *dōrea* occurs in Ephesians and elsewhere in the Pauline corpus [Rom 5:5-17; 2 Cor 9:15]) and is not based on human accomplishment. (The various uses of the preposition *ek* [of] in vv. 8-9 refer to origin or cause, i.e., faith is not caused by, nor does it draw its origins from, humans.) There is no place for human self-assertion. The mention of grace reinforces this point (see the notes on 2:5). "Grace" (e.g., Rom 3:24; 11:6), "faith" (e.g., Gal 2:16), "gift" (e.g., Rom 3:24), "works" (v. 9; cf. Gal 2:16; 3:2-5), and "boast" (v. 9; cf. Rom 3:27; 4:2) are all key concepts in the undisputed letters of Paul. The opposition between faith and works in vv. 8-9 is fundamental to Paul's message. It is important to note, however, that in the undisputed letters this terminology is not given the broad scope it has in Ephesians; in the undisputed letters it is used specifically to describe the meaning of life in Christ in

relation to the Jewish Law: justification by faith as opposed to the works of the Law (e.g., Gal 2:16; 3:2-5, 9-10; Rom 3:27, 28; see the notes and interpretation below). In Ephesians "works" stands for human accomplishment in general. On references to salvation as opposed to justification in Ephesians see the notes on 2:5.

10. *For we are his handiwork, created in Christ Jesus for good works:* To a certain extent v. 10 acts as a corrective to the previous verse. Salvation is not based on human accomplishment (v. 9), but works remain very important. The undisputed letters of Paul do not contain the precise phrase "good works," but a similar idea occurs in 2 Cor 9:8 and in 2 Thess 2:19 (cf. Col 1:10). Emphasis on good works is characteristic of the Pastoral Epistles and other post-Pauline works (cf. 1 Tim 2:10; 5:10, 25; 6:18; Titus 2:7, 14; 3:8, 14; Acts 9:36; Heb 10:24; cited in Lincoln [1990] 115). The recipients of Ephesians have been created in Christ Jesus for good works. The term "handiwork" *(poiēma)* is used in the LXX to describe creation itself (Pss 9:14; 14:25; cf. Rom 1:20). That the formation of believers is tied to God's very act of creation is implied by 1:4, which describes them as chosen in him before the foundation of the world. However, the subsequent reference to creation in Jesus Christ probably means that what is primarily in view here is the identity of believers as a new creation (Gal 6:15; 2 Cor 5:17). Christ is the agent through whom God conducts this re-creation of believers. Such a notion may prepare the way for the proclamation in 2:11-22 of the new reality created in Christ Jesus (see Perkins 64).

which God prepared beforehand in order that we might walk in them: The idea of good works being prepared by God beforehand is in keeping with the strong focus on God's sovereignty and initiative throughout Ephesians and especially in the blessing of 1:3-14. It is interesting to note that the only other use of the verb *proetoimazō* (to prepare beforehand) is in conjunction with predestination: Rom 9:23. The main point is that good works flow naturally from God choosing to save us; in fact God has prepared the works themselves beforehand for believers. This statement eradicates any thought of the irrelevance of works based on v. 9. In essence, good works emerge as the purpose of God's election. The mention of walking in good works recalls the reference to walking *(peripateō)* in 2:2. Just as a way of life defined the past existence of believers living in a sinful world, walking in good works now constitutes an announcement of God's purpose for the world. Ethical conduct is of great importance in Ephesians (see the interpretation below, and the notes and interpretation on 4:1–6:20).

INTERPRETATION

Ephesians 2:1-10 offers a very good illustration of why Ephesians is often viewed as a composite of traditional elements. It combines Jewish apocalyptic motifs (2:5-7), ancient cosmology (2:2), and conventional Jewish notions of Gentile sinfulness (2:2-3). Although the idea of heavenly enthronement with Christ is clearly attested in later Gnostic writings (e.g.,

Treatise on the Resurrection 45), it is probable that Jewish apocalyptic writings rather than Gnostic thought offer the more immediate sources of influence. These works speak of the righteous sharing in the kingdom and sitting on heavenly thrones (e.g., Dan 7:22, 27; Wis 3:8; 5:15, 16; *1 Enoch* 108:12; *Apoc. Elijah* 5.36-39; *T. Job* 33.3-5; *Asc. Isa.* 9:18; cf. Matt 19:28; 1 Cor 6:2; Rev 3:2, cited in Lincoln [1990] 107). In contrast to Ephesians, however, these works tend to focus especially on the future dimension of this reign. The QL, on the other hand, offers especially interesting parallels to the realized eschatological perspective of Ephesians while at the same time it uses many apocalyptic motifs:

> I thank thee, O Lord, for thou hast redeemed my soul from the Pit, and from the Hell of Abaddon Thou hast raised me up to everlasting height. . . . I walk on limitless level ground and I know there is no hope for him whom Thou has shaped from dust for the Everlasting Council. Thou has cleansed a perverse spirit of great sin that it may stand with the host of the Holy ones, and that it may enter into community with the congregation of the Sons of Heaven. (1QH 3:19-22; Vermes 197–98)

In addition to the influences from the broader social world in which Ephesians was composed, investigators intent on uncovering the traditional features of Ephesians have discussed the role of liturgy. The language and structure of vv. 4-7, 10 have convinced many that these verses draw their origin from a traditional hymn—perhaps a hymn of initiation. Similarly, scholars have pointed to connections between this section and the language of baptism. It is almost beyond question that the recipients would have recalled their baptism as they heard 2:1 and 2:5-6 proclaimed in the midst of the *ekklēsia*. Dying and rising were metaphorical descriptions of the experience of baptism. Yet the question of whether the language comes directly from baptismal proclamations is far more difficult to answer. The issue of the relationship between Colossians and Ephesians immediately arises (the same holds true with respect to the influence of the apocalyptic motifs as described above). For example Eph 2:1, 5 are very closely related to Col 2:13, and Eph 2:6 has much in common with Col 3:1-3 (see the notes above). It is possible that Colossians and Ephesians are drawing independently from the same liturgical traditions. But even if it is the case that the author of Ephesians is drawing immediately from Colossians and reinterpreting the text it is important to realize that it is highly likely that language with strong liturgical echoes would only be chosen if it had particular relevance for the recipients of Ephesians. Finally, as will be discussed further below, analysis of the use of tradition within Ephesians must take into account the linking of various Pauline motifs in Eph 2:8-10, which suggests the development of a Pauline message for a new day.

A strong then/now contrast operates throughout 2:1-10 (cf. 2:11-13). This contrast can also be seen in the undisputed letters of Paul (e.g., Rom 5:8-11; Gal 1:23; 4:3-7) and is especially prominent in Colossians (1:21, 22; 2:13; 3:7, 8). However, in Ephesians the past existence of believers, the world without Christ, and even the cosmos itself with its various realms are sometimes depicted in very pessimistic terms. The language in 2:1-3 and 6:10-17 constitutes strikingly strong statements of the dire state of existence without Christ and of humanity's utter helplessness. Evil has an ethical dimension that the description of the immorality of the past existence of believers in 2:3 illustrates clearly. But evil also transcends the ethical patterns of everyday life, for it is the dominion of "the ruler of the power of the air" (2:2). Believers must stand ready to do battle with the cosmic powers of this present darkness (6:12). It is important to recognize that in the case of 2:1-3 such statements prepare the way for the bold proclamation that believers have been raised with Christ. The dark and ominous language sets the stage for a celebration of the recipients' heavenly status. Moreover, there are texts in Ephesians that suggest universal salvation (1:23) and Christ's abolition of all human differences (2:11-22). Nevertheless, in comparison to Colossians in particular, and perhaps even to the undisputed letters of Paul, Ephesians displays a greater awareness of evil and greater encouragement to separate from a nonbelieving world.

In sociological terms Ephesians recommends a strongly "sectarian" response to the wider social order. The typology of sects by Bryan Wilson can be helpful in shedding light upon the particular kind of response Ephesians demonstrates. In order to classify a wide range of sectarian phenomena Wilson developed a seven-part typology based on studies of various sects including many Third World religious movements. Wilson's description of the "conversionist" (see the notes and interpretation on Col 4:2-6), "revolutionist" (or millennial; see Esler [1994] 72–73), and "introversionist" (see Esler [1994] 70–91) responses to the world exhibited by various sects has been especially influential in social-scientific interpretation of the NT. It is important to realize that typologies, like other social-scientific models, are artificial constructions, deliberately simplified and rendered general enough to be able to assist in the analysis of complex data. They are based on observations of a wide variety of phenomena and do not correspond perfectly to any one historical moment. In comparing specific early Christian groups to Wilson's ideal types the investigator will inevitably note not only points of similarity but also points of contrast. It is also possible that aspects of the evidence will correspond best to one sect type while other aspects will correspond best to another sect type. But it is precisely because it reveals not only similarities, but also incongruities, that comparison of historical evidence to the typology is so useful as a heuristic device. Such comparison can help illuminate the particular response to the world displayed by Ephesians, as well as its overall significance.

If one considers Ephesians in relation to the sectarian responses to the world listed above, it is the introversionist response that is most useful in elucidating what is distinctive about Ephesians in the Pauline corpus:

> The third response is to see the world as irredeemably evil and salvation to be attained only by the fullest possible withdrawal from it. The self may be purified by renouncing the world and leaving it. This response might be an individual response, of course, but as a response of a social movement it leads to the establishment of a separated community preoccupied with its own holiness and its means of insulation from the wider society. Even if the ideology posits only its future realization, in practice, salvation is sociologically present endeavor. The community itself becomes the source and seat of all salvation. Explicitly this prospect of salvation is only for those who belong. (Wilson [1975] 23–24)

Wilson's description can help us to see the social dynamics revealed by 2:1-10 more clearly. The text begins with denouncement of the world as irredeemably evil (2:1-3). Withdrawal from the world takes place through a transformation from death to life and a process of heavenly exaltation (2:4-7). Christ experiences heavenly enthronement (1:20) and believers are raised up with him and seated with him in heavenly places "in Christ Jesus" (2:6). Ephesians 2:6 implies that in a very important sense the community as the body of Christ itself becomes the source and seat of all salvation. Believers are found in Christ Jesus; they are located in him and are identified with him. To concentrate on ecclesiology—to pay special attention to the identity and holiness of the church—is a natural counterpart to this self-understanding. Ephesians continues to speak of the future dimensions of salvation (e.g., 2:7), but, as 2:6 illustrates so well, salvation has become sociologically a present endeavor.

Recently commentators have been intrigued by parallels with the QL, which display a similar introversionist response (on introverted sectarianism at Qumran see Esler [1974] 70–91). We might consider, for example, the following text where death and life are also symbols of entrance into the community: "For the sake of Thy glory Thou hast purified man of sin . . . that bodies gnawed by worms may be raised from the dust . . . that he may stand before Thee with the everlasting host . . . to be renewed together with all the living" (1QH 11:10-14; Vermes 222). The author of Ephesians distances believers from a sinful humanity by employing such designations as "children of wrath" (2:3) and "sons of disobedience" (2:2). Very similar terminology occurs in the QL: "sons of darkness" (1QS 1:10; 1QM 1:7, 16; cf. 1QS 3:21; 1QH 5:7), yet it is important to recognize that some texts in Ephesians moderate the strong introversionist tendencies that the document shares with the QL. As a whole the document reflects some of the tensions that are typical of a conversionist response to the world and are frequently demonstrated by Pauline churches (see M. Y. MacDonald [1988] 32–42). Texts that call for world rejection are found in a work that also displays great interest in universal mission (e.g., Eph 3:8-13; 6:19-20). The household code of 5:21–6:9 encourages a way of life that allows believers to remain physically integrated within the dominant society while permitting opportunities for evangelization. Such an ethical stance may well have been designed to defuse rising tension between the church and the world (see the notes and interpretation on 5:21-29). Thus in drawing upon Wilson's typology for the analysis of Ephesians we should be careful not to jump to conclusions about a perfect representation of Ephesians in any one "type," but be aware of the particular response to the world exhibited by Ephesians that transcends the limits of the typology.

When Ephesians is compared to the other works in the Pauline corpus and to Colossians in particular it becomes apparent that the pendulum has swung in the direction of greater introversion in a movement that nevertheless remains committed to universal salvation. Ephesians appears to reflect a situation in which believers are feeling threatened by evil spiritual forces that rule "this world" with all its immoral passions (on the powers see the notes and interpretations on 1:15-23). In reaction to such menacing powers the lines of the community are being drawn more forcefully. Moreover, the heavenly exaltation of believers represents triumph over menacing powers. As has been frequently noted, the statement that God has seated believers with Christ in the heavenly realm is a truly remarkable claim expressing a strong perspective of realized eschatology. Colossians 3:1-3 prepares the way for such a statement, but does not go so far as to state explicitly that believers share in the triumph of Christ's heavenly ascent. Colossians 3:3-4 assigns a future aspect to the resurrection life of believers, but Eph 2:7 contains only a general reference to "the ages to come," which remain important for God's plan of salvation.

Ephesians reveals the conviction that believers have already escaped to a higher world, and there are strong indications that the experience of transcendence is tied to the rituals of the community. Even the use of the verb *sygkathizō* (to sit down with) in v. 6 may have suggested the idea of a common meal (cf. Luke 13:29). Many commentators have understood 2:5-6 as rooted in the experience of baptism on account of the references to death, rebirth, and rising (see the notes). Anthropologists have observed the prominence of symbols of death and rebirth in initiation rites throughout the world (see the notes on Col 3:1-4). While the experience of baptism is no doubt related to these verses it is not quite as prominent as in the parallel text of Col 2:10-13. The emphasis on the heavenly exaltation of believers suggests the experience of visionary phenomena (see the notes and interpretation on 1:15-23). Ephesians 2:1-10 recalls the experience of entry into the community and rejection of the outside world. It may well be that visions were a fundamental part of the experiences that led the recipients of Ephesians to enter the community. Other texts in the NT associate visions with conversion and entry into the community (e.g., Acts 9–10). It is especially striking that the proponents of the false teaching in Colossae seem to have recommended ascetic practices, an initiation rite whereby the candidate experienced visions (implied by the phrase "entering into the things that he has seen"), and the worship of angels as a means of attaining divine fullness and warding off evil forces (Col 2:18; see the notes on 2:18, and the notes and interpretation on Col 2:16-23). While Ephesians and Colossians clearly reflect a very similar theological and ethical stance, it seems that the author of Ephesians was more open to visionary phenomena (see the notes on Eph 1:15-23). Even the consummation of salvation that will occur in the ages to come is depicted as a type of visual display (see the notes on 2:7).

In response to a context in which believers are strongly experiencing the threat of evil cosmic forces Eph 2:8-10 brings together many of the key Pauline beliefs and reinterprets them. In keeping with the ideas introduced in ch. 1 these verses stress that all is dependent on God's initiative, was prepared beforehand by God, and takes place through God's agent, Christ. Faith in Christ is a gift and even the good works that set believers apart from the sons of disobedience were prepared beforehand by God. Commentators have frequently been struck by the author of Ephesians' general contrast of faith and works with no specific reference to the situation that made it necessary for Paul to address the relationship between the works of Jewish Law and faith in Christ. Ephesians speaks to a situation where the struggle to introduce Gentile members into the church without requiring them to keep those aspects of the Law that traditionally separated Jews from Gentiles (e.g., male circumcision and food laws) appears to have subsided (see also the notes and interpretation on 2:11-22). The works of the Jewish Law no longer seem to be of major concern. Most scholars believe that Ephesians was composed about 90 C.E., a period when a new generation of believers was being integrated into the Pauline churches under new circumstances.

Insights from the sociology of knowledge can be valuable in shedding light on the transformation of Pauline symbolism that occurs in this new context. According to the analysis of Berger and Luckmann it is only by attaining a certain objective quality and becoming detached from their original social setting that symbols have the power to survive their creator into the next generation (see the interpretation on 1:3-14; M. Y. MacDonald [1988] 90–91). Symbols lose some of their original content, but become more flexible and adaptable. Language is passed down to a new generation and a reconstruction of the original processes that led to the formation of beliefs becomes unnecessary. "Faith versus works" becomes a general means of speaking about the giftedness of salvation as opposed to human accomplishment. By drawing upon the time-honored symbols of the Pauline movement the author of Ephesians offers encouragement in a new setting: Created by God, owned by God, dependent upon God, and loved by God, the recipients of Ephesians have nothing to fear from either the sons of disobedience or the evil powers that rule their lives. They have been rescued by grace.

FOR REFERENCE AND FURTHER STUDY

Barton, Tamsyn. *Ancient Astrology.* London and New York: Routledge, 1994.
Lincoln, Andrew. "Ephesians 2:8-10—A Summary of Paul's Gospel," *CBQ* 45 (1983) 617–30.
Schlier, Heinrich. *Christus und die Kirche im Epheserbrief.* Tübingen: Mohr, 1957.
Tannehill, Robert C. *Dying and Rising with Christ: a Study in Pauline Theology.* BZNW 32. Berlin: A. Topelmann, 1967.
Wilson, Bryan R. *Magic and the Millennium; A Sociological Study of Religious Movements of Protest Among Tribal and Third-World Peoples.* London: Heinemann; New York: Harper & Row, 1973; repr. St. Albans: Paladin, 1975.

18. *The Unity of Jews and Gentiles Created by Christ* (2:11-22)

2:11. Therefore, remember that you were once Gentiles in the flesh, the ones being called the uncircumcision by those called the circumcision, in the flesh made by hands, 12. that you were at that time without Christ, having been alienated from the commonwealth of Israel and strangers to the covenants of promise, having no hope and without God in the world. 13. But now in Christ Jesus you who were once far off have become near through the blood of Christ. 14. For he is our peace; in his flesh he has made both one and has broken down the dividing wall, the hostility, 15. having abolished the law of the commandments and regulations, in order that the two he might create in himself into one new person, making peace, 16. and might reconcile both in one body to God through the cross, putting the hostility to death in himself. 17. And he came and preached peace to you who were far off and peace to those who were near 18. for through him we both have access in one Spirit to the Father. 19. So then you are no longer strangers and aliens, but you are fellow-citizens with the saints and members of the household of God, 20. having been built upon the foundation of the apostles and prophets, Christ Jesus himself being the cornerstone, 21. in whom the whole structure, being fitted together, grows into a holy temple in the Lord, 22. in whom you also are being built up together into a dwelling place for God in the Spirit.

NOTES

2:11. *Therefore, remember that you were once Gentiles in the flesh:* "Therefore" *(dio)* links this phrase to the previous section. In 2:1-10 the salvation of believers by God through Christ is proclaimed. Ephesians 2:11-22 announces the consequences of that salvation for the social plane: "therefore." Moreover, the then/now contrast of the previous section continues here and is powerfully introduced by the imperative present verb, "remember" *(mnēmoneuete)*. The expression "Gentiles in the flesh" makes it clear that Ephesians is addressed to a Gentile audience, or at least to a Gentile majority. The circumstances of their past are recalled in 2:12, 19, and 3:1. The Paul of Eph 2:11 speaks as the representative of Jewish Christianity. His main interest is in proclaiming the achieved unity of Jew and Gentile in the church. He announces in 2:18: "through him we both have access by one Spirit to the Father." The you/we contrast is also plainly evident in 1:12-13 (see the notes on 1:12).

the ones being called the uncircumcision by those called the circumcision, in the flesh made by hands: This phrase recognizes the importance of male circumcision as a sign of Jewish identity in the Greco-Roman world. It may also represent an acknowledgment of tension between social groups. The alienation once experienced by Gentiles involved being labeled as outsiders by Jews (or perhaps by Jewish believers who were opposed to Paul's views on Gentiles and the Jewish Law). They were called "the uncircumcision" *(akrobystia)*. This is a term Paul uses frequently in his letters in both a figurative and a literal sense to explain the significance of faith in Christ (e.g., Rom 2:25-29; 4:10-12; 5:6). It is employed as a way of speaking about the Gentiles in general in Rom 3:30; 4:9; Gal 2:7; and especially Col 3:11, which describes the abolition of differences between Jews and Gentiles in Christ with the same terminology that occurs here: circumcision and uncircumcision. The author of Ephesians may have been influenced by the use of this expression in Colossians. It is also valuable to compare the text to Col 2:11 where the opposite expression to "circumcision, in the flesh made with hands" occurs. Colossians 2:11 refers to a "circumcision made without hands" apparently as a metaphor for baptism (see the notes). It is interesting to note that *cheiropoiētos* (made with hands) is used in the LXX to describe idols (e.g., Isa 2:18; 10:11; see also the interpretation below). Ephesians 2:11 stresses the physicality of circumcision. Given Col 2:11 and the criticism by the author of Colossians of physical rites in general, it is possible that Eph 2:11 was intended to be an implicit criticism of the Jewish rite of circumcision (see the notes and interpretation on Col 2:8-23). "In the flesh" recalls the use of the expression in the previous verse. The circumstances of Jews and Gentiles without Christ are evidently being equated.

12. *that you were at that time without Christ, having been alienated from the commonwealth of Israel:* Hoti (that) occurs at the beginning of this verse as in 2:11, indi-

cating that the clause is also connected to the verb "remember" in v. 11. Some English translations repeat the verb (e.g., NJB) in order to make this clear. This verse continues to expound on the previous existence of Gentile believers. As in 2:1-3, it is depicted in the most pessimistic terms. The imagery suggests the circumstances of a dispossessed people. *Politeia* can mean citizenship, but it is best to translate the term here as "commonwealth." The Gentile recipients of Ephesians would have associated the term with the state or the body politic and may well have understood the alienation as being paramount to exclusion from any protection offered from Rome's political might. It may also be that this verse reflects OT notions of Gentile exclusion (e.g., Exod 19:6; Pss 80:8-9, 105; cited in Perkins 68). The underlying assumption in 2:12 is that Gentile believers are now part of the commonwealth of Israel. In other words, the author of Ephesians seems to be equating Israel with the church. This is a striking development in relation to the undisputed letters of Paul. With the possible exception of Gal 6:16, Paul does not employ the term "Israel" to refer to the community of believers in Christ. His letters sometimes suggest that he considered believers to be the true Israel (e.g., Galatians 3; Romans 4; Romans 9), but it is plainly evident that Paul realizes Israel exists also outside the group. On the one hand, in Rom 9:6 he states that not all who descended from Israel actually belong to Israel (Rom 9:4), but on the other hand he speaks of the inherited privileges of the Israelites (Rom 9:4) and also of the failure of Israel, who pursued righteousness based on the Law, to attain righteousness (Rom 9:31). In other words, Paul's discussion reveals an awareness that there are real Israelites, real Jews, who are not in Christ (see E. P. Sanders [1983] 173–75). In contrast, Eph 2:11-22 seems to simply appropriate the language of Jewish nationhood for describing church identity (see the interpretation below).

and strangers to the covenants of promise, having no hope and without God in the world: The then/now contrast in this passage can be seen especially clearly by comparing 2:12 to 2:19. In both verses the term "strangers" *(xenoi)* is employed. The plural expression "covenants" no doubt refers to the several OT covenants that are sometimes enumerated together (e.g., Lev 26:42; cf. Rom 9:4). The covenants are based on God's promise. Paul frequently refers to the promise or promises of God (e.g., Rom 4:13; 9:4; Gal 3:16-29). In 1 Thess 4:13 he describes outsiders as those without hope. The expression "without God" is a translation of the Greek *atheoi* (literally "atheists"). What is being claimed is that believers were once such outsiders to the realm of salvation that they literally had no religion (cf. Gal 4:8). The notion that the Gentiles are ignorant of God is closely related to this idea (cf. LXX Jer 10:25; 1 Thess 1:9; 4:5; Gal 4:8; cited in Perkins 69). *Atheos* appears nowhere else in the NT or LXX. It is a term used to describe the godless or impious. It is sometimes used to refer to those who have never heard of the gods, but it also refers to those who reject the gods and their laws (BAGD 20). In the Greco-Roman world its usage is tied to the neglect of religious rites that were seen as fundamental to the welfare of the state. Evidence from the second century onward indicates that Christians themselves were accused of being atheists for refusing to participate in traditional religious practices. "Atheist" was used to label Christians as outsiders within the broader social order (e.g., *Mart. Pol.* 3; 9.2; Justin Martyr, *Apol.* 1.6.1; 13.1.) Although the evidence comes from later than the period of Ephesians it is not beyond the realm of possibility that the language used by the author of Ephesians to describe the previous life of Gentile believers is similar to the language employed by nonbelievers to critique the church. Believers may have been labeled atheists even if outsiders associated them closely with Jews, for there is evidence that Jews were also called atheists in the Greco-Roman world (Josephus, *C. Apion* 2.148). Second-century Christians likewise used the term to describe pagans (e.g., *Mart. Pol.* 9.2; Clem. Al. *Paed.* 3, 11, 80).

13. *But now in Christ Jesus you who were once far off have become near through the blood of Christ:* The passage moves from describing the past existence of believers (then) to a celebration of their present circumstances (now). The use of the expression *en Christō* is striking. Verses 11-12 described how believers were once located outside the realm of salvation but are now inside that realm—in Christ (see the notes on 1:1). The blood of Christ has created the new reality. Once alienated from the people of God, the Gentiles have been brought near. The blood of Christ is most likely a reference to the cross of Christ. Ephesians 1:7 speaks of "redemption through his blood, the forgiveness of trespasses." The author of Ephesians may have been influenced in vv. 13-14 by Col 1:20: "and through him to reconcile all things to himself, making peace through the blood of his cross." Similarly, Rom 5:8-11 describes the reconciliation to God that takes place through the blood of Christ (cf. 2 Cor 5:18-20). Some have argued that perhaps the rite of circumcision has influenced the author's choice of words here: It is the blood of Christ rather than the circumcision made with hands (v. 11) that creates the new order. Verses 13-14 and the similar text in v. 17 contain echoes of Isa 57:19 and possibly also Isa 52:7 (cf. Zech 6:15). Isaiah 57:19 reads: "Peace, peace, to the far and the near, says the Lord; and I will heal them" (NRSV). Originally those who were "far" were exiled Jews, but later rabbinic interpretations associate them with Gentile proselytes (see Barth [1974] 276–79). Although it is impossible to be certain, such an interpretation of Isa 57:19 may have been current in Paul's day. Moreover, frequently in the OT Gentiles are described as those who are far off (e.g., Deut 28:49; 29:22; 1 Kgs 8:41). While it does not refer specifically to the inclusion of Gentiles, the QL describes entry into the group in terms of the "bringing near"of members (e.g., 1QS 11:13; 1 QH 14:13-14; cited in Taylor and Reumann 49). In 1QS 9:15-16 the phrase refers to joining the sect and, by implication, increasing the distance from other Jews (Perkins 69–70).

14. *For he is our peace; in his flesh he has made both one:* The shift from the second person plural to the first person plural in this verse offers an indication that a new section of the passage is beginning. In fact many scholars (e.g., Schille 23–27; J. T. Sanders [1965] 216–18) have understood vv. 14-18 as a fragment of an early Christian hymn on account of such features as the frequent repetitions ("peace" is mentioned four times), the presence of literary patterns (e.g., note how "peace" and "hostility" alternate in vv. 14-16), and the formulaic phrases (the influence of a baptismal formula in v. 15). There have also been several

suggestions concerning the interpolations made in the hymn by the author of Ephesians. For example, "through the cross" (v. 16) is commonly regarded as a later addition. Translations vary as to whether the phrase *tēn echthran en tę sarki autou* (the hostility in his flesh) should be included in v. 14 or whether it constitutes the beginning of v. 15, introducing the notion of abolishing the Law. A comparison of the NRSV and NIV translations offers a good illustration of the two possible interpretations. Syntactical considerations, including the awkwardness of having objects of the verb "to break down" found on either side of it, suggest the latter option might be preferable (see Lincoln [1990] 124). Yet, although the "wall" (v. 14) and the "Law" (v. 15) are very closely related, the wall seems to be a more vivid symbol of hostility than of the *Law* (see the notes below). Thus "hostility" should probably be understood as being in apposition to the dividing wall and the phrase should be included as part of v. 14. "He" refers to Christ (cf. 2:16-18). "In his flesh" recalls Col 1:22 and suggests that through Christ's death a new order has arrived, involving salvation for the Gentiles (cf. Gal 3:13; Rom 7:4). The notion of making both one recalls 1:10 and anticipates 2:15 (see the notes). On possible allusions to Isa 57:19 in this verse see the notes on 2:13.

and has broken down the dividing wall, the hostility: The dividing wall (literally "the dividing wall of the fence": *to mesotoichon tou phragmou*) is most likely the partition that separated the Gentiles from the inner courts of the Jerusalem Temple (see the use of temple imagery in vv. 20-22). The verb *lyo* (to break down) is used to describe the destruction of the Temple (e.g., Matt 24:2; 26:61). If, as is being argued in this commentary, Ephesians was composed after the destruction of the Jerusalem Temple in 70 C.E., the imagery may have had special relevance for the recipients. Moreover, the author of Ephesians may have understood the breaking down of the Temple wall as a vindication of Paul's message concerning the salvation of the Gentiles (Kitchen 65). It should be noted, however, that the specific expression in Eph 2:14 is not found in the contemporary Jewish evidence; Josephus uses the term *dryphaktos* rather than *phragmos* (cf. Matt 21:33) for the balustrade (*Ant.* XV 417; see Barth 263-64, 282-91). The Greek noun *mesotoichon* occurs nowhere else in the NT and refers to a partition inside a house. Although the Temple wall remains the most likely possibility, the questions concerning how one should understand the expression have given rise to alternate interpretations. Houlden (290-91), for example, has suggested that it refers to the barrier that divides the spheres of heaven and earth (cf. *1 Enoch* 14:9). Such a notion may not be entirely absent from this verse since Ephesians envisions salvation as a journey of heavenly ascent (see the notes and interpretation on 1:15-23). The dividing wall is closely associated with the Jewish Law and some have argued that the "wall" is actually a reference to the Law and not to the partition that separated the Gentiles from the inner courts of the Jerusalem Temple (see the notes on 2:15; see also Lincoln [1990] 141). For a good illustration of how the dividing wall might be a symbol of hostility *par excellence* one might consider the famous inscription (discovered in 1871) concerning the separation of the court of the Gentiles from the other courts and inner sanctuary at the Jerusalem Temple:

"No man of another race is to enter within the fence and enclosure around the Temple. Whoever is caught will have only himself to thank for the death that follows" (cited in Lincoln [1990] 141; cf. Acts 21:27-31; 10:28).

15. *having abolished the law of the commandments and regulations:* Some translations begin v. 15 earlier (see the notes on 2:14). The breaking down of the wall is closely associated with abolishing the Law. An interesting Jewish text from the second century B.C.E., the *Epistle of Aristeas,* actually depicts the Law in terms of a protective barrier: "the legislator . . . being endowed by God for the knowledge of universal truths, surrounded us with unbroken palisades and iron walls to prevent our mixing with any other peoples . . . thus being kept pure in body and soul . . . and worshiping the only God omnipotent over creation" (*Ep. Arist.* 139; cited in Perkins 71). Perkins has suggested that the unusual phrase "dividing wall of the fence" in v. 14 may draw its origins from a phrase like "palisades and wall" in the *Epistle of Aristeas* (71). Moreover, she concludes that the wall of v. 14 should probably be understood as a metaphor for the Law (see also Lincoln [1990] 141), but this seems to be overstating the case (see the notes on 2:14). To speak of abolishing the Law is very strong language and departs from the statements about the Law found in the undisputed letters of Paul (cf. Rom 3:31). This has led some commentators to suggest that only parts of the Law (e.g., those aspects that visibly separated Jew from Gentile and not laws governing morality) are in view (e.g., Hendricksen 135). But there is very little support for the idea of the Law being divisible in Jewish texts (see Perkins 72). Moreover, the long expression, literally "the law of the commandment [expressed] in regulations," strengthens the impression that the whole Law is intended.

There may even be some pejorative undertones in this description of the Law. Ephesians may have been influenced by Col 2:20 where the term *dogmata* (regulations) clearly carries negative connotations—though in Col 2:14 (cf. 2:20) it refers to ascetic regulations rather than to the Torah *per se* (Lincoln [1990] 142). In describing the Law so negatively the author of Ephesians probably has in mind the way the Law contributes to hostility (see also the notes on 2:14). The way of life of the Jews based on the Law led to animosity against them in Greco-Roman society (e.g., Tacitus, *Hist.* 5.1-13) and Jewish authors in turn defended their laws (e.g., Josephus, *C. Apion* 2.146). Moreover, the focus on the creation of a new person later in this verse would naturally encourage categorical statements: Everything associated with the past is understood in terms of a flawed existence.

in order that the two he might create in himself into one new person, making peace: This phrase contains two notions also found in v. 14: "peace" and "making two into one." Ephesians 2:10 prepares the way for this phrase, for it refers to believers being created in Christ Jesus. It is in keeping with Paul's Adam christology in which Adam is the representative of the old order and Christ is the representative of the new order who incorporates believers into his body (e.g., 1 Cor 12:12, 13; 15:22, 45-49; Gal 3:27-28; Rom 12:5; Col 3:10-11; cited in Lincoln [1990] 143). Colossians 3:10 also refers to creation of a new person and the author of Ephesians was probably influenced by this text. Colossians 3:10-11, like Gal 3:27-28, appears to draw its origins from a traditional baptismal formula that celebrates the new creation in terms of unity and the abolition of differences, groups, and categories of persons (including the differences between Jew and Gentile). In seeking to shed light on the origins of Gal 3:27-28 Dennis R. MacDonald has pointed to the following saying from the *Gospel of the Egyptians*, a saying attributed to Jesus and cited by Clement of Alexandria: "When you tread upon the garment of shame and when the two are one and the male with the female neither male nor female" (Clem. Al. *Strom.* 3.13.92; see D. R. MacDonald [1987] 1–63. For other citations of this saying and further historical explanation see the notes and interpretation on Col 3:5-17). In Gnostic circles this saying was associated with asceticism and a return to a perfect androgynous state—a restoration of the person to the state prior to alienation from God.

It is interesting to note that Ephesians also refers to making two (Gentiles and Jews) into one. There is no evidence that such language is associated with sexual asceticism in Ephesians. In fact, Ephesians strongly encourages marriage. However, the unity of the sexes was clearly understood by the author of Ephesians as powerful imagery for speaking about the relationship between God and the human community. (See the notes and interpretation on Eph 5:21–6:9.) In 2:15 the author of Ephesians is drawing on traditional language associated with baptism that was interpreted in early Christianity as describing the "newness" of the community in various ways—the new creation that resulted from Christ's work and that transcended old divisions and categories. The author of Ephesians does not speak directly of baptism here, but such language must have conjured up images of baptism in the minds of the recipients (*pace* Perkins 73–74).

16. *and might reconcile both in one body to God through the cross, putting the hostility to death in himself:* The reference to peace in the previous verse prepares the way for the mention of reconciliation. Peace is also a theme in the hymn of Col 1:15-20, which describes the process of reconciliation. The verb "to reconcile" (*apokatallassō*) does not occur frequently in Pauline literature (2:16; Col 1:20, 22; *katallassō*: Rom 5:10; 2 Cor 5:18-20; see the notes on Col 1:20). The body (of Christ) is the first of several metaphors for the church used in this passage. The way in which this familiar Pauline symbol for the church is fused with "building" metaphors (vv. 20-21) is a particularly striking feature of the text. The verse repeats many of the same ideas found in v. 14. There is a second reference to "hostility," and the mention of what has been accomplished through the cross (cf. Col 1:20) corresponds to what has been achieved "in his flesh" (v. 14). This verse is also very closely related to Col 1:20-23. Both texts stress the importance of the physical death of Christ for the cosmic restoration that has occurred. Differences in the way the body symbolism is used in both passages can alert us to the slightly different perspectives of Colossians and Ephesians. Colossians 1:22 refers to "the body of his flesh through his death"; this is clearly a reference to the physical body of Christ that underwent suffering. In Eph 2:16 the absence of a direct reference to the physical body of Christ implies that the one body (comprised of the unity of Jew and Gentile) should be

understood as a metaphor for the church (cf. Eph 1:23; on the notion of "one body" as a means of describing the church see Col 1:18 and Eph 4:4). Ephesians shares Colossians' interest in a cosmic restoration that occurs through Christ, but implicates the church more directly in that process.

17. *And he came and preached peace to you who were far off and peace to those who were near:* In contrast to the hostility between groups and alienation described in vv. 11-12, Christ brings a message of peace. "You who were far off" refers to the Gentiles and "those who were near" refers to the Jews. This verse contains an allusion to Isa 57:19 and Isa 52:7 (cf. Zech 6:15; see the notes on 2:13). It is not entirely clear whether the peace that was preached by Christ refers to reconciliation with God or to the relationship between the two groups. The fact that the preaching is apparently delivered to each group separately may suggest the former (see Lincoln [1990] 148). However, for the author of Ephesians this experience of reconciliation to God clearly had important implications for how the groups should relate to one another. There has been a good deal of discussion about which part of Christ's ministry is described by the clause "and he came and preached" (see the summary in Barth 294). The earthly ministry of Jesus, the proclamation of Jesus after the resurrection, and the preaching of the resurrected Christ through the apostles have all been proposed. Given the broad—even cosmic—perspective of vv. 14-16 it seems inappropriate to pin the preaching down to one specific moment. The clause most likely refers to the whole of Christ's saving work. The second reference to "peace" is omitted in the Textus Receptus (following several later witnesses) probably because it was considered to be redundant. However, its presence is also strongly supported ($\mathfrak{P}^{46}$ ℵ A B D F G P it^{d,g} vg cop^{sa,bo} goth arm eth *al*). Moreover, it should also be noted that the second "peace" adds to the weight of the author's statement and is in keeping with the twofold reference to peace in LXX Isa 57:19 (see Metzger 602; Lincoln [1990] 124).

18. *for through him we both have access in one Spirit to the Father:* This verse contains ideas similar to those in v. 16; both verses emphasize the involvement of both groups and the fact that contact with God occurs through Christ. "One body" and "one Spirit" are listed together in 4:4. It is impossible to determine whether "in one Spirit" means that access to God takes place through the Spirit or in (the community of) the Spirit. But as with the expression "in Christ," the instrumental and locative senses are probably very closely related. On the Spirit see also 1:3, 17; 4:4-6. The use of the term "access" *(prosagōgē)* is especially interesting. It is a term that appears infrequently in the NT (cf. Rom 5:2; Eph 3:12). This term has political connotations. It can be used to refer to an audience with an emperor (e.g., Xenophon, *Cyr.* 1.3.8; 7.5.45). The supplicant would appeal to the powerful patron for benefits (see Perkins 74). The cognate verb *(prosagō)*, however, appears in the LXX in conjunction with cultic interests. It refers to unhindered access to the sanctuary as the place of divine presence (LXX Lev 1:3; 3:3; 4:14; cited in Lincoln [1990] 149). It may be that the term is intended to tie together notions of access to political powers with access to the divine. In so doing it challenges the expectation that only the privileged will have access to the domain of governors, princes, and kings (earthly referents

for the heavenly realms?). Moreover, Gentiles now have access to the divine favor Jews alone once enjoyed.

19. *So then you are no longer strangers and aliens:* With this verse the passage begins a new section, signaled by the return to "you" in contrast to the "we" of vv. 14-18 and in keeping with vv. 11-13. In many respects the final section of vv. 19-22 corresponds to the first section of the passage, vv. 11-13. The final section responds to the plight of the past existence of believers by describing the new reality with a composite of metaphors. Verse 12 states that believers were once strangers *(xenoi),* but in this verse they are told that they are no longer strangers and aliens *(paroikoi).* Salvation is presented in terms of rescue from lost nationhood and homelessness. The terms "strangers" and "aliens" are very closely related in ancient literature (used interchangeably in the LXX) and it is impossible to distinguish precisely between the meanings in Ephesians. The word *paroikoi* literally means sojourners or resident aliens. It may have been used in order to emphasize what it meant to be a stranger. The experience of being outside the realm of salvation was like being homeless in a foreign land. *Paroikoi* also occurs in 1 Pet 2:11; 1 Peter has important points of contacts with Ephesians (see the interpretation below). See also the use of the terms "aliens" (sojourners) and "strangers" in the *Epistle to Diognetus* cited below.

but you are fellow-citizens with the saints and members of the household of God: Verse 19 is designed to respond to the problem outlined in v. 12. Believers are told that they are no longer alienated from the commonwealth of Israel. They are no longer outsiders. They do not share the lot of disenfranchised foreigners and resident aliens who only participate in some of the benefits of the land. Rather they are now full citizens with legal rights. Although it is usually not apparent from the English translations, v. 12 and v. 19 are linguistically related: The term "fellow-citizen" *(sympolitēs)* is a cognate of the term "commonwealth" *(politeia).* Two metaphors for the church are closely related in this verse. In keeping with v. 12, the notion of the church as the spiritual Israel—a holy nation—underlies the first part of the verse, but the description of the new reality shared by believers moves into a proclamation that believers are members of the household of God. The church as the "household of God" must have been a powerful metaphor, for it related the experience of salvation to the physical gathering place of first-century believers—the local house (cf. Gal 6:10). The expression also appears in 1 Peter and in the Pastoral Epistles, works that also come from the later decades of the NT era (1 Pet 4:17; cf. 1 Pet 2:5; 1 Tim 3:15). Household language is found throughout Ephesians as a way of describing the relationship between believers and God (cf. 1:5; 3:14-15; 5:21–6:9).

If it were not for the mention of the household of God in this verse it might be best to understand the "saints" as a reference to the Jews or to Jewish believers in Jesus (i.e., the Gentile believers would be sharing in their lot). "The saints" or "the holy ones" was used in various Jewish texts as a designation for the righteous (see the notes on 1:18). But because the household of God is a broad concept referring to the totality of believers (Gentiles and Jews), it is best to understand "saints" as a reference to all believers (on saints see also the notes and interpretation on Eph 1:1-2). There is also a third possibility that cannot be ruled out completely. Some Jewish texts refer to angels as "the saints" or "the holy ones" (see the notes on 1:18). Given the emphasis in Eph 2:6 on believers partaking of the heavenly realms it is possible that the author has heavenly citizenship in mind. Once again, however, the reference to the household of God makes it very difficult to exclude human membership among the saints. It may be that for both the author and the recipients of Ephesians the concepts of heavenly citizenship with the angels and citizenship among the holy believers in Jesus had merged to a considerable extent.

20. *having been built upon the foundation of the apostles and prophets, Christ Jesus himself being the cornerstone:* The reference to the household of God in the previous verse introduces a series of very interesting architectural metaphors. Believers were once without Christ (v. 12), but now they live within a structure with Christ Jesus himself being the cornerstone. In general, throughout 2:20-22 the author of Ephesians seems to have been influenced by 1 Cor 3:9-17. The image of members of the community being shaped into a building with Christ as the cornerstone also appears in 1 Pet 2:4-6 (cf. 1 Cor 3:10-11; Isa 28:16; Ps 118:21-23). There has been considerable debate concerning whether the term *akrogōniaios* refers to the cornerstone of the foundation of a building (e.g., Mitton [1973] 112–14; McKelvey 352–59) or whether it actually refers to the stone that crowns the building—the capstone or keystone (e.g., Lincoln [1990] 154–55; Jeremias 154–57). There are good arguments in support of both interpretations. Among the strongest in favor of the latter interpretation is the fact that the notion of Christ as the top stone would fit with the emphasis throughout Ephesians on the exaltation of Christ (e.g., 4:16) and the idea of Christ as head of the body (1:22). In my opinion, however, there are several important reasons why "cornerstone" is to be preferred. These include the use of the term in LXX Isa 28:16, the foundational role given to Christ in 1 Cor 3:10-11, and the fact that it is difficult to make sense of the role of the prophets and apostles if Christ is not the base for the foundation (see also the notes on 2:21).

Although a few scholars have viewed the mention of prophets as a reference to OT prophets, most commentators have understood early church prophets to be primarily in view. The reference to "apostles and prophets" in 3:5 and 4:11 supports this contention. Moreover, the Acts of the Apostles (a work that has important points of contact with Ephesians; see the interpretation below) shares a similar interest in prophets and apostles. Luke paints a picture of apostles (those who had known the historical Jesus), elders (authoritative local leaders), and prophets (wandering teachers) sharing in the leadership of the early church. In Acts the prophets are wandering charismatic teachers who are connected to the Jerusalem church (Acts 11:27-28; 15:22, 27, 32; 21:10-11). Acts 13:1 lists Paul and Barnabas as members of a group of prophets and teachers who are leaders of the church at Antioch; they are set apart for their mission to the Gentiles through the action of the Holy Spirit (Acts 13:2-4). Although Acts is reluctant to attribute the title "apostle" to Paul, he is unquestionably an apostle in Ephesians (1:1; 3:1-13). Like Acts, however, Ephesians stresses the importance of the witness of apostles and prophets (there is no mention of elders, but the household code may represent an indirect legitimization of male householders to act as local leaders; see the notes and interpretation on 5:21–6:9). The content of 2:11-22 suggests that the author of Ephesians considered the witness of this group to be central to the development of the Gentile mission.

21. *in whom the whole structure, being fitted together, grows into a holy temple in the Lord:* The transition from v. 20 to v. 21 conveys an image of the harmonious growth of the church (cf. Eph 4:15-16). On "in whom" see the notes on 2:22. The fact that the building is understood as still growing offers support for the translation of *akrogōniaios* as "cornerstone" and not "capstone"; for Christ to be understood as the stone that crowns the building would not be in keeping with the image of sustained growth in v. 21 (see the notes on 2:20). The use of the temple metaphor is similar to the Qumran community's understanding of itself as God's temple (cf. 1QS 5:5-6; 8:4-15; 9:3-8; 11:7-8; 1 Cor 3:16; 6:19-20). On the implications of the reference to the temple in Ephesians see also the note on v. 14 and the interpretation below. The definite article *hē* (the) in the expression *pasa hē oikodomē* (the whole structure or building) is absent from many important witnesses (ℵ* B D G K Ψ 33 614 1739* *Byz Lect* Clement *al*). The shorter reading is probably to be preferred because it is the more difficult reading (it is actually possible also to translate the expression as "every building" in the sense of every local congregation) and the longer version may easily have arisen from the efforts of copyists to clarify the sense (Metzger 603; Lincoln [1990] 124). Despite the ambiguity inherent in the Greek expression *pasa oikodomē* it should probably be understood as a reference to the universal church, consistent with the interests of Ephesians as a whole (see the full discussion in Lincoln [1990] 156). The term *oikodomē* does occur in 1 Cor 3:9 to describe the local Corinthian community. In Eph 4:12, 16, 29 it means "upbuilding" in the sense of ethical edification.

22. *in whom you also are being built up together into a dwelling place for God in the Spirit:* The articulation of the temple metaphor continues from v. 21. "In whom" *(en hō)* could refer to "the Lord" or "a temple" in the previous verse, but the more likely explanation seems to be that it acts as a parallel to the opening in v. 21, and thus in both cases the expression refers to Christ Jesus in v. 20 (see Lincoln [1990] 158). The body metaphor (v. 16) has merged with architectural imagery in order to create a vision of a human spiritual dwelling. The believers (including both Jews and Gentiles) are living stones that are being built up together into a growing structure (cf. 1 Pet 2:5). The verb *synoikodomeō* (to build up together) occurs only here in the NT (cf. 4:16). The prefix *syn* underlines the fact that the building takes place as part of a joint communal effort. *Katoikētērion* is found elsewhere in the NT only in Rev 18:2 where it is used to describe Babylon as a dwelling place for demons. However, it is used in the LXX to refer to God's heavenly abode (1 Kgs 8:39, 43, 49) and to God's dwelling place in the temple in Jerusalem (1 Kgs 8:13). The physical temple was traditionally understood as a dwelling place for God, but now a spiritual temple exists in the shape of a community of believers. Emphasis on this spir-

itual entity is in direct contrast to the emphasis on the physical barriers that once separated Jews and Gentiles. While believers are now in the Spirit, identity was once defined by means of circumcision in the flesh made by hands (v. 11). As is frequently the case in Ephesians (cf. 1:3, 13, 14), it is not completely clear whether *en pneumati* should be taken as a reference to the Holy Spirit (e.g., NAB; NJB) or whether it should be understood as a more general reference to a spiritual dwelling place for God (e.g., NRSV; REB). The role assigned to the Spirit in v. 18, however, suggests that the former is more likely. The idea of the indwelling of God's Spirit in the community described as a temple is also found in the undisputed letters of Paul (1 Cor 3:16; 6:19-20).

INTERPRETATION

The theme of unity holds the various sections of Ephesians together. Among the passages that have received the most attention in Ephesians are the great "unity" texts of Eph 2:11-22 and Eph 5:22-33, both of which use a series of metaphors to explore the relationship between the human and the divine. Most commentators have understood Eph 2:11-22 as comprised of three major sections: vv. 11-13, vv. 14-18, and vv. 19-22. There is a close relationship between the first and the last parts in that the last part seems to respond to the plight of past existence outlined in the first (see the notes). Many commentators have argued that in vv. 14-18 the author of Ephesians draws upon a hymn to Christ that resembles Col 1:15-20. As in other passages, the author of Ephesians makes use here of traditional elements to build arguments and make proclamations. In addition to the hymnic elements, the influence of Col 1:21-23 and of Isa 52:7 and Isa 57:19 has been judged to be of paramount significance for the shape of the passage as it now stands (see the notes on 2:13, 16, 17). Like Eph 2:1-10, Eph 2:11-22 articulates a very strong contrast between a pre-Christian past (then) and the present life of believers (now). In articulating this contrast, however, 2:11-22 concentrates much more specifically on the historical plane: the unity between Gentiles and Jews. It is this focus on the historical plane that has led commentators to turn to Eph 2:11-22 most frequently when seeking to reconstruct the communal situation that inspired Ephesians.

For the reader who comes to 2:11-22 with knowledge of the undisputed letters of Paul (especially Galatians and Romans), the arguments seem immediately familiar. It is not surprising that many, therefore, have seen in these texts a continuation of Paul's interest in integrating the Gentiles into the church, and have concluded that some problem involving the unity of Gentiles and Jews underlies the text. That the recipients of Ephesians are Gentiles (or constitute a Gentile majority) is stated explicitly for the first time in v. 11. Scholars who believe (as is also the position in this commentary) that Ephesians is deutero-Pauline are virtually unanimous in holding that the author of Ephesians was a Jewish Christian; Eph 2:11-22 has figured prominently in this contention. The you/we contrast in the text (see the notes), the use of Scripture, and especially the author's interest in clarifying the relationship between the Gentile believers and Israel have been judged to be especially significant. As Paul had done for a previous generation of believers, this Jewish Christian author needed to describe how Jewish Christians and Gentile Christians were now united into one body, the household of God, the holy temple in the Lord.

Although Eph 2:11-22 might seem at first glance to constitute essentially a repetition of the Pauline message found in earlier letters, scholarly analysis of the text has highlighted important differences of perspective and has raised several difficult questions concerning the intention of the passage. First, it is important to note that there is no consensus concerning why the author of Ephesians needed to proclaim that the estrangement of Gentiles had been overcome with a resultant unity of Gentiles and Jews. Was the author responding to a Jewish Christian minority who argued that their heritage accorded them certain privileges? Were Gentiles beginning to ignore the Jewish roots of the church? Is there truly evidence in Ephesians for a social problem involving the relationship between Jews and Gentiles, or could the unity teaching be serving an entirely different purpose? In seeking to extract information about the social setting of Ephesians from 2:11-22 one encounters the same problem that recurs throughout Ephesians: the work simply resists being pinned down to any one historical situation. There is no direct evidence in Ephesians of conflict concerning Jewish-Gentile relations such as one finds in Galatians, for example. Even though Ephesians speaks of "circumcision" (v. 11) and the "law" (v. 15), these terms are included without providing evidence of specific issues involved in the conflict. It is striking to compare Ephesians in this respect to Colossians—where particular Jewish practices are at the heart of a controversy (e.g., Col 2:16). In fact, the unity of Jew and Gentile is presented as an achieved reality in 2:11-22 and one gets the impression that any conflict having to do with how Gentiles should be admitted into the church is long past.

One of the most popular and plausible proposals concerning the circumstances of 2:11-22 is that emphasis on the unity between Jew and Gentile in the text stems from a need to remind Gentile Christians of their Jewish heritage. In other words, the dangers expressed by Paul in Rom 11:17-24 have come true: Gentile Christianity has become successful and Gentile Christians are in danger of ignoring their continuity with Jewish Christianity and Israel. Perhaps Jewish Christians are being pushed aside or ignored (e.g., Käsemann [1968] 291; Sampley 158–63). But, as noted above, one of the main problems with such a proposal is that there is no direct evidence for tension between Jews and Gentiles in the community.

Moreover, because 2:11-22 proclaims the inclusion of Gentiles into an entity that transcends the historical Israel (see further below) it is conceivable that it might have increased Gentile arrogance should the problem have existed. There are no specific efforts here to deflate Gentile pride as there are in Romans 11. Nevertheless, aspects of the texts do suggest the idea of Gentiles sharing in the heritage of Israel (vv. 12-14) and that the author of Ephesians was trying to define the identity of a Gentile church in light of its Jewish roots (see Lincoln [1990] 153). In fact, the use of the metaphor of a spiritual Israel to define the church (see the notes on 2:12 and 2:19) might well have bolstered the identity of the church in important ways.

Ephesians reflects a setting in the churches of Asia Minor near the end of the first century when Gentile Christians probably greatly outnumbered Jewish Christians and exchanges between believers and Jewish communities may well have been limited (J. T. Sanders [1993]). However, by the end of the first century Jews and Christians coexisted in the cities of Asia Minor, which by and large would have had much larger and more influential Jewish communities (see Perkins 31–32, citing Feldman 73). Given the importance attached to honor in the Greco-Roman world it may have been quite natural to appeal to the Jewish community on a symbolic level as a way of establishing the prestige and boundaries of the new community. Even if there were very little explicit dialogue between Jews and Christians, the identification of the church with Israel (vv. 12, 19) might represent an attempt for Christians to orient themselves in relation to issues of Jewish nationhood such as the destruction of the Jerusalem Temple. The struggling sect would be simultaneously drawing on the benefits of continuity with Israel and at the same time justifying its superiority as a new creation in Christ: "he who has made both one and has broken down the dividing wall."

To understand Eph 2:11-22 as offering insight into specific tensions between Jewish and Gentile Christians is probably to go beyond the evidence. However, one is left with the question of the purpose of 2:11-22 for community life. In what sense would the recipients of Ephesians have found this text relevant for their lives? In my view there are two possibilities that are not mutually exclusive. The first constitutes a variation on the theory that the text responds to Gentile arrogance in the face of a dwindling Jewish Christian minority. A comparison of Ephesians to two works that are similar to it in many respects—Acts and 1 Peter—suggests that while Ephesians no longer reflects tensions concerning the incorporation of Gentiles into the church, it may well be seeking to encourage harmonious relations between Jews and Gentiles.

There is strong evidence that the issue of how Jews and Gentiles should live together in Christ had not been completely settled in the latter decades of the first century. The Acts of the Apostles, a work that bears a striking resemblance to Ephesians in language and style, is very interesting to consider in this regard (Mitton [1973] 15–17). The author of Acts is deeply concerned with the important part played by Israel in God's plan of salvation. However, the frequent depiction of Jewish rejection of the gospel, culminating in a turning to the Gentiles (e.g., Acts 13:46), may speak to an increasing Gentile membership in the community. Philip Esler has concluded that Acts recounts the story of the early church in order to serve the needs of a mixed community of Jews and Gentiles. He has argued that an effort to instill harmonious relations between the groups is especially visible in passages that exhibit concern for table fellowship (e.g., Acts 10:1–11:18; 15:20, 29; 16:14-15, 25-34; 18:7-11; 27:33-38). First Peter also offers many interesting parallels to Ephesians (Mitton [1973] 17–18). For example, like Eph 2:11-22, 1 Peter includes the image of community members being shaped into a building with Jesus as the cornerstone (cf. 1 Pet 2:4-6; Eph 2:18-22) and also relates the process of entry into the church to the experience of being a resident alien (1 Pet 2:11; Eph 2:19). Like Ephesians, 1 Peter highlights former Gentile ignorance and isolation from Israel (1 Pet 1:14, 18; 2:10; 4:2-4). Those who were once not a people are called the people of God (1 Pet 2:10). John H. Elliott (1982) has argued that 1 Peter addresses a mixed audience of former Jews and Gentiles in Asia Minor (45). The mixed character of the church has become an important concern and the theological break with Judaism requires justification (Elliott [1982] 85).

Studying points of contact between Ephesians and other works that come from the latter decades of the first century can be very suggestive regarding the general state of affairs addressed by Ephesians. Although there was probably no crisis concerning the relationship between Jews and Gentiles in the church, unity between the groups was something that required repeated encouragement. While Ephesians clearly addresses an audience made up predominantly of Gentiles it is important not to overstate the case for Gentile interests in the community. Ephesians abounds with Jewish concepts and traditions. It is difficult to imagine the author of Ephesians addressing the community as the only Jewish Christian connected to the community. The Jewish Christian perspective is very much alive in Ephesians even if the numbers of Jewish believers in the church may be dwindling rapidly.

In addition to encouraging harmonious relations between Jews and Gentiles in the church, Eph 2:11-22 might have server broader purposes. The metaphorical language is highly flexible and adaptable. In fact, this text offers a good illustration of the power of the imagery of Ephesians to transcend its historical referents. For example, walls mean barriers in most social contexts. We in the modern world might read 2:14 and immediately think of the tearing down of the Berlin Wall. Within a first-century context the breaking down of the dividing wall might have had strongly cosmological connotations. For those who had just been reminded of their heavenly exaltation (2:6), v. 14 may well have called to mind the breaking through of the cosmic wall between heaven and earth (*1 Enoch* 14:9; *3 Apoc. Bar.* 2:1, 2; *T. Levi* 2.7). For those who were crossing barriers en route to heavenly places a spiritual Israel transcending the historical Israel may have seemed a most appropriate metaphor for the church. In other words it is important to realize that the majestic proclamations in 2:11-22 might encode a variety of religious messages. The encouragement of unity might also have had broad applications. The tremendous achievement of unity between Jews and Gentiles could inspire harmony in community life at all levels. The points of contact between 2:11-22 and 5:21-33 (see the notes and interpretation on 5:21–6:9) indicate that the Ephesian message of unification was being applied so broadly that it extended from the expanse of the cosmos to the smallest social unit—the marriage at the center of a household. Moreover, as will be discussed further below, the manner in which unity-generating language intersects with the then/now pattern in 2:11-22 suggests that cohesion is being encouraged in reaction to the evil outside world where believers once lived.

The language in Ephesians about the unity of Gentile and Jew has become detached from the conflict situation where it was born (Paul's struggle to secure the admission of Gentiles without requiring works of the Law) and is being applied to a new situation. In the process it has gained an objective quality. Sociologists have noted that this "objectification" is typical of the need to transfer traditions and institutions to a new generation. It is only by achieving a certain objective quality that symbol systems can survive beyond the period of their creation (see the notes and interpretation on 2:1-10). There is in fact a hint in 2:11-22 that the setting of Ephesians is the generation following the disappearance of the first witnesses, authorities, and apostles. The mention of apostles and prophets in 2:19-20 reflects the perspective of a "built up" church looking back to its origins. The implication is one of considerable distance between the addressees and the earliest leaders (see Mitton [1973] 111). In this new setting language about Jews and Gentiles is being used in a surprising and sometimes shocking way. Most Christians in the world today would be very reluctant to appropriate the language of Jewish nationhood to describe the church as does the author of Ephesians in v. 12 and v. 19. There is a sense in which Israel has become a metaphor for the church. According to v. 12 the Gentiles were once alienated from the commonwealth of Israel, but according to v. 19 this is no longer the case. The Gentiles share in the salvation history that once belonged to Israel alone. But the verses between 12 and 19 prevent one from concluding that we have here the same notion we find in Romans 11: Believers constitute a remnant of Israel to which Gentiles have been added.

The author of Ephesians stops short of taking the argument for continuity with Israel to its logical conclusion. Instead the metaphors switch from proclaiming continuity to announcing discontinuity. Israel becomes a metaphor for a recreated unified entity ("one new person," v. 15), brought about through Christ's agency that has transcended the historical Israel. The church has become a distinct entity separate from both Judaism and other groups in the Greco-Roman world. Ultimately "Israel," like "body," "building," and "temple," serves as a metaphorical description of this new entity. Unlike Romans 9–11, Eph 2:11-22 is not concerned with the situation of the Jews who are not part of the church.

The way the author of Ephesians treats Israel seems quite surprising for a Jewish Christian. The very strong statement in v. 15 about Christ having abolished the Law is particularly striking. Such a statement departs from what is found in the undisputed letters of Paul (see the notes on 2:15) and offers a further indication of a break between the church and Judaism. It is somewhat ironic, then, that Jewish literature is increasingly being recognized as offering the most important background for understanding Ephesians. The QL offers probably the most important parallels to the religious concepts in Ephesians and it has been suggested that the author was a Jew whose sectarian piety was close to that of the Essenes (Perkins 30). Not only is the reference to the spiritual temple in keeping with the QL (see the notes on v. 21), but Pheme Perkins has drawn attention to a series of texts connecting "building a 'wall,' that is sectarian legal interpretation, and separation" (Perkins 72; e.g., CD 4:12, 19). The wall and the Law are very closely related in 2:14-15. Ephesians reflects a perspective that is sociologically quite "introversionist" (displaying a very strong sense of separation from the outside world) like the communal reality reflected in the QL (see the notes and interpretation on 1:15-23; 2:1-10). The author may be adopting an approach learned in the midst of Jewish sectarianism and applying it to a new situation.

As we seek to understand the social setting of Ephesians it is useful to consider the reconstruction of the context of 1 Peter offered by John H. Elliott. Elliott (1982) has dated 1 Peter provisionally between 73 and 92 C.E., the period in which Ephesians most likely was also composed. He has described a probable setting for the document involving social tensions created by population movement and the meeting of diverse cultures in the provinces of Asia Minor (Elliott 59–73). Although 1 Peter, like Ephesians, comes from a period before any direct confrontation between Rome and church communities, Elliott nevertheless feels justified in speaking about a crisis. Note how he draws attention to the reference to "resident aliens" in 1 Pet 2:11; the same term occurs in Eph 2:19:

It was a time when the expansion of the Christian movement in Asia Minor and its growing visibility as a distinct socio-religious entity was being encountered with suspicion, fear and animosity. Spread throughout all of the provinces north of the Taurus, the sect had attracted rural as well as urban elements of the population, former Jews as well as a predominant number of pagans. Living on the margin of political and social life, these *paroikoi,* "resident aliens" no doubt had seen in this new salvation movement new opportunity for social acceptance and improvement in their economic lot. Coming from the already suspect ranks of strangers, resident aliens and lower classes, however, these "Christ-lackeys" gained only further disdain for the exotic religion they embraced. Sporadic local outbreaks of slander and abuse had led to the suffering of these Christians here as elsewhere throughout the world. (Elliott [1982] 83–84)

In this commentary it is being argued that Ephesians reflects a setting where believers are feeling strongly threatened by external forces (see the notes and interpretation on 1:15-23). In addition to the threat of hostile cosmic powers (cf. 1:21; 2:2), it is highly likely that the community was experiencing tension in relation to outsiders of the type described by Elliott. The strong then/now contrast operating throughout 2:11-22 reinforces the boundaries between the church and the outside world. However, there are further indications in the text of mounting difficulties in the church's interaction with the outside world. The unusual use of the term *atheos* (atheist, being without God) to refer to the past existence of believers may offer evidence of a response to nonbelievers who had previously applied the derogatory label to church members (see the notes on 2:12). The term was frequently employed in polemical exchanges among pagans, Jews, and Christians in the Greco-Roman world. Furthermore, the overcoming of hostility between Jews and Gentiles is mentioned twice (2:14, 16), but this may have served to offer hope for Christ to overcome hostility between social groups more generally (see the notes on 2:15). To be sure, the image of growth in vv. 21-22 calls to mind the expansion and success of the church despite possible obstacles. But as has frequently been noted by commentators, this growth is vertical rather than horizontal. The holy temple is being built up into the heavenly realms. It may be that growth imagery seemed highly applicable to the lives of these early Christians even if at the time of composition of Ephesians they were not experiencing tremendous success in winning new members.

In order to understand the type of response to society exhibited by Ephesians one should pay special attention to how architectural imagery is used. The fusion of the Pauline notion of the body of Christ with architectural metaphors suggests a critique of conventional designations of sacred space. The community has rejected the usual architectural markers of identity. The erection of important buildings was an important way of demonstrating one's honor and status in the ancient world and was integral in gaining access to power. For example, the cities of Asia Minor aimed to secure imperial favor by seeking to build a temple to Augustus (Perkins 75, citing Faust). Ephesians suggests that increasingly the community on earth sees a true reflection of itself in a heavenly congregation —a heavenly temple (cf. 1QS 11:7, 8). Even the description of circumcision as "made by hands" (v. 11) may be closely related to belief in the heavenly abode. The Jerusalem Temple in the NT is frequently described as that which is "made with hands" and is understood as a symbol of the old order (Acts 7:48; 17:24; Heb 9:11, 24; Mark 14:58). Andrew Lincoln has made an important point about the significance of the spiritual temple described in Ephesians: "The emphasis on God's presence in the Spirit can provide a reminder that when we talk of the 'spiritualization' of the concept of the temple, we are not talking of invisibility or immateriality but of the reality of men and women forming the eschatological people of God, dominated by his living power and presence in the Spirit" (Lincoln [1990] 158). Lincoln is no doubt correct in his identification of the main goal as the "spiritualization" of the temple, but it is important to realize that the concomitant invisibility and immateriality of the holy temple had important social consequences for the community. It facilitated their integration into mainstream society. They did not withdraw into the desert or erect "some strange place of their own" (*Diogn.* 5.2) in order to build an alternate society, but continued to live in the world as though they did not belong to the world. This is very similar to the approach to society advocated in Colossians (see the notes and interpretation on Col 2:16-23; 3:18–4:1), but in Ephesians the notion of a "heavenly" withdrawal is even more pronounced. Although Ephesians displays no explicit interest in the local arrangements of meeting, the use of the household for church gatherings facilitated this physical integration into mainstream society. The "household of God" metaphor may reflect this reality. The community resembled a typical household group and lived in households, but its true essence was that of the household of God. In its attitude toward earthly citizenship and detachment from the structures of power that defined civic life Ephesians is in keeping with the second-century early Christian work called the *Epistle to Diognetus*:

> For the distinction between Christians and other men, is neither in country nor language nor customs. For they do not dwell in cities in some strange place of their own, nor do they use any strange variety of dialect, nor practice an extraordinary kind of life. This teaching of theirs has not been discovered by the intellect or thought of busy men, nor are they the advocates of any human doctrine as some men are. Yet while living in Greek and barbarian cities, according as each obtained his lot, and following the local customs, both in clothing and food and in the rest of life,

they show forth the wonderful and confessedly strange character of the constitution of their own citizenship. They dwell in their own father-lands, but as if sojourners *(paroikoi)* in them; they share all things as citizens, and suffer all things as strangers *(xenoi)*. Every foreign country is their fatherland, and every fatherland is a foreign country. (LCL *Diogn.* 5.1-5)

FOR REFERENCE AND FURTHER STUDY

Elliott, John H. *A Home for the Homeless.* Philadelphia: Fortress, 1981.

Faust, Eberhard. *Pax Christi et Pax Caesaris: Religionsgeschichtliche, traditions-geschichtliche und sozialgeschichtliche Studien zum Epheserbrief.* NTOA 24. Fribourg: Universitätsverlag; Göttingen: Vandenhoeck & Ruprecht, 1993.

Gärtner, Bertil. *The Temple and the Community in Qumran and the New Testament: A Comparative Study in the Temple Symbolism of the Qumran Texts and the New Testament.* MSSNTS 1. Cambridge: Cambridge University Press, 1965.

Jeremias, Joachim. "Eckstein–Schlusstein," *ZNW* 36 (1937) 154–57.

Käsemann, Ernst. "Ephesians and Acts," in Leander E. Keck and J. Louis Martyn, eds., *Studies in Luke-Acts.* London: SPCK, 1968, 288–97.

Martin, Ralph P. *Reconciliation: A Study of Paul's Theology.* Atlanta: John Knox, 1981.

McKelvey, R. J. "Christ as the Cornerstone," *NTS* 8 (1962) 352–59.

Meeks, Wayne A. "In One Body: The Unity of Humankind in Colossians and Ephesians," in Wayne A. Meeks and Jacob Jervell, eds., *God's Christ and His People: Studies in Honour of Nils Alstrup Dahl.* Oslo, Bergen, and Tromsö: Universitetsforlaget, 1977, 209–21.

Roetzel, Calvin J. "Jewish Christian–Gentile Christian Relations: A Discussion of Ephesians 2, 15a," *ZNW* 74 (1983) 81–89.

Sampley, J. Paul. *"And the Two Shall Become One Flesh": A Study of Traditions in Ephesians 5:21-33.* MSSNTS 16. Cambridge: Cambridge University Press, 1971.

Sanders, E. P. *Paul, the Law, and the Jewish People.* Philadelphia: Fortress, 1983.

Sanders, Jack T. "Hymnic Elements in Ephesians 1–3," *ZNW* 56 (1965) 214–32.

_____. *Schismatics, Sectarians, Dissidents, Deviants: The First One Hundred Years of Jewish-Christian Relations.* Valley Forge: Trinity Press International, 1993.

Schille, Gottfried. *Frühchristliche Hymnen.* Berlin: Evangelische Verlagsanstalt, 1965.

19. *The Apostle as Interpreter of the Divine Mystery* (3:1-13)

1. Because of this I, Paul, the prisoner of Christ Jesus on behalf of you Gentiles—2. if, as I suppose, you have heard of the stewardship of the grace of God given to me for you, 3. that the mystery was made known to me by revelation, as I have previously written briefly. 4. Whereby, when

you read, you will be able to comprehend my insight into the mystery of Christ, 5. which in other generations was not made known to the sons of men as it has now been revealed to his holy apostles and prophets by the Spirit. 6. that the Gentiles are now co-heirs, co-members of the body, and co-sharers of the promise in Christ Jesus through the gospel, 7. of which I became a minister according to the gift of the grace of God given to me according to the working of his power. 8. To me, the very least of all the saints, this grace was given to preach the unsearchable riches of Christ to the Gentiles. 9. and to make all see what is the plan of the mystery hidden for ages in God who created all things 10. in order that the manifold wisdom of God might now be known through the church to the rulers and authorities in the heavenly places, 11. according to the eternal purpose that he carried out in Christ Jesus the Lord, 12. in whom we have boldness and access in confidence through faith in him. 13. Therefore, I ask you not to lose heart over my afflictions on your behalf, which are your glory.

NOTES

3:1. *Because of this I, Paul, the prisoner of Christ Jesus on behalf of you Gentiles:* This verse appears to be an interrupted thought (there is no verb) that is resumed again in the prayer of Eph 3:14-19. Verse 14 includes the same introductory formula as v. 1: *toutou charin* (because of this; by reason of this. The expression is found elsewhere in the NT only in Titus 1:5). "This" refers to the description of the achieved unity of Jew and Gentile in 2:11-22. Verses 15-18 consider Paul's mission and authority as an apostle. He is called "the prisoner" (literally "the one who is in bonds," *ho desmios*) also in 4:1 (cf. Eph 3:1; 6:20). The use of the definite article may indicate a special significance being attached to Paul's role: he is *the* prisoner—the apostolic witness *par excellence*. He is depicted in Ephesians as being literally in captivity, but the expression "prisoner of Christ Jesus" is intended to highlight the true meaning of this imprisonment: he is under Christ's power and control; he is bound to Christ (cf. Phlm 1, 9). Beginning with the emphatic "I, Paul," this section includes a repeated emphasis on Paul's authority. Such terms as "I," "me," and "my" are employed throughout (cf. 3:2, 3, 4, 7, 8, 13). A link between what Paul has accomplished for the Gentiles and Christ's work is suggested by the use of the term *hyper* (on behalf of: cf. 3:13; Col 1:24). The same term is also employed to refer to Christ's work (cf. Eph 5:2, 25; see Taylor and Reumann 54). The phrase "you Gentiles" also occurs in 2:11.

2. *—if, as I suppose, you have heard of the stewardship of the grace of God given to me for you:* Ephesians 3:1-13 is closely related to Col 1:23-29. This close relationship is clearly visible in this verse. Both Col 1:23 and this verse open with the expression *ei ge* (if indeed). The context determines whether it constitutes an expression of doubt or a confident assumption (BDF 454 [2]). The context here suggests the latter. The author of Ephesians is using the expression to commu-

nicate assumed knowledge: "I suppose" or "for surely you" (e.g., NRSV; REB). The phrase suggests a certain amount of distance between Paul and the recipients of the work, for it is difficult to make sense of Paul making such an assertion to a community he knew so well. The phrase makes most sense if Ephesians was addressed to a community or communities of believers whom Paul did not know personally. Both Col 1:23 and Eph 3:2 include the expression "you heard" or "you have heard" *(ēkousate)*, although in Col 1:23 it is used specifically to refer to the gospel. Colossians 1:25 speaks of the "stewardship *[oikonomia]* of God given to me for you." This is the only instance of the term *oikonomia* in Colossians; it refers to the commission God gave Paul to become an apostle. (See the notes on Col 1:25; for a full discussion of the meaning of the term *oikonomia* in Ephesians see the notes on 1:10.) *Oikonomia* occurs three times in Ephesians (1:10; 3:2, 9). A distinctive feature of the use of the term in Ephesians is that it is closely associated with notions of God's plan for the universe. In fact, in 1:10 and 3:9 it is best translated simply as "plan." In 3:2 it is closer in meaning to the usage in Col 1:25, but 3:3-13 makes it clear that the author is concentrating on how Paul's role brings God's plan to fruition. Grace is a frequent theme in Ephesians (e.g., 2:5-8). In the undisputed letters of Paul "grace" *(charis)*—God's free gift—is a term frequently used to describe the nature of the apostle's commission (e.g., Gal 2:9; 1 Cor 3:10; 15:10; Rom 1:5; 12:3, 6; 15:15). In the parallel expression of Col 1:25 the term "stewardship" seems to function as the equivalent of "grace," but in 3:2 grace is mentioned explicitly. In contrast to Col 1:25, "given to me for you" now modifies grace rather than stewardship (see Lincoln [1990] 174).

3. *that the mystery was made known to me by revelation, as I have previously written briefly:* This verse recalls Eph 1:9 and contains terminology similar to Rom 16:25-27 and Col 1:26-27. *Mystērion* (mystery) is a central theme in Ephesians (cf. 1:9; 3:3-10; 5:32; 6:19). As in Colossians, it refers generally to the revelation in Christ that was once hidden. Such ideas draw their origins from Jewish apocalypses. (For a full discussion of the meaning and background of the term see the notes on 1:9, and the notes and interpretation on Col 1:26-27; cf. 1 Cor 2:7-10.) In contrast to Colossians, however, the content of the mystery is often defined very precisely in Ephesians (see the notes on 1:9-10; 2:6, 9) and plays a key role in ecclesiological statements (3:4-6; 5:32). Revelation *(apokalypsis)* is a central term for describing disclosure of the divine mystery (cf. 1:18 and 3:5 where the cognate verb occurs; for the notion of revelation in the undisputed letters of Paul see Gal 1:12, 16; Rom 16:25-27). The verb *gnorizō* (to make known) is also frequently employed throughout Ephesians to speak of the revelation of divine mystery (cf. 1:9; 3:3, 5, 10; 6:19). "As I have previously written briefly" probably refers back to Eph 1:9-10 and perhaps also to 2:11-22 (given that the unity of Jew and Gentile is integral to the definitions of the mystery found in 2:6). There have been other proposals, however. The similarity between this verse and Rom 16:25-27 (a passage with a complex textual history) has prompted the suggestion that Eph 3:3 actually refers back to Rom 16:25-27; this has been understood as supporting the theory that Romans 16 was originally addressed to Ephesus (Davies 568). Others have argued that

the phrase refers to Paul's earlier letters and in the use of the phrase have found support for the theory that Ephesians served as an introduction to the Pauline corpus (Goodspeed 41–42; Mitton [1951] 233–36). These theories, however, are highly speculative and are not accepted by most scholars today. The majority of commentators understand the phrase to be a reference back to what the author previously wrote in Ephesians.

4. *Whereby, when you read, you will be able to comprehend my insight into the mystery of Christ:* Although in Greek vv. 2-7 form one long sentence, a new sentence has been introduced into the English translation for the sake of clarity. This verse is awkward to translate into English, but its meaning is clear. There is reference to what the apostle has previously written (see the notes on 3:3). The description of the mystery in 3:4b-5 (on "mystery" see the notes on 3:3) follows Col 1:26 very closely. The expression "the mystery of Christ" recalls the equation of "mystery" with "Christ in you" in Col 1:27 (cf. Col 4:3). In Ephesians knowledge, wisdom (1:17-18), and insight are highly prized attributes of the believers. (The word for insight is *synesin;* a synonym of the term, *phronēsis,* occurs in 1:8. *Synesin* is mentioned in Col 1:9; 2:2.) These attributes seem to have played a role in the experience of spiritual illumination or inner enlightenment that underlies Ephesians (see the notes on 1:17-18). It is interesting to note the way Paul's role is presented here. Whereas earlier in the epistle the believers share these attributes, in this text it is Paul who has immediate access to insight into the mystery of Christ. He is the interpreter of the insight for the sake of the community (see the interpretation below). The specific content of Paul's insight is spelled out in v. 6.

5. *which in other generations was not made known to the sons of men:* This verse follows the wording of Col 1:26 closely, but there are also similar ideas expressed elsewhere in the NT. For example, the notion of God's plan being unknown to people of other times but now being made manifest is also found in 1 Pet 1:10-12. Such proclamations celebrating a great contrast between then and now are probably rooted in a ritual setting where new life was experienced and celebrated (see the notes on Col 1:26). The text offers one of many examples in Ephesians of the theme of hiding and revealing (see the notes on 1:15-23). The verb "made known" also occurs in v. 3. Colossians 1:26 refers to what has been hidden throughout the ages and from generations, but in Eph 3:5 only the generations are mentioned. Ephesians 3:9 describes what was hidden "for ages." Only Ephesians includes the expression "the sons of men" (a Hebraism meaning "humankind," e.g., LXX Gen 11:5; Ps 11:1).

as it has now been revealed to his holy apostles and prophets by the Spirit: This is the second reference to revelation in this passage, but in this case it is the verb *(apokalyptō)* rather than the noun that occurs. In contrast to Col 1:26 where the revelation is given to all the saints this verse continues the more limited focus of v. 4 and describes revelation as the attribute of the apostles and prophets. This is the second mention of apostles and prophets in the epistle (cf. 2:20; 4:11). It is even clearer than in the case of 2:20 that this is a reference to the central witnesses and charismatic teachers of the early Christian movement and does not include OT prophets (on apostles and prophets see the notes on 2:20).

In the Greek text the word "his" *(autou)* actually divides "apostles" and "prophets" and is not found at the end of the expression as one might expect if it modified both terms; this may suggest that "holy" is a designation for the apostles and not the prophets (i.e., "his holy apostles" and also the prophets). In contrast to the undisputed letters of Paul where "holy" is consistently used to describe all believers (Col 1:26 also speaks of all believers as "the saints" or "the holy ones"), we have here an indication of the special status of the apostles. This may reflect a setting in a new generation of the Pauline movement when it became important to stress the foundational role of the apostles (cf. Ign. *Magn.* 3:1, which refers to "holy presbyters"; see Lincoln [1990] 179; Gnilka [1980] 167). The stark contrast between then and now is in keeping with the focus on the church as a new creation in 2:11-22 (see the notes and interpretation).

Some commentators have seen a certain inconsistency between v. 3 and v. 5 because in v. 3 Paul alone receives the mystery whereas in v. 5 it is revealed to a larger group. However, the purpose of grounding the church in the authority of the holy apostles and prophets is probably both to establish Paul's (a central member of the group of holy apostles) authority over the addressees and to reinforce the authority of early church teachers by connecting them with Paul (see the interpretation below). This is one of many references to the Spirit in Ephesians (see the notes on 5:18). The Greek text might be translated literally as "in spirit" *(en pneumati)*, but it clearly refers to agency: by the Spirit. It is not completely clear whether the phrase modifies only the prophets (prophets in the Spirit; cf. 1 Thess 5:19-20; 1 Cor 12:9-10) or whether it modifies the verb "revealed" and thereby refers to the inspiration of both the holy apostles and the prophets. The usage in 1:17 suggests the latter; it refers to the agency of revelation: by the Holy Spirit (cf. 2:22; see Lincoln [1990] 180). The parallel text of Col 1:26 does not include a reference to the Spirit and this may offer further support for the contention that Ephesians is open to ecstatic experiences of the Spirit (see the notes and interpretation on 1:15-23).

6. *that the Gentiles are now co-heirs, co-members of the body, and co-sharers of the promise in Christ Jesus through the gospel:* This is perhaps the most concise expression of the Christian message found in Ephesians. Verse 6 describes the content of the mystery that Paul interprets for believers (see the notes above). It is essentially a summary of the teaching found in 2:11-22. A closely related description of the mystery is found in 1:10, but in 2:6 it is framed more in terms of the results on the historical plane than in grand cosmological terms. The emphasis on the equal participation of Gentiles and the joining together of Jew and Gentile is often weakened by English translations. In the Greek text the same prefix *(syn)* is attached to the three nouns (co-heirs, co-members, and co-sharers). Many *syn*-expressions also occur in 2:19-22. This verse repeats concepts that have previously been introduced. On "the inheritance" see the notes on 1:14 and 1:18. On "the body" see the notes on 1:23. "The promise" is mentioned earlier in 2:12 in a context that underlines the previous alienation of the Gentiles: "they were once strangers to the covenants of promise" (see the notes), but now they are co-sharers. It should be noted that the term *syssōmos*

(co-member of the body) does not appear elsewhere in ancient literature and seems to have been invented by the author to highlight the creation of a new reality in the church (Lincoln [1990] 180). The expression "in Christ" (see the notes and interpretation on Eph 1:1-2) probably modifies all three descriptions of the Gentiles. They are a new creation united in the sphere of Christ.

7. *of which I became a minister according to the gift of the grace of God given to me according to the working of his power:* The self-description of the apostle as a minister *(diakonos)* recalls both Col 1:23 and 1:25. The syntax and use of terminology in general more closely resembles Col 1:25 but, as in Col 1:23, Paul here is described as a minister *(diakonos)* of the gospel (not of the church as in 1:25). *Diakonos* (minister or servant) was a term used by Paul to describe his own leadership role as well as those of his fellow workers and local leaders. It later came to designate the office of deacon, but it should not be understood in that titular sense here. *Diakonos* was used in the ancient world generally to describe an agent of a high-ranking person who acted as an intermediary (see the summary of the evidence in the notes on Col 1:7 and Col 1:23). This notion may underlie Eph 3:1-13, for Paul is clearly being presented as an agent of God. The mention of the "gift of the grace of God given to me" repeats many of the thoughts found in 3:2, but adds "gift" *(dōrea)* instead of stewardship. As an intermediary between the patron God and the community Paul is the bearer of an important gift. Verse 8 announces that this gift is conveyed in the form of preaching. The expression "the working of his power" (the power of God) reinforces the notion of revelation and spiritual inspiration that runs through this passage. Very similar terminology is found in Eph 1:19: "the surpassing greatness of his power for us who believe, according to the working of his mighty strength," but in 1:19 it is the power of God working through all believers that is in view. Ephesians 3:7 seems to be especially closely related to Col 1:29, which addresses Paul's apostleship directly: "For this I also labor, struggling with his energy powerfully working within me" (cf. Col 2:12). Note, however, that in contrast to Col 1:29, in Eph 3:7 there is no allusion to Paul's suffering and struggles.

8. *To me, the very least of all the saints, this grace was given to preach the unsearchable riches of Christ to the Gentiles:* The notion that Paul's mission is based on God's gift of grace (see the notes on 3:7) is further emphasized. Colossians 1:27 also speaks of riches (cf. 1:7, 18; 2:4, 7; 3:16) and of the proclamation to the Gentiles, and Col 1:26 refers to "saints." However, unlike Colossians, Ephesians includes the image of Paul as a redeemed persecutor (see the interpretation below). There is no doubt that Paul considered this to be an integral part of his identity (1 Cor 15:8-11; cf. Phil 3:5-11). The expression "very least of all the saints" rather than the usual "least of the apostles" may suggest a great solidarity between the apostle and believers, but it may simply represent the influence of Col 1:26, where "saints" also occurs. Given the important role assigned to Paul in this passage as the interpreter of the mystery for believers, it remains striking that there is such insistence on his being the "very least" (the Greek term *elachistoteros* implies great emphasis) among the saints (fellow believers). Pheme Perkins has put forward an interesting interpretation: "The

expression may be dictated by the rhetorical requirements of self-praise. By having Paul deprecate his own achievement, Ephesians has him magnify the graciousness of the divine benefactor who has given him the task of preaching the gospel" (Perkins 84, citing Schnackenburg [1991] 136). It is not entirely clear whether "riches of Christ" should be taken as a subjective genitive (the riches belonging to and bestowed by Christ) or as an objective genitive (Christ himself constitutes the riches) but, given the previous uses of the term "riches" in Ephesians and in Col 1:27 and 2:3, the latter seems far more likely (Lincoln [1990] 183–84). "Unsearchable" in this context means vast or unfathomable (cf. Rom 11:33).

9. *and to make all see what is the plan of the mystery hidden for ages in God who created all things:* This verse is subject to a variety of manuscript variations. Many important manuscripts do not have "all" *(pantas)* following "to make see" *(phōtisai)*. That *phōtisai* would appear alone without the expected accusative would be highly unusual and therefore it is difficult to accept the shorter reading as original. It is also difficult to explain the shorter reading unless there was an accidental omission. Moreover, if "all" were not original one would have expected a variety of alternative readings as is usually the case in such circumstances, but there are no variant readings. On balance it is best to understand "all" as originally part of the text. Two other textual problems are far less difficult to solve. A few manuscripts replace *oikonomia* (plan) with *koinōnia* (fellowship). But since *oikonomia* already occurs in v. 2 there seems to be no good reason for accepting the much-less-well-attested alternate reading. Finally, "created" *(ktisanti)* is followed in a good number of witnesses by "through Christ Jesus" *(dia Iēsou Christou)*. But since there is no compelling explanation for the omission of these words if they were part of the original text, the shorter reading is to be preferred (see Metzger 603). The verb *phōtisai* means literally to "give light to" or "to enlighten." Thus Paul's mission is to make all see. His purpose in the world is in keeping with the purpose of the *logos* as defined by John 1:9: "The true light, which enlightens everyone, was coming into the world" (NRSV). Similar terminology occurs in 1:18 where it refers to the spiritual illumination of believers (see the notes). Taken together 1:18 and 3:9 offer strong evidence that visionary phenomena are of great significance in the communal context of Ephesians (see the interpretation below, and the notes and interpretation on 1:15-23). This is the second instance of *oikonomia* in this passage. (It is translated as "stewardship" in 3:2.) In this verse, however, it clearly means "plan" as in 1:10, and not "commission" as in Col 1:25 and perhaps also 3:2 (see the notes on 1:10 and 3:2). The secret plan of God is being revealed. The hiding/revealing motif permeates Ephesians and there are two expressions of it in this passage: v. 5 and vv. 9-10. Ephesians 3:9-10, like 3:5, appears to have been influenced by Col 1:26. One would actually have expected the mention of "ages" in 3:5, but it is carried over to 3:9 (see the notes on 3:5). The Greek text reads literally "from the ages" *(apo tōn aiōnōn)*. The *aiōnes* are mentioned frequently in Ephesians (1:21; 2:2, 7) and the term could refer to cosmic powers (corresponding to the rulers and authorities in v. 10; cf. Schlier [1957] 153–58; see the notes on 2:2), but the presence of the term "now" *(nyn)*

in v. 10 strongly suggests a temporal meaning as in Col 1:26. The description of the mystery as hidden in God recalls the description of believers in Col 3:3 as having their lives hidden with Christ in God. On the use of the term "mystery" *(mystērion)* in Ephesians see the notes on 1:9.

10. *in order that the manifold wisdom of God might now be known through the church to the rulers and authorities in the heavenly places:* The revelation schema in this passage seems to operate in terms of two distinct stages. Verse 5 announces the hidden mystery now revealed to a select group, the holy apostles and prophets (of which Paul is clearly the most important member). Verses 9-10 announce the transition from that limited scope to the universal church and ultimately to the whole cosmos. The apostle Paul, as the interpreter of the mystery, plays a fundamental role in that transition. Underlying v. 10 is a vision of expansion. In the typical fashion of Ephesians, however, the verse leaves the realities of earthly evangelization behind to make an astounding claim. The purpose of Paul's mission is ultimately to make the manifold wisdom of God known to the rulers and authorities *(tais archais kai tais exousiais).* It is through the church, the recreated unity of Jews and Gentiles resulting from Paul's mission, that it will be accomplished.

In Ephesians the "rulers and authorities" are cosmic powers (see the notes on 1:21). Both here and especially in 6:12 they are identified as malevolent forces. "The heavenly places" is an expression that occurs in the NT only in Ephesians. It is both a realm of heavenly transcendence where Christ dwells with believers and a sphere that remains subject to the hostile influence of cosmic powers (see the notes on 1:3). The vision presented here of the ultimate goal of Paul's mission has to do with demonstrating God's superior power over these cosmic forces. The term *polypoikilos* (manifold) serves to highlight that superiority. It means literally "many-sided," "many-colored," or "comprehensive"—in this case of much more intricate design than humans can appreciate. Wisdom and mystery (NRSV: that which is secret) are linked together in 1 Cor 2:6-8, and according to Eph 1:8 and 17 wisdom is a gift that God bestows on believers. The description of the wisdom of God has to do with divine purpose operating in creation and throughout history in a multifaceted way (cf. Wis 7:22; see Lincoln [1990] 188).

11. *according to the eternal purpose that he carried out in Christ Jesus the Lord:* This verse has points in common with the opening blessing of 1:3-14, which underlines God's initiative and purpose for the world. The term "purpose" *(prothesis)* also occurs in 1:11, and a cognate verb "to set forth or to plan" *(protithēmi)* in 1:9. The Greek text refers literally to "the purpose of the ages" *(prothesin tōn aiōnōn).* This is the second reference to "ages" *(aiōnes)* in this section and, as is also the case in 3:9, it has a temporal meaning.

12. *in whom we have boldness and access in confidence through faith in him:* This verse and the following one resonate with the values of ancient Mediterranean culture. *Parrēsia* (boldness) is a term that occurs frequently in ancient literature to describe the rights of citizens to speak freely, especially before people of high rank. It can also mean a valued openness between friends and sometimes suggests a certain fearlessness, as in the case of 6:19-20 (see also Col 2:15 where

Christ strips the powers and rulers and makes a public example of them "boldly"). The term can also refer to dealings with God, in particular to access in prayer and within a cultic setting (e.g., Philo, *Her.* 5-7; Heb 4:16; 10:19; see BAGD 630–31). The term "confidence" *(pepoithēsis)* reinforces the idea of boldness. It is a word that appears a few times in the NT, but only in the Pauline epistles and especially in 2 Corinthians. Although it can be used to describe the apostle's relationship with God in 2 Cor 3:4, it is used most frequently by Paul in an effort to secure good relations with the Corinthians (2 Cor 1:15; 8:22; 10:2; Phil 3:4). The use of "boldness" and "confidence" to describe ideal dealings between people and God represents the appropriation of values from the world of interpersonal relationships to define human-divine relations (Reese 9). These values are essential for preserving the core values of honor and shame in the Mediterranean world (see the notes on 3:13). The term "access" *(prosagōgē)* also occurs in 2:18 (see the notes). There it refers to access to the Father of both Gentiles and Jews. Access to the Father is also in view here. The Greek expression *pisteōs autou* (literally "faith of him") is ambiguous. It most likely means through believers' faith in Christ (cf. 1:13, 15, 19; 2:8), but it is also possible that it refers to the faith of Christ (Christ's own faithfulness).

13. *Therefore I ask you not to lose heart over my afflictions on your behalf, which are your glory:* With the previous verses the recipients of Ephesians have received insight into the mystery of God's plan for the universe. Paul's role in revealing that mystery has been explained. Therefore *(dio)* they should not lose heart. The use of the verb *aiteō* (to ask) provides a transition to the prayer in 3:14-21; *aiteō* is used in the NT in conjunction with supplication (e.g., Mark 11:24; John 14:13; 15:16; 16:24, 26). There are many similarities between this verse and Col 1:23-29. Although in that passage the term used is "sufferings" rather than "afflictions," both Col 1:24 and Eph 3:13 state that the apostle endures pain on behalf of believers. "Affliction" *(thlipsis)* occurs in both Col 1:24 and Eph 3:13. This term is regularly used in the undisputed letters of Paul (e.g., Rom 5:3; 8:35; 2 Cor 1:4, 8; 2:4; 4:17; 6:4; 7:4; see the full discussion in the notes on Col 1:24). However, in Col 1:24 the afflictions belong to Christ: "in my flesh I am filling up what is lacking in Christ's afflictions, on behalf of his body, which is the church." This verse has inspired a good deal of scholarly comment and it becomes immediately clear that such a strong statement about the meaning of Paul's suffering is absent from Ephesians. Nevertheless, Paul's sufferings are called the Ephesians' glory (glory is also mentioned in Col 1:27; cf. Eph 1:6, 12, 14, 17, 18; 3:16, 21). As in Col 1:24, they take place for the sake of the church. This assessment of Paul's suffering, which might strike modern people at first glance as an unfortunate "glorification" of suffering, needs to be understood in light of the values of honor and shame in the Mediterranean world. Paul is embedded within a broader community and his sufferings have become a means through which the community's honor (reputation) is externally manifested (cf. 2 Cor 1:6; 4:12). First-century cultural norms require external manifestations of honor. Afflictions can act as external manifestations of honor because in Pauline Christianity they have come to symbolize the promise of salvation. Suffering will be followed by glory (e.g., Rom 8:17-18).

Ephesians 3:1 introduces a prayer that is interrupted and taken up again at 3:14. Rather than being an inconsequential digression, however, Eph 3:1-13 serves as an important bridge between remembrance of the alienation and subsequent salvation experienced by the Gentile recipients of the letter in chs. 1–3 and the ethical exhortations beginning in ch. 4. It is Paul the prisoner, minister, and apostle—the revealer of the mystery of Christ (3:4)—who has the unquestionable authority to challenge believers to lead a life worthy of their calling (4:1).

This section offers some of the strongest evidence for the dependence of Ephesians on Colossians. Ephesians 3:1-13 employs many of the terms and ideas found in Col 1:23-28. In addition to the discussion of the various points of overlap listed in the notes above, readers may consult one of the many charts of parallels that have been drawn up by commentators (e.g., for English translations see Perkins 79–80; for the Greek text see Lincoln [1990] 169). This is not to suggest, however, that the author of Ephesians has simply taken over what was found in Colossians. Rather there are several distinctive features of 3:1-13. First, although the notion of Paul as the revealer of mystery also underlies Col 1:23-28 this idea is developed significantly by the author of Ephesians. Second, there is a greater interest in the role and identity of the church in Eph 3:1-13 than in Col 1:23-28. Finally, Ephesians is distinctive in including a focus on the unity of Jew and Gentile (3:6; in keeping with 2:11-22) and in discussing the role of the holy apostles and prophets (3:5) in God's plan of salvation.

As in Col 1:23-28, the main theme of Eph 3:1-13 is Paul's apostolic authority. Both texts are in keeping with the undisputed letters of Paul in underscoring what might be described in sociological terms as Paul's charismatic authority (see the notes on 1:1-2 and Col 1:1-2). Phrases such as "the stewardship of the grace of God given to me for you" (3:2), "the mystery that was made known to me by revelation" (3:3), and "a minister according to the gift of the grace of God given to me according to the working of his power" (3:7) indicate that Paul's authority is based on a divine commission. Although the text appeals to commonly held cultural values and employs rhetorical strategies to enhance Paul's status, ultimately the sanction for the apostle's authority comes from God rather than from tradition or convention. A particularly interesting aspect of this presentation of the apostle in 3:1-13 is the development of Paul's identity as a type of "seer." Not only is Paul the recipient of revelation as in the undisputed letters (e.g., Gal 1:12), but he is also presented as the interpreter and mediator of that revelation to the community: "you will be able to comprehend my insight into the mystery of Christ" (3:4). Pheme Perkins has drawn attention to several texts from the QL where the role of the teacher is presented as that of seer:

> The "I" of the Essene teacher is described as mediating the divine illumination he received from God to the community through his teaching, "like perfect dawn you have revealed yourself to me with your light" (1QH 12 [=4]:6); "you exhibit your power in me and reveal yourself in me with your strength to enlighten them" (1QH 12:23); "through me you have enlightened the face of the Many . . . for you have shown me your wondrous mysteries" (1QH 12:27). Comparison with Essene language indicates that "all" stands in place of its designation for those illuminated through the Teacher, "the many." (84)

These texts offer a valuable backdrop for understanding the presentation of Paul's role in 3:1-13. His mission is "to make all see what is the plan of the mystery hidden for ages in God who created all things." In terms of enlightenment there are interesting points of contact between the presentation of Paul's role and the description of being a believer in 1:17-18. Having described the experience of faith in earlier sections of the epistle, the author now underlines Paul's fundamental part in leading believers to this experience. It is being argued in this commentary that Ephesians reflects a type of spirituality that is open to visionary phenomena and ecstatic experiences of the Spirit. Believers are depicted as engaged in a journey of heavenly ascent (see the notes and interpretation on 1:15-23). Paul facilitates this process. He builds a church whose ultimate purpose is to make the manifold wisdom of God known to the rulers and authorities in the heavenly places (v. 10).

Despite the points of contact between Ephesians (and Colossians) and the undisputed letters of Paul in the idea of Paul as a charismatic leader, there are clear indications that Paul's authority is becoming routinized; there are early signs of a greater appeal to tradition and the apostle's authority is becoming linked to emerging authority structures in the community. Ephesians 3:13 contains idealized images of the apostle that are also present in Acts and other deutero-Pauline writings, works that are rooted in a situation following the death or disappearance of Paul (see de Boer). Paul's authority is asserted with great confidence and there does not seem to be the same need to defend the claim to apostleship that one frequently detects in the undisputed letters. There is no need, for example, to explain his former life in Judaism as in Gal 1:13-17. The commendation of Paul's special status does not seem to have been provoked by the type of historical disputes that echo throughout the undisputed letters. As in Paul's earlier letters, there is considerable interest in his suffering, but the irony of the cross is not articulated in the same way. Rather we have here a more idealized suffering apostle. He speaks with authority: "I,

Paul the prisoner." There may be some irony inherent in the fact that Paul's triumph is announced in the context of bondage, but it has less to do with the nature of the gospel message itself than with bolstering the confidence of the community. Paul's afflictions are the community's glory: they represent an assertion of the community's honor in a hostile world (see the notes on 3:13).

While it clearly has important points of continuity with the contents of the undisputed letters of Paul, Eph 3:1-13 contains elements of a traditional portrait of the apostle that is being made to speak to a new generation of believers. Martinus de Boer has identified six images of Paul that emerge in Colossians, Ephesians, Acts, and the Pastoral Epistles. Paul is (1) *the* apostle (or, in Acts, *the* missionary) (2) to the Gentiles (3) who brought the gospel to the whole world (4) and suffered to make this possible. He is (5) the redeemed persecutor and (6) the authoritative teacher of the church (see de Boer 370). All six of these categories are evident in 3:1-13 (in contrast, Colossians lacks category 5). But the way in which categories 3, 5, and 6 operate within Ephesians deserves special comment.

That Paul brought the gospel to the whole world is announced in a very interesting way in this passage. There is a chain of events that emerges here. The mystery of Christ that was previously unknown has now been revealed to the holy apostles and prophets. Paul is clearly the most important member of this group: he makes all see (v. 9). The implication is that his evangelical efforts lead to the building of a universal church. But, as is typical of Ephesians, the text quickly leads the hearer away from a historical focus to consider the whole cosmos. As is also the case in 1:22, which contains the first mention of the church in the epistle, the second reference to the *ekklēsia* is to an entity that transcends the human community. The church announces God's wisdom to the spiritual powers that inhabit the heavenly places (see the notes on 1:3, 20-21). Making this happen is the goal of Paul's universal mission.

Given the great importance of Paul's role as the revealer of the mystery of Christ, it is striking to find the kind of strong statement of Paul's identity as a redeemed persecutor that one finds in 3:8: he is the very least of all the saints. It has been suggested, however, that this text is best understood in light of the rhetorical requirements of self-praise (see the notes on 3:8). Similar statements can be found in the writings of Ignatius of Antioch at the beginning of the second century; he also composed letters in the context of "bondage." It is interesting to compare Eph 3:8 to the conclusion of Ignatius' letter to the Ephesians, where he uses an expression that corresponds to "the very least of all the saints" (*tǭ elaschistoterǭ pantōn hagiōn*): "Pray for the Church in Syria, whence I am led a prisoner to Rome, being the least of the faithful who are there [*eschastos ōn tōn ekei pistōn]*, even as I was thought worthy to show the honor of God." (Ign. *Eph.* 21:2, LCL). A fuller statement of self-effacement is found in Ign. *Eph.* 13:1: "I do not give you commands as if I were some one great, for though I am prisoner for the Name, I am not yet perfect in Christ Jesus; for I do but begin to be a disciple, and I speak to you as my fellow learners" (LCL). Ritva Williams has studied this passage in light of Plutarch's treatise "On Praising Oneself Inoffensively" in the hope of shedding light on the meaning of Ignatius' self-deprecating tendencies (Williams 132–45). Her findings can also illuminate Eph 3:8. She notes that Plutarch sets out very specific circumstances in which individuals can engage in self-praise, including the need to raise confidence among one's friends and fellow citizens in times of crises (*Moralia* 7, 15.544D–16.545D, LCL). Self-praise should bring advantage to one's audience rather than to oneself (*Moralia* 7, 22.547F).

Ephesians 3:1-13 functions rhetorically as an exercise in self-praise even if (as is being argued in this commentary) it was written in Paul's name. Paul himself is presented as the speaker. That this exercise takes place in a time of fear and that there is a need for encouragement is made explicit especially at the beginning and end of the passage. Paul writes as a prisoner and he writes to comfort believers in light of what has happened to him (and perhaps also in light of the tribulations they themselves endure). What believers have achieved as a result of Paul's mission is expressed in the conventional categories associated with the rights of citizens to free speech and open expression: they have boldness and confident access to God (see the notes on 3:12). Paul's efforts are not based on self-interest. In fact, Paul's afflictions represent the glory of believers.

In addition to the circumstances during which self-praise is acceptable Plutarch outlines specific techniques of self-praise. For example, self-praise can be made less offensive by ascribing some of the honor linked with one's accomplishments to the gods (*Moralia* 7, 11.542E), by making references to one's faults, and by stressing that one's status has been the result of much hardship and danger (*Moralia* 7, 13.543F–14.544D). The Paul of Ephesians stresses his dependence on God in the same breath as he makes a self-effacing comment in 3:8. Paul preaches because he has received the grace of God. The description of Paul as the very least of all the saints recalls his previous life as a persecutor of the church; it characterizes his past life as replete with the most serious flaws. The idealized image of the suffering apostle in Eph 3:1-13 adds credence to the teaching of one who claims to be the interpreter of the mystery of Christ. It is important to realize that the portrait of Paul in Eph 3:1-13 draws upon conventional cultural values and is developed using rhetorical strategies designed to win an audience. As it became increasingly important to present Paul as a hero to new generations, such reliance on traditional means for establishing authority may well have become more important (see also the notes and interpretation on Col 1:24–2:7).

The sixth image identified by de Boer as central to the presentation of Paul in deutero-Pauline literature and Acts needs to be considered carefully in relation to Ephesians. Tracing Paul's role as *the* authoritative teacher in Ephesians can help one to see how Paul's charismatic authority is becoming increasingly tied to emerging authority structures in the community. Ephesians 3:3 communicates the expectation that what Paul previously wrote in the letter will have taught the community something important. Readers will be able to comprehend his insight into the mystery of Christ (v. 4). As an interpreter of revealed mystery Paul not only communicates prophetic utterances but also interprets their meaning and teaches their significance. That Paul is not only *a* teacher but actually *the* authoritative teacher is suggested by the privileged position he occupies as the one "who makes all see what is the plan of the mystery." The repeated use of the first person in 3:1-13, coupled with the fact that the work is presented as coming from Paul alone and not Paul and one or more co-worker(s) as is usually the case in Pauline epistles, serves to reinforce this privileged position (see also the notes and interpretation on 1:1-2).

Yet, despite Paul's unique role, his status is articulated in relation to a broader group of teachers: the holy apostles and the (early church) prophets (see the notes on 3:5 and 2:20). The way the text simultaneously reinforces Paul's role while at the same time underscoring the authority of a broader group (of which Paul is clearly a member) has seemed puzzling to commentators. Since one would expect Paul to include himself in the group of apostles (cf. 1 Cor 4:9), it is somewhat surprising to find a reference to "*his* holy apostles" (v. 5). It has seemed strange that a text clearly intended to stress Paul's authority mentions a broad group of early church leaders in a manner that suggests a certain temporal distance between the composition of Ephesians and the birth of the church. The text may reflect a desire to stress the foundational role of this group. Moreover, the merging of Paul's authority with the authority of the holy apostles and prophets may have served as an effective means of tying the authority of current church teachers to the authority of foundational leaders (cf. 2:20). The third and final reference to apostles and prophets occurs in a text concerned with the organization of the community. In Eph 4:11 we find a list of various ministries that are all in one way or another connected with teaching (see the notes on 4:11). These ministries are central to warding off false teaching (cf. 4:13-16). In the commentary on Colossians I argued that one of the most important means of guaranteeing the survival of the Pauline churches after Paul's disappearance was reinforcement of the authority of Paul's fellow workers, including highlighting their close relationship with the apostle (see the notes and interpretation on Col 1:3-

8; 4:7-18). Ephesians makes little reference to Paul's coworkers (see 6:21-24). Instead there seems to be an attempt to link the crucial role of teacher in the community with the privileged position of Paul as *the* authoritative teacher in the church. One wonders whether the way Paul's leadership is presented in 3:1-13 may actually reflect some of the qualities that were considered desirable in church teachers at the end of the first century in the churches of Asia Minor. Did they act as seers? Were visions among the gifts of the Spirit demonstrated by community teachers who were among the recipients of Ephesians?

While the authority of the apostle Paul is clearly the main theme of Eph 3:1-13, it is important to consider what the text implies concerning the life of the church. As has frequently been noted in this commentary, the identity of the church is of paramount significance in Ephesians. The reference to the church in 3:10 must therefore be studied carefully. Although, as noted previously, any reconstruction of the communal circumstances underlying Ephesians must remain highly tentative, it seems relatively certain that Ephesians spoke to a community that felt threatened by external forces (see the notes and interpretation on 1:15-23). Ephesians 3:10 is ultimately about the defeat of cosmic powers—hostile spiritual forces that dwell in the heavenly realms. It is through the church that the wisdom of God will be announced to these spiritual forces. If one considers carefully what is being claimed here, the significance of the identity of the church for the life of the cosmos becomes clear. The church exists because Paul communicates and interprets the revealed mystery. This mystery is defined in terms that recall 2:11-22: "the Gentiles are now co-heirs, co-members of the body, and co-sharers of the promise in Christ Jesus through the gospel" (3:6). The church demonstrates the mystery; it demonstrates the power of God through Christ in creating the equal participation of the Gentiles and the joining together of Jew and Gentile in one universal church. This reality, which is not only historical but also of cosmic significance, will do more than allow for inclusion and harmony between people; it will transform the universe: "He has made known to us the mystery of his will, according to his good pleasure that he set forth in him, as a plan for the fullness of time, to sum up all things in Christ, the things in the heavens and the things on the earth" (1:9-10; cf. 1:22-23).

FOR REFERENCE AND FURTHER STUDY

Boer, Martinus C. de, "Images of Paul in the Post-Apostolic Period," *CBQ* 42 (1980) 359–80.

Caragounis, Chrys C. *The Ephesian Mysterion: Meaning and Content.* CB.NT 8. Lund: Gleerup, 1977.

Davies, Llynfi. "I Wrote Afore in a Few Words (Eph 3.3)," *ExpT* 46 (1934–35) 568.

Marrow, Stanley B. "*Parrhesia* and the New Testament," *CBQ* 44 (1982) 431–46.

Minear, Paul S. "The Vocation to Invisible Powers: Ephesians 3:8-10," in idem, *To Die and to Live: Christ's Resurrection and Christian Vocation*. New York: Seabury, 1977, 89–106.

Reese, James M. "Assertiveness," in John J. Pilch and Bruce J. Malina, eds., *Biblical Social Values and their Meaning: A Handbook*. Peabody, Mass.: Hendrickson, 1993, 9–11.

Williams, Ritva H. *Charismatic Patronage and Brokerage: Episcopal Leadership in the Letters of Ignatius of Antioch*. Doctoral Dissertation, University of Ottawa, 1997.

20. *Prayer and Doxology* (3:14-21)

14. Because of this I bow down on my knees before the Father 15. from whom every family in heaven and on earth is named, 16. that he may grant you according to the riches of his glory to be strengthened with power through his Spirit in the inner self, 17. that Christ may dwell through faith in your hearts, rooted and grounded in love, 18. that you may have strength to comprehend with all the saints what is the breadth and length and height and depth 19. and to know the love of Christ that surpasses knowledge, in order that you may be filled to all the fullness of God. 20. Now to him who has the power to do far more beyond all that we ask or think, according to the power operating in us, 21. to him be glory in the church and in Christ Jesus throughout all generations, for ever and ever. Amen.

NOTES

14. *Because of this I bow down on my knees:* Ephesians 3:14 takes up the thought that was interrupted at 3:1. The same introductory formula is repeated: *toutou charin* (because of this, for this reason). "This" refers to the description of the unity of Jew and Gentile in 2:11-22, which has been accomplished through Paul's preaching. However, the digression concerning the nature of Paul's mission in 3:1-13 needs also to be kept in mind here. Readers have heard that this new creation has been achieved because of the revelation made to Paul to carry out God's plan. It is as the authoritative teacher and apostle that he now falls before God to pray that the recipients receive the most profound of spiritual gifts. The prayer takes up many elements of the intercession found in 1:16-23. The usual Jewish position for prayer was standing (e.g., Mark 11:25; Luke 18:11, 13), but prostration is not unknown in the Bible. Gentiles might have associated it especially with the stance one must adopt before a king (Thurston

117). For references to prayer in the kneeling position in the Bible (most likely prostrate with face on the ground) see 1 Kings 8:54; 1 Chr 29:20; Dan 6:10; Mark 1:40; 10:17; Matt 17:14; Luke 22:41; Acts 7:60; 9:40; 20:36; 21:5). To bow down on one's knees is more closely associated with homage or worship than prayer in the other occurrences of the expression in the Pauline corpus (e.g., Rom 14:11; Phil 2:10), but intercessory prayer and homage probably go together in this text (Lincoln [1990] 202).

before the Father 15. *from whom every family in heaven and on earth is named:* God is called "Father" also in 1:2, 3, 17; 2:18; 4:6; 5:20; 6:23. Some manuscripts add "of our Lord Jesus Christ" after "Father" ($\aleph^c$ D G K Ψ 88 614 Byz Lect it^{d,g,61} vg syr^{p,h} goth arm *al*). But since there would be no good reason to omit the words, the shorter reading probably represents the original. The longer reading probably resulted in an attempt to harmonize the text with 1:3 and other similar passages (see Metzger 604). The Greek text contains a play on words that is masked by the English translation. The Greek word for family *(patria)* derives from the Greek word for Father *(patēr)*. The concept of family (a clan or extended family, not a nuclear family) is obviously so important that it derives its very name from God's name (see the interpretation below). The identity of the Father shapes the identity of the family. Naming in the Hebrew Bible is an act that establishes God's dominion (Ps 147:4; Isa 40:26; Gen 2:19-20). Although some commentators have understood the expression *pasa patria* to mean the whole family, such an interpretation would require the presence of a definite article. A very similar expression to "in heaven and on earth" occurs in 1:10 (on heaven see the notes on 1:3). As in 1:10 and in keeping with the NT generally, heaven is in the plural *(en ouranois:* in heavens), but 1:10 contains a definite article *(epi tois ouranois:* in the heavens). As elsewhere in Ephesians, this text connects the earthly community to a heavenly (angelic?) community; the church transcends the historical realm. In referring to the heavenly family the author most likely has in mind the company of angels (including both good and hostile angelic beings; see the notes and interpretation on 1:15-23). The phrase "sons" or "children" of angels is found in 1 *Enoch* 69:3, 4; 71:1; 106:5 (cited in Lincoln [1990] 202). To say that the heavenly community takes its name from the Father may be an assertion that the spiritual beings that inhabit the heavenly realms are also subject to God (see the notes on 3:10). Those tempted to call upon the names of these spiritual beings in the context of magical practices would be reminded of God's superior power (see the notes on 1:21; and see Arnold [1989] 54–56, 58–59).

16. *that he may grant you according to the riches of his glory to be strengthened with power through his Spirit in the inner self:* Verses 16-17 introduce the first of three main prayer requests, each beginning with *hina* (that, in order that). Riches and glory are both terms that have already appeared frequently in Ephesians. There have been references to the "riches of grace" (1:7; 2:7; 3:8) and to the "glory of grace" (1:6; cf. 1:12, 14). As is also the case with "riches of glory" (cf. Rom 9:23; Col 1:27), these expressions are typical of a liturgical style. The verb *krataioō* (to strengthen) only occurs here, but cognate nouns also occur at 1:19 and 6:10. In 1:19 "might" is used to speak about the superiority of God's

power bestowed upon believers in relation to the cosmic powers. In 6:10 the need for a defensive might that comes from being empowered by the Lord is expressed even more strongly (see the interpretation below). Power is conveyed through the Spirit. This is one of several references to the Spirit in Ephesians (cf. 1:13-14; 2:22; see also the notes on v. 17 below). "The inner self" *(eis ton esō anthrōpon)* is an expression that occurs in the undisputed letters of Paul (cf. Rom 7:22-23; 2 Cor 4:16). In ancient literature, including Gnostic literature, the expression plays a part in dualistic notions of identity (see the full discussion in Lincoln [1990] 204), but no dualism is in view here. The expression corresponds to the reference to "heart" in v. 17 (see the notes). In 2 Corinthians 4 there is also a connection between the transformation of the heart and the inner self (cf. 4:6, 16: here Paul uses the expression to describe the true identity of the believer, which is not visible by sight). It has sometimes been suggested that the "inner self" corresponds to the "new humanity" of 4:24 (e.g., Schlier [1957] 169), but this has not won wide approval among commentators (for a detailed discussion of the meaning of the "inner self" see Bouttier 157–58).

17. *that Christ may dwell through faith in your hearts, rooted and grounded in love:* In many respects this verse acts as a parallel to and interprets the previous verse. The "indwelling" of Christ is that which strengthens believers. Similar concepts occur in 2:22, which describes the indwelling of God's Spirit in the community. The mention of the heart recalls 1:18 where reference to the heart is made in a description of spiritual enlightenment. In the ancient world the eyes and the heart together are central to expressions of commitment; they represent the zone of human capacity for thought, judgment, and emotion (Malina [1993] "Eyes–Heart" 63–67). "Rooted and grounded" recalls similar expressions found elsewhere in the Pauline literature (e.g., 1 Cor 3:6-12; Col 2:7). Here it recalls the architectural metaphors of 2:19-22 (see the interpretation below) and in particular the idea of the church being built on a foundation of the apostles and prophets with Christ himself as the cornerstone. The use of the verb *katoikeō* (to dwell, to inhabit, to settle permanently) is closely related to such spatial and residential images. The Greek syntax allows for the phrase "rooted and grounded in love" to be understood in a couple of different ways. It may in fact be a result clause, providing the condition for the next petition. This is how the RSV understands the phrase: "that you, being rooted and grounded in love, may have the power to comprehend." But it is probably best to view the phrase as a subsidiary request. The wish is that the community be rooted and grounded in love (see Lincoln [1990] 197). Love is a frequent theme in Ephesians (e.g., 1:15; 2:4; 3:19). It is not entirely clear whether believers' love or God's love through Christ is primarily in view here, but the two notions are in any case closely related.

18. *that you may have strength to comprehend with all the saints:* The second of three main prayer requests is introduced here. All three begin with *hina* (that, in order that). As in v. 16 there is terminology of power and strength. The verb *exischuō* (to be strong enough) occurs only here in the NT. Verses 16-17 tell about believers becoming empowered, but v. 18 describes the purpose of that

empowerment. In v. 19 the verb "to comprehend" or "to seize" *(katalambanō)* essentially serves as a synonym of "to come to know," "to perceive" *(ginōskō)*. "The saints" *(hoi hagioi*, literally "the holy ones") usually refers to believers in Ephesians and may well do so here: all the saints (the universal church; cf. 1:15; 3:8; 6:18). It may in fact prepare the way for the specific reference to the church in v. 21. However, it is also possible that the expression is used here as in some Jewish texts to refer to the angelic hosts (see Dahl [1975] 73). Ephesians may even be drawing upon a Jewish liturgical fragment. As noted previously, "the saints" may refer to angels in 1:18 (see the notes). Thus the recipients of the work, who are described as seated in the heavenly places in Christ Jesus (2:6), would essentially be invited to share in the knowledge enjoyed by the heavenly hosts.

what is the breadth and length and height and depth: This expression occurs frequently throughout ancient literature and is used in a variety of ways. It appears for example in the OT, Jewish literature, Stoic philosophy, Hermetic writings, the Greek Magical Papyri, and later church writings. In this case it is not certain to what these dimensions refer (see the summary of references and possible interpretation in Schnackenburg 150). Among the most intriguing interpretations is that it refers to the cosmic dimensions of the cross, an idea found in early Christian literature (e.g., Schlier [1957] 174). However, such an interpretation is hard to accept in light of the one mention of the cross in Eph 2:16 where the cross clearly does not have these symbolic proportions. The dimensions do, however, recall the architectural metaphors of Eph 2:19-22. It has even been suggested that this phrase is a metaphorical reference to the dimensions of the Jerusalem Temple (e.g., Ezek 40:1–43:12) or to the New Jerusalem (e.g., Ezek 48:16-17; Rev 21:6-27; for similar imagery employed to describe the church see *Herm. Vis.* 3.2.5). If it is a reference to a specific heavenly entity this would fit especially well with the interpretation of "saints" as angelic hosts (see the notes above). But such specificity is not really supported by the text. It seems more likely that the measurements are being used in a more general sense to refer to the vastness of the love of Christ that transforms the universe (3:17, 19) or to the fullness of God (v. 19). The verse recalls the idea that only God's wisdom can comprehend the cosmos (Job 11:7-9; cf. Sir 1:1-10; cited in Perkins 90). Indeed, in Eph 3:10 the role of the church is defined as making the wisdom of God known in the heavenly places. Perkins (citing Betz) has also drawn attention to the fact that "the four dimensions are named in a prayer that the magician is to say in order to draw down and retain divine light (PGM IV 970–85)" (Perkins 92; see Arnold [1989] 89–96). The recipients of Ephesians, who may well have been tempted to engage in such magical practices, are being told that such power comes only through the Holy Spirit (3:16).

19. *and to know the love of Christ that surpasses knowledge:* In Ephesians knowledge is a central attribute of believers. Cognates of the verb "to know" *(ginōskō)* occur also in 1:9, 17; 3:4-5; 4:13 (see also the notes on v. 18). The knowledge that is prized here is clearly not knowledge of complicated philosophical thought or cosmic speculation, but knowledge of the love of Christ that transcends

purely human knowing and is, in fact, immeasurable. The author has apparently pushed one step further the notion of the vastness of the wisdom of God that underlies v. 18. Knowledge of the love of Christ is perhaps best described as a perception or awareness that comes through an inner awakening of the Spirit (vv. 16-17). This is the second reference to love in this section. While in v. 17 the reference is somewhat ambiguous (see the notes on v. 17), in this case there is no doubt concerning the type of love: it is the love of Christ, that is, the love belonging to Christ, which he bestows on believers. Love is mentioned frequently in Ephesians (e.g., 1:15; 2:4; 3:17). The Greek expression *to hyperballon* (the surpassing, or the exceeding) has already been employed twice previously in the work (1:19 and 2:7); in both cases the expression is used to highlight the powerful transformation God has brought about in believers.

in order that you may be filled to all the fullness of God: This is the third of the three main prayer requests in this section introduced with *hina* ("that," "in order that"; see the notes on 3:16). The fullness *(plērōma)* and the concept of filling figure prominently in the theology of Colossians and Ephesians (cf. 1:23; Col 1:19; 2:9). Since the term *plērōma* occurs in Gnostic speculation, interpreters who argue that Ephesians needs to be understood against a Gnostic background attach special significance to this verse. But even if (as is the case in this commentary) one does not view Gnosticism as the most illuminating background against which to evaluate Ephesians, it may well be that the terminology had special significance for believers living in a syncretistic religious environment. In 1:23 the term "fullness" is used to describe the church —that which is filled by Christ (see the notes on 1:23 and Col 1:19 for a full discussion of the term). In this case the usage resembles that in Col 2:9, which speaks of the fullness of God dwelling in Christ bodily (cf. Col 1:19). Likewise, in Col 2:10 believers are described as having been filled in him. In keeping with the frequent emphasis on the sovereignty of God, Eph 3:19 speaks directly of God. The verb "to fill" *(plēroō)* is in the passive voice (that you may be filled); the implication is that God is doing the filling. God is in control of the process that leads ultimately to believers' being filled "to all the fullness of God."

Although the reading adopted here *(hina plērōthēte eis pan to plērōma tou theou)* is well attested in both Western and Alexandrian witnesses, there are several manuscript variations. The most important of these omits *-te eis: hina plērōthę pan to plērōma tou theou* (in order that all the fullness of God may be filled up; 𝔓[46] B 462 cop[sa]). This variation may have resulted either from an attempt to offer an easier syntactical construction or on account of theological problems caused by the notion of humans possessing the fullness of the deity (see Lincoln [1990] 196–97; Metzger 605). Although English translations consistently render the phrase as "with all the fullness of God" in an effort to avoid awkward constructions (cf. NRSV; REB; NAB; NJB), "with" does not really capture the force of the preposition *eis*. *Eis* means literally "to" or "into" and conveys movement toward a goal: "being filled up to the measure of God's fullness" (Lincoln [1990] 214; see also the notes on 4:13). While it departs in some respects from the literal meaning of the Greek text, the translation offered by Schnackenburg aims to convey this sense of progression toward a goal: "that you may enter into the total fullness of God" (144). There is actually a progression of thought from v. 14 to v. 19 involving the role of God as the creator and sustainer of the universe. Verse 14 describes the origins of humanity as resting in God and v. 19 describes union with God as the ultimate goal of humanity.

20. *Now to him who has the power to do far more beyond all that we ask or think:* The bold prayer request in v. 19 gives rise to a concluding doxology in this section, giving glory to God. What is being requested concerning the unity of humanity and God naturally leads to a proclamation of God's power. Doxologies are found frequently in both Jewish and early Christian literature. They often occur at the end of letters (e.g., Rom 16:25; Phil 4:20; 2 Tim 4:18; Heb 13:21; 1 Pet 5:11). They follow a predictable form: the person for whom the praise is intended is named, and this is followed by the praise itself (often including the word "glory"). They also include an eternity formula (e.g., forever and ever) and frequently end with "amen" (see the notes on v. 21). Doxologies are not usually linked to prayers, but a fairly close parallel to the prayer and doxology in Eph 3:20-21 is found in Phil 4:19-20 (see Perkins 93). Philippians 4:19 comes close to a prayer request: "And my God will fully satisfy every need of yours according to his riches in glory in Christ Jesus. To our God and Father be glory forever and ever. Amen" (Phil 4:19-20 NRSV). The Greek text is often translated as "to him who is able" (*tǭ de dynamenǭ*; e.g., REB; NAB), but this masks the fact that the verb is a cognate of the word "power" *(dynamis)* found in the following phrase. A rare adverb, *hyperekperissou* (far more than, or superabundantly; cf. 1 Thess 3:10; 5:13), is used to describe the infinite magnitude of God's power. With this verse the community is drawn into the act of prayer ("all that we ask or think") following the report of Paul's prayer in 3:14-19. Because it seems to be redundant, a good number of witnesses ($\mathfrak{P}^{46}$ D E F it[d,g] vg Ambrosiaster) omit *hyper* (beyond).

according to the power operating in us: This clause qualifies "has the power to do." God's power working in us does more than we ask or think. Norbert Baumert has argued that the clause should be taken with "ask or think"; thus the meaning would be that God is able to do more even than the extent of God's own power working within us (276–79). However, the syntax favors the more usual interpretation and Baumert's proposal has not won wide approval among commentators (see Lincoln [1990] 215–16). The phrase recalls the prayer requests in v. 16 that believers be strengthened with power *(dynamis)* and in v. 19 that believers "be filled to all the fullness of God." The term "power" is a cognate of the verb that occurs previously in the verse (see the notes above). In the prayer report found in Eph 1:15-23 there is a similar reference to the power of God. In 1:19-20 the power of God that transforms the life of believers is said to be working in Christ. Here it is said to be working or operating *(energeō)* within believers.

21. *to him be glory in the church and in Christ Jesus throughout all generations, forever and ever. Amen:* This is the only doxology (see the notes above) in the NT that

contains both the phrase "in the church" and "in Christ Jesus." To be in Christ Jesus in Pauline literature is to be in the church (see the notes on 1:3), and so it is probably best not to think of a clear distinction between "in the church" and "in Christ Jesus." However, the expression may recall the idea that the church is Christ's body, ruled by Christ Jesus as its head (cf. 1:22-23). The church is a very important theme in Ephesians and it is significant that the author of Ephesians chooses to mention the church at the closing of the first part of the epistle. The reference to eternity is typical of doxologies, though the expression "forever and ever" is unusual among NT doxologies in combining a singular and a plural (literally "of the age of the ages" [*tou aiōnos tōn aiōnōn*]). In the NT both terms are typically found in the plural, but the combination of singular and plural does occur in the LXX Dan 3:90; 7:18 (cited in Lincoln [1990] 217). The term "ages" (*aiōn*) has already occurred in 1:21; 2:7; 3:9, 11. This is the only NT doxology that contains the word "generation" (*genea*), although the term does occur in some early Christian doxologies (e.g., 1 *Clem.* 63:1; *Mart. Pol.* 21). The reference to the generations recalls 3:5 and is in keeping with the mention of families in vv. 14-15. The concluding "amen" is a usual feature of NT doxologies (see the notes on v. 20). It provides a very clear ending to the first part of the epistle. Although doxologies are usually found at the end of letters (see the notes on vv. 20-21), this is not always the case. As with the doxology in Rom 11:36, Eph 3:20-21 marks the end of the theological section of the letter. The remainder of the work will concentrate more extensively (though not exclusively) on ethics.

INTERPRETATION

Ephesians 3:14-21 is the second prayer-report found in the epistle. There is also such a report in 1:15-23. As discussed further below, it has much in common with 3:14-21 (see the notes and interpretation on 1:15-23). Consisting of one long sentence in Greek, 3:14-21 has a clearly detectable structure. After a brief introduction of the prayer-report in vv. 14-15 (taking up the thought introduced in 3:1), there are three main prayer requests, each introduced by *hina* ("that," "in order that") in v. 16, v. 18 and v. 19b. Verse 17a is parallel to the previous verse, while v. 17b is best understood as a subsidiary request, closely related to the previous one. Verses 20-21 constitute a doxology (see the notes on 3:20-21) that repeats many of the themes found in the prayer-report, including the dwelling of the power of God within believers. The doxology marks the end of the first half of the letter.

The previous section ended with a proclamation that believers in Christ now have bold access to God the Father. The prayer-report of 3:14-21 offers an example of what this bold access looks like. The effect of the three requests is like that of a musical crescendo building up to a triumphant proclamation of the power of God. The first request is for believers to be strengthened through the Spirit in their inner selves (v. 16). In the second request that strength serves as the basis for believers' receiving knowledge. The hope is that they will comprehend with all the saints—the universal church (perhaps including the heavenly hosts; see the notes on v. 18)—the extent of what God has accomplished in the cosmos, revealed especially in the love of Christ. Although love is a frequent theme in Ephesians, this special focus on knowing the love of Christ sets 3:14-21 apart from the prayer-report of 1:15-23. The third request offers the loudest example of boldness. The prayer is that believers themselves be "filled up to all the fullness of God." They should experience the power of God to the fullest. This is certainly among the strongest expressions of the desire for human union with God in all the NT. It is not surprising that this leads to a doxology in vv. 20-21: a glorification of God. God is praised in a repetitive fashion to emphasize that God is able to do "far more beyond what we ask or think." The fact that the church has an important role to play in the glorification of God is an especially noteworthy feature of the Ephesian doxology.

There is a great emphasis in Ephesians on the power, sovereignty, and majesty of God. The prayer-report of 3:14-19 actually contains a progression of thought that mirrors the progression from the blessing of 1:3-14 to the doxology of 3:20-31. Like 1:4-6, 3:14-18 extols God as the author of creation, but in 3:19 the line of thought moves from humanity's origins in God to a description of the ultimate goal of humanity as "being filled to all the fullness of God." This movement toward a goal is anticipated to a certain extent by Eph 1:23, which describes the church as the "fullness of the one who fills all in every way." Colossians 2:9 (this section of Ephesians appears to be dependent upon Col 1:29–2:10) describes the fullness of the Godhead dwelling bodily in Christ, but in Eph 3:19 the focus is on how the fullness of God shapes the lives of believers directly. Andrew Lincoln (1990) has usefully summarized the theological problem raised by 3:19: "So bold is the request, in fact, that it might well leave the modern Christian asking whether there is any difference in the kind of fullness of deity that dwelt in Christ and that which is available to believers" (215). An awareness of the liturgical background of Ephesians, however, can explain why the first section of Ephesians culminates in such a bold claim, one that does not appear to be the least bit interested in fine points of dogma.

Liturgical forms heavily influence the first three chapters of Ephesians. This is particularly true of the opening and closing of this first segment of the epistle. The structure and language of the opening blessing in 1:3-14, the thanksgiving and prayer-report of 1:15-23, and the prayer-report and doxology of 3:14-21 all draw their origins from the prayer and worship of the community (see J. T. Sanders [1965] 214). The anthropologist Clifford

Geertz has explained the importance of rituals (consecrated behavior such as baptismal rites, the singing of hymns, communal prayer) for the creation of religious beliefs. Not only do participants celebrate what they believe in the midst of ritual, but they also formulate beliefs there and then. In ritual performances one discovers a source of authority that transforms human experience; one accepts the lordship of something other than one's self (Geertz 25, 34). According to Geertz rituals are both a model of what is believed and a model for believing it. In other words, people attain their faith as they portray it (Geertz 29; see M. Y. MacDonald [1988] 62–63). Ephesians 3:14-21, with its climactic request to be "filled to all the fullness of God," offers us a window into this process. During community prayer those who petition God may well lose all reserve in the face of the majesty of God. They are perhaps overcome by what God has accomplished through Christ for believers. The theological perspective of 3:14-21 is not the fruit of "detached" intellectual scholarship. It is rooted in powerful experiences of the Spirit (v. 16) in the midst of ritual.

The very act of the community gathering together is an example of ritual: behavior set apart for contact with the sacred. There may in fact be a reflection of the significance of this meeting together in vv. 14-15. As noted above, the Greek text of these verses includes a play on words that is often masked by English translations. The Greek word for family *(patria)* derives from the Greek word for father *(patēr)*. The identity of the father shapes the identity of the family. Although Ephesians does not refer to local meetings of church groups in the houses of particular church members, this familial setting must naturally have occurred to the recipients of the letter who heard of "the Father from whom every family in heaven and on earth is named." The household churches resembled the extended families of the ancient world. Preferring to adopt a universalistic perspective (see the notes and interpretation on 1:1-2), the author of Ephesians does not choose to address the circumstances of a particular community. Yet family life (no doubt including life in the house church) colors the author's description of the union between humanity and divinity. This is especially evident in Eph 5:21–6:9 where the foundational institution of the family (marriage) is presented as reflecting the relationship between Christ and the church. In this section of the epistle, however, the author is not primarily interested in earthly relationships or in the earthly arrangements of meeting. The expression "every family in heaven and on earth" connects the earthly community to a heavenly community that probably includes the angelic hosts. The authority of God the Father extends not only over humans, but also over spiritual powers (see the notes on 3:15). In many respects the description of bold access to the Father in 3:12 prepares the way for the presentation of God here. Ephesians 3:12 reflects notions concerning the rights of citizens to address people of high rank, such as a powerful patron or head of the household (see the notes). In Eph 3:14-15 God is presented in that role. God is the cosmic Father and patron of all who should be approached on bended knee (v. 14).

There is a sense in which Paul appears as a mediator between the church and God in Eph 3:14-21. With his authority as the Apostle to the Gentiles rendered beyond question by 3:1-13, he now prays that church members will receive the most profound spiritual gifts (cf. 1:17). As is also the case in the prayer of 1:15-23, Paul's prayer in 3:14-21 is for the spiritual illumination of believers, described as "knowledge of the love of Christ" (3:19). Underlying Eph 1:15-23 is the notion of a journey of heavenly ascent with the ultimate destination being the heavenly places where Christ sits (1:20; cf. 2:6; see the notes and interpretation on 1:15-23). This idea of a heavenly ascent is not as clearly evident in 3:14-21, but the text does envisage sacred space along similar lines. The passage should actually be considered in relation to 2:19-22 where architectural metaphors reveal a rejection of conventional ideas of sacred space, including buildings and physical arrangements for meeting (see the notes and interpretation on 2:11-22). Both the expressions "every family in heaven and on earth" (v. 15) and "the breadth and length and height and depth" (v. 18) describe the realm of God's power as having both horizontal and vertical dimensions. The prayer is that believers will seize that power and experience it to the fullest (vv. 18-19). They live in a sacred community whose boundaries transcend the horizontal and merely earthly realm.

Ephesians 3:16-17 should probably be taken as an indication of openness to powerful experiences of the Spirit (see also the notes on 5:18). These powerful experiences may well have involved visions (see the notes on 1:15-23). The experience of enlightenment leads to a type of knowing (vv. 18-19; cf. 1:18). Knowledge is highly prized in Ephesians, but it clearly does not involve esoteric speculation; rather it is a profound awareness of the love of Christ. In arguing that "the saints" in 3:18 should be understood as referring to the whole church and not the angels Lincoln has rightly observed: "The comprehension the writer desires for his readers is not some esoteric knowledge on the part of individual initiates, not some isolated contemplation, but the shared insight from belonging to a community of believers" ([1990] 213). In response to Lincoln it should be noted that, even though knowledge may be presented as universally available, the knowledge shared by believers is at the heart of what leads them to set themselves apart from the broader social order. It is central to the self-definition of the church. This is true whether "the saints" refers to the whole church or to the "angels." Believers are essentially being invited to share in the knowledge enjoyed by the heavenly hosts (see the notes on 3:18). The focus of knowledge and illumination in Ephesians plays an important role in encouraging a response to the world that is quite introversionist;

there is a tendency to reinforce the boundaries of the community against external threats and a strong sentiment of ultimately belonging to another world (see the notes and interpretation on 1:15-23; 2:1-10).

It is not surprising, therefore, that the doxology of Eph 3:20-21 makes explicit mention of the church (cf. Eph 1:22-23). The role of the church is inseparable from the role of Christ through whom God makes the divine purposes known in the world. The *ekklēsia* is caught up in a cosmic drama. The goal of the church is to make known the manifold wisdom of God to the rulers and authorities in the heavenly places (3:10). The church is central to the glorification of God. It sings of God's exalted status and bestows honor upon God. Why, one might ask, does God require this type of glorification? In the NT world claims of worth must be publicly acknowledged. The public display implied by the phrase "to him be glory in the church and in Christ Jesus" is a culturally appropriate way of acknowledging the status and ultimate authority of God (see Plevnik 95–96).

Behind the great emphasis on the power of God and on the empowerment of believers in Eph 3:14-21 one detects a certain insecurity. It is being argued in this commentary that Ephesians responds to a context in which believers are feeling strongly threatened by external forces, including spiritual powers. The reference to the dominion of the Father extending over heavenly families may be designed to reassure believers that the spiritual beings inhabiting the heavenly realms are also subject to God (see the notes on 3:15 and 3:10). It may be that the recipients of Ephesians were tempted to engage in magical practices in order to guarantee their protection (see the notes on 1:21; 3:15, 18; and see Arnold [1989]). The prayer of Eph 3:14-21 could not make the point more forcefully: these measures are not necessary. Paul's prayer on behalf of believers functions rhetorically to secure their good will and to offer the strongest possible reassurance against any cosmic or societal threat. It serves as a very effective transition to the second half of the letter, where the author will give directions concerning how the recipients should live.

For Reference and Further Study

Arnold, Clinton E. *Ephesians, Power and Magic: The Concept of Power in Ephesians in Light of its Historical Setting.* MSSNTS 63. Cambridge: Cambridge University Press, 1989.

Baumert, Norbert. *Täglich Sterben und Auferstehen: Der Literalsinn von 2 Kor 4, 12-5, 10.* StANT 34. Munich: Kösel, 1973.

Betz, Hans Dieter, ed. *The Greek Magical Papyri in Translation.* Vol. 1, Texts. Chicago: University of Chicago Press, 1986.

Dahl, Nils A. "Cosmic Dimensions and Religious Knowledge (Eph 3:18)," in E. Earle Ellis and Erich Grässer, eds., *Jesus und Paulus. Festschrift für Werner*

Georg Kummel zum 70. Geburtstag. Göttingen: Vandenhoeck & Ruprecht, 1975, 57–75.

Malina, Bruce J. "Eyes–Heart," in John J. Pilch and Bruce J. Malina, eds., *Biblical Social Values and Their Meaning*. Peabody, Mass.: Hendrickson, 1993, 63–67.

Plevnik, Joseph. "Honor–Shame," in ibid. 95–104.

Sanders, Jack T. "Hymnic Elements in Ephesians 1–3," *ZNW* 56 (1965) 214–32.

21. *The Unity of the Spirit* (4:1-16)

1. I beseech you therefore, I, the prisoner in the Lord, to walk in a manner worthy of the calling with which you have been called 2. with all humility and gentleness, with patience, bearing with one another in love, 3. being eager to keep the unity of the Spirit in the bond of peace: 4. one body and one Spirit, as you were also called in the one hope of your calling, 5. one Lord, one faith, one baptism, 6. one God and Father of all, who is above all and through all and in all. 7. But to each one of us grace was given according to the measure of Christ's gift. 8. Therefore it says: "When he ascended on high, he made captivity captive; he gave gifts to human beings." 9. Now, "he ascended," what does it mean except that he also descended into the lower parts of the earth? 10. The one who descended is also the one who ascended far above all the heavens in order that he might fill all things. 11. And it was he who gave the apostles, the prophets, the evangelists, the pastors and teachers 12. for the equipping of the saints, for the work of ministry, for the building up of the body of Christ. 13. until we all arrive at the unity of faith and of the knowledge of the Son of God, at the mature person, at the measure of the stature of the fullness of Christ, 14. so that we may no longer be children, being tossed and carried along by every wind of teaching, by human trickery, by craftiness, in the scheming of error, 15. but speaking the truth in love, we may grow in every respect up into him who is the head, Christ, 16. from whom the whole body, joined and brought together by every ligament that gives supply, according to the proper working of each part, promotes the body's growth in building itself up in love.

NOTES

1. *I beseech you therefore, I, the prisoner in the Lord:* The ethical admonitions that begin here and continue to the end of the epistle commence with the same introductory term as is found in Rom 12:1: *parakalō* (I beseech or exhort you; cf. 1 Thess 4:1). Although a new section of Ephesians begins here, this opening phrase clearly relates the exhortations to the previous sections. The thought

that is interrupted in 3:1 and taken up again at 3:14 also contains Paul's self-description as "the prisoner." However, 3:1 has "prisoner of Christ Jesus." The meaning of the expression in this case is roughly the same, but "in Christ"—incorporation into Christ—stresses the communal significance of the experience to a greater extent (on "in Christ" in Ephesians see the notes and interpretation on 1:1-2). "Therefore" *(oun)* connects the phrase to the previous section and in particular to the doxology of Eph 3:20-21 celebrating the magnitude of God's power. As is frequently the case in Paul's letters, the indicatives that describe the nature of salvation lead to imperatives of ethical exhortation (see Furnish 224–27).

to walk in a manner worthy of the calling with which you have been called: The verb *peripateō* (literally "to walk"; cf. 2:2, 10; 4:17; 5:2, 8, 15) is often used to refer to how one conducts one's life. Therefore it is frequently translated "to live." However, the more literal translation better captures the active dimension of the term. It refers to active commitment to a way of life. As is suggested by the use of the word in the Pauline epistles with respect to behavior in relation to outsiders, *peripateō* refers to behavior that is publicly visible and demonstrates the honor of community members. The verb figures prominently in attempts to distinguish the ethical comportment of believers from the nonbelieving world (see the notes on 2:2). The mention of one's calling evokes the emphasis on being called or chosen by God in the blessing of 1:3-14 (cf. 1:4, 5, 12). The great emphasis on God's initiative that runs through the first part of Ephesians is here directly related to ethics. Being called or chosen by God implies an appropriate way of life. The use of the term "worthy" *(axiōs)* is very similar to the usage in 1 Thess 2:12 (cf. Phil 1:27; Col 1:10).

2. *with all humility and gentleness, with patience, bearing with one another in love:* These virtues are all also found in Col 3:12-13. Only Ephesians, however, has "in love." In Col 3:12 believers are described as having been loved by God, and love is described as the most important Christian virtue in Col 3:14. As is typically the case in Ephesians, emphasis falls upon the love shared between believers. The importance of love as a characteristic of community life is made especially clear by the final two verses of this section (see the notes on vv. 15-16). As in Col 3:12, "humility" *(tapeinophrosynē)* is obviously a positive attribute, but in Col 2:18 and 2:23 the same Greek word is best translated as "self-abasement" and refers to the activity of false teachers. Given the content of Eph 4:1-16 the reference to humility deserves special attention. This text calls for unity in light of a diversity of gifts. Humility is what diffuses the spirit of competition. In the Greco-Roman world generally humility was associated with servility (cf. Epictetus, *Diss.* 1.9.10; 3.24.6), but the OT speaks of God exalting the humble. It is particularly interesting to note that Matthew presents the qualities of both humility and gentleness as embodied in Jesus: "Take my yoke upon you, and learn from me; for I am gentle and humble in heart" (Matt 11:29 NRSV; see Lincoln [1990] 235–36). The call to bear with one another in love also takes on special significance given the previous passages in Ephesians. Bearing with one another means that differences based on status and ethnic origin must be alleviated. Ephesians 2:11-22 describes the unity of

Jew and Gentile as the pinnacle of God's accomplishments in Christ. Gentleness (cf. Gal 5:23; 6:1; 1 Cor 4:21; Col 3:12) and patience (Gal 5:22; 2 Cor 6:6; Col 3:12) are frequently included in Pauline lists of virtues.

3. *being eager to keep the unity of the Spirit in the bond of peace:* As is also the case with the previous participle, "bearing with one another," so here "being eager" is gramatically dependent on the verb "to walk" in v. 1. However, it can also be taken as an imperative and is translated as such in some versions: "Take every care to preserve" (NJB; cf. REB). "Bond" *(syndesmos)* also occurs in Col 3:14 where love is described as "the bond of completeness." The bond in this case is "the bond of peace." There may be an echo here of the apostle's self-designation as the prisoner in the Lord (he is literally "in bonds"; see Perkins 96). The expression is in keeping with the usage found in some philosophical writings where it refers to the bond that unites virtues. The Pythagoreans, for example, regarded friendship as the bond of all virtues (see Bruce [1984] 156). Peace here serves the bonding function, holding tight against any aggression, division, or arrogance. The dative expression "in the bond" should probably be taken as a dative of agency. The bond of peace is the means through which the unity of the Spirit is maintained. Peace has already emerged as a central aspect of the gospel message in Eph 2:11-22. In fact, the word appears four times in 2:14-17. In the undisputed letters of Paul peace is presented as a gift of the Spirit (e.g., Gal 5:22; Rom 8:6; 14:17; 15:13). The unity-generating function of this "peace" is especially evident in 2:17: "And he came and preached peace to you who were far off and peace to those who were near." The mention of those who were far off and those who were near is a metaphorical reference to the Gentiles and the Jews (see the notes on 2:17). The mention of unity in 4:3 is intended to link daily community life to the momentous achievement of God in uniting Jew and Gentile in Christ. The term "unity" *(henotēs)* occurs in the NT only here and in 4:13, but it is used extensively by the second-century bishop Ignatius of Antioch for ecclesiological purposes (e.g., Ign. *Eph.* 4:1-2; 5:1; for a full list of references see Schnackenburg 164). The Spirit is of central significance in Ephesians (see the notes on 4:4).

4. *one body and one Spirit, as you were also called in the one hope of your calling:* Although it is not included in the Greek text, many modern English translations include the words, "There is" (introducing a new sentence) for the sake of clarity (e.g., NRSV; REB; NJB). The ethical exhortations of vv. 1-3 give rise to a confessional statement in vv. 4-6 that draws upon language closely associated with baptism (see the notes on v. 5). The liturgical context is suggested by the poetic repetition of the term "one" throughout vv. 4-6 (and later "all" in v. 6), making this one of the most beautiful texts in all of the NT. It is sometimes suggested that vv. 4-6 actually constitute a self-contained confession or hymn (Barth 429), but because of the likely dependence upon 1 Cor 12:13 (itself probably a baptismal formula) and Col 3:15 it seems best to think of liturgical echoes in the text rather than a self-contained liturgical unit. The dependence upon Col 3:12-15 that begins at 4:2 is maintained in this verse. Colossians 3:15 speaks of those who "were called into one body." The notion of being called

has already figured prominently in 4:1, and "the body" will be mentioned again at v. 12 and vv. 15-16 (cf. 1:23; 5:23). "The body" is clearly a reference to the universal church. As is also the case with the previous verse, there are connections between 4:4 and the content of 2:11-22; 2:18 also refers to the one Spirit who plays a fundamental role in the process of believers gaining access to the Father. The Spirit is central to the process of calling believers into community. Here also, because it is placed in apposition to the expression "one body," we should understand the Spirit as being central to the very process of creating the boundaries of the community. Ephesians 1:18 contains the phrase "the hope of his calling." Although it refers directly to God's (his) calling, the meaning is essentially the same. "Your calling" refers to the calling that believers have received from God. In both instances hope is presented as an object to be seized: eternal life. Such use of the word "hope" is typical also of Colossians (cf. Col 1:5, 23, 27). Elsewhere in Ephesians "hope" does have the future connotations that appear in the undisputed letters of Paul (e.g., 1:12-14), but here the emphasis is on how hope shapes the present life of believers.

5. *one Lord, one faith, one baptism:* This sounds very much like the baptismal formula. The change in gender for the term "one" *(heis, mia, hen)* is especially striking, reinforcing the comprehensiveness of the proclamation. On the liturgical echoes in 4:4-6 see the notes on v. 4. There are many allusions to baptism in Ephesians (cf. 1:11-14; 2:1-6; 4:22-24, 30; 5:25-27). The specific mention of baptism here and the strong influence of baptismal language throughout 4:4-6 offers a very good example of a central feature of both Colossians and Ephesians. Remembrances of the event of baptism play a special role in encouraging a particular kind of behavior in Christ. The ethical exhortations of vv. 1-3 lead naturally into the baptismal language of vv. 4-6 (see the interpretation below). The "Lord" is clearly the Lord Jesus Christ (cf. Phil 2:11; 1 Cor 8:6; 12:3), though the absence of the specific name is striking (perhaps reflecting contemporary liturgical usage). In many respects vv. 5-6 seem to offer a summary of 1 Cor 8:6: "there is one God, the Father, from whom are all things and for whom we exist and one Lord, Jesus Christ, through whom are all things and through whom we exist" (NRSV), yet these concepts take on a particular significance in the context of Ephesians. The proclamation of "one Lord" is made in light of the celebration of the triumph of Christ over all other "lords" in 1:21 and the vision of Jew and Gentile united in one Lord in 2:11-22. The reference to "one faith" may well reflect a growing awareness of the need to assert the unity of the church in the face of "false teaching." (This need can be seen especially clearly in the writings of Ignatius of Antioch at the beginning of the second century.) Although Ephesians offers no evidence of the type of serious problem with false teaching we find in Colossians, the work nevertheless offers strong warnings against its dangers in this section (4:14; see the interpretation below).

6. *one God and Father of all, who is above all and through all and in all:* On the reference to "one God and Father of all" see the notes on v. 5. Previous verses in this section recall the description of the unity of Jews and Gentiles that God

has accomplished in Christ, but this text draws one's attention back to previous proclamations of God's sovereignty and of God's role in uniting the cosmos through Christ (e.g., 1:10, 20-23). There are cosmological texts that praise the power that rules and permeates the universe in terms similar to Eph 4:6 (e.g., Marcus Aurelius, *Medit.* 4.23: "all things are from you, all things are in you, all things are to you"; cited in Lincoln [1990] 240). Scholars, however, are divided as to whether this cosmological meaning is intended in Ephesians. Some take the "all" references as masculine and therefore as meaning "believers," pointing back to the ecclesiological tone of the previous two verses (e.g., Schnackenburg 167). But others prefer to take the "all" references as neuter and as preserving the cosmological connotations visible in the parallels from ancient literature (e.g., Lincoln [1990] 240). Indeed, the neuter gender seems to be more likely because of both the literary parallels and the previous proclamations of God's role in uniting the cosmos cited above. God's activity in uniting the cosmos and in uniting the church by giving it Christ as its head are clearly related but distinguishable lines of thought in Ephesians. The fourfold repetition of *panta* (all) is typical of a liturgical style (cf. Rom 11:36). On the liturgical echoes in this verse see the notes on v. 4; for assertions of monotheism in the undisputed letters of Paul see Rom 3:30 and 1 Cor 8:5-6 (cf. Deut 6:4). Two explanatory glosses are part of the manuscript tradition for this verse. Some witnesses, including the Textus Receptus, have "all of you," whereas other witnesses (D F G K L Ψ 181 326 917 920 it^{d,g} vg syr^{p,h} goth arm *al*) have "all of us." It is clear, however, that these glosses were added to make "all" refer to believers. The reading adopted here has strong support ($\mathfrak{P}^{46}$ ℵ A B C P 082 33 88 104, etc.; see Metzger 604).

7. *But to each one of us grace was given according to the measure of Christ's gift:* The confession of unity in vv. 4-6 sets the stage for the treatment of the diversity of gifts and ministries in one body that begins here and continues to the end of v. 16. The notion of "giving" serves as a special link between 4:7, the citation from Scripture in 4:8, and the interpretation that runs from 4:9 to 4:11. This verse and what follows are unique in the NT in stressing the specific role of Christ as the giver of a gift (or gifts), but they nevertheless have much in common with Rom 12:5-8 and 1 Cor 12:27-28. It is interesting to note that God's gift of grace *(charis),* which is clearly associated with Paul's unique role as the apostle in 3:1-13, is here described as bestowed upon all believers. Very similar terminology occurs in 3:7: "of which I became a minister according to the gift of the grace of God given to me" (cf. 3:2, 8 where the word "grace" is used in a similar fashion). "Grace" itself implies the notion of gift (God's free gift), but like 3:7, Eph 4:7 contains the specific word "gift" *(dōrea;* cf. Acts 2:38; 8:20; 10:45; 11:17). This word is functionally the equivalent of the word for "gift" *(charisma)* that occurs in 1 Cor 12:4 and Rom 12:6. In the NT both *dōrea* and *charisma* are associated with gifts of the Spirit. Here *dōrea* refers to Christ's gift, but the notion of the Spirit's agency is not necessarily excluded (Lincoln [1990] 241). The use of the term "measure" *(metron)* in v. 13 and especially in v. 16 suggests that grace has been given according to the measure or proportion deemed appropriate for each of us. The main point in vv. 11-16 is that all the

gifts are needed for the proper functioning of the body (cf. Rom 12:3 and 1 Cor 12:11).

8. *Therefore it says: "When he ascended on high, he made captivity captive; he gave gifts to human beings":* Although Ephesians contains many scriptural allusions, this verse contains the first of only two scriptural quotations ("it" refers to Scripture here; cf. 5:14). The second citation is found in Eph 5:31. Yet the reference to Ps 68:18 (LXX Ps 67:19) in 4:8 is unusual. There has been a shift from the second person singular to the third person (see the detailed discussion in Lincoln [1990] 242–43). As is made clear by the relationship with the previous verse, the Psalm has also been altered to read "he [Christ] gave gifts" instead of "you [God] received gifts." This alteration is in keeping with rabbinic Jewish traditions that took the passage as a reference to Moses ascending Mount Sinai (often interpreted as an ascent to heaven) and subsequently giving the Law to the people (e.g., *T. Dan* 5.10, 11; *Midr. Tehillin* on Ps 68:11; *Abot R. Nat.* 2.2a). The author of Ephesians takes the psalm as referring to Christ and seems to understand him as the new Moses. "He made captivity captive" is a very strong expression implying the total defeat of Christ's enemies. "Captivity" (or "the captives") probably refers to the spiritual powers that Christ, who now is enthroned in heaven and sits at God's right hand, defeats. Thus the expression recalls such texts as 1:21-23 and anticipates the battle imagery of 6:10-20. Some witnesses have "and he gave gifts," but "and" *(kai)* seems to have been added to smooth out an awkward Greek construction. The reading adopted here is very well attested (see Metzger 605).

9. *Now, "he ascended," what does it mean except that he also descended into the lower parts of the earth?:* Psalm 68:18 is interpreted as referring to Christ. Taken together with v. 8, the vision is one of both descent and ascent. The Greek text does not specify whether ascent preceded descent or vice versa. Obviously in an effort to lend greater precision to the verse, some witnesses have *prōton* after *katebē* (he descended first). The reading adopted here is, however, strongly supported ($\mathfrak{P}^{46}$ ℵ* A C* D G 1739 *al*; see Metzger 605). Lincoln offers the following convincing explanation for the details of the interpretation of Ps 68:18: "since the psalm mentions only an ascent in connection with the giving of gifts, the writer felt it necessary to show that the ascent also implies a descent in order to establish his point that Christ who ascended is the giver of gifts in the Church" ([1990] 226). The main interpretative difficulties have to do with the meaning of "descended into the lower parts of the earth." It might refer to a descent into Hades (the abode of the dead; cf. Acts 2:27, 31; Rom 10:7; Phil 2:10; 1 Pet 3:19; 4:6). However, despite the fact that Ephesians distinguishes between "the air" and the heavenly realms (Eph 2:2), there are no clear references to an underworld or regions below the earth (in contrast to Phil 2:10). It seems more likely that this expression refers to the Incarnation. In that case the expression "of the earth" *(tēs gēs)* would be understood as an appositional genitive (the lower parts, i.e., the earth). Christ's incarnation is followed by his ascent (his resurrection and/or ascension). There are other texts in the NT in which such ascent/descent imagery is used to describe Christ's exaltation (e.g., John 3:13; Acts 2:34). If one understands the expression "of the

earth" as an appositional genitive it is also possible that descent refers to the coming down of the exalted Christ in the Spirit. In that case the gift of the Spirit is presented as what follows the resurrection/ascension of Christ. In favor of this interpretation are references to the Spirit in vv. 3-4, the importance of the Spirit in Pauline notions of gifts (e.g., 1 Corinthians 12), and the close association between life in the Spirit and union with Christ in Ephesians (e.g., 1:13; 3:16-17; 4:30; see the full discussion in Lincoln [1990] 244–47).

10. *The one who descended is also the one who ascended far above all the heavens in order that he might fill all things:* The ambiguity with respect to the order of the descent and ascent are maintained in this verse (see the notes on v. 9). The idea of a heavenly journey in this verse recalls similar notions earlier in the epistle. Ephesians 1:23 describes the church as Christ's fullness and presents Christ as the one who is completely filling the cosmos: "the one who fills all in every way" (see the notes; cf. 3:19). "All things" refers to the cosmos. Christ draws all things into himself, uniting all things. The author aims to unite this notion of divine initiative with the idea of the giving of gifts that shape community life (see v. 11 below). In keeping with Hebrew thought the NT refers to heaven in the plural: "the heavens." It is interesting to note that Ephesians can present Christ both as exalted in heaven (1:20; 6:9) and as transcending heaven, ultimately transcending the created universe (Lincoln [1990] 248).

11. *And it was he who gave:* Among similar texts in Pauline literature Ephesians is unique in stressing the direct role of Christ in the giving of gifts (see the notes on v. 7). After the Scripture citation and interpretation in vv. 8-10 this verse picks up again on the thought introduced in v. 7 (which has now been explained and justified). A single sentence in Greek runs from v. 11 to the end of v. 16. The translation of the verse adopted here follows Lincoln ([1990] 249). On the basis of the usual meaning of the Greek expression *tous men . . . tous de* both Lincoln ([1990] 249) and Schnackenburg (180) have challenged the frequent rendering of the verse in which the article *tous* is translated as "some" rather than as "the" (e.g., NRSV: "The gifts he gave were that some would be apostles"). The author's grammatical construction actually implies a straightforward list. A literal translation of the Greek text of v. 11 suggests that Christ actually gives these leaders to the community. What is implied is that the gifts the ascended Christ gives to believers for service to the church have led to the creation of apostles, prophets, evangelists, pastors, and teachers. It is interesting to note that all the ministries listed perform functions of preaching and/ or teaching (see the notes and interpretation below). Although the list has much in common with similar lists in the undisputed letters of Paul (e.g., Rom 12:5-8 and 1 Cor 12:28), it reveals even less than they do about the differentiation of roles. For example, there are no references to the more practical functions of administration or caring for the needs of the poor.

the apostles, the prophets, the evangelists, the pastors and teachers: "Apostles and prophets" are listed together twice previously in Ephesians, where they are presented as central witnesses and charismatic teachers of the early Christian movement (2:20 and 3:5; note however that it is possible, though unlikely, that in 2:20 OT prophets are in view; see the notes on 2:20). They play a founda-

tional role (cf. 1 Cor 12:28). Their importance is highlighted in this verse in
that they are listed first. Apart from this, however, there is nothing revealed
about their significance. In fact, the tendency to group them together with
other similar leaders suggests an effort on the part of the author to legitimize
the role of the teacher-preacher generally in the community (see the interpretation below). The terms "evangelist" *(euaggelistēs)* and "pastor" *(poimēn)* have
no counterpart in the undisputed letters of Paul. However, in Acts 21:8 Philip
is described as an evangelist. He is presented as a wandering teacher (cf. Acts
8:5, 40). In 2 Tim 4:5, Timothy is instructed to do the work of an evangelist.
This involves perseverance in the face of false teaching (2 Tim 4:1-4).

Although it is less explicit in the textual evidence, the role of pastor may
also be connected to teaching. A cognate verb occurs in Acts 20:28 *(poimainō)*
where "shepherding" is given as one of the tasks of the elders of Ephesus (cf.
1 Pet 5:2; John 21:16). Shepherding involves protecting the community from
false teaching (Acts 20:29-31). The term "teacher" *(didaskalos)* is third in Paul's
list of 1 Cor 12:28, following the apostles and prophets (cf. Rom 12:7; Acts 13:1;
1 Tim 3:2; 5:17; Titus 1:9). The significance of its presence in this list is heightened by the mention in 4:14 of the threat of being carried away by false teaching. It is not clear why the definite article is missing before "teachers,"
apparently grouping pastors and teachers together. While it has been suggested that these offices were identical (Barth 438–39), it is more likely that
they were understood as closely related. A good teacher was perhaps often a
good pastor for the community (nurturing and protecting the community
from unhealthy influences).

12. *for the equipping of the saints, for the work of ministry, for the building up of the body
    of Christ:* This verse supplies the reason for Christ's giving of gifts—the giving
    of the apostles, the prophets, and so on (see v. 11). Grammatical considerations
    affect translation here. There are three prepositional phrases in this verse; the
    first one begins with *pros* (for) and the next two have *eis* (for or to). Most mod-
    ern translations understand the first and second prepositional phrases as re-
    lated (e.g., NRSV: "to equip the saints for the work of ministry, for building up
    the body of Christ") and the work of ministry becomes the responsibility of all
    believers. But as Lincoln (1990) notes, there are no grammatical or linguistic
    grounds for taking the first two phrases as related (he believes that the change
    of preposition is only a variation in style), and all three phrases should be
    taken as referring to the "ministers" named in v. 11 (see the full discussion in
    Lincoln [1990] 253; see also Schnackenburg 182–84). Thus more responsibility
    is actually being given the ministers than many modern translations suggest.
    This is the only use of the noun *katartismos* (the equipping) in the NT. The term
    appears in medical treatises to refer literally "to the setting of a bone"
    (BAGD). This is in keeping with the body imagery in this verse. The presence
    of this term gives the work of the various leaders a very practical appearance:
    they engage in the practical preparation or training of the saints. This empha-
    sis on the practical continues with the next phrase: "for the work of ministry
    or service" *(diakonia)*. In 1 Cor 12:4-5 differing ministries are linked to gifts of
    the Spirit and in Rom 12:7 ministry or service *(diakonia)* is itself listed as a par-

ticular gift of the Spirit. The "saints" or "holy ones" *(hagioi)* are all believers making up the church. It is a term that occurs frequently in Ephesians (e.g., 1:1, 15, 18; 2:19; 3:8; on "saints" see the notes on Eph 1:1). The notion of upbuilding *(oikodomē)* the body also occurs in 4:16. Paul uses the concept often in 1 Corinthians to stress the importance of love shaping the relationship between church members (1 Cor 8:1; 10:23; 14:3-4). This is the second reference to the body in this passage. Unlike in 4:4, however, here the body is specifically identified as the body of Christ (cf. 4:15-16; see the notes on 4:4).

13. *until we all arrive at the unity of faith and of the knowledge of the Son of God, at the mature person, at the measure of the stature of the fullness of Christ:* This verse links the work of the ministers (vv. 11-12) with the goal of the existence of the church as a whole. The Greek text literally refers to the mature man, the adult male *(anēr)*, but because of the contrast with children introduced in the next verse it is best to understand the term as a general reference to persons. A very similar expression to "the mature man" *(andra teleion)* is found in Col 1:28: "That we may present every person perfect *(anthrōpon teleion)* in Christ." In Col 1:28 the adjective *teleios* is best understood as referring to one made perfect in Christ (see the notes on 1:28) rather than to maturity in faith. In Ephesians the adjective refers to maturity in the sense also found in 1 Cor 14:20. Following the lead of Col 3:10, Eph 2:15 speaks of the new person *(kainon anthrōpon)* referring to the creation that results from the new unity between Jew and Gentile. Since 4:13 refers to all believers it seems likely that, like "the new person" of 2:15, the "mature person" is a corporate entity rather than an image of individual perfection. This is further supported by the reference to the unity of faith and of the knowledge of the Son of God (cf. Col 2:2, 3). The unity of the knowledge of God is the full knowledge that creates oneness (on knowledge see also 1:17-19; 3:16-19). The mention of the "Son" of God is found frequently in Pauline epistles (e.g., 1 Thess 1:10; Gal 1:16; 1 Cor 1:9; Rom 1:3), but occurs only here in Ephesians. As in made clear by vv. 15-16, the community as a whole is growing into Christ—attaining the measure of the stature of the fullness of Christ. The threefold repetition of *eis* (at or to) suggests movement toward a goal. The fact that in this verse a future goal is in view offers evidence for a future dimension of Christian life to counterbalance the frequent emphasis upon the present in Ephesians. In fact, unity of faith appears as a present reality in 4:4-6. On the concept of "measure" *(metron)* see the notes on v. 7 and v. 16.

14. *so that we may no longer be children, being tossed and carried along by every wind of teaching, by human trickery, by craftiness, in the scheming of error:* On the contrast between maturity and being like children when it comes to faith see the notes on v. 13. The verb *klydōnizomai* means literally to be tossed by waves. The vision of instability is very similar to that presented in Jas 1:6-8 where cognates of this verb and the term "wind" *(anemos)* occur: "But ask in faith, never doubting, for the one who doubts is like a wave *(klydoni)* of the sea, driven *(anemizomenǭ)* and tossed by the wind, for the doubter, being double-minded and unstable in every way, must not expect to receive anything from the Lord" (NRSV; cf. Ps. 107:23-27; Isa 57:20-21; Jude 12, 13; Heb 13:9; see the

interpretation below). The presence of such terms as "fullness" *(plērōma)* and the concept of the mature (or perfect) person (v. 13) have sometimes led to the suggestion that this verse responds to a specific Gnostic teaching (e.g., Pokorný 78). But the presence of such terminology can be accounted for in other ways, including the probable dependence of Ephesians upon Colossians. This verse is one of only two places in the epistle where the problem of false teaching is actually addressed specifically (cf. Eph 5:6-13). While it represents one of the issues underlying Ephesians it clearly does not represent the main focus of the epistle. In this way Ephesians is quite different from Colossians, which expresses similar sentiments but gives detailed attention to the problem of false teaching (cf. Col 2:8-23). Colossians 2:4 warns of those who "may deceive you with persuasive speech." Deceit and trickery are frequently associated with false teaching in the NT writings of the later decades of the first century and the beginning of the second century C.E. (e.g., Acts 20:29-30; 1 John 4:6; 1 Tim 4:1; 2 Tim 3:13; 2 Pet 2:18; 3:17). The reference to human trickery *(kybeia)* is especially interesting. As in Col 2:8 and 2:20-22, to call the effort "human" is a means of labeling it as untrustworthy. *Kybeia* literally means "dice playing" and is found only here in the NT. Its use underlines the importance of deception as a value in the New Testament world. Jerome Neyrey explains its significance as follows: "New Testament people . . . experienced a world of masquerade and deception, in which people both deceived others and expected to be deceived in return. It was a world of flatterers, spies, hypocrites, and disguised demons. 'Do not be deceived' was a serious, but common, watchword, even for members of the church (Matt 24:4; Mark 13:5; Luke 21:8; 1 Cor 6:9; Jas 1:16)" ("Deception" [1993] 42).

15. *but speaking the truth in love, we may grow in every respect up into him who is the head, Christ:* The call to speak in truth is in contrast to the deception of false teaching (v. 14). But this is speaking the truth in the manner of a believer—characterized by love (on love see the notes on v. 16). Christ is depicted as the head of the body also in 1:22-23 (see the notes; cf. 5:23). The identification of Christ as the head of the body sets Colossians and Ephesians apart from the undisputed letters of Paul (cf. Col 1:18; 2:10; see also the interpretation below). The image of the community growing up into Christ recalls the similar use of the verb *auxanō* (to grow) in Eph 2:21.

16. *from whom the whole body, joined and brought together by every ligament that gives supply:* This verse is notoriously difficult to translate into English (e.g., note the redundant second reference to the body), even though its meaning is fairly straightforward. The relationship between phrases is complex as the author apparently tries to tie together the major themes in this section and elsewhere in Ephesians. It should also be noted that v. 16 echoes the teaching in Col 2:19, which appears in the context of the response to the false teaching (see the discussion of the relationship in Schnackenburg 189). The reference to "the whole body" recalls v. 4 and v. 12. The same verb *synarmologeō* (to join or to fit together) is used in conjunction with the architectural imagery to describe the church as the holy temple in 2:21. "Brought together" recalls the use of the same verb in Col 2:19 (cf. Col 2:2). The Greek text refers literally to "every liga-

ment of supply" *(pasēs haphēs tēs epichorēgias)*, which means the ligaments giving supply: functioning to provide connections between the parts of the body (Lincoln [1990] 263). Schnackenburg has proposed that the ligaments or joints *(haphē)* are a metaphor for the ministers listed in v. 11; they provide connections between the various parts of the body and are integral to the ability of the body to move and grow (189). Schnackenburg's proposal is somewhat speculative. However, his suggestion is in keeping with the emphasis on the importance of the role of these ministers for the life of the church that runs throughout 4:11-16.

according to the proper working of each part, promotes the body's growth in building itself up in love: The Greek text might be translated literally as "according to the working in measure of each part." The term "working" *(energeia)* also occurs in 1:19 and 3:7. The presence of the word "measure" *(metron)* is often masked by English translations, but it relates the verse to v. 7 (see also v. 13) where we find the notion of grace being given according to the measure or proportion deemed appropriate for each person. Such balance is needed for the proper working of the body. Ultimately each member performs acts of service that are appropriate for him or her. Love is a central theme in Ephesians (cf. 1:4, 15; 2:4; 3:18-19; 4:2, 15). The notion of building up the body in love is in keeping with the vision of community in the undisputed letters of Paul (see the notes on v. 12; see also 2:21). Love ensures proper growth, which is viewed here as ongoing. The concept of growth is also found in v. 15 (see the notes).

INTERPRETATION

Ephesians 4:1-16 marks the beginning of the second half of the epistle, the ethical exhortation segment. With a strong plea from the prisoner of the Lord—a title that ties this section to the reinforcement of Paul's authority in 3:1-13—the passage begins with ethical instruction in 4:1-3 (vv. 2-4 are heavily dependent on Col 3:12-15). This ethical teaching will be developed in far greater detail in the next section where a deliberate attempt is made to outline a way of life that separates believers from nonbelievers (4:17–5:20). Ephesians 4:1-16 barely introduces the ethical teaching before leading the reader into the confessional statement of 4:4-6, celebrating unity in the most poetic terms. This is followed by what is essentially an explanation of the origins of this unity in 4:7-16: it is the result of Christ's giving gifts to believers. The explanation involves an intriguing midrash on Ps 68:18 (vv. 8-10) and a description of the work of various ministers (vv. 11-13). In the end we are presented with a vision of a harmonious church (the body of Christ) ruled by Christ as its head. It is a church that enjoys growth and is building itself up in love.

There are many fascinating features of this text that have captured the attention of interpreters. For example, the references to the persons of the Trinity in vv. 4-6 have been of great interest. This text refers to the Father,

Son, and Spirit, but in the reverse order of the classical creeds (see R. R. Williams [1954–55]). Moreover, the proclamations in v. 4 begin not with God but with the unity of the church (one body). This is not surprising, however, given that in this section the author of Ephesians is mainly concerned with the nature of the church. References to the Spirit, to the Lord, and to God the Father serve to articulate the identity of the church as a unified whole that ultimately draws its origins from divine oneness. In moving from church to God the Father the author takes believers through a progression of thought from daily community existence to experiences of the Spirit to identification with Christ in baptism to beholding divine transcendence.

In vv. 4-6 one senses the powerful experience of worship of NT Christians. Many commentators have argued that vv. 4-6 are infused with liturgical echoes and perhaps even include a baptismal proclamation (v. 5). But there may be less obvious indications that the text is tied closely to the rituals and the experiences of the Spirit in the community. Here it is particularly interesting to consider the ascent/descent theme in 4:8-10. In rabbinic tradition Psalm 68 was associated not only with Moses' ascent of Sinai but also with a heavenly ascent in which he received the Torah and various heavenly secrets. It may be that a type of Moses mysticism was current in Asia Minor when Ephesians was composed (see the notes on v. 8 and the full discussion in Lincoln [1990] 243). Against such a background the author of Ephesians insists that it is Christ who ascends and descends, giving gifts to believers. Elsewhere in Ephesians, however, believers are depicted as sharing in Christ's journey and one wonders whether the psalm and its interpretation recalled powerful experiences of enlightenment (perhaps visions) experienced as a heavenly ascent (e.g., 2:5-6). It is true that there is nothing in the text to support the contention that believers are being promised access to esoteric wisdom, but 4:13 presents the unity of the knowledge of the Son of God as the goal of church existence. There is a divine knowing at the heart of the formation of communities.

Clinton Arnold (1989) has noted the importance of the concept of descent into the underworld in certain initiation rites of the mystery cults (e.g., the Mysteries of the Idaean Dactyls) of the ancient world. He understands the reference to descent into the lower parts of the earth (v. 9) as speaking of the underworld, and the notion of making captivity captive as a reference to Christ's defeat of hostile spiritual powers (see the notes on v. 8). Thus he views Eph 4:8-10 as an attempt to establish Christ's supremacy over all the powers of evil, including the so-called underworld deities (Arnold [1989] 56–58). Arnold's interpretation of 4:8-10 is dependent on a particular reading of the text that is by no means self-evident. For example, it is being argued in this commentary that it may well be best to understand the descent of v. 9 as a reference to the coming down to earth of the exalted Christ in the Spirit (see the notes on v. 9). But Arnold has made a valuable contribution in highlighting the points in common between the language of Eph 4:8-10 and the language of mystery cults. He reminds us that the recipients of Ephesians probably associated such terminology with rites of various forms, those they may have left behind and perhaps also those they continued to share as believers. The concepts of coming down and going up, closely tied to images of life and death, are associated with Christian rituals. We might consider, for example, the strong baptismal overtones of 2:1-6, where such symbolism is at work. It is possible that ascent and descent were central to the worship of the community in other ways. It is being argued in this commentary that Ephesians displays a significant openness to visionary phenomena and powerful experiences of the Spirit (see the notes and interpretation on 1:15-23; 4:17-5:20). In this passage the Spirit is specifically mentioned in vv. 3 and 4 and, as noted above, the descent of the exalted Christ in the form of the Spirit may well be the true meaning of "he also descended into the lower parts of the earth" (v. 9).

The main theme of Eph 4:1-16 is the unity of the church in one Spirit. The author has several strategies for encouraging this unity. At the outset the author turns to ethical exhortation. Given the repetition of the word "love" (vv. 2, 15, 16), it is evident how important love is to this vision of relations between believers. There is even the suggestion of a reversal of cultural expectations governing relationships. This can be seen especially in the call for "humility," a concept closely associated with servility in ancient society (see the notes on 4:2). Moreover, the competition and deception that characterize the marketplace of philosophies and new religions in the ancient world have no place in the lives of believers. In contrast to the human trickery of false teachers, believers are to speak the truth in love (vv. 14-15). As is discussed further below, a second strategy adopted by the author to encourage unity is to argue that gifts have been given to the church according to the measure or proportion deemed appropriate for each member. This allows for the harmonious functioning of the whole body. It is within the discussion of Christ's giving of gifts that the Paul of Ephesians sets his explanation of the importance of various ministers to the functioning of the body (vv. 11-13). Finally, the concept of the "head" plays a central unity-generating function. Christ is joined to the community as its head and ensures its well being, but he also governs the body (and indeed rules the universe: Eph 1:21-23). A model of community is developing in which some will be given authority over others (see further below and 5:21-6:9).

Why was it necessary to encourage unity so strongly? There is in fact a certain urgency implied by the use of the participle "being eager" (v. 3).

Believers are to make every effort to preserve the unity of the Spirit. I have argued previously that the author of Ephesians' interest in the identity of the church is rooted in the need to defend the church in light of some external threat—menacing spiritual powers and increasingly hostile reactions from the outside world (see the notes and interpretation on 1:15-23; 2:1-10; 6:10-20). Encouragement of cohesion becomes a strong defensive stance. The way the unity of the church is tied to God's power in uniting the cosmos in vv. 4-6 suggests invincible power. The unity of the church must be manifested publicly and boldly; a united body does indeed have the capacity to make the manifold wisdom of God known to the powers in the heavenly places (3:10). As the church became increasingly threatened by deviance from within and persecution from without the focus on unity seems to have increased in early Christianity. The concept is central, for example in the writings of Ignatius of Antioch. At the beginning of the second century Ignatius linked unity with communion with God:

> Therefore it is fitting that you should live in harmony with the will of the bishop, as indeed you do. For your justly famous presbytery, worthy of God, is attuned to the bishop as the strings to a harp. Therefore by your concord and harmonious love Jesus Christ is being sung. Now do each of you join this choir, that by being harmoniously in concord you may receive the key of God in unison, and sing with one voice through Jesus Christ to the Father, that he may both hear you and may recognize, through your good works, that you are members of his Son. It is therefore profitable for you to be in blameless unity, in order that you may always commune with God." (Ign. *Eph.* 4:1-2; LCL)

For Ignatius unity involves acceptance of a hierarchical system of church leadership with the bishop at its head. Ephesians does not yet call for acceptance of such a system. Each of the ministers takes a part in the integrated whole of the church (v. 11). Nevertheless, a careful analysis of 4:11-16 reveals an unmistakable interest in reinforcing the leadership of the ministers. If indeed Ephesians is deutero-Pauline it responds to a context in which the church is struggling with the disappearance of the charismatic leader, Paul. We have seen that Colossians responds to the problem of succession and the crisis of authority by reinforcing the authority of Paul's fellow workers. In the language of Weberian sociology, there has been an effort made to guarantee the survival of the movement by reinforcing the authority of the staff of the charismatic leader. Indeed it is likely that Paul's fellow workers had a stake in doing this themselves (see the notes and interpretation on Col 1:3-8; 4:7-18). Something slightly different appears to be going on in Ephesians. Here Paul's vision of ministry based on the gifts of the Holy Spirit is given new meaning. As in Paul's undisputed letters, we still have the notion of divine gifts being offered in differing quantities and according to need. We hear of a variety of gifts working together to create a harmonious whole. But according to vv. 10-11 Christ himself is the giver of gifts and the gifts are the various ministers themselves. Scholarly attempts to distinguish between the various ministers listed in v. 11 have only been marginally successful. When the text is compared to other texts in the NT where the terms occur a tremendous amount of overlap in function emerges (see the notes on v. 11). All are engaged in teaching or preaching in one form or another. The charism associated with leadership in Paul's churches is apparently being routinized; it is becoming attached to an established teaching leadership (on routinization see the notes and interpretation on Col 1:1-2). The recipients of Ephesians are being reassured that these ministers are gifts that Christ himself gives to the community. Verse 12 explains why these gifts are given to the community (see the notes on v. 12) and v. 13 ties their ministry to the goal of the church's continued existence. It is even possible that the author of Ephesians means for us to understand that these teachers are the ligaments holding the body of Christ together (see the notes on v. 16).

Ephesians 4:1-16 offers us a window into the transitional period between the early stages of the church when Paul conducted his ministry and later church periods when hierarchical ministry came to be understood as central to the life of the church in some communities (see the Ignatian correspondence). The apostles and prophets were charismatic teachers who were central to the leadership of the church in Paul's day. Taken together, the references in 2:20; 3:5; and 4:11 suggest that the apostles and prophets are viewed as laying a foundation for the type of ministry practiced at the time of Ephesians; they seem to belong to the past (although some church leaders claimed the title "prophet" into the second century: *Did.* 11–13; 15:1-2; *Herm. Man.* 11). It is likely that by listing the evangelists, pastors, and teachers beside the apostles and prophets the author of Ephesians seeks to bolster the authority of the evangelists, pastors, and teachers. They may be performing the ministry once performed by apostles and prophets. Although the text itself is silent on the matter one wonders whether there has been a shift away from an itinerant leadership of apostles and prophets to a resident leadership (see Horrell; see also the notes and interpretation on 5:21–6:9).

Ephesians does not seem to be responding to a specific crisis of false teaching, but the presentation of such teaching as a definite threat in 4:14 implies that there is a general problem. The unity of one faith must be preserved (4:5). As the ocean imagery of 4:14 suggests, there seems to be a general fear of instability. The ministers will help the body hold tight in face of a storm. The ministers will prepare believers, serve believers, and generally build up the body of Christ (v. 12). The church members themselves must be equipped. They must be mature in faith; they must lack the vulnerability of a young child. In the following section both the dangers threatening believers and the attributes of a mature faith are spelled out in considerable detail.

FOR REFERENCE AND FURTHER STUDY

Bony, Paul. "L'Épître aux Ephésiens," in idem, et al., *Le ministère et les ministères selon le Nouveau Testament: Dossier exégétique et réflexion théologique. Sous la direction de Jean Delorme.* Paris: Editions du Seuil, 1974, 74–92.
Cambier, Jules. "La Signification Christologique d'Eph IV.7-10," *NTS* 9 (1962/63) 262–75.
Horrell, David G. "Leadership Patterns and the Development of Ideology in Early Christianity," in idem, ed., *Social-Scientific Approaches to New Testament Interpretation.* Edinburgh: T & T Clark, 1999, 309–37.
Furnish, Victor P. *Theology and Ethics in Paul.* Nashville: Abingdon, 1968.
Malina, Bruce J. "Humility," in John J. Pilch and Bruce J. Malina, eds., *Biblical Social Values and Their Meanings: A Handbook.* Peabody, Mass.: Hendrickson, 1993, 107–108.
Meeks, Wayne A. "In One Body: The Unity of Humankind in Colossians and Ephesians," in Wayne A. Meeks and Jacob Jervell, eds., *God's Christ and His People: Studies in Honour of Nils Alstrup Dahl.* Oslo, Bergen, and Tromsö: Universitetsforlaget, 1977, 209–21.
Neyrey, Jerome H. "Deception," in Pilch and Malina, eds., *Biblical Social Values and Their Meaning* (1993) 38–42.
Smith, G. V. "Paul's use of Psalm 68:18 in Ephesians 4:8," *JETS* 18 (1975) 181–89.
Williams, R. R. "Logic Versus Experience in the Order of Creedal Formulae," *NTS* 1 (1954-55) 42–44.

22. *The Sons of Disobedience and the Children of Light* (4:17–5:20)

17. This therefore I say to you and testify in the Lord, that you must no longer walk as the Gentiles walk, in the futility of their minds, 18. darkened in their intellects, alienated from the life of God through their ignorance, on account of the hardness of their hearts. 19. Having ceased to care, they have given themselves to licentiousness for every work of impurity with greed. 20. But that is not how you learned Christ, 21. if indeed you heard of him and were taught in him, as truth is in Jesus, 22. that, as regards your former conduct, you should put off the old person, corrupted by the passions that come from deceit, 23. and be renewed in the spirit of your mind, 24. and put on the new person created according to God in righteousness and true holiness. 25. Therefore, putting off falsehood, let each person speak the truth to his neighbor, because we are all members of one another. 26. Be angry, but do not sin; do not let the

sun set on your anger, 27 and do not make room for the devil. 28. No longer let the thief steal, but rather let him labor, doing good work with his own hands, in order that he may have something to share with the one in need. 29. Let no foul language come out of your mouths, but only what is good for building up as the need arises, in order that it may give grace to those who hear. 30. And do not grieve the Holy Spirit of God, in whom you were sealed for the day of redemption. 31. All bitterness, rage, wrath, shouting, and slander must be removed from you with all malice. 32. And be kind to one another, compassionate, forgiving one another, just as God in Christ forgave you. 5:1. Therefore be imitators of God as beloved children, 2. and walk in love, as Christ loved us and gave himself up for us, as a fragrant offering and sacrifice to God. 3. But immorality and every kind of impurity or greed must not be mentioned among you, as is fitting among saints, 4. nor obscenity, foolish talk, or coarse jesting, which are out of place, but rather thanksgiving. 5. Be sure of this, that no immoral, impure, or greedy person (that is to say, an idolater) has any inheritance in the kingdom of Christ and of God. 6. Let no one deceive you with empty words; because of these things the wrath of God is coming upon the sons of disobedience. 7. Therefore do not be partakers with them. 8. For you were then darkness, but you are now light in the Lord. Walk as children of light, 9. for the fruit of the light is in all goodness and righteousness and truth, 10. discovering what is pleasing to the Lord. 11. And take no part in the unfruitful works of darkness, but rather expose them, 12. for it is shameful even to speak of the things being done by them in secret. 13. But everything exposed by the light becomes visible, 14. for everything that becomes visible is light. Therefore it says, "Awake O sleeper, and rise from the dead, and Christ will shine on you." 15. Watch carefully, therefore, how you walk, not as unwise people, but as wise, 16. making the most of the time, because the days are evil. 17. Therefore do not be foolish, but understand what is the will of the Lord. 18. And do not get drunk with wine, in which is debauchery, but be filled with the Spirit, 19. speaking to one another in psalms and hymns and spiritual songs, singing and chanting to the Lord in your heart, 20. always giving thanks for everything in the name of our Lord Jesus Christ to God the Father.

Notes

17. *This therefore I say to you and testify in the Lord:* This section repeats the emphasis on ethics in 4:1-16. The word "therefore" in fact connects the phrase to the previous passage. The image of the harmonious body in 4:15-16 provides justification for the very strong appeal in this verse for the community to separate itself from the Gentiles. The importance of what Paul is about to say ("this") is stressed by means of the use of the verb "testify" (*martyromai*), essentially repeating the idea that Paul is about to make a weighty proclamation (cf. 1 Thess 2:12).

that you must no longer walk as the Gentiles walk: The verb *peripateō* ("to walk,"
cf. 2:2, 10; 5:2, 8, 15) is often used to refer to how one conducts one's life and is
usually translated "to live." However, the more literal translation of the verb
is being adopted in this commentary in order to capture the active dimension
of the term. In the Pauline epistles *peripateō* refers to behavior that is publicly
visible and demonstrates the honor of community members. As is the case in
the verse, the verb figures prominently in attempts to distinguish the ethical
comportment of believers from the nonbelieving world (see the notes on 2:2).
One can see this, for example, in Col 3:7, and Eph 4:17-24 seems to be dependent on Col 3:5-10 (though the order of the verses in Colossians is not followed;
see the notes below). The reference to the Gentiles recalls Jewish attempts to
distinguish their way of life from the immorality of non-Jews. In fact 4:17–5:20
reflects the influence of Jewish ethical teaching (see the notes below; on the
similarity between this section and the QL see especially Kuhn). Here the term
"Gentile" essentially serves as a label for all those who are outside the church
(i.e., excluding Gentiles who have become members of the church). The effort
to be clear about this point may explain the textual variant that arose in some
witnesses including the Textus Receptus: *ta loipa ethnē* (the rest of the Gentiles). But since the reading adopted here is the more difficult one and is well
attested it is usually preferred (see Metzger 605).

in the futility of their minds, 18. *darkened in their intellects, alienated from the life of
God through their ignorance, on account of the hardness of their hearts:* Taken together these expressions are meant to cover the whole of the person's thinking
and emotions—all of the person's identity—turned against God. Very similar
terminology is found in Rom 1:21: "though they knew God, they did not
honor him as God or give thanks to him, but they became futile in their thinking, and their senseless minds were darkened" (NRSV; cf. Wis 13:1). The depiction of the Gentile world here has points of contact with both Jewish
literature and early Christian depictions of former existence. (On futility see
for example 1 Pet 1:18; *Did.* 5:2. On the darkened mind see Josephus, *Ant.*
9.4.3; 1QS 3:3.) Life without Christ is described in similar terms in 2:3, 11-12
and darkness is again taken up as a theme in Eph 5:11. On Gentile ignorance
see Wis 13:1, 8, 9; 1 Pet 1:14. Hardness of heart is presented here as the reason
for Gentile ignorance (i.e., the Gentiles themselves are to blame). The association of the mind with the heart (in fact the LXX frequently uses "understanding" and "heart" interchangeably) is in keeping with biblical thought
generally where the "eyes-heart" is often understood as the zone of emotion-
fused thought (Malina [1993] "Eyes–Heart" 63–64). To have a "hardened
heart" is to have turned oneself away from God (e.g., Mark 3:5; 6:52; 8:17; John
12:40; cf. Ps 95:8; Isa 6:10). The idea of hardness or petrification here serves as
a good introduction to the mention of callousness in the next verse. Nonbelievers are viewed as being in direct contrast to believers, about whom the author prays: "that the God of our Lord Jesus Christ, the Father of Glory, may
give you a spirit of wisdom and of revelation in full knowledge of him. I pray
that, the eyes of your heart having been enlightened, you may know what is
the hope of his calling, what are the riches of the glory of his inheritance

among the saints" (1:17-18). The notion of alienation also occurs in 2:12 ("alienated from the commonwealth of Israel"; see the notes). Here the circumstances of the Gentiles are presented as even more dire. Gentiles are alienated from the very life of God.

19. *Having ceased to care, they have given themselves to licentiousness for every work of impurity with greed:* In the Greek text one sentence runs from v. 17 to the end of v. 19. A new sentence has been introduced into the English translation for the sake of clarity. The sentence actually begins with the preposition "who," which may in fact be intended to add emphasis to the previous statement about Gentile hardness of hearts ("who indeed having ceased to care"; BAGD 587). The Gentiles are accused here of callousness. This is the only use of the verb *apalgeō* (literally "to cease to feel pain") in the NT. The Gentiles' attitude leads them to a complete loss of moral restraint. As in the case of vv. 17-18, this verse reiterates the ideas found in Rom 1:21-32. Here the parallel is Rom 1:24: "Therefore God gave them up in the lusts of their hearts to impurity, to the degrading of their bodies among themselves" (NRSV). But in contrast to Rom 1:21-32 there is greater emphasis on the moral culpability of the Gentiles: it is not God but the Gentiles themselves who give themselves up to immorality (see Lincoln [1990] 279). As the comparison to Rom 1:24 makes clear, Eph 4:19 probably refers primarily to sexual immorality (on impurity *[akatharsia]* referring to immoral sexual conduct see also 1 Thess 4:7; Gal 5:19; 2 Cor 2:21; on licentiousness *[aselegia]* see Rom 13:13; 1 Pet 4:3). In fact, idolatry and sexual immorality were the two most frequently listed vices of the Gentiles in Jewish literature (e.g., Wisdom 13–14). It is interesting to note that impurity *(akatharsia)* is listed together with idolatry in 5:5 (impurity is also mentioned in 5:3). Idolatry, impurity, and greed are also linked together in Col 3:5 and the author of Ephesians is probably dependent on this text. Often the expression *en pleonexią* (with greed) is taken as qualifying "every work of impurity" and understood as referring to excessive desire (e.g., NAB: "the practice of every kind of impurity to excess"). But given the references in 5:3, 5 and Col 3:5, it is probably best to understand it as a distinct vice. Greed, perhaps involving the pursuit of business transactions, may have brought with it the dangers of apostasy (see the interpretation below).

20. *But that is not how you learned Christ:* A new sentence begins here in the Greek text. This phrase provides the transition from vv. 17-19, describing the state of nonbelievers, to vv. 21-24, describing the existence of believers. Learning Christ means learning traditions about Christ; a similar expression occurs in Acts 5:42 ("teach and proclaim Jesus as the Messiah"). Colossians 1:6-7 speaks of "learning" the gospel. But these traditions clearly include an ethical imperative; they demand a certain type of walking: active devotion to a way of life (see the notes on 4:17). The tone here is one of exclamation. With this verse and the following one the author aims to draw the audience into the discussion by reminding them of what they have already been taught.

21. *if indeed you heard of him and were taught in him, as truth is in Jesus:* The rhetorical purpose of the expression *ei ge* (if indeed) is to remind the audience of what surely they have already heard (e.g., NRSV; see the notes on 4:20). The

purpose of the clause that begins with "as" *(kathōs)* is apparently that the gospel tradition is summed up in Jesus (Lincoln [1990] 283). It should be noted, however, that the relationship between *kathōs* and what precedes it has been debated (in some translations the term "as" disappears completely) and doubts have been raised about whether "truth" *(alētheia)* can serve as the subject of a clause since it lacks a definite article (see for example the NJB where truth appears as the direct object of "were taught": "you were taught what the truth is in Jesus"). But for convincing arguments in favor of the reading adopted here see the extensive discussion in Lincoln [1990] 280–82. This is the only place in Ephesians where the name Jesus occurs by itself, and indeed the use of the name alone is fairly rare in the undisputed letters of Paul (e.g., 1 Thess 1:10; 4:14; Gal 6:17; 1 Cor 12:3; 2 Cor 4:5, 10-11, 14; 11:4; Rom 8:11). It has often been noted that the Pauline epistles make very little mention of the teaching of the earthly Jesus. Verses 20-21 may include a reference to this teaching. The expression "as truth is in Jesus" has been understood in this sense (see Schnackenburg 199). It has also been suggested, however, that the clause was intended to respond to Gnostic false teachers who drew a sharp distinction between the heavenly Christ and earthly Jesus (Schlier [1957] 217). Among the many objections that have been raised against this theory the most important is that nowhere else in Ephesians is there direct evidence of a problem with Gnosticism. In the end the expression remains somewhat cryptic and the reference to "in Jesus" may simply be a stylistic variation of "in Christ," but it clearly implies some type of prior instruction about Jesus. This is the first of three references to truth in this section (cf. 4:24, 25). It recalls the mention of truth in Eph 1:13, which also refers to what is heard: "you also have heard the word of truth, the gospel of your salvation" (cf. Col 1:5). Moreover, speaking in truth is the hallmark of the believer who has the stamina to stand firm against the winds of false teaching (Eph 4:14-15). There is a growing importance being attached to the truth of the gospel message—the reliability of the apostolic tradition. Similar trends can be detected in the Pastoral Epistles, where there is great emphasis on truth (e.g., 1 Tim 2:4, 7; 3:15; 4:3; 6:5; 2 Tim 2:15, 18, 25; 3:7, 8; 4:4; Titus 1:1, 14).

22. *that, as regards your former conduct, you should put off the old person, corrupted by the passions that come from deceit:* The three infinitive verbs in vv. 22-24 *(apothesthai* [put off], *ananeousthai* [be renewed], and *endysasthai* [put on]) are dependent on "you were taught" (v. 21) and have the force of an imperative (see the full discussion of the grammatical issues and problems of translation relating to the three infinitives in Lincoln [1990] 283–84). The reference to former "conduct" or "way of life" *(anastrophē)* recalls the use of the cognate verb "to live" *(anastrephō)* in 2:3, a passage that also refers to the previous existence of believers. Similarly, 2:3 also speaks of passions *(epithymia;* cf. Gal 5:16, 24; Col 3:5). As a whole, vv. 22-24 are closely related to Col 3:8-10. Putting off the old person and putting on the new person (cf. Rom 6:6) is a reference to baptism— a rite that is of central significance in Ephesians (e.g., 1:11-14; 2:1-6; 4:4-6, 30; 5:25-27). Garment imagery reflecting the process of disrobing and robing during the course of the ritual also occurs in the undisputed letters of Paul (e.g.,

Gal 3:27; 1 Thess 5:8; Rom 13:12-14) and is of prime importance in Col 3:8-10. It should also be noted that the idea of putting on virtues (e.g., Philo, *Conf. Ling.* 31) and putting off vices (*Ep. Arist.* 122) was widespread in Greco-Roman literature. The expression *tēs apatēs* (literally "of deceit"; cf. 2 Thess 2:10; Col 2:8) is often taken as a genitive of quality (e.g., NAB: deceitful desires), but it is probably best to understand the expression as a genitive of origin, explaining the basis of the lusts and placing more weight on deceit itself. This is in keeping with the QL, which employs contrast between truth and deceit as a way of distinguishing the community from outsiders (1QS 4:2–5:10; see Perkins 108; Lincoln [1990] 271). While the specific term is not used, the underlying problem with false teachers is nevertheless their propensity for deception (4:14).

23. *and be renewed in the spirit of your mind:* The ethical exhortations in Romans begin with a similar expression: "Do not be conformed to this world, but be transformed by the renewing of your minds" (Rom 12:2 NRSV). Ephesians is probably also influenced by Col 3:10, which speaks of believers being renewed in knowledge. Believers are in direct contrast to Gentiles, who are described as walking in the futility of their minds. The present tense implies that renewal is ongoing. Elsewhere in Ephesians "spirit" *(pneuma)* refers to the Holy Spirit who shapes the life of believers (e.g., 1:17; 3:16; 4:3; 5:18; 6:18). Many commentators have been convinced, therefore, that 4:23 refers to the Holy Spirit (e.g., Schnackenburg 200). But because the reference is clearly to the spirit of *your* mind the expression is probably a means of describing the innermost self (Lincoln [1990] 287; cf. 3:16).

24. *and put on the new person created according to God in righteousness and true holiness:* On the association of putting off and putting on the new person through baptism see the notes on 4:22. To speak about the new person being created according to God is to make a very strong statement about the transformation that occurs in baptism. "According to God" could be according to the will of God, but the parallel text of Col 3:10 makes it more likely that God's likeness is in view (cf. NRSV; REB). Col 3:10 speaks of "the new self, which is being renewed in full knowledge according to the image of its creator." However, the absence of the word "image" from Ephesians is significant. It means that a more direct emphasis is being placed on the ethical stance of believers. To be created according to God is to live in righteousness and true holiness. Both righteousness and holiness are characteristics of God (LXX Ps 144:17; Deut 32:4; cf. Luke 1:75) and, in the words of 5:1, believers must become imitators of God. Here Ephesians departs somewhat from the undisputed letters of Paul where "righteousness" *(dikaiosynē)* is generally used to speak about humanity's right relationship with God. Here "righteousness" represents the pinnacle of human virtues in imitation of God. On truth and its relationship to deceit see the notes on vv. 21-22.

25. *Therefore, putting off falsehood, let each person speak the truth to his neighbor:* Verses 17-24 set out the contrast between the life of the Gentiles (and, by implication, the previous existence of believers) and life in Christ. The same pattern continues here with a balancing of specific vices to be put off by virtues to be

adopted. Verses 25-29 mention four specific vices. The first of these is lying or falsehood (*pseudos;* cf. Col 3:8-9). The verb "to put off" also occurs in v. 22 to describe the shedding of one's previous existence—the old man or the old self. (Although a literal translation of the participle has been adopted here it is also possible to translate the verb in this case as an imperative; cf. REB; NJB.) In keeping with Greco-Roman moral teaching we find a reference to putting off the vices associated with that past existence. The importance assigned to truth as a distinguishing feature of community life recalls the QL, where truth is frequently distinguished from falsehood or deceit (1QS 5:10; 1QH 1:26, 27, 30); this contrast is central to the description of the two ways in 1QS 4:2-26 (see the notes on 1:24; Lincoln [1990] 288–89). This is the third reference to "truth" in this section (cf. 4:21, 24). Some have argued that the author of Ephesians is actually citing the words of Zech 8:16: "These are the things that you shall do: Speak the truth to one another, render in your gates judgements that are true and make for peace" (NRSV; see, for example, Kitchen 87). It should be noted, however, that the author of Ephesians cites the OT directly only rarely, and it may be that the allusion to Zechariah reflects a general familiarity with Jewish ethical tradition where the words of Zechariah were cited (cf. *T. Dan* 5.2; Lincoln [1990] 300).

because we are all members of one another: This is the first of several clauses in vv. 25-29 offering the motive for the rejection of vices: Lying must be avoided because it breaks down the solidarity of the community. As the notes above make clear, Eph 4:25 offers one of many examples of the incorporation of traditional ethical material into the epistle. However, the second part of the verse offers a clear indication that the author shapes this material to address the specific circumstances of the community (see the interpretation below). The theme of unity, which is so central to this work, is brought to bear upon the traditional material. There is clearly a link being drawn with the discussion in 4:1-16, and particularly with the image of the body in 4:12, 15-16 (cf. 5:20; 1 Cor 12:12-27; Rom 12:4, 5). Ephesians 4:15 identifies "speaking the truth in love" as key to building up the body.

26. *Be angry, but do not sin; do not let the sun set on your anger:* It is interesting to compare this verse to Col 3:8, where anger is prohibited. Ephesians seems to acknowledge the existence of anger. The opening of the verse, which includes the words of Ps 4:4 (LXX Ps 4:4; see the notes on v. 25 about the possibility of the indirect influence of Scripture on the author of Ephesians), should, however, by no means be taken as encouragement to be angry. Rather, the imperative verb probably reflects the use of a Semitic idiom meaning, "if you do get angry, do not let it lead to sin" (see Mitton [1976] 168; see REB). The perspective is in keeping with the NT attitude toward anger. The existence of anger is acknowledged but in most cases it is not in keeping with God's purposes: "let everyone be quick to listen, slow to speak, slow to anger; for your anger does not produce God's righteousness" (Jas 1:19-20 NRSV; cf. Matt 5:21-22). In the ancient world sunset was thought of as an important end point for a variety of activities. Statements of the importance of the need for reconciliation before sunset occur elsewhere in ancient literature (e.g., Plutarch, *Moralia* 488C; CD

7:2, 3). It is possible that the author of Ephesians is drawing here upon a traditional maxim.

27. *and do not make room for the devil:* The word "devil" (*diabolos;* literally "the slanderer") does not appear in the undisputed letters of Paul. It is used a second time in Eph 6:11 (cf. 2:2) and appears quite frequently in the NT literature of the later decades of the first century. Believers are often warned against entrapment by the devil (e.g., 1 Tim 3:7; 2 Tim 2:26; 1 Pet 5:8). *Topos* means literally a place or room in which to live, stay, or sit. Here the term is being used metaphorically to warn against the opportunities the devil might have to exert influence (BAGD 822). A similar usage appears in Rom 12:19 where believers are instructed to leave room for the wrath of God. Anger is presented in v. 27 as creating the right conditions for the devil to do his work (cf. *Herm. Man.* 5.1.3). The spatial connotations of the language of v. 27 are particularly interesting given the composite of architectural and body metaphors in 2:19-22 (cf. 3:17-18; 4:15-16). The community itself is a sacred space whose boundaries may be violated by the devil.

28. *No longer let the thief steal, but rather let him labor, doing good work with his own hands:* The clause "doing good work with his own hands" (*ergazomenos tais idiais chersin to agathon*) is subject to a variety of manuscript variations having to do with the sequence of words and the possible omission of words (most notably *idiais* [his own]). As regards the word sequence, the order adopted here has strong support. It is difficult to decide whether *idiais* was added in order to harmonize the verse with 1 Cor 4:12 or whether it was originally part of the work and deleted by scribes on the basis of perceived superfluity, but the fact that it has fairly strong support in the manuscript tradition suggests that the longer reading is to be preferred. The omission from some versions of either *to agathon* (the good thing) or *tais chersin* (with the hands) was probably the result of perceptions concerning the incompatibility of manual labor with what is good (see Metzger 605–606; Lincoln [1990] 292–93). Stealing is the third of four vices that are described in vv. 25-29 (cf. 1 Cor 6:10; 1 Pet 4:15). To labor, "doing good work with one's own hands," sounds like one of the ideals expressed by Paul concerning his own apostleship (e.g., 1 Thess 2:9; 1 Cor 4:12). The author of Ephesians applies this ideal to all community members. Recipients were probably familiar with this aspect of the apostle's life and would have recognized it as an ideal to emulate. In fact, in 2 Thess 3:6-11 the apostle's own example becomes a model for the self-sufficiency of the community (cf. 1 Thess 4:11-12). Perhaps dependency on wealthy patrons was leading believers to compromise their commitments to the one God. There is clearly a connection in these texts between self-sufficiency and the reputation of the church in the larger community. It may be that theft was a particularly serious temptation for slave members of the community (cf. Phlm 18; Titus 2:10; see Gnilka [1971] 271; Perkins 109). The believing slaves of nonbelieving masters were in an especially dangerous position with respect to relations between the church and the outside world.

in order that he may have something to share with the one in need: As in v. 25, we have here a clause supplying the motive for the avoidance of vice and the living out of virtue. The function of the clause is made clear by the term *hina* (in order that). Working with one's own hands will result in having enough to share with those in need. Although they are not connected directly with the issue of work there are passages in the undisputed letters of Paul that encourage sharing with those in need (e.g., Rom 12:13; 2 Cor 9:6-12). Some early Christian works deal explicitly with the reality of differences based on wealth (e.g., *Herm. Vis.* 3.5-6). The author of the Pastoral Epistles calls the prosperous "to do good, to be rich in good works, generous and ready to share" (1 Tim 6:18; cf. 1 Tim 6:17-19).

29. *Let no foul language come out of your mouths, but only what is good for building up as the need arises:* A very similar expression occurs in Col 3:8: "filthy language (*aischrologia*) out of your mouths." A synonym of *aischrologia* occurs here, *logos sapros*, which literally means speech that is rotten or decayed (e.g., Matt 7:17; 12:33; 13:48; Luke 6:43). Here the term is used figuratively to refer to foul, corrupt, or evil language and conjures up images of the physical deterioration of the body. Its metaphorical use is very much in keeping with the values of the ancient Mediterranean world where special significance is attached to the mouth as a boundary of the human body. Purity is protected by carefully controlling what goes into the mouth (food) and what goes out (speech; cf. Prov 10:31-32; 12:17-19; McVann 25. On inappropriate use of the mouth causing concern in community life see Jas 3:1-12 and 1 Tim 5:13). Appropriate language protects the community; it builds it up. The use of the noun *oikodomē* (upbuilding, edification) recalls its usage in 4:12 and 4:16 to speak of the upbuilding of the body in love. As in v. 25, traditional ethical ideals are being employed in conjunction with concepts that are central to the author of Ephesians' attempt to encourage the cohesion of the group. Some manuscripts have "for the building up of faith" instead of "for the building up of need," but the reading adopted here has very strong support. *Pros oikodomēn tēs chreias* (literally "for the building up of need") is an awkward construction (perhaps influenced by the reference to need *[chreia]* in the previous verse) and is subject to different interpretations. It might be rendered as "for the building up of that which is necessary" (objective genitive). For discussion of the grammatical considerations and justification for the reading adopted here (genitive of quality) see Lincoln [1990] 305–306 and Schnackenburg 209.

in order that it may give grace to those who hear: Like v. 28, v. 29 contains a purpose clause (*hina*, in order that) explaining the motive for avoiding the vice. The expression *dō charin* might be translated accurately as "benefit" (e.g., Lincoln [1990] 292; the NJB: "do good to your listeners"). However, the more literal translation of *charis* as "grace" better illustrates the points of contact between this verse and other passages that illustrate the importance attached to grace in Ephesians. There is a connection between the gift of salvation imparted by God and the human gift that seems to be in view here (see BAGD 877–78). Human words can further God's plan.

30. *And do not grieve the Holy Spirit of God, in whom you were sealed for the day of redemption:* This verse seems to interrupt the list of specific vices and virtues that runs from 4:25 to 5:2. It may be that the relationship between v. 30 and

v. 29 is like the relationship between v. 27 and v. 26, in which case v. 30 would be spelling out the consequences of using foul language. The Holy Spirit plays a key role in Ephesians (e.g., 1:17; 3:16; 4:3; 5:18; 6:18) and the work reflects considerable openness to ecstatic experiences of the Spirit (see the notes on 5:18-19). The verb *sphragizō* (to seal or mark with a seal) also occurs in 1:13 and this verse recalls the ideas found in 1:13-14: "were sealed with the promised Holy Spirit which is the pledge of our inheritance toward redemption as his possession to the praise of his glory" (see also 2 Cor 1:21-22; for a full discussion of the significance of "seal" see the notes on 1:13). As is also the case in 1:13, the concept of the seal refers to God's pledge to complete the bestowing of the gifts of salvation, of which believers have already received the first installment. Ephesians 1:3 speaks of "redemption," but 4:30 of the "day of redemption" (a formulation for the Last Day that is unique to Ephesians). It is even clearer than in the case of 1:13-14 that despite some tendencies in the direction of "realized eschatology" Ephesians continues to assign a future dimension to salvation that is in keeping with the undisputed letters of Paul (see also 1:14; 2:7; 5:5, 27; 6:8, 13). The verb *lypeō* means literally "to grieve or pain," but in this case it has the sense of vex, irritate, offend, or insult (BAGD 481). The warning that believers should not grieve the Spirit of God suggests that they might offend the holy presence dwelling in the community (cf. 2:20-22; CD 5:11-12; 7:2). In the *Damascus Document* there is a connection drawn between defiling one's holy spirit and the sins of the tongue (CD 5:11-12). The phrase "do not grieve the Holy Spirit of God" resembles the words of Isa 63:10.

31. *All bitterness, rage, wrath, shouting, and slander must be removed from you with all malice:* Ephesians 4:26 already has warned against anger, but this verse admonishes against the various manifestations of anger. With the exceptions of "bitterness" and "shouting" the vices are also listed in Col 3:8. Bitterness *(pikria)* is also listed as a vice in Rom 3:14 and a cognate verb occurs in the instructions concerning the treatment of wives by their husbands in Col 3:19: husbands should not be embittered against their wives. The word for "rage" *(thymos)* is very closely related in meaning to "wrath" *(orgē)*, but the former perhaps refers more precisely to an outburst of anger (BAGD 365). The terms appear together very frequently (e.g., Rom 2:8; Rev 16:19; 19:15). This is the only case in the NT where "shouting" *(kraugē)* is named as a vice, but the term occurs elsewhere to refer to a yell or cry (Matt 25:6; Luke 1:42; Acts 23:9; Heb 5:7; Rev 21:4). "Slander" *(blasphēmia)* points to how anger can destroy relationships between people (cf. Mark 7:22 par.; 1 Tim 6:4; 2 Tim 3:2). "Malice" *(kakia)* refers to wicked intent (cf. 1 Cor 5:8; 14:20; Rom 1:29; Eph 4:31). The strength of the verb "to remove" *(airō)* can be sensed especially clearly by means of comparison to 1 Cor 5:2 where it occurs as part of the injunction to remove the incestuous believer from the midst of the community. The idea is that the community must be purged of such vices.

32. *And be kind to one another, compassionate, forgiving one another, just as God in Christ forgave you:* These virtues are intended to create conditions in the community that are exactly opposite to the angry circumstances described in v. 31. Kindness, compassion, and forgiveness are all mentioned in Col 3:12-13 (see

the notes on those verses). Colossians expresses the call for mutual forgiveness in slightly different language: "as the Lord forgave you, so also you must" (perhaps alluding to the Lord's Prayer; see Matt 6:9-15). While Colossians refers to Christ's forgiveness, in this verse the focus is on God's forgiveness (cf. Luke 6:36) in Christ. The first part of Ephesians concentrates heavily on what God has accomplished through Christ and the language of this verse is in keeping with this interest. Some manuscripts have "forgave us" (*hēmin*) instead of "forgave you" (*hymin*), but the reading adopted here has strong support (𝔓⁴⁶ ℵ A G P 81 614 etc.), and is in keeping with the parallel text of Col 3:13 and with the consistent use of the second person plural since v. 29 (see Metzger 606; Lincoln [1990] 293).

5:1. *Therefore be imitators of God as beloved children:* Although it is sometimes taken as marking the beginning of a new paragraph (see Barth 555), it is more likely in this case that "therefore" (*oun*) connects this exhortation to the previous verse. The call to be imitators of God flows naturally from what has previously been asserted about what God has done in Christ. Because God forgives in Christ believers should be imitators (*mimetēs*) of God as God's beloved children. In Paul's letters believers are frequently called children of God (e.g., Gal 4:5-6; Rom 8:15; Phil 2:15) and this notion probably also underlies the reference to adoption as sons in Eph 1:5. This is the only call to "imitate" God in the whole of the NT (cf. Matt 5:48); it recalls the strong statement of believers' being created according to God in v. 24. Yet the notion of imitating God is rooted in the OT notion of following God (e.g., Exod 13:21-22; Num 14:24; Deut 1:30-33; Isa 40:3-5). The undisputed letters of Paul speak of believers as imitators of Christ (1 Thess 1:6; 1 Cor 11:1) and of the apostle (1 Thess 1:6; 2 Thess 3:7, 9; 1 Cor 4:16; 11:1). Believers can even be encouraged to imitate other churches (1 Thess 2:14). "Imitation" was also part of the language of Hellenistic mystery cults. But the reference to beloved children suggests that the more immediate influence on the author is the frequent theme of ancient ethical teaching: emulation of one's father's virtues (e.g., Pseudo-Isocrates, *Demonicus* 9–11; cited in Perkins 113–14). Philo of Alexandria uses the language of imitating God to describe acts of kindness and forgiveness (*Spec. Leg.* 4.72-3; see Lincoln [1990] 310–11 for further references to Hellenistic Jewish writings where the specific terminology is used).

2. *and walk in love, as Christ loved us and gave himself up for us, as a fragrant offering and sacrifice to God:* The verb *peripateō* ("to walk," often translated as "to live" [see the notes on 4:17]; cf. 2:2, 10; 4:17; 5:2, 8, 15) recalls the call to no longer walk as the Gentiles do in 4:17. In contrast to behavior that would shame the community, believers are invited to engage in behavior that will mirror its true essence (on walking in love see Rom 14:15). The idea of Christ setting an example continues the line of reasoning that begins at 4:32. God and Christ provide examples for believers to emulate (the shift from God to Christ may have been inspired by the description of God's forgiveness in Christ in 4:32). Love is a central theme in Ephesians. God's love is described in 2:4 and there are many references to the love shared by believers (see the notes on 1:4). Love is what defines the nature of the community (4:16). The theme of Christ's exem-

plary love is developed extensively in the exhortations concerning marriage in 5:25-27. Some have seen an echo of an early church hymn (including an allusion to Isa 53:6, 12 where the notion of sacrificial death is prominent) in "as Christ loved us" (see Barth 557; cf. Gal 1:4; 2:20), and commentators generally view the formulation as traditional. Christ's sacrificial death has already been highlighted in 1:7 and 2:13. The symbol of a fragrant offering is a traditional means of describing a sacrifice that is pleasing to God (e.g., Exod 29:18; Lev 2:9, 12; Ezek 20:41). Paul uses very similar language in Phil 4:18: "I have received from Epaphroditus the gifts you sent, a fragrant offering, a sacrifice acceptable and pleasing to God" (NRSV). As in the previous verse there are manuscript variations having to do with the use of the pronouns. The evidence supporting "loved you" *(hymas)* and "loved us" *(hēmas)* is evenly balanced. However, since the external evidence is much stronger in the case of "for us" *(hēmōn)* than "for you" *(hymōn)*, "us" is probably to be preferred in the first instance as well (see Metzger 606–607). The change of pronoun may have resulted from the incorporation of a traditional formulation.

3. *But immorality and every kind of impurity or greed must not be mentioned among you, as is fitting among saints:* A vice list begins here and continues to the end of v. 7. (This vice list is balanced by the list of appropriate behaviors in 5:18-20.) The repetition here of two of the vices singled out in 4:19 and the recurrence of all three in v. 5 give the impression of insistence on the need to purify the community from any corrupting influences. On impurity and greed see the notes on 4:19. "Impurity" has sexual connotations (see the notes on 4:19) and "immorality" *(porneia)* refers to sexual immorality (especially adultery and intercourse with prostitutes; e.g., 1 Cor 5:1; 6:12-20; 7:2). Immorality and impurity are frequently placed together in vice lists (Col 3:5; Gal 5:19; 2 Cor 12:21; 1 Thess 4:3, 7). It may be that the greed in view here is sexual greed. Influenced by the command against coveting a neighbor's wife, greed and fornication are closely associated in Jewish ethical teaching (e.g., *T. Levi* 14.5-6; *T. Jud.* 18.2; 1QS 4:9-10; *CD* 4:15-18). But it is also possible that the accumulation of wealth is viewed as the source of pollution. Greed could lead believers to cultivate friendships and associations with pagans in the name of business and ultimately lead them into situations where their commitment to life in Christ was compromised (see the notes on 4:19 and the interpretation below). What believers do with their bodies can pollute the whole. The mouths of believers must also be carefully controlled; the implication is that talking about such acts is tantamount to encouraging them. The assertion that these things must not even be mentioned in the community points to the potential for pollution inherent in speech (see the notes on 4:29). The expression "as is fitting among saints" points to the existence of standards: lines separating the pure and holy community from the outside world. Here the use of the term "saints" *(hagioi,* literally "the holy ones" and sometimes meaning the angels) for believers is most appropriate.

4. *nor obscenity, foolish talk, or coarse jesting, which are out of place, but rather thanksgiving:* The idea of the polluting potential of speech introduced in the previous verse is developed further here. This verse also recalls the reference to foul

language in 4:29. The fact that there are three warnings against the dangers of inappropriate speech in this section (cf. 4:29; 5:6) is striking. "Obscenity" (*aischrotēs*) is a word that occurs only here in the NT (though a very similar term, *aischrologia*, appears in Col 3:8, implying that obscene speech is also in view here). This is also the case with "foolish or silly talk" (*mōrologia*) and coarse jesting (*eutrapelia*). This last term is especially interesting. In ancient literature it is used generally in a positive sense to mean wittiness (BAGD 327), but here it clearly has strongly negative connotations. The usual means by which one demonstrates verbal superiority have no place in this community characterized by love. The final clause instructs believers concerning what should come out of their mouths: thanksgiving (*eucharistia*)—what is good for building up (v. 29). Thanksgiving is a priority that runs throughout Ephesians (cf. 1:3-23). This no doubt serves as an introduction to the focus on worship in 5:18-20. For thanksgiving as the opposite of foolish speech see 1QS 10:21-23.

5. *Be sure of this, that no immoral, impure, or greedy person (that is to say, an idolater) has any inheritance in the kingdom of Christ and of God:* The introductory formula announces a solemn proclamation. It actually contains two words for "know": the second person plural (*iste*) of the verb "to know" (*oida*) and the present participle (*ginōskontes*) of the verb "to know" (*ginōskō*). *Iste* is usually understood as an imperative and the addition of the participle is understood as a Hebraism intended to convey emphasis. In this verse the vices of v. 3 are personalized and denounced in the strongest possible terms. Immorality, impurity, and greed are associated with idolatry in Jewish ethical teaching (e.g., Wis 14:12; *T. Jud.* 19.1; 23.1; *T. Reub.* 4.6; Philo, *Spec. Leg.* 1.23, 25), but here it is probably the greedy person specifically who is being called an idolater (for grammatical considerations see Lincoln [1990] 316–17; cf. Col 3:5; *T. Jud.* 19.1; Philo, *Spec. Leg.* 1.23, 25). The effort to clarify the relationship between idolaters and other sinners probably lies behind the alteration of *ho estin* (that is to say) to *hos estin*. In the latter case the masculine relative pronoun would agree with the noun that it qualifies. However, the use of the neuter by no means rules out the possibility that it is the greedy person specifically who is the idolater (BDF 132 [2]). Moreover, the neuter *ho* has much stronger manuscript support ($\mathfrak{P}^{46}$ℵ B F G Ψ 33 81 424ᶜ 915 1175 1319 1739 2005 2127 it vg goth *al*; Lincoln [1990] 316–17). Paul can speak in similar terms of exclusion from the kingdom in Gal 5:19-21 and 1 Cor 6:9-10. The expression "the kingdom of Christ and of God" occurs only here in the NT, though there is a similar expression in Rev 11:15. There is no question of two different kingdoms. The expression has probably been influenced by the mention of God in Christ in 4:32 and the references to God and Christ in 5:1-2.

6. *Let no one deceive you with empty words:* This is the third reference to the dangers of inappropriate speech in this section (cf. 4:29; 5:4; cf. Col 2:4, 8). Here the focus is on the relationship between speech and deception. Similarly 4:25 warns against deception and 4:14 against the craftiness of false teachers. It is most unlikely that 5:6 addresses a specific problem with false teachers, however. In this verse the vices of the Gentiles generally are in view—Gentiles who perhaps in various ways were challenging the validity of Christian alle-

giance with "empty words." The reference to deceit calls to mind the light/ darkness dualism of the QL and anticipates the use of such imagery in vv. 8- 14. The agent of deceit is described as the "angel of darkness": "In the hand of the Prince of Lights is dominion over all the sons of justice; they walk on paths of light. And in the hand of the Angel of Darkness is total dominion over the sons of deceit" (1QS 3:20-22; cited in Perkins 117). On the cultural expectation of deception see the notes and interpretation on Col 3:5-17.

because of these things the wrath of God is coming upon the sons of disobedience: In the parallel text of Col 3:6 various vices (cf. Col 3:5, similar to the list in Eph 5:3-5) provide the basis for the very similar assertion: "Because of these things the wrath of God is coming" (upon the sons of disobedience; the manuscript tradition is divided with respect to the inclusion of the last clause: see the notes on Col 3:6). Ephesians 4:31 warns against *orgē* (wrath) and a cognate term appears in 4:26 in the context of the injunction against anger that begins "be angry *(orgizesthe)*, but. . . ." As in Col 3:6, wrath in Eph 5:6 is not a human emotion, but a way of speaking about God's future judgment (BAGD 578–79). It is interesting to note that in contrast to Col 3:6 and Eph 5:6, Rom 1:18-32 concentrates on the present dimension of wrath. Both Colossians and Ephesians tend to emphasize the present dimensions of salvation, but here we probably have a reference to the future (see also the notes on Col 3:6). In the case of Ephesians it is important to note that this is the second such reference in this section (cf. 4:30). The expression "sons of disobedience" is also found in 2:2, and it recalls the designations found in the QL (e.g., 1QS 1:10; 3:21). Ephesians 2:3 refers in a similar fashion to the "children of wrath." This is very strong insider/outsider language relegating all nonbelievers to the realm of sin.

7. *Therefore do not be partakers with them:* Verse 6 provides the justification for the call for separation from the Gentiles found here *(oun* [therefore] makes this relationship clear). The noun *symmetochos* (joint sharer or partaker) is found only here and in 3:6 in the NT. In 3:6 the mystery of Christ is defined in terms of believers becoming partakers in salvation, but in 5:7 the focus is on the exclusion of nonbelievers from the realm of salvation (cf. 2 Cor 6:14–7:1). In 3:6 Gentile believers are described as co-sharers (with the Jews) of the promise of Christ.

8. *For you were then darkness, but you are now light in the Lord. Walk as children of light:* This is one of the several statements in this passage of the contrast between the previous existence of believers and their new identity. The actual terminology of then/now is found in 2:1-22 and its use here in conjunction with the darkness/light contrast functions as a remembrance of conversion and suggests a baptismal setting (cf. Col 1:12-13). The darkness/light imagery recalls the QL (1QM 1:1-16; 3:6, 9; 13:16; 14:17; 1QS 1:9, 10; 3:13, 19-21, 24, 25; see Kuhn 122–24; see also the notes on 5:6). Such imagery occurs very frequently in the Johannine literature (e.g., John 1:4, 5, 7-9; 1 John 1:5; 2:8) and it is also found in the undisputed letters of Paul (1 Thess 5:5; 2 Cor 4:4, 6; 6:14; Rom 13:12, 13). The verb *peripateō* ("to walk," often translated "to live") occurs in this section also at 4:17, 5:2, and 5:15. It is a manner of describing the publicly visible orientation that believers adopt in the world (see the notes on 4:17

and the interpretation below). The association of the verb with the darkness/light imagery makes clear the emphasis on what is publicly apparent: Christians are to carry themselves like a beacon witnessing to the identity of the saints. Darkness was associated with the previous existence of believers (and the present condition of non-Christians) in 5:18. It is striking that the previous lives of believers are not described as "in darkness" or characterized by darkness, but as actually constituting darkness itself. The reference to "children of light" recalls the previous description of believers as children in 5:1.

9. *for the fruit of the light is in all goodness and righteousness and truth:* The reading adopted here is supported by early and diverse witnesses. But some witnesses, including the Textus Receptus, have *pneumatos* (spirit) instead of *phōtos* (light). While it may be argued that the reading adopted here resulted from an attempt to harmonize this verse with the preceding one, it is more likely that the inclusion of *pneumatos* was the result of an attempt to harmonize the verse with Paul's use of the very similar expression in Gal 5:22: "the fruit of the spirit" (*ho de karpos tou pneumatos;* see Metzger 607). As in Gal 5:22, virtues constitute the fruit (cf. Phil 1:11). "The fruit" is a metaphorical means of describing that which grows from Christian conversion. The light manifests itself in tangible and visible ethical conduct (see the interpretation below). The list of ethical virtues recalls the reference to righteousness and true holiness in 4:24 (see the notes; cf. 1QS 1:5). Truth emerges in this text as a key marker of Christian identity (cf. 4:21, 24, 25). What is good is listed as a fruit of the Spirit in Gal 5:22 (cf. Rom 15:14; 2 Thess 1:11) and Col 1:10 speaks of bearing fruit in every good work. Interestingly, the Greek text of this verse contains no verb; thus modern translators insert the verb "to be" or what is understood as its equivalent (e.g., NRSV: "the fruit of the light is found in"; NJB: "the effects of the light are seen").

10. *discovering what is pleasing to the Lord:* The verb *dokimazō* means literally to put to the test or to examine (BAGD 202). Here it refers more specifically to the process of learning or discovering. The implication is of active engagement in the ethical arena where discernment is necessary. Choices and decisions are sometimes difficult as one walks as a believer in the world and the believer must take on responsibility. *Dokimazō* was a key concept in Stoic ethics, where discernment was described as an activity of reason (e.g., Epictetus, *Diss.* 1.20.7; 2.23.6, 8; 4.5.16; 4.6.13; 4.7.40; cited in Lincoln [1990] 328). Romans 2:18 presents Jews who are instructed in the Law as capable of such discernment (cf. Rom 12:2; 1 Thess 5:21; Phil 1:9-10). In Pauline literature what is pleasing to God or to the Lord is frequently listed as a goal of Christian living (e.g., Rom 12:2; 2 Cor 5:9; Col 3:20).

11. *And take no part in the unfruitful works of darkness, but rather expose them:* Verses 8-10 describe the life of the children of light, whose fruit is made visible by means of virtues. Here the call to separate oneself from the unfruitful works of darkness (i.e., the way of life of nonbelievers) is followed by an encouragement of behavior that leads to a different type of visibility. Believers are called to bring to light or to expose (*elegchō;* cf. 5:13) the sins of the Gentiles—expose them for what they really are. The verb *elegchō* can have slightly different

meanings in the NT and there may be some echoes of these various meanings at work here. It can mean "to reprove" or "to correct," as it clearly does in the instruction concerning church discipline in Matt 18:15. Particularly interesting for Ephesians, however, is the use of the term in 1 Cor 14:24, where it refers to the act of convincing (see BAGD 249). Paul describes the possibility of nonbelievers' witnessing early church prophecy and becoming convinced. In other words, the term has evangelical connotations. Ephesians seems much less interested in evangelization and much more defensive in relation to the outside world than does Paul in 1 Cor 14:24. Nevertheless, the attitude recommended in Eph 5:11 is not one of fearful withdrawal but of bold confrontation and, if the occasion should arise, of active opposition. There is no question of compromise, however. The term *sygkoinōneō* (take part), which is quite rare in the NT (cf. Rev 18:4; Phil 4:14), means to participate in a given reality, to be connected with something: to have fellowship with. But with strong language that recalls the sentiments of 5:7 believers are instructed to reject any such association.

12. *for it is shameful even to speak of the things being done by them in secret:* The mention of secrecy is in keeping with the reference to works of darkness in the previous verse. Given the sexual connotations associated with many of the vices (see the notes on 5:3), it is likely that indecency and sexual immorality are largely in view here. It is interesting to note that second-century pagan critics accused Christians of engaging in secret immoral acts (see M. Y. MacDonald [1996] 49–126). The speech of Marcus Cornelius Fronto (100–166 C.E.) recorded by the Christian apologist Minucius Felix (200–240 C.E.) offers an especially good example:

> they have formed a rabble of blasphemous conspirators, who with nocturnal assemblies, periodic fasts, and inhuman feasts seal their pact not with some religious ritual, but with desecrating profanation; they are a crowd that furtively lurks in hiding places, shunning the light; they are speechless in public but gabble away in corners. . . . They recognize each other by secret marks and signs; hardly have they met when they love each other, throughout the world, uniting in the practice of a veritable religion of lusts. (*Octavius* 8–9)

It is highly likely that such rumors circulated about early Christian groups determined to set themselves apart from others even in the first century C.E. Perhaps in response to accusations against early Christians, Eph 5:12 accused the Gentile population of secretive, immoral acts. The notion that speaking about such acts is tantamount to participating in them is also found in 5:3, as is the implicit relationship between pollution that occurs through the mouth and sexual immorality (see the notes). The use of the adjective *aischros* (shameful) is particularly appropriate in this context. It refers to loss of honor—loss of all reputation in the eyes of others. To engage in shameful behavior is to violate the boundaries of the pure community. Very often descriptions of what is shameful or honorable are expressed in terms of gender. (On the values of honor and shame see the notes and interpretation on Col 1:3-8.) In the undisputed letters of Paul *aischros* is used to describe the consequences of a woman cutting her hair (1 Cor 11:6) and with reference to women speaking in church (1 Cor 14:35).

13. *But everything exposed by the light becomes visible, 14. for everything that becomes visible is light:* On the idea of exposure see the notes on 5:11. The meaning of these somewhat repetitive assertions is not immediately clear, but it is perhaps best not to press this highly metaphoral language too hard for precise meaning. The wide potential applications of light/darkness imagery allow the author of Ephesians to lead the reader from the idea of the light (believers) exposing the works of darkness for what they really are to the role of the light (Christ) in leading to conversion (see the notes below). The first clause in v. 14 allows for the transition between these two thoughts. In contrast to the secretive nonbelievers, the Christians are illuminated and visible. Their fruit—their moral way of life—is visible for all to see. To become "light" is to be transformed. One senses a possible interest in evangelization that is also found in v. 11 (see the notes).

Therefore it says, "Awake O sleeper, and rise from the dead, and Christ will shine on you": Here an early Christian hymn is cited. (There has in fact been extensive debate among scholars concerning the background of the quotation; for a good summary of the debate see Schnackenburg 228–29.) The same introductory formula is used with respect to the Scripture citation in 4:8. The reference to waking up and rising from the dead is probably an allusion to baptism and it is likely that this hymn was associated with baptism (Rom 6:4-13). Indeed, light and baptism are linked together in the NT and early Christian literature (e.g., Heb 6:4; 10:32; Justin Martyr, *Apol.* 1.61.12, 13; 65.1). Rescue from a past existence of sin is suggested by the metaphorical reference to death—a theme that occurs elsewhere in the epistle (Eph 2:1, 5; cf. Col 2:13). The call to remain awake also evokes the vigilance required for the Day of the Lord (1 Thess 5:5-8; Rom 13:11-14). Commentators have frequently suggested that the hymn contains an allusion to Isa 60:1: "Arise, shine; for your light has come and the glory of the Lord has risen upon you." To speak of Christ shining means that there is clearly a relationship between this hymnic fragment and vv. 8-13, where the darkness/light motif figures prominently, but the precise nature of the relationship is not entirely clear. The structure suggests that the fragment is intended to justify the previous assertions in some way, but the connection is obscured by the fact that in the previous verses the believers themselves are the light whereas here Christ is the light. There are many places in the NT where Christ is depicted as light (e.g., Luke 2:32; John 1:4, 5, 9; Rev 1:16). In the broadest terms it seems that the new identity adopted by believers—they have been illuminated by Christ—is the basis for their relationship with the outside world and their treatment of the works of darkness (see also the notes on 5:13-14a). Moreover, given the allusion to baptism, the believers' identification with Christ is probably to be assumed. To have Christ shine upon one is probably to have experienced the light conveyed by the example of fellow believers.

15. *Watch carefully, therefore, how you walk, not as unwise people, but as wise, 16. making the most of the time, because the days are evil:* From the darkness/light con-

trast in 5:8-14 the text moves on to consider the unwise/wise contrast—one that is common in Jewish ethical teaching (e.g., Prov 4:10-14; 1QS 4:23-24). As in v. 8, the verb *peripateō* ("to walk," often translated "to live") occurs. This is the final instance of the verb in this section; it was found previously in 4:17; 5:2, 8. It occurs frequently in Pauline literature in the context of instructions intended to guide believers' dealings with the nonbelieving world (see the notes on 4:17); it is found in the parallel text of Col 4:5: "Walk in wisdom toward outsiders, making the most of the time" (cf. Col 1:9-10). Like Colossians, Ephesians assigns a positive role to wisdom in Christian existence, but Ephesians lacks the specific concern for guiding the exchanges between believers and nonbelievers that one finds in Colossians. Colossians 4:5-6 reveals an awareness of the perilous nature of exchanges with outsiders, but also an awareness of the potential for dialogue (see the notes and interpretation on Col 4:5-6). In comparison, Eph 5:15-16 reveals a stronger sentiment of being set apart from nonbelievers. There is no talk of the delicate maneuvers being required for exchanges with the Gentiles. Instead, the recipients are simply instructed to act as wise people—presumably separating themselves from the unwise—because the days are evil (see the interpretation below).

Like Colossians, Ephesians speaks of "making the most of the time." While in Colossians this expression may have some eschatological overtones (see the notes on Col 4:5 for a full discussion of the meaning of this expression), it is used primarily to encourage the use of every opportunity to evangelize. In contrast the use of the expression in conjunction with "the days are evil" in Ephesians suggests that eschatological interests are at the forefront. In the undisputed letters of Paul the word "time" *(kairos)* frequently refers to eschatological time (e.g., 1 Cor 4:5; 7:29; 2 Cor 6:2) and stresses the eschatological urgency of Paul's mission (e.g., Rom 11:13-15). Although it is unusual in the context of Ephesians, a sense of imminent expectation is revealed in 5:17. In the face of evil, surrounded by the unwise, believers are to stand prepared and to make use of every opportunity to emulate the example of Christ. Some texts have *pōs akribōs* (how carefully), suggesting that "carefully" should modify "walking" rather than watching. But the reading adopted here *(akribōs pōs)* has much stronger support. The manuscript variation may have occurred because *pōs* was accidentally omitted and reinserted again. A few manuscripts include the word *adelphoi* (brothers) in this verse (see Metzger 608; Lincoln [1990] 337).

17. *Therefore do not be foolish, but understand what is the will of the Lord:* The reference to evil days in the previous verse provides the justification for this exhortation. This is made clear by the use of "therefore" *(dia touto)*. Although the term "foolish" *(aphrōn)* is not employed earlier, previous warnings against ignorance (4:17-21) and foolish talk (5:4) prepare the way for this exhortation. The word *aphrōn* occurs quite frequently in the undisputed letters of Paul (Rom 2:20; 1 Cor 15:36; 2 Cor 11:16, 19; 12:6, 11). Particularly interesting is Paul's ironic use of the term in the context of his dispute with apostolic rivals. He must render himself foolish in order to compare himself with these rivals (cf. 2 Cor 12:11). The use of *aphrōn* in Ephesians is closer to that in Rom 2:17-20, where Paul describes the appropriate qualities of a Jew instructed in the Law.

There are also points of contact between Rom 2:17-20 and Eph 5:10 (see the notes). Like 5:17, 5:10 is concerned with understanding what is the will of the Lord.

18. *And do not get drunk with wine, in which is debauchery, but be filled with the Spirit:* The first part of the verse contains an allusion to Prov 23:31, but it is likely that its influence on the author of Ephesians was indirect; the injunction was a regular part of Jewish ethical teaching and is actually linked with debauchery in *The Testaments of the Twelve Patriarchs* (cf. *T. Iss.* 7.2, 3; *T. Jud.* 11.2; 12.3; 13.6; 16.1; cited in Lincoln [1990] 340). Paul associates drunkenness with debauchery in Rom 13:12-13 and sobriety with light in 1 Thess 5:6-8 (cf. 1 Cor 5:11; 6:10). The term "debauchery" (*asōtia*; cf. Titus 1:6; 1 Pet 4:4) here is a synonym for "licentiousness" in 4:19. This verse has sometimes been understood as an attempt to distinguish the Spirit-induced ecstasy of the early Christians from the frenzies of such pagan cults as that of Dionysius (see Rogers). The author of Ephesians may have been attempting to ensure that believers in no way partook in behavior that emulated the activities of these cults, but we may also have here an indirect acknowledgment that the worship of the early Christians was understood by outside observers as similar to other cults considered suspect in the ancient world (note also the impression recorded in Acts that believers filled with the Spirit were drunk; cf. Acts 2:4, 13, 15). Similar dynamics may have been at work in 5:12 (see the notes) in the exhortation to avoid things done in secret. The Spirit plays a central role in Ephesians (see the notes on 4:30) and is clearly linked to the worship of the community in the following verse.

19. *speaking to one another in psalms and hymns and spiritual songs, singing and chanting to the Lord in your heart:* These activities flow from being filled with the Spirit. The role of the Spirit is highlighted in vv. 18-19 to a greater extent than in the parallel text of Col 3:16. This, along with the emphasis on the role of the Spirit throughout the epistle, suggests a great openness to manifestations of the Spirit in the midst of the community. The expression "speaking to one another" suggests an intimate, spontaneous atmosphere for worship (see Thurston 137). In Col 3:16 the instructional potential of such exchanges is brought out (see the notes on Col 3:16). The importance of hymnic material for the author of Ephesians is illustrated by the incorporation of such material into the epistle (e.g., 5:14). It is impossible to distinguish precisely between psalms, hymns, and spiritual songs. The last term implies inspiration by the Spirit and may actually refer to the gift of tongues (cf. 1 Cor 14:15; note, however, that although the term "spiritual" only agrees in gender with "songs" it is possible that it refers to all three activities; see BDF 135 [3]). "Psalms" probably includes psalms from the biblical psalter. It is likely that in the singing and chanting traditional elements such as Jewish liturgical materials were combined with ecstatic, innovative tendencies. In contrast to Col 3:16, which has "as you sing with gratitude in your hearts to God," Ephesians speaks of "singing and chanting to the Lord (i.e., Christ; cf. 4:17) in your heart." It is impossible to distinguish between the use of the verb *ǎdō* ("sing"; cognate of "song") and *psallō* ("chant"; cognate of "psalm"; cf. NJB). Some commentators

(e.g., Barth 584; cf. NAB) have argued that the latter term includes making instrumental music, but the contemporary usage of the word makes it much more likely that it refers to "making melody" (NRSV) by means of singing (see BAGD 891). The close relationship between Col 3:16 and Eph 5:19 has figured prominently in explanations of the manuscript variations. A shorter reading found in a variety of texts, omitting *pneumatikais* (spiritual; $\mathfrak{P}^{46}$, B, it^d, Ambrosiaster), is sometimes judged to be original in view of a possible attempt to harmonize Eph 5:19 with Col 3:16. However, it seems more likely that the shorter reading resulted from a scribal error caused by the eye skipping from the ending of "song" *(-ais)* to the ending of "spiritual" *(-ais)* with the consequent mistaken deletion of "spiritual." The attempt to harmonize the two verses does, however, explain the long reading in A, which includes *en chariti* (with gratitude; see Metzger 608; Lincoln [1990] 337).

20. *always giving thanks for everything in the name of our Lord Jesus Christ to God the Father:* The notion of thanksgiving plays an important role in both Colossians and Ephesians and is closely associated with liturgical traditions (see the notes on 5:4). Here the author of Ephesians is influenced by both Col 3:15 and 3:16 where notions of thanksgiving and gratitude occur respectively. The instructions to give constant, comprehensive thanks are similar to those found in 1 Thess 5:18. Although the author of Ephesians concentrates in much more depth on ethics than on worship in 4:17–5:20, vv. 18-20 make it clear that behavior during worship is also an important part of no longer walking as Gentiles do (4:17) and of keeping on the right path as children of God. Some manuscripts have the unusual expression "Father and God" *(patri kai theǭ)*, but the reading adopted here *(theǭ kai patri)* is much more widely supported (cf. Metzger 608; cf. 1:3; 4:6).

INTERPRETATION

It is difficult to know how to divide this long passage into sections. There is very little justification on grammatical, linguistic, or thematic grounds for doing so (see Thurston 128). Nevertheless, many commentators have attempted such divisions. Andrew Lincoln ([1990] 274), for example, divides the long passage into four pericopes, noting the importance of the verb "to walk" *(peripateō;* see the notes on 4:17) in each: 4:17-24 (cf. 4:17); 4:25–5:2 (cf. 5:2); 5:3-14 (cf. 5:8); and 5:15-20 (cf. 5:15). This approach no doubt has merit and it is clear that the author of Ephesians seeks to highlight several aspects of how members of the community are to walk as believers in the world. Perhaps, above all else, it allows for practical management of the discussion. But in my view the many points of overlap among the verses in this section mean that it is better, though admittedly somewhat impractical, to treat this passage as a whole. Treating 4:17–5:20 as a whole allows one to see more clearly how two related goals shape the exhortation. The purpose of the exhortation is to instill nothing less than repulsion for the way of life of nonbelievers and to encourage unity among believers through the adoption of ethical virtues and the practice of harmonious worship.

To assess the significance of the instructions in 4:17–5:20 is, however, no easy task. Perhaps nowhere else in the epistle is the dependence on tradition so apparent. Most obviously, Ephesians here relies heavily on Colossians (Eph 4:17-24 = Col 3:5-10; Eph 5:3-8 = Col 3:5-8; Eph 5:15-20 = Col 3:16-17; 4:5). There also seems to be some reworking of material from the undisputed letters of Paul (e.g., Eph 4:17-19 = Rom 1:21, 24). As the notes above make clear there is also significant correspondence between this passage and Greco-Roman moral codes, Jewish ethical teaching, and in particular the teaching found in the QL. For example, as is also true of the QL, truth emerges as a hallmark of the community set apart from the world. In fact, the very structure of the exhortation appears to be traditional. The text is structured according to the theme of the "two ways" (virtue and vice) that is found in the QL (e.g., 1QS 3–4; especially 4:2-26) and in early Christian works (e.g., *Did.* 1–5; *Barn.* 18–20). Throughout the text the author balances prohibitions (the ways that must be rejected) against positive alternatives (the ways that should be adopted; e.g., 4:22-32; 5:3-5). All this means that scholars have generally been reluctant to look to the list of virtues and vices to provide information about the community (e.g., Perkins 105).

While conclusions must remain tentative, a socio-historical approach demands that we consider the relationship between even highly conventional teaching and social setting. We may do this by looking for indications of where the author of Ephesians apparently shapes or departs from tradition and by attempting to understand the implications for community life of the values encoded in traditional teaching. For example, 4:25 clearly incorporates traditional material about the importance of avoiding falsehood, but the second half of the verse, which provides the motivation for avoiding this vice, offers an indication of the author's particular interests. The reference to being "members of one another" ties the exhortation to the previous section (4:1-16) and relates the exhortations to the general concern for unity that runs throughout Ephesians (see the notes on 4:25). A similar case might be made for the reference to "upbuilding" in 4:29. The ethical exhortations of 4:17–5:20 are tied together by a fervent desire to encourage the cohesion of the community. As is discussed further below, so fervent is this desire that there is good reason to suspect that Ephesians responds to strong perceptions concerning threats to community life.

Sometimes evidence concerning the social setting of Ephesians can be detected by paying attention to subtle differences between Ephesians and parallel texts from Colossians and the Pauline literature generally. One of the most striking features of 4:17–5:20 is the sharp, uncompromising distinction between those inside the church and those outside (see also the notes and interpretation on 2:1-10). As is illustrated above, similar teaching occurs in Colossians and elsewhere in the undisputed letters of Paul. But when 4:17–5:20 is considered as a unit one is struck by the length of the exhortation devoted to encouraging separation and one senses a great emphasis on solidarity in the face of menacing evil. In the undisputed letters of Paul the only text that matches the strength of the sentiment in 5:7 (cf. 5:11; see the notes on 5:7 and 5:11) about the need to separate from the Gentile world is 2 Cor 6:14–7:1, a text commonly regarded as an interpolation. A comparison of 5:15-16 to Col 4:5 is also instructive for gaining a sense of the intensity of world rejection one detects in Ephesians. Colossians 4:5-6 reflects an awareness of the perils involved in exchanges with the nonbelieving world but leaves the door open for dialogue. In contrast, Eph 5:15-16 makes no mention of exchanges with outsiders and sets the instructions concerning walking wisely within the context of eschatological woes: Walking wisely is necessary because the days are evil! The community is vulnerable; its boundaries must be protected. The community may even be violated by the devil (see the notes on 4:27).

In this commentary it is being argued that in comparison to Colossians and the undisputed letters of Paul, Ephesians demonstrates a much stronger sense of introversion (see the notes and interpretation on 1:3-14, 15-23; 2:1-10). The Pauline mission continues to be presented as universal in scope, and expansion remains an ideal (e.g., the hope of conversion underlies the focus on the light in 5:8-14). But for the moment at least the community is adopting an increasingly defensive strategy in relation to nonbelievers. As has frequently been noted, in many respects the ethos here resembles that of the QL. But Pheme Perkins has written in an interesting way of possible differences of perspective between the two:

> In the Essene case, the call for separation from the "sons of darkness" has a clear sociological meaning. Persons become members of a new community with its own interpretation of the Mosaic Law, ritual calendar, worship, and detailed instructions governing the lives of members. Contact with outsiders is limited. It would be natural to read Ephesians as requiring a similar withdrawal, except that the letter nowhere hints at the kind of social structures required to sustain such a move. Therefore the dissociation required in this passage seems to apply primarily to the activities that characterized the lifestyle of non-Christians. The emphasis on "fruit of the light" and "pleasing to the Lord" in verses 9-10 suggests that a Christian's general conduct is in view. (118)

In discussing the social structures required for withdrawal Perkins identifies what might be described in sociological terms as the mechanisms required for the establishment of sectarian identity. She is right to take note of a significant difference between Ephesians and the QL. Ephesians lacks evidence of the clearly articulated, visible, physical measures to encourage segregation that we find in the QL. But it is possible that the act of withdrawal, though different, is equally intense. General ethical conduct is understood as a sign of a new identity. Compared to other ethical teaching in Pauline literature, including Colossians, the attention given in Ephesians to a distinct way of life is striking. It seems that the loss of boundary markers associated with Judaism (e.g., circumcision) is being compensated for by detailed attention to ethical boundaries. It is probably not reading too much into the text of 4:17–5:20, with its many allusions to baptism and transformation, to sense a fear of forgetting the parameters of identity and ultimately a fear of assimilation. Moreover, it must be remembered that the ethical stance operates in conjunction with religious symbolism that reinforces the idea that believers already inhabit the heavenly realm. They are in the world but not of it (see the notes and interpretation on 1:15-23; 2:1-10).

Social interaction with outsiders must have been affected in many more ways than simply the rejection of certain aspects of the lifestyles of nonbelievers. There were many aspects of daily life, including business dealings and dependence on wealthy patrons, that presented opportunities for compromising one's commitment to the one God. In the list of vices (4:19; 5:3, 5) there is repeated emphasis on the avoidance of greed. Early Christian literature links the preoccupation with pagan friends and the accumulation of wealth with apostasy (e.g., *Herm. Sim.* 4.5; 8.8.1-2; 9.20.1; *Herm. Vis.* 3.6.5; see the notes on Eph 4:28 and the interpretation of Col 3:5-17). The special concern with appropriate speech that emerges time and again in 4:25–5:12 also deserves special attention. Speech is presented as integral to the true essence of the community, and one wonders whether the vices of tongue that the author associates with the nonbelieving world (e.g., 5:4, 6) are based on a communal experience of slander (on rumors see further below). Rooted in a first-century Mediterranean context, Eph 4:17–5:20 links the honor of the community with the public demonstration of its reputation. (See the notes and interpretation on Col 1:3-8 and Col 3:5-17, which include a discussion of the important role sexual conduct played in the preservation of honor.) Believers must walk in the world as children of light (5:8). Interaction between believers and nonbelievers may be tense and more restricted than before, but believers must ensure that the demeanor of the community—its public persona—mirrors its true essence. The risks of polluting influences are very high. It is in light of such values that one must understand the solemn proclamation of exclusion in 5:5: "Be sure of this, that no immoral, impure, or greedy person (that is to say, an idolater) has any inheritance in the kingdom of Christ and of God."

Finally, it is important to note that 4:17–5:20 presents the alternative to "no longer walking as the Gentiles do" not only in terms of ethics but also in the form of recommendations concerning worship. Behind the call to engage in worship, which is opposite to the drunkenness and debauchery of the Gentiles, there is clearly an attempt to demarcate the difference between early Christian ritual and the rites of other cults. It may well be that Christians are themselves being accused of disorderly and immoral activities. It is clear that the worship of the community must maintain certain standards, but we find no attempt here to quiet early Christian worship. Gentiles may engage in secret activities and indeed early Christians may themselves be subject to such accusations, but secrecy is not an ideal in the community, which nevertheless demonstrates a very strong commitment to separating itself from the wicked world. Believers are to be filled with the Spirit. Community members speak to one another by means of psalms, hymns, and spiritual songs. The picture is one of intimate worship that includes spontaneous outbursts of the Spirit's power (see the notes on 5:12, 18-20). The remarks of the second-century critics of Christianity demonstrate that the worship of the early Christians was a key aspect of the group's visibility. It is particularly striking, for example, to note the correspondence between the wording of Eph 5:19-20 and Pliny's impressionistic report about Christians that they meet together "on a certain day before daylight to sing a song with responses to Christ" (Pliny, *Epistles* 10.96.7; see Lincoln [1990] 356). Given the boldness in worship that is commended in 5:18-20 it is not surprising that the believers are being prepared with battle imagery to face evil (cf. 6:10-20).

The sharp, uncompromising distinction between believers and non-believers of Eph 4:17–5:20 can seem shocking to modern readers, but it is very important to understand the function of such language in a first-century church setting. The use of such "sectarian" labels as "sons of disobedience" and "children of light" is rooted in an attempt to delineate and protect the boundaries of a new community. Amid probable rumors of debauchery and secrecy, and hostile reactions from outsiders, believers struggled to survive in household groups throughout the eastern Mediterranean. (On the apologetic function of Ephesians see the notes and interpretation on 5:21–6:9.) They were convinced that they now belonged to a perfected creation through Christ (4:20-24) and presented the alternative to this in the strongest possible terms. There is no question that such categorical thinking has no place in the modern church's response to the world, but many of the virtues and vices listed in this passage have a timeless importance for setting the ethical standards in Christian churches. In the early church context perhaps the most remarkable aspect of this teaching is that while it encouraged a strong separation from nonbelievers the author of Ephesians intended this separation to be lived out by

Christians who remained physically integrated within the broader community. (This will become evident in the subsequent examination of 5:21–6:9.) The model of the Christian household presented in 5:21–6:9 in many ways matches the conventional standards of the day. However, as will be discussed further in the next section, the author of Ephesians was convinced that living according to this model was a central aspect of no longer walking as the Gentiles walk.

For Reference and Further Study

Best, Ernest. "Ephesians: Two Types of Existence," *Int* 48 (1993) 39–51.
Kuhn, Karl Georg. "The Epistle to the Ephesians in the Light of the Qumran Texts," in Jerome Murphy-O'Connor, ed., *Paul and Qumran: Studies in New Testament Exegesis*. London: Geoffrey Chapman; Chicago: Priory, 1968, 115–31.
Malina, Bruce J. "Eyes–Heart," in John J. Pilch and Bruce J. Malina, eds., *Biblical Social Values and Their Meaning*. Peabody, Mass.: Hendrickson, 1993, 63–67.
McVann, Mark. "Communicativeness (Mouth–Ears)," in ibid. 25–28.
Minucius Felix, Marcus. *The Octavius of Marcus Minucius Felix*. Translated by G. W. Clarke. ACW 39. New York: Newman, 1974.
Murphy-O'Connor, Jerome. "Truth: Paul and Qumran," in idem, ed., *Paul and Qumran: Studies in New Testament Exegesis* (1968) 179–230.
Rogers, Cleon L. Jr. "The Dionysian Background of Eph 5:18," *Bibliotheca Sacra* 136 (1979) 249–57.
Suggs, M. Jack. "The Christian Two Way Tradition: Its Antiquity, Form, and Function," in David E. Aune, ed., *Studies in the New Testament and Early Christian Literature: Essays in Honor of Allen P. Wikgren*. NTS.S 33. Leiden: E. J. Brill, 1972, 60–74.
Wild, Robert A. "Be Imitators of God: Discipleship in the Letter to the Ephesians," in Fernando F. Segovia, ed., *Discipleship in the New Testament*. Philadelphia: Fortress, 1985.

23. *The Households of Believers* (5:21–6:9)

21. Be subject to one another out of reverence for Christ. 22. Wives, be subject to your husbands as to the Lord, 23. for the husband is the head of the wife as also Christ is the head of the church, himself savior of the body. 24. But as the church is subject to Christ, so also the wives ought to be to the husbands in everything. 25. Husbands, love your wives, just as Christ loved the church and gave himself up on behalf of her, 26. in order that he might sanctify her, cleansing her by the washing of the water by the word, 27. in order that he might present the church to himself in

splendor, without spot or wrinkle or any such thing, that she might be holy and without blemish. 28. In the same way, husbands ought to love their wives as their own bodies. He who loves his wife loves himself, 29. for no one ever hated his own flesh, but nourishes and cherishes it, as also Christ does the church, 30. because we are members of his body. 31. "For this reason a man shall leave his father and his mother and be joined to his wife, and the two will become one flesh." 32. This is a great mystery, but I am speaking about Christ and the church. 33. In any case, each one of you should love his wife as himself and the wife should fear her husband. 6:1. Children, obey your parents in the Lord, for this is right. 2. "Honor your father and your mother," which is the first commandment with a promise 3. "in order that it may be well with you and that you may live long on the earth." 4. And fathers, do not provoke your children to anger, but bring them up in the discipline and admonition of the Lord. 5. Slaves, obey your masters according to the flesh, with fear and trembling, with simplicity of heart, as to Christ, 6. not with eyeservice as people-pleasers, but as slaves of Christ, doing the will of God with all your heart, 7. serving as slaves with enthusiasm, as for the Lord and not for human beings, 8. knowing that each person will be paid back from the Lord for whatever good is done, whether he is a slave or free. 9. And masters, do the same thing to them, stopping the threatening, knowing that both they and you have a master in heaven and with him there is no partiality.

NOTES

21. *Be subject to one another out of reverence for Christ:* Commentators are divided as to whether it is best to discuss this verse in conjunction with the previous section or whether it should be taken as introducing a new section. The matter is not easy to decide. The verse is grammatically connected to what comes before. It actually begins with a participle of the verb *hypotassō* (to be subject or subordinate to someone else), here rendered as an imperative, but literally, "submitting." Thus the relationship between v. 20 and v. 21 might be expressed as follows: "always giving thanks for everything . . . submitting to one another." These verses are grammatically dependent on the verb found in 5:18: "Be filled." But v. 21 is thematically related to what comes next. The call to be subject to Christ introduces the notion of subordination that is so central to the household code that follows. Moreover, 5:22 relies on 5:21 to supply its verb (see the notes below). The advantage of reading 5:21 in relation to 5:20 is that it brings out the fact that submitting to one another is understood as central to a way of life that sets believers apart from the Gentiles (cf. 4:17). It has even been suggested that the whole of the household code material needs to be understood as closely linked to the ethical exhortations in 4:17–5:20 (e.g., Lincoln [1990] 338 understands 5:15–6:9 as a unit). Still, the household code stands out as a self-contained unit, influenced by tradition in both form and content. Because of the close relationship of v. 21 to this material it seems best

to understand v. 21 as an introduction to the passage. The respect and obedience one owes to the head of the household is to be shown to Christ. This is suggested not only by the use of the verb "to submit" (see the notes on v. 22), but also by the call for such submission to be reverent (*en phobō*; literally "in fear"). Such an expression clearly reflects the OT notion of fear of God (e.g., Ps 36:2; cf. Rom 3:18), but some ancient philosophers taught that a wife must fear her husband (e.g., Xenophon, *Concerning Household Management* 7.25; Pseudo-Aristotle, *Concerning Household Management* III.144.2; cf. 1 Pet 3:2) and this idea is also found in 5:33. The call for mutual submission sets the tone for the teaching that follows, qualifying all calls for submission as rooted in reverence for Christ.

22. *Wives, be subject to your husbands as to the Lord:* After a transitional, introductory verse the household code proper begins. Similar codes are found elsewhere in the NT and early Christian literature (cf. Col 3:18–4:1; 1 Pet 2:18–3:7; 1 Tim 2:8-15; 3:4; 6:1-2; Titus 2:1-10; 3:1; Ign. *Pol.* 4:1–5:1; Pol. *Phil.* 4:2–6:1). In content these codes closely resemble traditional expositions of the topos "concerning household management" found in the teaching of various philosophers from Aristotle onward. The form of the codes is also heavily influenced by tradition. They are structured according to a predictable schema in which pairs (wives-husbands, children-parents, slaves-masters) are assigned reciprocal responsibilities. (For a full discussion of the origin and structure of the household codes see the notes on Col 3:18 and the interpretation of Col 3:18–4:1.) Typically the address ("wives") is followed by an imperative (here implied by the use of the verb in the previous verse). In fact, in many manuscripts the verb is missing and the verse is thus dependent on the participle found in the previous verse (see the notes on 5:21). However, some manuscripts have a form of the verb *hypotassō* (to be subject or subordinate to someone else; see the notes on v. 21) inserted after either "wives" or "husbands." The shorter reading adopted here is probably to be preferred since the longer versions are easily explained in light of an attempt to clarify the meaning of the verse (see Metzger 609). Although the language is not identical, the verse closely resembles Col 3:18. In both cases *hypotassō* is used of the relationship between husbands and wives, as is also the case elsewhere in the NT (cf. Titus 2:5; 1 Pet 3:1). Outside the NT the verb is used to describe a wife's submission to her husband in Plutarch, *Advice to the Bride and Groom* 33 (*Moralia* 142E) and in Pseudo-Callisthenes, *Historia Alexandri Magni* 1.22.4 (cited in Lincoln [1990] 367). The expression "as to the Lord" (i.e., wives should submit to their husbands as they do to Christ) constitutes a motivation or justification clause that is typical of household codes. This clause receives further expansion in vv. 23-24. On the similarities between v. 22 and v. 24 see the notes on v. 24.

23. *for the husband is the head of the wife as also Christ is the head of the church:* Picking up on v. 22b, this verse provides a theological justification for the call for wives to submit to their husbands. The link between the two verses is made clear by the use of *hoti* (for). A central aspect of this justification is the analogy between Christ-church and husband-wife. Introduced at this point, the analogy is also of key importance in subsequent verses. It draws its origins from

the use of marriage as a metaphor for God's relationship with Israel through-out the book of Hosea and elsewhere in the Hebrew Bible (e.g., Ezek 16:8-14). The notion of Christ as head of the church-body has already been introduced in the epistle (cf. 1:22-23; 4:15-16). Here it is employed in conjunction with the idea, reminiscent of Paul's justification for the attire of women in the assembly in 1 Cor 11:2-16, that the husband is the head *(kephalē)* of his wife. The word *ekklēsia* (church) occurs six times in 5:22-33; there are nine occurrences of the word in Ephesians as a whole (see Best [1998] 534).

himself savior of the body: This is the only place in the NT where Christ is de-scribed as the savior *(sōtēr)* of the body, but Paul uses the title "savior" for Christ in Phil 3:20. The uniqueness of the expression "savior of the body" has been understood by some commentators as an indication that the author of Ephesians knew of an early version of a Gnostic redeemer myth in which the preexistent Sophia falls and is saved through union with a redeemer in a heavenly syzygy (e.g., Schlier [1957] 266–76; Fisher 186–94). Such ideas can been seen, for example, in the *Exegesis on the Soul:* "For they were originally joined to one another when they were with the Father before the woman led astray the man, who is her brother. This marriage has brought them back to-gether again and the soul has been joined to her true love, her real master, as it is written, 'For the master of the woman is her husband'" *(Exeg. Soul.* 133. 4-10; cited in Perkins 133). But there are problems with the theory of a Gnostic background for Ephesians. Gnostic texts tend to cite material that also appears in Ephesians 5, but it is by no means clear that Ephesians 5 was itself influ-enced by earlier forms of Gnostic myths. These myths tend to present the church as a preexistent entity, and this idea plays very little part in Ephesians. The work contains only a very general conception of the participation of believers in God's preordained plan of salvation (see the notes on Eph 1:4). Moreover, Ephesians does not speak of the soul's reunion with a heavenly spouse, but focuses instead on the cross as the center of unity and restoration (cf. 2:1-10, 14; 5:2; for further discussion of problems with a Gnostic back-ground to Ephesians see Perkins 133 and Lincoln [1990] 362–71). Commenta-tors are divided as to whether this description of a "savior" in 5:23 applies only to Christ or whether it also applies, by analogy, to the husband. The syn-tax allows for the former interpretation (see Lincoln [1990] 370, who notes in particular the place and force of *autos* [himself]) and it is certainly less trouble-some in a modern context. However, given first-century Mediterranean values, it is difficult to imagine that listeners would have broken down the analogy at this point. Christ defines the very identity of the body. Christ protects the body and rescues it. These ideas resonate with the Mediterranean values of honor and shame. In daily interactions men become the defenders of honor; they protect the reputation of women who in turn must display appropriate "shame" (i.e., concern for their reputations; see also the notes on vv. 25-27 and the interpretation below). For the use of the concept of salvation within dis-cussions of marriage see 1 Cor 7:16 and Tob 6:18.

24. *But as the church is subject to Christ, so also the wives ought to be to the husbands in everything:* The development of the theological justification for v. 22 continues

with this verse. It is in fact the mirror image of the previous verse. The result is the A-B-B-A pattern that is very common in the NT (marriage—relationship between Christ and the church—relationship between Christ and the church—marriage). *Hypotassō* (to be subject) occurs for the second time in this section. Here the church's relationship with Christ acts as the model for the wife's subordination. The nature of that relationship has already been extensively discussed. Among other things this is a church that relies on Christ for its growth (4:15-16) and imitates Christ's love (5:2). What this means in practical terms for the husbands' treatment of their wives is spelled out in vv. 25-33. But the call for submission of wives to husbands "in everything" (inspired by the notion of the obedience believers owe to Christ) is a very strong plea reinforcing the patriarchal authority of the husband. The traditional structures of the household are reinforced even though the nature of the relationship between husband and wife is understood as transformed by love (see the notes and interpretation below).

25. *Husbands, love your wives, just as Christ loved the church and gave himself up on behalf of her:* As is typical of household codes, the coordinate responsibilities of the husband are spelled out here. The opening exhortation follows Col 3:18 exactly, but the call not to be embittered against wives in Col 3:19 is replaced by a much longer motivating clause having to do with the nature of Christ's love for the church. Love is a central theme in Ephesians (e.g., 1:4; 3:17) and the reference to Christ's love builds naturally on the ideas introduced in the previous verse. In particular, 4:25 recalls the description of Christ's giving of himself and sacrifice that are presented as the model for believers' love in 5:2 (cf. Gal 2:20). This verse offers perhaps the strongest indication of the transformation of the marriage relationship that occurs in Christ. Where one would have expected emphasis on the role of the husband as "ruler" of his wife, the emphasis lies on the "paradigmatic love relationship of Christ to the church" (see Schüssler Fiorenza 374).

26. *in order that he might sanctify her, cleansing her by the washing of the water by the word:* The first of three *hina* (in order that) clauses occurs here, spelling out the purpose of Christ's love for the church (see also the notes on v. 25). The role of the husband in relation to his wife is seen as analogous to the role of Christ who sanctifies (*hagiazō*; makes holy) the church. We can sense the general influence of OT notions of sanctification: setting a holy people apart. Believers are frequently described as saints or holy ones *(hagioi)* in Ephesians (e.g., 1:1, 4; 2:19; 5:3). The preparation of a Jewish woman for marriage by washing with water (Ezek 16:9; cf. Ezek 16:8-14) is juxtaposed with the ritual of baptism (cf. 1 Cor 6:11; Titus 3:5; Heb 10:22). In all likelihood the expression "with the word" refers to the name of Christ spoken in the midst of baptism (e.g., Acts 2:38; Jas 2:7), but it is also possible that the expression is more loosely connected to the notion of cleansing and means simply the gospel message (cf. 6:17; see Lincoln [1990] 376). The analogy draws strongly on the cultural values of honor and shame (see the notes on v. 27 and the interpretation below).

27. *in order that he might present the church to himself in splendor, without spot or wrinkle or any such thing, that she might be holy and without blemish:* Notions of

cleansing and sanctifying are developed further in this verse. There are two *hina* (in order that, that) clauses spelling out the purpose of Christ's love for the church (as in v. 26; see the notes above). The opening of the verse recalls the language of 2 Cor 11:2, where Paul envisions the Corinthian congregation as a bride: "I feel a divine jealousy for you, for I promised you in marriage to one husband, to present you as a chaste virgin to Christ" (NRSV). The picture of a bride being presented in splendor recalls the notion of the beautiful bride of Ezek 16:10-14 (see the notes on v. 26). This verse offers an especially good example of how the teaching on marriage in Ephesians 5 reveals the influence of the Mediterranean values of honor and shame. The active role of Christ (and of Paul in 2 Cor 11:2) and the passive position of the woman-church are in keeping with the role of the Mediterranean male as protector of the honor of women. The chastity of women is understood as a resource that must be carefully protected. Anthropologists have noted the tendency in Mediterranean societies for social groups (e.g., households, villages) to be viewed as symbolically female. Just as the purity of the woman must be guarded, so too must boundaries of the community be protected. The idea of a woman-church reflects such values (see the interpretation below). The notion of a woman-church as a pure creation—holy and without blemish—also recalls the ethical exhortations of 4:17–5:20 that reject any impurity and call believers "to put on the new person created according to God in righteousness and true holiness" (4:24).

28. *In the same way, husbands ought to love their wives as their own bodies. He who loves his wife loves himself:* In vv. 26-27 the focus is mainly on the relationship between Christ and the church, with marriage being used as a metaphor for explaining the nature of this divine union. Attention turns back to the marriage relationship here with the relationship between Christ and the church as the model to emulate ("in the same way"). The first part of the verse essentially repeats v. 25a, but the reference to husbands loving their wives as their own bodies builds on the notion of Christ as the savior of the body-church in v. 23 (see the notes). The author's frequent allusions to Hebrew Scripture continue in this verse. The commandment to love one's neighbor as oneself in Lev 19:18 underlies the exhortations in 5:28-30. Love was introduced in v. 25, but with this verse the author amplifies its centrality for the life of the couple. Notions of the concord of the married couple were common in ancient literature. In a manner that resembles the ideas in Ephesians 5 to a certain extent, the second-century author Plutarch states that a husband should not rule his wife the way a master rules his property, but the way the soul rules the body (Plutarch, *Praec. Conj.* 142; for other points of contact between Plutarch and Ephesians see the interpretation below). Although Ephesians resembles Plutarch in the sense that it presents the treatment of the wife in terms of caring for what is intimately one own—one's very body—Ephesians does not share Plutarch's interest in the soul-body distinction.

29. *for no one ever hated his own flesh, but nourishes and cherishes it, as also Christ does the church:* Read in conjunction with v. 28, this verse anticipates the quotation of Gen 2:24 in v. 31: "and the two will become one flesh." What it means for

the husband to love himself and, by implication, his wife is explained. The verse has to do with adopting a proper attitude to the physical body (*sarx* [flesh] is the equivalent of *sōma* [body] here; cf. 1 Cor 6:16). Any ascetic extremism—a serious problem in Colossians (see the notes and interpretation on Col 2:6-23)—is ruled out. It should be noted that in some early Christian texts the marriage metaphor could be employed to justify sexual asceticism (see the discussion in Fox 370–74). This appears to be the case, for example, with the second-century text called *2 Clement*, which is dependent on Ephesians: "if any of us guard her [the Church] in the flesh without corruption, he shall receive her back again in the Holy Spirit" (*2 Clem.* 14:3; cf. 14:1–15:1; on asceticism in *2 Clement* see Dennis R. MacDonald 42–43). In Ephesians 5 marriage clearly involves physical union and the perspective of Ephesians is at some distance even from the preference for celibacy expressed by Paul in 1 Corinthians 7. The perspective of Ephesians in fact resembles the proclamation made in Heb 13:4: "Let marriage be held in honor by all, and let the marriage bed be kept undefiled; for God will judge the fornicators and adulterers" (NRSV). The author of Ephesians expresses these ideas with language and values that would have been very familiar to a first-century audience. "Nourish" and "cherish" are concepts that have turned up together in an ancient marriage contract (see Gnilka 264). The concept of nourishing is also used with respect to children in 6:4.

30. *because we are members of his body:* This explains why Christ loves the church. The notion of the church as the body of Christ is central in Ephesians and in this section has already figured prominently in v. 23 and v. 29. The introduction of the first person plural, "we are," is striking. It draws the recipients of the letter specifically into the argument. The ethical exhortations concerning marriage have a direct bearing on the Ephesians as they participate in this church—this sacred body—that is nourished and cherished by Christ. The reading adopted here is strongly supported ($\mathfrak{P}^{46}$ $\aleph$* A B 33 81 1739* cop^{sa,bo}). However, there is also considerable evidence for longer readings, especially "of his flesh and of his bones." These readings seem, however, to have been formulated in light of Gen 2:23 (Gen 2:24 is cited in the next verse; see Metzger 609; Lincoln [1990] 351).

31. *"For this reason a man shall leave his father and his mother and be joined to his wife, and the two will become one flesh":* This is a quotation from Gen 2:24. The purpose of the quotation appears to be threefold. Most obviously it explains the origin of the union of man and woman in marriage and establishes that this union is from God but, as the following verse makes clear, the quotation is also being employed to shed light on the mysterious relationship between Christ and the church. Moreover, the quotation from Genesis—one of the few direct quotations from Scripture in the epistle—also serves to place marriage (both human marriage and the divine-human union) unquestionably within God's plan of salvation for the universe. (For a full discussion of the significance of the passage from Genesis see Sampley 51–61, 110–14, 146.) Verses 28-29 anticipate the reference to Genesis by introducing the concept of "flesh" (see the notes). However, it has been argued that the passage actually informs

the whole of the teaching on marriage in Ephesians, including the proactive and protective role of the husband and the reactive role of the wife (see Tanzer 339; cf. Gen 2:18-25).

32. *This is a great mystery, but I am speaking about Christ and the church:* There is some uncertainty as to what exactly constitutes the mystery here. Does it refer to marriage between man and woman, only to Christ and the church, or to both? The apparent lack of clarity may be due to the close association between the two in the author's own mind. Given the use of the marriage metaphor throughout 5:22-33, it seems best to assume that the term "mystery" encompasses both human marriage (seen as a reflection of divine reality) and the relationship between Christ and the church. The term "mystery" *(mystērion)* is central in Ephesians and is strongly associated with the revelation of the will of God (1:9; 3:3; 4:9; 6:19; see the full discussion in the notes on 1:9). Two characteristic features of the use of the term "mystery" in Ephesians are evident here. First, the content of the mystery in Ephesians tends to be defined fairly precisely. Although the exact shape of the mystery in this verse is not completely evident to us it is clear that the author had something specific in mind. Second, "mystery" is closely associated with the identity of the church. For example, in 3:6 the mystery of Christ is defined as the unification of Gentiles with Jews; the Gentiles have now become joint sharers of the promise in Christ Jesus through the gospel.

There is clearly also a special connection between 3:6 and 5:32 in that both link mystery to unity, another key theme in Ephesians. The construction *egō de legō* (but I am speaking) is emphatic, and some commentators have argued that the author of Ephesians may be countering certain interpretations of Gen 2:24 that were current in early Christian circles. Some Gnostic texts present the division of Adam and Eve in Gen 2:22-23 as the source of death and suffering and offer salvation as reunification and a return to androgynous perfection (see Pagels). In some circles reunification may have been acted out in a bridal chamber ritual involving sexual intercourse, but in other circles similar imagery was used to justify the renunciation of sexual relations. Some texts echo Ephesians by speaking in terms of "mystery" (e.g., *Gos. Phil.* 64; 70; 82). The *Gospel of Thomas* records a saying attributed to Jesus in which he speaks of making the two one and making the male and female one, so that there is no longer any male and female (see *Gos. Thom.* 22; see also the notes and interpretation on Col 3:5-17). Although these documents come from the second or third century, recent research has demonstrated the probability that androgynous interpretations of Genesis were current in Paul's day (see Dennis R. MacDonald).

33. *In any case, each one of you should love his wife as himself and the wife should fear her husband:* The conjunction *plēn* can have an adversative sense (but). However, it can also be used to round off a discussion (at any rate, in any case), and this rendering seems best, given the content here. The term is used to alert the reader that a summary of what has come before is beginning. The exhortation to the husbands essentially repeats what is found in v. 25 and v. 28; like v. 28 we have an allusion to Lev 19:18. The exhortation to wives repeats the instructions

of 5:22 even though different terminology is used. Here wives are instructed to "fear" *(phobeō)* their husbands, evoking the call to be reverent *(en phobǭ;* literally "in fear") to Christ in 5:21 (hence the REB translates 5:33 as "the wife must show reverence for her husband"). Many commentators prefer "respect" to "fear" as a translation for 5:33. In our modern context one can certainly respect someone without being subordinate to that person, but there is no question that the subjection of wife to husband is in view in this verse. (On the concept of wives fearing their husbands in ancient literature see the notes on v. 21.) Ephesians 5:22-33 includes much theological reflection, but this verse, with its clear connection to v. 22, reminds us that the most important purpose of the exhortation is to describe the shape of marriages between believers. Such marriages must include the loving treatment of wives by their husbands but clearly also involve the subordination of wives to their husbands.

6:1. *Children, obey your parents in the Lord:* From the consideration of marriage in 5:22-33 the household code moves on to treat the second pair of relationships, children and parents. The exhortation concerning this pair is much briefer than the previous treatment of marriage. It is interesting to note that the children are addressed directly; the expectation is that they will be part of the audience when the letter is read aloud. As in Col 3:20, children are instructed to obey *(hypakouō).* Although sometimes commentators have tried to distinguish the meaning of this verb from *hypotassomai* (be subject), used with respect to wives in 5:22, in actual fact the two verbs can be used interchangeably in the NT (cf. 1 Pet 3:5-6). The imperative is amplified by a further expression, as is frequently the case with household codes. However, it is by no means certain that "in the Lord" *(en kyriǭ)* was part of the original text. The phrase is absent from several early witnesses (B D* G it[dg] Marcion Clement Tertullian Cyprian Ambrosiaster; see Metzger 609). Some have felt that the expression may have been added to harmonize the verse with 5:22, but then it is difficult to understand why *hōs tǭ kyriǭ* would not have been used as in 5:22. It has also been suggested that "in the Lord" may have been added on account of an attempt to harmonize the verse with Col 3:20, but in Colossians the expression occurs at the end of the theological justification ("for this is pleasing in the Lord") and one would, therefore, have expected it to be added to the end of this verse as well. These problems, coupled with the fairly strong support for the longer reading, suggest that the longer reading should be preferred (see Metzger 609; Lincoln [1990] 395).

Obedience in the Lord means that the obedience of children to their parents takes on new meaning: it manifests the nature of the commitment to the Lord and to life in the Lord. The obedience of children is central to both Jewish (e.g., Philo, *Spec. Leg.* 2:225-36; see also the notes on 6:2) and Greco-Roman ethical teaching (e.g., Dionysius of Halicarnassus, *Rom. Ant.* 2.2.26.1-4; for further citations and a full discussion of the evidence see Lincoln [1990] 400–401). Paul identifies being rebellious toward parents as one of the sins of the Gentiles in Rom 1:29-31.

for this is right: "For this is right" (literally "this is righteous" *[dikaion]*) constitutes an appeal to tradition: this is the way that God has ordained and that has been acknowledged as correct down through the ages. It provides the justification or motivation for the call to obedience. In this way it resembles "for this is pleasing in the Lord" in Col 3:20 (cf. 5:10). It should be noted that 5:9 lists righteousness *(dikaiosynē)* as one of the fruits of the light: one of the ethical markers that set believers apart from nonbelievers in the world.

2. *"Honor your father and your mother," which is the first commandment with a promise,* 3. *"in order that it may be well with you and that you may live long on the earth"*: This citation of the fourth commandment (Exod 20:12; cf. Deut 5:16) expresses the call to obedience in a different form. The citation is divided into two parts, apparently to lay emphasis on the theological motivation: the promise. The nature of the promise is spelled out in v. 3. Exodus 20:12 actually has "in the land that the Lord your God is giving you," but this is replaced by "on the earth," making the citation universally applicable and not tied exclusively to a promised land. What has puzzled commentators most about this verse is why the fourth commandment is here called the first "with a promise." An earlier commandment (forbidding the making of graven images) speaks of a jealous God who punishes disobedience but promises rich rewards to the obedient (cf. Exod 20:4-6). It seems reasonable to surmise that this commandment is the first that contains a promise. However, it has been argued that it does not in fact include a promise, but rather a promise forms part of the explanation of God as a jealous God. According to this line of reasoning the fourth commandment would actually be the first "with a promise" (Mitton [1976] 212). Commentators have been struck by the references to well-being and long life in this verse, and have argued that they indicate deutero-Pauline authorship; the citation seems incompatible with the sense of imminent expectation of the *parousia* that permeates the undisputed letters of Paul, but since the author of Ephesians is citing traditional material here it is probably imprudent to draw conclusions about a dwindling of imminent expectation based on this verse.

4. *And fathers, do not provoke your children to anger, but bring them up in the discipline and admonition of the Lord:* As in Col 3:21, in contrast to the reference to parents in the previous verses we have a reference to the father alone. But since the exhortation is designed to warn fathers against being too harsh, the specific reference to fathers is quite appropriate; it reflects the extreme authority given to fathers over their children in Greco-Roman society (see the full discussion in the notes on Col 3:21). Warnings against excessive severity in dealing with children can be found in ancient literature (e.g., Pseudo-Plutarch, The *Education of Children* 8F; *Pseudo-Phocylides* 207; cited in Perkins 138). The instruction not to provoke children to wrath *(parorgizō)* recalls the similar exhortation in Col 3:21, "do not provoke your children" *(erethizō)*, though different terms are used. A cognate noun of the verb used in 6:4 is found in 4:26: "do not let the sun set on your anger *(parorgismos)*." The verb *ektrephō* (to bring up) also occurs in 5:29 where it is best translated as "to nourish" and refers to the treatment of wives by their husbands. The Greek term *paideia* means discipline or training. It can refer specifically to the upbringing of a child or to the instruction or orientation of an adult. Second Timothy 3:16 names "training in righteousness" as one of the purposes of Scripture. In Heb 12:8 the discipline of

children is used as a model for the way God deals with believers. *Nouthesia* refers to admonition, teaching, or correction that can be verbal (Titus 3:10) or written (1 Cor 10:11). The expression "in the discipline and admonition of the Lord" offers a very good example of a typical feature of household codes: traditional values and ideals are interpreted in light of the experience of being in the Lord. Some have understood "of the Lord" as a subjective genitive, implying that this is the discipline that the Lord himself imparts (via the fathers), but others understand it to be a genitive of quality, in which case the expression would mean Christian instruction in general—the training and teaching that involves emulating the Lord and hearing his words. On the important role of the household setting for teaching in early Christianity see the interpretation below.

5. *Slaves, obey your masters according to the flesh, with fear and trembling, with simplicity of heart, as to Christ:* Instructions concerning the third pair of relationships in the household code (slaves and masters) begin here. The length of the exhortation is approximately the same as that directed to children and parents and both make use of the verb "obey" *(hypakouō).* There are many similarities with the teaching concerning slaves in Col 3:22–4:1, by far the longest section of the Colossian household code. The expression "masters according to the flesh" also occurs in Col 3:22 and probably means earthly masters (see the full discussion in the notes on Col 3:22). Because the word for "master" and "lord" is the same in Greek *(kyrios),* the author of Colossians is able to link the notion of serving an earthly lord with serving a heavenly Lord. This is less in evidence in Ephesians (though it does come into play in vv. 7-9). Yet the reference to fear does link earthly masters with the Lord. Fear has been identified earlier as an appropriate demeanor for wives to adopt in relation to their husbands (5:33), and the same Greek term *(phobos)* occurs in 5:21 concerning reverence toward Christ. Similarly, Col 3:22 states that slaves should fear the Lord. "Fear and trembling" is found three times in the undisputed letters of Paul (1 Cor 2:3; 2 Cor 7:15; Phil 2:12). The expression "with simplicity of heart" is also found in Col 3:22, where it refers to the kind of single-mindedness involved in total commitment (see the notes on Col 3:22 for a full discussion of the expression). "As to Christ" offers the motivation and justification for the instruction to slaves. In their relationship to their masters, slaves are to emulate their obedience to Christ.

6. *not with eyeservice as people-pleasers, but as slaves of Christ, doing the will of God with all your heart:* The first clause is identical to that in Col 3:22. In ancient literature *ophthalmodoulia* (eyeservice) is found only here and in Col 3:22. It refers to service conducted only when the master is watching, or perhaps service designed especially to catch the master's attention (see the notes on Col 3:22). The term "people-pleasers" *(anthrōpareskoi)* appears in the NT only here and in Col 3:22, and refers to those who curry favor (see the notes on Col 3:22). The implicit contrast is between slaves of human masters (those who are only people-pleasers) and slaves of Christ. The expression "slaves of Christ" essentially restates the command found at the end of the previous verse for slaves to emulate their relationship with Christ in obeying their earthly masters.

These slaves will then be carrying out God's will. "With all your heart" might be translated literally as "from the soul" (*ek psychēs*). A literal translation into English, however, might lead to the mistaken conclusion that the soul is the essence of the human person confined within the body; the soul here is not some disembodied spirit. Rather the soul is understood in the biblical sense as the inner source of a person's thinking and doing; the expression is meant to convey total commitment (on the soul see the notes on Col 3:23). The expression is the functional equivalent of simplicity of heart in v. 5. (For a similar association of heart with soul see Deut 6:5.) The need for the full commitment of slaves could not be expressed in stronger terms than in vv. 5-6.

7. *serving as slaves with enthusiasm, as for the Lord and not for human beings:* This verse picks up many of the ideas of the previous verse and is very similar to Col 3:23. The reference to enthusiasm might be translated literally as "with goodwill" (*met' eunoias*) and it is a typical virtue of slaves that emerges in ancient literature. The call for enthusiasm is very close in meaning to the reference to service "with all your heart" in v. 6 and "with simplicity of heart" in v. 5. The verb *doulouō* (to serve as a slave) recalls the notion of being slaves of Christ in the previous verse. This verb is employed figuratively in Paul's letters to stress the true nature of the believers' loyalty (e.g., Rom 7:6 NRSV: "But now we are discharged from the law, dead to that which held us captive, so that we are slaves [*doulouō*] not under the old written code but in the new life of the Spirit"). The identical expression "as for the Lord and not for human beings" is found in Col 3:23. In the context of Ephesians the expression develops the notion of slaves of Christ (v. 6) one step further. This is the first time in this section that the word "Lord" is used for Christ in the exhortations to slaves. The point is that believers serve the true Lord in serving their earthly lords. Their service is ultimately for the Lord and not for human beings. The literal translation "human beings" for *anthrōpoi* captures the universal intent. In Greek there is a verbal connection between "people-pleasers" in v. 6 and "human beings" in v. 7.

8. *knowing that each person will be paid back from the Lord for whatever good is done, whether he is a slave or free:* Verses 8-9 largely summarize the content of Col 3:24–4:1. Colossians 3:24 promises slaves that they will receive the reward of "inheritance," a metaphorical way of speaking of salvation that draws upon the notion of believers' adoption as children of God. It is a concept that occurs frequently in Ephesians (e.g., 1:14, 18; 5:5), but it is not made explicit here. Nevertheless, we do find a connection being drawn between service as a slave and the promise of salvation. The focus is on complete salvation, including the benefits of divine judgment at the end. Colossians 3:25 has "for the wrongdoer will be paid back for what was done wrong." In Colossians the emphasis is on punishment for disobedience, whereas in Ephesians it is placed more directly on the reward for obedience, yet the main point is the same: receiving fitting payment for one's behavior. The verb *komizō* means to get back, to be requited for, or to be paid back (see the notes on Col 3:25). The final clause has the effect of rendering the status of those who are slaves and those who are free ultimately equal before God (cf. Gal 3:28; 1 Cor 12:13). This prepares the way for

the next verse and, in particular, for the proclamation in v. 9 that "there is no partiality."

9. *And masters, do the same thing to them, stopping the threatening:* As was previously the case with respect to their role as husbands, householders are being reminded of their fundamental obligations and invited to mirror the behavior of the Lord in their treatment of their slaves. This might well involve paying slaves back for whatever good they do. The command to "stop the threatening" (the participle has the force of an imperative here) is similar to the plea found in Col 4:1 to treat their slaves justly and fairly (on calls for the just treatment of slaves in antiquity see the notes on Col 4:1; on avoiding anger and rage when dealing with slaves see Seneca, *Ira.* 3.24.2; 3.32.1; see Wiedemann 179–80). Masters are to develop a positive relationship with slaves, apparently based more on rewarding good behavior than on punishing or frightening with threats.

knowing that both they and you have a master in heaven and with him there is no partiality: These clauses contain the motivation for treating slaves well. The author takes full advantage of the double meaning of *kyrios* ("lord" and "master") to link the role of the Lord and the role of the earthly master. Therefore it is best in this case to translate the reference to the Lord as "master in heaven." The clause "there is no partiality" is also found in Col 3:25, where its purpose is primarily to motivate slaves by warning them of the dangers of doing wrong and encouraging them with the promise of God's justice (see the notes on Col 3:25). Here it refers more directly to the equal status of slaves and masters before God (see the notes on Eph 6:8). With God's judgment there is no favoritism. On the term "partiality" *(prosōpolēmpsia)* see the notes on Col 3:25.

INTERPRETATION

The origin and function of the NT household codes is discussed extensively in the notes and interpretation on Col 3:18–4:1 (see also the detailed treatment of slavery in early Christianity). Readers should consult this earlier section in conjunction with the interpretation of Eph 5:21–6:9 offered below. Here I will concentrate on what is distinctive to Ephesians in household teaching.

What sets Ephesians most obviously apart from other NT household codes is the great attention given to marriage and the use of marriage as a metaphor for the relationship between Christ and the church (5:22-33). The implications of this long exhortation will be discussed in detail below, but it is important to begin our discussion with some less obvious but potentially very important distinctions between the Colossian and Ephesian household codes.

The Colossian household code is inserted rather abruptly within that epistle; there is no effort made to integrate the traditional material within the larger work. This is clearly not the case with Ephesians. Ephesians 5:21

is a transitional verse that is intended to link the household teaching with the ethical teaching concerning walking in the world in a manner distinct from the Gentiles that begins in 4:17 and is resumed in 6:10 (see the notes on 5:21 and 6:10). This has important implications for the purpose of the household code in Ephesians. Despite its obvious points of contact with the ethical teachings of Jews and Gentiles in the Greco-Roman world the code is clearly understood by the author as a central means of setting believers apart from those around them (see further below). Moreover, at several junctures in the code the author highlights themes that have been prominent earlier in the epistle such as unity, love, the meaning of baptism, the body of Christ, and the identity of believers as the holy ones set apart from all impurity (see the notes).

The literary antecedents to the NT household codes connect household teaching to the welfare of the state, and they tend to present the household as a microcosm of the state (see the interpretation of Col 3:18–4:1). It is not terribly surprising, therefore, that in the NT as well household ethics are sometimes linked to commands to respect government authorities (e.g., 1 Pet 2:13-14; cf. 1 Tim 2:1-7; Titus 3:1-11). Ephesians does not speak of government authorities, but it demonstrates points of contact with ancient texts that draw connections between the household and the state. Household relations are understood as reflecting a wider social reality: the obedience of wife to husband is viewed as a reflection of the obedience of church to Christ. Thus the author of Ephesians is not only making a statement about the shape of Christian marriage but is also using the ethical exposition to make statements about the identity of the wider social group—the church—and about the relationship between this group and the social order in general.

Often the appearance of the household codes in the NT has been explained in terms of a need for apology. As early church groups came to be increasingly visible and viewed with suspicion there was a need to explain the nature of the groups to the outside world. As the theory goes, this need produced greater encouragement of traditional values and patterns of living within church circles. Whereas celibacy, which questions the social order, was clearly preferred by Paul in 1 Corinthians 7, in Ephesians 5 we find an unmistakable endorsement of marriage and the role of the *paterfamilias* as head of the household.

The apologetic theory has, however, been questioned with respect to Ephesians (e.g., Tanzer 330). Unlike other documents, in particular 1 Peter, there is no direct evidence that Ephesians was written under circumstances in which believers were called upon to explain their beliefs to outsiders. Moreover, in contrast to Col 4:5-6, the parallel text of Eph 5:15-16 shows no explicit interest in dialogue with outsiders. Ephesians directs its household code toward believers and seems especially concerned with encouraging internal cohesion via the marriage metaphor. However, to say "this ethic describes a well-ordered Christian household independent of the views or actions of outsiders" is probably to overstate the case (*pace* Perkins 140). When we examine the social consequences of the household code of Ephesians the perspective of outsiders is unavoidable.

The historian of antiquity Peter Brown has spoken eloquently about the social consequences of the household code in Ephesians. He argues that by presenting relations between husbands and wives as a reflection of the relationship between Christ and the church the author of Ephesians was providing "an image of unbreakable order that the pagan world could understand. In the church, as in the city, the concord of a married couple was made to bear the heavy weight of expressing the ideal harmony of a whole society" (Brown 57). Ephesians 5:22-33 calls believers to match or exceed the highest ethical ideals of the day. It is very difficult to tell whether the image of marriage contained in the text would have won the hearts of nonbelievers, but it is clear that the Ephesian household teaching would have allowed believers to become integrated within a Greco-Roman city. Since the text reveals very little about social setting any reconstruction of the circumstances underlying Ephesians must remain highly speculative; however, there are several indications that it was composed in light of a perceived threat (see especially the following discussion of 6:10-18). In comparison to other Pauline works Ephesians suggests greater introversion with respect to the outside world. Even its household teaching is presented as part of a plan for believers to set themselves apart from nonbelievers (4:17–5:20). It seems ironic, then, to find such clear correspondence between this teaching and traditional values and ethics. But, as is often forgotten, one of the means of encouraging greater introversion is to recommend a stance that renders believers invisible within a given social setting (see also the interpretation of Col 3:18–4:1). It may not be appropriate to call Eph 5:21–6:9 apologetic, but it is probable that the household code was part of a defensive strategy in dealing with the Gentile world.

The teaching on marriage in Eph 5:22-33 is very different from that in 1 Corinthians 7 where Paul's preference for celibacy—with its inevitable confrontation of the standards of the world—renders invisibility impossible. While sexual renunciation was by no means unknown in the ancient world, marriage was widely viewed as a civic duty for the majority of the population. Scholarly investigations of the use of Gen 2:24 in Eph 5:31 and the reference to a great mystery in 5:32 have noted important points of contact between Eph 5:22-33 and Gnostic and early church circles where sexual asceticism flourished (see the notes above). It has sometimes been argued that Ephesians responds to the devaluation of sexual relations within marriage. Such arguments must remain tentative, however. Although there is a general reference to opponents in 4:14 the author of Ephesians says nothing explicitly about those who reject marriage. Still, it is clear that living out marriage according to traditional patterns is understood as an indicator of the church's participation in the body of Christ. Moreover, given the importance of remembrances of baptism for the author of Ephesians, the conflation of the image of the pure bride with the symbols of baptismal purification—the washing of the water by the word—in Eph 5:26-27 needs to be considered carefully. The interplay between this association and the allusion to the Jewish practice of purifying the bride with water in preparation for marriage (Ezek 16:9) only reinforces the holiness of the union. There is little doubt that being clothed in the new self, created according to the likeness of God, means embracing a Christian marriage that includes physical union (Eph 4:24).

Given the preponderance of ascetic currents in early Christianity there is good reason to believe that the author of Ephesians was distancing the community from those currents, even if they were not an immediate threat. Elsewhere I have explained the emphasis on marriage in Ephesians in terms of the development of endogamy rules (for marriage within a group) in early Christian literature (see M. Y. MacDonald [1994] 107–15). Sociological analysis of religious sects has proven to be an invaluable tool in the study of early Christianity and has already served us well in our analysis of Colossians and Ephesians (see the notes and interpretation on 1:15-23; 2:1-10). Bryan Wilson's work on sects has stressed the fact that in order to draw the faithful apart sects require various means of insulation from the external world (e.g., rules governing personal deportment, interpersonal relationships, social involvement). Endogamy rules are one type of mechanism serving this purpose (Wilson [1967] 37). The shape of these rules varies from group to group. They may include, for example, an attempt to exercise control over a leader's choice of wife (Wilson [1967] 152–53). Members may describe their endogamy rules in terms of social protest against the practices of outsiders and/or as a testimony to the unity that exists within their own group (see Isechei 169–70). For the present study it is particularly interesting to note that easily identifiable rules of marriage and courtship can become the focus of public hostility (see Robertson 86).

Among the letters of Paul 1 Thess 4:4-5 stands out as an attempt to use marriage between believers as an indicator of behavior that sets believers apart from Gentiles: "that each one of you know how to take a wife for himself in holiness and honor, not with lustful passion, like the Gentiles who do not know God" (alternate translation of the Greek text presented in the notes to the NRSV; cf. 2 Cor 6:14–7:1). Nevertheless, 1 Cor 7:12-16 makes it clear that marriage between believers and nonbelievers exists within the church because sometimes only one partner has accepted the faith. However, while it cannot be determined with absolute certainty, it is probable that Paul's instructions in 1 Cor 7:39 are meant to encourage widows who choose remarriage to marry fellow believers (i.e., new marriages should only be in the Lord). Ephesians 5:22-33 reflects further on the significance of marriage between believers. The text sanctifies marriage between believers within a broader context explicitly concerned with distinguishing Christians from nonbelievers (4:17-24). By the time Ignatius, Bishop of Antioch, cites Eph 5:22-33 at the beginning of the second century C.E. marriage guidelines have become full-blown endogamy rules. Marriages must take place with the permission of the bishop (Ign. *Pol.* 5:1-2). Episcopal sanction serves to ensure that marriages take place within the boundaries of the church.

Within early Christianity marriage practices provide measures to encourage group cohesion; reflection about marriage can serve as a way of thinking about the place of the community in the broader social world. In exploring the relationship between marriage and communal identity it is useful to consider how Eph 5:22-33 reflects Mediterranean values of honor and shame (see the notes and interpretation on Col 1:3-8). In this text the church is presented as a "pure bride," reflecting deeply rooted values in the ancient Mediterranean world that associate a woman's purity and circumspect behavior with the preservation of the reputation of the household, and identifying the husband as the active defender of the honor of the household. But rather than seeing the obedient wife simply as a static image of a pure church, recent anthropological discussion of women and gender in modern Mediterranean societies has been exploring how women's bodies function symbolically in the maintenance of household and group boundaries and in the mediation between realms. One anthropologist working on rural Greece has called a woman's body "the symbol of family integrity and purity, and, more generally, of society as a whole" (Dubisch 208).

The use of the female body as a symbol for the church is a significant part of early Christian history; it expresses the drawing of boundaries between a sacred community and a world full of lust (Eph 5:26-27). How this symbolism was related to the actual lives of married early Christian women is more difficult to discern. We know that wives who entered the church without their partners acted as mediators between the realm of the church and the realm of the world. The hope was that wives would lead their husbands to the Lord by means of model behavior (cf. 1 Pet 3:1-6; 1 Cor 7:12-16), and the NT tells of faith spreading from women to their children (2 Tim 1:5). Moreover, given the household setting of early Christian group meetings, it is also important to keep in mind that women's lives and work played an integral part in ensuring that groups had the necessary infrastructure for survival.

There are aspects of the text that are widely recognized by modern Christians as having continuing validity: the transformative power of love, the importance of using one's relationship with the Lord as a means of discerning how to treat others, and the value assigned to marriage in general (sometimes forgotten in a church eager to encourage celibacy). In addition, the author of Ephesians clearly understands household relations as having been transformed in Christ (see the notes on 5:25). Moreover, anthropological studies remind us that it is erroneous to conclude that hierarchical authority structures such as those presented in Eph 5:21–6:9 (where the head of the household has authority over subordinate members) necessarily mean that subordinate members of the household were without influence. Nevertheless, it is important to acknowledge that the text presents a vision of household relationships, rooted in an ancient setting, that is considered unjust today (and, in the case of slavery, completely immoral).

Attempts by commentators to take the partriarchal sting out of Eph 5:22–6:9 have generally proved unconvincing (see, for example, Schnackenburg 246, and the response by Tanzer 334). The primary purpose of Eph 5:21–6:9 is to provide theological justification and motivation for the subordination of wives, children, and slaves to the head of the household. Feminist interpreters have drawn attention to the problematic use of marriage as a metaphor for the relationship between divinity and humanity that forms part of this theological justification. The problem stems from the fact that it is the husband who is understood as representing God or Christ while the wife is a symbol of the human community. When the metaphorical nature of the language is forgotten there is the potential for abuse: the text can seem to justify male impunity in the face of female fallibility. In my view Eph 5:21-33 can speak to a modern context only if the interpreter makes the potentially problematic nature of the text clear and makes every effort to understand its meaning in an early church context. It is only then that one might begin to discern the elements of the text that have a timeless value.

For Reference and Further Study

Balch, David L. "Household Codes," in David E. Aune, ed., *Greco-Roman Literature and the New Testament: Selected Forms and Genres*. SBS 21. Atlanta: Scholars, 1988, 25–50.

_____. "Neophythagorean Moralists and the New Testament Household Codes," *ANRW* II 26.1. Berlin: Walter deGruyter, 1992, 380–411.

Brown, Peter. *The Body and Society: Men, Women, and Sexual Renunciation in Early Christianity*. New York: Columbia University Press, 1988.

Dubisch, Jill. *Gender and Power in Rural Greece.* Princeton: Princeton University Press, 1986.

Isechei, Elizabeth. "Organisation and Power in the Society of Friends, 1852–59," in Bryan R. Wilson, ed., *Patterns of Sectarianism: Organisation and Ideology in Social and Religious Movements.* London: Heinemann, 1967, 182–210.

MacDonald, Dennis Ronald. *There is No Male and Female: the Fate of a Dominical Saying in Paul and Gnosticism.* Philadelphia: Fortress, 1987.

MacDonald, Margaret Y. "The Ideal of the Christian Couple: Ign. Pol. 5.1-2 Looking Back to Paul," *NTS* 40 (1994) 105–25.

Miletic, Stephen F. *"One Flesh": Eph 5.22-24, 5.31: Marriage and the New Creation.* AnBib 115. Rome: Pontifical Biblical Institute, 1988.

Pagels, Elaine. "Adam and Eve: Christ and the Church," in A.H.B. Logan and A.J.M. Wedderburn, eds., *The New Testament and Gnosis: Essays in Honour of Robert McL. Wilson.* Edinburgh: T&T Clark, 1983, 146–75.

Robertson, Roland. "The Salvation Army: The Persistence of Sectarianism," in Bryan R. Wilson, ed., *Patterns of Sectarianism* (1967) 49–105.

Sampley, J. Paul. *"And the Two Shall Become One Flesh": A Study of Traditions in Eph 5:21-33.* Cambridge: Cambridge University Press, 1971.

Schüssler Fiorenza, Elisabeth. *In Memory of Her: A Feminist Theological Reconstruction of Christian Origins.* New York: Crossroad, 1983.

Wiedemann, Thomas, ed. *Greek and Roman Slavery.* London: Croom Helm, 1981.

Wilson, Bryan R. *Patterns of Sectarianism: Organisation and Ideology in Social and Religious Movements.* London: Heinemann, 1967.

24. *Doing Battle with Evil* (6:10-20)

10. Finally, be empowered in the Lord and in his mighty strength. 11. Put on the whole armor of God in order that you may be able to stand against the craftiness of the devil. 12. For our battle is not against blood and flesh, but against the rulers, against the authorities, against the cosmic rulers of this darkness, against the spiritual forces of evil in the heavenly places. 13. Therefore take up the whole armor of God in order that you may be able to stand firm on the evil day, and having done everything, to stand. 14. Stand, therefore, having belted your waist with truth and having put on the breastplate of righteousness, 15. and having fitted your feet with the readiness of the gospel of peace, 16. with all of these, having taken up the shield of faith, with which you will be able to put out all the flaming arrows of the evil one. 17. And receive the helmet of salvation and the sword of the Spirit, which is the word of God, 18. through every prayer and petition, always praying in the Spirit, and to this end being watchful in all perseverance and petition concerning all the saints, 19. and for me, in order that speech may be given to me when I open my mouth, to make known with boldness the mystery of the gospel, 20. for

which I am an ambassador in chains, in order that I may speak of it boldly as it is necessary for me to speak.

NOTES

10. *Finally, be empowered in the Lord and in his mighty strength:* "Finally" *(tou loipou)* signals the conclusion of the ethical exhortations that began at 4:1 (BAGD 480). Some commentators prefer the alternate and more usual translation of *tou loipou* as "from now on, in the future" (e.g., Barth 759–60; cf. Gal 6:17), but the fact that the present and future are both in view suggests that the translation adopted here is more likely (see Schnackenburg 271, n. 1; Lincoln [1990] 441). The verse recalls Col 1:11 and brings the theme of divine power (cf. 1:19-21; 3:16, 20) back into the discussion. The apostle's wish for believers is expressed with terminology that is very similar to the description of the basis of Paul's ministry in 3:7: "I became a minister according to the gift of grace of God given to me according to the working of his power." For the expression "in the Lord" see also 2:21; 4:17; 5:8; 6:1, 21.

11. *Put on the whole armor of God in order that you may be able to stand against the craftiness of the devil:* Ephesians 4:24 speaks of putting on a new humanity. To "put on the whole armor of God" is another way of speaking about the transformation that believers must undergo. The Greek term for "the whole armor" *(panoplia)* is the one typically employed for the full armor of a foot soldier (e.g., Polybius 6.23; Thucydides 3.114). The mention of God's armor reflects OT ideas (e.g., Isa 11:5; 59:16-17). Paul drew upon such notions elsewhere in his letters even if he did not develop them with the detail of Ephesians (e.g., Rom 13:11-14; 1 Thess 5:1-11; 2 Cor 10:3-6). Moreover, the metaphorical use of battle language was quite common in the religious and philosophical thinking of the day. Cynic and Stoic philosophers, for example, could use battle imagery to describe the fortification of a wise man's soul in a manner similar to Paul's pronouncement in 2 Corinthians: "we do not wage war according to human standards; for the weapons of our warfare are not merely human, but they have divine power to destroy strongholds. We destroy arguments and every proud obstacle raised up against the knowledge of God, and we take every thought captive to obey Christ" (2 Cor 10:3-5 NRSV; see Seneca, *Const. Sap.* 6.8. For battle imagery in the QL see especially 1QM; 1QH 3:24-39; 6:28-35). The notion of standing against a perceived threat also occurs in vv. 13 and 14. The metaphorical use of battle imagery is not surprising in the Roman world, given the fact that military might was strongly evident. Certainly first-century recipients of Ephesians would have envisioned the might of a Roman soldier even if their struggle were against a cosmic and not a purely human enemy. Given the frequent stress on the present triumph of believers in Ephesians (e.g., 2:6) it is striking here that believers are unmistakably told they must prepare for the future. It should be noted, however, that the picture presented is of a soldier waiting attentively, not of a soldier provoking aggression. This is the second reference to the devil in the epistle

("Satan" is the usual term in the undisputed letters of Paul). The devil is mentioned in 4:27 and there is a probable reference to the devil in 2:2, which speaks of "the ruler of the power of the air" (see the notes). As in 4:27, the devil is presented as wily, seeking out opportunities to trap believers. In 4:14 "craftiness" *(methodeia)* is attributed to the false teachers, illustrating the close connection in the author's mind between the earthly experience of evil and the workings of evil cosmic powers (see also the notes below).

12. *For our battle is not against blood and flesh, but against the rulers, against the authorities, against the cosmic rulers of this darkness, against the spiritual forces of evil in the heavenly places:* There is actually greater manuscript evidence for the alternate reading "your *(hymin)* battle." But because the natural tendency of scribes would have been to harmonize the verse with the use of the second person plural in the rest of the paragraph, "our *(hēmin)* battle" is the more difficult reading and should be preferred (see Metzger 610). Given that 6:10 marks the start of the conclusion of the ethical exhortations beginning at 4:1, it is somewhat ironic that the battle is described as "not against blood and flesh" (the terms are in the reverse order of what one would normally expect; see also Heb 2:14). Ephesians 4:17 calls for behavior that sets believers apart from nonbelievers and is very much concerned with human virtues and vices. But in this verse believers are told that their battle is really about nothing earthly at all. In fact, Eph 6:12 figured in Gnostic theories concerning the soul being trapped in a world created by the evil creator and his subordinate powers *(Hyp. Arch.* 86, 20–25; cited in Perkins 144). Comparison of the text to 1:21; 2:2; and 3:10, where similar terminology occurs, makes it clear that the members of the community are presented as doing battle with malevolent spiritual powers (see the notes on 1:21). It is impossible to distinguish precisely between these powers and, indeed, the author seems less interested in this than in labeling all of them as equally sinister. The point is that these spiritual powers are still capable of exerting influence in the world; they are the real cause of evil. They are far more terrifying than any earthly enemy, and believers must be prepared to defend themselves against them. That there is an implicit relationship between an evil earthly world and the evil forces that control it is made clear by the expression "the cosmic rulers of this darkness." "Darkness" has already been used twice before in the epistle to refer to the past existence of believers (5:8) and to describe the deeds of the Gentiles that must not be allowed to infiltrate the church (5:11). In essence "darkness" refers to the world dominated by evil; "the cosmic rulers of this darkness" describes the world under the grip of those cosmic powers.

The term "cosmic ruler" *(kosmokratōr)* occurs only here in Ephesians. It appears also in the magical papyri and in Mandean Gnosticism and draws its origins from astrological discussions where it refers to the role of the sun and planets in shaping earthly events (see Lincoln [1990] 444). In the magical papyri such gods as Sarapis and Hermes receive this designation, and the second century *Testament of Solomon* employs the term to refer to evil spirit powers (see Arnold [1989] 65–67; Lincoln [1990] 444). "Spiritual" *(pneumatikos)* has been used twice before in the epistle as an adjective in a positive sense (cf.

1:3 and 5:19). The neuter construction *ta pneumatika* here means literally "the spiritual things" (cf. Rom 15:27; 1 Cor 9:11), but because it is modified by "of evil" it is clear that evil spiritual powers are once again in view. On the expression "heavenly places"—unique to Ephesians—see the notes on 1:3 (cf. 1:20; 2:6; 3:10).

13. *Therefore take up the whole armor of God in order that you may be able to stand firm on the evil day, and having done everything, to stand:* "Therefore" *(dia touto)* indicates that the author is resuming what he has previously said; hence there is a good deal of repetition of the content of vv. 10-11 here. The military metaphor is highly developed. The verb used to describe the act of taking up the armor of God was commonly used for putting on one's armor before battle. The meaning of "the evil day" is not entirely clear. It could refer to a powerful encounter with evil that believers might experience in their everyday lives. It could also refer to a strong temptation they must guard against. Given the imagery of cosmic battle and the points of contact with Paul's letters it seems likely that the eschatological battle at the end of time is primarily in view here (e.g., 1 Thess 5:2-4; 1 Cor 7:26; 2 Thess 2:3-12) or perhaps even the last day— the day of the Lord. The future is clearly very important in this verse but the present is also crucial: as the similar expression in 5:16 makes clear, "the days are evil!" (see Taylor and Reumann 88). The phrase "having done everything" is somewhat vague. It suggests that all necessary preparations have been made: believers are fully armed with ethical virtue and empowered by God.

14. *Stand, therefore, having belted your waist with truth and having put on the breastplate of righteousness:* The verb "stand" also occurs in vv. 11 and 13. (Verse 13 also has "stand firm.") In this case it is repeated immediately after the previous use in v. 13. The image of an armed soldier introduced in v. 11 is developed further with a list of the specific parts of the armor. The description reflects OT traditions. For example, Isa 59:17 has "He put on righteousness like a breastplate" (NRSV; cf. Wis 5:18; 1 Thess 5:8). Similarly, in Isa 11:5 the messianic figure has a belt of righteousness and faithfulness. Like 4:24 and 6:14, this verse speaks of putting on *(endyō)* the signs of a new identity. The verse recalls the ideas found in 5:8-9. There believers are instructed to "walk as children of light, for the fruit of the light is in all goodness, and righteousness, and light." Truth is an especially important sign of the new identity of believers (cf. 4:25; 5:9). Ephesians also speaks of the truth of the gospel (cf. 1:13; 4:21, 24), but it is likely that "truth" in 6:14 is a virtue that believers must demonstrate.

15. *and having fitted your feet with the readiness of the gospel of peace:* The image here is of the proper footwear worn for battle: a leather sandal or short boot that sometimes included nails to act as cleats. Instead of such earthly shoes designed for the sure footing of the soldier believers are to be fitted with the readiness of the gospel of peace. *Hetoimasia* (readiness) suggests a state of preparation for combat. Once again there are scriptural echoes: "How beautiful upon the mountains are the feet of the messenger who announces peace, who brings good news, who announces salvation" (Isa 52:7 NRSV; cf. Rom 10:15). The LXX version of this passage has literally "preaches the gospel of peace"; thus "gospel" and "peace" are brought together just as in Ephesians.

Peace is a central theme in Ephesians (cf. 1:2; 2:14, 15, 17; 4:3; 6:23). "Gospel" occurs in 1:13 and 3:6. The identification of the soldier with Christ is suggested by the description in 2:14 of Christ as "our peace."

16. *with all of these, having taken up the shield of faith, with which you will be able to put out all the flaming arrows of the evil one:* Wisdom 5:19 speaks of holiness as an invisible shield and there are frequent references in the OT to God as a "shield" (e.g., Gen 15:1; Pss 5:12; 18:30; 28:7). This verse relies heavily on images from warfare in the ancient world. The *thyreos* was a long oblong shield designed to protect the whole body. Flaming arrows were commonly used in the ancient world in attacks on besieged cities; they could render shields useless, causing soldiers to flee in terror (Thucydides, *The Peloponnesian War* 2.75, 5; cited in Perkins 147). It is possible that the recipients of Ephesians associated the arrows with verbal attacks they had experienced at the hands of nonbelievers (cf. Prov 26:18). The QL speaks of the fiery words that the wicked speak against God as "arrows." In one particularly close parallel to Ephesians the righteous person's testimony to the truth about God leads to a barrage of attacks against him: "they loose off arrows without any cure; the tip of the spear, like fire which consumes trees" (1QH 10:23-26). Taken together with v. 15, which speaks of the gospel of peace, v. 16 may envision the message of Christ being spoken by believers and provoking assaults from the wicked (see Perkins 147). The evil one is the devil (cf. 2 Thess 3:3; the expression does not occur in the undisputed letters of Paul). But as Eph 2:2 (where the devil is described as the ruler of the power of the air) makes clear, the work of the devil is closely associated with the activities of wicked unbelievers in Ephesians: "in which you once walked according to the age of this world, according to the ruler of the power of the air, of the spirit who now works in the sons of disobedience."

17. *And receive the helmet of salvation and the sword of the Spirit, which is the word of God:* The Roman soldier received his helmet from an attendant, who usually placed the helmet on the soldier's head and handed him his sword (a short weapon used in close combat). After a series of participles in vv. 14-16, which describe effort on the part of the soldier, he is presented in v. 17 as a passive recipient of the final pieces of his equipment. There is a shift from the participles to the imperative of the verb *dechomai* (receive). Salvation and the word of God are what God gives and the believer receives (see Wild [1984] 297). The reference to the "helmet of salvation" is an echo of Isa 59:17 (cf. Wis 5:18; 1 Thess 5:8). "The sword of the Spirit" recalls the many previous references to the Spirit in Ephesians (1:13, 17; 2:2, 18, 22; 3:5, 16; 4:3, 4, 23, 30; 5:18; 6:18). The sword is further described as the word of God. The term for "word" here (*rēma*) refers to what is spoken (in contrast, 1:13 has *logos*). There is a metaphorical reference to using the spoken word of God as a means to attack the enemy (note that in Acts 6:13 *rēma* is used in the context of making threats against something).

18. *through every prayer and petition, always praying in the Spirit, and to this end being watchful in all perseverance and petition concerning all the saints:* Ephesians 6:18-20 is closely related to Col 4:2-4, where prayer is also recommended in con-

junction with being watchful. The close relationship between the battle imagery and the material on prayer is suggested by the use of *dia* (through). The
battle is spiritual. This verse illustrates vividly that the battle against evil that
believers face has nothing to do with engaging in violent acts. The stance is
rather one of passive resistance. Equipped with the virtues of God and having
received the benefits of salvation and the word of God, believers are to turn
their attention to prayer. Once again the Spirit figures prominently (see the
notes on 6:17). The reference to prayer in the Spirit recalls the reinforcement in
5:18-20 of the importance of worship in the community as well as the general
emphasis on prayer throughout the epistle (cf. 1:15-23; 3:14-21). Being watchful implies having an attitude of readiness as in v. 15. There is a general association of prayer with perseverance and watchfulness in the NT. Prayer that is
constant and watchful does not fail in the face of temptation (e.g., Mark 14:38;
Luke 21:36; 1 Pet 4:7). Watchfulness is understood to be an appropriate attitude as the end of all things draws near (1 Thess 5:6, 10; 1 Pet 4:7). "All the
saints" is a means of referring to all believers (see the notes on 1:1).

19. *and for me, in order that speech may be given to me when I open my mouth, to make
known with boldness the mystery of the gospel:* Very similar concepts, though expressed slightly differently, occur in Col 4:3: "at the same time pray also for us,
in order that God may open a door to us for the word, to speak of the mystery
of Christ for which I am in prison." The hope is that Paul will be able to preach
even when he is in captivity. On prison posing no hindrance for the word of
God see also Phil 1:12-14 and 2 Tim 2:9 (see the notes on Col 4:3). Ephesians
departs from Colossians, however, in expressing the prayer not only that Paul
be enabled to speak but also that his speech might be powerfully inspired
(that speech be given to me when I open my mouth; cf. Ps 78:2; Ezek 3:27;
33:22; Dan 10:16) and that he speak with boldness (*en parrēsią*; see also the
notes on 6:20). There is also mention of "boldness" in 3:12 in conjunction with
the nature of Paul's role. *Parrēsia* is a word that occurs frequently in ancient literature to describe the rights of citizens to speak freely, especially before
people of high rank. It refers to openness and can sometimes suggest a certain
fearlessness (see the notes on 3:12). Its use in Eph 6:19 in conjunction with
mystery (*mystērion*) indicates that Paul is the bold revealer of the mystery of
the gospel. A central theme in Ephesians, mystery (*mystērion*) is here closely
associated with notions of the mystery of God's will in 1:9, 10 and with the
church proclaiming the mystery in 3:10. Earlier in the epistle there were references to "the gospel of your salvation" (1:13) and "the gospel of peace" (6:15).

20. *for which I am an ambassador in chains, in order that I may speak of it boldly as it is
necessary for me to speak:* This verse reiterates the image in the previous verse of
the apostle who proclaims the gospel boldly. It picks up on Paul's claim that
he is an ambassador for Christ in 2 Cor 5:20; the notions of ambassador and
prisoner occur together in Phlm 9. Ambassadors were official representatives
of the emperor. Paul uses the term "ambassador" to stress that he is God's or
the gospel's official representative (cf. 3:7-8). There is tremendous irony in the
claim that Paul is an ambassador in chains. It is important to keep in mind the
wretched conditions of an ancient prison. Here an official who normally has

immunity in the face of the enemy is presented as in captivity and bound up like a criminal in chains. For "chains" as a means of expressing Paul's imprisonment see Acts 28:20 and 2 Tim 1:16. The same sense of duty or compulsion to speak is expressed in Col 4:4.

INTERPRETATION

Andrew Lincoln has offered an insightful interpretation of both the form and the function of Eph 6:10-20. He argues that this passage actually serves as the conclusion not only for the ethical exhortation that begins at 4:1 but also for the letter as a whole. Studied from the perspective of rhetorical analysis Ephesians may be understood as "a persuasive communication that would be read aloud to its recipients," and 6:10-20 constitutes the work's *peroratio:*

> In the *peroratio* (cf. Quintillian 6.1.1) an author not only sought to bring his address to an appropriate conclusion but also to do so in a way which would arouse the audience's emotions. According to Aristotle, (*Rhet.* 3.19) the *epilogos*—his equivalent term—had four parts: making the audience well-disposed toward the speaker and ill-disposed towards any opposition, magnifying or minimizing the leading facts, exciting the required kind of emotion in the hearers, and refreshing their memories by means of recapitulation. (Lincoln [1990] 432)

Lincoln notes that this particular *peroratio* has the form of a "call to battle" and has much in common with the speeches of generals before battle. In bringing together OT traditions with a well-known hortatory form the author of Ephesians crafts a very effective *peroratio:*

> It . . . dwells on the need for valor with its exhortations to be strong, prepared and alert, and to stand firm. It points out the dangers and strengths of the enemy. It braces its soldiers for successful outcome of the battle by reminding them of the superior strength, resources, and equipment they possess. It makes clear not only that they have God on their side but also that he has put his own full armor at their disposal. It gives them a model for triumph in an embattled situation by bringing to their consciousness the boldness and freedom of proclamation of the imprisoned apostle. (Lincoln [1990] 433–44)

As Lincoln's analysis suggests, the fact that Ephesians ends with this call to battle needs to be considered carefully as we try to understand the implications of Ephesians for the life of the community. In keeping with the typical features of the *peroratio* the concluding section of Ephesians seeks to encourage the community's disdain for the enemy. The author of Ephesians is certainly convinced that believers are menaced by outside forces (see the notes and interpretation on 1:15-23). That the evil powers are spiritual agencies and not human authorities is communicated especially strongly by 6:12, where the conflict is said to be not against blood and flesh but against spiritual powers. In the past the recipients of Ephesians may well have employed magical practices to deal with such menacing forces and were perhaps inclined to consider returning to them. For such people Eph 1:21-23 has already conveyed an important message: Christ's power transcends these spiritual forces and fills the universe (Arnold [1989] 56). With Eph 6:10 the focus is once again on the power of Christ strengthening believers, but as the culmination of the ethical teaching that begins at 4:1, Eph 6:10-20 offers practical suggestions for ensuring one's protection against the menacing forces. One is to be armed with virtues. The crowning touches of one's armor are the helmet of salvation and the sword of the Spirit—the sword that is the word of God (v. 17). One's stance should involve prayer and watchfulness (v. 18). One should remain open to experiences of the Spirit (vv. 17 and 18; see the interpretation of 1:15-23). Against such protection the evil one will be powerless.

While they do not refer to earthly enemies *per se*, it is important to recognize that the spiritual powers in Ephesians are understood as deeply affecting the society in which believers live. This is illustrated clearly by 2:1-3, where the outside world is depicted as dominated by the "ruler of the power of the air" (2:1; see the notes and interpretation on 2:1-10. Ephesians 6:16 speaks of the evil one; in both cases the devil is probably in view). This dominion causes great moral decay (2:3) and the only real defense against it is God's armor of ethical and spiritual virtues (6:14-17). In their daily lives believers struggle against the spiritual forces of evil in the heavenly places. Thus in Ephesians the present state of society is understood as the result of a cosmic struggle that is overcome for believers by means of a new life with Christ in the heavenly places (cf. 1:20; 2:6). What is experienced on the earthly plane has a cosmic referent. Furthermore, how one lives on the earthly plane finds its true significance in the heavenly places. Ephesians was in all likelihood composed in an atmosphere of great consciousness of evil and strong commitment to separation from outsiders. There is no evidence that believers are experiencing persecution from political powers, but there are suggestions that they are experiencing increasing hostility from nonbelievers as their forays into society at large become increasingly problematic (see the notes and interpretation on 1:2-14; 2:1-10). On the basis of 6:15-16, for example, it is likely that the message of Christ announced by believers has been provoking verbal assaults from the wicked (see the notes above).

Like Ephesians as a whole, 6:10-20 reflects tension between a victory already won against evil (cf. 2:6) and the continuing influence of menacing powers. The underlying assumption is that believers will undoubtedly ultimately triumph, yet the menacing powers are still capable of making their way into the lives of believers and of interfering with the progress of the gospel before they are defeated once and for all. In light of this ongoing threat it is especially important that the *peroratio* of 6:10-20 instill appropriate emotions in its audience. It must strengthen believers in the face of hostility, but it must also reassure them of their strong position and offer comfort in the face of possible suffering. The reassuring and comforting elements of the section become especially clear in 6:18-20 as the symbolism shifts from the believer as armed soldier to the image of the suffering apostle (see the similar combination of images in 2 Cor 10:1-10). Paul is an "ambassador in chains"; his true identity as God's representative is not thwarted by the inhuman conditions of an ancient prison.

Read from a sociological perspective Eph 6:10-20 might be understood as a strongly sectarian response, encouraging increasing distance and caution with respect to the outside world. The battle imagery draws sharp boundaries between believers and all enemies. According to the author there is no doubt that the Gentile, nonbelieving world is in the grip of evil spiritual powers that can still make inroads into the community (e.g., 4:17-24). When Ephesians is compared to the other works in the Pauline corpus, and to Colossians in particular, it becomes apparent that the pendulum has swung in the direction of greater introversion in a movement that nevertheless remains committed to universal salvation (see the notes and interpretation on 2:1-10). The prayer is that the apostle will be able to speak of the mystery of the gospel boldly and openly even from a prison setting. But in daily life believers are to have the demeanor of armed soldiers of God. They must be cautious and protect themselves. The message is one of endurance in the face of hostility.

FOR REFERENCE AND FURTHER STUDY

Arnold, Clinton E. *Ephesians, Power and Magic: The Concept of Power in Ephesians in the Light of Its Historical Setting.* MSSNTS 63. Cambridge: Cambridge University Press, 1989.

Wild, Robert A. "The Warrior and the Prisoner: Some Reflections on Ephesians 6:10-20," *CBQ* 46 (1984) 284–98.

25. *Conclusion: Personal Matters and Final Blessing* (6:21-24)

21. In order that you may know the news about me, what I am doing, Tychicus, the beloved brother and faithful minister in the Lord, will tell you all the news. 22. I have sent him to you for this very purpose, in order that you may know how we are and that he may encourage your

hearts. 23. Peace be to the brothers, and love with faith from God the Father and our Lord Jesus Christ. 24. Grace be to all those who love our Lord Jesus Christ in immortality.

NOTES

6:21. *In order that you may know the news about me, what I am doing, Tychicus, the beloved brother and faithful minister in the Lord, will tell you all the news:* There is a very close relationship between 6:21-22 and Col 4:7-9. Both speak of Tychicus with similar terminology. In contrast to Eph 6:21, however, Col 4:7 calls Tychicus not only a beloved brother and faithful minister but also a fellow slave in the Lord. "Beloved brother and faithful minister" is an example of the "language of belonging" that is typical of Pauline Christianity (see the notes and interpretation on Col 1:1-2). The term "minister" (*diakonos*, sometimes also translated "helper") should be understood as an important leadership designation but it does not refer to the office of deacon that the term later came to designate. Tychicus is the only individual mentioned in Ephesians other than Paul. The fact that Tychicus is mentioned only in the Acts of the Apostles (Acts 20:4) and in letters usually considered deutero-Pauline suggests that he may have become involved only in the final stages of Paul's ministry (cf. Col 4:7-8; 2 Tim 4:12; Titus 3:12). References to him in these works may be intended to legitimize his role as an authentic representative of the apostle (see the notes on Col 4:7). The mention of Tychicus has been understood as adding support to the theory that the letter was originally intended for Ephesus (see the notes on 1:1). In the Pastoral Epistles he is presented as the emissary to Ephesus and Crete (2 Tim 4:12; Titus 3:12; but see the notes on 6:23). "The news" (literally "the things") may refer to the conditions of Paul's imprisonment or to other personal details. This somewhat repetitive verse underlines the fact that the Ephesians are to know all about Paul (see also the notes on Col 4:9).

22. *I have sent him to you for this very purpose, in order that you might know how we are and that he may encourage your hearts:* No new sentence begins in the Greek, which reads literally "whom I have sent," but a new sentence is introduced into the English translation for the sake of clarity. This verse is identical to Col 4:8. The aorist tense of the verb *pempō* (to send) suggests that Tychicus is the bearer of the letter. This use of the epistolary aorist can also lead to the translation of the verb as "I am sending" (see the notes on Col 4:8). Paul's mission is presented in Col 2:1 as encouraging or comforting (*parakaleō*) the hearts of believers. Tychicus is being presented as Paul's emissary who comforts believers in Paul's absence. We should not think of the reference to the "heart" purely in terms of emotional support. Given the way the heart could be presented as the center of both thought and emotion it is best to think of Tychicus fostering the commitment of believers as a whole (see the notes on Col 3:15).

23. *Peace be to the brothers, and love with faith from God the Father and our Lord Jesus Christ:* After following Colossians closely in vv. 21-22, Ephesians departs significantly from Colossians in its closing wish of peace and benediction.

Although the reference is literally to "the brothers" *(tois adelphois)*, it should be understood as embracing the whole community (e.g., NRSV; REB). Peace and love are both important themes in Ephesians. The reference to "peace" and "grace" (vv. 23-24) recalls the opening, where the terms are in the reverse order (cf. Eph 1:2). Although the wish for peace does not occur at the end of Colossians it is found in the majority of Pauline letters (e.g., Rom 15:33; 2 Cor 13:11; Phil 4:7, 9; 1 Thess 5:23; 2 Thess 3:16). The wish for peace in 6:23 has most in common, however, with the wish for peace in Gal 6:16, which is also expressed in the third person. "God the Father and our Lord Jesus Christ" are depicted here as bestowing love (see also v. 24) with faith. The use of the third person gives the impression of a generalized greeting, adding to the impression that Ephesians was originally a circular letter intended for a broad audience.

24. *Grace be to all those who love our Lord Jesus Christ in immortality:* Paul's letters typically bestow grace (of our Lord Jesus Christ) as part of the closing (cf. 1 Cor 16:23; 2 Cor 13:14; Gal 6:18; Phil 4:23; 1 Thess 5:28; 2 Thess 3:18; Phlm 25). The closing greeting of Colossians is particularly brief: "Grace be with you" (Col 4:18). The unusual last phrase of Ephesians is subject to different translations. The true significance of the final expression "in immortality" or "in incorruptibility" *(en aphtharsią)* is far from clear. It has often been understood as modifying "love." Thus the NRSV has "Grace be with all who have an undying love for our Lord Jesus Christ" (cf. REB). But the majority of commentators hold that the expression actually modifies "grace" (i.e., grace that is imperishable; see the summary of the debate in Lincoln [1990] 467–68). Grace is presented in 2:7 as extending into eternity. Since Ephesians highlights the enthronement of believers with Christ in the heavenly places (2:6) and generally presents believers as engaged in a journey of heavenly ascent, it is particularly appropriate that the epistle ends with a mention of immortality (cf. 1 Cor 15:42, 53-54; 2 Tim 1:10). The mention of peace, love, grace, and faith recalls the themes introduced in the opening blessing of 1:3-14 (Taylor and Reumann 94). Although the evidence for the reading adopted here is significantly stronger, it should be noted that the Textus Receptus and other texts add the liturgical "Amen" *(amen)* at the end of this verse in order to harmonize 6:24 with the liturgical ending of the first half of the letter (3:21; see Metzger 610).

Interpretation

The very close relationship between Col 4:7-8 and Eph 6:21-22 has been judged by many commentators as offering strong evidence in favor of deutero-Pauline authorship. Here the literary dependence of Ephesians on Colossians becomes almost indisputable. (Note, however, that Ernest Best [1998] has argued that it is ". . . as probable that [the author of Colossians] used Ephesians as the reverse" [613]. But the single and somewhat artificial mention of Tychicus in Eph 6:21-22 makes more sense if the author of Ephesians worked from the author of Colossians' vivid references to fellow workers and greetings in Col 4:7-18 than the reverse. See further below.) Up to this point it has seemed that the author of Ephesians was familiar with Colossians and borrowed many of its concepts and terms, but there were also significant differences between parallel passages. The relationship between Colossians and Ephesians could be explained on the basis of general familiarity with Colossians on the part of the author of Ephesians. The author could have been reproducing main ideas on the basis of memory. But here the correspondence between the two works is almost verbatim. As has frequently been pointed out by commentators, the writer of Ephesians reproduced thirty-two words found in the same order in Colossians. There are only a very few minor departures from Colossians (see the notes above). Particularly telling is the fact that the author of Ephesians maintains the change in number from "news about me, what I am doing" (v. 21) to "how we are" (v. 22). This shift makes sense in the context of Colossians since Timothy is presented as the co-sender of the epistle (Col 1:1) and there is great emphasis on Paul's coworkers in general (e.g., Col 4:10-17). However, the shift seems out of place in Ephesians, which concentrates so deliberately on the authority of the apostle alone (e.g., 1:1; 3:1-4). Yet it should be noted that Tychicus is presented as being with Paul at the time of the composition of Ephesians, so it would be an exaggeration to say that the shift makes no sense at all.

It is difficult to know what to make of the reference to Tychicus in 6:21-22. The dependence of Eph 6:21-22 on Col 4:7-8 gives the impression that the references to him are artificial. Some have understood them in terms of the literary devices of pseudonymity (cf. 3:1-13; 4:1; see Lincoln [1990] 468). The frequent references to Tychicus in deutero-Pauline literature, however, suggest that Tychicus was well known in the communities that remained devoted to Paul's leadership even after his imprisonment and death (see the notes on 6:21). The reinforcement of the authority of Paul's fellow workers surfaces in these works as one of the means through which Pauline Christianity was able to survive the disappearance of its central leader (see the notes and interpretation on Eph 4:7-18). It has even been suggested that Tychicus was himself the author of Ephesians and sought to remind readers of the close relationship he had with Paul by citing the words of Colossians (e.g., Mitton [1976] 230).

As is typical of Pauline works, the closing of Ephesians includes a wish for peace and a benediction (6:23-24). Peace and grace (though in the reverse order) are also part of the initial greeting (1:2). But the closing remarks of 6:23-24 are unusual in that instead of the second person plural (cf. Rom 15:33; 1 Cor 16:23-24; Gal 6:18; Phil 4:21-23) they are expressed in the third person, which gives the impression of a greater distance between the author and the recipients of the letter and thus suggests a wider audience. This is very much in keeping with the somewhat magisterial tone of

Ephesians and the interest in the universal church, and it fits with the theory that the epistle was originally intended for several congregations.

As noted above, the final two verses bring together many key themes of the epistle in a very brief space. The focus on God's gifts of love with faith, and on grace in general, points back to the first part of the epistle where the importance of God's initiative is underlined. Peace is the result of the unifying process in Christ through which God makes the divine mysteries known (cf. 2:14-17; 3:3-6). Love also plays a central role in the ethical exhortations of the second half of the epistle; it is the defining feature of believers, the means through which they emulate Christ (e.g., 5:2). The last word, "immortality," has not been used previously in Ephesians, but it nevertheless summarizes the promise of the epistle as a whole: a life with Christ (2:6) that stretches into eternity.

For Reference and Further Study

Weima, J.A.D. *Neglected Endings: The Significance of Pauline Letter Closings.* JSNT.S 101. Sheffield: JSOT Press, 1994.

INDEXES

SELECTED SCRIPTURAL CITATIONS

5:7	309		2:4-6	249, 254
6:1	141		2:5	248, 250
6:2	100		2:9	205
6:4	217, 316		2:10	76, 254
6:11	85		2:11	248, 254, 256
8:5	110		2:13-14	160, 337
8:10	71		2:15	162
9:10	100		2:17	157
9:11	258		2:18	157
9:14	72		2:18–3:7	153, 162, 326
9:24	258		3:1	168, 326
10:1	110		3:1-2	157, 162
10:12	219		3:1-6	157, 162, 168, 340
10:19	267		3:2	60, 157, 326
10:22	85, 328		3:5-6	154, 332
10:32	217, 316		3:6	157, 169
11:27	58		3:14	157
11:31	180		3:15-16	162, 174
11:35	52, 200		3:19	290
12:8	333		4:2-4	254
13:4	330		4:3	303
13:9	293		4:4	318
13:13	179		4:6	290
13:21	279		4:7	170, 347
			4:8	61
James			4:12-19	175
1:6-8	293		4:15	307
1:16	294		4:17	248
1:19-20	306		5:2	292
1:22	87		5:8	170, 307
2:7	328		5:9	88
2:17-26	101		5:11	279
3:1-12	137, 308		5:12	43
3:14	137			
4:11	110		*2 Peter*	
5:12	60		2:4-10	73
			2:10	60
1 Peter			2:13	158
1:1	17, 193		2:18	294
1:3-12	197		3:10	97
1:10-12	262		3:12	97
1:14	254, 302		3:15-16	16
1:14-25	76		3:17	294
1:17	157			
1:18	254, 302		*1 John*	
1:19	72		1:5	313
1:20	198		1:6	137

SELECTED REFERENCES TO OTHER LITERATURE

Early Jewish Literature

2 Apoc. Bar.
48:42–52:7	131
78:2	32, 192

3 Apoc. Bar.
2:1	255
2:2	255

1 Enoch
1–36	224
14:9	114, 244, 255
46:3	86
47:1-4	79
49:1-4	60
51	50
63:3	81
69:3	275
69:4	275
71:1	275
71:1-17	112
104:11-13	81
106:5	275
108:12	235

2 Enoch
20:1	60
22:4-7	112
61:10	60

3 Enoch
	112

Abot de-Rabbi Nathan
2.2a	290

Apocalypse of Abraham
	112

Apocalypse of Elijah
5.36-39	235

Ascension of Isaiah
	112
9:18	235

Epistle of Aristeas
122	305
139	245

Josephus, *Against Apion*
1.54	97
2.146	245
2.148	243
2.206	155
2.217	155
2.199–216	161

Josephus, *Antiquities of the Jews*
9.4.3	302
12.5.4	113
18.11	97
XV 417	244

Josephus, *Bellum Judaicum* (Jewish War)
2.119	97

Jubilees
6:34-8	110

Midrash Tehillin
Ps 68:11	290

Early Christian Literature

INDEX OF AUTHORS

INDEX OF SUBJECTS